GONDOLIN PRESS

Fr. Paul L. Kramer, B.Ph., S.T.B., M. Div., S.T.L. (Cand.)

ON THE TRUE AND THE FALSE POPE

TO DECEIVE THE ELECT

VOLUME TWO

THE CASE AGAINST BERGOGLIO

gondolin press

ON THE TRUE AND THE FALSE POPE – *Paul Kramer*

© **Gondolin Institute LLC**
1915 Aster Rd.
60178 Sycamore IL

www.gondolinpress.com
info@gondolinpress.com

ISBN 978-1-945658-25-9 *(hard cover)*
ISBN 978-1-945658-26-6 *(soft cover)*

All the literary and artistic rights are reserved. The rights for translation, electronicstorage, copy and total or partial adaptation, by any equipment, (including microfilm and photostats) are reserved for all countries. The publisher is available to untraceable rights holders.

First Edition: November 2021
Printed in U.S.A.

PREFACE

For seven years, since the election by the cardinals of Jorge Mario Bergoglio in 2013, there is a grave "constitutional crisis" in the Church — a crisis specifically regarding the divine constitution of the Church which allows for there to exist only one exclusive holder of the Petrine *munus*. While the majority of Catholics do not understand the nature of the problem, and are therefore not even aware of its existence, there are enough voices being heard in various parts of the Catholic world which give evidence to the reality that there exists in the Church a disputed papacy — not openly disputed by the claimants themselves, but the dispute exists between those who recognize "Francis" and those who recognize Benedict XVI as the valid holder of the papal office. Some are convinced that Francis is the pope, others believe that Benedict XVI is still the sole legitimate holder of the Petrine *munus*, and many are not sure which is the true pope. While the vast majority of bishops (whose positions of authority and source of income depend on their remaining subject to Francis), do not question (at least in public[1]) that Francis is the pope, yet there exists a great number of lay Catholics, and even some bishops who do question Bergoglio's validity; and even if he should resign tomorrow, there would remain the problem of the doubtful validity of his successor. It is my hope that this volume will shed sufficient light on the question in order that the pastors of the Church will be able to orient themselves towards solving what may turn out to be, and already shows signs of becoming the gravest crisis in the entire bimillennial history of the Church. There has not been a situation in any way analogous to the present one since the attempt by Emperor Constantius to establish a co-papacy between Pope Liberius and the Arian leaning, Antipope Felix II in the year 357. Fortunately for the Church in that century, neither Liberius nor the Roman clergy were in any manner disposed to accept such an unorthodox arrangement which would have brought about the defection of the Church from

---

[1] Even some cardinals have expressed their doubts privately about the validity of Bergoglio's claim. For obvious reasons, their names cannot be mentioned here.

her divine constitution. Felix was driven out and lived the remainder of his life in retirement. Today there are two claimants who each, in some manner, lay claim on some aspect of the Petrine *munus*. However, a former pope — one who has validly renounced the office, is incapable of retaining any aspect of the Petrine *munus*, because as a former pope, he is simply and absolutely no longer pope. In contrast, a bishop who resigns from his office as ordinary of a diocese remains a bishop, and therefore is capable of retaining some relation with his former diocese as "Bishop Emeritus" in virtue of the episcopal *munus* that remains with him as a successor of the Apostles even as a retired bishop without ordinary jurisdiction. Thus, the present situation of the Church, in which there is one man (Bergoglio), who is generally acknowledged to wield the papal jurisdiction, and another (Benedict XVI), who renounced his active ministry without entirely renouncing his mandate (what he calls his *Auftrag* in German, which in Latin is *munus*), which he received upon accepting his election to the papacy, is anomalous. Such an arrangement cannot validly exist in the Church. There is only one indivisible Petrine *munus* in the Church which is held exclusively by the individual who is validly constituted as the successor of Peter in the Supreme Pontificate. For so long as the pope retains any claim on that *munus*, it cannot be validly passed on to a successor; and if he would validly resign his office, one who is a formal heretic cannot validly receive that *munus* and succeed him in the papacy. In the pages of this volume which follow, it is explained and proven in the light of Church doctrine, that Benedict XVI did not validly renounce the Petrine *munus*, and the man elected by the cardinals to be his successor, Jorge Mario Bergoglio, was not validly elected pope, and is in fact, a heretic, and as such, is an incapable subject of holding the office of the papacy.

PART ONE

DOCTRINAL SUMMARY

«In tantum enim fides mihi necessaria est ut cum de cæteris peccatis solum Deum judicem habeam, propter solum peccatum quod in fide committitur possem ab Ecclesia judicari. Nam *qui non credit, iam iudicatus est*. (Joh. 3:18)»

Innocentius III — *SERMONES DE DIVERSIS*. – *Sermo II* «IN CONSACRATIONE PONTIFICIS MAXIMI»

This shorter volume is being presented in the place of the more comprehensive examination originally planned on of the case of the two claimants to the Petrine *munus* — that of the one who is in my judgment the true Pope, Benedict XVI, and of the other — the *certain* heretic, who is therefore a *certain* antipope, Jorge "Francis" Bergoglio. The overriding consideration for replacing the originally planned volume with this shorter revision and completion of the doctrine elaborated in *Volume One*, and its application to the claims of Benedict and Bergoglio on the Petrine *munus*, is that by the time I would have finished the more lengthy work I had planned, the question of which of the claimants has the valid claim will probably be moot, although the problem of succession would remain even if Bergoglio would die or resign before Pope Benedict vacates the office. Secondly, in order that all of what I wrote in Volume One might be of some immediate benefit to the Church, I have summarized the main points of that doctrine in a compressed form, and I have added new argumentation explicating points which were only touched upon in the first volume, such as the essential distinction between episcopal and primatial power, so as to make the Church's doctrine on the question of papal deposition more easily and clearly understandable not only to those members of the clergy who have not studied the question in depth, but to the general reader as well. In this volume I will also touch upon the new objections being made by Bishop Athanasius Schneider as well as others, who ought to know better, but appear to not have examined the theological issues concerning the question of papal heresy and renunciation of the papacy in any great depth.

First, the questions on judging a pope must be clearly formulated and answered, and then the proofs will follow:

Dubium 1: Can a true and certain pope be judged a heretic by the Church?

Resp. Negative. It is claimed by some that a true and certain pope can be judged for heresy, but cases of heresy, since they are concerned with matters of faith can only be settled with finality by an infallible papal judgment. Only the pope, because he succeeds Peter not merely as an apostle in the manner that other bishops are successors of the Apostles, but because he succeeds Peter as *Cephas* in his function as the infallible *Rock* foundation of the Church, and as head of the Church over all the bishops, possesses the *singular power* to judge infallibly, which even all the bishops together without the pope do not possess; for which reason judgments in matters of faith are ultimately reserved to him alone, and his definitive judgment is final.[2] An "imperfect ecumenical council" is incapable of judging on a matter of faith infallibly, and therefore cannot definitively judge with finality whether a pope's opinion is heresy, and from there determine that the pope is indeed a contumacious heretic. The definitive and final settling of cases involving matters of faith and morals are reserved to the pope's infallible judgment; and before such final judgment is made, the case remains without a definitive judgment. Only if a pope has infallibly judged the case and condemned the heretic, can a person then be said to be definitively condemned with finality as a heretic by the Church. Until such judgment is made, one can always appeal to the pope's judgment to whose final judgment all such cases are reserved. If the accused is himself a true and certain pope, then the final decision is reserved to himself alone. Hence, a true and certain pope cannot be judged by the Church. Only a *manifest heretic*, or one who is *certainly a heretic*, because he is morally certain to

---

[2] Concilium Lugdunense II — «*si quæ de fide subortæ fuerint quæstiones, suo debent judicio definiri*»; *Summa Theol.* II^a II^æ q. 1 a. 10 — «*Ad illius ergo auctoritatem pertinet editio symboli, ad cuius auctoritatem pertinet finaliter determinare ea, quae sunt fidei, ut ab omnibus inconcussa fide teneantur. Hoc autem pertinet ad auctoritatem summi Pontificis, ad quem maiores et difficiliores Ecclesiae quaestiones referuntur, ut dicitur in Decretalibus extra, de Baptismo, cap. majores.*»

be a heretic who remains incorrigible while violently suspect of heresy, can be judged to be no pope because of his evident heresy, because a heretic is an incapable subject of the papacy, and the Church, being indefectible, has the infallible power to distinguish between a true and false pope — i.e. to recognize a true pope and reject a false pope who from the beginning of his claimed pontificate was never a true pope.

If an "imperfect council" presumes to judge a true and validly reigning pope guilty of heresy, the pope as supreme judge possesses the right and the power to overrule the council and judge the matter with *infallibility* and *finality*. No council can arrogate the power to itself to nullify or suppress the pope's right of primacy to judge the case as the supreme, final, and infallible judge, and then presume to arrogate to itself the supreme power to judge the pope's opinion heretical with finality, and compel the pope with coercive juridical force to submit to the judgment of the Council. For so long as an "imperfect council" does not receive a grant of jurisdiction from the Supreme Pontiff, it has no ecclesiastical jurisdiction — no power to judge or decide anything — and any judgment it would make would not be final, but would be subject to the pope's supreme power to judge with finality. Without a grant of jurisdiction from the pope, the Council's judgments would be nothing but a collective private judgment of the aggregation of individuals that comprise the gathering. Even the totality of the bishops of the Church cannot judge against a true and valid pope because he is the supreme and final judge in virtue of the "full and supreme jurisdiction" of his Primacy over the universal Church. The totality of bishops do not possess the power to judge a pope, or juridically condemn his opinion as heretical. The reason for this is that the authority of bishops is the ordinary episcopal power first received not immediately from Christ but indirectly from God through the Apostles — a power which, after the death of the Apostles is juridically derived from the pope's supreme power, and is granted to bishops in hierarchical subordination to the supreme power, and which is common to all diocesan ordinaries as successors of the Apostles. The *apostolic power* was *extraordinary*, and not passed on by the Apostles to their successors, but the Apostles conferred *episcopal jurisdiction* on their successors, which is a power exercised by the bishops only over their own subjects. The Petrine authority, which is an *ordinary and singular power* conferred directly by Christ on Peter alone, is a distinct power from the apostolic authority that was *extraordinary*, and was common to all the Apostles. The Petrine authority is the power of a full and supreme Primacy of jurisdiction over the whole Church, which Peter exercised over all the other Apostles and bishops. Unlike the extraordinary apostolic power common to all the Apostles which was not passed on to the bishops, the Primacy St. Peter received from Christ was ordinary, and is passed on to Peter's successors who receive it directly from Christ, whereas the episcopal jurisdiction is not conferred immediately by Christ on the bishops, but is received mediately, and in hierarchical subordination to the pope, and is juridically derived from and dependant on the pope's full and supreme jurisdiction.

The Church can unanimously reject a man's claim on the papacy and declare him to be no pope because he is a known heretic. That does not require a juridical condemnation of heresy, but only a cognitive recognition and clear general acknowledgment by those who comprise the body of the true Church, of the invalidity of the heretic's claim on the office in view of the certain fact of heresy, as happened at the Council of Constance in the case of Pedro de Luna ("Benedict XIII"). The Church has this power, as Gregory XVI explains in the passage quoted below, because the sheep have from Christ the grace to hear the voice of the shepherd and flee the stranger. (John 10:5)

Dubium 2: Can a true and certain pope fall into formal heresy and be judged to have fallen from the papacy by the Church?

Resp. Negative. If there is no certain pope among doubtful claimants, the Church possesses the infallible power to resolve the doubt, and judge which, if any, is a true pope, because it is contrary to the divine constitution of the Church that there can exist in the Church the contradiction of a visible head, i.e. one who is visible as such as head, who remains unknown, and therefore not visible as *head* — and therefore *invisible as head* due to the uncertainty as to whether or not he is a true pope. If a claimant is a heretic, the Church can judge him to be an *incapable subject* of the papacy and no pope at all. Even if he would have been at some time generally and reputed to be pope (but not with unconditional and exclusive unanimity), if his heresy were so clearly manifest, with total certitude, the judgment against him would consist of a general and unanimous rejection, such as the rejection by the Roman Church of Antipope Felix II, (who had never gained general acceptance in the first place), and the judgment of the Council of Constance rejecting the claim of "Benedict XIII". In such a case (as history proves) the juridical declaration of vacancy, or the universal acceptance of the heretic's rival claimant necessarily follows the general non-juridical recognition of the fact of nullity of the heretic's claim. But the possibility for an indubitable pope to fall into heresy and lose office *ipso facto* exists only as a pure hypothesis, because if a true pope were to fall into formal heresy, the Church would be deprived of her foundation in which exists the infallible power of the head of the Church to juridically render a final and definitive judgment to condemn the heresy in such a case, firstly, because in such cases, in which the matter and the form of heresy are not absolutely and manifestly certain, a judgment would require the pope's infallible power of the primacy to judge the case in order that the case be definitively settled with finality, and secondly; because even if the heresy is manifest, (as was the case with Arius) if such a one had been a valid pope before falling into heresy, having been validly constituted as head of the Church, there would exist no supreme power to juridically resolve the case with finality, and thereby convict him by judicial power and declare him with supreme judicial power to have fallen from the supreme pontificate, without his having any right to appeal to any supreme jurisdiction to resolve the case. Such a supreme jurisdiction does not exist in any other individual or body but only in the Roman Pontiff in virtue of his primacy. Furthermore, if it would be suspected that the pope has fallen into formal heresy, there would no longer exist an infallible means to determine the matter, and then, based on that judgment, bind the pope with juridical finality to that judgment. Without the pope's definitive and infallible judgment and supreme jurisdiction, a council cannot definitively condemn a proposition and juridically convict the fallen pontiff. That can only be brought about by means of the full and supreme jurisdiction of the primacy — *no other means suffices to convict heretics.*[3] Even the case of heresy so manifest as that of Arius

---

[3] Alfonso Maria de' Liguori, *Vindiciae pro suprema pontificis potestate adversus Iustinum Febronium,* Torino, 1832, p. 13.

was only able to be definitively adjudicated by a pope, but if Arius himself had been the pope when he began teaching heresy, there would have been no one else with the supreme authority to infallibly judge and condemn his teaching, bind him and the whole Church coercively to the judgment, and convict him of heresy for having rejected the judgment. Even if a council would judge that the pope has fallen into a previously condemned heresy, the pope, to whose authority judgment in all matters of faith are reserved, could issue a solemn judgment to the contrary — and then there could arise the dilemma of whose judgment is to be followed, the pope's or the council's. If the council's judgment would be correct, then the pope would forfeit his primacy and cease to be pope; but if the council's fallible judgment is erroneous, then the pope retains his primacy and office; and then there would be no authority on earth to judge between them. It is only for the reason that a true pope cannot defect from the faith that it can be concluded that a public heretic, or one later discovered to be a heretic, was never a true pope; so that a council would have the right to condemn him, and the final outcome of the process would necessarily have to be left to divine providence. Even a council's judgment would not be infallible in such a case, and therefore the doubt could only be definitively resolved by a subsequent universal and peaceful acceptance of a claimant.

However, for so long as a man is validly constituted in the papacy, the infallible power to judge with finality exists singularly and exclusively in virtue of his supreme authority as successor of Peter in the primacy, and not in all the bishops collectively, who do not receive any share in the Petrine primatial power from Christ, nor have they received it from the Apostles, who themselves possessed no share in it. Accordingly St. Thomas did not even see fit to dignify the question on papal heresy by mentioning it, yet he did answer it perfectly without even directly addressing the question of papal heresy by explaining in all-embracing general terms (in the passages I cite in this work) why it is that any prelate would lose his jurisdiction automatically if he were to fall into the sin of public heresy, and that it pertains exclusively to the pope's authority to determine with finality the Church's judgment on all matters of faith. Considering the huge quantity of *Summæ* of the Decretists commenting on the *Canon si papa* in the *Decretum Gratiani*, it is remarkable that St. Thomas did not treat specifically on the question of papal heresy, but only on correction of a pope for his misdeeds.[4] He obviously had too much contempt for the question of a pope becoming a heretic, even to mention it, but the disdainful silence of the "Dumb Ox" on the specific question of papal heresy bellows even more loudly than the erudition of all those who comprise that vast majority of theologians who correctly hold that a true pope is protected by divine grace from ever falling into formal heresy. Thus, St. Alphonsus, who ranked St. Thomas first among all theologians, concurs entirely with the strictly implied teaching of Aquinas that the pope being the final and infallible judge cannot become a heretic, for which reason Alphonsus says that God would not permit a pope to become a heretic, even as a private person,[5] because as a heretic, he would cease to be pope, and there would be no infallible judge to define the matter and condemn the heretic, and the Church would be deprived of its foundation. Therefore he explains:

> Since therefore Peter is the rock, or is the foundation of the Church, he cannot fail; otherwise, if the foundation could fail, the Church could one day fail; but this is impossible, because of the promise already made in the same place: *Et portæ inferi non prævalebunt adversus eam.* And if Peter cannot fail, neither can the Pontiffs his successors fail; since Jesus Christ having promised that hell will never prevail against the Church, the promise must necessarily be understood as made forever, as long as the Church lasts. Nor, does it avail to say that the promise was not made directly to Peter, but to the Church, while it was made to Peter as the representative of the Church. But if by the rock we must mean the Church, then must we say that the Church is the foundation of the Church? Or that there are two churches, one of which is the foundation, and the other is the building? The truth is that Peter was constituted by the Lord as the foundation of the Church for the good of the same,

---

[4] *Commentarium in IV Sententiarum,* Dist. 19, q. 2, art. 2 — «Quamvis autem praelati sint corripiendis a subditis; non tamen est eis poena infligenda, sed recurrendo ad superiorem denuntiando; vel, si non habet superiorem, recurrat ad Deum, qui eum emendet, vel de medio subtrahat»

[5] Alfonso Maria de' Liguori, *Verità Della Fede*, Tomo Secondo, Monza, 1823, Parte III. Capo. VIII. p. 157 — «Iddio non mai permetterà che alcuno de' Pontefici Romani, anche come uomo privato, diventi eretico né notorio, né occulto.».

hence Peter was given to be *Saxum inmobile molem continens*, as wrote. S Augustine (*Serm. De Cath.*): Unmovable stone, not subject to wavering; for, as well warns Origen (*in Matth.* 16.): *Si prævalerent* (portæ inferi) *adversus petram, in qua fundata Ecclesia erat, contra Ecclesiam etiam prævalerent.* [If the gates of hell would prevail against the rock, on which the Church was founded, they would also prevail against the Church.] So that the firmness of foundation was directly given to Peter and indirectly to the Church, since it is true that the foundation supports the house, not the house that supports the foundation.[6]

MANIFEST HERETIC AND SUSPECTED HERETIC

Heresy is manifest if the fact is **seen** as *evidenter verum* that both the opinion is heresy, and that it is held with pertinacity. If it concerns a truth not yet explicitly defined nor known as manifestly evident through its principles, (such as was the case with John XXII), then pertinacity, i.e. the *form* of heresy cannot be definitively established In such a case until a true and certain pope rules with infallible finality on the *matter* of the question. A perfect example of such a doctrine

---

[6] Alfonso Maria de' Liguori, *Verità Della Fede*, Tomo Secondo, Monza, 1823, pp. 161-163 — «Giacché dunque Pietro è la pietra, o sia il fondamento della Chiesa, egli non può mancare; altrimenti, se potesse mancare il fondamento, potrebbe un giorno, mancare anche la Chiesa; ma ciò è impossibile, per la promessa già fatta nello stesso luogo: *Et portæ inferi non prævalebunt adversus eam.* E se Pietro non può mancare, né anche possono mancare i Pontefici suoi successori; poiché avendo promesso Gesù Cristo che contro la Chiesa non prevarrà mai l'inferno, la promessa dee necessariamente intendersi fatta per sempre, finché durerà la Chiesa. Ne vale dire che la promessa non fu fatta direttamente a Pietro, ma alla Chiesa, mentre fu fatta a Pietro come rappresentante la Chiesa. Ma se per la pietra si dee intender la Chiesa, dunque dobbiam dire che la Chiesa è il fondamento della Chiesa? O che vi sono due Chiese, di cui una è il fondamento, e l'altra è l'edificio? La verità si è che Pietro fu costituito dal Signore fondamento della Chiesa per bene della medesima, onde a Pietro fu dato l'esser *Saxum inmobile molem continens, come scrisse.* S. Agostino (Serm. de Cath.): pietra immobile, non soggetta a vacillare; poiché, come bene avverti Origene (*in Matth.* 16.): *Si prævalerent* (portæ inferi) *adversus petram, in qua fundata Ecclesia erat, contra Ecclesiam etiam prævalerent.* Sicché la fermezza di fondamento direttamente fu data a Pietro e indirettamente alla Chiesa essendo vero che il fondamento sostiene la casa, non la casa sostiene il fondamento.»

that is implicitly contained in a previous definition but not in a manner that is manifestly evident is the dogma of the Assumption of the Blessed Virgin Mary. Peter Seewald relates in *Benedikt XVI — Ein Leben*:

> The dogma published on All Saints Day, November 1, 1950, about the physical assumption of Mary into heaven caused additional excitement in Munich. While in the rest of Catholic Germany Pius XII. met with great approval, the relationship of the Munich theological faculty to Rome was regarded as chilled. "The answer from our teachers was strictly negative," reported Ratzinger. Both Söhngen and Schmaus expressed their disapproval in response to a worldwide survey initiated in advance by the Curia. It did not refer so much to the content of the new dogma — in prayer practice, for example in the rosary, the bodily assumption of Mary into heaven had long been spoken of — but to the dogmatization itself. An expert on patristic research had proven that the teaching of the bodily assumption of Mary before the 5th century was completely unknown. It is therefore not possible to assign them to the "apostolic tradition". Ratzinger saw things differently than his professor, at least in the years that followed. If tradition is understood as a living process in which the Holy Spirit continues to familiarize the Church with the truth, tradition should not be restricted to apostolic tradition.

Of course, Ratzinger was correct, as can be gathered from the teaching of Pius XI, who explained in *Mortalium Animos* that what is solemnly defined is not something invented, but is already *implicitly contained* in the deposit of revelation: «But in the use of this extraordinary teaching authority no newly invented matter is brought in, nor is anything new added to the number of those truths which are at least implicitly contained in the deposit of Revelation, divinely handed down to the Church: only those which are made clear which perhaps may still seem obscure to some, or that which some have previously called into question is declared to be of faith.»[7] It is not

---

[7] PIUS PP. XI LITTERAE ENCYCLICAE *MORTALIUM ANIMOS*, 6 January 1928 — «Quo quidem extraordinario magisterii usu nullum sane inventum inducitur nec quidquam additur novi ad earum summam veritatum, quae in deposito Revelationis, Ecclesiae divinitus tradito, saltem

necessary for a doctrine to be explicitly set forth in Scripture or taught explicitly by the Fathers in order that it be implicitly contained in the deposit of revelation and definable; nor does there exist a necessary condition that there be seen a strict logical implication from premise to conclusion so that the dogma to be defined would follow necessarily and obviously from the principles in which it is implicitly contained. Accordingly, the dogma of the Assumption can be considered to be already implicitly contained in the deposit of revelation. Thus, in Luke 1:28 we read, "And the angel being come in, said unto her: Hail, full of grace, the Lord is with thee: blessed art thou among women." The expression 'Hail, full of grace' is St. Jerome's translation/interpretation of the Greek expression Χαῖρε, κεχαριτωμένη contained in the verse, which employs the perfect feminine singular mediopassive participle, which the Evangelist uses to express a fullness of grace existing in a state of consummate perfection. On the foundation of St. Thomas' teaching on *Galatians 5*, it can be argued that grace is a certain beginning of glory in us (quædam inchoatio gloriæ in nobis *II^a-II^{ae} q. 24 a. 3 ad 2*); and that the end must correspond with the principle (finis respondet principio *I^a II^a Q. 1 a. 8*)[8] so that in that principle which is a fullness of grace there exists the full and infallible potentiality for the consummate perfection of glory of that which although not yet attained *in statu viæ*, already exists potentially in the principle. That glory which is the consummation of grace (gloria, quae nihil est aliud quam gratia consummata. *I^a q. 95 a. 1 arg. 6*), for Mary is the consummate perfection of the fullness of grace, which consists in the perfection of glory corresponding not merely to the potentiality of some degree of grace existing in her soul, but to the potentiality of the fullness of grace, which overflows even to the body — the consummation of which is the maximum glory which can exist in a creature, and therefore necessarily excludes any privation whatsoever of soul or body. The state of separation of the soul from the body is in the nature of a privation and penalty, and therefore is a state that cannot

---

implicite continentur, verum aut ea declarantur quae forte adhuc obscura compluribus videri possint aut ea tenenda de fide statuuntur quae a nonnullis ante in controversiam vocabantur.»

[8] *Summa Theol.* I^a q. 103 a. 2 co. — «cum finis respondeat principio, non potest fieri ut, principio cognito, quid sit rerum finis ignoretur.»

co-exist with the consummation of the fullness of grace which was the singular privilege granted by God to Mary.

In order to understand how the Blessed Virgin's "fullness of grace" was consummated by her bodily assumption into heaven, it is necessary to consider the relation of that fullness of grace to the fruits it produced, and the twofold nature of the spiritual goods which the Apostle calls "fruits". St. Thomas comments on the verse of *Galatians 5*, ("But the fruit of the Spirit is, charity, joy, peace, patience, benignity, goodness, longanimity, Mildness, faith, modesty, continency, chastity." [9]), and he points out that the Apostle first «enumerates the spiritual goods which he calls "fruits."» And he explains that:

> "Fruit" is said in two ways: namely, as something acquired, for example, from labour or study — "The fruit of good labours is glorious" (Wis 3:15) — and as something produced, as fruit is produced from a tree: "A good tree cannot bear evil fruit" (Mt 7:18). Now the works of the spirit are called fruits, not as something earned or acquired, but as produced. Furthermore, fruit which is acquired has the character of an ultimate end; not, however, fruit which is produced. Nevertheless, fruit so understood implies two things: namely, that it is the last thing of the producer, as the last thing produced by a tree is its fruit, and that it is sweet or delightful: *"His fruit was sweet to my palate"* (Cant 2:3). So, then, the works of the virtues and of the spirit are something last in us. For the Holy Spirit is in us through grace, through which we acquire the habit of the virtues; these in turn make us capable of working according to virtue. Furthermore, they are delightful and even fruitful: *"You have your fruit unto sanctification,* i.e., in holy works (Rom 6:22). And that is why they are called fruits. But they are also called "flowers," namely, in relation to future happiness; because just as from flowers hope of fruit is taken, so from works of the virtues is obtained hope of eternal life and happiness. And as in the flower there is a beginning of the fruit, so in the works of the virtues is a beginning of happiness, which will exist when knowledge and charity are made perfect.[10]

---

[9] *"Fructus autem Spiritus est caritas, gaudium, pax, patientia, benignitas, bonitas, longanimitas, mansuetudo, fides, modestia, continentia, castitas."*

[10] *Super Gal.*, cap. 5 *l.* 6 — «Respondeo. Dicendum est quod fructus dicitur dupliciter, scilicet ut acquisitus, puta ex labore vel studio, Sap. III, 15: *bonorum laborum gloriosus est fructus,* et ut productus, sicut fructus

He then explains why «the Apostle calls the effects of the flesh "works," but the fruits of the spirit he calls "fruits." For it has been pointed out that a fruit is something ultimate and sweet, produced from a thing.» — «For God planted in human nature certain seeds, namely, a natural desire of good and knowledge, and He added gifts of grace: And therefore, because the works of the virtues are produced naturally from these, they are called "fruits,"» From there it follows, «It is plain, therefore, from what has been said, that the works of the virtues are called fruits of the spirit, both because they have a sweetness and delight in themselves and because they are the last and congruous products of the gifts.» Thus there is the relation between the fruits produced, in which there is a beginning of beatitude, and the ultimate fruits acquired from the first fruits or flowers, which are enjoyed in eternity: «But they are also called "flowers," namely, in relation to future happiness; because just as from flowers hope of fruit is taken, so from works of the virtues is obtained hope of eternal life and happiness.»

That relation is of the principle to its end: "the beginning of anything is always ordained to its completion; as is clearly the case in effects both of nature and of art. Wherefore every beginning of perfection is ordained to complete perfection which is achieved

---

producitur ex arbore. Matth. c. VII, 18: *non potest arbor bona fructus malos facere*. Opera autem spiritus dicuntur fructus non ut adepti sive acquisiti, sed ut producti; fructus autem qui est adeptus, habet rationem ultimi finis, non autem fructus productus. Nihilominus tamen fructus sic acceptus duo importat, scilicet quod sit ultimum producentis, sicut ultimum quod producitur ab arbore est fructus eius, et quod sit suave sive delectabile. Cant. II, 3: *fructus eius dulcis gutturi meo*. Sic ergo opera virtutum et spiritus sunt quid ultimum in nobis. Nam spiritus sanctus est in nobis per gratiam, per quam acquirimus habitum virtutum, et ex hoc potentes sumus operari secundum virtutem. Sunt etiam delectabilia, et sunt etiam fructuosa. Rom. VI, 22: *habetis fructum vestrum in sanctificationem*, id est in operibus sanctificatis, et ideo dicuntur fructus. Dicuntur etiam flores respectu futurae beatitudinis, quia sicut ex floribus accipitur spes fructus, ita ex operibus virtutum habetur spes vitae aeternae et beatitudinis. Et sicut in flore est quaedam inchoatio fructus, ita in operibus virtutum est quaedam inchoatio beatitudinis, quae tunc erit quando cognitio et charitas perficientur.»

through the last end."¹¹ As in the order of nature, likewise in the order of grace: "while those that are assigned as rewards, may be either perfect happiness, so as to refer to the future life, or some beginning of happiness, such as is found in those who have attained perfection, in which case they refer to the present life. Because when a man begins to make progress in the acts of the virtues and gifts, it is to be hoped that he will arrive at perfection, both as a wayfarer, and as a citizen of the heavenly kingdom."¹²Thus the relation between grace and glory: "grace and glory are referred to the same genus, for grace is nothing else than a beginning of glory in us."¹³

That relation between principle and end existed most perfectly in the Blessed Virgin from the first principle, which was the fullness of grace of Immaculate Conception, to its consummation in her glorious Assumption. Thus, St. Thomas explains:

> The Blessed Virgin is said to be full of grace in three things. First, as to the soul, in which she had the fullness of grace. God, in fact, gives grace for two things, namely, to do good and to avoid evil; and, as to these two things, the Blessed Virgin had the most perfect grace. After Jesus Christ, she avoided sin in a more perfect way than any other saint. [...] This is why it is written in the Book of Songs, chapter IV: "*You are all beautiful, my beloved, there is no defilement in you.*" Saint Augustine says, in his book of Nature and Grace: *If, except the holy virgin Mary, we asked all the saints who have lived here below whether they have been without sins, they would cry out with one voice: If we say that we are without sin, we are deceiving ourselves, the truth is not in us. So except, I say, this holy Virgin, from whom, for the honour of the Lord, when it comes to sin, I don't want to talk at all. We know that she was*

---

11 *Iᵃ IIᵃᵉ* q. 1 a. 6 — «semper inchoatio alicuius ordinatur ad consummationem ipsius; sicut patet tam in his quae fiunt a natura, quam in his quae fiunt ab arte. Et ideo omnis inchoatio perfectionis ordinatur in perfectionem consummatam, quae est per ultimum finem.»

12 *Iᵃ IIᵃᵉ* q. 69 a. 2 — «Ea vero quae ponuntur tanquam praemia, possunt esse vel ipsa beatitudo perfecta, et sic pertinent ad futuram vitam, vel aliqua inchoatio beatitudinis, sicut est in viris perfectis, et sic praemia pertinent ad praesentem vitam. Cum enim aliquis incipit proficere in actibus virtutum et donorum, potest sperari de eo quod perveniet et ad perfectionem viae, et ad perfectionem patriae.»

13 *IIᵃ-IIᵃᵉ* q. 24 a. 3 ad 2 — «gratia et gloria ad idem genus referuntur, quia gratia nihil est aliud quam quaedam inchoatio gloriae in nobis.»

given more grace to overcome sin in whatever form it presented itself; she deserved to conceive and give birth to him who, as it is established, was not defiled by any sin.[14]

Not being defiled by any sin, the perfection of her works exceeded that of all the angels and saints:

> The Blessed Virgin even practiced all the virtues in a perfect way; for the other saints, they practiced some in a more special way; one practiced above all humility, the other, chastity, another, mercy; this is what makes them given as models of particular virtues: thus Blessed Nicholas is a model of mercy, etc. But the Blessed Virgin is the model of all virtues, because in her you will find a model of humility. It is written in Saint Luke, chapter I: "*Behold the handmaid of the Lord;*" and further: "*He regarded the humility of his servant.*" She is a model of chastity: "For I have not known man;" she is the model of all the virtues, as is sufficiently clear. So therefore she is full of grace, both to do good and to avoid evil. In the second place, she was full of grace regarding the overflow of the soul with the flesh or body. For it is great in any saint to have received enough grace to sanctify the soul; but the soul of the Blessed Virgin was so full, that from her soul grace was poured out on the flesh, to the point that, from this same flesh, she conceived the Son of God; and therefore Hugo of Saint-Victor says: "*Because the love of the Holy Ghost burned in her heart, that is why he worked wonderful things in her flesh, to the point that God and man would be born from her.*" It is written in Saint Luke, chapter I: "*The Holy One born of you will be called the Son of God.*" Thirdly, regarding the pouring out of grace on all the other men. It is something great for each saint, when he has enough grace to be sufficient for the salvation of several men; but

---

[14] **Expositio Salutationis Angelicae** — «Dicitur autem beata virgo plena gratia quantum ad tria. Primo quantum ad animam, in qua habuit omnem plenitudinem gratiae. Nam gratia Dei datur ad duo: scilicet ad bonum operandum, et ad vitandum malum; et quantum ad ista duo perfectissimam gratiam habuit beata virgo. Nam ipsa omne peccatum vitavit magis quam aliquis sanctus post Christum. [...] Unde Cant. IV, 7: *tota pulchra es, amica mea, et macula non est in te*. Augustinus in libro de natura et gratia: *excepta sancta virgine Maria, si omnes sancti et sanctae cum hic viverent, interrogati fuissent utrum sine peccato essent, omnes una voce clamassent: si dixerimus quia peccatum non habemus, ipsi nos seducimus, et veritas in nobis non est. Excepta, inquam, hac sancta virgine, de qua propter honorem domini, cum de peccato agitur, nullam prorsus volo quaestionem habere. Scimus enim quod ei plus gratiae collatum fuerit ad peccatum ex omni parte vincendum quae illum concipere et parere meruit quem constat nullum habuisse peccatum.*»

when one would have so much that it would suffice for the salvation of all men, that is the maximum; and this is in Christ and in the Blessed Virgin. In all kinds of perils you can, in fact, obtain salvation from the glorious Virgin. Whence it says in the Book of Canticles, chapter IV: "*A thousand shields*, that is to say, *a thousand remedies are suspended against perils*, etc." You can also have her for support in any work of virtue; and this is what is said in Ecclesiasticus, chapter XLIV: "*In me is all hope of life and of virtue.*" So she is full of grace, and she surpasses the angels by the fullness of grace, and for that she received the name of Mary, which we interpret as illuminated in oneself. This is why Isaiah says in chapter LVIII: "*He will fill your soul with splendor,*" she will serve as light to others throughout the universe, and for that she is compared to the sun and the moon.[15]

---

[15] ***Expositio Salutationis Angelicae*** — «Ipsa etiam omnium virtutum opera exercuit, alii autem sancti specialia quaedam: quia alius humilis, alius castus, alius misericors; et ideo ipsi dantur in exemplum specialium virtutum, sicut beatus Nicolaus in exemplum misericordiae et cetera. Sed beata virgo in exemplum omnium virtutum: quia in ea reperis exemplum humilitatis: Luc. I, 38: *ecce ancilla domini*, et post, vers. 48: *respexit humilitatem ancillae suae*, castitatis, *quoniam virum non cognosco*, vers. 34, et omnium virtutum; ut satis patet. Sic ergo plena est gratia beata virgo et quantum ad boni operationem, et quantum ad mali vitationem. Secundo plena fuit gratia quantum ad redundantiam animae ad carnem vel corpus. Nam magnum est in sanctis habere tantum de gratia quod sanctificet animam; sed anima beatae virginis ita fuit plena quod ex ea refudit gratiam in carnem, ut de ipsa conciperet filium Dei. Et ideo dicit Hugo de s. Victore: *quia in corde eius amor spiritus sancti singulariter ardebat, ideo in carne eius mirabilia faciebat, intantum quod de ea nasceretur Deus et homo*. Luc. I, 35: *quod enim nascetur ex te sanctum, vocabitur filius Dei*. Tertio quantum ad refusionem in omnes homines. Magnum enim est in quolibet sancto, quando habet tantum de gratia quod sufficit ad salutem multorum; sed quando haberet tantum quod sufficeret ad salutem omnium hominum de mundo, hoc esset maximum: et hoc est in Christo, et in beata virgine. Nam in omni periculo potes salutem obtinere ab ipsa virgine gloriosa. Unde Cant. IV, 4: *mille clypei*, (idest remedia contra pericula), *pendent ex ea*. Item in omni opere virtutis potes eam habere in adiutorium; et ideo dicit ipsa, Eccli. XXIV, 25: *in me omnis spes vitae et virtutis*. Sic ergo plena est gratia, et excedit Angelos in plenitudine gratiae; et propter hoc convenienter vocatur Maria quae interpretatur illuminata in se; unde Isai. LVIII, 11: *implebit splendoribus animam tuam*, et illuminatrix in alios, quantum ad totum mundum; et ideo assimilatur soli et lunae.»

Having produced the spiritual fruits of consummate perfection unhindered by any sin, the Blessed Virgin was immune from all penalty so that the fruits produced in this world correspond to the consummate glory obtained by her merits through her fullness of grace:

> Likewise regarding the penalty. Three curses were pronounced against men because of sin. The first was pronounced against the woman, which is that she would conceive in corruption, that her gestation would be painful, and that she would give birth in pain. But the Blessed Virgin was immune to this, because she conceived without corruption, her gestation was full of consolation, and she gave birth to the Saviour with joy. It is said in Isaiah, chapter XXXV: "*It will grow and it will sprout in the outpouring of joy and praise.*" The second was pronounced against the man, and that is that he would eat his bread by the sweat of his brow. The Blessed Virgin was exempt from this curse, because, as the Apostle says, Epistle to the Corinthians, chapter VII: "*Virgins are free from the cares of the world, they are concerned only with the service of God.*" The third was common to man and woman, that is, they would become dust; and the Blessed Virgin was preserved from it, because she was taken up with her body into heaven. It is said, Psalm CXXXI: "*Arise, Lord, to enter into your rest, you and the ark of your sanctification.*"[16]

Thus, from the revelation given in Scripture, it is proven *ex ratione* that the dogma of the Assumption, even if not manifestly, is implicitly contained in the revelation made by the angel to Mary. The denial of such a doctrine before its solemn definition is not an act of heresy.

---

[16] ***Expositio Salutationis Angelicae*** — «Item quantum ad poenam. Tres enim maledictiones datae sunt hominibus propter peccatum. Prima data est mulieri, scilicet quod cum corruptione conciperet, cum gravamine portaret, et in dolore pareret. Sed ab hac immunis fuit beata virgo: quia sine corruptione concepit, in solatio portavit, et in gaudio peperit salvatorem. Isai. XXXV, 2: *germinans germinabit exultabunda et laudans*. Secunda data est homini, scilicet quod in sudore vultus vesceretur pane suo. Ab hac immunis fuit beata virgo: quia, ut dicit apostolus, I Cor. VII, virgines solutae sunt a cura huius mundi, et soli Deo vacant. Tertia fuit communis viris et mulieribus, scilicet ut in pulverem reverterentur. Et ab hac immunis fuit beata virgo, quia cum corpore assumpta est in caelum. Credimus enim quod post mortem resuscitata fuerit, et portata in caelum. Psal. CXXXI, 8: *surge, domine, in requiem tuam; tu, et arca sanctificationis tuae*.»

The denial of a doctrine that can be manifestly and immediately seen to be contained in a defined truth of faith constitutes an act of heresy insofar as it is a denial of an evident or manifest dogma.

If the suspected heretic is a pope, then he simply cannot be judged for holding a suspect opinion if the opinion, i.e. the *matter* has not yet been definitively judged to be heretical — and only a pope can make that final determination of the matter. If the matter can be plainly *seen* to be heretical to the degree that it is known immediately with absolute certitude (such as a verbatim negation of an already defined dogmatic formula), or clearly seen to be heretical through its principles as manifestly evident by strict logical implication, (such as the pre-Nicene denial of the coeternity, uncreatedness and equality of the divine persons in the Trinity), then pertinacity can be established by the simple verification of obstinacy in the suspect's holding of that heretical belief. Thus, Arius was already validly judged a heretic by a regional council before his error was definitively condemned by means of the solemn profession of Nicea, because the full divinity of Christ could already be plainly seen as evidently and necessarily contained in its principles, namely, the primary truths of faith already professed in the Apostles' Creed and all the most primitive credal formulae, so that Arius could be seen to have asserted heresy against what was already known to be an evident dogma even before the solemn profession of Nicea.

Heresy is indeed manifest if it is explicitly asserted against a primary truth or a principal mystery of faith, but the question inevitably arises: Where does one draw the line between what is principal and primary and what is not? And more importantly, *Who* has the authority to draw that line and determine that matter with finality other than the pope? And who would have the jurisdiction to judge with juridical finality and infallible certitude that the pope's pertinacity has resulted in the *ipso jure* loss of office? Since only a pope would have the power to make these judgments, if the pope himself were to fall from office *ipso facto* by his own act of heresy, the Church would be deprived of the foundation of its infallibility without which a definitive judgment of the case could not be reached. The Church, therefore, while it has the authority to judge bishops, has no juridical power to judge that a true pope has actually fallen from the papacy, but it has the infallible power to judge only *doubtful popes* or *pertinacious heretics* — and accordingly, to judge that a heretic is not a true pope because of manifestly evident heresy. If both the fact of the matter of heresy and its pertinacity are not certain and evident, then a judgment of heresy will not be certain, and no judgment against the suspected *doubtful pope* will be possible, unless he persists incorrigibly in *violent suspicion*, which would establish *moral certitude of pertinacity*. Thus, it is only in this limited and qualified sense that it can be stated that a pope can be judged for heresy, because such manifest heresy itself would prove that the man, as a heretic, never was pope and is incapable of holding the papal office. But there can be no judgment against the suspect's claim on the papacy if the matter of heresy is neither defined nor evident, and consequently a judgment on the matter could not be made until a true and certain pope will eventually issue a final definitive judgment on the doctrine itself, as happened after the death of John XXII. In the case of John XXII, the judgment in the form of a solemn dogmatic definition by his successor, Benedict XII, determined with finality that the previous pope's doctrine was heretical, but John escaped condemnation because of the absence of pertinacity, as well as there not having yet been a definitive papal judgment of the question, namely, *whether or not the souls of the departed that had already completed purgation enjoy the beatific vision before the general judgment*, although the matter already pertained to the universal and ordinary magisterium. On that case, Roberto de Mattei relates:

> The error according to which the Beatific Vision of the Divinity would be conceded to souls not after the first judgment, but only after the resurrection of the flesh was an old one, but in the XIII century it had been rebutted by St. Thomas Aquinas, primarily in *De veritate* (q. 8, a. 1) and in the Summa Theologica (I, q. 12, a. 1). When John XXII re-proposed this error, he was openly criticized by many theologians. Among those that intervened in the debate, were Guillaume Durand de Saint Pourcain, Bishop of Meaux (1270-1334), who accused the Pope of re-proposing the Catharist heresies, the English Dominican Thomas Waleys (1318-1349), who, as a result of his public resistance underwent trial and imprisonment, the Franciscan Nicola da Lira (1270 -1349) and Cardinal Jacques Fournier (1280-1342), pontifical theologian and author of the treatise *De statu animarum ante generale iudicium*.
>
> When the Pope tried to impose this erroneous doctrine on the Faculty of Theology in Paris, the King of France, Philip VI of Valois,

prohibited its teaching, and, according to accounts by the Sorbonne's Chancellor, Jean Gerson [even] reached the point of threatening John XXII with the stake if he didn't make a retraction. John XXII's sermons *totum mundum christianum turbaverunt*, so said Thomas of Strasburg, Master of the Hermits of Saint Augustine (in Dykmans, *op. cit.*, p. 10).

On the eve of John XXII's death, he stated that he had expressed himself simply as a private theologian, without any binding to the magisterium he held. Giovanni Villani reports in his Chronicle, the retraction the Pope made on his thesis on December 3rd 1334, the day before his death, at the solicitation of Cardinal Dal Poggetto, his nephew, and some other relatives.

On December 20th 1334, Cardinal Fournier was elected Pope, taking the name of Benedict XII (1335-1342). The new Pontiff wanted to close the issue with a dogmatic definition, the constitution, *Benedictus Deus* of January 29th 1336, where he expresses thus: "*We, with apostolic authority, define the following: According to the general disposition of God, the souls of all the saints [...] already before they take up their bodies again and before the general judgment, have been, are and will be with Christ in heaven [...] and these souls have seen and see the divine essence with an intuitive vision and even face to face, without the mediation of any creature.*" (Denz-H, n. 1000). It was an article of faith referred to again on July 6th 1439, by the Bull, *Laetentur coeli* at the Council of Florence (Denz-H, n. 1305).[17]

What is most noteworthy in this account is the observation that, "When the Pope tried to impose this erroneous doctrine on the Faculty of Theology in Paris, the King of France, Philip VI of Valois, prohibited its teaching, and, according to accounts by the Sorbonne's Chancellor, Jean Gerson, [even] reached the point of threatening John XXII with the stake if he didn't make a retraction." The king understood only too well that a universally held revealed truth of the ordinary magisterium is an article of faith which must be held *de fide*, and that a non-infallible papal teaching that contradicts an evident dogma of the ordinary magisterium is a heresy that must be categorically rejected; and that even a pope who would remain obstinate in such heresy is to be condemned by the Church and be handed over to the secular power for punishment. Accordingly, Bishop Gerson, himself a prominent theologian whose own theology

---

[17] Roberto de Mattei, *A POPE WHO FELL INTO HERESY, A CHURCH THAT RESISTED: John XXII and the Beatific Vision*.

would undoubtedly be supportive of the king's position, saw fit to call attention to it.

That it was already an evident dogma of faith professed by the Roman Church since antiquity is plainly evident in the testimony of the liturgy, which, as Pius XI explained, is the most important organ of the *ordinary magisterium*.[18] Most notably there are many prayers which can be found throughout the Roman Missal, some of which are very ancient, which petition the intercession of the saints. The foundation of the Church's belief in the power of the intercession of the saints has always been the belief that the saints have already entered eternal life in the beatific presence of God and the divine Saviour, with whom they can therefore intercede face to face on behalf of their suppliants. The testimony of this belief is not only found in the ancient liturgy of the Church, but is carved in the very stones of ancient Rome as well. At the early burial site of Sts. Peter and Paul at the *Memoria Apostolorum* at the cemetery *ad Catacumbas*, which today lies under the Church of S. Sebastiano on the via Appia, dating approximately from the mid-third to early fourth century, there are found many graffiti invoking their intercession, such as *"Paule et Petre petite pro Victore"* ("Paul and Peter intercede for Victor."); and "Πέτρε Παίτρε μνημόνευαι | Τιμοκράτην καὶ Εὐ|τυχείαν κινα(?) καὶ | ἐσώρα(?)" ("Peter, Peter, remember Timokrates and Eutychia, and...")[19] Another testimony to the ancient belief that the blessed souls of the faithful departed already enjoyed the *refrigerium* of heaven, i.e. the fruition of eternal life which consists in the beatific vision, is inscribed in the ancient tomb of the Caetenni, excavated under St. Peters Basilica in the last century. On that tomb there was engraved the inscription, "ANIMA DULCIS GORGONIA". Thomas J. Craughwell relates, «Two Christian emblems were incised into the

---

[18] Thomas A. Thompson, *MARIAN STUDIES—LITURGY*, Marian Studies, Vol. 50 [1999], Art. 16 — «"A larger view of the role of liturgy was stated by Pius XI in 1935; in a private audience to Dom B. Capelle, he asserted that the liturgy was the most important organ of the ordinary magisterium of the Church.⁴" [⁴ *Documenta Pontificia ad instaurationem liturgicam spectantia* (1903-1953) (Bibliotheca "Ephemerides liturgicae," 6; Roma: Edizioni liturgiche, 1953), 70 (#25 liturgia, Didascalia Ecclesiae).]»

[19] University of Oxford, *The Cult of the Saints in Late Antiquity*: http://csla.history.ox.ac.uk/record.php?recid=E05087.

marble: two doves bearing olive branches, the symbol of peace, flanked by the phrase, "Sleep in peace." To the left of the inscription is a woman drawing water from a well, an early Christian sign of eternal life.»[20] In *Die Gräber der Apostelfürsten St. Peter und St. Paul in Rom*,[21] Engelbert Kirschbaum mentions that the woman in the image is holding an amphora of water drawn from the well, which symbolized the *refrigerium* that the blessed souls were believed to receive upon entering heaven after their departure from this world. Craughwell adds, "Vatican archaeologists estimated that the Caetenni had erected their family tomb sometime between AD 130 and 170, and that it had been in use for approximately two hundred years." So we have the most ancient testimony that it was indeed and always has been the faith of the Roman Church that the blessed souls of the faithful departed have already gained possession of eternal life — the *refrigerium* which essentially consists in the beatific vision: "Now this is eternal life: That they may know thee, the only true God, and Jesus Christ, whom thou hast sent." (John 17: 3) Nevertheless, since even such an evident dogma as this had not yet been solemnly defined by the extraordinary magisterium, no one was able to point out to John XXII a solemn definition or a solemn anathema against his own belief which would have sufficed to establish pertinacity if he would still refuse to abandon his error. He remained unconvinced by the arguments of the theological faculty of the University of Paris, and even those of Cardinal Jacques Fournier, the papal theologian who became Pope Benedict XII, and who as pope defined against John's error. The *Catholic Encyclopedia* relates:

> In December, 1333, the theologians at Paris, after a consultation on the question, decided in favour of the doctrine that the souls of the blessed departed saw God immediately after death or after their complete purification; at the same time they pointed out that the pope had given no decision on this question but only advanced his personal opinion, and now petitioned the pope to confirm their decision. John appointed a commission at Avignon to study the writings of the Fathers, and to discuss further the disputed question. In a consistory held on 3

---

[20] Thomas J. Craughwell, *St. Peter's Bones — How the Relics of the first Pope Were Lost and Found... and Then Lost and Found Again*, New York, 2013, pp. 4-5.
[21] Scheffler Verlag, Herdecke, 1959.

January, 1334, the pope explicitly declared that he had never meant to teach aught contrary to Holy Scripture or the rule of faith and in fact had not intended to give any decision whatever. Before his death he withdrew his former opinion, and declared his belief that souls separated from their bodies enjoyed in heaven the Beatific Vision.

What this historical episode shows is that a dispute between a true and certain pope who materially errs against faith and even the most eminent theologians who oppose him cannot be resolved by a decision made by anyone other than the pope, because, as St. Alphonsus wrote, «We repeat here that memorable judgment of Cyprian: *For neither from anywhere else have heresies arisen, or have schisms been born, than from there that the Priest of God is not obeyed, and besides one is considered in the Church at the same time priest and judge in the place of Christ. Lib. 1. ep. ad Corn. papam.* Note, *one priest the judge in the place of Christ.*»[22] Even a point that has already been solemnly defined can be misinterpreted in such a manner that it would necessarily require an additional exercise of the supreme magisterium to resolve it — and until then it would be argued back and forth with one side saying that the new interpretation is heretical and the other claiming it is not — and such a dispute could only be judged with finality by that *one priest who is the judge in the place of Christ*. Now, as Ballerini points out,[23] that

---

[22] Alfonso Maria de' Liguori, *Vindiciae pro suprema pontificis potestate adversus Iustinum Febronium*, Torino, 1832, p. 31 — «Repetamus hic memorabilem illam Cypriani sententiam: *Ne que enim aliunde hæreses obortæ sunt, aut nata schismata, quam inde quod sacerdoti Dei non obtemperatur; nec unus in ecclesia ad tempus sacerdos, et ad tempus judex vice Christi cogitatur. Lib. 1. ep. ad Corn. papam.* Nota, *sacerdos unus judex vice Christi.*»

[23] From *Wikipedia*: Pietro Ballerini — "Born 7 September 1698; died 28 March 1769, after completing his studies both at college and the seminary was chosen principal of a classical school in Verona. He attracted the attention of Pope Benedict XIV, who commissioned him to prepare an edition of St. Leo's works in refutation of the defective one published by Quesnel. After almost nine years of labour in which he enjoyed free access to all the libraries of Rome, Pietro brought out his work in three volumes (Rome, 1753-57) reproducing the entire edition of Quesnel together with elaborate refutations and additions (Migne, *Patrologia Latina*, LIV-LVI). The third volume is a profound study of the sources of canon law. He also published two works against Febronius on papal power, *De vi*

one priest is the pope,[24] so therefore, if he is the one whose personal opinion offends against the rule of faith, there will be no other judge in the whole Church who can judge the dispute other than himself, because opinions are definitively and finally judged to be heresies only when they are infallibly condemned by the pope. St. Alphonsus explains, "It is so true; for, if the infallibility in matters of faith are removed from the supreme pontiff, no other means suffices (as we will see below) to convict heretics."[25] Only the pope possesses the power to judge infallibly in matters of faith, and *no other means suffices to convict heretics*.

* * *

If the one at the top who is in reality a false pope, but is widely perceived, even by a majority to be a true pope, will cause a schism in the greater part of the Church by his heresy, then after the defection of the greater part, the smaller portion of what formerly comprised the entire Body before the defection which retains the visible form of the Church will then be accordingly judged and recognized to be the whole Church, in virtue of its visible adherence to the apostolic tradition evident in the integral profession of every article of faith held in previous ages: *ubique, semper et ab omnibus*. Thus, even if a vastly greater portion of the Church would defect from that faith together with their false pope into heresy, it would be evident that it is not the true Catholic Church, because the visible form of the true Catholic

---

ac ratione Primatus Romanorum Pontificum (Verona, 1766), and *De potestate ecclesiastica Summorum Pontificum et Concilorum generalium* (Verona, 1765)."

[24] Pietro Ballerini, *De Vi Ac Ratione Primatus Romanorum Pontificum Et De Ipsorum Infallibilitate Iin Definiendis Controversiis Fidei*, Monasterii Westphalorum 1845, c. 13. §. 3., num. 13, p. 116 — «Hic autem unus sacerdoa aut Episcopus, non quivis particularium ecclesiarum Episcopus esse potest, qui in solum suum particularem gregem jus habeat, sed unus est summus sacerdos Romanus Episcopus, cui tota Ecclesia, ac totius Ecclesiae unitas commissa est.»

[25] Alfonso Maria de' Liguori, *Vindiciae pro suprema pontificis potestate adversus Iustinum Febronium*, Torino, 1832, p. 13 — «Idque nimis verum est; nam, sublata infallibilitate circa res fidei a pontifice romano, nullum suppetit medium (ut infra videbimus) ad hæreticos convincendos.»

and Apostolic Church would be absent from it. The true Church of Christ is that one which professes the faith taught by Christ. *Vera enim Ecclesia est, quae profitetur Christi fidem.*[26] The true faith is found only in that Church where there can be seen *Agreement in doctrine with the ancient Church*[27]; and that agreement must be of an *uninterrupted duration from antiquity.*[28] It does not suffice for a Church to be judged Catholic merely on the criteria of its material visibility and universality, and that with its heretical leader it has materially and temporally succeeded from the apostolic Church that preceded it; because even if it enjoys greater visibility and universality, it visibly lacks the form of the Church if it does not exhibit the recognisable attributes of holiness, apostolicity of doctrine, and unity which are essential marks of recognition plainly visible in the Holy Roman Catholic and Apostolic Church. *For*, as Bellarmine says, *"the true Church is said to be apostolic, according to the testimony of Tertullian (lib. de praescript.) not only because of the succession of bishops from the apostles, but also because of the consanguinity of doctrine, as he says, because plainly it retains the doctrine which the apostles handed down."*[29] If any infallible dogma or moral truth is reformed, abolished, or in any manner changed; or if the essence of the sacraments would be changed, then the ecclesial communities which embrace those changes can be visibly seen to separate from the Catholic Church, because they lack the visible form by which the true Church can be easily recognised, and the reputed "pope" who would presume to institute those heretical reforms would, by the very act of institution, demonstrate with absolute certitude that he is not a valid pope.

Even if he would err obstinately against faith only in his personal opinions, as a manifest heretic, he would demonstrate the evident fact of the nullity of his claim on the papacy. Those who argue that a true pope can fall into heresy as a private person but not as pope, and that

---

[26] S. Robertus Bellarminus, *De Ecclesia Militante*, cap. xv.

[27] S. Robertus Bellarminus, *De Notis Ecclesiæ*, cap. ix. — «Conspiratio in doctrina cum Ecclesia antiqua.»

[28] *Ibid.* cap. vi. — «Duratio diuturna, nec unquam interrupta.»

[29] *De Notis Ecclesiæ*, cap. ix. — «Vera enim Ecclesia dicitur apostolica, teste Tertull. lib. de praescript. non solum propter successionem episcoporum ab apostolis, sed etiam propter doctrinae consanguinitatem, ut ipse loquitur, quia videlicet doctrinam retinet, quam apostoli tradiderunt.»

he, while still pope, can be judged by a council, destroy their own argument; because as pope he cannot err in his judgment, and it is reserved to his authority to pronounce that infallible judgment with finality.[30] If a validly reigning pontiff could be judged by a council for heresy, the divinely instituted supreme authority of the ecclesiastical monarchy would be subverted and destroyed by being made ultimately subject to the aristocratic authority of the bishops assembled in a council — an aristocratic authority which would be the worst possible for the Church, as St. Robert Bellarmine explains: *"Democracy is the absolutely worst governance: nevertheless aristocracy is seen to be more pernicious for the Church. Indeed the supreme evil for the Church is heresy: heresy is stirred up by higher-ups rather than by common men. Certainly nearly all the heresiarchs, were either bishops or priests; accordingly some heresies are as factions of the leaders, without which there would not be rebellions of peoples in the Church. But factions never arise more easily and more frequently than when the higher-ups rule, as can be established not only by experience and by the testimony of the philosophers, but even by the admission of Calvin himself in lib. 4. Institut. cap. 20. §. 8."*[31]

As pope, a true and certain pope's judgment cannot fail. The council's judgment can fail, even if the agreement of the bishops is unanimous, but it cannot prevail in a truly ecumenical council, as Bellarmine explains: *"For even if the greater part should resist the better; as*

---

[30] Concilium Lugdunense II — «*si quæ de fide subortæ fuerint quæstiones, suo debent judicio definiri*»; *Summa Theol.* II^a II^æ q. 1 a. 10 — «*Ad illius ergo auctoritatem pertinet editio symboli, ad cuius auctoritatem pertinet finaliter determinare ea, quae sunt fidei, ut ab omnibus inconcussa fide teneantur. Hoc autem pertinet ad auctoritatem summi Pontificis, ad quem maiores et difficiliores Ecclesiae quaestiones referuntur, ut dicitur in Decretalibus extra, de Baptismo, cap. majores.*»

[31] S. Robertus Bellarminus, *De Romano Pontifice*, lib. i. cap. viii — «Quarto, tametsi Dimocratia est absolute pessimum regimen: tamen Ecclesiæ perniciosior esse videtur Aristocratia. Siquidem summum Ecclesiæ malum hæresis est: hæreses autem ab Optimatibus potius, quam a plebeis hominibus excitantur. Certe Hæresiarchæ fere omnes, aut Episcopi, aut Presbyteri fuerunt; itaque sunt hæreses quædam quasi Optimatium factiones, sine quibus nullæ essent in Ecclesia populorum seditiones. Factiones autem nunquam facilius, & frequentius oriuntur, quam cum Optimates regunt, ut non solum experimento, & Philosophorum testimonio, sed etiam Calvini ipsius confessione lib. 4. Institut. cap. 20. §. 8. comprobari potest.»

happened at the Ariminese and second Ephesian councils, nevertheless it never prevails; for later the acts of such councils are nullified by him to whom it befits from his office to confirm the brethren, in such a manner as we see took place in the aforementioned Ariminese and Ephesian II councils."[82] *"You will say: All questions will be brought to an end by a general Council: all will acquiesce to the majority of bishops. But even in a general Council the majority can err, if there lacks the authority of the supreme Pastor, as is proven by the experience of the Ariminese and Second Ephesian Councils."*[83] In matters of faith, the judgment of an imperfect council is binding neither on the pope nor the rest of the Church, since, as Bellarmine explains: "For it is necessary, that all the faithful hold the same in matters of faith: *There is one God, one Faith, one Baptism.* Ephes. 4. **But there cannot be one Faith in the Church, if there is not one supreme Judge, to whom all are bound to acquiesce.**"[34] All have the right to appeal to the pope against the sentence of bishops or any other tribunal. According to those who heretically hold that a certainly valid pope can be judged for heresy by his subordinates, it is only the pope himself who is denied this right of appeal to an infallible papal judgment, without which the **final determination of the Church's judgment** cannot be reached (St. Thomas, *Summa Theologiae* I^a II^{ae} q. 1 a. 10), as St. Thomas explains: «*To publish a new edition of the symbol belongs to* **that authority which is empowered to decide matters of faith finally**, *so that they may be held by all with unshaken faith. Now this belongs to the authority of the Sovereign Pontiff,* "*to whom the more important and more difficult questions*

---

[32] S. Robertus Belarminus, *De Conciliorum Auctoritate,* cap. ix — «Nam etiamsi major pars resislat meliori; ut factum est in concilio ariminensi et ephesino II. tamen nunquam vincit; mox enim irritantur ejusmodi conciliorum acta ab eo, cui convenit ex officio fratres confirmare, quemadmodum in praedictis conciliis ariminensi et ephesino, II. factum videmus.»

[33] Bellarminus, *De Romano Pontifice,* lib. i. cap. ix. — «Dices: terminabuntur quaetiones a Concilio generali: omnes enim majori parti Episcoporum acquiescent. At etiam in Concilio generali major pars potest errare, si auctoritas desit summi Pastoris, ut experimento comprobatum est Ariminensis & Ephesini 2. Concilii.»

[34] *De Romano Pontifice lib. i. cap. ix* — «Necesse est enim, ut omnes Fideles idem omnino sentiant in rebus Fidei: *Est enim unus Deus, una Fides, unum Baptifma,* Ephes. 4. at una Fides in Ecclesia esse non potest, si non sit unus summus Judex, cui omnes acquiescere teneantur.»

that arise in the Church are referred," as stated in the Decretals *[*Dist. xvii, Can. 5]*. Hence our Lord said to Peter whom he made Sovereign Pontiff (Lk. 22:32): "I have prayed for thee," Peter, "that thy faith fail not, and thou, being once converted, confirm thy brethren." The reason of this is that **there should be but one faith of the whole Church**, according to 1 Cor. 1:10: "That you all speak the same thing, and that there be no schisms among you": **and this could not be secured unless any question of faith that may arise be decided by him who presides over the whole Church**, so that the whole Church may hold firmly to his decision. Consequently **it belongs to the sole authority of the Sovereign Pontiff** to publish a new edition of the symbol, **as do all other matters which concern the whole Church**, such as to convoke a general council and so forth.»

* * *

There are two extreme positions on the question of papal deposition which still manage to acquire adherents even in our time. The first is the belief that if a pope would become a manifest formal heretic, he would remain in office, and could not be deposed in any manner whatever. This opinion is entirely discredited and is followed by no theologians of repute since the Dominican, Fr. Marie Dominique Bouix in the nineteenth century. This opinion contains within itself the implicit heresy of asserting that a manifest heretic, remaining as the head of the Church would therefore still be a member of the Church. This error is founded on the failure to distinguish between a *certain pope* and a *doubtful pope,* believing that whoever is reputed by the vast majority in some general but not necessarily unequivocal or exclusive manner to be the pope, is therefore to be regarded as certainly in possession of the rights of the primacy, and therefore cannot be judged or deposed. **The second is the heretical belief that a true and valid pope who falls into formal heresy would continue in his office and remain in possession of the Petrine *munus* until he is *judged by the Church* to be a heretic**; and only then he would either fall from office, or would have to be deposed by the authority of the Church. It is properly a heresy because it was solemnly defined at Vatican I that there exists only one *total fullness of supreme power* (totam plenitudinem huius supremae potestatis), which is *universal* — over the entire world, which consists in the Roman Pontiff's **universal primacy of jurisdiction** over the entire *oecumene* (οἰκουμένη = the entire inhabited world); for which reason, there exists only one **supreme ecumenical authority** over the Church which subsists entirely in the *"full and absolute jurisdiction"* (Pius XII, *Vacantis Apostolicæ Sedis*) of the pope — which therefore in strict logic categorically excludes the possibility of any ecumenical power existing in the episcopal authority, even of the entire body of bishops gathered together in a council in opposition to the pope. Hence, the mere notion of an "imperfect ecumenical council" exercising an ecumenical authority in opposition to the **supreme and absolute ecumenical authority of the pope** is *per se* contradictory and **heretical**. On this point, Bishop Schneider rightly observes, "The eventual condemnation of a pope in the case of heresy by a so-called imperfect Council of bishops corresponds to the thesis of mitigated Conciliarism." This heresy is founded on the failure to distinguish between a *certain heretic* and a *suspected heretic*. If the *indicia*,[35] which are the words and deeds constituting probative evidence of crime, establish indisputably certain guilt, proving that a man reputed to be pope is a *public heretic*, then there is no need for a juridical process to determine whether or not there exists a presumption of nullity of his claim on the papacy, and prove what the *indicia* already prove beyond all shadow of doubt. In the presence of such indisputable proof, there would also be absolutely no need for canonical warnings,[36] because canonical warnings are proper only to a superior,

---

[35] P. Francesco Bordoni, *Sacrum Tribunal Iudicum In Causis Sanctæ Fidei Contra Hæreticos Et Hæresi Suspectos*, Romæ, 1648, cap. x. p. 223 — «Indicium est signum probativum inducens iudicem in cognitionem delicti… [idest] ex verbis, vel factis.»

[36] P. Francesco Bordoni, *Manuale Consultorum In Causis S. Officii contra Hæreticum pravitatem refertum quamplurimis dubiis novis, & veteribus resolutis*, Parmæ, 1693, p. 35 — «Quaeritur 6. An ad Pertinaciam requiratur praevia monitio… & nihilominus in sua Opinione persistens incipiat tunc esse pertinax, & formalis Haereticus? R. Nullam require monitionem, sed esse Haereticum formaliter hoc ipso, quod aserit aliquo pro vero, quod scit esse contra Fidem, in hoc enim formaliter consistit Pertinacia, quae non datur sine Scientia illius obiecti, contra quod est ipsa Pertinacia, quae includit Scientiam, ergo frustra praemonetur, qui scit se scire illud, cui adversatur; monitio enim fit ignorantibus, non scientibus.»

and are administered by a superior at the initial phase of a penal process.[37] Warnings are necessary at the beginning of a penal process when there is at least a mild suspicion, in order to sufficiently establish a *presumption of guilt*; and if the suspect remains obstinate after unheeded warnings, *pertinacity* is thereby proven. Since certain *indicia* of formal heresy constitute *per se* **certain and plainly obvious proof** beyond all shadow of doubt that the individual in question is indeed guilty of the crime of heresy, there is in the presence of such existing proof absolutely no need to prove by means of warnings what is already proven, nor even less, to establish a presumption of guilt when manifestly evident proof of guilt already exists. Thus, if a man is not merely a suspect, but the certain *indicia* of heresy prove absolutely that he is a formal heretic, by the fact alone of those *certain indicia*, it is absolutely proven beyond all shadow of doubt that he is indeed a heretic and not a true pope. Correction and admonitions are generally necessary, but the necessity is a *relative necessity* which is not absolute. It is for this reason De Lugo[38] in *disp. XX, sect. IV, n. 157-158*, explained, "For if it could be established, [...] given that the doctrine is well known, given the kind of person involved and given the other circumstances, that the accused could not have been unaware that his thesis was opposed to the Church, he would be

---

[37] In the 1907 edition of the *Catholic Encyclopedia*, it is explained that **Canonical Admonitions** are «"A preliminary means used by the Church towards a suspected person, as a preventive of harm or a remedy of evil" (Burtsell).» The article quotes an Instruction of Pope Leo XIII which states that, "Among the preservative measures are chiefly to be reckoned the spiritual retreat, admonitions, and injunctions." This Instruction specifies further that, "the canonical admonitions may be made in a paternal and private manner (even by letter or by an intermediary person), or in legal form, but always in such a way that proof of their having been made shall remain on record." And then then it is explained that these admonitions are to be issued, "after an investigation to be made by one having due authority, with the result of establishing a reasonable basis for the suspicion."

[38] Juan de Lugo y de Quiroga (1583 - 1660) was an eminent Spanish Jesuit theologian and canonist. *Wikipedia* says of him, «In moral theology he put an end, as Ballerini remarks, to several disputed questions. St. Alphonsus de Liguori did not hesitate to rank him immediately after the Doctor of the Church St. Thomas Aquinas, "post S. Thomam facile princeps", and pope Benedict XIV called him "a light of the Church".»

considered as a heretic from this fact". If an explicitly revealed and defined dogma is universally known by all, even the most ignorant, whether it be solemnly defined or known by all to be defined by the ordinary and universal magisterium, and it is directly and immediately denied, then the heresy would be manifestly evident on its face. It is only when there exists a reasonable and founded *doubt* based on *indicia* which establish *suspicion of heresy* that an *inquest* would be required to determine whether or not the *indicia* establish a **presumption of nullity** of the suspect's claim on the pontificate and a **presumption of vacancy** of the Apostolic See, and then, proper canonical admonitions can be administered to ascertain whether or not there is pertinacity. Such would be the case when an *article of faith*, such as the dogma of the universality of the Church is *implicitly or practically denied*, as happened in the case of Antipope Benedict XIII (Pedro de Luna), who adamantly asserted before the representatives of the Council of Constance that the Church existed only in Paniscola, an assertion which strictly implies a defection of the Church from her universality; for which reason the council administered corrective warnings to him to verify his pertinacity before declaring that **he had already separated himself from the Church and lost all office and ecclesiastical dignity previous to the issuance of the declaration**, as the declaration of the council itself stated, and as Ballerini and Gregory XVI explained in the passages I cited in Volume One. As I pointed out in Volume One, Jorge Bergoglio's deliberate, conscious and blatant rejection of the most basic dogmas of the Catholic faith have been asserted so explicitly and repeatedly that there is absolutely no doubt about his pertinacity. His disbelief is pertaining more to the species of apostasy rather than heresy, because he has on numerous occasions manifested that his faith is not in God, but in some other sort of "god" — in a Teilhardian demiurge — a world-soul that is more akin to the Hegelian *Absolut* than to the God and Father of Our Lord Jesus Christ, who together with the Son are infinitely, eternally, and perfectly One in the supremely simple *actus purus* of unity in the Holy Ghost.

If on the basis of sufficient *indicia* there exists already according to juridical standards a strong presumption of nullity, only then could the claimant, after a first correction, be issued not just a corrective warning, but proper a *canonical admonition*, which would be necessary to verify with absolute certitude the already morally certain fact of **pertinacity**. If the *indicia* suffice only to establish a *light suspicion*, then he would still enjoy the presumption of innocence, and therefore a presumption of a valid claim on the papacy, and would accordingly need to be administered correction, but not *canonical admonitions*. The reason for this is that unlike *vehement* or *violent* suspicion, *"Light* suspicion admits of no conclusion, because it is based on absolutely insufficient *indicia.*"[39]

The first extreme position is the opinion which seems to be supported by Bishop Athanasius Schneider, and the second is the heresy of John Salza and Robert Siscoe. Bishop Schneider begins his article, On the Question of the True Pope,[40] with the words, "The hypothesis of the possibility of a heretical pope derives from the Decree of Gratian (dist. XL, cap. 6, col. 146) from the twelfth century," but then forgetting that all of the main exponents of "the opinion of the automatic loss of the papacy for heresy," such as St. Robert Bellarmine, St. Alphonsus de' Liguori, Don Pietro Ballerini, Pope Gregory XVI all considered it, to use Ballerini's words, to be no more than a "mere hypothesis,"[41] and that they also professed their belief in the impossibility that a true pope could ever become a heretic, Bishop Schneider then asserts entirely without foundation: "such an opinion contains a contradiction and reveals a hint of crypto-conciliarism." As will become evident, there is neither a contradiction nor any hint of crypto-conciliarism in the opinion, as I will amply prove in this volume. Bishop Schneider then goes on to suggest that "the Magisterium of the Church, since Popes Pius X and Benedict XV, has seemed to reject such an opinion, as the formulation of the spurious decree of Gratian was eliminated in the *Code of Canon Law 1917.*" In fact, the canon was not "eliminated" from

---

[39] The Rev. P, Chas. Augustine, O.S.B., D.D., *A COMMENTAY ON THE NEW CODE OF CANON LAW.*, Vol. VIII, St. Louis and London, 1922, pp. 284.

[40] *LATIN MASS*, Vol 29, No.2 — Summer 2020.

[41] Pietro Ballerini, *De Potestate Ecclesiastica. Summor. Pont. Et Conc. Gen.* Cap. IX § II. Augsburg, 1770, pp. 129 — «Quid igitur in mera hypothesi laboremus pluribus.»

ecclesiastical law, because it never had any force of law to begin with.⁴²
There was never any statute or decree of canon law applicable to a
case of papal heresy, because the Church does not legislate for merely
hypothetical eventualities, and the possibility of a true pope falling
into heresy is indeed that — just a mere hypothesis, as will be
explained. On these points, Bishop Schneider's observations only
serve to underscore the observation made by St. Thomas in one of
his commentaries, where he says that a brighter light from farther
away penetrates more deeply than a dimmer light. I think that after
reading this volume, all will agree that on this point of doctrine, such
Doctors of the Church as St. Robert Bellarmine and St. Alphonsus
de' Liguori are brighter lights than Bishop Schneider. Bishop
Schneider's mistake is rooted in an imprecise and restrictive usage of
the word "pope" which fails to critically distinguish adequately
between a true and certain pope on the one hand, and a "doubtful
pope" (papa dubius) on the other. The former must always be
regarded, as a dogmatic fact, to be the holder of the primacy; while
the latter's claim, according to all the theologians, falls under the
jurisdiction of the Church: *Papa dubius, papa nullus.* The opinion that
Bishop Schneider characterizes as form of "crypto-Conciliarism" is
in fact, not only supported by Innocent III, but it can be seen after
careful examination to be the doctrinal position of that same pontiff,⁴³
which was subsequently developed theologically and elaborated
according to its variations in the following centuries by some of the

---

⁴² «It was about 1150 that the Camaldolese monk, Gratian, professor of theology at the University of Bologna, to obviate the difficulties which beset the study of practical, external theology (theologia practica externa), i.e. canon law, composed the work entitled by himself "Concordia discordantium canonum", but called by others "Nova collectio", "Decreta", "Corpus juris canonici", also "Decretum Gratiani", the latter being now the commonly accepted name. In spite of its great reputation the "Decretum" has never been recognized by the Church as an official collection.» — *Catholic Encyclopedia*

⁴³ Cf. Ballerini, *De Pot. Ecc.* p. 127 footnote 1: (1) — «Favet huic sententiæ Innocentius III. sermone tertio habito die suæ conscerationis scribens; *In tantum fides mihi necessaria est, ut, cum in cæteris peccatis Deum judicem habeam, propter peccatum, quod in fide committitur, possim ab Ecclesia judicari.* Vide Sylvium in 2. 2. S. Thomæ tom. 3. q. 39. art. 3. conclus. 2.»

most eminent theologians and doctors — St. Robert Bellarmine, St Alphonsus de Liguori, St. Francis de Sales[44], Pietro Ballerini, Pope Gregory XVI, just to mention a few. According to these Doctors, a heretic pope, 1) "ceases by himself to be Pope and head, in the same way as he ceases to be a Christian and a member of the body of the Church; and for this reason he can be judged and punished by the Church" [Bellarmine][45], 2) that "by his public pertinacity... he

---

[44] I have quoted the relevant texts of the named authors in Volume One, with the exception of St. Francis de Sales, who wrote: "Under the ancient law the High Priest did not wear the Rational except when he was vested in the pontifical robes and was entering before the Lord. Thus we do not say that the Pope cannot err in his private opinions, as did John XXII; or be altogether a heretic, as perhaps Honorius was. Now when he is explicitly a heretic, he falls ipso facto from his dignity out of the Church, and the Church must either deprive him, as some say, or declare him deprived, of his Apostolic See, and must say as St. Peter did: Let another take his bishopric (Acts I). When he errs in his private opinion he must be instructed, advised, convinced; as happened with John XXII, who was so far from dying obstinate or from determining anything during his life concerning his opinion, that he died whilst he was making the examination which is necessary for determining in a matter of faith, as his successor declared in the *Extravagantes* which begins Benedictus Deus." [St. Francis de Sales, *The Catholic Controversy*, Part II, art. VI, Ch. 14 (Tan Books), p. 388] "En l'ancienne loy le grand pretre ne portait pas le rational si non quand il estoit revestu des habits pontificaux et qu'il entroit devant le Seigneur. Ainsi ne disons nous pas que le pape en ses opinions particulieres ne puisse errer comme fit Jean XXII, ou etre du tout heretique comme peut etre fut Honorius. Or quand il est heretique expres 'ipso facto' il tombe de son grade hors de l'Eglise et l'Eglise le doit ou priver comme disent quelques uns, ou le declarer prive de son siege apostolique et dire comme fit St. Pierre: Episcopatum eius accipiat alter. Quand il erre en sa particuliere opinion il le faut enseigner, adviser, convaincre comme on fit a Jean XXII le quel tant s'en faut qu'il mourut opiniatre ou que pendant sa vie il determina aucune chose touchant son opinion, que pendant qu'il faysoit l'inquisition requise pour determiner en matiere de foy, il mourut, au recit de son successeur en l'Extravagante qui se commence 'Benedictus Deus.'"

[45] *De Romano Pontifice*, lib. II cap. xxx — «papam haereticum manifestum per se desinere esse papam et caput, sicut per se desinit esse christianus et membrum corporis Ecclesiae; quare ab, Ecclesia posse eum judicari et puniri.»

declares himself to be a heretic, i.e. to have withdrawn from the Catholic faith and the Church by his own will, so that no declaration or sentence from anyone would be necessary,"[46] "that he by his own will departed", and is "severed from the body of the Church, and has in some manner abdicated the Pontificate"[47] — i.e. that he "*ipso facto* by his own will *abdicated* the primacy and the pontificate",[48] [Ballerini]; 3) "For the rest, if God should permit that a Pope should become a notorious and contumacious heretic, he would cease to be Pope, and the pontificate would be vacant" [St. Alphonsus de Liguori][49]; 4) "Whence he could be considered, as Ballerini observes, as a public schismatic and heretic, and in consequence, and to have fallen by himself from the pontificate, if he had been validly elevated to it"[50], and therefore, "the deposition is not a prescription against... the current representation of the Church in the Pope recognized as such, but only against the person, who was before adorned with papal

---

[46] Pietro Ballerini, *DE POTESTATE ECCLESIASTICA SUMMORUM PONTIFICUM ET CONCILIORUM GENERALIUM*. Verona, 1768, Caput IX. §. II. p. 128 — «hac sua publica pertinacia... semetipsum palam declarat haereticum, hoc est a fide catholica, & ab Ecclesia voluntate propria recessisse, ita ut ad eum praecidendum a corpore Eccleaiae nulla cujusquam declaratio aut sententia necessaria sit.»

[47] *Ibid.* — «ne aliis perniciem afferret, in publicum proferenda esset ejus hæresis, & contumacia, ut omnes similiter ab eo caverent, sicque sententia, quam in se ipsum tulit, toti Ecclesiæ proposita, **eum sua voluntate recessisse, & ab Ecclesiæ corpore declararet avulsum, atque abdicasse quodammodo Pontificatum**»

[48] *Ibid.* p. 138 — «ipso facto sua voluntate primatu & pontificatu exauctoratus.»

[49] *Verità Della Fede*, Opera Del Beato Alfonso Maria de' Liguori, Tomo Secondo, Monza, 1823, Parte Terza - Contro i Settarj, Capo. VIII, n. 10. p. 157 — «Del resto, si Dio permettesse che un papa fosse notoriamente eretico e contumace, egli cesserebbe d'essere papa, e vacherebbe il pontificato.»

[50] D. Mauro Cappellari ora Gregorio XVI, *Il trionfo della santa sede e della chiesa contro gli assalti dei novatori*, Venezia, 1832, PRELIMINARE § LIV. p. 46-47: «Ond ' è che poteasi, come osserva il Ballerini, considerarlo quale pubblico scismatico e eretico, ed in conseguenza per se decaduto dal pontificato, se anche ad esso fosse stato validamente innalzato.»

dignity."⁵¹ [Gregory XVI]). The passage in its context reads as follows: "Even so that it could be for a moment, that the Church has the authority to depose the Pontiffs: what then?... In fact, by ceasing in this hypothesis the deposed Pope to be a true Pope, the deposition is not a prescription against the rights of the Primacy, and therefore against the current representation of the Church in the Pope recognized as such, but only against the person, who was before adorned with papal dignity..."⁵² Gregory XVI, in the passage just cited, explicitly cites Ballerini's doctrine as the basis for his own position on this question; and Ballerini's teaching is most clearly stated in the following passage:

> «For any person, even a private person, the words of Saint Paul to Titus hold: *"A man that is a heretic, after the first and second admonition avoid: knowing that he that is such a one, is subverted, and sinneth, being condemned by his own judgment."* (Tit. 3, 10-11). He undoubtedly, who having been once or twice corrected, does not repent, but remains obstinate in a belief contrary to a manifest or defined dogma; by this his public pertinacity which for no reason can be excused, since pertinacity properly pertains to heresy, **he declares himself to be a heretic, i.e. to have withdrawn from the Catholic faith and the Church by his own will, so that no declaration or sentence from anyone would be necessary**. Conspicuous in this matter is the explanation of St. Jerome on the commended words of Paul. *Therefore, by himself [the heretic] is said to be condemned, because the fornicator, adulterer, murderer, and those guilty of other misdeeds are driven out from the Church by the Priests: but heretics deliver the sentence upon themselves, departing from the Church by their own will: this departure is seen to be the condemnation by their own conscience.* Therefore a Pontiff, who after such a solemn and public admonition from the Cardinals, Roman Clergy, or even a synod would maintain himself hardened in heresy, and have openly departed from the Church, according to the precept of Paul he

---

⁵¹ *Ibid.* Capo XXIII. p. 270 — «non è la deposizione una prescrizione... contro l'attuale rappresentanza della Chiesa nel Papa per tale riconosciuto, ma soltanto contro la persona, che era prima ornata di papal dignità.»

⁵² *Ibid.* pp. 269-270: «Tuttavolta sia pure così per un momento, ed abbia pure la Chiesa l'autorità di deporre i Pontefici: che perciò?... Infatti, cessando in questa ipotesi il Papa deposto di essere vero Papa, non è la deposizione una prescrizione contro i diritti del Primato, e quindi contro l'attuale rappresentanza della Chiesa nel Papa per tale riconosciuto, ma soltanto contro la persona, che era prima ornata di papal dignità...»

would have to be avoided; and lest he bring ruin to the rest, his heresy and contumacy would have to be publicly pronounced, so that likewise all could keep clear of him, and thus the sentence which he brought upon himself, made known to the whole Church, that he by his own will departed, would declare him to have separated from the body of the Church, and **in some manner to have abdicated the Pontificate**, which no one holds or can hold, who is not in the Church.» [53]

Ballerini elaborates further on this point:

The present question can only refer to that case in which the Pope, deceived by private judgment would believe, and pertinaciously contend something contrary to any defined or evident article of faith, which is properly heresy. In this case (which, granted that it be from a definition of faith and is most foreign to our thesis, however by the protection of God I trust will never happen) not a few even of the defenders of pontifical authority (1) assert the right of a general council over a Pope deviating from the faith, but whom they propound to be a heretic;

---

[53] Ballerini, *De Pot. Ecc.* Caput IX. §. II. pp. 128-129: «*Quemcumque vel privatum respiciunt illa Pauli ad Titum: Haereticum Hominem post unam et alteram correptionem devita, sciens quia subversus est, qui ejusmodi est, et delinquit, cum sit proprio judicio condemnatus.* Qui nimirum semel & bis correctus non resipiscit, sed pertinax est in sententia dogmati manifesto aut definito contraria; hac sua publica pertinacia, cum ab haeresi proprie dicta, quae pertinaciam requirit, excusari nulla ratione potest; tum vero semetipsum palam declarat haereticum, hoc est a fide catholica, & ab Ecclesia voluntate propria recessisse, ita ut ad eum praecidendum a corpore Eccleaiae nulla cujusquam declaratio aut sententia necessaria sit. Perspicua hac in re est S. Hieronimi ratio in laudata Pauli verba, *Propterea a semetipso dicitur esse damnatus, quia fornicator, adulter, homicida, et cetera vitia per sacerdotes ex Ecclesia propelluntur: haeretici autem in semetipsis sententiam ferunt, suo arbitrio de Ecclesia recedentes: quae recessio propriae conscientiae videtur esse damnatio.* Pontifex ergo, qui post solemnem & publicam Cardinalium, Romani Cleri, vel etiam synodi monitionem se se obfirmatum praeferret in haeresi, & de Ecclesia palam recessisset, iuxta praeceptum Pauli esset vitandus; & ne aliis perniciem afferret, in publicum proferenda esset ejus haeresis, & contumacia, ut omnes similiter ab eo caverent, sicque sententia, quam in se ipsum tulit, toti Ecclesiae proposita, cum sua voluntate recessisse, & ab Ecclesiae corpore declararet avulsum, atque abdicasse quodammodo Pontificatum, quo nemo fruitur, nec frui potest, qui non sit in Ecclesia.»

because they believe such a Pontiff by the heresy itself to be severed and cut off from the foundation of the Church which is faith, and consequently from the Church itself, and to have utterly fallen from the Pontificate, and in this hypothesis it will be the right of the general council over him, who is no longer the Pontiff, nor does he possess the primacy.[54]

Ballerini also made the very important observation that there is no intrinsic reason which would necessitate that it always be a council to resolve the issue of a heretical pope. If the Church of Rome could settle the matter adequately by setting the intruder aside, then there would be no need to prolong the dire crisis by waiting for the opportune time to convene an ecumenical council — which could even take many years with catastrophic results caused by the undue delay. On this point he wrote:

> But why is it to be believed, that the remedy is to be expected from the not so easily done convocation of a general synod, when a most present and gravest of all dangers for the faith, which, impending from a Pontiff espousing heresy even in his private judgment, would not be able to be endured through lengthy delays? In such a crisis for the faith, cannot even inferiors warn their superior by fraternal correction, resist him to the face, and subdue; and, if need be, refute and drive him to the recovery of his good sense? The Cardinals, who are there to advise him, will be able to do it; the Roman Clergy will be able to; even a Roman

---

[54] Ballerini, *Ibid.* pp. 127-128: «Ad eum itaque casum tantummodo præsens quæstio referri potest, quo Papa privato judicio deceptus crederet, & pertinaciter propugnaret aliquid contrarium cuipiam articulo fidei evidenti, aut definito, quod haeresis proprium est. Hoc autem in casu (quem, licet a definitione fidei & a nostro proposito alienissimum, Dei tamen praesidio numquam eventuram confido) non pauci etiam ex ipsis Pontificiae auctoritatis vindicibus (1) jus generalis concilii in Papam a fide devium, seu haereticum asserunt; quia credunt talem Pontificem ex ipsa haeresi ab Ecclesiae fundamento, quod est fides, & consequenter ab ipsa Ecclesia sejunctum atque praecisum, a Pontificatu penitus decidisse, hacque in hypothesi jus generalis concilii fore in eum, qui Pontifex amplius non est, nec primatu fruitur.»

synod, if it is judged to be expedient, having been convened, will be able to.[55]

By the late 19th Century, Fr. Sydney Smith SJ (in 1895) testified to the fact that Ballerini's opinion, that a manifestly heretical pope would cease automatically to be pope, and that only a declaratory sentence on the one who was no longer pope would need to be pronounced, had already become the *common opinion* of theologians: "[I]t has been generally held that, given the possibility of a personally heretical Pope, he would *ipso facto* cease to be Pope by ceasing to be a member of the Church. The Church in that case, as represented by the Cardinals or otherwise, could on due information of the fact pass a declaratory sentence on one who being no longer Pope was no longer its superior, and then take measures to remove him from the see in which he had become an intruder."[56] Franz Xavier Wernz S.J., reputed by some to be the most illustrious canonist of the 20th Century, in his *Jus Canonicum*, revised by Pedro Vidal S.J., taught: «453. By heresy which is notorious and openly made known. The Roman Pontiff should he fall into it is by that very fact even before any declaratory sentence of the Church deprived of his power of jurisdiction. (*Per haeresim notoriam et palam divulgatam R. Pontifex si in illam incidat, ipso facto etiam ante omnem sententiam declaratoriam Ecclesiae sua potestate iurisdictionis privatus existit*)»[57] He goes on to explain, «Concerning this matter there are five Opinions...» and he elaborates: «The fourth opinion, with Suarez, Cajetan and others, contends that a Pope is not automatically deposed even for manifest heresy, but that he can and must be deposed by at

---

[55] *Ibid.* p. 128 — «Cur vero in præsentissimo omniumque gravissimo periculo fidei, quod ex Pontifice hæresim privato licet judicio propugnante impendens, diuturniores moras non pateretur, remedium ex generalis synodi non ita facili convocatione expectandum credatur? Nonne etiam inferiores quicumque in tanto fidei discrimine superiorem suum correctione fraterna commonere queunt, in faciem eidem resistere, atque revincere; &, si opus sit, redarguere ac ad resipiscentiam urgere? Poterunt id Cardinales, qui ipsi a consiliis adstant; poterit Romanus Clerus; Romana etiam synodus, si expedire judicetur, congregata poterit.»

[56] Sydney F. Smith S.J. Catholic Truth Society, London, 1896, *Dr. Littledale's Theory of the Disappearance of the Papacy*.

[57] Wernz-Vidal, *Jus Canonicum* (1938) Chapter VII.

least a declaratory sentence of the crime. 'Which opinion in my judgment is indefensible', as Bellarmine teaches.» And then, «Finally, there is the fifth opinion — that of Bellarmine himself — which was expressed initially and is rightly defended by Tanner and others as the best proven and the most common. For he who is no longer a member of the body of the Church, i.e. the Church as a visible society, cannot be the head of the Universal Church. But a Pope who fell into public heresy would cease by that very fact to be a member of the Church. Therefore he would also cease by that very fact to be the head of the Church.» Note especially the words, *"But a Pope who fell into public heresy would cease by that very fact to be a member of the Church. Therefore he would also cease by that very fact to be the head of the Church."* Dr. Edward Peters J.C.D., in *A Canon Lawyer's Blog*[58] attests to the fact that the opinion that a heretic pope would remain in office until even a merely declaratory sentence would result in his loss of office has been entirely abandoned where he says, «I know of no author coming after Wernz who disputes this analysis [of Wernz and Vidal]. See, e.g., Ayrinhac, CONSTITUTION (1930) 33; Sipos, ENCHIRIDION (1954) 156; Regatillo, INSTITUTIONES I (1961) 299; Palazzini, DMC III (1966) 573; and Wrenn[59] (2001) above. As for the lack of detailed canonical examination of the *mechanics* for assessing possible papal heresy, Cocchi, COMMENTARIUM II/2 (1931) n. 155, ascribes it to the fact that law provides for common cases and adapts for rarer; may I say again, heretical popes are about as rare as rare can be and yet still be. In sum, and while additional important points could be offered on this matter, ***in the view of modern canonists from Wernz to Wrenn***, however remote is the possibility of a pope actually

---

[58] https://canonlawblog.wordpress.com/2016/12/16/a-canonical-primer-on-popes-and-heresy/.

[59] «Wrenn, writing in the CLSA NEW COMM (2001) at 1618 states: "Canon 1404 is not a statement of personal impeccability or inerrancy of the Holy Father. Should, indeed, the pope fall into heresy, it is understood that he would lose his office. To fall from Peter's faith is to fall from his chair."» An earlier edition of that same commentary says, "Communion becomes a real issue when it is threatened or even lost. This occurs especially through heresy, apostasy and schism. Classical canonists discussed the question whether a pope, in his private or personal opinions, could go into heresy, apostasy or schism."

falling into heresy and however difficult it might be to determine whether a pope has so fallen, **such a catastrophe, Deus vetet, would result in the loss of papal office.**» Note the words, "*I know of no author coming after Wernz who disputes this analysis,*" and, "*in the view of modern canonists from Wernz to Wrenn… such a catastrophe, Deus vetet, would result in the loss of papal office.*"

Interestingly (if I may briefly digress), Salza & Siscoe have completely inverted the truth in this matter and say that the opposite is true: "But notwithstanding the different opinions regarding precisely when and how a Pope falls from office, the *unanimous* opinion is that the Pope loses the pontificate *after* the Church (a general council) establishes the crime of heresy (and probably after the Council issues the declarative sentence)."[60] And they go on to say that "The rejection of the unanimous opinion is clearly not the fruit of sound, scholarly research of the question, but rather a rash and superficial judgment based, in many cases, on snippets read on the internet".[61]

John of St. Thomas testifies to the fact that the doctrine which holds that a heretic pope is to be removed is the common teaching of theologians and also of many jurists (Quæ est communis sententia theologorum, et multorum etiam juristarum.)[62], and that *the doctors are united in teaching* that a heretic pope is to be deposed,[63] and therefore it is not a mere opinion but a matter of divine and Catholic faith.[64] He

---

[60] John F. Salza and Robert J. Siscoe, *TRUE OR FALSE POPE? - Refuting Sedevacantism and other Modern Errors*; STAS Editions, St. Thomas Aquinas Seminary 21077 Quarry Hill Road, Winona, Minnesota 55987, 2015, p. 346.

[61] *Ibid.* p. 361.

[62] John of St. Thomas, *Cursus Theologicus II-II De Auctoritate Summi Pontificis, Disp. II, Art. III, De Depositione Papae*, p. 256.

[63] *Ibid.* p. 251 — «Circa causam hæresis multa disputant theologi, et jurispperiti, quæ ad longum prosequi locus non est; **est autem concors doctorum sententia propter hæresim posse papam deponi.**»

[64] Pius PP. IX, 21 Decembris, 1863, *Epistula Tuas Libenter* — «Namque etiamsi ageretur de illa subiectione, quae fidei divinae actu est praestanda, limitanda tamen non esset ad ea, quae expressis, oecumenicorum Conciliorum aut Romanorum Pontificum, huiusque Apostolicae Sedis decretis definita sunt, sed ad ea quoque extendenda quae ordinario totius

then cites the passage of St. Paul which says that the heretic is to be avoided:

> The reason is that we are bound to separate ourselves from heretics I Timoth. III: *Hæreticum, hominem post primam et secundam correptionem devita*. However he who remains in the pontificate is not to be avoided, but rather the Church is bound to be united to him and be in communion, or he must be deposed from the pontificate. The first is tantamount to the evident destruction of the Church, and brings in the intrinsic risk of going astray in the whole of the government of the Church, if the Church is obliged to follow a heretical head: indeed since a heretic is an enemy of the Church, for this by natural law the Church can act against the pope, namely by right of defence, she can defend herself from her enemy, which a heretic pope is; therefore to act against him; therefore it must be undoubtedly the second namely, that such a pope be deposed.[65]

Moynihan mentions that there was such "a tradition already prevalent as far back as the seventh century."[66] The doctrine that any prelate can be judged for heresy by his inferiors has been asserted since the late Patristic period, namely, by St. Isidore of Seville, "the last scholar of the ancient world" (c. 560 – 4 April 636); and the proposition that the pope can be judged for heresy was already

---

Ecclesiae per orbem dispersae magisterio tanquam divinitus revelata traduntur, ideoque universali et constanti consensu a catholicis Theologis ad fidem pertinere retinentur.»

[65] John of St. Thomas, *Op. cit.* p. 51 — «Ratio est, quia ab hæreticis tenemur nos segregare I ad Timoth. III: *Hæreticum hominem post primam et secundam correptionem devita*. At vero qui manet in pontificatu non est vitandus, sed potius illi uniri, et communicare tenetur Ecclesia tamquam supremo capiti suo; ergo si papa est hæreticus, vel tenetur Ecclesia illi communicare, vel debet a pontificatu deponi. Primum autem est in evidentem Ecclesiæ destructionem, et importans intrinsece periculum errandi in toto regimine ecclesiastico, si Ecclesia teneatur sequi caput hæreticum: immo cum hæreticus sit Ecclesiæ hostis, hoc jure naturali potest Ecclesia agere contra papam, scilicet jure defensionis, quia defendere se potest ab inimico suo, qualis est papa hæreticus; ergo et agere contra illum; ergo secundum omnino debet fieri scilicet, quod talis papa deponatur.»

[66] James M. Moynihan, STL, JCD, *Papal Immunity and Liability in the Writings of the Medieval Canonists*, Gregorian University Press, Roma 1961, p. 33.

explicitly asserted by St. Columban (540 – 21 November 615). In the year 636, St. Isidore wrote in his *Sententiarum,* Lib. II, c. 39, "The rulers therefore are to be judged by God, and by no means are to be judged by their subjects... but if the rector strays from the faith, then he is to be accused by his subjects; but for objectionable moral behaviour he is more to be tolerated rather than to be segregated from the people."[67] Moynihan relates that at the time when rumours were circulating against the orthodoxy of Pope Boniface IV (608-615), St. Columban wrote to him, assuring him that he believed none of it, but the saint was careful to add: «For if these things are certain rather than fables, then vice versa your children have become the head, but you the tail (Deut. 28:44) which is even painful to say, and for that reason those who have preserved the orthodox faith will be your judges, whoever they may be, even if they are seen to be your juniors — those orthodox and true Catholics, who have neither received nor defended any heretics or suspected heretics at any time, but have persevered enduringly in the zeal of the true faith.»[68] With the words, *"neque hæreticos neque suspectos aliquos";* the saint makes it clear that the subjects have the right in conscience to judge and reject (literally to not receive[69]) not only superiors who are notoriously *manifest heretics,* but also those who positively manifest themselves to be reasonably considered *suspected heretics.* The Fifth Lateran Council in the Ninth

---

[67] *Ibid.* p. 27 — «Rectores ergo a Deo judicandi sunt, a suis autem subditis nequaquam judicandi sunt... Quod si a fide exhorbitaverit rector, tunc erit arguendus a subditis; pro moribus vero reprobis tolerandus magis distringendus a plebe est.»

[68] «Si enim hæc certa magis quam fabulosa sunt, versa vice filii vestri *in caput* conversi sunt, vos vero in *caudam* (Deut. 28, 44); quod etiam dici dolor est: ideo et vestri erunt judices qui semper orthodoxam fidem servaverunt, quicumque illi fuerint, etiamsi juniores vestri videantur. Ipsi autem orthodoxi et veri catholici, qui neque hæreticos neque suspectos aliquos aliquando receperunt neque defenderunt, sed in zelo veræ fidei permanserunt.»

[69] St. Columban's use of the term *"receperunt"* in the phrase, *neque suspectos aliquos aliquando receperunt neque defenderunt,* is a clear allusion to the apostolic teaching that heretics and infidels are to be absolutely shunned and avoided, "If any man come to you, and bring not this doctrine, receive him not into the house, nor say to him, God speed you." (II John 10)

Session (*Bull on the Reform of the Curia*) ruled, "All false Christians and those with evil sentiments towards the faith, of whatever race or nation they may be, as well as heretics and those stained with some taint of heresy, or Judaizers, are to be totally excluded from the company of Christ's faithful and expelled from any position, especially from the Roman curia, and punished with an appropriate penalty."[70] Pope Innocent III, taught (*Sermo IV. IN CONSECRATIONE PONTIFICIS),* "Since the Roman Pontiff has no other superior than God… who could cast him out or trample him under foot?… But he ought not vainly flatter himself because of his power… because the less he is judged by men, the more he is judged by God. I say the less, because he can be judged by men, or rather he **can be shown to be already judged**, if he should wither away into heresy; because «*he who does not believe has already been judged (John III)*»"[71] From this papal teaching, supported by the unanimous teaching of theologians, it can be seen to be theologically certain that a pope can be judged for heresy. If the act of heresy is external it is judicable as a crime. The pope's external act of heresy is *judicable*; but it is also infallibly taught that a true pope is **injudicable**. Therefore if the pope is a heretic he is not a true pope, because as a heretic he is **judicable**, and therefore; the teaching of Innocent III on this point of judging a heretic pope is only capable of being logically understood in a qualified manner, insofar as the heretic in question, as a heretic, is either no longer pope or never was a valid pope. St. Alphonsus,

---

[70] «Et ut omnes ficti christiani ac de fide male sentientes cuiuscumque generis aut nationis fuerint nec non haeretici seu aliqua haeresis labe polluti vel Iudaizantes a christi fidelium coetu penitus eliminentur et a quocumque loco et praesertim a Romana curia expellantur ac debita animadversione puniantur statuimus ut contra eos diligenti inquisitione ubique et in dicta curia maxime procedatur per iudices per nos deputandos et eius criminis reos et legitime convictos debitis poenis puniri relapsos vero absque ulla spe veniae aut remissionis affici volumus.»

[71] «Unde, cum Romanus pontifex non habeat alium dominum nisi Deum… quis potest eum foras mittere aut pedibus conculcari?… Verum non frustra sibi blandiatur de potestate, neque de sublimitate vel honore temere glorietur; quia quanto minus judicatur ab homine, tanto magis judicatur a Deo. Minus dico; quia potest ab hominibus judicari, **vel potius judicatus ostendi**» – *Sermo IV. IN CONSECRATIONE PONTIFICIS.*

following exactly the doctrine of St. Robert Bellarmine's *fifth opinion*, pronounces on the question of judging a pope, saying: "We answer, that if ever a pope as a private person would fall into heresy, then he would immediately fall from the papacy; for since he would be outside the Church, he could no longer be the head of the Church. Whence in that case the Church would have to not in fact depose him, because no one has power over the pope, but declare him to have fallen from the pontificate."[72] Thus, the proposition that a heretic can be judged and removed from the papal throne cannot be considered a cryptic form of Conciliarism because it is infallibly taught by the magisterium of the Church.[73]

Salza & Siscoe on the other hand, (and all who unwittingly have been led into heresy by them), hold to an opinion known as *Mitigated Conciliarism,* which is a heresy, because it is logically reducible to the radically heretical error of *Conciliarism,* insofar as it professes that the Church represented by an *imperfect council* has the authority to judge a validly reigning pope with finality for heresy, thus effectively ascribing to a council the *supreme authority* to act as the *final arbiter in a matter of faith* against the pope, which in this case would consist in the question of the doctrinal orthodoxy of the pope's opinion; whereas it is a solemnly defined dogma that the pope as the **supreme judge** is the *final arbiter* in absolutely **ALL** disputes concerning doctrine of faith or morals. A council cannot judge a true and valid pope's opinions, and thereby subject the pope's beliefs to the "judgment of the Church" because it is defined *de fide* in *Pastor Æternus* that the pope as the holder

---

[72] Alfonso Maria de' Liguori, *Vindiciae pro suprema pontificis potestate adversus Iustinum Febronium*, Torino, 1832, p. 142 — «Respondemus, quod si unquam papa ut privata persona in hæresim incideret, tunc ipse statim a papatu decideret; cum enim tunc esset extra ecclesiam, ecclesiæ caput amplius esse non posset. Unde eo casu ecclesia deberet, non quidem eum deponere, quia nemo supra papam jus habet, sed eum a pontificatu lapsum declarare.»

[73] St. Robert Bellarmine, *De Romano Pontifice, lib. ii cap. xxx* — «expresse habetur... apud Innocentium serm. 2. de consecr. Pontif... non possumus negare, quin Hadrianus cum Romano Concilio, immo & tota Synodus VIII. generalis senserit, in caussa haeresis posse Romanum Pontificem judicari.» Having been unanimously taught by theologians, in accordance with *Tuas Libenter* (quoted above) this doctrine must be qualified as *de fide divina et catholica.*

of the primacy possesses ***"the full and supreme power of jurisdiction over the whole church"*** (plenam et supremam potestatem iurisdictionis in universam Ecclesiam), whose primacy comprehends "the supreme power of magisterium"[74] and is therefore the **"supreme judge"** (docemus etiam et declaramus, eum esse iudicem supremum) — the *final arbiter* to whose authority it pertains to definitively determine the Church's judgment on all questions of faith with *finality*. (***si quae de fide subortae fuerint quaestiones, suo debent iudicio definiri***). St. Alphonsus de Liguori expounds on this point:

> 11. What's more we have it defined by the council that the Pope has the *fullness of power*, or the *supreme* power in the Church. In the Second Council of Lyon, where there were 500 bishops, under Gregory X. in the year 1274 against the heresy of the Greeks, that the Holy Spirit does not proceed from the Son, in the profession of faith that was made publicly in the council by the legates of the emperor Michael Paleologus it was said: *This Holy Roman Church possesses the supreme and full primacy and authority over the whole Catholic Church, which it recognizes in truth and humility to have received with the fullness of power from the Lord himself in St. Peter, chief of the Apostles. And just as more than the others it is bound to defend the truth of the faith, thus if there will have arisen questions of faith, by its judgment they must be defined etc.*[75] Then it explained in what the fullness of power consists: *The fullness of power consists in admitting other Churches to a share in the responsibility... saving always its own prerogatives established both in general councils as well as in some others.* This profession of faith was then accepted by the whole council, and this was the first constitution that was made in the council, it being said by the Fathers: *By the above written truth of faith, as it*

---

[74] *Pastor Æternus*, Caput IV — «Ipso autem Apostolico primatu, quem Romanus Pontifex tamquam Petri principis Apostolorum successor in universam Ecclesiam obtinet, supremam quoque magisterii potestatem comprehendi, haec Sancta Sedes semper tenuit, perpetuus Ecclesiae usus comprobat»

[75] I have followed the uncorrupted text in my translation: «*Ipsa quoque S. Romana Ecclesia summum et plenum primatum et principatum super universam Ecclesiam catholicam obtinet, quem se ab ipso Domino in B. Petro, Apostolorum Principe, sive vertice, cujus Rom. Pontifex est Successor, cum potestatis plenitudine recepisse veraciter, et humiliter recognoscit. Et sicut præ ceteris tenetur fidei veritatem defendere, sic et si quæ de fide subortæ fuerint quæstiones, suo debent judicio definiri etc.*» [cf. *Opuscula Ad Hierarchicam Ecclesiæ Constitutionem Spectantia* – Venetiis 1790, p. 193]

has been fully read, and faithfully explained, we recognize the true, holy, catholic and orthodox faith, and we receive, and by the mouth and heart confess, what the Holy Roman Church truly holds, and faithfully teaches and preaches. Note the words referred to above: *If there will have arisen questions of faith, by its judgment they must be defined.* This was also previously said in the Nicene Council I. (between Canons 19. and 29.): *All bishops… are to appeal to the Apostolic See, in order that they* (as it always was) *be upheld, defended, and freed, to whose disposition the ancient authority of the Apostles and their successors, and the canons reserved all major Ecclesiastical cases.* We add what was said in the Viennese General Council in the year 1307 under Clement V. with the contribution of about 300 bishops: *It pertains only to the Apostolic See to pronounce on questions of faith.* Whence St. Cyril wrote: *Just as from the Father all power was given to Christ and to no other, so the supreme responsibility of the Church was committed to Peter and to his successors and to no other. Lib. Thesaur. tom. 2.*[76]

---

[76] *Verità Della Fede*, Opera Del Beato Alfonso Maria de' Liguori, Tomo Secondo, Monza, 1823, Capo IX. pp. 171-172 — «11. Di più abbiamo definito da' concilj che il Papa ha la *pienezza della potestà*, o sia la potestà *suprema* nella Chiesa. Nel Concilio Lugdunese II, ove furono 500 vescovi, sotto Gregorio X dell'anno 1274 contro l'eresia de' Greci, che lo Spirito Santo non proceda dal Figliuolo, nella professione di fede che si fece pubblicamente nel concilio da' legati dell'imperator Michele Paleologo si disse: *Ipsa quoque S. Romana Ecclesia summum et plenum primatum et principatum super universam Ecclesiam catholicam obtinet, quam se ab ipso Domino in B. Petro, cujus Rom. Pontifex est superior, cum potestatis plenitudine recepisse veraciter et humiliter recognoscit. Et sicut præ ceteris tenetur fidei veritatem defendere, sic et si quæ de fide subortæ fuerint quæstiones, suo debent judicio definiri etc.* Indi spiegossi in che consistesse la pienezza di potestà: *Potestatis plenitudo consistit, quod Ecclesias ceteras ad sollicitudinis partem admittit… sua tamen observata prærogativa, et tum in generalibus conciliis, tum in aliquibus aliis semper salva.* Questa professione di fede fu poi accettata da tutto il concilio, e questa fu la prima costituzione che nel concilio si fece, dicendosi da' Padri: *Suprascripta fidei veritate, prout plene lecta est, et fideliter exposita, veram, sanctam, catholicam et orthodoxam fidem cognoscimus, et acceptamus, et ore ac corde confitemur, quod vere tenet, et fideliter docet et prædicat S. Romana Ecclesia.* Si notino le parole di sopra riferite: *Si quæ de fide subortæ fuerint quæstiones, suo debent judicio definiri.* Il che fu anche prima detto nel Concilio Niceno I (tra i Canoni 19. e 29.): *Omnes episcopi… Apostolicam appellent Sedem, ut ab ea (sicut semper fuit) fulciantur, defendantur, et liberentur, cujus dispositioni omnes majores Ecclesiasticas causas antiqua Apostolorum, eorumque successorum, atque canonum auctoritas reservavit.* Si aggiunge quel che si disse nel Concilio generale Viennense nell'anno 1307 sotto Clemente V. col concorso di 300 vescovi in

It is only if the pope's opinions, being *indicia* of heresy, were to qualify him as a *suspect of heresy*, that those opinions themselves would render doubtful the validity of his pontificate. In such a case it would fall within the jurisdiction of the Church to determine whether or not the suspect is *pertinacious,* and therefore disqualified by heresy from holding office as an *incapable subject* of the papacy, or just a valid pope who holds an honestly mistaken opinion, as was the case with Pope John XXII. The heresy of *Mitigated Conciliarism* is particularly worrisome because it has spread rampantly among those faithful and clergy who constitute what is commonly referred to as the *traditional movement*, as I explained in Volume One. The two zealots who have led so many priest, faithful, and even some bishops into this heresy, are the authors of the infamous heretical volume which explicitly promotes this heresy against which I wrote in Volume One of this work. Those two authors are none other than John Salza and Robert Siscoe.

The two extreme opinions outlined above correspond to the third and fourth opinions according to St. Robert Bellarmine's classification of the five historical opinions on the question of the deposition of a pope for heresy. Briefly, those five opinions are:

1) That the pope simply cannot become a formal heretic, and therefore cannot be deposed for heresy.
2) That a pope who even internally falls into formal heresy is immediately deposed by God and ceases to be pope.
3) That a pope who is even a manifest heretic is not deposed *ipso facto* and cannot be deposed by the Church.
4) That a manifest heretic does not fall from the pontificate by himself *ipso facto*, but must be judged by the Church to fall from office.
5) That a manifest heretic ceases by himself to be pope *ipso facto*, for which reason he may be judged and punished by the Church.

---

circa: *Dubia fidei declarare ad Sedem dumtaxat Apostolicam pertinere.* Onde scrisse S. Cirillo: *Sicut Christo a Patre omnis potestas et nulli alteri data est, sic Petro ejusque successoribus, supremam Ecclesiæ curam, nullique alteri commissam. Lib. Thesaur. tom. 2.*»

My examination of the "five opinions" can be found in Volume One of this work. Here are some general observations on them: Opinion No. One is the only possible true opinion, while No. Five is valid only as a pure hypothesis. Opinions 2, 3, and 4 are false opinions which either lead to heresy or are founded on unstated heretical premises. I say that No. One is the only possible true opinion because the others all are irresolvably problematic, as I have explained. Briefly, it is the infallible teaching of the Church that the pope is the supreme judge whose power of jurisdiction is absolute and universal, and cannot be judged by anyone. If the pope could fall into heresy, *he would have to be judged and deposed*, because it is a revealed truth of faith that *all heretics are to be excluded from ecclesial communion*. Therefore, if a pope were to become a heretic, then the pope who by divine law can never be judged by anyone would by divine law need to be judged by his subordinates who may never judge the pope. If a pope could become a heretic, then there would exist an unresolved contradiction in the divine positive law itself with no clear remedy being provided for a problem which by its very nature is so grave that it would absolutely need to be provided for if such an eventuality as a heretic pope would be permitted by divine providence. It is inconceivable and contrary to reason that a God of infinite wisdom would not have wisely provided a remedy for such an eventuality if such thing would actually be permitted to occur; otherwise, God could be accused of not having sufficiently provided the Church with a remedy for such a catastrophe which if unremedied would lead to the defection of the Church, by allowing a lawless destroyer and a rebel against the eternal truths to govern the Church as the supreme legislator, teacher and ruler. The fact that God, who provides all that is necessary prescribed no remedy for this maximum necessity in the deposit of revelation, by itself sufficiently proves that God will never allow such an eventuality as a heretic pope to take place.

Number Two is clearly false, because it would destroy the divine constitution of the Church: 1) because it would be impossible for the Church to judge that the pope has fallen from the pontificate, with the result that the body of the Church would be left headless by being united to a false head. 2) Even worse, if an internal heretic invisibly ceased to be pope, no one would know that he is no longer the pope, and that he is no longer protected by divine assistance from defining false dogmas. If he would invent some new error against the faith, not yet condemned by the Church as a heresy, he could define it as a dogma, and there would be no pope to condemn it. There would be no way to distinguish between a true dogma defined by a true pope, and a false dogma defined by a false pope. There would exist no means by which the false dogma could be infallibly condemned by the Church, and be recognized by the whole Church as infallibly condemned. The attribute of infallibility would cease to exist in the Church. Therefore, even a secret heretic, who has not yet externally denied any already defined dogma, would be able to cause the defection of the Church without there being a remedy by inventing and defining a new heresy. Thus, there would no longer exist a means by which the infallible rule of faith could be authoritatively proposed, which would amount to a defection of the Church from her divine constitution. Number Three is false, because, (as I have proven in Volume One), it is *de fide* that a public heretic is severed from membership *ipso facto* by the very nature of heresy, and loses office *ipso jure*; but a public heretic who remains pope while no longer a member would still be the chief member; and he would still hold office even after losing his office *ipso jure*. The consideration of these absurdities proves that the opinion is against the Catholic faith; yet, this opinion is still popular among many ignorant Catholics.

Opinion Number Four is heretical, because it attributes to the pope's inferiors a power to judge him who is absolutely immune from judgment; and to act as final arbiter in a dispute on a matter of faith, which pertains exclusively to the full and supreme jurisdiction of the Roman Pontiff as the *supreme judge of all disputes*. Opinion Number Five as a pure hypothesis is valid for the reasons explained by St. Robert Bellarmine. It is not founded on any heretical premise, nor does it logically imply any heresy. Nevertheless, since divine revelation has not prescribed any clear remedy for dealing with such an eventuality, and opinions remain divided on how the Church would resolve such a crisis, it is clear that divine revelation itself does not envisage that such an eventuality will ever happen. If a pope were manifestly and certainly a formal heretic, (which he would be if he were to unequivocally assert that God is not a perfect Trinity, or that Jesus Christ was a mere man and nothing more), it would be patently obvious that he is not a Christian, and therefore not a pope of the

Catholic Church. However, if his heresy would be only *materially* public but *formally* occult; then there would exist a doubt whether he was a formal heretic or not. It is of divine law that all known heretics are to be cast out and excluded from the Church's communion, but if the suspect would still be pope even as a heretic, then by his primatial right of injudicability he could not be subjected to a canonical examination and judged, and the doubt about his heresy could then never be resolved, and it would be impossible for the Church to execute the absolute and unconditional divine precept to cast out heretics from her midst. It is only if the heretic, even before conviction, is already no pope, that the divine command can be observed. Thus it is evident, that a heretic, whether occult or manifest is absolutely and simply an incapable subject of the papacy.

From the above considerations, and from what I have documented and proven in the first volume of this work, it is established that the Church's doctrine on papal heresy and deposition can be summed up in the following eight points:

1. A **valid pope *jure divino*** cannot be **tried or judged**, therefore a true and certain pope **cannot be judged or deposed**.
2. All heretics **without exception** are to be excluded from communion *jure divino*, and therefore deposed from office.
3. Therefore, a heretic pope must be excluded, and accordingly, must be deposed, as Pope Innocent III teaches in unanimity with the teaching of theologians — thus, it is *theologice certum* that a heretic pope cannot be tolerated but must be deposed.
4. Therefore it follows that a heretic pope is already no pope, even before conviction — an **incapable subject** of the papacy. He may be judged, deposed and punished.
5. **Anyone** who presents the *certain indicia of heresy* is a formal heretic and no pope, who places himself outside the Church and incurs the penalty of excommunication *latae sententiae* prescribed in Canon 1364 §1, which corresponds to Canon 2314 of the 1917 Code. Anyone who presents the **vehement** or **violent** *indicia of suspected heresy*, according to the degree of suspicion is *presumed guilty* unless in the penal process it can be shown to appear otherwise. In virtue of the *indicia* against him,

such a one would be a doubtful pope. Such suspects fell under the provisions of cann. 2315 ss. In the 1917 Code, which prescribed for the entire Latin Rite the penal process to be followed for *suspected heretics*. The process outlined in the new Code is not specific and comprehensive as it was in the 1917 Code, but in the 1983 Code, rather than one uniform process prescribed for the universal Church, there is, according to the principle of subsidiarity, allowance given for variation in particular law regarding the precise measures to be applied in the process.[77]

6. A certain formal heretic whose pertinacity is already immediately manifest is to be deposed straightaway without trial. He is condemned by his own judgment.
7. Since a heretic is an incapable subject of the papacy, a suspected heretic reputed to be pope is a doubtful pope and is accordingly presumed to be no pope. He is to be first corrected, then warned, and if he still remains incorrigible, he is to be deposed.
8. One who is vehemently or violently suspected of heresy, being therefore a doubtful pope *on the basis of probable cause of heresy*, must be judged on the presumption of being no pope, and deposed if he remains incorrigible; because in doubt, the Church has the authority to determine if a man is a legitimate pope or not, and to judge and condemn all heretics.

Since the pope's *full and supreme jurisdiction* is defined *de fide* to be a *total fullness of supreme power*, it is *de fide* that any exception to that power

---

[77] "Se regulan todos aquellos supuestos de hecho delictuosos que, por su gravedad, requieren una tipificación penal, y que, por la universalidad de sus efectos criminosos, interesa que sean incluidos en el derecho común, dejando para la legislación particular aquellos supuestos que inciden en un ámbito más reducido. Se conjugan así el principio de subsidiariedad y la necesidad de arbitrar los instrumentos coercitivos mínimos de carácter universal, «sin los cuales la Sociedad eclesiástica no podría permanecer, ante la ingerencia de los enemigos que violan la libertad de la Iglesia y arrasan con el escándalo el bien de las almas» (*Praenotanda*, cit. en el comentario a este Libro)." — *Código De Derecho Canónico Edición Bilingüe Y Anotada Universidad De Navarra*, Facultad De Derecho Canónico, Sexta edición revisada y actualizada, p. 849.

is totally excluded. This, as is explained below, can be seen from the essential difference in the primatial power which in its very nature is supreme, and is a different power than the episcopal power of the bishops which exists essentially as a *subordinate power* to the *total and supreme power* of the pope. The *episcopal power* is common to all bishops (including the pope) who are all equally successors of the Apostles, but episcopal power in its very nature is solemnly defined as existing in *hierarchical subordination* to the supreme power of the pope who succeeds Peter, not merely as a successor of Apostles, but succeeds Peter in the primacy as the supreme head over all bishops and dioceses, who therefore receive their grant of jurisdiction directly from the pope and only indirectly from God. The *Petrine primacy* which constituted Peter as supreme head of the Church over all the other Apostles, is passed on to Peter's successor, who receives it not from the Church, but directly from Christ at the instant he accepts his election and becomes Christ's vicar on earth, and is thereby constituted as supreme head of the Church over all the other bishops. To assert an exception is heresy. Since it is defined *de fide* that the pope is the supreme judge in all cases in matters of faith or morals, he is the supreme judge in all cases without exception, and is therefore the final arbiter in all disputes in matters of faith without exception.[78] It

---

[78] Constitutio Dogmatica «*Pastor Æternus*» Concilii Vaticani I: «Et quoniam divino Apostolici primatus iure Romanus Pontifex universæ Ecclesiæ præest, docemus etiam et declaramus, **eum esse iudicem supremum** fidelium (Pii PP. VI Breve, *Super soliditate* d. 28 Nov. 1786), et *in omnibus causis ad examen ecclesiasticum spectantibus* ad ipsius posse iudicium recurri (Concil. Oecum. Lugdun. II); ***Sedis vero Apostolicæ, cuius auctoritate maior non est, iudicium a nemine fore retractandum, neque cuiquam de eius licere iudicare iudicio*** (Ep. Nicolai 1 ad Michælem Imporatorem). ***Quare a recto veritatis tramite aberrant, qui affirmant, licere ab iudiciis Romanorum Pontificum ad oecumenicum Concilium tamquam ad auctoritatem Romano Pontifice superiorem appellare.*»; «Approbante vero Lugdunensi Concilio secundo, Graeci professi sunt: Sanctam Romanam Ecclesiam **summum et plenum primatum** et principatum super universam Ecclesiam catholicam obtinere, quem se ab ipso Domino in beato Petro Apostolorum principe sive vertice, cuius Romanus Pontifex est successor, **cum potestatis plenitudine recepisse** veraciter et humiliter recognoscit; et ***sicut prae ceteris tenetur fidei veritatem***

strictly follows from this premise that the Church possesses absolutely no power to judge a valid pope for heresy or for any other crime. Since the Church possesses the power to judge all heretics *jure divino*, without exception, in judging a pope a heretic, she can only judge that the heretic being judged is really not a valid pope; because if he were still the pope even as a heretic, as pope he would remain in possession of the primacy, which constitutes him as the supreme, final and infallible judge in all disputes concerning matters of faith. From this premise it follows strictly that for so long as a man is pope, he cannot become a formal heretic. If he could be simultaneously both a valid pope and a heretic, he would retain absolute power of jurisdiction, and could never be judged for so long as he is pope. However, it is against faith to say that a heretic cannot be judged by the Church and excluded from communion with her. The constant Catholic doctrine, commonly taught by theologians for centuries, and taught by Pope Innocent III, that as a heretic a pope can be judged and deposed proves absolutely that the heretic who would be so judged would be no valid pope at all: A heretic is *absolute et simpliciter* an intrinsically incapable subject of the papacy. Hence, it is not only that the public heretic is incapable of assuming the papacy for having severed himself from the body of the Church, but even the occult heretic is incapable of assuming it because the papacy and heresy are intrinsically incompatible, and therefore are incapable of existing simultaneously in the same subject. A pope cannot become a formal heretic and still remain pope because if that were possible, it would mean that as pope the heretic could never be judged for so long as he remains pope, but if a pope could become a formal heretic, but not a manifest heretic, and if he would cease automatically to be pope, it would ultimately deprive the Church of the power to determine whether or not the reputed pope is a true and valid pope; and the reason for this is that when evidence of heresy might emerge, it would be sometimes impossible according to mere juridical standards of judgment, to conclusively determine guilt or innocence of formal heresy, and therefore it could not be known with any certitude whether the pope has fallen into heresy and ceased to be pope, and

---

defendere, sic et, si quae de fide subortae fuerint quaestiones, suo debent iudicio definiri.»

accordingly to be judged and deposed by his former subjects; or if he has only materially erred in a matter of faith, and thus being innocent of formally defecting into heresy, to have retained the papal office and primacy with its absolute right of injudicability. If he could fall from office because of secret heresy, or heresy that is evident to some degree but cannot be absolutely proven, he would lose his papal infallibility, and then it could not be known whether his final judgment would be infallible and with jurisdiction, or if the council's judgment against him would be the true judgment. There would exist no infallible means to resolve the question and determine whether or not the suspect in question remains a valid pope or has fallen from the pontificate. It is as I stated in Volume One, that except for a clear-cut case of manifestly formal heresy, or one that is at least morally certain by way of a clear-cut and incorrigible *violent suspicion of heresy* based on verified factual *indicia*, it would really be impossible to determine if a materially heretical pope is guilty of formal heresy and falls from office or if he remains pope — and even then, there would not exist a certain infallible primatial power to judge him with finality. Only an infallible remedy prescribed by divine law could resolve the uncertainty that would be created by the need for such a judgment, in order to prevent the defection of the Church from her divine constitution which would result from the Church being separated from her head, and from the loss of infallibility caused by the opposing judgments of a doubtful pope and an imperfect council, neither of which could be known with certitude to be infallible. No remedy has been provided by God in the deposit of revelation, as Suárez observed,[79] yet, the same Suárez rightly argues, "*natural reason teaches thus; for it is not credible that Christ left the Church destitute of any remedy*

---

[79] R. P. Francisci Suarez, *Opera Omnia*, Paris 1863 (Vivés), *Tomus Doudecimus, Tractatus Primus, De Fide Theologica. Disputatio X. De Summo Pontifice, Sect. VI.* p. 316 — «Et infra agentes de pœnis hæreticorum alios referemus, ac generaliter ostendemus jure divino non privari quempiam dignitate et jurisdictione ecclesiastica propter culpam hæresis; nuuc breviter ratio a priori redditur, quia cum ea sit gravissima pœna, ut ipso facto incurratur, oportet jure divino expressam esse; nullum autem jus tale invenitur, quod vel generaliter id statuat de hæreticis, aut specialiter de episcopis, aut specialissime de Papa; nec item certa traditio de eo habetur.»

*for so great a peril";*⁸⁰ and Melchior Canus observes: "Inasmuch as God promised firmness of faith to the Church, He cannot be wanting to it [...] Nor can it be doubted that what happens in natural things, the same occurs in supernatural; namely, that he who gives the end gives the means to the end."⁸¹ Therefore, ***since no remedy has been provided by God in divine positive law for this absolute necessity, this absolute necessity to judge a pope for heresy cannot ever arise***. Thus, as I proved in Volume One, on the one hand, a true pope cannot become a heretic, even if he might appear to be one; and on the other, a heretic, by the certain fact of his formal heresy, proves he is not a valid pope. Thus, it is evident that the Church can never judge a validly reigning pope, but only a doubtful one as Bellarmine, Ballerini, St. Alphonsus, and Gregory XVI teach.

I will elaborate these points in the course of this doctrinal summary and answer the latest objections of the two front men of the Masonically oriented Bergoglian regime — the propagandists of the heresy of **Mitigated Conciliarism**, John Salza and Robert Siscoe who stoutly assert Bergoglio's bogus claim on the papacy as valid, while continuing to perversely propagate the heretical belief that **the Church can juridically judge a certain and valid pope while he is still in office as the holder of the Petrine *munus*, and *depose him for the crime of heresy*.**

Even after I clearly exposed and refuted the heresy of their opinions on this point in Volume One of this work, John Salza, in a recent interview has announced his intention to co-author with Robert Siscoe a three volume work in defence of their heresy. He declared in the interview that there is yet new material they have found in the writings of St. Robert Bellarmine which fully vindicate all they have written previously on the question of papal deposition.

---

⁸⁰ *Ibid.* p. 318 — «rationem naturalem ita docere, quia non est credendum Christum destituisse Ecclesiam omni remedio in tanto periculo; quod vero adduxi maxime accommodatum apparet causæ de qua disputamus.»

⁸¹ «Cum Ecclesiæ fidei firmitatem fuerit pollicitus, deesse non potest quominus tribuat Ecclesiæ preces, cæteraque præsidia, quibus hæc firmitas conservatur. Nec vero dubitari potest, quod in rebus naturalibus contingit, idem in supernaturalibus usu venire; ut qui dat finem, det consequentia ad finem. — Melchior Canus, *De Locis Theol.*, lib. v. cap. 5, pp. 120, 131, Venice, 1776.» [Vide: Cardinal Manning, *The Vatican Council and its Definitions*, p. 115.]

What they have previously written can be summed up in their own heretical words: «After the Church establishes that the Pope is guilty of the crime of heresy, she renders a judgment of the same (and, as we will see, this is to be done during an "imperfect" ecumenical council).»[82] In his article in *The Remnant* (Nov. 18, 2014), Siscoe heretically asserted: «The Church must render a judgment before the pope loses his office.» In view of their adamant entrenchment in a heresy which they profess and propagate with such a fanatical zeal that it has led a great number of Catholics into heresy, I will present here in this volume a more concise exposition of the Church's teaching on the Primacy and papal heresy than what I elaborated in Volume One. Simply stated, it is a heresy to say that a true and valid pope can ever be judged by anyone for any crime whatsoever ***including heresy***, because *Pastor Æternus* defined the pope as **the supreme judge in all cases that refer to ecclesiastical examination**: «iudicem supremum… in omnibus causis ad examen ecclesiasticum spectantibus» As the *supreme judge*, it pertains to the pope's authority to determine the Church's judgment with finality, as Pope Gregory XVI explained, citing St. Thomas; so it is quite impossible for there to be an authoritative judgment against the pope in matters of faith, since the final determination of the Church's judgment in matters of faith can only be made by the pope.[83] The passage of St. Thomas which Pope Gregory quotes reads in English, "To his authority belongs the promulgation of the creed, to whose authority it pertains to DETERMINE WITH FINALITY the matters of faith, so that they may be held by all with unshakable faith." (*Summa Theol.* II^a - II^æ q. 1 a. 10) He who is solemnly defined to be the **"supreme judge"** who possesses the **"total fullness of supreme power,"** cannot be judged by the Church, because it pertains to *his* authority as *"the supreme judge of disputes"*[84] to freely confect by *his* definitive judgment, the final determination of the Church's judgment

---

[82] *TRUE OR FALSE POPE?* - p. 331.

[83] D. Mauro Cappellari ora Gregorio XVI, *Il trionfo della santa sede e della chiesa contro gli assalti dei novatori*, Venezia, 1832 p. Capo V, p. 123 "Ad illius ergo auctoritatem pertinet editio symboli, ad cuius auctoritatem pertinet FINALITER DETERMINARE ea, quae sunt fidei, ut ab omnibus inconcussa fide teneantur." [*Summa Theol.* II^a - II^æ q. 1 a. 10]

[84] *Ibid.* p. 123.

in all matters pertaining to faith. **This one consideration by itself amply suffices to demolish all arguments which, *by way of exception*, attribute a power to the pope's inferiors to judge *the reigning pontiff* for the crime of heresy**, since it is *de fide definita* that the pope possesses *absolute et simpliciter* a full and absolute jurisdiction over a council and the whole Church. Such an absolute fullness of jurisdictional power in which the primacy essentially consists, by its nature excludes all possibility of any exception of even the slightest degree, since admitting an exception to that full and supreme power would concede to a council a supreme power directly opposed to the very nature of the total fullness of supreme power which constitutes the essence of the primacy. Indeed, the primacy itself would be negated and destroyed if a synod or council, or the College of Cardinals could ever exercise a final, and therefore a supreme authority to juridically judge a validly reigning pope, and depose him directly, *or to juridically declare him a heretic* and depose him indirectly, by instrumentally and dispositively causing him to fall from office by introducing a disposition that would separate him from the Church or the Church from him. If such an exception to the primacy's *full and supreme power of jurisdiction* were to exist, then the primacy itself would not be able to exist according to its solemnly defined nature as a total fullness of supreme power. As I will explain below, the theories for such an *indirect deposition* as proposed in the writings of Cajetan, John of St. Thomas, and Suárez, are premised upon there being placed an *act of jurisdiction* — a **juridical** judgment against the *full and supreme jurisdiction* of the Primacy. Nevertheless, heretical arguments are difficult to suppress even when the argument itself has been demolished, because trying to suppress heretical arguments is like trying to kill Rasputin. A clean shot to the heart with a lead bullet did not put him away — and a clean thrust of the sword of truth through the heart of the false doctrine does not extinguish the perversity of rebellion against divine revelation which inhabits the heart of the heretic.

Some readers have asked me why I spend so much time refuting such blighters as Salza & Siscoe; and the answer is that they are not just the pseudo-intellectual yobs that any competent theologian easily recognizes them to be; but they assert their doctrinal errors with such consummate sophistry, that the crude fallacies that form the foundation of their heretical arguments are usually only detected by the astute reader who is consciously seeking out these fallacies in their writings. They are verbal con-artists who are good at what they do, (like the crooks who are told by the police that they are "good") — thus, their readers are seduced by their errant reasoning constructed from carefully crafted arguments, which can most accurately be characterized as a form of *Fundamentalism*, because the predominant characteristic of their arguments is oversimplification — an oversimplification which they deliberately employ to divert the attention of their readers away from the clearly demonstrated proofs which expose the hollow superficiality of their false arguments and the errant conclusions they lead to; in order to invert the truth in the minds of their readers, and put darkness in the place of light – a practice which is so odious in the sight of God, that He curses those who employ it: *Woe to them that put darkness for light.* (Isaiah 5:20) However, the main purpose of this volume is not to refute the errors of those who assert that a true and certain pope can be judged a heretic by the Church; or that a man reputed to be pope who would manifest the pertinacity of heresy, (who would therefore not be a true pope but only a *putative pope*) cannot be judged by the Church to be no pope. That I have amply proven in the first volume. Here I will only deliver the *coup de grâce* to this latest strain of the Conciliarist heresy advocated by Salza & Siscoe, which they propagate in order to provide cover and apparent legitimacy to the faux pontificate of the heretic Jorge Bergoglio, and by way of extension to legitimize the *Masonic* pan-Christian and pan-religious *Reformation* for which Bergoglio was installed to consummate, in order to bring about the completion of the work begun by Luther and the Protestant Reformers; which was to establish a *counter-church* based on the ancient heresy of *Gnosticism* — a *new religion* founded on the "Ancient Mysteries" of Freemasonry.

However, the primary purpose of the first part of this volume is to briefly elaborate the teaching of the Church on *the nature of ecclesiastical authority* insofar as it applies to the Church's power *to determine infallibly and judge between multiple claimants to the papal throne,* **or to judge on the legitimacy of a doubtful pope who is reputed to be the valid pontiff — a putative pope.** In the second part, I will apply this doctrine to the claims on the Petrine *munus* of Jorge Bergoglio and Joseph Ratzinger; and I will prove that Bergoglio is a formal heretic, and therefore an *incapable subject* of the papacy, and therefore *not a valid pope*; while, Joseph Ratzinger (Pope Benedict XVI), according to the standards of canonical tradition, does not present in his doctrines any certain *indicia* of formal heresy which would constitute proof sufficient to disqualify him from holding the Petrine office. A brief but concise exposition on the nullifying canonical defects of Benedict's renunciation will also be included this volume, which will demonstrate that **Benedict XVI, even as Pope Emeritus remains in full possession of the Petrine munus**, so that upon his death, the Apostolic See will become vacant, and it will then be necessary for a new pope to be elected. However, if after a thorough examination of the question of validity of his resignation, there should remain an unresolvable and founded *positive and probable doubt* in the minds of the legitimate pastors of the Church about the validity of Benedict's renunciation — **and if Pope Benedict would still refuse to resolve that doubt by means of an unequivocal declaration**; then, in this eventuality it would be necessary for the Church to proceed to the election of a new pope.

However, for the Church to have authority in such a case of doubt about the legitimacy of a claimant, there must not merely be some degree of founded *positive and probable doubt*, but the doubt must be such as would make it impossible to recognize any of the claimants as certainly a valid pope. If a pope is a true pope validly elected, his election cannot be nullified by a council, nor can his primacy be removed, as Ballerini explained: «*The same primacy exists in every Pontiff who is true and legitimate, even if because of ambiguous circumstances it is not ascertained who among the contenders is the legitimate and true pope. This ignorance could indeed excuse those whose due efforts do not arrive at a true Pontiff in reality invincibly unknown to them; but as simple ignorance impairs no right, and cannot impair him who is a true and legitimate Pontiff, albeit unknown to others, accordingly it does not nor can it grant any right over him even to an ecumenical council: undoubtedly the right of the primacy always remains in reality with a true and legitimate Pontiff, who always, being superior to the whole Church and whatever council by this right of the primacy, is removed from the jurisdiction of those others.*»[85] In fact, as Bordoni[86] explains, even if faced with war or other imminent dangers, or an opposing party supported by the secular powers, the pope is morally bound to resist any such attempt that would coerce his resignation or nullify his primacy with all his might, even unto death, rather than allow a schism to be brought about by ceding the rights of the papacy to a demonstrably illegitimate intruder.[87] The proposition that a council could nullify the election of a true and valid pope or deprive him of his jurisdiction directly opposes the solemn definition of the Primacy which infallibly declared in *Pastor Æternus* that the Primacy consists of the *"full and supreme power of jurisdiction"* (plenam et supremam potestatem

---

[85] *De Potestate Ecclesiastica Summorum Pontificum Et Conciliorum Generalium*, Auctore Petro Ballerinio Presbytero Veronensi, Augustæ Vindelicorum (Augsburg), 1770, p. 132 — «Idem vero primatus inest cuivis Pontifici, qui verus & legitimus sit, etiamsi ob ancipites circumstantias non constet, quis inter contendentes sit legitimus et verus. Hæc enim ignorantia potest quidem excusare eos, qui verum re ipsa Pontificem sibi invincibiliter ignotum debitis oficiis non prosequuntur; at sicut simplex ignorantia nihil juris adimit, aut adimere potest ei, qui re ipsa verus & legitimus Pontifex sit, licet aliis ignotus, ita nihil juris tribuit, aut tribuere potest in ipsum concilio quamvis œumenico: semper nimirum jus primatus manet re ipsa vero legitimoque Pontifici, qui semper hoc primatus jure re ipsa toti Ecclesiæ, & cuivis concilio superior, a jurisdictione istorum subtrahitur.»

[86] Father Francesco Bordoni of Parma († 1671), theologian, jurist, and historian, was the most notable Franciscan friar of his time, and was described by the Franciscan historian Luke Wadding as «vir doctus varioque scientiarum genere ornatus.» He was a man of vast culture, whose writings span multiple genres — a dogmatic and moral theology, canonical, historical, literary, and hagiographical. Fr. Bordoni was a theological consultor for the City of Parma and Synodal Examiner, and later Minister General of the Order (1653-1659). He was also a Marian Doctor and zealous defender of the Immaculate Conception.

[87] P. Francesco Bordoni, *Sacrum Tribunal Iudicum In Causis Sanctæ Fidei Contra Hæreticos Et Hæresi Suspectos*, Romæ, 1648, p. 150 — «Tum quia verus Papa pro viribus usq. ad mortem tenetur tueri unitatem Ecclesiæ in suo capite legitimo nullum permittendo schisma in Ecclesia Dei; per renuntiationem autem permitteret schisma, ergo nullatenus renuntiare potest. Tum quia hoc renuntiare esset cedere iura Papatus intruso, quod fieri non potest, cum sit contra omnia iura, quod non Papa notorie habendus sit pro vero Papa.»

iurisdictionis) and the *"total fullness of this supreme power"* (totam plenitudinem huius supremae potestatis). Against this solemn definition, John Salza and Robert Siscoe heretically assert on page 392 of *True or False Pope?* — "But in a case in which there is no peaceful and universal acceptance of an elected Pope, if the Church were to later nullify the election (e.g., by an act of deposition by an imperfect council, if the man were still living), this act would not infringe upon the Church's infallibility concerning dogmatic facts."[88] Once a man is validly elected and accepts his election, he is the pope, regardless of whether or not he is universally and peacefully accepted. No council has ever nullified the election of a true and valid pope on the pretext that he was not universally and peacefully accepted by the Church. Even the Council of Constance in its depositions did not nullify the election of any valid pope, but as Ballerini observed, "One sees by what means the divine providence employed the synod of Constance to end the most tenacious schism, so that that synod did not need to exercise any power of jurisdiction by its authority to depose any true, albeit unknown, actual Pontiff."[89] Such an act which would separate the head of the Church from the members of the mystical body, being opposed to the divine constitution of the Church, would bring about the destruction of the Church by decapitating the body, and therefore is impossible. In virtue of the Church's attributes of *Infallibility* and *Indefectibility,* the Church is infallibly protected by divine providence from such an occurrence ever taking place, because the pope as visible head of the Church participates in the headship of the invisible principal Head of the Church, Our Lord Jesus Christ who cannot be separated from the body; and who invisibly directs the affairs of the Church through his *vicar,* the Pope, and the pope's hierarchical subordinates. The invisibility of the Head presiding over the visible head and the members makes his governance of the Church no less real; and if He were visible, we would see Him visibly directing and governing the whole Church on earth, as St. Robert Bellarmine

---

[88] Salza & Siscoe, *Op. cit.* p. 392.

[89] Ballerini, *Op. cit.* p. 138 — «Vides interim, quibus modis divina providentia usa est ad abolendum per Constantiensem synudum pertinacissimam schisma, ut ne opus esset eamdem synodum quiquam juris exercere ad deponendum sua auctoritate quempiam verum, licet ignotum, actualem Pontificem.»

explained in *De Conciliorum Auctoritate Caput XV*, in his third argument proving that "The supreme pontiff is the head of the whole Church":

> Third, the pope is the immediate vicar of Christ, according to the cited Council of Lyon and Florence, as well as the Council of Constance, session. 8, where was condemned the heresy of Wycliff who said the pope is not the immediate Vicar of Christ. Nor do the adversaries deny it; therefore he presides over all in the place of Christ, over whom Christ invisibly presides, and over whom he would visibly preside, if he were visibly present, not only over the particular churches but even over the whole universal Church, and general councils; therefore the pope presides over the universal Church.[90]

The Pope as the visible head of the Church, participating in the headship of Christ, also shares in His kingship, as Pope Gregory XVI explains:

> And in truth why is it maintained that the Pope is a true monarch? For those reasons, in fact, which together make him subject to many laws. In fact, it is not said that he is such, except for the following reasons: I. God gave him the task of moderating and correcting the abuses, as well as of punishing the abuses of his own cooperators in the episcopate, giving him the authority to depose them if they are contumacious, as St. Bernard attests, writing to Eugene: *Nonne, si causa extiterit, Tu episcopo coelum claudere, Tu ipsum ab episcopatu deponere etiam, et tradere Satanae potes (1)?* and as was verified, by the testimony of Natale Alessandro, in the deposition of Antimus bishop of Constantinople, and in the subsequent replacement of Menna, made by Pope Saint Agapitus: *Primatum gloriosius exercere non potuit romanus Pontifex, quam CP. Patriarcham haereticum exauctorando, et in eius locum alium ordinando, idque nulla synodo convocata* (1). II. Because he is constituted by Christ, the universal and

---

[90] *De Conciliorum Auctoritate,* cap. xv. p. 65 — «Tertio, papa est immediatus vicarius Christi, ut habetur in concilio lugdunensi et florentino citatis, neenon in concilio constantiensi, sess. 8. ubi damnatur haeresis Wiclefi dicentis, papam non esse immediatum Christi vicarium. Neque id adversarii negant; ergo praeest iis omnibus loco Christi, quibus Christus ipse invisibiliter praeest, et quibus etiam praeesset visibiliter, si visibiliter adesset: Christus autem praeest; et praeesset visibiliter, si adesset visibiliter, non solum Ecclesiis particularibus, sed etiam toti Ecclesiae universali, et generalibus conciliis; igitur etiam papa praeest Ecclesiae universali.»

authoritative defender of the rights of others, as Saint Athanasius reminded Felix, the supreme pontiff: *Ob id vos praedecessoresque vestros in summitatis arcen constituit Deus, ut nobis succurratis.* III. Because he is the head and father of all Bishops even when they are congregated, as the Chalcedonian Council names him in its letter to St. Leo: *Summitas tua filiis quod deest adimpleat.* IV. Because he has the right to propose, establish and authorize the norm of true belief, that is, because, as St. Thomas says, *ad ipsum pertinet editio symboli*, and he is the only one, with whom not to gather is to be dispersed, and with whom not to agree is the same as declaring oneself a follower of the Antichrist, as is rightly expressed by Saint Jerome, who wrote to Saint Damasus: *Quicumque tecum non colligit, spargit: qui tecum non est, Antichristi est.* V. Finally the Pope says it of himself and is a true monarch, because to him is committed the care of the whole fold of Christ.[91]

The pope's supreme power over the Church is a participation in the supreme power over the Church exercised by Christ himself. On this supreme power of Christ, Pius XI taught, «The foundation of this power and dignity of Our Lord is rightly indicated by Cyril of Alexandria. "Christ," he says, "has dominion over all creatures, a dominion not seized by violence nor usurped, but his by essence and by nature." His kingship is founded upon the ineffable hypostatic union.»[92] «He is the Head of the Church in his own right;» Canon Smith explains — «Peter and his successors, only in virtue of the power received from him. Thus the Pope is the Vicar (*i.e.* representative), not the successor, of Christ. Christ is Head as Redeemer and Mediator of all men; "and therefore," writes Pius XII, "this Body has only one principal Head, namely Christ, who, continuing himself to govern the Church invisibly and directly, rules it visibly through his personal representative on earth."»[93] This absolute spiritual power is entirely distinct from the pope's temporal power, as Fr. Denis Fahey explains, "The Temporal Sovereignty of

---

[91] D. Mauro Cappellari ora Gregorio XVI, *Il trionfo della santa sede e della chiesa contro gli assalti dei novatori*, Venezia, 1832, Preliminare, §. LXII. pp. 52-53.

[92] *Quas Primas* Pius XI, Dec. 11, 1925.

[93] Canon George F. Smith, D.D., Ph.D., *The Teaching Of The Catholic Church*, London, Second Edition, 1952, XX THE CHURCH ON EARTH, PART II, THE JURIDICAL STRUCTURE OF THE CHURCH, § VIII: THE POPE: THE VICAR OF CHRIST, p. 720.

the Pope in the Vatican State is completely different from his Indirect Power in temporal affairs. It is, however, a consequence of the Pope's participation in the Spiritual Kingship of Christ as His Vicar on earth."[94] The doctrine on the divinely instituted papal monarchy, briefly capsulized in this work, was fully elaborated in the works of St. Robert Bellarmine, primarily in *De Romano Pontifice*.

* * *

I have mentioned in Volume One that Pope Benedict XVI as holder of the Petrine *munus* still retains the power by divine right to designate the electors of his successor, and to declare Jorge "Francis" Bergoglio deposed. Benedict XVI, constituted by God as an *absolute monarch* over the Church, possesses this power by divine right because to him who is pope is committed the care of the whole Church, as St. Robert Bellarmine explains in the cited passages below. Unfortunately, Pope Benedict's own words constitute the most clear indication that he has no intention to ever again exercise the power of the primacy that remains with him by divine right. However, in the eventuality that the pastors of the Church would have a founded doubt about the legitimacy of the claim of Jorge Bergoglio to the Petrine *munus* as well as the validity of Pope Benedict's ambiguous but continuing claim on it, then, **in the uncertainty and in the reasonable and founded positive doubt of the legitimacy of the claims on the *munus*, it is infallibly certain that the pastors of the Church would have the right and the power to resolve the doubt.** That this power is *infallible* is proven by John of St. Thomas where he says, "I add, however, it seems likely that this case is impossible, namely that the Church would judge not to be pope, one who is truly the pope, this would be for the whole Church to be deceived by making a judgment in a most grave matter which affects the body of the whole Church, even as the Church cannot be deceived in judging the canonization of some saint, likewise in condemning someone as a heretic and deposing him from the pontificate, it does

---

[94] Rev. Denis Fahey, C.S.SP., B.A., D.Pa., D.D. Professor of Philosophy and Church History, Senior Scholasticate, Blackrock College, *The Kingship of Christ According to the Principles of St. Thomas Aquinas*, Dublin 1931.

not seem the Church can err, nor be permitted by God, that she would judge him not to be pope, he who in reality is the pope."[95] Therefore, if it would eventually emerge that there is no certain pope, the pastors of the Church would then have to proceed to the election of a new pope. Pope Gregory XVI explained that this was within the power of the Church to do, and was actually done in the similar case of Antipope Benedict XIII who maintained his claim after the abdication of Pope Gregory XII:

> «The Council therefore had the whole foundation for judging that his proponents themselves had known the illegitimacy and nullity of his assumption to the Apostolic See: nor, on the other hand, should it cooperate in the continuation of the schism, leaving him in the peaceful possession of his alleged pontificate. In this hypothesis, therefore, it had all the right, I will say indeed, the obligation to provide for the security of the whole Church with the deposition of Benedict, without being able to infer from this, that it had an equal right to depose an evidently legitimate Pope. In fact, it pronounced and carried out its final sentence, not on the basis of its authority over the Pope, but on the founded supposition that he was not [the pope]: in which case the power of the Church is evidently certain, as much as it is clearly certain that Jesus Christ, wanting *immutable, visible and perpetual* government, founded for the safety of the faithful, must have provided the Church with all means, which are necessary in order not to be governed by an illegitimate leader. Therefore he must infallibly have conferred on it the right to the power, in the uncertainty and in the reasonable and founded doubt of the legitimacy of a Pope, to proceed to the election of another. And this, above all, if that one, whose legitimacy is reasonably suspect, did not allow it to be molested in a thousand ways, so that God should have to

---

[95] *Cursus Theologicus II-II De Auctoritate Summi Pontificis, Disp. II, Art. III, De Depositione Papae*, p. 256—«Addo tamen verisimilibus videri illum casum impossibilem esse, quod scilicet Ecclesia judicet aliquem non esse pontificem, qui vere in re sit pontifex, hoc esset falli Ecclesiam universalem inferendo judicio circa rem gravissimam, quæ et totum Ecclesiæ corpus tangit, ita quod sicut Ecclesia falli non potest in judicando canonizationem alicujus sancti, ita in condemnando aliquem tamquam hæreticum, et deponendo illum a pontificatu, non videtur errare posse Ecclesiam, nec permitti a Deo, ut judicet non esse pontificem illum, qui vere in re pontifex est.»

be accused of not having sufficiently provided for its indefectibility, if in such circumstances it did not have the appropriate faculties.»[96]

Bordoni argued similarly, explaining that since God does not fail to provide for his Church in necessity, in virtue of his words in Matthew, "I am with you all days even until the end of the world," the Lord would not fail to provide the Church with all that is necessary; and thus, by His authority which was conferred not only on Peter the head but on all the apostles, when it is necessary, and which is of maximum necessity in such cases as a heretic pope or an uncertain pope, the Church would be in a most dire state if it would not have a remedy, by which it could come into knowledge of its true spouse and head; or if it had no means to depose the intruders and acquire a true and legitimate head. Therefore, in virtue of Christ's promise, God cannot fail to provide a remedy.[97] When there exists such a doubt, Bordoni explains, "Since in doubt it is presumed that there is no Pontiff, and therefore a Council is to be convened, so that they [the doubtful popes] be deposed, and a legitimate Pontiff be elected, lest the Church remain without a head, and the sheep without a Pastor."[98] It is to be noted, however, (and is explained below) that this power is not a supreme authority suppletively conferred by God as an exception in exceptional circumstances, since the supreme authority pertains essentially and exclusively to the Primacy, which was conferred singularly upon Peter and his successors; but that power exists in virtue of the attributes of *indefectibility* and *infallibility* of

---

[96] Gregorio XVI, *Op. cit.* p. 46

[97] Bordoni, *Sacrum Tribunal Iudicum,* cap. VI, p. 151: «Tum quia, Deus in necesariis non deest Ecclesiæ suæ, cum dixerit per Matth. extremis verbis. Ecce ego vobiscum sum omnibus diebus usque ad consumationem sæculi… quæ necessitas maxime accidit in his duobus casibus de Pontifice hæretico, & incerto, cum enim caput dolet, eius membra languent & tabescunt, ac valde infelix esset Ecclesia, si nullum haberet remedium, per quod posset venire in cognitionem veri sponsi, & capitis sui, aut si nullum haberet medium, quo sibi acquirere posset verum, & legitimum superiorem, depositis adulteris, & intrusis.»

[98] *Ibid.* p. 159 — «quia in dubio præsumitur nullum adesse Pontificem, ac proinde Concilium congregandum est, vt deponantur, & legitimus eligatur Potifex, ne Ecclesia remaneat sine capite, & oues sine Pastore.»

the Church, by which the members are provided with all necessary means to remain perpetually united to their legitimate head, and therefore to be able to designate and recognize the head and subject themselves to him, but not to depose him. Therefore, whenever there is a certain pope, the authority of the entire episcopate united to the head exists entirely in *hierarchical subordination* to the pope's supreme authority; since the supreme authority of the head is not conferred suppletively by way of exception on the bishops of the Church in virtue of their totality, but that supreme authority belongs exclusively to the certain holder of the Primacy. Only when there exists a founded and probable doubt about a papal claimant's legitimacy does it fall within the jurisdiction of the entire episcopate united in a council to resolve the doubt. Thus far, however, Pope Benedict has sufficiently maintained his claim on the papal *munus* to the extent that it cannot be judged to be a doubtful or uncertain claim. Benedict XVI remains in possession of the *munus* and the Primacy which belong by divine right to him as the holder of the Petrine *munus*, as will be explained in Part II. Since one can prudently foresee that Pope Benedict will most probably not exercise his primacy for the remainder of the duration of his pontificate, it will most likely be necessary for the Church to resolve the issue of succession after Benedict's death by ruling on the invalidity of Jorge Bergoglio's claim on the papacy.

* * *

John Salza and Robert Siscoe, the authors whose heretical articles have appeared in *The Catholic Family News* and in *The Remnant*, have continued to defend Bergoglio's illegitimate claim on the papacy by attacking the dogma of the primacy. It is their position that even as a public heretic manifestly guilty of formal heresy, Bergoglio would remain validly constituted in the papacy until judged guilty of heresy by the Church; but that can never happen, since if Bergoglio was indeed a valid pope, he could never be judged, because the Church has solemnly defined that the jurisdictional power of the primacy is absolute — a *total fullness of supreme power*. In their immense confusion, Salza & Siscoe posted an article on their website, *Fr. Kramer's Canonical Confusion,* in which they continue to attack the dogma of the primacy by reiterating their heretical assertions which attribute **to a council the power to act as the supreme judge and final arbiter on a matter of faith in a case of heresy against a validly reigning pontiff.** It is yet another patent attempt to vindicate their heretical Conciliarist belief, by caricaturizing my arguments and then attacking the caricature. It is a masterpiece of sophistry in which their deception is very craftily concealed; but their intention is transparent — they are again attempting to justify their heretical belief that the Church has the power to judge and convict a validly reigning and certain pontiff for the crime of heresy. Although their arguments are founded on the crudest of fallacies, due to their subtle and crafty employment of the methods of sophistry, the logical incoherence of their position is not always immediately apparent to readers, even to some who have completed some formal education in philosophy and theology but do not read astutely; and for that reason, the heresy has spread widely among traditional Catholics, even among the clergy. Against their heretical opinion, I have conclusively argued in the first volume of this work with irrefutable proofs, and have demonstrated that the Church teaches *de fide*: 1) That a manifest public heretic, entirely by his own action and without any judgment by ecclesiastical authority, ceases to be a member of the Church, and renders himself incapable of holding ecclesiastical office; and as a consequence thereof loses any ecclesiastical office he may have held *ipso jure*; 2) That a true and certain pope who has not lost office *ipso jure* by publicly defecting from the Catholic faith, possesses an absolute judicial immunity in virtue of his Primacy for so long as he remains in office, and therefore, in virtue of his *total fullness of supreme power*, cannot be judged or deposed for heresy or any other crime by his inferiors in the Church.

Their article begins with a quotation of my words: "A public heretic is one who obstinately denies or doubts a revealed truth which must be believed with divine and Catholic faith in such a manner that is publicly known or will soon be publicly known. Such a heretic is by canonical definition a public heretic, who is *ipso facto* separated from the body of the Church, and loses ecclesiastical office *ipso jure*." My words which state precisely what is set forth in the Code of Canon Law were followed by Siscoe's inane comment: "Father, with all due respect, that is so manifestly absurd on its face, and so easily shown to be false when considered in light of the historical practice of the Church, that it is difficult to believe you actually wrote it." So, Siscoe is saying that a proposition whose conclusion follows from premises strictly formulated according to definitions taken straight out of the Code of Canon Law is "manifestly absurd on its face". Heresy is defined in Canon 1325, §2[99] of the 1917 Code, and in Canon 751[100] of the 1983 Code. According to these canons, heresy is defined as the obstinate post baptismal denial or doubt by one who retains the name of Christian, of any divinely revealed truth which must be believed with divine and Catholic faith. An act is defined in canon law as *public* exactly as I explained in my reply to Siscoe. I have explained this point at some length in both my first volume of this work and in my replies to Siscoe; but Salza & Siscoe resort to a corrupt lawyer's trick, which is to refuse even to acknowledge the fact that I replied to their objection — deliberately setting about to create the impression in the minds of their readers that Fr. Kramer is at a loss to reply to it. A *public heretic* is one whose obstinate heresy is *public*, according to the definition of *public* as the term is defined in canon law. I have argued at great length and demonstrated beyond any reasonable dispute that it pertains to the nature of heresy that it is essentially an act of defection from the Catholic faith; and according to both the 1917 and 1983 Code of Canon Law, the *ipso jure* loss of office is the statutory effect of the *fact* of a public defection from the Catholic faith. What this means (and is explicitly stated in the canons) is that all ecclesiastical offices are lost automatically *by operation of the law itself* by the very fact of the defection; and it is strictly in accordance with the definition of the expression, '*ipso jure*', that whatever is effected *ipso jure* takes place **by operation of the law itself** before any declaratory sentence is issued by ecclesiastical authority, so that the declaration only declares juridically what has already happened by operation of the law.

---

[99] «Post receptum baptismum si qui, nomen retinens christianum, pertinaciter aliquam ex veritatibus fide divina et catholica credendis denegat aut de ea dubitat, haereticus… est.»

[100] «Can. 751 — Dicitur hæresis, pertinax, post receptum baptismum, alicuius veritatis divina et catholica credendæ denegatio, aut de eadem pertinax dubitatio; apostasia, fidei christianæ ex toto repudiatio.»

What I have said previously on this topic is that Salza & Siscoe err in their belief that "only notorious heretics are excluded from the body of the Church"; and hence, a pope's heresy would need to be *public and notorious*; and therefore, it would need to actually be widely known throughout the Church, for a pope to cease to be a member of the Church; and even then, they do not concede that such a pope would lose office without first being judged by the Church. In their article, *RESPONSE TO FR. KRAMER'S ERROR ON "NOTORIOUS BY FACT"*, they quote a passage of Fr. Dominique Boulet of the SSPX out of context: "For the criminality of a Pope's heresy to be legally recognized, such that his heresy would be canonically Notorious, not only would a knowledge of his heresy [the material aspect] have to have spread widely through the Church, as we have seen above, but it would also have to have been widely recognized as a morally imputable crime [the formal aspect]." For a pope's heresy to be legally recognized as a *public and notorious*, i.e. *notorious by fact*, it would indeed need to have been spread widely through the Church — but it would not need to be widely diffused for his heresy to be considered *public* according to the letter of ecclesiastical law. Such an opinion as that of Salza & Siscoe is based on an antiquated notion of *public delict* that was held by some canonists before the codification of Canon Law in the 1917 Code made that opinion obsolete by defining what the law intends by the term *public*. The canonically obsolete expression employed by Salza & Siscoe, *"public and notorious"*, was taken by them straight out of the writings of John of St. Thomas, who formulated his opinion on this point centuries before the term *public* was legally defined in the Code. The highly authoritative 1952 canon law commentary of the Faculty of Canon Law of the Pontifical University of Salamanca, explains that in the legislation previous to the 1917 Code, there was not yet the clear and uniform concept of *public delict*.[101] From what is set forth in the

---

[101] Miguelez – Alonso – Cabreros; *Código de Derecho Canónico – Bilingüe y Comentado*; Madrid, 1952, p. 785 – "En el derecho anterior al Código no era claro ni uniforme el concepto de *delito público*. Hoy la publicidad puede risultar de dos capítulos: o porque ya está divulgado el delito, o porque hay peligro próximo de divulgación. 1.° *Está ya divulgado* el delito, cuando una parte notable de la comunidad tiene conociemiento del *hecho* y de su carácter *delictivo*. Con la palabra «comunidad» pretendemos designar aquí no

text of the canon and in the expert commentary, it is clear that according to the specifications of the canon in question that for the crime or the fact to be considered public, knowledge of the heresy would not have to actually be publicly known, but there would only need to be the proximate danger of it becoming known; and the proximate likelihood that it would be divulged and widely diffused, would not have to be the danger of a divulgation that would be diffused widely throughout the greater portion of the whole Church in order for it to be considered "public". As I demonstrated irrefutably in my first volume of this work, quoting the verbatim text of the canons, and the most authoritative commentaries on the canons; that for a crime or a sin to be *public*, it suffices that the knowledge of the act be public or *likely to soon become public* (canon 2197. 1°, "*Delictum est publicum, si iam divulgatum est aut talibus contigit aut versatur in adiunctis ut prudenter iudicari possit et debeat facile divulgatum iri*"; and a crime is *notorious by fact* (canon 2197. 3°) if the knowledge of the fact of the crime and its imputability are, 1) public (*si publice notum sit*), and, 2) that the crime is committed under such circumstances that it cannot be concealed by any subterfuge, nor excused by any excuse admitted in laws (*in talibus adiunctis commissum, ut nulla tergiversatione celari nulloque iuris suffragio excusari possit*). Similarly, for the imputability to be *notorious*, I prove in my first volume that Salza & Siscoe go far beyond the letter of the law and what is explained in the authoritative commentaries, specifying gratuitously and arbitrarily their own highly restrictive conditions, which according to them, must be verified for the fact of the crime of heresy and its imputability to be qualified as

---

precisamente una sociedad perfecta, una diócesis, una religion o una ciudad; sino un núcleo de fieles que pueden más directamente experimentar daño del delito o de su divulgacion, v. gr., una parroquia o una casa religiosa. En qué proporción hayan de estar los que conocen el delito para que pueda decirse que «una parte notable de la comunidad» tiene conocimiento de él, no puede definirse taxativamente… 2.° *Peligro de divulgación* no es lo mismo que «possibilidad de prueba» en el fuero externo. [...] En más: tratándose de una communidad algo numerosa, pueden conocerlo seis u ocho personas, y no considerarse el delito ni divulgado ni en peligro de divulgación. Las cualidades y circumstancias de las personas son las que hay que apreciar en cada caso, más que el numero de las mismas."

notorious by fact.¹⁰² For an ecclesiastical officeholder to be severed from the body of the Church and to lose office, it suffices that the *fact* of defection from the faith be *public*, and thus it suffices that the publicity of the act conforms to the same conditions specified for a public delict in canon 2197. 1°. In their *Formal Reply*, Salza & Siscoe erroneously declare: "If the culprit's heresy is not deemed to be notorious by fact, however, he must be formally judged and declared a heretic by the Church (rendering him notorious by law) before he is legally separated from the Body of the Church." The proposition is plainly opposed to the magisterium and the letter of canon law, according to which It suffices that the defection into heresy be *public* for the juridical bond to be visibly severed, and for the loss of office to take place *ipso jure*. (*CIC* 1983 Canon 194 § 2; *CIC* 1917 Canon 188. 4°) I have fully explained the matter in the first volume of this work.

Salza & Siscoe then object by quoting the opinion of Fr. Klekotka¹⁰³: "We must note however cases of tacit resignation ipso jure enumerated in canon 188. The provisions of this canon apply to all offices and therefore per se even to bishoprics. *The only probable case of such tacit resignation with the bishop would be public apostasy* and hence as a crime we treat of it here. It must be noted however that this *must be public and certain*." One must carefully take note of Fr. Klekotka's phraseology, "the only **probable** case", he says, "**would** be public apostasy" – he does **not** say that the canon under consideration is **not applicable** to cases of simple heresy, since according to the letter of the law, the *fact* of public defection from the faith *per se* suffices to

---

¹⁰² Salza writes, "pertinacity is established only if the Pope were to renounce the Church as the RULE of faith by PUBLIC PROFESSION"; and again, he and Siscoe state, "… if a Catholic leaves the Church and becomes a professed atheist, or publicly joins a Protestant or Sedevacantist sect, he thereby ceases to be a member of the Body of the Church by his own act, since public apostasy, heresy and schism do sever juridical bonds which are necessary for a Catholic to retain visible union with the Church." Pertinacity, as the Church understands it, is simply this: the persistence in an error in faith even after it has been sufficiently explained so as to convince a reasonable man. This is how it is explained by all the canonists and theologians, such as St. Alphonsus, Fr. Francesco Bordoni, Fr. Charles Augustine, etc.

¹⁰³ Fr. Peter Klekotka, *Diocesean Consultors* (1920), p 161.

effect the *ipso jure* loss of office; and heresy is according to its nature a defection from the faith. However, the reason why the only *probable* case would be public apostasy is that the *fact* of apostasy is usually more plainly obvious; whereas the *pertinacity* of heresy is difficult to verify in the vast majority of cases, since heretics are notoriously evasive, and they do their utmost to conceal the *dolus*[104] of their heresy; so that it is very rare that their heresy is committed with evident pertinacity and in such a manner that can be said to be "committed under such circumstances that it cannot be concealed by any subterfuge, nor excused by any excuse admitted in laws." (Canon 2197. 3°) Nevertheless, in such cases of simple heresy (as heresy is defined in canon law and in theology) in which the pertinacity is plainly and certainly manifest, (which is to say, *public and certain*), then the letter of the law strictly and properly applies *ipso jure* as provided in the canon. Thus, the objection they also make, that I, "seek out the most broad interpretation" of the canon in violation of the canonical principle, "favorable things are to be given a broad interpretation, while odious ones are to receive a strict interpretation," is plainly deceitful and false, as is obvious from their own words by which the accuse me of "interpreting the phrase 'public defection from the faith' as equivalent to the definition of a 'public heretic,' which they ludicrously claim I "invented"; whereas in fact, I have rigorously adhered to the usage of the terms as they are defined in canon law as can be gathered from the examination of these terms elaborated in Volume One. It is Salza & Siscoe, in fact, who are inventing their own definitions of terms. Indeed, as I have amply demonstrated in the first volume, they totally disregard the definitions of terms, such as *judgment'*, and employ the usage of terms in the manner of Humpty Dumpty ("When I use a **word**," Humpty Dumpty said, in rather a scornful tone, "it means just what I choose it to mean—neither more nor less.") According to them, public heresy is not an act of public defection from the faith unless one joins another religion or explicitly renounces the Catholic faith. On page 281 of their book, «"*public heresy" and "public defection from the faith" are two different things*». The sophistry is patent in the logical fallacy which they deliberately

---

[104] In canon law, *dolus* is defined as the deliberate will to violate a law – «*deliberata voluntas violandi legem*» (*CIC 1917*, Canon 2200).

employ; since, while *public heresy* is indeed one form of defecting from the faith, it is not an *equivalent term*. Defection from the faith is a broader term which includes not only heresy, but apostasy as well. However, in explaining that they are *two different things,* they falsely assert that *public heresy* is not included among the acts which constitute a *defection from the faith*.

Their argument is an artifice of sophistry which is an example of one the classic types of verbal fallacy systematized and catalogued by Aristotle in his Sophistical Refutations (*De Sophisticis Elenchis*). An example of this kind of fallacy is, 1) "Corsicus is different from Socrates"; 2) "Socrates is a man"; 3) "therefore Corsicus is different from a man".[105] Now, in their latest article they repeat the same falsehood founded on the same fallacy they employed in their book, saying that the provision for tacit loss of office for defection from the faith refers to "a cleric who leaves the Church and joins a non-catholic sect". Such a one, they say, "is considered to have "tacitly renounced" his office, according to canon 188.4"; however, from this premise it does not follow that "one who tacitly renounces his office" means "one who openly leaves the Church or joins another religious organization"; because defection from the faith is not limited to these acts, but includes all acts which are in their nature a defection from the faith. Hence, "one who tacitly renounces his office" is one who commits any act which conforms to the definition of '*public defection from the faith*', and not only one who apostatizes, explicitly renounces the Church, or joins a heretical sect. On page 139 of *The Renunciation of an Ecclesiastical Office*, Fr. Gerald McDevitt writes: "The defection of faith must be public. It is to be noted immediately that **adherence to or inscription in a non-catholic sect is not required to constitute the publicity that the canon demands.**" The Very Rev. H. A. Ayrinhac comments on Canon 2197 in his *General Legislation in the New Code of Canon Law* (pp. 349-350), that public defection from the faith means: "Public defection from the faith, by formal heresy or apostasy, with or without affiliation with another religious society. The offense must be public, that is, generally known or liable to become so before

---

[105] Bustamente, Thomas; Dahlman, Christian, eds. (2015). *Argument types and fallacies in legal argumentation.* Heidelberg: Springer International Publishing. p. x. ISBN 978-3-319-16147-1.

long. (Can. 2197)" Nor is it required that one formally declare oneself to have left the Church. John P. Beal, in the *New Commentaru on the Code if Canon Law* explains, "A formal act [i.e. a declaration that one has left the Church] is not required for the defection in canon 194; the only requirement is that it be public (known or likely to become known).[114] Neither is it required that the officeholder join another religion, although this could be an objective indication of defection. [[114] Socha, in *Münster Com, 194/2—3; Urrutia*, n. 925, confuses this with "notorious".]"[106] At this point, the Salza-Siscoe artifice of sophistry becomes transparent, because it is indeed true that one who joins a sect can be said to have defected from the faith, but from that fact it does not logically follow that defection from the faith is defined as joining a non-Catholic sect, explicitly renouncing the Catholic faith, or leaving the Church by means of a formal declaration to that effect. Public defection from the faith, according to the learned commentators I have quoted, is accomplished by any act which is *public*, and which is in the nature of a defection from the faith such as *formal heresy*. Indeed, joining a heretical sect and public heresy are not equivalent terms; and joining a heretical sect is an example of defection from the faith, but it does not follow logically from these premises that *public defection from the faith* means *joining a non-catholic sect*; or that public heresy is *not* an example of *public defection from the faith*. Similarly, *"public heresy"* and *"public defection from the faith"* are *two different things* insofar as they are not entirely equivalent and identical, but it does not follow logically that just because they are not identical, i.e., since public heresy is not defined as an equivalent term, that therefore, public heresy is not in the nature of a defection from the faith. This kind of fallacy is one that is chronically and deliberately employed by Salza and Siscoe for the purpose of deceiving their readers and leading them into error and heresy.

Salza & Siscoe resort to the identical type of verbal trickery when they claim that the term "manifest heretic", as it was applied to a hypothetical case of a heretical pope in Bellarmine's day, referred only to the members or founders of heretical sects, but not to all those heretics generally whose acts of formal heresy are public and whose pertinacity is manifest. The proposition is evidently absurd on its face,

---

[106] John P. Beal, *New Commentary on the Code of Canon Law*, pp. 226-227.

since the mere fact that the theologians of the period, in treating on the question of the deposition of a manifestly heretical pope, were clearly speculating about whether or not a pope who would still maintain the pretence of being a Catholic and the head of the Church can be deposed, plainly rules out that the question even concerned the case of a pope who would openly leave the Church and join some heretical sect. There was not even any debate on the question of a pope who would leave the Church and declare himself to no longer be Catholic. No theologian in the history of the Church has ever claimed that if a pope had openly defected into paganism, like Julian the Apostate — or if a pope would have become a Calvinist minister, that he would still be the pope of the Catholic Church. The question of judging a manifestly heretical pope as it was treated by canonists and theologians since the hypothesis was first formulated by Gratian, concerned not a pope who openly rejects the Church or leaves it to join some other religion, but rather, as can be seen already from Gratian's formulation, it concerns a pope who ostensibly remains in the Church as pope, but who deviates on some article of faith: "Here no mortal presumes to rebuke his faults, because he, the one who is to judge all, is to be judged by none, *unless he be found straying from the faith*; for whose enduring steadfastness the whole body of the faithful the more earnestly prays the more they realize that, after God, their salvation depends on his own."[107] No Catholic on earth would think for a moment that his salvation would depend in any manner whatever on a pope who left the Church to become a Protestant. It was precisely for the reason that the "manifest heretic" pope would at first appear ostensibly to still be in the Church that that theologians like Bellarmine, Ballerini, and the others, spoke of the need for corrections or warnings in order to render manifest the pertinacity of the already evident material heresy of a pope who would still claim to be Catholic. This by itself already demonstrates absolutely that the term was not applied restrictively to mean only those who joined or founded sects, or openly left or rejected the Church; because it

---

[107] «Huius culpas istic redarguere presumit mortalium nullus, quia ipse judicaturus a nemine est judicandus, *nisi deprehendatur a fide devius;* pro cuius perpetuo statu universitas fidelium tanto instantius oratquanto suam salute post Deum ex illius incolumitate animadvertunt propensius pendere.» [Vide – Moynihan, *Op. cit.* pp. 26 - 27]

patently pertains to the nature of ecclesiastical warnings that they are given with the threat to separate from the Church those dissenters who still maintain the pretence of belonging to the Church, if they will remain obdurate in their pertinacity; and it would be absurd to threaten with exclusion someone who has already expressly declared his wilful departure and has in fact already left. Thus it can be easily seen that the term "manifest heretic" has always been properly understood not only to refer to one who has openly rejected the Church, but also to one whose objective heresy and subjective pertinacity in the disbelief of some dogma are plainly obvious and *certain* — or as Bellarmine explains in his refutation of Cajetan's 'fourth opinion': one is a manifest heretic "after he appears manifestly pertinacious," and hence the injunction: "that the heretic is to be avoided after two warnings, that is, after he appears to be manifestly pertinacious". (*hæreticum post duas correptiones, idest, postquam manifeste apparet pertinax, vitari*) This is undoubtedly how Pietro Ballerini understood it when he said of a pope who "*remains obstinate in a belief contrary to a manifest or defined dogma*", that he, "by this his public pertinacity which for no reason can be excused, since pertinacity properly pertains to heresy, *he declares himself to be a heretic, i.e. to have withdrawn from the Catholic faith and the Church by his own will, so that no declaration or sentence from anyone would be necessary*", and "that he by his own will departed, making known to be severed from the body of the Church, and *in some manner to have abdicated the Pontificate*, which no one holds or can hold, who is not in the Church.» [108] Thus it is absolutely clear

---

[108] *De Potestate Ecclesiastica Summorum Pontificum Et Conciliorum Generalium*, Auctore Petro Ballerinio Presbytero Veronensi, Augustæ Vindelicorum (Augsburg), MDCCLXX, Cap. IX. § II. pp. 128-129 – «*Quemcumque vel privatum respiciunt illa Pauli ad Titum: Haereticum Hominem post unam et alteram correptionem devita, sciens quia subversus est, qui ejusmodi est, et delinquit, cum sit proprio judicio condemnatus.* Qui nimirum semel & bis correctus non resipiscit, sed pertinax est in sententia dogmati manifesto aut definito contraria; hac sua publica pertinacia, cum ab haeresi proprie dicta, quae pertinaciam requirit, excusari nulla ratione potest; tum vero semetipsum palam declarat haereticum, hoc est a fide catholica, & ab Ecclesia voluntate propria recessisse, ita ut ad eum praecidendum a corpore Eccleaiae nulla cujusquam declaratio aut sententia necessaria sit. Perspicua hac in re est S. Hieronimi

and unmistakable according to the mind of Ballerini, that what he says of the pope who "by his public pertinacity... declares himself to be a heretic, i.e. to have withdrawn from the Catholic faith and the Church by his own will,"[109] is identical to Bellarmine's meaning in *De Romano Pontifice lib. ii cap. xxx*, where he speaks of a *"manifest heretic pope"*; as one who is a manifest heretic, "after he appears manifestly pertinacious," saying, "a manifest heretic pope ceases by himself to be pope and head, just as he ceases to be a Christian and a member of the Church".[110] They most evidently do not employ the term in a manner that would restrict its meaning only to a pope who openly renounces the Church or joins a heretical sect, but they most obviously refer to one who still maintains the pretence of *remaining in the Church as its head, while plainly manifesting his formal heresy by obstinately denying some article of faith externally as a fact which is seen as evidently true.* Thus, to understand what is meant by the term "manifest heretic", one must bear in mind Bellarmine's juristic distinction between what is *evidently true* and what is *evidently credible.*

Bellarmine explains that, "evidently true and evidently credible are not the same thing. What is evidently true is seen, either in itself or in

---

ratio in laudata Pauli verba, *Propterea a semetipso dicitur esse damnatus, quia fornicator, adulter, homicida, et cetera vitia per sacerdotes ex Ecclesia propelluntur: haeretici autem in semetipsis sententiam ferunt, suo arbitrio de Ecclesia recedentes: quae recessio propriae conscientiae videtur esse damnatio.* Pontifex ergo, qui post solemnem & publicam Cardinalium, Romani Cleri, vel etiam synodi monitionem se se obfirmatum praeferret in haeresi, & de Ecclesia palam recessisset, iuxta praeceptum Pauli esset vitandus; & ne aliis perniciem afferret, in publicum proferenda esset ejus haeresis, & contumacia, ut omnes similiter ab eo caverent, sicque sententia, quam in se ipsum tulit, toti Ecclesiae proposita, cum sua voluntate recessisse, & ab Ecclesiae corpore declararet avulsum, atque abdicasse quodammodo Pontificatum, quo nemo fruitur, nec frui potest, qui non sit in Ecclesia.»

[109] Pietro Ballerini, *DE POTESTATE ECCLESIASTICA SUMMORUM PONTIFICUM ET CONCILIORUM GENERALIUM.* Verona, 1768, Caput IX. §. II. p. 128 — «hac sua publica pertinacia... semetipsum palam declarat haereticum, hoc est a fide catholica, & ab Ecclesia voluntate propria recessisse, ita ut ad eum praecidendum a corpore Eccleaiae nulla cujusquam declaratio aut sententia necessaria sit.»

[110] «*Papam hæreticum manifestum* per se desinere esse Papam & Caput, sicut per se desinit esse Christianus & membrum corporis Ecclesiae.»

its principles. Evidently credible is that which is seen neither in itself nor in its principles, but it has so much weighty testimony, that any sensible man reasonably ought to believe it; so that if a judge sees a man get killed by a robber, or mortally wounded who then dies afterwards, he has evidence of the truth that that robber is a murderer; but if he does not actually see the bloodshed take place, but he does have twenty most serious witnesses who say they did see it, he has evidence of credibility."[111] *Indicia* which are evidence *per se* of formal heresy constitute evident truth of heresy. One who exhibits such *indicia* is a **manifest heretic**, because the *indicia* by themselves immediately render the fact of formal heresy immediately seen as evidently true *per se* or in its principles. *Indicia* which render the heresy visible not in itself, but from its principles to the extent that the fact and *dolus* of heresy are judged to be evident by certain arguments and proofs, and accordingly judged through *knowledge of the cause*, are also properly *indicia* of formal heresy, but are not by themselves immediately evident *indicia* of *manifest heresy*. Such heresy becomes manifest only upon being proven to be certainly true, and as such, becomes evidently true when *pertinacity becomes manifestly evident*. No matter how evidently credible would be a charge of heresy, based on credible *indicia,* but without any plainly evident fact of both matter and pertinacity, there is not manifest heresy, but only suspicion. A suspect of heresy, no matter how grave the suspicion may be, is not a manifest heretic; but if there are certain and evident *indicia* of formal heresy, that evident truth of formal heresy qualifies the offender as a **manifest heretic**. Similarly, one who remains obstinate after correction in *violent suspicion of heresy* is a certain heretic with a moral

---

[111] *De Notis Ecclesiæ* cap. iii. P. 109 — «non quidem efficiunt evidenter verum, ipsam esse veram Dei Ecclesiam; sed tamen efficiunt id evidenter credibile; nec enim est idem evidenter verum, et evidenter credibile. Nam evidenter verum dicitur, quod vel in se, vel in suis principiis videtur; evidenter credibile illud dicitur, quod non videtur nec in se, nec in suis principiis, habet tamen tot, et tam gravia testimonia, ut quilibet vir sapiens merito id credere debeat; ut si judex videat hominem a latrone occidi, vel vulnerari laethaliter, et postea mori, habet evidentiam veritatis, quod ille latro sit homicida; si autem caedem fieri non videat, sed habeat viginti testes viros gravissimos, qui dicunt se vidisse, habet evidentiam credibilitatis.»

certitude that approximates manifest heresy to a degree of virtual equivalence.

It is also quite obvious that by the way John of St. Thomas employed the term *manifest heretic*, he did not intend it to denote only the members or founders of heretical sects; as it is plainly evident from his words that when using this term he is not speaking restrictively of one who has formally defected from the Church, and who has publicly declared himself outside the Church, and is therefore not only outside the Church *per se,* but also *quoad nos*; but he says the *manifest heretic* is still a member of the Church *quoad nos* until he has been declared a non-Christian by ecclesiastical authority — expressly distinguishing between those who declare themselves outside or have openly left the Church and are therefore outside the Church *qouad se* and *quoad nos;* and the *manifest heretics* who although outside the Church *quoad se,* maintain the pretence of still being Catholics, and therefore remain members of the Church *quoad nos* until they are judged by the Church.[112] In spite of the explicit distinction made by John of St. Thomas, Salza & Siscoe still assert this humbug that according to the authors of the time, the term *"manifest heretic" refers only to those who explicitly renounced the Church or joined heretical sects.*

---

[112] *Cursus Theologicus II-II De Auctoritate Summi Pontificis,* Disp. II, Art. III, *De Depositione Papae,* XXVI, p. 263: «Nec Hieronymus quando dicit hæreticum per se discedere a corpore Christi, excludit ipsum Ecclesiæ judicium præsertim in re tam gravi, qualis est depositio papæ, sed criminis judicat qualitatem, quod per se sine alia censura superaddita excludit ab Ecclesia, dummodo tamen per Ecclesiam declaretur; licet enim ex se sepatet ab Ecclesia, tamen quoad nos non intelligitur facta separatio sine ista declaratione. Et similiter ad rationem respondetur, quod non Christianus, qui quoad se, et quoad nos Christianus non est, non potest esse papa, si tamen quoad se Christianus non sit, quia fidem amisit; quoad nos autem adhuc non fit juridice declaratus, ut infidelis, vel hæreticus, quantumcumque manifestus sit secundum privatum judicium, adhuc quoad nos est membrum Ecclesiæ, et consequenter caput. Requiritur ergo judicium Ecclesiæ, quo proponatur, ut non Christianus, et evitandus, et tunc desinit quoad nos esse papa, et consequenter antea non desierat etiam in se, quia omnia quæ faciebat erat valida in se.»

John of St Thomas explains, "It is responded that a heretic is to be avoided because of two corrections juridically made and by the authority of the Church, and not according to private judgment; for there would follow a great confusion in the Church if it would suffice that this correction be made by a private man, and that the manifestation of heresy were to be made but not declared by the Church, and proposed to all that they avoid the pontiff, all being bound to avoid him".[113] It is self-evident from the author's words themselves that the "manifest heretic" (*hæreticus, quantumcumque sit manifestus*) spoken of here as to be avoided is one who has not formally declared himself to have left the Church, joined a sect, or to have explicitly rejected her authority, but is one who maintains the pretence of remaining inside the Church as a member in good standing who respects her magisterial authority while at the same time obstinately rejecting some article of faith while still claiming to be a Catholic. It is precisely because such a manifest heretic who still maintains the pretence of being a faithful Catholic would, in the author's opinion, be a source of "great confusion" to many if his heresy would not be juridically declared by the Church; whereas one who publicly and unambiguously manifests the will to be separated from the Church is understood by all to be outside the Church in such a manner that there cannot be any confusion in anyone's mind about his departure from the Church. Such a one, is recognized in law as a heretic *quoad nos*, because his heresy is *public and notorious* and is *juridically notorious by fact*. Consequently, it is abundantly clear and obvious that even according to the authors of the sixteenth and seventeenth centuries, the term "manifest heretic" did not denote only those who had

---

[113] *Ibid.* — «XXVI. Respondetur hæreticum esse evitandum propter duas correctiones juridice scilicet factas, et ab Ecclesiæ auctoritate, et non secundum privatum judicium; sequeretur enim magna confusio in Ecclesia si sufficeret hanc correctionem esse factam ab homine privato, et quod facta manifestatione hæresis non tamen declarata ab Ecclesia, et proposita omnibus ut evitent pontificem teneri omnes illum evitare, nec enim omnibus fidelibus potest esse publica hæresis papæ, nisi ex relatione aliorum: requiritur ergo quod sicut Ecclesia designando ipsum omnibus juridice ipsum ut electum proponit, sic declarando et proponendo eum ut hæreticum evitandum eum deponat.»

openly rejected the Church or became members of other denominations.

Fr. Gerald McDevitt elaborates on the canonical meaning of defection from the faith in canon 188. 4° on pp. 136-140 of *The Renunciation of an Ecclesiastical Office*:

> «Since it is not only incongruous that one who has publicly defected from the faith should remain in an ecclesiastical office, but since such a condition might also be the source of serious spiritual harm when the care of souls is concerned, the Code prescribes that a cleric tacitly renounces his office by public defection from the faith. Prior to the Code the law imposed a privation of office and benefice on a cleric for such a crime. This penalty was certainly imposed upon those clerics who were publicly guilty of heresy and of apostasy, but because of two apparently contradictory laws it was disputed whether the penalty applied also to those who were publicly guilty of schism. The present law attaches a tacit renunciation instead of a privation of office to a public defection from the faith. Since canon 188, n. 4, uses a general terminology, it necessary to determine the meaning of defection of faith and also to determine the extent of publicity that is required if the act of defection is to become the basis for a tacit renunciation of office.
>
> Since three specific crimes, namely, heresy, apostasy and schism, will enter this discussion, it is necessary to give the definitions of them as found in the Code. These definitions are contained in canon 1325, §2, which reads as follows:
>
> Post receptum baptismum si quis, nomen retinens christianum, pertinaciter aliquam ex veritatibus fide divina et catholica credendis denegat aut de ea dubitat, haereticus; si a fide Christiana totaliter recedit, apostata; si denique subess renuit Summo Pontifici aut cum membris Ecclesiae ei subiectis communicare recusat, schismaticus est. These definitions are quite clear. Apostasy is a total defection from the faith, while heresy is only a partial defection, but as MacKenzie remarks (The Delict of Heresy in Its Commission, Penalization, Absolution, The Catholic University of America Canon Law Studies, n. 77 (Washington, D.C.: The Catholic University of America, 1932), p. 19), they are essentially the same, since the rejection of any one truth involves the same blasphemous attitude towards God that is involved in a denial of all the truths.
>
> The authors are not in agreement as to whether schism is to be included in the meaning of the term "defection of faith," as used in canon 188, n. 4. Augustine, Blat, Toso and Coronata do not regard

schism as constituting a defection from the faith as understood in canon 188, n. 4. since schism as such does not essentially militate against the possible retention of the faith even in its entirety. Maroto, Vermeersch-Creusen, Cocchi and Sipos, on the other hand, consider schism pure and simple as sufficient to constitute a defection from the faith and hence to call for the application of the sanction enacted in canon 188, n. 4. Heneghan includes those who are guilty purely of schism in his interpretation of the clause, "qui notorie aut catholicam fidem abjecerunt," in canon 1065, § 1. The expression which Heneghan interprets in this manner is substantially the same as the expression employed in canon 188, n. 4, which reads as follows: "A fide catholica publice defecerit."

According to the strict interpretation of the words contained in canon 188, n. 4, and of the definition of schism, it must be admitted that the canon does not indisputably comprehend the condition of pure schism, since in its essence schism does not denote defection from the faith, but rather connotes a violation of obedience and charity. However, one could doubt that the law intends to exclude the consideration of schism from this canon, for in canon 2314, §1, n. 3, which provides penalties for the public adherence to a non-catholic sect, cognizance is taken of canon 188, n. 4, with the words "firmo praescripto can. 188, n. 4." Since the wording of canon 2314, § 1, n. 3, applies to a schismatical sect as well as to a heretical one, and since the application of canon 188, n. 4, is confirmed in this canon, on could reasonably be led to conclude that the wording of canon 188, n. 4, means to comprise also the condition of pure schism.

In practice it will be extremely rare that a case of pure schism will arise, for almost invariably and all but inevitably some heresy will be joined to it. This is especially true since the time of the solemn definition of the primacy and the infallibility of the Roman Pontiff. If, however, there should arise a case of pure schism on the part of a cleric, the writer believes that the cleric would not lose his office by a tacit renunciation since the sanction of canon 188, n. 4, is of but doubtful efficacy in view of its questionable comprehension of the condition of pure schism, and especially since the effective application of that sanction involves the forfeiture of a vested right.

The defection of faith must be public. It is to be noted immediately that adherence to or inscription in a non-catholic sect is not required to constitute the publicity that the canon demands. The defection must be public according to the definition of publicity which is found in canon 2197, n. 1:

Delictum est publicum, si iam divulgatum est aut talibus contigit aut versatur in adiunctis ut prudenter iudicari possit et debeat facile divulgatum iri.

The authors are in agreement that this is the type of publicity postulated for making the defection a public one. Thus the defection from the faith may be public by reason of the fact that it is already known to a notable part of the community. The law does not prescribe any special number as being necessary to constitute a notable part of the community. Determination of this point is left to man's prudent judgment. Besides being public by reason of actual divulgation, the defection from the faith may be public also because of the fact that the circumstances force one to conclude that it will be easily divulged in the future. Thus if even only a few loquacious persons witnessed the defection from the faith, or if the sole and only witness was a taciturn person who later threatened to divulge the crime because of an enmity that has arisen between him and the delinquent, the delict would be public in the sense of canon 2197, n. 1.

A cleric, then, if he is to occasion the tacit renunciation of his office, must have defected from the faith by apostasy or heresy in a public manner according to the explanation just given. Since the writer holds the opinion that tacit renunciation is not of the nature of a penalty, he holds also that the prescriptions of canon 2229 concerning excusing causes with reference to latae sententiae penalties do not apply to the case of a tacit renunciation of office on the part of a cleric who has perpetrated the act which is mentioned in canon 188, n. 4. Thus the writer believes that even if it were thinkable that a cleric was excused from incurring excommunication involved in a defection from the faith in view of the prescriptions of canon 2229, § 3, n. 1, he still would lose his office by a tacit renunciation. In this regard a tacit renunciation is like an irregularity, which, while in many respects it looks like a penalty, is nevertheless not a penalty in a truly canonical sense.»

Any confusion that there may have previously existed on this point is entirely cleared up in the 1983 Code, which speaks not only of defection from the faith as effecting loss of office, but of defection from communion with the Church (*a communione Ecclesiæ*), which takes place by an act of heresy, schism or apostasy.

The same kind of artifice of deception as that described above is again employed by Salza & Siscoe in expressing their false doctrine on *canonical* or *ecclesiastical warnings*. First they say, "The Church is a juridical institution with laws and procedures governing how heretics are to be ***deprived*** of their office. In a case such as you described above, the Church would first ***juridically determine*** that the *matter* (the proposition, as such) was *heresy*, as opposed to a lesser error. The culprit would then be issued a ***canonical warning*** providing him ample opportunity to renounce the heresy, BEFORE any loss of office would take place." What they are describing here is the procedure that must be followed in a case of ***penal deprivation of office***, which is not the process prescribed for *tacit renunciation of office* (188.4°) or *removal*, (as it is called in the new Code), which is *automatic*, because it takes place *ipso jure*; and for which *no canonical warnings are prescribed*. Canonical warnings, as I have explained at some length in Volume One, are the first stage of the penal process, and can only be administered by a *superior* with *jurisdiction* to ***judge***. In a case of heresy it is first necessary to *judge* that the *matter* is heresy and only then to warn the subject, and then, if the subject remains obstinate, to judge and punish the subject. For the *Church* to *juridically determine* that the *matter* is heresy, the *Church* must first *judge* that the matter is heretical. As I explain below, it is solemnly defined *de fide* by the First Vatican Council that the ***final determination*** of the Church's ***judgment*** concerning of all matters of faith, pertains exclusively to the authority of the **Roman Pontiff**, who is the holder of the ***universal primacy of jurisdiction***, by which he exercises the *"total fullness supreme power"*, ***"not only in matters of faith and morals, but also in those which concern the discipline and government of the church dispersed throughout the whole world"*** — (*Pastor Æternus*). As I have amply documented in Volume One, it pertains to the authority of the pope, who, by the supreme authority of Christ, is appointed as the ***"supreme judge"*** to make these ***judgments*** and to juridically warn and judge all, and be judged by none, because, (as St. Thomas explains the doctrine later defined at Lyon II and at Vatican I), *to his authority it pertains to DETERMINE WITH FINALITY the matters of faith, so that they may be held by all with unshakable faith. (Summa Theol.* II^a - II^æ q. 1, art. 1). Hence, St. Thomas explains, "A subject is not competent to administer to his prelate the correction which is an act of justice through the coercive nature of punishment: but the fraternal correction which is an act of charity is within the competency of everyone in respect of any person towards whom he is bound by charity, provided there be something in that person which requires correction." (*I^a - II^a q. 33 a. 4*) A valid pope, therefore, can only be *corrected* by his inferiors in the Church, but it is beyond the jurisdiction of anyone or any group, even a council, to administer *ecclesiastical warnings* to a validly reigning pope, since such warnings pertain to the jurisdiction of a superior.

Then they again resort to verbal sleight of hand, referring to an act of ***fraternal correction of a pope*** as an ***ecclesiastical warning***: "In the case of a Pope, the ***warning*** is not an act of jurisdiction, but an obligation of charity (fraternal correction), as Bellarmine explains". However, a *fraternal correction* is not a *warning* made by the *Church,* as is clear from the passage of Bellarmine they quote.[114] I already pointed out to Siscoe that "The Fifth Lateran Council defined that the pope possesses **absolute** power over a council, so there exists no possibility for canonical warnings to be administered to a pope, nor to **legally establish charges against a reigning pontiff**." Although that definition was not technically a *solemn definition of the extraordinary magisterium*, it was, nevertheless sufficiently solemn and definitive expression of the pope's supreme magisterium and of the ordinary and universal magisterium to qualify as a revealed truth of divine and Catholic faith, and thus to be ascribed the note of infallibility, as is evident from the text of the decree itself[115]: "*For it is clearly established that only the contemporary Roman pontiff, as holding authority over all councils, has the full right and power to summon, transfer and dissolve councils. This we know not only from the witness of holy scripture, the statements of holy fathers and our predecessors as Roman pontiffs, and the decisions of the sacred canons, but*

---

[114] «"Peter allowed himself to be reprimanded by Paul because that was not a juridical censure, but a Fraternal correction. For, as Augustine says in letter 19 to Jerome, and Gregory in homily 18 on Ezekiel, Paul does not reprimand Peter, as a superior judges inferiors with authority, but as inferiors sometimes correct their superiors out of charity." (De Romano Pontifice, lib. 2, cap. xxvii).»

[115] In the same manner as the pronouncement of Pope John Paul II against the ordination of women was ruled by the Sacred Congregation for the Doctrine of the Faith to be sufficiently solemn to be ascribed the note of *infallible*, the definitive character of this even more solemn pronouncement of the Fifth Lateran Council was already sufficiently solemn to be qualified with the theological note of *infallible* at the time it was made. After the solemn definition of the Primacy in 1870, it is indisputably *de fide definita*.

also from the declarations of the same councils. Some of this evidence we have decided to repeat, and some to pass over in silence as being sufficiently well known."[116] [Fifth Lateran Council, Session 11, Tanner translation) On the *de fide* nature of this pronouncement, St. Alphonsus points out: "St. Antoninus (part. 3. tit. 23. cap. 3. §. 3.) did not hesitate to write: *But neither can appeal be made to a general council against a pope, because the pope is superior to every council; nor does it have the power, whatever it does, unless by the authority of the Roman Pontiff it be given force and confirmed. Therefore to think that a council can be appealed to against a pope is heretical.*"[117]

It was precisely at this point of the discussion that Siscoe replied, "In the case of a Pope, the warning is not an act of jurisdiction, but an obligation of charity (fraternal correction)". Indeed, the correction is not an act of jurisdiction, and for that reason, it is not a *canonical* or *ecclesiastical warning* – **It is not an official act of the CHURCH.** An *ecclesiastical warning* is a *canonical admonition* administered with authority by the *Church*. Not only do the inferiors lack the authority to canonically admonish their superior, *which by definition is an act of jurisdiction of a superior*, but their act is not an act of the *Church*, because the *Church* does not consist of the members without their head, but is composed of the members together with the head; without which the Church is not constituted as such, as is explained later below. As I explained above, the necessity to correct or admonish a heretic is established by canonical doctrine and tradition to be a *relative necessity*. It is not an absolute necessity, as is plainly gathered from the eminent authorities I cited; but Salza & Siscoe draw from the verse of St. Paul, and the passages of Bellarmine and Ballerini, an absolute necessity, interpreting the texts against the mind of the Church in the crudely simplistic manner so typical of fundamentalists. The method of

---

[116] «cum etiam solum Romanum pontificem pro tempore existentem tamquam auctoritatem super omnia concilia habentem conciliorum indicendorum transferendorum ac dissolvendorum plenum ius et potestatem habere nedum ex sacrae scripturae testimonio dictis sanctorum patrum ac aliorum romanorum pontificum etiam praedecessorum nostrorum sacrorum que canonum decretis sed propria etiam eorumdem conciliorum confessione manifeste constet quorum aliqua referre placuit reliqua vero utpote notoria silentio praeterire.»

[117] Alfonso Maria de' Liguori, *Vindiciae pro suprema pontificis potestate adversus Iustinum Febronium*, Torino, 1832, p. 164.

sophistry they employ is not so crude as their fallacy. It is a Hegelian dialectical artifice used by Lenin and the Communists, which is characterized in the words of Vladimir Lenin, "It is necessary sometimes to take one step backward to take two steps forward."[118] First they assert the absolute necessity of admonitions, and cite the verse of St. Paul to Titus and the texts of Bellarmine and Ballerini. Then they refer in passing to the exception mentioned by De Lugo; and then they re-assert the absolute necessity for warnings with a fallaciously flimsy argument. Thus, exactly in the manner of Masons and Marxists, they achieve the apparent inversion of the truth by means of a Hegelian "negation of the negation".[119] It is not surprising that Salza employs the same methodology as did Lenin — Like Vladimir Lenin, John Salza was also initiated into the Scottish Rite of Freemasonry. Salza, a former instructor on Masonic ritual, was initiated into the thirty-second degree. and Lenin was an initiate of the thirty-third degree. Fr. Manfred Adler explains, "Lenin and

---

[118] The phrase is an inversion of the title of a book Lenin wrote in 1904, Шаг вперед, два шага назад (One Step Forward Two Steps Back). Karl Marx, who was a practicing Satanist, was particularly given over to the practice of inversion. As I have shown in Volume One, Salza and Siscoe have perfected the art of inversion of truth, inverting the proper sense of Catholic teaching and of Catholic authors.

[119] "The law of the negation of the negation, which Hegel used as the fundamental law for the construction of his whole system of thought, has a far wider sphere of application in the system of nature. This law really expresses the fundamental form of development in nature. The opposing forces at work in every single thing bring, about constant changes in its constitution. These changes accumulate in quantity until, at a certain determinate stage in the process of development, a distinct qualitative transformation or leap occurs. The thing loses its original identity and passes over into its opposite. But the evolutionary process does not halt at the point of simple negation. The new form of material existence is no less self-contradictory than the old and subject to the same internal restlessness. The first negation in turn undergoes self-differentiation and division until it, too, passes into its own opposite and thereby becomes negated. The final result of this process is called the negation of the negation, a synthetic unity which has discarded the transitional forms but preserved within itself the essential content of both sides of the contradictory whole." — Wm. F. Warde (pseudonym of George Novack), *Engels on Dialectics of Nature* (December 1940)

Trotsky, the fathers of the Russian October Revolution, were not only passionate Communists, but were enlightened Freemasons as well. They belonged to the thirty-third degree of the Scottish Rite."[120] On the cited page of Adler's work one reads the following: "As the Bolshevist Revolution was victoriously brought to completion in 1917, Brother Rozieres delivered an address in praise of the two glorious high-degree brothers on December 24, 1917 in Paris at the Lodge, *Art et Travail*." In a biographical note in Salza's very sanitized exposé on Masonry,[121] which leaves out all mention of the Sect's history of crimes and devilry, one reads, «*He was a member of James M. Hays Lodge #331 and Nathan Hale Lodge #350 in Milwaukee, Wisconsin where he served as Junior Deacon, Senior Deacon and Junior Warden. The Grand Lodge of Wisconsin awarded Salza a Proficiency Card which authorized him to teach Masons how to perform the Three Degrees of Freemasonry. In addition to teaching Freemasonry's degrees in schools of instruction, Salza proposed many changes to Wisconsin's Masonic ritual which were adopted by the Grand Lodge of Wisconsin. Salza also performed in major degree roles in the Scottish Rite of Freemasonry and the Ritualistic Divan of the Ancient Arabic Order Nobles of the Mystic Shrine.*» Thus it is no surprise that Salza & Siscoe employ the same deceitful artifices of inversion and deception as did Lenin, such as altering and manipulating the meaning of words, and demonizing opponents, and especially following the dictum of Lenin: "Telling the truth is a petty-bourgeois prejudice. Deception, on the other hand, is often justified by the goal."[122]

Siscoe then objects further, «No bishop or priest in 2000 years of Catholicism has lost his office, ipso jure, for merely doubting a dogma with obstinacy, in a manner that "will soon become" publicly known. That's not how it works. The Church is a juridical institution with laws and procedures governing how heretics are to be deprived of their office. In a case such as you described above, the Church would first juridically determine that the *matter* (the proposition, as such)

---

[120] Manfred Adler, Die *Antichristliche Revolution der Freimaurerei*, p. 47. cf. Adler provides the reference: G. Frei, *Das Wirken der Finsternis — heute*, o. O. u. o. J., p. 5.

[121] Masonry Unmasked—*An Insider Reveals the Secrets of the Lodge*, 2007.

[122] Quoted by Albert Weeks, professor at New York University, in *The long shadow of Lenin's 'worse is better'*. (The Christian Science Monitor / April 23, 1980).

was *heresy*, as opposed to a lesser error. The culprit would then be issued a canonical warning providing him ample opportunity to renounce the heresy, BEFORE any loss of office would take place.» In this passage, Siscoe cunningly conflates *loss of office* (Can. 194), which is found in Book 1 under GENERAL NORMS, CHAPTER II, "LOSS OF ECCLESIASTICAL OFFICE", under the heading of "Removal" (Article 3) with *penal deprivation of office* (Can. 196), which is found under the heading of "Privation" (Article 4). Canon 196 explains, «Privation from office, namely, a penalty for a delict, can be done only according to the norm of law. §2. Privation takes effect according to the prescripts of the canons on penal law.» Salza & Siscoe then quote an excerpt from *The Delict of Heresy* (1932), by Fr.Eric MacKenzie, which explains the *penal process* for *deprivation of office*. I have explained at length in my first volume exactly how *loss of office for defection from the Catholic faith* takes place *ipso facto* by operation of the law itself (*ipso jure*), and how *penal deprivation of office* is inflicted according to the prescribed procedures. They, however, refuse to take cognizance of what I have explained in order to create the impression that I am at a loss to provide a logically coherent response; and instead they again trot out their favourite canard; which is to say that I am merely repeating a Sedevacantist argument: «It appears that you have fallen for the Sedevacantist error of combining the definition of the sin of *heresy* with the canonical definition of *public* and concluding that one who meets the *combined meaning* of the two has "publicly defected from the faith," and lost his office, *ipso facto*, according to canon 188.4 (which is no longer on the books). Even a cursory reading of the approved commentaries on canon 2314 (1917 Code) should enable you to see the embarrassing absurdity of that Sedevacantist error.» Again, their argument rests on a conflation of the *penal process* prescribed in Can. 2314 with the administrative *ipso jure* provision decreed in Canon 188.4°. They then resort to an outright lie, claiming that I, "continue to insist that the two canons are identical"; i.e. the two canons on loss of office, Canon 188.4° in the 1917 Code, and Canon 194 §1 –2 in the 1983 Code; whereas what I actually wrote is that, "Although Canon 188.4° is no longer in force, its *identical provision* is found in Canon 194 of the 1983 Code."

Thus, what I actually explained was not that the *canons* of the two codes are identical, but that the *ipso jure* **provision** for loss of office *set forth in those canons* for defection from the faith is *identical* – and it is indeed identical in both – virtually word for word.[123] What is different in the two canons is that the prescribed process for dealing with the defection juridically is different: In the old Code, it was dealt with by a penal process; while in the 1983 Code, an administrative declaration is prescribed. I have fully elaborated this point in the first volume of this work. Similarly, they accurately quote me saying that the declaration is a judicial act requiring jurisdiction; but then they speciously claim that *"*A pope cannot be judged with a coercive judgment while he remains pope, but he can be judged with a discretionary judgment, as Bellarmine *and everyone else* admits.*"* However, as I explain below, a discretionary judgment can have no juridical effect on a pope, and the simple act of discretion which establishes a crime in the minds of men is not a juridical act, but is a natural personal act of private persons exercising the human faculty of judgment, which, when expressed as a *discretionary judgment* of an *arbiter*, is not in the nature of a judgment of the *Church*. As is explained below, to be a valid *judgment of the Church*, the judgment must be a **juridically declared act** — and to be juridically declared it must be pronounced by one who possesses the jurisdiction to issue a *judgment* (even if the judgment is not pronounced in the judicial forum) — and only then would such a declaration be a *judgment of the Church*.[124] A *discretionary judgment* is not a *judicial act*, and therefore, it is not a *juridical act*, as Salza & Siscoe falsely assert in their online tract:

> A pope cannot be judged with a coercive judgment while he remains pope, but he can be judged with a discretionary judgment, as Bellarmine *and everyone else* admits. A discretionary judgment is a *legal* judgement, but one that lacks any coercive force. The *nature* of the

---

[123] In both codes, the loss of office for **defection from the Catholic faith** takes place *ipso jure*: 1) **IPSO JURE LOSS OF OFFICE:** "Can. 188.—Ob tacitam renuntiationem ab **ipso iure** admissam **quaelibet officia vacant ipso facto**" "Can. 194 — § 1. **Ipso iure ab ecclesiastico officio amovetur**" 2) **FOR DEFECTION FROM THE CATHOLIC FAITH:** "Can. 188.— ... si clericus: [...] 4° **A fide catholica publice defecerit**"; "Can. 194 — § 1. ... 2° qui **a fide catholica** aut a communione Ecclesiae **publice defecerit**".

[124] Bordoni, *Op. cit.* cap. VI, p. 154.

judgment is merely to decide or determine facts, not to punish or impose penalties. Bellarmine explains that a discretionary judgment is the form of judgment used by an Arbitrator, not a judge in the true sense of the word. He also lists many Popes who were indeed judged in this manner, including Leo IV who willingly submitted to the judgment of the Emperor and agreed to obey whatever was decided.

Since a discretionary judgment does not include any coercive force it is not, *of its nature,* forbidden in the case of a Pope. This is the form of judgment the Church would exercise in the case of a Pope who was accused of heresy. The Church would investigate charges and reach a verdict (discretionary judgment); Christ would authoritatively depose the Pope by severing the bond that unites the man to the office; then the Church would judge and punish the pope (coercive judgment). As we will see later, this is how Bellarmine himself says the process would unfold, in quotations that you will never find on a Sedevacantist website.

Here again Salza & Siscoe deceptively apply the Humpty Dumpty rule of sophistry: "When I use a word, it means just what I choose it to mean". They say "a discretionary judgment is a *legal* judgment," in the sense that the discretionary judgment would be a *verdict*: "The Church would investigate charges and reach a verdict (discretionary judgment)". Now this is absolutely false, and is directly contrary to what Bellarmine actually wrote, but they give it the appearance of truth by fraudulently interpreting Bellarmine's uncited and unreferenced words in a manner that falsify his meaning. ***A discretionary judgment is not a legal verdict of the Church***, first, because, lacking jurisdiction, it is not *judicial*; and second, in the case of a pope, it would not be a judgment of the Church, but only of part of the Church, namely, the *inferior* part, with the principal part, the HEAD, being excluded.[125] Furthermore, as is explained below, if the pope as the head of the Church were to be excluded from making the FINAL DETERMINATION of the judgment, it would not be a judgment of the Church.

---

[125] *De Conciliorum Auctoritate,* Cap. xviii. p. 70 – «Si accipiatur Ecclesia sine papa, falsum est illam esse totum, non enim est totum, sed pars, et quidem major, quam caput, magnitudine molis, minor autem magnitudine virtutis, sive auctoritatis, ut patet in quolibet corpore. Quod autem adversarii dicunt, auctoritatem capitis manere in Ecclesia suppletive, jam est refuta tum antea.»

What Bellarmine actually says on this point is, "The Supreme Pontiff cannot commit to a council or to any man a coercive judgment over himself, but only a discretionary one."[126] He then expounds on the distinction between the two: "First, in perfect judgment, there are found two elements. First, the power to examine the case, and to discern and to judge what ought to be done. Second, the power to compel the one who falls under the case to observe the sentence brought against him."[127] "Both," he explains, "are found in one who is properly a judge, who is the head [of government], or a magistrate (*praetor*) appointed by the head."[128] – "But in *arbiters,* only the first is found, to whose sentence men are bound to abide out of natural law, because we are bound to keep promises, but not by force of the sentence, because arbiters cannot coerce."[129] Now, according to Lewis & Short, an *arbiter* is "*he that is appointed to inquire into a cause in an actio bonae fidei* (i. e. who decides acc. to equity, while the *judex* decides acc. to laws)"[130] The authors also note that, "In the time of Cicero, when, acc. to the Lex Aebutia, the decisions were given in definite formulae of the praetor, the formal distinction between judex and arbiter disappeared". Now, when, Bellarmine says of arbiters, "to whose sentence men are bound to abide out of natural law, because we are bound to keep promises," he is clearly using the term as it is understood according to its primary meaning in English, given by *Wiktionary* as, "A person appointed, or chosen, by parties to determine a controversy between them". Bellarmine then explains

---

[126] Cap. xviii p. 69. «Summus pontifex non potest committere, neque concilio, neque ulli homini supra se judicium coactivum, sed tantum discretivum.»

[127] *Ibid.* – «Nota, in judicio perfecto duo quaedam reperiri. Primo, potestatem discutiendi caussam, et discernendi ac judicandi quid agendum sit. Secundo, potestatem cogendi eum, qui cecidit caussa, ad obtemperandum sententiae contra se latae.»

[128] *Ibid.* – «Utrumque invenitur in judice proprie dicto, qualis est princeps, vel praetor a principe constitutus.»

[129] *Ibid.* – «Primum autem solum reperitur in arbitris, quorum sententiae etiam si teneantur homines stare ex jure naturae, quia tenemur servare promissa; non tamen ex vi sententiae, quia non possunt arbitri cogere.»

[130] *A Latin Dictionary* — Charlton T. Lewis, Ph.D. and. Charles Short, LL.D. Oxford. Clarendon Press. 1879.

why a discretionary judgment can never be binding on a pope: "First, because the power of the pope over all is of divine law, as is evident; and the pope cannot dispense from divine law. Second, because an inferior cannot make a judgment that is reserved to one who is higher."[131] He concludes the argument saying, "And the judgment in the case of a pontiff is reserved to God, as we have taught above."[132]

Salza & Siscoe then absurdly claim that the Church has actually made "discretionary judgments" on popes; but the *Church* has never juridically pronounced a "discretionary judgment" against any reigning pontiff or anyone else, because a *judgment*, according to its proper and primary meaning, is not discretionary but *judicial*. A judgment, in order to be a juridically valid *judgment*, requires the jurisdiction of a superior. That it is impossible for any kind of judgment made by the pope's inferiors, whether coercive or discretionary, to cause the pope to fall from office either directly or dispositively becomes plainly obvious when one considers the *nature* of judgment. The primary meaning of *iudicium*, according to Lewis & Short, is *"a judgment,* i. e. *a judicial investigation, trial; a judicial sentence"*. So, when we speak of a *judgment of the Church*, whether it be declaratory or penal, the term properly designates *a judicial sentence*. The nature of judgment is expressed in the legal adage, *"Judicium est quasi juris dictum"* – which means that judgment is a "a declaration of the law" (*Black's Law Dictionary*, Second Edition 1910); or a "a command of the law" (*Ballentine's Law Dictionary*, 1916). Such a declaration or command properly pertains to the authority of a *judge*. St. Thomas teaches that the word *judgment* properly expresses the act of a judge acting in his capacity as a judge: *"iudicium proprie nominat actum iudicis inquantum est iudex."* (*II^a – II^a q. 60 a. 1*) Therefore, Bordoni, citing the sources of jurisprudence, explains, that "every act in order to be juridical and

---

[131] *De Conciliorum Auctoritate,* Cap. xviii p. 69 — «Primo, quia potestas papae super omnes, est de jure divino, ut patet. At non potest papa dispensare in jure divino. Secundo, quia non potest inferior committere alicui judicium reservatum superiori.»

[132] *Ibid.* — «At judicium in caussa ponificis est reservatum Deo, ut supra docuimus.»

valid essentially depends on jurisdiction."[133] Such an act which is proper to the office of a judge is not a mere act of discretionary judgment but, as Ballerini explains, "Judgment properly so called is delivered when one pronounces a sentence based on knowledge of the cause".[134]

The nature of discretion is different: "Judgment is objective; discretion is subjective. Forming a judgment means taking a decision; so legal rules of decision-taking apply."[135] In their authoritative work, *A Latin Dictionary*, Lewis and Short give the non-juridical meaning of *judicium* as, "The power of judging, judgment, discernment"; and cite Cicero's usage, «*"studio optimo, judicio minus firmo praeditus,"* Cic. Or. 7, 24".» In this non-juridical sense they explain that *judicium* refers to discretion, citing Cicero again: «*"si quid mei judicii est,"* if I can judge of it, Cic. Fin. 2, 12, 36: *"videor id judicio facere,"* i.e. with discretion, good judgment, id. Q. Fr. 3, 1, 5, § 18.» Discretionary judgment is subjective, it is a judgment which is decided according to equity — it is not a juridical ruling. It is not *judicial*. It does not declare the command of the law by one who acts in the capacity of a *judge* who decides according to *the law*. In a deposition from office, the judgment cannot be merely discretionary, but to be a *judgment of the Church*, it must be *judicial*, and therefore must be a proper *judicial sentence* of a *judge* acting with the jurisdiction of a *superior*, or at least *a judgment pronounced administratively outside of the judicial forum by a superior in possession of judicial power*. A mere *declaration* made without judicial power is not in the nature of a juridical act — it is neither a judgment of the Church nor an official act of Church authority: It is nothing. It is *tamquam non existens*. There does not exist in the divinely constituted *monarchy* of the Church a *separation of powers* such as is found in a *republic*, where the legislative, executive and judicial powers are located in their respective branches of government. In the papacy there exists

---

[133] Bordoni, *Op. cit.*, p. 158 — «omnis actus vt sit iuridicus, & validus essentialiter dependet a iurisditione. Bald. in *l. omne verbum, C. com. de legat.* Alex. *lib.*4. *confil.* 52. *num.*30. ex Rota Roman. *vol.* 1. *decis.*451. *nu.* 2.»

[134] *De Potestate ecclesiastica summorum Pontificum et Conciliorum generalium*, Augsburg, 1770, Cap. II p. 30 — «Judicium enim proprie dictum tunc fertur, cum quis ex causae cognitione sententiam pronuntiat.»

[135] F. A. R. Bennion, *Understanding Common Law Legislation*, Chapter: 13 *The nature of judgment*, Oxford University Press, p.111.

the totality of the power of governance, which subsist in the Primacy. In Canon Smith's *The Teaching of the Catholic Church*, it is explained that, "To enable the Church to carry out Christ's commission of leading mankind to salvation she has been vested by him with a threefold power, corresponding to his own office of Prophet, Priest and King: that of teaching, her doctrinal authority; that of order, her ministerial authority; that of government, her jurisdictional authority."[136] The total fullness of that threefold power subsists in the pope's *"full and absolute jurisdiction"* (Pius XII, *Vacantis Apostolicæ Sedis*), which is **"ordinary and immediate** *both over all and each of the* **churches** *and over all and each of the* **pastors and faithful"** (*Pastor Æternus*). **The bishops as** *ordinaries* **in their respective dioceses also possess that threefold power, but in** *hierarchical subordination* **to the supreme power of the Roman Pontiff. There simply does not exist any separate power in the Church outside of the hierarchical subordination to that supreme power, whereby the pontiff could be judged for heresy by the totality of the bishops in a council.**[137] **The Church possesses absolutely no power to judge the pope, but can only judge whether or not a doubtful pope's election was valid. As is explained above and elaborated below, only when** there exists a *presumption of vacancy* founded on the reasonable doubt that the man in question is a true pope, i.e., a doubt that his

---

[136] Canon George F. Smith, D.D., Ph.D.,*The Teaching Of The Catholic Church*, London, Second Edition, 1952, XX THE CHURCH ON EARTH, PART II, THE JURIDICAL STRUCTURE OF THE CHURCH, § VII: PRELIMINARY: THE AUTHORITY OF THE CHURCH, p. 710.

[137] *De Conciliorum Auctoritate, cap. xvi.* p. 66 — «Nam Christus legitur quidem dedisse Petro claves regni coelorum, Matthaei 16. et eumdem praefecisse ovili suo, Joan. ult. Dedit etiam apostolis caeteris potestatem praedicandi, baptizandi, peccata, dimittendi, et alia quaedam faciendi, quae ad munus episcopale spectant, sed hanc potestatem Christus singulis dedit ita ut potuerit quisque eorum illa omnia exercere sine congregatione aliorum, ut notum est: At quod ipsi Ecclesiae, idest, fidelium universitati in se, idest, ratione suae totalitatis aliquid potestatis tribuerit, nusquam legitur; immo e contrario legimus, praecipi populus, ut obediant, et subjaceant pastoribus suis, Hebr. 13. et alibi. Quod si Ecclesiae universitati non est data ulla auctoritas, ergo neque concilio generali, quatenus Ecclesiam universalem repraesentat.»

election is valid, does it pertain to the jurisdiction of the Church to decide the question. Such a presumption exists when there are sufficient *incidia* of heresy to establish doubt of validity of a claimant's election, since a heretic, being an incapable subject, is incapable of assuming the papacy; and once the papacy is validly assumed, the pope cannot fall into heresy, because, "the Pope by his own nature can fall into heresy, *but not when there is posited the singular assistance of God which Christ obtained for him by his prayer*: but Christ prayed *that his faith not fail*, not lest he would fall into other vices."[138] If it can be proven that the suspect is certainly a heretic, it is thereby proven that either he has fallen from office and is no pope, or he was never a true pope to begin with, and consequently was invalidly elected, for which reason he can be judged and deposed. This opinion was already expressed in the thirteenth century by Bernard of Parma in the *Glossa Ordinaria*, with the words, «Et sic nulla exceptione potest opponi sibi nisi de haeresi, xl *si papa* (D. XL, c. 6)».[139] If he is manifestly and certainly a heretic beyond all shadow of doubt, being condemned by his own judgment, he is no pope and can be deposed without a trial in accordance with the doctrine of Bellarmine, Ballerini and Gregory XVI, since, whether or not he ever was pope, as a manifest heretic he would be no pope and therefore *minor quolibet catholico*.

---

[138] St. Robert Bellarmine, *De Romano Pontifice*, lib. iv, cap. vii – «Respondeo ad primum argumentum: inde recte colligi, posse Papam ex natura sua incidere in haeresim, non tamen posita singulari Dei assistentia, quam Christus oratione sua illi impetravit: oravit autem Christus, ne deficeret Fides ejus, non autem ne incideret in alia vitia.»

[139] "The decretal [of Gregory IX] stated that no exception of invalidity could be brought against a pope who had been elected by a two-thirds majority of the college of cardinals. Bernard qualified this statement saying that an exception of heresy may be alleged. In this case, then, an *exceptio* would be an allegation that a pope's election had been invalidated by the fact of his heresy and that consequently he had never been a true pope, or that he had ceased to be one. On the other hand an *accusatio* is a form of procedure which involves a criminal indictment necessitating a trial in the strict sense of the term. Thus does Bernard allow of an *exceptio*, but not of an *accusatio* in the case of papal heresy." — James M. Moynihan, STL, JCD; *Papal Immunity and Liability in the Writings of the Medieval Canonists*, Gregorian University Press, Roma 1961, p. 114.

Salza & Siscoe play fast and loose with legal definitions which for them, mean whatever they want them to mean or not to mean. In the footnote on page 275 of their *magnum opus*, Salza & Siscoe most ignorantly declare: "***A merely declaratory sentence of the crime is not a juridical act.***" A *declaratory sentence*, however, since it is a clear cut example of administration of the law, to wit, a *public judgment of the Church*, it is a *juridical act*,[140] the execution of which pertains to the administrative power.[141] Administrative acts are *juridical acts*.[142] To *establish the crime* means to prove that the facts, which are the *indicia* of crime, constitute probable cause of crime. To *establish the crime* is not to make a *judgment*, but judgment is only made when the sentence is pronounced on the basis of the established *indicia*; since *judgment* properly expresses the act of a judge acting in his capacity as a judge, which is to declare the law or a command of the law, such as a *penal* or *declaratory sentence* by which the judge declares that the accused is proven guilty on the basis of the *indicia*. Siscoe attempted to obfuscate this point by explaining to me in an email how merely *establishing the crime* constitutes a judgment of the Church, writing: "We did not falsify the teaching of Ballarini. *(sic)* In the book, we state over and

---

[140] *Merriam-Webster*, **juridical**: "of or relating to the administration of justice or the office of a judge". According to the *Oxford Dictionaries*, 'juridical' means: "relating to judicial proceedings and the administration of the law."

[141] *Vocabulario De Significaciones De Derecho Canónico* (Universidad de Sevilla), pp. 119, 120 — "POTESTAD ADMINISTRATIVA. Funciòn de gobernar, inspirar, guiar e incluso santificar. En este sentido, poseen la potestad administrativa no sòlo los que ya tienen la potestad ejecutiva sino incluso el legislador. Es que, en la Iglesia, el legislador no sòlo legisla sino que a veces desempeña funciones que estrictamente pertenecen a la potestad ejecutiva. P. e: el obispo ecònomo. La diferencia fundamental entre la potestad ejecutiva y la administrativa está en que esta última se refiere a la administraciòn de toda la Iglesia mientras que la potestad ejecutiva es parte de la potestad administrativa porque sirve para urgir el uso y la aplicaciòn de las leyes. En consecuencia, poseen la potestad administrativa los moderadores supremos (superiores y superioras generales) de los institutos de vida consagrada e incluso, de las sociedades de vida apostòlica."

[142] *Ibid.* p.5 — "ACTOS ADMINISTRATIVOS. Son los actos jurídicos puestos por la autoridad que posee la potestad administrativa. CC. 16 &3, 479 &1. (Cf. Potestad administrativa)."

over again that the pope will not lose his jurisdiction until the Church establishes the crime (that is the phrase we use). The Church "establishes the crime" by judging that the doctrine he professes is qualified as heretical (not a lesser error), and then issuing one or more ecclesiastical warnings. If the pope remains hardened in heresy in the face of these warnings, he publicly **reveals his pertinacity and thereby manifests his heresy** (since heresy requires pertinacity). This is an indirect judgment of the Pope which reveals that "he is already judged" (by God). All of this precedes the loss of papal jurisdiction for an heretical Pope. That is how we explain it in the book, and it is exactly how Ballerini explains it." So, for Salza & Siscoe, the bishops in council silently listening to a pope abdicate his office by professing formal heresy in their presence is a *judgment of the Church*; but for them, the council's "*declaratory sentence of the crime is not a juridical act.*"!

The motive for all this nonsensical absurdity is to make it appear that a manifest heretic would not fall from office until **after the judgment** of the Church. It is plainly obvious that in twisting Ballerini's words in order to make them appear to conform to their own contrivance, they have twisted them beyond the breaking point. Ballerini in the above cited passage says of the hypothetical fallen pope, that, "the sentence which he brought upon himself," would be "made known to the whole Church," and would declare, "that he by his own will departed, would declare him to have separated from the body of the Church, and in some manner to have **abdicated** the Pontificate". It is for this reason he explains it would be declared after the fact of defection that, "such a Pontiff **by the heresy itself to be severed and cut off** from the foundation of the Church which is faith, and consequently from the Church itself, **and to have utterly fallen from the Pontificate**," and having fallen from the pontificate, "it will be the right of the general council over him, **who is no longer the Pontiff, nor does he possess the primacy.**" Now an act of *abdication* does not in any way depend on a dispositive act of judgment by the pope's inferiors for the abdication to validly take effect. It is universally agreed by theologians and canonists, that a papal *abdication* happens **entirely by itself**, and in no way depends on the pope's inferiors to take effect. Against the plain and obvious sense of these words, which clearly explain that the Church would judge the heretic **after he had fallen from the papacy by himself,** Salza & Siscoe justify their own heresy against the dogma of the primacy, which ascribes to the pontiff the full and supreme jurisdiction to determine the Church's judgment on faith and morals with finality, by attributing to Ballerini the opinion that, "the pope will not lose his jurisdiction until the Church establishes the crime… **by judging that the doctrine he professes is qualified as heretical,**" and "This is an indirect judgment of the Pope," and, "All of this precedes the loss of papal jurisdiction for an heretical Pope." Siscoe has stated explicitly in this passage that *the council's judgment qualifying the pope's doctrine as heretical* **"precedes the loss of papal jurisdiction" — thus heretically attributing to an imperfect council a power of its own by which it could pre-empt and thereby usurp the primatial function of exercising the supreme power to judge a matter of faith with finality!** The clear words of Ballerini (cited above) pronounce against this concocted contrivance, (which Salza & Siscoe invented in order to establish the right of a council to judge a validly reigning pope for the crime of heresy), stating that, "undoubtedly the **right of the primacy always remains in reality with a true and legitimate Pontiff,** who **always, being superior to the whole Church and whatever council by this right of the primacy, is removed from the jurisdiction of those others.**" Pope Gregory XVI understood this well enough, so that he commented on Ballerini, saying, "Whence he could be considered, **as Ballerini observes… to have fallen by himself from the pontificate,**" and therefore, the judgment of deposition would not be made against "the current representation of the Church in the Pope recognized as such, **but only against the person, who was before adorned with papal dignity.**" Clearly, for Salza & Siscoe, who think they understand Ballerini better than Pope Gregory XVI understood him, the word "judgment" means whatever they want it to mean, but according to them, it is I who invent definitions!

Even the term "indirect judgment" is an expression Siscoe abusively derives from John of St. Thomas, since for John of St. Thomas, the judgment consists of a proper juridical deposition in which the heretic pope would be convicted in a trial for the crime of heresy, but not judged directly: "And neither is the pope directly judged for heresy, but since from Scripture and divine law the Church is bound to segregate herself and not communicate with heretics, for that reason with the declaration having been made that he is a heretic, the Church cannot regard him as the head, since she cannot communicate with him, but a head that is not united to the body, and with which it cannot communicate, is not a head."[143] However, in order to segregate herself and not communicate with heretics, the Church declares heretics guilty of heresy and excommunicates them for the crime, and only then declares them *vitandi*. The Church's juridical declaration of heresy is in its nature a *direct judgment*, because it is either a *proper judgment made with jurisdiction over the one who is judged*, or it is nothing — it is simply not a judgment of the Church at all if it is not a proper and direct judgment. What John of St. Thomas also overlooked is that if the pope would visibly defect into heresy, he would already *ipso facto* no longer be in communion with the members, having severed the bond of faith, and being therefore no longer united to the body as a member, he would already no longer be the head, and no longer being the head, he would no longer be pope; but would be *minor quolibet catholico* even before the declaration, which, if made against a validly reigning pontiff still holding office, would be null and void for lack of jurisdiction. Since the declaration of heresy requires jurisdiction over him who is declared a heretic, which jurisdiction is lacking in the pope's inferiors; even a supposedly indirect judgment made against the pope in this manner would be a juridical nonentity (in canonical language, *habetur pro infecto*), which therefore, being juridically non-existent (*tamquam non existens*), would be incapable of acting as a dispositive cause to effect his fall from office, which therefore would necessarily take place either *ipso facto*, before all judgment, or not at all.

For so long as a man is the pope, he absolutely can be judged by no one on earth. Bellarmine sets forth the doctrine: "The Supreme Pontiff is *simpliciter et absolute* above the universal Church, and above

---

[143] *Cursus Theologicus II-II De Auctoritate Summi Pontificis*, Disp. II, Art. III, *De Depositione Papae*, p. 257 — «Et neque propter hæresim directe judicatur papa, sed quia ex Scriptura, et jure divino Ecclesiæ tenetur segregare se, et non communicare hæretico, ideo facta declaratione quod sit hæreticus Ecclesia non potest ipsum respicere ut caput, quia non potest ei communicare, caput autem cui corpus non est unitum, et cui non communicat, non est caput.»

a general council, so that he does not recognize any judgment over him on earth."[144] He demonstrates this point in chapter seventeen of *De Conciliorum Auctoritate*[145] with such forceful arguments, that they

---

[144] *De Conciliorum Auctoritate*, Cap. xvii. p. 66 – «*Summus pontifex simpliciter et absolute est supra Ecclesiam universam, et supra concilium generale, ita ut nullum in terris supra se judicium agnoscat.*»

[145] *De Conciliorum Auctoritate*, Cap. xvii. p. 66-67 — «Haec etiam est fere de fide; et probatur primo ex duabus praecedentibus: nam si papa est caput Ecclesiae universae etiam simul congregatae, et Ecclesia universa etiam simul congregata non habet ullam potestatem ratione suae totalitatis; sequitur papam supra concilium esse, et supra Ecclesiam, non contra. Secundo probatur ratione, in Scripturis fundata; nam omnia nomina, quae in Scripturis tribuuntur Christo, unde constat eum esse supra Ecclesiam, eadem omnia tribuuntur pontifici. Ac primnm, Christus est paterfamilias in domo sua, quae est Ecclesia, pontifex in eadem est summus oeconomus, idest, paterfamilias loco Christi. Lucae 12. *Quis est fidelis dispensator, et prudens, quem constituit Dominus super familiam suam etc.* Hic enim per dispensatorem, sive oeconomum, ut graece habetur, intelligunt episcopum. Ambrosius in hunc locum, et Hilarius, et Hieronymus in cap.24. Matth. ubi similis habetur sententia. Et quamvis Patres non loquantur expresse de episcopo romano, tamen sine dubio sententia Scripturae illa est; ut episcopi particulares sunt summi oeconomi in suis Ecclesiis, ita esse episcopum romanum, in Ecclesia universa. Unde Ambrosius in illud 1. Tim. 3. Ut scias quomodo te oprrteat conversari in domo Dei etc. *Domus Dei.* inquit, *Ecclesia dicitur*, cujus hodie rector est Damasus. Et Chrysostomus lib. 2. de sacerdotio circa iniitium, hunc ipsum locum: *Quis est fidelis servus etc.* de Petro exponit. Quod autem oeconomus summus sit supra familiam, et ab ea judicari, ac puniri non possit, patet ex hoc eodem loco, Dominus enim ait: *Quem constituit Dominus super familiam suam.* Et ibidem: *Quod si dixerit servus ille in corde suo, moram facit Dominus meus venire et coeperit percutere servos, et ancillas, edere, et bibere, et inebriari, veniet Dominus servi illius in die, qua nom sperat, et dividet eum, partemque ejus cum infidelibus ponet.* Ubi vides Dominum servare suo judicio servum illum, et non committere judicio familiae. Idem etiam docet usus omnium familiarum: nulla enim familia est, in qua liceat inferioribus famulis etiam simul congregatis punire, vel expellere oeconomum, etiamsi pessimus sit, id enim ad solum Dominum totius familiae pertinet. Alteruin momen Christi est pastor. Joannis 10. *Ego sum pastor bonus etc.* Idem communicat Petro, Joan. ult. *Pasce oves meas.* Constat autem pastorem ita praeesse ovibus, ut nullo modo ab eis judicari possit. Tertium est: Caput corporis Ecclesiae, Ephes. 4. idem communicat Petro, ut habemus in concilio chalcedonensi, act. 3. ubi

formed the basis of Ballerini's doctrine on the Primacy as a distinct and superior power to that of a council, which in turn was soon after affirmed as a dogma of the universal magisterium by Pius VI in *Super Soliditate,* and then became the theological foundation for the dogmatic definition of *Pastor Æternus* on the Primacy.[146] Since this point was solemnly defined *de fide* in the definition of the Primacy in 1870, there is no need to argue the point; but Bellarmine provided his pre-1870 argument on these lines: "This is nearly de fide; and is proven from the two preceding points: for if the pope is the head of the whole Church congregated together, and the whole Church congregated together does not have any power by reason of its totality; it follows that the pope is over a council, and over the Church, and not the contrary."[147] The reason why the pope is absolutely above the Church is that ecclesiastical jurisdiction was not given by Christ to the Church, but was given immediately to St. Peter and the Apostles. Ballerini, following the doctrine of Bellarmine, set forth in chapter sixteen of *De Conciliorum Auctoritate*[148] (*Summa potestas*

---

legati sententiam pronunciant in Dioscorum, et in epist. concilii ad Leonem. Porro caput a membris regi, et non ea potius regere, contra naturam est. sicut etiam est contra naturam, quod membra sibi caput praecidant, cum forte graviter aegrotat. Quartum est: Vir, seu sponsus, Ephes. 5. *Viri diligite uxores vestras, sicut Christus dilexit Ecclesiam, et tradidit seipsum pro ea, etc.* Idem convenit Petro, nam in concilio generali lugdunensi, ut habetur cap. *Ubi periculum,* de elect. in 6. loquens concilium de electione romami pontificis: *Acceleret,* inquit, *utilis per necessaria totius mundi provisio, idoneo celeriter eidem Ecclesiae sponso dato.* Est autem contra apostolum Ephes. 5. et contra naturae ordinem, ut sponsa praesit sponso, et non potius subsit. Probatur secundo ex verbis expressis conciliorum et pontificum...»

[146] Indeed, the Vatican Council practically took the title of Ballerini's work on the Primacy, *De Vi Ac Ratione Primatus Romanorum Pontificum,* for chapter three of *Pastor Æternus,* DE VI ET RATIONE PRIMATUS ROMANI PONTIFICIS.

[147] *De Conc. Auct.* cap. xvii. p. 66.

[148] *De Conc. Auct.* cap. xvi. p. 66 — «Non habet Ecclesia hanc auctoritatem a seipsa, nec ab alio; igitur nullo modo habet. Quod a seipsa, non habeat, manifeste probat discrimen, quod est inter regnum Christi et regna caetera; non enim est Ecclesia tale regnum, qualia sunt regna hujus mundi, in quibus summa potestas est in rege, sed a populo profecta et derivata, et proinde radicaliter et suppletive eadem potestas est in regno.

Nam in regno Christi summa potestas est in Christo, et non derivata ullo modo a populo. In regnis enim hoinmmum, potestas regis est a populo, quia populus facit regem, qui alioqui esset homo privatus, sicut caeteri; omnes enim homines naturaliter sunt liberi et aequales, nec posset unus caeteris imperare, nisi illi se ei subjicerent, et super se potestatem ei concederent.

At Christus est Deus et homo et quatenus Deus, est naturaliter Dominus, et rex omnium creaturarum; quatenus homo habet a Deo omnem potestatem, nec ipse ab Ecclesia factus est rex, sed ipse potius fecit Ecclesiam esse suum regnum. Apoc.5. *Fecisti nos Deo nostro regnum.* Hinc est, quod in Scriptura, regnum Christi, quod est Ecclesia, ne putaretur tale. qualia sunt caetera, comparatur etiam familiae, Matlh. 24. *Quis est fidelis servus, et prudems, quem comstituit Domimus, super familiam suam.* Et Hebr. 3. Moyses erat fidelis in tota domo Dei tamquam servus, Christus autem erat fidelis in tota domo sua tamquam Dominus. Constat enim patremfamilias non habere a familia ullam auctoritatem, sed ex se; quia non ipse a familia constituitur pater, sed ipse facit sibi familiam gignendo filios, emendo servos. Unde paterfamilias, etiamsi pessimus sit, numquam potest a familia judicari, vel expelli, sicut potest rex quando degenerat in tyrannum. Comparatur etiam ovili, Joan. 10. Item corpori et sponsae, Ephes. 4. el 5. ut in telligamus,quod sicut non accipit auctoritatem pastor ab ovibus, nec caput a corpore, nec vir ab uxore, ita neque Christus ab Ecclesia.

Ex his habemus Ecclesiam ex se nullam habere auctoritatem, sed omnem esse in Christo, et iis, quibus Christus eam communicavit. Quod autem non habeat ab alio, nimirum a Christo, probatur. Nam Christus legitur quidem dedisse Petro claves regni coelorum, Matthaei 16. et eumdem praefecisse ovili suo, Joan. ult. Dedit etiam apostolis caeteris potestatem praedicandi, baptizandi, peccata dimittendi, et alia quaedam faciendi, quae ad munus episcopale spectant, sed hanc potestatem Christus singulis dedit ita ut potuerit quisque eorum illa omnia exercere sine congregatione aliorum, ut notum est: At quod ipsi Ecclesiae, idest, fidelium universitati in se, idest, ratione suae totalitatis aliquid potestatis tribuerit, nusquam legitur; immo e contrario legimus, praecipi populis, ut obediant, et subjaceant pastoribus suis, Hebr. 13. et alibi. Quod si Ecclesiae universitati non est data ulla auctoritas, ergo neque concilio generali, quatenus Ecclesiam universalem repraesentat. Ergo in concilio non est auctoritas summa, sive papalis, sed tantum episcopalis, seu archiepiscopalis, prout sunt personae, quae ibi conveniunt. Siquidem summa, seu papalis auctoritas non ponitur in concilio ab adversariis, nisi quatenus concilium gerit vicem Ecclesiae universae. Si ergo Ecclesia universa, secluso papa, non habet papalem auctoritatem, ergo multo minus concilium habet.»

ecclesiastica non est in Ecclesia, vel concilio. remoto papa, aut formaliter, aut suppletive.) explains:

> Ecclesiastical jurisdiction takes its origin from Christ, who immediately handed it over to St. Peter and the Apostles, when he gave to them together with the keys of the kingdom of heaven the power to bind and loose, which power is the same as jurisdiction; and for which reason these are of divine right. This power or jurisdiction was immediately handed over to St. Peter and the Apostles for the building and good of the Church; and was given before Christ ascended into heaven, and (I) before the Church was built by the same Apostles: thus it cannot be said to have been given immediately to the Church, so that Peter and the Apostles had received it from the Church, who received it from Christ himself as the words of the Gospel testify.[149]

In the footnote (I) Ballerini explains further, "(I) Thus St. Cyprian writing in Epistle 73 *Ecclesia una est, & super unum qui & claves ejus accepit, Domimi voce fundata*, judges Peter to have received from Christ the keys of the Church, or Ecclesiastical jurisdiction, but the words of Christ themselves mean that the keys were not handed over to the Church, since after the words *Ecclesiam meam* he did not say *to her,* but TO THEE *I will give the keys of the kingdom of heaven.*"[150] St. Alphonsus

---

[149] Ballerini, *De Potestate Ecclesiastica*, CAPUT I. § I. pp. 1-2. — «Jurisdictio Ecclesiastica a Christo ducit originem, qui eamdem S. Petro & Apostolis immediate tradidit, quando ipfis una cum clavibus regni cœlorum dedit potestatem ligandi atque solvendi, quas potestas idem est ac jurisdictio; ac propterea hæc in origine est juris divini. Hæc quidem potestas, seu jurisdictio S. Petro & Apostolis immediate tradita fuit in ædificationem & bonum Ecclesiæ; at tradita antequam Christus incœlum ascenderet, & (I) antequam ab iisdem Apostolis ipsa ædificaretur Ecclesia: ac proinde dici non potest immediate collata eidem Ecclesiæ, quæ nondum ab illis erat ædificata, nec ita immediate tradita Ecclesiæ dici potest, ut illam Petrus & Apostoli acceperint ab Ecclesia, quos ab ipso Christo eam accepisse Evangelica verba testantur.»

[150] *Ibid.* p.2. — «(I) Ita sane S. Cyprianus scribens in epist. 73. *Ecclesia una est, & super unum qui & claves ejus accepit, Domimi voce fundata*, Petrum claves Ecclesiæ, seu jurisdictiunem Ecclesiasticam a Christo accepisse iudicat, antequam idem Christus super ipsum ædificaret Ecclesiam- Petro quidem, non autem *Ecclesiæ* claves a Christo traditas, ipsa Christi verba palam

taught in his answer to the Febronians: "They say that Christ granted the keys also to the other apostles, saying: *Amen, dico vobis, quæcumque alligaveritis super terram, erunt ligata et in coelo: et quæcumque solveritis super terram, erunt soluta et in coelo.* Matth. 18. 18. But what stands in the way of this? We have already said above, the apostles received immediately from Christ a power indeed equal, and which Peter received, as the first founders of the Gospel; but all of them were subject to Peter as the head, and chief, as all the Fathers proclaim."[151] Bellarmine explained it in such terms that in what manner Peter bore the figure of the Church he accordingly received the keys immediately from Christ: "But we believe Peter in the prior manner bore the person of the Church: thus undoubtedly, that he truly, and principally, and immediately had received the keys, and by receiving them at the same time signified the universal Church afterward to receive [them]."[152] So it is that Christ handed no ecclesiastical power to the Church, but to Peter was given the full power of the primacy, and to the apostles the power was given to exercise jurisdiction in hierarchical subordination to that primacy; whence the whole Church congregated together, whose jurisdiction, according to its very nature exists in hierarchical subordination to the pope's primacy of jurisdiction, has absolutely no power whatsoever to judge or to depose a validly reigning pontiff. That the members should overrule the head or cut off the head is

---

signifcant, cum post verba *Ecclesiam meam* non dixerit *Ei*, sed *TIBI dabo claves regni cœlorum.*»

[151] Alfonso Maria de' Liguori, *Vindiciae pro suprema pontificis potestate adversus Iustinum Febronium*, Torino, 1832, Cap. II p. 34 — «Dicunt, quod Christus etiam aliis apostolis in alio loco claves tradidit, dicens: *Amen. dico vobis, quæcumque alligaveritis super terram, erunt ligata et in coelo: et quæcumque solveritis super terram, erunt soluta et in coelo.* Matth. 18. 18. Sed hoc quid obstat? Jam supra diximus, apostolos immediate a Christo potestatem quidem æqualem ac Petrum recepisse, tamquam primos Evangelii fundatores; sed omnes ipsos fuisse Petro subjectos ut capiti, et principi, prout cuncti patres eum proclamant.»

[152] *De Romano Pontifice lib. I cap. xii* — «Nos vero priore modo Petrum Ecclesiae personam gessisse credimus: ita nimirum, ut ipse vere, & principaliter, ac (ut ipsi loquuntur) immediate claves acceperit, & simul eas accipiendo significaverit, universam Ecclesiam suo quodam modo postea accepturam.»

against nature: "Moreover, for the head to be ruled by the members, and not rather that they be ruled by the head, is against nature, just as it is also against nature that the members cut off the head, when perchance it would gravely be ill."[153]

For these reasons Bellarmine explains it is only when the pope is *dubius* or is *no pope*, that a council can judge who is the pope or provide a true shepherd for the Church.[154] And further down on the page he clarifies, "For **a doubtful pope is considered no pope**, and thus, to have power over him is not to have power over the pope."[155] For this reason, Bellarmine explains in CAPUT ix. (*De utilitate vel etiam necessitate celebrandorum comciliorum*) of *De Concilliis et Ecclesia,* that one of the reasons which would necessitate the convening of a council would be "suspicion of heresy in the Roman Pontiff if it should happen"[156]. Bordoni also explains that only a true and certain pope is above a council, but doubtful popes and pertinacious heretics (because they are incapable subjects) are subject to a council: *solus verus & indubitatus Papa est supra Concilium, et non alii de quibus dubitatur, ergo subijciuntur Concilio.*[157] In such situations as these, according to the most eminent authorities, **the apostolic see is considered vacant**, and it is precisely when in such a case if the pope were to be discovered to be an obstinate heretic, the judgment [in the words of Pope Gregory XVI] would not be made against the actually reigning pope, "but only

---

[153] *De Conciliorum Auctoritate,* Cap. xvii. — «Porro caput a membris regi, et non ea potius regere, contra naturam est, sicut etiam est contra naturam, quod membra sibi caput praecidant, cum forte graviter aegrotat.»

[154] *De Conciliorum Auctoritate,* Cap. xviii p. 71 — «Nam etsi concilium sine papa non potest definire nova dogmata fidei, potest tamen judicare tempore schismatis, quis sit verus papa, et providere Ecclesiae de vero pastore, quando is nullius, aut dubius est, et hoc est quod recte fecit concilium constantiense.»

[155] *Ibid.* – «Nam dubius papa habetur pro non papa, et proinde habere super illum potestatem, non est habere potestatem in papam.»

[156] *De Concilliis et Ecclesia,* CAPUT ix. p. 20 — «Quarta causa est suspicio haeresis in romano pontifice, si forte accideret.»

[157] Bordoni, *Op. cit.* cap. vi. p. 149.

against the person who was before adorned with the papal dignity."[158] Thus, for this reason that the see would be presumed vacant, Bellarmine says, "In which case a council can examine the case of the pontiff, and if it should find that the pope is really an infidel, it can declare him outside the Church, and condemn him." [159] St. Alphonsus explains, «*For a better understanding of what will be said here, it is useful to premise three things for certain. The first, that any ecumenical, or general council, to be legitimate must be convened by the Pope. [... p. 159] 2. The second thing is certain that when in times of schism it is doubted who the true Pope is, in this case the council can be convened by cardinals and bishops; and at the same time each of the elected is bound to adhere to the definition of the council, because then the Apostolic See is held as vacant. And the same would be the case if the Pope fell notoriously, and pertinaciously into some heresy. Although then, as others say better, it would not be the Pope deprived of the pontificate by the council as his superior, but would be immediately stripped of it by Christ, thus becoming in fact an incapable subject and fallen from his office.*»[160] Later in the same chapter he clarifies further: «*God has given the power to elect the Pope to the Church, that is, to the college of cardinals, or to the council in the case of a doubtful or heretical Pope, but not yet the papal power. They oppose for 6.°: but if the council can depose the heretical Pope, it can also depose him in other crimes equally*

---

[158] D. Mauro Cappellari ora Gregorio XVI, *Il trionfo della santa sede e della chiesa contro gli assatti dei novatori*, Venezia, 1832, p. 270 — "ma soltanto contro la persona, che era prima ornata della papal dignità".

[159] *De Conciliorum Auctoritate*, Cap. xviii p. 69 – «in quo casu potest conicilium discutere caussam pontificis, et si inveniat, revera esse infidelem, potest declarare eum esse extra Ecclesiam, et sic damnare.»

[160] Alfonso Maria de' Liguori, *Verità Della Fede*, Tomo Secondo, Monza, 1823, Capo IX. pp. 158-159: «Per maggior intelligenza di quello che qui si dirà, giova premettere tre cose per certe. La prima, che ogni concilio ecumenico, o sia generale, per esser legittimo dee esser convocato dal Papa. 2. La seconda cosa certa si è che quando in tempo di scisma si dubita chi sia il vero Papa, in tal caso il concilio può esser convocato da' cardinali e da' vescovi; ed allora ciascuno degli eletti è tenuto di stare alla definizione del concilio, perché allora si tiene come vacante la Sede Apostolica. E lo stesso sarebbe nel caso che il Papa cadesse notoriamente, e pertinacemente in qualche eresia. Benché allora, come meglio dicono altri, non sarebbe il Papa privato del pontificato dal concilio come suo superiore, ma ne sarebbe spogliato immediatamente da Cristo, divenendo allora soggetto affatto inabile e caduto dal suo officio.»

pernicious to the Church; and from this they deduce that the council is above the Pope. But it is answered that heresy alone, not the other crimes already make the Pope incapable for his office; so in case the Pope is a heretic, it is not that the council is superior to the Pope (**how then can it be above the Pope, if there is no Pope?**): *then the council declares the Pope fallen from the pontificate, as he who cannot be anymore a doctor of the Church, holding a false doctrine.*»[161] Thus, (the Holy Doctor concludes, as quoted above): "We answer, that if ever a pope as a private person would fall into heresy, then he would immediately fall from the papacy; for since he would be outside the Church, he could no longer be the head of the Church. Whence in that case the Church would have to not in fact depose him, because no one has power over the pope, but declare him to have fallen from the pontificate."

On the point of the authority of the Church to judge whether or not a man is a legitimate pope, Pope Gregory XVI explains:

«... it is clearly certain that Jesus Christ, wanting *immutable, visible and perpetual* government, founded for the safety of the faithful, must have provided the Church with all means, which are necessary in order not to be governed by an illegitimate leader. **Therefore he must infallibly have conferred on it the right to the power, in the uncertainty and in the reasonable and founded doubt of the legitimacy of a Pope, to proceed to the election of another.** And this, above all, if that one, whose legitimacy is reasonably suspect, did not allow it to be molested in a thousand ways, so that God should have to be accused of not having sufficiently provided for its indefectibility, if in such circumstances it did not have the appropriate faculties ... [In these cases] **the Church carries**

---

[161] Alfonso Maria de' Liguori, *Verità Della Fede*, Tomo Secondo, Monza, 1823, Capo IX. pp. 206 - 207: «Iddio ha data la podestà di eleggere il Papa alla Chiesa, cioè al collegio de' cardinali, o al concilio nel caso di Papa dubbio o eretico, ma non già la podestà papale. Oppongono per 6.°: ma se il concilio può deporre il Papa eretico, può anche deporlo negli altri delitti egualmente perniciosi alla Chiesa; e da ciò deducono essere il concilio, sopra del Papa. Ma si risponde che la sola eresia, non già gli altri delitti rendono il Papa inabile al suo officio; onde in caso che il Papa sia eretico, non è che il concilio sia superiore al Papa (come allora può esser sopra del Papa, se non vi è Papa?): allora il concilio dichiara il Papa decaduto dal pontificato, come colui che non può esser più dottore della Chiesa, tenendo una falsa dottrina.»

out its final sentence, not on the basis of its authority over the Pope, but on the well-founded assumption that such was not [the pope]: in which case the power of the Church is evidently certain...»[162]

If in the case of an obstinate public heretic, in which, according to the *indicia* of formal heresy established by canonical tradition and the jurisprudence of the Roman Church, the matter of the heresy would be indisputably certain and the pertinacity likewise indisputably manifest, then the pertinacity itself would constitute absolutely certain proof that the man is not a true pope, and it would then be known with certitude that the papal see is vacant. In his answer to the question, "Whether a council can depose a pope," (*An Concilium possit deponere Papam.*), Bordoni responds, saying that *a pertinacious heretic is already judged by God, because He who does not believe is already judged, and is to be declared by the Council to be deposed and deprived of the papacy; for it is necessary that the judgment of God be published by the ministry of men, and this is most aptly done by a Council, which is the supreme tribunal* **when the papal see is vacant.**[163] Bordoni explains that it is precisely in such a case, like

---

[162] D. Mauro Cappellari ora Gregorio XVI, p. 46 — «... è certo, che Gesù Cristo, volendo *immutabile, visibile e perpetuo* il governo da se fondato per la sicurezza dei fedeli, deve aver provveduta la Chiesa di tutti quei mezzi, che son necessarii per non lasciarsi governare da un capo illegittimo. Quindi deve infallibilmente averle conferito il diritto di potere nell'incertezza e nel dubbio ragionevole e fondato della legittimità di un Papa, procedere all'elezione di un altro. E ciò soprattutto se quello, la cui legittimità è ragionevolmente sospetta, non lasciasse di molestarla in mille guise, cosicché accusar dovrebbesi Iddio medesimo di non aver sufficientemente provveduto alla sua indefettibilità, se in tali circostanze fornita non l'avesse delle opportune facoltà [...] (In questi casi) la Chiesa esegue la sua sentenza finale, non sull'appoggio della sua autorità sopra il Papa, ma sulla fondata supposizione che tale non fosse: nel qual caso è evidentemente certa la potestà della Chiesa...»

[163] Bordoni, *Op. cit.* p. 149: «Pertinax [hæreticus] vero a Deo etiam iudicatus ex illo Ioan. 3. *Num.* 18. *Qui vero non credit, iam iudicatus est*, a Concilio **declaratur depositus**, & privatus Papatu, nam necessarium est, quod Dei iudicium publicetur ministerio alicuius hominis, sed nullus aptius, & congruentius assignatur, quam Concilium, quod est supremum tribunal, quando vacat Papale.»

that one hypothesized in this cited passage of Pope Gregory XVI, (about which Gregory said that Christ, "must infallibly have conferred the right to the power" on the Church to resolve the issue of a heretic's claim on the papacy), that the immediate assistance of the Holy Ghost would suffice even during the *sede vacante* for the council to proceed infallibly in deposing a doubtful pope for reason of heresy or schism.[164] But contrary to the opinion of Bordoni, Bellarmine rightly argued that the infallibility (that would exist in such a case of deposing a heretic) does not extend to defining in matters of faith, since that pertains exclusively to the primatial power of the pontiff.[165]

St. Alphonsus explains it is certain that for an ecumenical council to be legitimate, it must be convoked by the pope; *but in such cases when it is doubtful who is the true pope, the council can be convoked by the cardinals, and by the bishops*; and then all the elected would be bound by the decision of the Council, *because in such a case the Apostolic See would be considered vacant.* [166] The Holy Doctor then continues in the next sentence, "The same would be in the case, if the pope were to fall

---

[164] *Ibid.* p. 163 — «Nec dicas, in eo casu Concilium esse sine Papa, ac proinde errare posse secundum Cordubam lib.4. q. 2. quia id procedit, quando Concilium congregatur irrationabiliter sine licentia Papæ non autem ex causa legitima deponendi illum ex hæresi, vel fchismate, in quo casu sufficit inmediata assistentia Spiritus Sancti.»

[165] *De Conc. Auct.* cap. xix p. 69 — «Non fuisse concilium constantiense, cum id asseruit hujusmodi, ut quaestiones de fide definire posset; nam inprimis non erat tunc generale concilium, cum tantum adesset tertia pars Ecclesiae, idest, ii tantum praelati, qui obediebant Joanni; nam qui obediebant Gregorio et Benedicto, repugnabant iis, quae a synmodo fiebant. Deinde non aderat tunc certus papa in Ecclesia, **sine quo dubia de fide definiri non possunt**, in concilio autem nullus erat papa. Joannes enim XXIII. qui concilium inchoaverat, jam inde recesserat, cum quarta sessio haberetur.»

[166] Alfonso Maria de' Liguori, *Verità Della Fede*, Tomo Secondo, Monza, 1823, Parte Terza. Capo IX. p. 159 — «La seconda cosa certa si è, che quando in tempo di Scisma si dubita, chi fosse il vero Papa, in tal caso il Concilio può essere convocato da' Cardinali, e da' Vescovi; ed allora ciascuno degli eletti è tenuto di stare alla definizione del Concilio, perché allora si tiene come vacante la Sede Apostolica.»

notoriously and pertinaciously in some heresy." Pope Gregory XVI explains why this is so:

> «In the times of the antipopes, as well as of the dead Pope, the form of the government ordained by Christ does not remain obscure, even in a case where there is founded doubt, so that it is not clear who should be venerated for Pope, yes in the case of sede vacante it happens in the Church what happens in different monarchies, in which in time of interregnum the government resides in some senate; as practiced also in the ancient Roman empire, in which the Roman senate commanded in time of interregnum; so in the mean while in those cases the government of the Church is aristocratic. But who does not know that this cannot be its natural state? Who can recognize it from the same dilligence that the Church gave to elect her head, suffering ill from remaining headless for a long time?»[167]

Jurisdiction is required for the declaration which follows upon a discretionary judgment for the judgment to be a juridical judgment of the Church; since *the judgment of the Church, even if merely declaratory, is a judicial act which requires jurisdiction in order for that declaration to be juridically valid.*[168] The objection that says in deposing a heretic pope who still holds office, a council's judgment expressed in a declaratory sentence

---

[167] D. Mauro Cappellari ora Gregorio XVI, *Op. cit.* p. 29 – «Nei tempi degli antipapi, come anche di Papa morto, non resta oscurata la forma del governo ordinato da Cristo, imperciocché sì nel caso in cui siavi dubbio fondato, per cui non si sappia bene chi debbasi venerare per Papa, sì nel caso di sede vacante succede nella Chiesa ciò che succede in diverse monarchie, nelle quali in tempo di interregno il governo risiede in qualche senato; come praticavasi pure nell'antico impero romano, nel quale il senato romano comandava in tempo d'interregno; quindi in quei casi il governo della Chiesa è intrattanto aristocratico. Ma chi non sa, che questo non può essere il suo stato naturale? Chi può riconoscerlo dalle stesse premure che dessi la Chiesa per eleggersi il suo capo, mal soffrendo di starsene acefala per lungo tempo?»

[168] Bordoni, *Op. cit.* p. 158 – «omnis actus vt sit iuridicus, & validus essentialiter dependet a iurisditione. Bald. in *l. omne verbum, C. com. de legat.* Alex. *lib.*4. *confil.* 52. *num.*30. ex Rota Roman. *vol.* 1. *decis.*451. *nu.* 2.»; *Ibid.*, p. 154 – «Numerantur autem tres actus, declarario hæresis, desitio Papatus, & eiectio extra Ecclesiam, qui omnes sunt iudiciales, ac proinde requirentes iurisdictionem in eo, qui illa tria præstare debet.»

would not exercise power of jurisdiction over the pope as a superior, is specious and fatally flawed insofar as every judgment, including one that is merely declaratory, hinges directly on the power of a true jurisdiction, without which the act cannot consist, since **the basis and foundation of judgment** is *jurisdiction*, so that a judgment lacking jurisdiction would be incurable and irreparable;[169] and, furthermore, no judgment whatsoever pronounced by a council would have any juridical effect unless it would be confirmed by the pope and promulgated by his order,[170] because it is *de fide definita* that the FINAL DETERMINATION of that judgment pertains exclusively to the supreme authority of the holder of the Primacy; who, in virtue of his "full and supreme jurisdiction" exercises the **"total fullness of supreme power"**. Ballerini explains that judges of a lower rank are subject, by their nature, to judges of a higher rank, without thereby ceasing to be true judges; thus Bishops are subject to the Pope without ceasing to be judges in their own dioceses, as the Pope is in the whole Church.[171] Thus, they are not independent judges, but subordinate judges according to the divinely instituted *hierarchical subordination* (non tamen independentes, sed subordinati, ea scilicet *hierarchica subordinatione*): "This subordination, while it excludes juridic equality between the inferior and the superior, since it is generally that the inferior, who is subordinate to the superior judge, cannot deliver a legitimate sentence against his judgment: then the more it is that the bishops subordinate to the supreme Pontiff, to whom Christ granted

---

[169] *Ibid.*, p. 154: «Deinde per illam quandam ordinationem factam a Concilio vel intelligitur vera, & propria potestas, & iurisdictio Concilii in Papam, [...] vel intelligitur aliquid aliud, quod tamen consonum non est, quia omnis actus iudicialis pendet a vera iurisdictione, sine qua nullus actus consistere potest, quia basis, & fundamentum iudicij reputatur iurisdictio Bald. *C. si a compet. iud. in Rubr.* Paris *de confidet. q.79. num. 22* ita quod defectus iurisdictionis dicicur insanabilis, & irreparabilis, ex Staphil. Sarnen, & Vantio ex eodem Parisio *num.* 24.»

[170] *CIC 1917*: «Can. 227. Concilii decreta vim definitivam obligandi non habent, nisi a Romano Pontifice fuerint confirmata et eius iussu promulgata.»

[171] Cf. *De Potestate Ecclesiastica Summorum Pontificum Et Conciliorum Generalium*, Auctore Petro Ballerinio Presbytero Veronensi, Augustæ Vindelicorum (Augsburg), MDCCLXX, Cap. II. § I., pp. 26-32.

the proper authority for the purpose of guarding unity especially in faith, cannot issue definitions in disagreements concerning faith, [...] without doubt that compliance of mind, which yet from the bishops themselves, even when they act as judges, to the divine as well as supreme authority founded on the promise of Christ is to be shown in hierarchical subordination." [172] Thus, on the basis of the supreme authority of Christ they must remain in *hierarchical subordination* even when acting in the capacity of judges — and thus, they do not have the power to **deprive the Pope of his authority to judge,** nor may they **impede his right to pronounce a definitive judgment,** since this power is his by **DIVINE RIGHT.** Therefore: «***One priest or Bishop must be recognized in the Church, with whom all must be in communion, in order that schisms be impeded, and to whom all adhere together in the unity of faith, so that the entrance of heresies may be stopped; and that in him and by him the unity of the whole Catholic Church may be protected. This one priest or Bishop, cannot be any one Bishop of particular churches, who would have authority only over his own flock, but is the Roman Bishop, the one high priest, to whom the whole Church, and the unity of the whole Church is committed.***»[173] IF THE POPE IS NOT THE ONE TO ISSUE

---

[172] Ballerini, *Op. cit.*, p. 29 – «Haec autem subordinatio, dum juris aequalitatem inter inferiorem & superiorem excludit, cum generatim efficit, ut inferior, qui superiori judici est subordinatus, nequeat contra istius judicium legitimam ferre sententiam: tum multo magis efficit, ne id possint Episcopi subordinati summo Pontifici, cui cum Christus in finem custodiendae unitatis praesertim in fide idoneam auctoritatem dedit, ut in dissensionibus circa fidem definitionem ederent, [...] eo nimirum mentis obsequio, quod etsi ab ipsis Episcopis, etiam cum judices agunt, *divinae aeque ac summae auctoritati Christique pollicitationi nixae*, hierarchica subordinatione praestandum est.»

[173] Ballerini, *De Vi Ac Ratione Primatus Romanorum Pontificum Et De Ipsorum Infallibilitate Iin Definiendis Controversiis Fidei*, Monasterii Westphalorum 1845, c. 13. §. 3., num. 13, p. 116 – «Agnosci igitur debet in Ecclesia unus sacerdos, vel Episcopus, cum quo omnes communicent, ut impediantur schismata, et cui in fidei unitate omnes cohaereant, ut haeresibus aditus intercipiatur; sique in illo, atque per illum tota catholicae Ecclesiae unitas vindicetur. Hic autem unus sacerdoa aut Episcopus, non quivis particularium ecclesiarum Episcopus esse potest, qui in solum suum particularem gregem jus habeat,

THE FINAL JUDGMENT, THE UNITY OF FAITH WILL BE DESTROYED, CAUSING THE DEFECTION OF THE CHURCH. Cardinal Manning explained, "It is *de fide*, or matter of faith, that the head of the Church, as such, can never be separated, either from the *Ecclesia docens*, or the *Ecclesia discens*; that is, either from the Episcopate or from the faithful."[174] **THIS IS PRECISELY THE HERESY OF JOHN SALZA AND ROBERT SISCOE.** *They received this heresy directly from the writings of John of St. Thomas.*

Manning then continues, "To suppose this, would be to deny the perpetual indwelling office of the Holy Ghost in the Church, by which the mystical body is knit together; the head to the Body, the Body to the head, the members to each other; and to "dissolve Jesus*" [* * St. John iv. 3, "Omnis spiritus qui solvit Jesum," &c.]. The Cardinal then concludes, "On this unity all the properties and endowments of the Church depend; indefectibility, unity, infallibility. As the Church can never be separated from its invisible Head, so never from its visible head."[175] This is so, Gregory XVI explains in the above cited passage, "**Because he is the head and father of all Bishops even when they are congregated**, as the Chalcedonian Council names him in its letter to St. Leo: *Summitas tua filiis quod deest adimpleat.* IV. **Because he has the right to propose, establish and authorize the norm of true belief**, that is, because, as St. Thomas says, *ad ipsum pertinet editio symboli*, and **he is the only one, with whom not to gather is to be dispersed, and with whom not to agree is the same as declaring oneself a follower of the Antichrist**, as is rightly expressed by Saint Jerome, who wrote to Saint Damasus: *Quicumque tecum non colligit, spargit: qui tecum non est, Antichristi est.*"

Without the FINAL DETERMINATION of the judgment coming from the supreme judge himself, there is no judgment of the Church, since a judgment of the bishops or the cardinals pronounced on a validly reigning pontiff while still in office is not in the nature of a judgment of the Church, and therefore cannot be considered to be

---

sed unus est summus sacerdos Romanus Episcopus, cui tota Ecclesia, ac totius Ecclesiae unitas commissa est.»

[174] Cardinal Henry Edward Manning, *The Vatican Council and its Definitions*, Second Edition, New York & Montreal, 1871, p. 112.

[175] *Ibid.* pp. 112-113.

a judgment of the Church, since it lacks that which is essential for such a judgment to be qualified as a judgment of the *Church*, namely, the ***jurisdiction*** which the head exercises over the members as their superior, but which the members as inferiors cannot exercise over the head.[176] St. Robert Bellarmine explains[177]: When we speak of judgment of the Church, St. John Chrysostom explains and Innocent III proves that by the word "Church" is meant the bishop, or the congregation of the faithful with their head, as is expressed in the letter of St. Cyprian, *Ecclesia est plebs sacerdoti adunata, et pastori suo grex adhaerens*. Thus, on the foundation of this principle Bellarmine continues: «Why in every bishopric the offenders are to be prosecuted before the Church and Bishop of the place, but if there is a bishop who is guilty, he could not be brought before his own Church, otherwise he would be brought before himself, since he is the head of the Church, but is to be brought before a Church that is higher, which is presided over by an archbishop or patriarch, but if the offender is the patriarch, he cannot be brought before his own Church, but to one that is greater, that is, to the Romans Church, or a general council, over which the supreme pontiff presides: but if the

---

[176] Bordoni, *Op. Cit.*, p. 155 – «omnis actus iudicialis semper exercetur per superiorem iudicem in inferiorem. personam, & subditam, ac non per inferiorem in superiorem, quia inferior nullam habet poestatem in superiorem.»

[177] *De Conciliorum Auctoritate, cap. xix.* – «Respondeo: Nomine Ecclesiae, vel intelligi episcopum, ut exponit hoc loco Chrysostomus, el Innoccntius III. cap. *Novit*, extra, de judiciis et praxis Ecclesiae demonstrat; quotidie enim episcopo denunciantur ii, de quibus Dominus ait *Dic Ecclesiae*; vel certe fidelium coetum cum suo capite. Nam ut Cyprianus ait in epistola ad Florentium, quae est nona lib. 4. *Ecclesia est plebs sacerdoti adunata, et pastori suo grex adhaerens*. Quare in quocumque episcopatu deferendi sunt peccatores ad Ecclesiam, et episcopum ejus loci, sed si is episcopus peccet, non potest deferri ad eam Ecclesiam, nisi debeat referri ad seipsum, cum ipse sit caput ejusdem Ecclesiae, sed deferendus est ad Ecclesiam aliquam altiorem, cui praeest archiepiscopus vel patriarcha: Si vero peccet patriarcha, deferri non potest ad Ecclesiam suam, sed ad majorem, idest, ad romanam Ecclesiam, vel generale concilium, cui summus pontifex praesidet: Quod si ipse summus pontifex peccet, judicio Dei reservandus est, non enim est ulla Ecclesia, ad quam deferri possit, eum sine ipso non inveniatur Ecclesia cum capite.» –

supreme pontiff himself is the one who is guilty, he is reserved to the judgment of God, for there is not any Church, to which he can be referred which without him there would be found a church with a head.» From this it follows strictly that a pope cannot be judged by the Church, because the pope has no superior but God. The bishops united in a Council are true judges, but as judges they are subordinate to the pope.

Bordoni elaborates further on this point:

> «Then, because no one can be deposed unless by their superior, deposition is an act of judicial jurisdiction exercised only by a superior, **but there is no superior over the Pope, apart from God**, and, therefore, **he can be deposed by no one, for he judges all, and is judged by no one**, *cap.Si Papa dift.* 40. *cap. Duo funt* [...] *dift.* 96. Firstly, because the members do not judge the head, from whom they have influx, whence members are understood to have been destroyed by their having destroyed the head, not the reverse, *l. cum in diuerfis ff. de relig.* [...] *fumpt. fin.* And members must follow the head, not head follow the members, *cap.* I. *dift.* 12. However, a Council is constituted of the members, whose head is the Pope as is proved in q.5. Therefore a Pope cannot be deposed by a Council. And in this there is no difficulty.»[178]

It could be argued, by citing Cajetan's specious objection (noted by Bordoni[179]), that the papacy itself is not destroyed when the head is destroyed by deposition, but while the papacy as an institution would not be destroyed (because it would still exist potentially in a successor), the papal dignity actually existing in the person as a habit would certainly be destroyed by an act of deposition, which unlike death or renunciation, would be an act of decapitation contrary to divine law, as Bellarmine points out:

> First, it is of natural law that putrid members be cut off, except the head. It is better to have a putrid head than none. But this solution is of

---

[178] *Sacrum Tribunal Iudicum In Causis Sanctæ Fidei Contra Hæreticos Et Hæresi Suspectos, Caput VI, De Sacriis Conciliis*, Romæ MDCXLVIII, p. 149.

[179] Bordoni, *Sacrum Tribunal*, Cap. VI, p. 157 — «deposito tamen Papa, falsum, est, non destrui dignitatem Papatus, contra Caiet, dicentem, amotionem Petri a, Papatu non esse destructionem Papatus, nec Petri, sed tantum illius coniunctionis...»

little value; for in natural bodies the head must be excepted, because it being amputated, the whole body dies. But the body of the Church does not die with the death of the pope; whence we see in temporal republics, if the king degenerates into a tyrant, although he is the head, he is deposed by the people and another is elected. Secondly I say, in a natural body and in temporal republics members infecting the whole body can be cut off, because upon the body itself they depend and have power: but the body of the Church is not of the same nature, whose head did not receive authority from the body but from God, just as it is not licit for a family to depose the chief householder, although he be the worst, because he is not appointed by the family but by the Lord.[180]

In the cited Question 5, Bordoni, following Bellarmine, explains the Catholic doctrine revealed in scripture and taught by the magisterium[181] and by all the great theologians of the Church, on the *divine constitution of the Church* as a *kingdom* whose ruling *monarch* is the Pope; as a *household* and *family* over which the Pope rules and commands with the authority of the *householder* and *father*, and as a *body*

---

[180] *De Conciliorum Auctoritate,* cap. xix. p. 71 — «Primo, de jure naturae esse, ut abscindantur membra putrida, sed excepto capite. Melius enim est habere caput putridum, quam nullum. Sed haec solutio parum valet; nam in corporibus naturalibus debet excipi caput, quia eo amputato, totum corpus moritur. At corpus Ecclesiae non moritur moriente papa; unde etiam videmus in rebuspublicis temporalibus, si rex degeneret in tyrannum, licet sit caput regni, tamen a populo deponi, et eligi alium. Dico ergo secundo, in corpore naturali et rebuspublicis temporalibus posse abscindi membra inficientia totum corpus, quia ab ipso corpore pendent, et vim habent: At non eadem ratio est corporis Ecclesiae, cujus caput non a corpore, sed a Deo auctoritatem accepit, sicut etiam non licet familiae deponere summum oeconomum, licet pessimum, quia non a familia, sed a Domino institutus est.»
[181] CONSTITUTIO DOGMATICA PASTOR AETERNUS, PIUS EPISCOPUS, SERVUS SERVORUM DEI, SACRO APPROBANTE CONCILIO — «Unum enim Simonem, cui iam pridem dixerat: Tu vocaberis Cephas (Ioan. I, 42), postquam ille suam edidit confessionem inquiens Tu es Christus, Filius Dei vivi, solemnibus his verbis allocutus est Dominus: Beatus es Simon Bar-Iona; quia caro, et sanguis non revelavit tibi, sed Pater meus, qui in cöelis est: et ego dico tibi, quia tu es Petrus, et super hanc petram aedificabo Ecclesiam meam, et portae inferi non praevalebunt adversus eam: et **tibi dabo claves regni coelorum.**»

to which the Pope is constituted by God as its *head*. Before him, Bellarmine expounded the same more thoroughly in *De Conciliorum Auctoritate cap. xvi*, explaining that the Church is according to divine revelation a monarchy, because it is the kingdom of Christ, who is the King over the universe, as is revealed throughout scripture; and therefore, the pope is a monarch, but unlike an earthly king, he cannot be deposed by men, because earthly kings receive their authority from God mediately through the consent of their subjects, and can therefore be deposed by them because of tyranny; but the pope receives his authority immediately from God, and therefore cannot be deposed by men. Nor, when the pope is lacking does this supreme monarchical power exist in the Church or in a council *suppletively* or *formally*, because authority in the Church as is taught in scripture, is not from the Church herself but exists totally in Christ and, to those to whom He communicated it *singly*, to be exercised singly, and not collegially in the Church by reason of her totality.[182] Therefore also, the argument based on an errant appeal to natural law[183] which says a validly reigning pontiff can be deposed from office by a council because of heresy is false and heretical, because the absolute power of the primacy is received by the pope immediately from God, and does not exist in any manner in the Church, nor is it in any way

---

[182] Bellarmine's complete and exhaustive expositions on the monarchical authority and supreme power of the primacy over the Church are contained in the first, second, and fourth books of *De Romano Pontifice*.

[183] Fr. Jean-Michel Gleize summarizes the natural law argument of Fr. Guillaume Devillers: "Now it is clear that revelation does not teach that [the deposal of the heretical pope would be necessary according to the teaching of Scripture and Tradition]. This is why the remaining option is to turn to the natural law. It is enough to apply the principle that the supernatural order presupposes the natural order. The Church is a society. Now, in every society, natural divine law requires that in a case of tyranny the citizens proclaim the dethronement of a power that may still be legal but has become illegitimate. And on the other hand this natural divine law which applies to the case of the city [= society] of the natural order remains valid also in the case of the Church, because she is a city in the supernatural order. This is why it is not only licit but necessary to depose a heretical pope, because that pope is to the Church what a tyrant is to natural society. And in order to do this, society receives in that case delegation from God." – *The Question of Papal Heresy* – Part 1.

derived from the Church. Therefore, a true and valid pope could only be deposed if he would already have ceased to be pope by himself by an act of tacit abdication because of public heresy, schism, or apostasy, as Bellarmine, Ballerini, Cappellari, St. Alphonsus, and several other notable theologians taught before *Pastor Æternus*; and as is taught with virtual unanimity after 1870 by theologians who admit at least the hypothetical possibility of a pope falling into public heresy. St. Alphonsus in the above cited passage stated categorically that a council cannot judge the pope for heresy, but could only declare that he had fallen from the pontificate. Like Bellarmine, he brought forth several proofs in his *Dissertatio de Pontificis Auctoritate* S. II. *De Auctoritate Pontificis supra Concilium,* explaining that a council can have no power over the pope, the last reason being that the Church is a monarchy:

> It is proven moreover from reason, because Monarchical Rule is the best among the others, as St. Thomas teaches in 4. contra Gentes c. 76. With these outstanding words: *The optimal rulership of the multitude is that it be ruled by one, for the peace and unity of the subjects is the end of rulership, the more appropriate cause of unity is one rather than many, whence Christ Jn. 10:16 said: And there will be made one sheepfold and one shepherd.* Calvin taught that Christ did not institute Monarchical Governance in the Church; but the opposite is commonly taught by Catholics with St. Cyprian; and Gerson wrote the same: *One who holds the contrary is a heretic; Christ did not constitute in the Church any other polity besides Monarchy.* In addition, if the rulership in the Church were not Monarchical, God would not have sufficiently provided for the good of the Church...[184]

---

[184] *Theologia Moralis, Dissertatio de Pontificis Auctoritate,* §. II. *De Auctoritate Pontificis supra Concilium* Tomus Primus Bassani (Bassano del Grappa) 1836, pp. 94-95 — «Probatur demum ex ratione, quia Regimen Monarchicum inter alia est optimum, ut docet D. Thom. in 4. contra Gentes c. 76. his præstantibus verbis: *Optimum Regimen multitudinis est, ut regatur per unum, pax enim, & unitas subditorum finis est Regiminis, unitatis autem congruentior causa est unus, quam multi, unde Christus. Jo. 10. 16. dixit: Et fiet unum ovile, & unus pastor.* Calvinus docuit Christum non instituisse Gubernium Monarchicum in Ecclesia; sed commununiter oppositum vere docent Catholici cum D. Cypriano; & idem Gerson scripsit: *Hereticum esse qui contrarium tenet; nullam aliam politicam constituit in Ecclesia Christus præter Monarchicam.* Adde si Regimen

Such an *ipso facto* fall from the pontificate followed by a deposition by a council is at least *hypothetically possible* because while in office, before being declared a heretic, the pope does have a Judge over him: «Before the Pope is declared a heretic, he is the Pope, therefore in this while he is still the Pope, he has a judge over him»[185] While he is pope, the pope as the Vicar of Christ, participates in Christ's kingship and headship over the Church, and therefore has only God over him as a Judge. For this reason, the successor of Peter in the Primacy can no more be judged by the bishops than Peter could have been judged by the other Apostles. Indeed, as *Vicar of Christ,* the pope, because of his participation in Christ's own headship over the Church as the supreme Monarch and Judge, he can no more be judged by his inferior members in the Church than Christ himself could have been judged by the apostles. Christ alone is the pope's judge for so long as he remains validly constituted as Pontiff. Hence, that Judge over the pope is not a Council, with jurisdiction by way of exception for heresy (as Bordoni and others believed before the definition of the Primacy in 1870 made that opinion dogmatically inadmissible), but that Judge can only be God, as is gathered even from Bordoni's own premise stated in the above cited passage, *"a pertinacious heretic is already judged by God"*, from which it follows that he, "is to be declared deposed by a council". He cannot be deposed by a council, but could only be declared by a council to already "be deposed".

Already centuries before Bellarmine, Bordoni or Cajetan, Innocent III taught, "the Roman Pontiff has no other superior than God"; and therefore, "He who judges is the Lord (I Cor. IV)"; for which reason, "The servant, according to the Apostle, «stands or falls by his lord» (Rom. xiv)."[186] However, as Innocent taught; and Bellarmine, Ballerini, St. Alphonsus, and Gregory XVI after him taught: once the pope would pronounce the judgment of God upon himself by obstinately professing heresy, he would fall from office by himself and could, in the words of Pope Innocent in the same sermon, "be shown to be already judged"; "cast out", "and trampled by men". By

---

in Ecclesia non esset Monarchicum, non satis a Deo Ecclesiæ bono provisum esset...»

[185] *Bordoni,* Op. cit. p. 154. – «antequam autem Papa declaretur hæreticus Papa est, ergo in hoc dum adhuc est Papa, supra se habet judicem.»

[186] Innocentius III — *Sermo IV. IN CONSECRATIONE PONTIFICIS.*

openly manifesting the *dolus* of his crime against divine law, he confesses the crime of heresy by which he defects from the faith and departs by himself from the Church; and thus shows himself to be "already judged" and is to be simply "cast out". Thus, Pope Innocent III teaches in *Sermo IV. IN CONSECRATIONE PONTIFICIS* that if a pope were to "wither away into heresy", "he can be judged by men, or rather can be shown to be already judged" – thus it is a papal teaching that a heretic pope is in reality no pope, and is therefore simply to be rejected like "salt that has lost its savour". He would be "already judged" and being already no longer pope, the already accomplished fact would only need to be juridically declared by the Church, since, as Bordoni explained: "for it is necessary that the judgment of God be published by the ministry of men, and this is most aptly done by a Council, which is the supreme tribunal when the papal see is vacant." The foundation of this doctrine is that God is both the Legislator of laws decreed to be observed in heaven and on earth; and the Judge over both the living and the dead, so that **those who publicly transgress divine law by declaring their own defection from the faith are publicly separated from the Church and condemned by their own judgment pronounced upon themselves in accordance with that divine law. It is for this reason that the lower tribunals would possess the jurisdiction to enforce the judgment of the *Supreme Judge* against the manifestly heretical pope who would impenitently declare his own crime before God and men.** The opposing opinion which held that even after pronouncing the judgment of God upon himself by obstinately professing heresy, the pope would remain in office until he is deposed or judged a heretic by the authority of the Church, was universally abandoned after the definition of the Primacy and Infallibility of the pope by the First Vatican Council in 1870, because that opinion directly opposes the dogma of the Primacy in that it subtracts from the Primacy the *"total fullness of supreme power"* in virtue of which the pope is the *supreme judge* of *disputes* concerning matters of faith; and the *"supreme judge of all cases that refer to ecclesiastical examination"* (*"not only in matters of faith and morals, but also in those which concern the discipline and government of the church dispersed throughout the whole world"* – *Pastor Æternus*). For so long as he is pope, it is solemnly defined that the final and infallible judgment of all matters of faith pertain to the pope's authority, so that no council may ever presume to depose a validly reigning pontiff for heresy with its own non-infallible judgment. It is precisely because the pope is appointed by Christ as the supreme and final judge in matters of faith, against whose judgment there can be no appeal, that he is endowed with the power, and therefore the right to judge infallibly. Therefore, if it were allowed by way of exception, that a pope could be judged for heresy by his inferiors while still validly holding the office of Supreme Pontiff, it would (as I explain below) irremediably destroy the very foundation of unity upon which the Church is built, since, as St. Cyprian teaches (*Lib*. 1. *ep. ad Corn. papam.*), all heresy originates out of the rejection of doctrinal judgments made by infallible papal authority. If that infallibility would be removed from the pope, or, if the pope's primacy would be altered, so that it would be *rendered inoperable* by personal heresy, as John of St. Thomas taught (see below), *then the pope's definition would not be infallible*; and **there would remain no infallible means to condemn heresy.**[187] **But to assert this, i.e.** *that the pope's definition would not be infallible*, **is heresy.**

Against the opinion that a heretic pope must be judged by the Church before he would fall from office there was already the teaching of Pope Innocent III, who taught in *Sermo III «IN CONSECRATIONE PONTIFICIS»*, that the pope is united to the Church in a spiritual matrimony (*Sic et Romanus pontifex sponsam habet Romanam ecclesiam*), and for so long as the pope is conjoined to the Church in matrimony, he cannot be judged, separated or deposed:

---

[187] Alfonso Maria de' Liguori, *Vindiciae pro suprema pontificis potestate adversus Iustinum Febronium*, Torino, 1832, p. 12 — "«Illud assero, et fidenter quidem assero, pestem eos ecclesiæ, et perniciem afferre, qui negant, romanum pontificem Petro fidei, doctrinæque auctoritate, succedere, aut certe adstruunt summum ecclesiæ pastorem, qui cumque ille sit, errare in fidei judicio posse. Utrumque scilicet hæretici faciunt: qui vero illis in utroque repugnant, hi in Ecclesia catholica habentur.» Hucusque Canus, ejusque dictis valde consonat famosa sententia s. Cypriani: *Neque enim aliunde hæreses ob ortæ sunt, quam inde quod sacerdoti Dei non obtemperatur, nec unus in ecclesia sacerdos, et ad tempus judeæ vice Christi cogitatur. Epist.* 3. *lib.* 2. *ad Cornel. Pap.* Idque nimis verum est; nam, sublata infallibilitate circa res fidei a pontifice romano, nullum suppetit medium (ut infra videbimus) ad hæreticos convincendos."

The pope has no superior but God (*post Deum alium superiorem non habet*) to judge him; thus, **"He is not deposed."**: Thus he explains, "But the sacrament between the Roman Pontiff and the Roman Church is so firm and stable that only by death are they ever separated from each other... he does not cede, he is not deposed; for «*he stands or falls by his own master*» (*Rom.* XIV). — «He who judges is the Lord» (I *Cor.* IV)."[188] However, Innocent explains at some length in the same sermon, that the matrimony can only exist between legitimate persons (*solus consensus inter legitimas personas efficit matrimonium*), and therefore, by the sin of infidelity, the spiritual matrimonial union between the Roman Pontiff and the Church would cease to exist; and thus the heretic, no longer a legitimate spouse, would cease to be pope, and could therefore be judged by men. Thus he explains:

> For reason of fornication the Roman Church could dismiss the Roman Pontiff. I do not mean carnal fornication but spiritual; and since it is not carnal but a spiritual union, that is because of the error of infidelity; because «he who does not believe has already been judged (*John* iii)»: and in this article is understood what is read in the Gospel, which you have heard: «You are the salt of the earth, but if the salt should lose its savour wherewith shall it be salted? (*Matth.* V.)»[189]

The reason for this, he explains in *Sermo II*, "Faith is so necessary for me, that while I have God alone for a judge; but for the sin committed against faith, I can be judged by the Church, because he

---

[188] *Sermo III «IN CONSECRATIONE PONTIFICIS»* — "Sacramentum autem inter Romanum pontificem et Romanam Ecclesiam tam firmum et stabile perseverat, ut non nisi per mortem umquam ab invicem separentur... Vir autem iste [Romanus Pontifex] alligatus uxori, [Ecclesiæ Romanæ] solutionem non quærit, non cedit, **non deponitur; nam «suo domino aut stat, aut cadit»** (*Rom.* XIV). — «Qui autem judicat, dominus est» (I *Cor.* IV)."

[189] Innocentius III — *Sermo III. «IN CONSECRATIONE PONTIFICIS»* — "Propter causam vero fornicationis Ecclesia romana posset dimmitere Romanum pontificem. Fornicationem non dico carnalem, sed spiritualem; quia non est carnale, sed spirituale conjugium, id est propter infidelitatis errorem; quoniam «qui non credit, jam judicatus est (*Joan.* iii)»: et in hoc articulo intelligitur, quod legitur in Evangelio, quod audistis: «Vos estis sal terræ, quod sis al evanuerit in quo salietur? (*Matth.* V.)»"

who does not believe has already been judged (John3: 18)"[190] Then in *Sermo IV* he qualifies more precisely in what manner the Roman Pontiff can be judged by the Church. He begins by saying that for prelates in general, "So then the sin of a prelate is harmful to others and is dangerous to himself. ... It is dangerous to himself, because *he would be good for nothing except to be cast out*, i.e., deposed from office, *and to be trampled by men*, i.e., despised by the people. Or *cast out and be trampled by men*, i.e. to be excommunicated and avoided." Then he adds, "As to how this could be understood in the case of any other prelate, that is clear enough. As to how it should be understood when it comes to the Roman Pontiff, however, that is not so obvious." He then explains why it is not so obvious, and the reason is that the pope has no superior on earth to condemn him: "The servant, according to the Apostle, «stands or falls by his master (Rom. xiv).» For which reason the same Apostle says; «Who art thou who judgeth the servant of another?» (Ibid.) Whence the Roman Pontiff has no master but God. Who, therefore, should a pope 'lose his savour', could cast him out or trample him under foot — since of the pope it is said 'gather thy case (causa) into thy fold' [fold of the toga over the breast]?" He then adds the qualification that the pope, if he falls into heresy, can be shown to be already judged, because the unbeliever is already condemned: "Truly, he should not flatter himself about his power, nor should he rashly glory in his honour and high estate, because the less he is judged by man, the more he is judged by God. I say less, because he can be judged by men, or rather, can be shown to be already judged, if for example he should wither away into heresy; because he who does not believe is already judged. In such a case it should be said of him: If salt should lose its savour, it is good for nothing but to be cast out and trampled by men."[191] By "cast out",

---

[190] Sermo II «*IN CONSECRATIONE PONTIFICIS MAXIMI*» — «In tantum enim fides mihi necessaria est ut cum de caeteris peccatis solum Deum judicem habeam, propter solum peccatum quod in fide committitur possem ab Ecclesia judicari. Nam qui non credit, iam iudicatus est. (Joh.3 18).»

[191] *Sermo IV* «*IN CONSECRATIONE PONTIFICIS*» — "Peccatum ergo prælati et aliis damnosum, et sibi est periculosum… Periculosum sibi; quoniam *ad nihilum valet ultra, nisi ut mittatur foras*, id est ab officio deponatur: *et conculcetur ab hominibus*, id est a populo contemnatur. Vel *mittatur foras, et*

Innocent means "deposed", and by "trampled by men, "despised by the people": (*mittatur foras, id est ab officio deponatur: et conculcetur ab hominibus, id est a populo contemnatur*).[192] This doctrine is the basis for what St. Robert Bellarmine teaches in *De Romano Pontifice lib. ii cap. xxx*: "Therefore the fifth opinion is true, a manifest heretic pope ceases to be pope and head, just as he ceases by himself to be a Christian and a member of the body of the Church, for which reason the he can be judged by the Church and punished. This is the view of all the ancient Fathers who teach that manifest heretics straightaway lose all jurisdiction."[193] In this manner, the pope, who has no judge but God, can be judged by men upon having ceased to be pope: "The

---

conculcetur ab hominibus, id est ut excommunicetur et evitetur… Qualiter ergo de quolibet alio praelato possit intelligi, satis apparet; sed qualiter intelligi debeat de Romano pontifice, non est adeo manifestum. Servus enim, secundum Apostolum, «suo domino stat aut cadit (Rom. xiv).» Propter quod idem Apostolus ait; «Tu quis es, qui judicas alienum servum?» (Ibid.) Unde cum Romanus pontifex non habeat alium dominum nisi Deum, quantumlibet evanescat, quis potest eum foras mittere, aut pedibus conculcare? Cum illi dicatur: «Collige causam tuam in sinum tuum?» Verum non frustra sibi blandiatur de potestate, neque de sublimitate vel honore temere glorietur; quia quanto minus judicatur ab homine, tanto magis judicatur a Deo. Minus dico; quia potest ab hominibus judicari, vel potius judicatus ostendi, si videlicet evanescat in haeresim; quoniam «qui non credit, jam judicatus est» (*Joan*. iii). In hoc siquidem casu debet intelligi de illo, *quod si sal evanuerit, ad nihilum valet ultra, nisi ut mittatur foras, et conculcetur ab hominibus*."

[192] Innocentius III — *Sermo IV. «IN CONSECRATIONE PONTIFICIS»*. It is to be noted that the expression, *id est ab officio deponatur*, in the passage where Innocent uses it, does not specifically refer to the deposition of a pope, but to prelates in general: "Peccatum ergo prælati et aliis damnosum, et sibi est periculosum… Periculosum sibi; quoniam *ad nihilum valet ultra, nisi ut mittatur foras*, id est ab officio deponatur: *et conculcetur ab hominibus*, id est a populo contemnatur." He adds, however, that while as pope he cannot be judged, if he falls into heresy, being already condemned, he is to be cast out and trampled by men.

[193] «Est ergo quinta opinio vera, papam hæreticum manifestum per se desinere esse papam et caput, sicut per se desinit esse christianus et membrum corporis Ecclesiæ; quare ab Ecclesia posse eum judicari et puniri. Hæc est sententia omnium veterum Patrum, qui docent, hæreticos manifestos mox amittere omnem jurisdictionem.»

foundation of this argument is that the manifest heretic is not in any way a member of the Church, that is, neither in soul nor body, and neither by internal nor external union."[194] Thus, *the heretic is judged by God*, but *the heretic pronounces sentence of self-condemnation with his own mouth* (Luke 19:22), as Bellarmine and Ballerini explain: Bellarmine — "Yet heretics are outside the Church, even before excommunication, and deprived of all jurisdiction, for they are condemned by their own judgment, as the Apostle teaches to Titus; that is, they are cut from the body of the Church without excommunication, as Jerome expresses it." *De Romano Pontifice, Lib. II, Cap. XXX.* Ballerini — "Conspicuous in this matter is the explanation of St. Jerome on the commended words of Paul. 'Therefore, by himself [the heretic] is said to be condemned, because the fornicator, adulterer, murderer, and those guilty of other misdeeds are driven out from the Church by the Priests: *but heretics deliver the sentence upon themselves*, departing from the Church by their own will: this departure is seen to be the condemnation by their own conscience.' ... and thus his sentence which he brought upon himself, would have to be publicly pronounced, made known to the whole Church, that he by his own will departed, making known to be severed from the body of the Church, and in some manner *to have abdicated the Pontificate*, which no one holds or can hold, who is not in the Church."[195] Commenting on Ballerini, Pope Gregory XVI explains, "Even so that it could be for a moment, that the Church has the authority to depose the Pontiffs: what then?... In fact, by ceasing in this hypothesis the deposed Pope to be a true Pope, the deposition is not a prescription against the rights of the Primacy, and therefore against the current representation of the Church in the Pope recognized as such, but only against the person, who was *before* adorned with papal dignity."[196] St. Alphonsus teaches similarly, stating, "if God allowed a Pope to be notoriously heretical and

---

[194] «Fundamentum hujus sententiæ est quoniam hæreticus manifestus nullo modo est membrum Ecclesiæ, idest, neque animo neque corpore, sive neque unione interna, neque externa.»

[195] Pietro Ballerini, *De Potestate Ecclesiastica. Summor. Pont. Et Conc. Gen.*, Cap. IX § II., Verona, 1765, pp. 128-9

[196] D. Mauro Cappellari ora Gregorio XVI, *Il trionfo della santa sede e della chiesa contro gli assatti dei novatori*, Venezia, 1832, p. 269-270.

contumacious, he would cease to be Pope, and he would vacate the Pontificate."[197]

The reason why a *manifest heretic* would fall from office entirely by himself *ipso jure* is because a manifest act of contumacious public heresy is itself an act of *pertinacity* which constitutes according to its very nature a public confession of guilt of the crime of heresy and an **admission of the *fact* of *defection from the Catholic faith***:

1) To be qualified as a *manifest heretic* the pope would have to manifest the *dolus* of crime, which in canon law is defined as the "deliberate will to violate the law" (*deliberata voluntas violandi legem*). Canon 2200 §1 of the 1917 Code of Canon Law defined the term and explained, that *dolus* is opposed by the lack of knowledge or liberty: "Dolus heic est deliberata voluntas violandi legem, eique opponitur ex parte intellectus defectus cognitionis et ex parte voluntatis defectus libertatis." Therefore, since *dolus* cannot be simply presumed outside of a penal process, the pope cannot simply be presumed to be a heretic on the sole basis that he speaks or acts in a such manner that exhibits the *indicia* of suspicion. In such a case in which the pope would manifest in his actions or words the factual evidence which constitute *indicia* of heresy sufficient to establish the crime as *probable*, he would only qualify as *suspect of heresy*. The matter of heresy is a proposition which asserts explicit heresy: "A heretical proposition is one which is formally and directly opposed to a proposition explicitly or implicitly revealed, and defined as such by the Church, which is therefore contradictory to the faith."[198] An example of such a heretical

---

[197] Alfonso M. De Liguori, *Verità Della Fede*, Tomo Secondo, Monza, 1823, Parte Terza - Contro i Settarj, Capo. VIII, n. 10. p. 157; *Verità della Fede*, Napoli, 1838, p. 455 – «Del resto, se Dio permettesse che un Papa fosse notoriamente eretico e contumace, egli cesserebbe d'essere Papa, e vacherebbe il Pontificato.» Before the precise distinction between *public* and *notorious* was formalized by the definitions of these terms in the 1917 Code, the terms were sometimes used interchangeably, as I have explained in Volume One.

[198] Cf. Ballerini, *De vi ac ratione primatus Romanorum Pontificum,* Elbert Wilhelm Westhoff, PRAEMONITUM IN NOVAM EDITIONEM, Monasterii Westphalorum, 1845, p. ix — «Propositio hæretica ea est, quæ formaliter et directe adversatur propositioni explicite revelatæ, vel implicite revelatæ et ut tali ab Ecclesia definitæ, cujus ergo contradictoria est a fide.»

proposition asserted against an *implicitly* revealed proposition would be the one I cited in Volume One, of Pedro de Luna's denial of the moral catholicity of the Church, for which he was declared a heretic in the thirty-seventh session of the Council of Constance for having denied the dogma *Unam Sanctam*.

2) The pope would qualify as a public *formal heretic* if the *dolus* is public and manifest: i.e., the heresy is professed in such a manner that it would be *certain* that he knowingly and freely asserted disbelief, with an act that explicitly, immediately, and directly opposes an article of divinely revealed truth which must be believed with divine and Catholic faith. I have explained in Volume One the conditions which must be fulfilled in order for it to be verified that the *indicia* which constitute evidence of heresy are to be qualified as certain *indicia* of *formal heresy*. If the certain *indicia* of formal heresy are manifested in such a manner that qualifies the act as *public*, as the term *public* is defined in canon law, then the act would be in the nature of a public profession of disbelief, an abjuration of the Catholic faith, and a public confession of guilt for the crime of heresy. In such an event as this, even if the man insists he is still a Catholic and not a heretic, his profession of disbelief by its very nature pleads guilty to the crime of heresy, and is an open admission of the *fact* of defection from the faith; and therefore, to effect his loss of office there is no need for a judge to pronounce a judgment of guilt, since, as Bellarmine says, "heretics are outside the Church, even before excommunication, and deprived of all jurisdiction, for they are condemned by their own judgment".[199] Indeed, in any jurisdiction whether ecclesiastical or secular, when the accused confesses his guilt for the crime, there is no longer any need for a **judgment** to be deliberated upon, and then decided upon by a **judge**, but the court simply proceeds to the penal sentencing. Thus, in the hypothetical case of a public heretic pope, he, by his own act of disbelief, declares himself in heresy and outside the Church; and being condemned by his own judgment, he desists by himself from the papacy; and ***losing all jurisdiction, he falls under the jurisdiction of the ecclesiastical authority,*** **and as a consequence thereof, he is excommunicated** ***latæ sententiæ***. It is at this point that a merely *declaratory sentence* would be pronounced by

---

[199] *De Romano Pontifice, lib. ii cap. xxx.*

the Church, confirming by juridical act that for having committed the crime of heresy, he has departed from the Church, forfeited his office, and incurred the penalty of excommunication. Hence, this is the teaching of Pope Innocent III: «Faith is so necessary for me that while for other sins I have only God for a judge, for only the sin committed against faith, I can be judged by the Church. For *he who does not believe, already has been judged.* (John 3: 18)»[200] Hence, while he is pope, even as *Vicar of Christ*, he does have a Judge over him — the divine Judge; and because he has God over him as a legislator and judge, by falling into heresy he would stand before that Judge and the whole Church self-condemned by his own judgment because *he who does not believe, already has been judged.* (John 3: 18) Thus by manifesting his obstinate and manifestly evident disbelief in a revealed dogma of faith that he as pope was bound by divine law to teach to the Church in God's name as Christ's representative, he would cease to be Christ's representative on earth by the very public fact that his contrary disposition to faith which is heresy, would manifest him to be the representative of disbelief against Christ, and thereby visibly deprive him of the form of the pontificate, which consists in the visible representation of the true faith he opposes, and thus render him manifestly opposed to the exercise of the *munus* of teaching the faith he now opposes, which he was bound by the law of Christ to teach.

But if a pope were capable of remaining in office and in possession of the *universal jurisdiction* of the Primacy even after falling into manifest heresy, so that he would need to be judged by the Church first before falling from office, he would never be able to be deposed from office because both the *supreme magisterial jurisdiction to* **judge the error in question** would be required, and the j*urisdiction of a superior over the* **person** would be required for a *juridical judgment* to be made against the heretic, since a deposition from ecclesiastical office could not take place without a *juridical judgment* of both the **doctrine** and the guilty **person**. Therefore a *judicial act* and of *jurisdiction* would be required to declare the pope a heretic even in order for it to act as a dispositive

---

[200] «In tantum enim fides mihi necessaria est ut cum de cæteris peccatis solum Deum judicem habeam, propter solum peccatum quod in fide committitur possem ab Ecclesia judicari. Nam **qui non credit, iam iudicatus est.** (Joh.3 18)» (*Sermo II* «IN CONSACRATIONE PONTIFICIS MAXIMI»)

cause of a heretical pope's fall from office. Such a juridical act could only be accomplished by a *judge;* and therefore, the *sine qua non* requirement for such a deposition to take place, would be a *judicial act which by its very nature can only be exercised by a superior over his inferior.*[201] This is plainly evident, firstly, in view of the fact that the *juridical declaration of heresy* by its nature is a **judgment**, because, as Ballerini says, "Judgment properly so called is delivered when one pronounces a sentence based on knowledge of the cause". A declaration of heresy is not a juridical judgment if it is not a **sentence** made by a **judge** acting with **jurisdiction to judge both the error in question and the guilt of the person who asserts it**. It must be made *with jurisdiction* regarding the cause (i.e., the juridically established *indicia* of heresy), without which it is not *juridical,* and not a *judgment,* but is nothing but a mere *assertion of an opinion* — a mere non-juridical conjecture, even if it would be pronounced by a self-appointed council against a pope. Such a declaration would be incapable of having any juridical effect, and would therefore not exercise *any power* to bring about the fall from office of a pope, *by which power* the Church could "induce a disposition incompatible with the pontificate" (XXVIII)[202], causing the "separation of this power [the primacy] from that person [the pope], by declaring him a heretic" (XXI)[203]. Therefore, for the declaration to be *juridical,* it would have to be a *judicial* pronouncement; which can only be made by a *judge* acting with the *jurisdiction of a superior in every respect.* Secondly, if the fall from the papacy can only take place upon an act of *juridical judgment of heresy,* then also for the same reason as for the declaration of heresy, the declaration of the *desisting of the pope from the papacy* would also require an act of a *judge* acting with the jurisdiction of a *superior* over the **person.** Thus, in a deposition there are enumerated three acts, 1) the declaration of heresy, 2) the desisting of the papacy in the person, and 3) penal expulsion from the Church; all of which are *judicial acts,* and therefore **require the power of jurisdiction in whoever would provide**

---

[201] Bordoni. cap. vi. p. 155.
[202] John of St. Thomas, *Op cit.* p. 264 — «Inducere dispositionem incompossibilem cum pontificatu.»
[203] *Ibid.* p. 260 — «Separationem hujus potestatis a persona, declarando illum pro haeretico.»

the act. [204] The deposition of a pope, therefore, would necessarily be a judicial act of jurisdiction, since, according to its nature, it cannot be done except by a judge; therefore, such a deposition could only be done by a superior who is over the pope as an inferior and subject, for which reason it matters little whether the power is called authoritative or ministerial, since *a deposition is a judicial act by its very nature exercised by a superior over an inferior.*[205]

This, as I have pointed out in Volume One, is the fatal flaw in all of the theories which merely posit a supposedly juridical declaration of heresy against the pope as a condition for his fall from office; or a proper deposition of the pope, which, according to the theory of Cajetan, is supposed to be brought about by means of what he speciously claimed would only be a *ministerial* act that exercises power not over the pope, but only over the conjunction by which the pope is joined to the papacy. Bordoni already pointed out in 1648 that "it matters little whether the power is called authoritative or ministerial, since a deposition is a judicial act by its very nature exercised by a superior over an inferior."[206] After all, according to Cajetan's conjunction theory, it is the *pope* who is being judged for the crime of heresy, and not the *conjunction* — and judging a man is not judging a conjunction; and judging him guilty of a *crime* is not ministerial but *judicial*; as is also the juridical act of merely declaring him a heretic, since juridically declaring a man a heretic according to law is properly an act of *judgment* according to its very nature (as explained above), which can only be performed by one who possesses the power of a *judge* acting with *jurisdiction,* even when that judgment is not rendered in a judicial forum, but through the executive power of one who also possesses judicial jurisdiction. Then Cajetan also denies that an

---

[204] Bordoni, *Op. cit.*, p. 154 – «Numerantur autem tres actus, declarario hæresis, desitio Papatus, & eiectio extra Ecclesiam, qui omnes sunt iudiciales, ac proinde requirentes iurisdictionem in eo, qui illa tria præstare debet.»

[205] *Ibid.* p. 155 — «depositio Papæ: est actus iudícialis, & jurisdictionis, quia nonnisi per iudicem fieri potest, secundum omnes, ergo huiusmodi depositio fit per superiorem in Papam tamquam inferiorem, ac subditum.»

[206] *Ibid.* — «parum ergo refert, quod ea potestas vocetur auctoritatiua, siue ministerialis, fi depositio est actus iudicialis ex sua natura exercitus a superiore in inferiorem.»

authoritative power is exercised in the deposition of a pope, insofar as it would not be exercised over a pope regarding the papacy, but over the conjunction; and therefore, Bordoni observed, it matters little whether that power by which a pope is deposed is called ministerial or authoritative; since supposedly nothing of it is exercised over the papacy but over the conjunction. However, even ministerial acts require jurisdiction, such as the election of a pope, and that jurisdiction is granted *jure pontificio*; and while the jurisdiction to elect a pope is granted by papal legislation in virtue of the pope's *full and supreme jurisdiction*, no power was ever granted to the pope's inferiors by Christ to dissolve of the conjunction between the pope and the papacy, because 1) as noted above, Christ conferred no ecclesiastical power directly on the Church, but the Church's power is dependent on and hierarchically subordinate to the pope's *fullness of power*, and; 2) while the power to bring about the not yet existing conjunction pertains to the Church, jurisdiction over the existing conjunction pertains not to the bishops or the cardinals, but to the full and absolute jurisdiction of the Roman Pontiff over the whole Church. Such a separation from the head brought about by the inferior members of the Church would oppose the absolute power of the primacy, which extends even over the conjunction, and would be essentially an act of destruction of the Church as divinely constituted, resulting in her defection through decapitation. Cajetan and John of St. Thomas attempt to circumvent this absolute necessity of jurisdiction over the person to be judged and deposed by asserting, "The power of the Church has for its object the application of the power of the pope to the person by designating him by election, and the separation of this power from the person, by declaring him a heretic and to be avoided by the faithful".[207] The humbug in these words is exposed in the assertion that *the power of the Church* consists in the "application of the power of the pope to the person by designating him by election", whereas the election applies no such power to the person, but merely designates the person to whom that

---

[207] *Cursus Theologicus II-II De Auctoritate Summi Pontificis, Disp. II, Art. III, De Depositione Papae*, XX. p. 260 — «potestas Ecclesiæ habet pro objecto applicationem potestatis papæ ad personam, designando illam per electionem, et separationem hujus potestatis a persona, declarando illum pro hæretico, et evitandi a fidelibus.»

power is to be applied immediately by God if the elected person consents to the election. On the basis of the heretically asserted existence of the Church's **power over the conjunction**, John of St. Thomas appeals to the authority of Cajetan saying, "that the Church is not above the pope absolutely, even in the case of heresy, whereas it *is above the conjunction of the pontificate with that person by dissolving it*, just as it united it at the election, and this power is ministerial".[208] Bellarmine already pointed out the fallacy of this proposition which asserts that the conjunction is made in the same way as it is dissolved, saying, "For while a thing is being made, the action is exerted on the matter of the thing that will be, not on the composite which as yet is not: but while a thing is being destroyed, the action is exerted over the composite".[209] Cajetan's proposition is heretical in that it directly opposes the dogma of the primacy which defined the "full and supreme jurisdiction" of the primacy as a *"total fullness of supreme power"*. The Church has the ministerial power to designate the person who may then be joined by God to the pontificate by the not yet existing conjunction, and thus receive immediately from God the absolute power of primacy not yet existing in the person at the time of election; but *it is heresy to attribute to the Church a power over the actually existing conjunction*, to dissolve it, because **the exercise of the Church's supposed power over the actual conjunction would directly oppose the *absolute power of primacy*** actually existing in the pope, since **the holder of the primacy possesses an *absolute power of jurisdiction* over the whole Church, and therefore also over the conjunction**. Against this *total fullness of power* of the *full and supreme jurisdiction* of the Roman Pontiff, there can exist no power of jurisdiction in the Church by which there can be introduced a disposition to dissolve the conjunction which remains under the pope's supreme jurisdiction; yet this is precisely the heretical thesis of Cajetan, which can clearly be

---

[208] *Ibid.* — «quod Ecclesia non est supra papam absolute etiam in casu hæresis, sed quod est supra conjunctionem cum ista persona dissolvendo illam, eo modo quo illam per electionem conjunxit, quæ potestas Ecclesiæ ministerialis est.»

[209] *De Rom. Pont. ii. xxx.* — «Nam dum res fit, actio exercetur circa materiam rei futuræ, non circa compositum quod nondum est: at dum res destruitur, exercetur circa compositum.»

seen to be heretical in the passage of Cajetan which Don Curzio Nitoglia quotes and comments on: «The substance of Cajetan's hypothesis can be summarized in the verse of *De comparata auctoritate* (Roma, Angelicum, 1936, a cura di V. Pollet, cap. XIX, p. 122, n. 269; cap. XX, p. 126, n. 276; cap. XX, p. 132, n. 207): "When the Pope is deposed, the power of jurisdiction is not taken away from the Papacy, but from this man by means of human judgment [...] The Pope neither *simpliciter* nor *secundum quid* has a superior on earth, but is under the instrumental and ministerial power of the Universal Church only as far as deposition or disjunction between the Papacy and the canonically elected person [...]. The Church does not have power over the Papacy, but it has power over the conjunction between Peter and the Papacy." That is, the power of the Church, in case of hypothetical heresy of the Pope, is authoritative (i.e. by its own virtue and as a principal cause) only on the union between the Papacy and the person canonically elected by the Conclave, while it is instrumental or ministerial (as an instrument in the hands of God) on the Papacy.»[210]

Most clearly the Church has no power from God whatsoever over the actually existing conjunction, because the Primacy, in which consists the *"total fullness of supreme power"*, is given to the pope directly by God, which, being a *total fullness,* leaves absolutely no power for the rest of the Church to exercise over the conjunction.

---

[210] «La sostanza della ipotesi del Gaetano è riassumibile nel versetto del *De comparata auctoritate* (Roma, Angelicum, 1936, a cura di V. Pollet, cap. XIX, p. 122, n. 269; cap. XX, p. 126, n. 276; cap. XX, p. 132, n. 207): *"Cum deponitur Papa, non aufertur potestas jurisdictionis a Papatu, sed ab hoc homine mediante judicio humano. [...]. Papa nec simpliciter nec secundum quid habet superiorem in terris, sed subest potestati instrumentali et ministeriali Ecclesiae Universali quoad solam depositionem seu disjunctionem inter Papatum et personam electam canonice. [...]. Ecclesia non habet potestatem supra Papatum, sed habet potestatem supra conjunctionem inter Petrum* [Eugenium, Georgium] *et Papatum"*. Ossia il potere della Chiesa, in caso di eresia ipotetica del Papa, è autoritativo (cioè per propria virtù e come causa principale) solo sull'unione tra il Papato e la persona eletta canonicamente dal Conclave, mentre è strumentale o ministeriale (come uno strumento in mano a Dio) sul Papato.» — *GIOVANNI DA SAN TOMMASO E LA DEPOSIZIONE DEL PAPA ERETICO* di Don Curzio Nitoglia.

Furthermore, it is absurd to say that the council exercises only a ministerial power in deposing a pope by exercising jurisdiction over the conjunction, since, **when the council declares the pope guilty of heresy, it is not judging the conjunction guilty of heresy but it is judging the PERSON — the PERSON who is THE POPE, whom it has not the *power to judge*;** for which reason a council's judgment of a validly reigning pope is **juridically *null and void*.** In Volume One I pointed out that, Cajetan's argument does not hold together, because, as Suárez observed, it maintained that a council would not be judging the pope as pope, but as a private person. In refuting Cajetan's opinion, Suárez explained that *it is precisely the dignity of the person invested with the primacy which strictly excludes that he can be personally judged by anyone*: "also because the Pope being superior insofar as he is Pope, is nothing else than that person by reason of the dignity to be exempt from all jurisdiction of another man, and to have jurisdiction in others, as is clear with whatever other dignity; and it is explained, for the pontifical dignity does not make an abstract or metaphysical superior, but really and in an individual a superior subject to none."[211] In vain John of St. Thomas deceitfully attempted to refute Suárez on this point by asserting that according to Cajetan, the judgment would not be an exercise of authority over the pope as pope, but only an exercise of jurisdiction over the conjunction, and of a ministerial power; since, as has been explained, it pertains to the nature of a judgment against a person that it is an act of jurisdiction

---

[211] R. P. Francisci Suarez, *Op. cit. Tomus Doudecimus, Tractatus Primus, De Fide Theologica. Disputatio X. De Summo Pontifice, Sect. VI. Tertium dubium*, p. 318: «At hinc oritur tertia dubitatio, quo jure possit ab illa congregatione Papa judicari, cum esset illa superior? Qua in re Cajetanus se mire vexat, ne cogatur admittere Ecclesiam vel Concilium stare supra Papam, in casu etiam heresis; tandem vero concludit supra Papam quidem stare, ut privatam personam, non ut papam; sed non satisfacit distinctio; nam eodem modo posset affirmari Ecclesiam judicare Papam valere, atque punire, non ut Papam, sed ut privatam personam; item quia Papam superiorem esse in quantum Papam, nihil est aliud quam eam personam ratione dignitatis esse exemptam ab omni jurisdictione hominis alterius, et habere jurisdictionem in alios, ut patet de quacumque alia dignitate; et explicatur, nam dignitas pontificia non facit superiorem abstracte et metaphysice, sed revera et in individuo superiorem nulli subjectum.»

of a superior exercising judicial power over that person, and hence, it cannot be maintained that such a judgment would be a merely ministerial act made without the jurisdiction of a superior. Thus, John of St. Thomas explained, "Suarez also in the often cited disputation, sect. VI, num. VII, attacks Cajetan for saying that in the case of heresy the Church is over the pope as a private person, not insofar as he is pope. Which however Cajetan did not say, that the Church is not above the pope absolutely even in the case of heresy, but is over the conjunction of the pontificate with that person by dissolving it, in that manner by which she conjoined it by election, which power is ministerial, for with respect to the pope only Christ the Lord is superior *simpliciter*."[212] Cajetan's own words expose the duplicity of John of St. Thomas, where Cajetan says, "When the Pope is deposed, the power of jurisdiction is not taken away from the Papacy, *but from this man by means of human judgment*," thus, insofar as Cajetan says that *by means of human judgment the power of jurisdiction is being taken away from this man*, Cajetan is saying that the Church *pronounces judgment on this man, the POPE*, and **by means of this human judgment** exercised **over the person of the pope**, the papal jurisdiction is being taken away from him.

For that to be possible, the jurisdictional power of a council to validly **judge a pope guilty** of **heresy** and **depose him** would necessarily have to be (even if only by way of exception) **a power which according to its very nature is formally *superior to the jurisdictional power of the primacy*** which ***exists in the person of the pope as a habit in a subject***, otherwise the council could not act juridically to judge and depose a pope unless formally its power were greater. This is plainly evident from reason because ***that which acts with power over another is of a greater force and power than the***

---

212 *Cursus Theologicus II-II De Auctoritate Summi Pontificis, Disp. II, Art. III, De Depositione Papae*, XX, p. 260 — «Suarez quoque disputatione sæpe citata, sect. VI, num. VII Cajetanum impugnat, quod dixerit Ecclesiam in casu hæresis super papam tamquam privatam personam, non in quantum papa est. Quod tamen Cajetanus non dixit, sed quod Ecclesia non est supra papam absolute etiam in casu hæresis, sed quod est supra conjunctionem pontificatus cum ista persona dissolvendo illam, eo modo quo illam per electionem conjunxit, quæ potestas Ecclesiæ ministerialis est, nam simpliciter superior solum est Chriastus Dominus respectu papæ.»

other over which it acts, so that it is able to overcome the power of that over which it acts. **Thus, if the Council** *by means of human judgment* **is to bring about the destruction of the habit of the pontificate in the Pontiff,** *its jurisdictional power to judge must be of a greater magnitude than the primatial power of the Pope.*[213] But the fullness of power of the primacy is infallibly defined to be **a** *"total fullness" — a "full and supreme jurisdiction"*, and therefore there exists no power on earth, not even by way of exception, that can bring about its removal from the person of the pope *by means of human judgment*, whether directly or dispositively, whether authoritatively or ministerially. **Therefore, to assert that such a power exists by which a disposition can be introduced to bring about the separation of the papacy from the pope by dissolving the conjunction between them is HERESY.**

John of St. Thomas sums up Bellarmine's refutation of Cajetan's deposition theory in No. XVII, and in No. XXVIII and XXIX[214] he

---

[213] Bordoni. p. 158 — «Sed numquid hæc potestas Concilii Papam deponedi est maior Papatus? Vtique, alioquin Concilium non potest agere in depositionem Pontificis, si in hoc casu non esset maioris potestatis, id enim quod agit in alterius destructionem maioris semper est virtutis, & potentiæ, vt passum superare possit, sic Concilium si habet destruere Pontificem maiorem Papa in hoc debet habere potestatem.»

[214] «XXVIII. Respondetur, quod aliter potest pontifex in episcopum quando ipsum deponit, aliter Ecclesia in pontificem: nam pontifex privat ipsum tamquam sibi subjectum, et habenten potestatem sibi subordinatam et dependentem, quam limitare, et coarctare potest, unde licet tollat episcopatum a persona, et non destruat episcopatum, tamen hoc tollit ex suprioritate quam habet ad personam, etiam ex parte potestatis sibi subordinatæ, ratione cujus illam amovet a persona, et non solum personam personam ab ipsa. Ecclesia vero tollit pontificatum ex superioritate ad potestatem ipsam, sed ex ministeriali, et dispositive potestate qua potest inducer dispositionem incompossibilem cum pontificatu, ut dictum est. XXIX. Ad confirmationem respondetur, papam dispone invitum ministerialiter, et dispositive ab Ecclesia, auctoritative a Christo Domino, unde ab ipso, non ab Ecclesia punitur proprie loquendo. Ad ultimum dicitur, quod qui potest in conjunctionem partium, potest in totum simpliciter, non tamen si ministerialiter solum, et dispositive possit in talem conjunctionem nisi in naturalibus, in quibus physicæ dispositions habent naturalem connexionem cum ipso esse totius, quod cum communicetur ab

responds with crudely fallacious, speciously contrived arguments, which do not hold up to critical scrutiny, in that the **ministerial and dispositive** *power to depose* an actually reigning valid pope, which he asserts as pertaining to the authority of the Church, by which authority is introduced a disposition incompatible with the pontificate, **simply does not exist**; because *the totality of ecclesiastical power* **exists in the primacy of the pontiff as a** *"total fullness of supreme power,"* **which would not be a total fullness of power if it were subject to limitations, such as an alteration or mutation brought about by heresy, which would render that** *"full and supreme jurisdiction"* **in some manner** *inferior to a power which in its very nature is hierarchically subordinate to it,* **which could then introduce a disposition** *incompatible with the absolutely superior supreme pontificate.* Thus, the very notion of a primacy that can be mutated and somehow rendered inferior to a subordinate power and subject to its judgment is logically opposed to the nature of the primacy solemnly defined as a *total fullness of supreme power,* which as such is **essentially** ***different power,*** **and is** ***of its very nature superior*** **to the power of the episcopacy**. Consequently, the power of the primacy, being dogmatically defined according to its very nature as total, full, supreme, and universal, is not subject to alteration, mutation, or diminution in any manner whatsoever by heresy; **but heresy, being directly and** *per se* **opposed to faith, is therefore opposed** *per se* **to the nature of the pontificate** which was instituted above all for the purpose of preserving and safeguarding the unity of the Church in the purity of the Catholic faith; so that heresy, as Bellarmine explains, would not alter the power of the primacy, but **would be the uttermost disposition for its destruction**, so that *it would cease to exist by itself, without any*

---

agente producente dispositions conjuncivas partium, simpliciter producit ipsum totum: in moralibus autem disposition, quæ fit ab aliquo, cum solum habeat morale conjunctionem cum forma, et quasi ex institutione voluntaria, qui disponit non censetur facere ipsum totum simpliciter, et auctoritative, sed quasi ministerialiter: sicut si pontifex alicui concedat, ut loca quæ designaverit habeant privilegia lucrandi indulgentias, et quæ declaraverit non habere, non habeant, designanatio, vel declaration ista non habet tollere, aut concedere indulgentias auctoritative et principaliter, sed ministerialiter solum.» [p. 264]

external agent; and in this manner, "a heretic pope without any other deposition would cease by himself to be Pope." — «Thenceforth, either Faith is *simpliciter* a necessary disposition for someone to be Pope, or only to be a good pope. If the first, then this disposition being removed by the contrary which is heresy, the Pope straightaway ceases to be Pope: nor can the form be conserved without the necessary dispositions... *Then,* those which have the uttermost disposition to destruction thereafter cease to be, without any external power, as is evident; therefore a heretic pope without any other deposition would cease by himself to be Pope.»[215]

It was Ballerini who explained that power which exists in the episcopacy, is according to its nature an essentially *different power* which is *hierarchically subordinate to the absolute power of the primacy*. The analogy of the ministerial power to grant indulgences John of St. Thomas uses to illustrate the principle explained in these paragraphs is not valid, in that the authority to exercise a ministerial power to grant the indulgences is conceded by a superior ecclesiastical authority; whereas the power to depose a pope ministerially is not conceded to the pope's inferiors by divine law, and cannot be conceded *jure pontificio* to a subordinate to be exercised against a pope, who possesses the *total fullness of supreme power*. Therefore, Bordoni rightly points out that "if the Council is to bring about the destruction of the Pontiff, *it must have a greater power than the Pope,*" but such a power greater than the absolute power of the primacy simply does not exist on earth.

Furthermore, Bordoni points out that **it is a deceitful contrivance to posit that conjunction to be brought about by the ministry of men through election in relation to the papal dignity and power**, since the electors only designate the person, upon whom God thereafter confers the dignity and authority, **so that the election is not the means, by which Christ bestows the papacy upon the elected**, but only the condition *sine qua non* with which God confers the papacy

---

[215] *De Rom. Pont. Lib. ii cap. xxx* — «Deinde. Vel Fides est dispositio necessaria simpliciter ad hoc ut aliquis sit Papa, vel tantum ad bene esse. Si primum; ergo ista dispositione sublata per contrariam quæ est hæresis, mox Papa desinit esse: neque enim potest forma conservari sine necessariis dispositionibus... *Deinde,* quae habent ultimam dispositionem ad interitum, paulo post desinit esse, sine alia vi externa, ut patet; igitur et Papa haereticus sine alia depositione *per se* desinit esse Papa.»

upon someone; and therefore, *the conjunction is not made by the ministry of the electors*, but immediately by God, lest it be said that the electors confer the papacy together with God, and thus make a man pope according to the nature of the pope.[216] Furthermore, because **if by the ministry of men, the papacy is joined to the elected man,** *the pope would no longer receive the dignity of the papacy immediately from God*, but also from men – **against the common doctrine of all canonists and theologians, and against the above cited teaching of Pius XII in** *Vacantis Apostolicæ Sedis*. And also *it would follow from there that the electors conjoin the papacy to the one they elect*, which is to confer upon him the dignity, like a whitewasher conjoining whiteness to a wall, and confer whiteness upon the wall; thus, likewise *by Cajetan's conjunction the electors can be said to confer the papacy on the pope, which is false*, because the electors designate the person, and *God, by himself immediately confers the dignity and jurisdiction*;[217] yet John of St. Thomas contradicts himself when he asserts on the one hand "the Church has the ministerial power of electing as far as the designating of the person, **but not in the conferring of power**, because this is done immediately by Christ"[218]; but at the same time he asserts the doctrine of Cajetan who says, "that the pope is truly deposed by the Church, and by authority... but that the Church is not above the pope absolutely even in the case of heresy, **but that** *she is above the conjunction* **with that person by dissolving it,** *IN THAT MANNER BY WHICH SHE CONJOINED IT BY ELECTION*,

---

[216] Bordoni, *Op. cit.* p. 156 — «Tum quia frustratorium est ponere eam coniunctionem ministerio hominum per illam electionem in ordine ad dignitatem, & potestatem Pontificiam, quia electores tantum designant personam, cui Deus postea confert dignitatem, & auctoritatem, ita quod electio, non est medium, quo a Christo tribuatur Papatus electo, fed tantum conditio sine qua non confert Deus Papatum alicui... ergo coniunctio hæc non fit ministerio electorum, fed immediate a Deo, ne dicamus electores conferre dignitatem Papatus electo simul cum Deo, & sic facere Papam in ratione Papæ.»

[217] *Ibid.* p. 156

[218] «Ecclesia habet ministerialem potestatem eligendi quoad designationem personæ, *non quoad collationem potestatis*, quia hæc fit immdiate a Christo» — p. 260.

which **power** is ministerial".²¹⁹ **Now to say, as John of St. Thomas explicitly asserts,** *that the Church conjoined the person to the papacy even ministerially is false*, **and to assert on the basis of this false premise that the Church** *is above the conjunction* **and therefore has the** *power to dissolve the conjunction* **is HERESY.**²²⁰ The Church only disposes the person to be joined to the papacy by God, but once disposed, the uniting of the matter and form is accomplished immediately by God alone. From the instant the pope-elect gives his consent to his election, **he receives immediately from God** the *"full and absolute jurisdiction over the whole planet"*;²²¹ for which reason, in virtue of the *"total fullness of supreme power,"* (Pastor Æternus) **the pope exercises** *absolute power of jurisdiction over the conjunction* **for so long as he is pope**. The conjunction, therefore, is destroyed only by death or valid resignation, as is explicitly set forth in *Universi Dominici Gregis*;²²² and in virtue of the *"full and absolute jurisdiction"* of the Primacy conferred immediately upon the pope by God, the conjunction is intrinsically incapable of being acted upon by any external dispositive agent acting ministerially, for which reason, papal loss of office is accomplished explicitly or tacitly by the pope *"sine alia vi externa"*;²²³ and therefore **by himself alone**. Thus it follows strictly, as Cardinal Billot observed in *Traité de l'Église du Christ*,

---

²¹⁹ «papa ab Ecclesia deponitur vere, et ex auctoritate [...] sed quod [Ecclesia] non est supra papam absolute etiam in casu hæresis, **sed quod est supra conjunctionem cum ista persona dissolvendo illam**, *eo modo quo illam per electionem conjunxit*, quæ **potestas** Ecclesiæ ministerialis est.» — p. 260.

²²⁰ Such a theory reduces the pope to the status of a prime minister voted into office by a council of ministers, who could then be voted out of office by a vote of no confidence by the same council of ministers. The Sacred College of Cardinals possesses no such power, but it exists absolutely in hierarchical subordination to the full and absolute jurisdiction of the Primacy.

²²¹ «Hoc consensu praestito ... illico electus est verus Papa, atque actu **plenam absolutamque iurisdictionem supra totum orbem** acquirit et exercere potest» [Constitutio Apostolica «*Vacantis Apostolicæ Sedis*» Pius XII, 8 December 1945.

²²² *Universi Dominici Gregis* explicitly states that the see becomes vacant *"after the death or valid resignation of the Pope."*

²²³ Bellarmine, *De Romano Pontifice lib. ii cap. xxx*.

question 14, thesis 29, part 2: *"The Church, or an ecclesiastical assembly, cannot perform any act upon the person of the pope, except for the election. And therefore, once the election is canonically terminated, the Church has nothing more to do until a new election takes place, which can occur only after the see becomes vacant."* Therefore, whoever says that the pope's inferiors, even the totality of the episcopate congregated together in a council, possess the power to dissolve the conjunction which joins the papacy to the person of the Supreme Pontiff, either directly or indirectly (by introducing a disposition to disjoin the conjunction), explicitly asserts heresy against the dogma of the Primacy, solemnly defined in *Pastor Æternus*, which infallibly set forth as *de fide definita* the **"total fullness of supreme power"** of the Primacy — a fullness of power which in virtue of its totality admits no share whatsoever to the pope's inferiors in the exercise of that supreme power by which the Roman Pontiff exercises exclusively a *"full and supreme power of jurisdiction"* (*Pastor Æternus*) — a *"full and absolute jurisdiction"* (*Vacantis Apostolicæ Sedis*) which he exercises even over the conjunction between the papacy and himself. Thus, the doctrine of John of St. Thomas on papal deposition based on the conjunction theory of Cajetan falls under the anathema of the First Vatican Council.[224]

Moreover, it is absolutely impossible for there to be a valid declaration or judgment of heresy pronounced on a reigning pontiff by his inferiors which would result in his loss of office, because the holder of the primacy possesses the exclusive and absolute authority as *supreme judge* to judge in all matters of faith and morals and in all disputes over matters of faith; and because the Church as a whole has been given no suppletive authority in virtue of its totality to exercise by way of exception the *supreme power* (which exists only in the primacy) to judge in matters of faith instead of the pope, in a manner

---

[224] *PASTOR ÆTERNUS:* «Si quis itaque dixerit, Romanum Pontificem habere tantummodo officium inspectionis vel directionis, non autem **plenam et supremam potestatem iurisdictionis in universam Ecclesiam, non solum in rebus, quae ad fidem et mores, sed etiam in iis, quae ad disciplinam et regimen Ecclesiae per totum orbem diffusae pertinent**; aut eum habere tantum potiores partes, non vero **totam plenitudinem huius supremae potestatis;** aut hanc eius potestatem non esse **ordinariam et immediatam sive in omnes ac singulas ecclesias, sive in omnes et singulos pastores et fideles; ANATHEMA SIT.**»

that would thereby effectively suspend the absolute power of the Primacy, and to judge against the *supreme judge*, whose supreme power of jurisdiction is *total* and *absolute*. Juridical judgment on a person can only be pronounced by a judge or by a tribunal of judges exercising power over a person who is subject to their jurisdiction. The objection that in deposing a pope, a council, a synod, or the cardinals, would pronounce judgment on a pope without directly exercise power over that pope is plainly fallacious and absurd on its face. **In his refutation of Cajetan's theory (Bellarmine's "fourth opinion"), Bellarmine explained that such an act of deposition requires an exercise of power over the pope: "For, if the Church deposes a Pope against his will, certainly it is over the Pope."** (Nam si Ecclesia invitum Papam deponit, certe est *supra Papam*.) Cardinal Billot, in his *Traité de l'Église du Christ*, question 14, thesis 29, part 2, explained against Cajetan why it cannot be legitimately objected, "that the deposal could still be understood not as the direct withdrawal of the papacy"; and the reason he gives is that given by Bellarmine and Bordoni: Such a deposal, says Billot, "corresponds to an act of jurisdiction and to the exercise of a power. This is why the objection's conclusion does not follow: just because the person of the pope can be designated by men, this does not mean that the latter have the legitimate power to dismiss the person of the pope from the papacy."[225] Such a power, Bellarmine explains, requires the jurisdiction of a superior: "for one to be deposed from the pontificate against his will is without a doubt a penalty; therefore, the Church deposing a Pope against his will, without a doubt punishes him; but to punish is for a superior and a judge". This *sententia* is echoed by Wernz & Vidal and is unanimously taught by canonists: "*For every judicial sentence of privation supposes a superior jurisdiction over him against whom the sentence is laid.*"[226]

Furthermore, the notion of a "judgment" or "declaration" posited in all of the theories which call for a either a juridical declaration or a judgment against the pope, without exercising jurisdiction over the pope, *is a contradiction in terms,* and is therefore *contrary to the nature of a*

---

[225] *Traité de l'Église du Christ*, question 14, thesis 29, part 2, pp. 605-606, nos. 940-941.

[226] Wernz-Vidal, *IUS CANONICUM II* (1928), n. 453.

juridical act, and consequently *is not a juridical act*, but is *"something else"*, as Bordoni explained, *"which is not holding together"*: «intelligitur aliquid aliud, quod tamen consonum non est».[227] Thus, the fallacy that underlies all of these theories (which directly contradict the dogmatic definition of the Primacy and are seen to be heretically opposed to the solemn anathema of *Pastor Æternus*), is their violation of the *principle of the excluded middle*: because they are all founded on the logically incoherent notion of a supposed juridical act which does not conform to the definition of a juridical act. This is also the error of Suárez, who explained that the Church would depose the pope but *not acting as a superior*, but the deposition would be accomplished by a *declaratory sentence pronounced upon him by the legitimate jurisdiction of the Church*: 1)"Therefore when the Church would depose a Pope, she would not do it as a superior, but by the consent of Christ the Lord she would juridically declare him to be a heretic, and thus unworthy of the pontifical dignity; and then ipso facto he would be immediately deposed by Christ, and being deposed he would remain inferior, and could be punished."[228] 2) "Thirdly I say, if the Pope is heretical and incorrigible, as soon as a declaratory sentence is pronounced by the legitimate jurisdiction of the Church, he ceases to be Pope."[229] In addition to Suárez's self-contradictory notion of a *juridical deposition pronounced by the* **legitimate jurisdiction** *of the Church but* **not acting as a superior**, there is also his self-contradictory notion of an ***immediate ipso facto deposition by Christ which would take place*** **mediately** *by the dispositive agency of a juridical declaration by the Church*. Now it pertains to the nature of an *ipso facto* action that it is not effected **mediately**, because what takes place *mediately* takes place by the instrumentality

---

[227] Bordoni, *Sacrum Tribunal Iudicum*, p. 154.

[228] R. P. Francisci Suarez, *Opera Omnia*, Paris 1863 (Vivés), *Tomus Doudecimus, Tractatus Primus, De Fide Theologica. Disputatio X. De Summo Pontifice, Sect. VI*. p. 318: «quando ergo Ecclesia Papam hæreticum deponeret, non ipsa tanquam superior id præstaret, sed ex consensione Christi Domini juridice declararet eum hæreticum esse, atque adeo prorsus indignum Pontificis dignitate; tuncque ipso facto immediate a Christo deponeretur, depositusque maneret inferior, ac posset puniri.»

[229] *Ibid.*p. 317 — «Dico tertio: si Papa sit hæreticus et incorrigibilis, cum primum per legitimam Ecclesiæ jurisdictionem sententia declaratoria criminis in eum profertur, desinit esse Papa.»

of another; whereas the very words *"ipso facto"* mean "by the fact itself", which logically excludes the mediation of any external agent, whether by direct causation or merely *indirectly* as a **dispositive** or **instrumental cause**. It is for this reason that Bellarmine, understanding perfectly the nature of an *ipso facto* action explained that the heretic's *ipso facto* deposition would take place **"by itself"** (*"per se"*), **"*sine alia vi externa*"**, and therefore, **without another deposition**, "*sine alia depositione*".[230] Therefore also, Salza's theory that the Church can judge the pope by *establishing the crime,* and Siscoe's errant notion that the pope can be judged and deposed by *indirect judgment,* are plainly **heretical** insofar as they posit the agency of dispositive and instrumental causes of a council acting with jurisdiction over the conjunction to cause the *separation of the Church from her head against his will, and therefore against the absolute power of his jurisdiction over the conjunction between himself and the papacy.* Both of these theories oppose the dogma of the primacy according to which the pope possesses a full and absolute jurisdiction over the whole Church, and therefore also over the conjunction.

DETAILED CRITIQUE OF THE CAJETAN-JOHN OF ST. THOMAS THEORY

It is precisely because Cajetan and John of St. Thomas in their deposition theories ascribe to a council a jurisdiction which pertains exclusively to the *full and supreme jurisdiction* of the Roman Pontiff, that the doctrine of John of St Thomas collapses upon itself and deviates into error (indisputable heresy as of 1870); and in so doing, he follows the heretical path marked out by Cardinal Cajetan:

> 1. «[XX] Cajetan said a manifest heretic pope is not deposed ipso facto, and that ***the pope is deposed truly by the Church and by authority*** [...] that the Church is not above the pope absolutely even in the case of heresy, whereas ***it is above the conjunction of the pontificate with that person by dissolving it, in that manner by which it united it at the***

---

[230] *De Romano Pontifice, lib. ii. cap. xxx.*

election, which power is **ministerial**, because, only Christ the Lord is *simpliciter* the superior of the pope.»[231]

Sed contra — The Church has no authority whatsoever to depose a pope, because it possesses jurisdiction neither over the pope, nor over the conjunction; and to say that it does, whether immediately or mediately, *directly opposes the totality of the jurisdictional power of the Primacy* defined in *Pastor Æternus*. Furthermore, while John of St. Thomas is correct insofar as he says *Suárez* maintained that if "a pope is a manifest heretic & declared incorrigible, he is deposed immediately by Christ the Lord, and not by any authority in the Church," he erred by attributing this opinion to Bellarmine, since **that is not what Bellarmine taught**. Bellarmine says nothing anywhere about any need for the pope to be declared incorrigible for him to fall from office; but rather, he says that once the pope manifests himself to be pertinacious, he immediately falls from office entirely by himself *ipso facto*; and not mediately by the dispositive agency of anyone else's declaration, but "*by himself*", and "without another external agent" (*sine alia vi externa*). John of St. Thomas was guilty of sloppy scholarship in his treatment of Bellarmine here, as he was in another passage earlier in the same paragraph where he said, "The other way of speaking is followed by Cajetan and explained at length by him; and he is quoted and attacked by Bellarmine in Book II, De Romano Pontifice, cap. XX, especially on two points, namely when Cajetan says that that a manifest heretic pope is not deposed ipso facto, and that the pope is deposed truly by the authority of the Church". It was not in *cap. xx* but in *cap. xxx* where Bellarmine refuted Cajetan's deposition theory.

2. «XXI. Therefore Cajetan's sentence is contained in three dicta. The first is that a heretic pope precisely by the fact itself of heresy is not

---

[231] *Cursus Theologicus II-II De Auctoritate Summi Pontificis, Disp. II, Art. III, De Depositione Papae*, XXI p. 260 — «Cajetanus dixerit papam hæreticum manifestum non esse ipso facto depositum, et papa ab Ecclesia deponitur vere, et ex auctoritate [...] sed quod Ecclesia non est supra papam absolute etiam in casu hæresis, sed quod est supra conjunctionem cum ista persona dissolvendo illam, eo modo quo illam per electionem conjunxit, quæ potestas Ecclesiæ ministerialis est, nam simpliciter superior solum est Christus Dominus respectu papæ.»

deprived of the pontificate, nor is he deposed: the second is, the Church has no power, nor superiority, even in the case of heresy over the pope, from the part of the power of the pope, as if there would be a power over the power in such a case, but in no way is the power of the Church above the power of the pope, and consequently neither over the pope absolutely: the third dictum is, *the power of the Church has for an object the application of the power of the pope to the person, designating him by election, and the separation of the power from the person, by declaring him a heretic, and to be avoided by the faithful*. Accordingly granted that the declaration is as an antecedent disposition, and being ministerial in relation to the deposition itself, but dispositively and ministerially even reaching the form, to the extent of controlling the disposition it reaches mediately in the form...»[232]

Sed contra — Again, the heresy in this text is clearly apparent in that the author attributes to the Church a **POWER** *having for an object* **THE APPLICATION OF THE POWER OF THE POPE, 1)** *designating him by election*, **2)** *the* **SEPARATION OF THE POWER FROM THE PERSON.** The Church designates the man by election, but **the application of the power of the pope to the person** is accomplished immediately, directly, and exclusively by God alone. This is absolutely clear from the fact that the power is received from God **not by means of the election, but by means of the** *act* **of consent** of the one who is elected pope: «*Hoc consensu praestito ... illico electus est verus Papa, atque **actu plenam absolutamque***

---

[232] *Ibid.* — «XXI. Igitur Cajetani sententis tribus dictis continetur. Primum est papa hæeticus per ipsum factum hæresis præcise non privatur pontificatu, nec deponitur: secundum est, Ecclesia nullam potestatem, nec superioritatem, etiam in casu hæresis habet supra papam ex parte potestatis papæ, quasi sit potestas supra potestatem etiam in tali casu, sed nullo pacto potestas Ecclesiæ est supra potestatem papæ, et consequenter neque supra papam absolute: tertium dictum est, potestas Ecclesiæ habet pro objecto applicationem potestatis papæ ad personam, designando illam per electionem, et separationem hujus potestatis a persona, declarando illum pro hæretico, etevitandi a fidelubus. Itaque licet declaratio criminis sit quasi dispositio antecedrns, et ministerialiter se habens ad depositionem ipsam, tamen dispositive, et ministerialiter attingit etiam formam, quatenus tenendo in dispositionem tendit mediate in formam.»

iurisdictionem supra totum orbem acquirit et exercere potest».[233] In the same manner as with the **applying of the power of the pope to the person**, which is accomplished directly and immediately by God, accordingly, the **SEPARATION OF THE POWER FROM THE PERSON** of the heretic would be accomplished directly and immediately by God, who alone *is above the conjunction of the pontificate with that person. God, who alone is above the conjunction, would dissolve it immediately upon the pope's consent to manifest heresy, in that same manner by which He conjoined the man and the papacy upon his election immediately* **BY MEANS OF THE ACT OF CONSENT GIVEN BY THE POPE-ELECT.** For so long as he is alive, the pope possesses the **full and absolute ecclesiastical power or jurisdiction**, so the bishops gathered in a council possess **no power to separate the power of the primacy from the pope by declaring him a heretic, and to be avoided by the faithful.** Thus, **the ecclesiastical power over the conjunction exists in the pope alone for so long as he is validly constituted in the papal office.** While John of St Thomas admits, "the Church has no power, nor superiority, even in the case of heresy over the pope, from the part of the power of the pope, as if there would be a power over the power in such a case, but in no way is the power of the Church above the power of the pope, and consequently neither over the pope absolutely," but by asserting that the power of the council to appropriate to itself the power to judge with supreme authority and finality against the pope in a matter of faith, thereby denying the pontiff's right inherent in his primacy to act as the supreme judge with the authority to determine all matter of faith with finality, is to assert "a power over the power in such a case," which would constitute a "power of the Church above the power of the pope," which would be a power "over the pope absolutely".

Therefore the pope could only lose his absolute jurisdiction in the same manner he received it directly from God — i.e., by his own action either by death or renunciation, since it is only by these acts that the necessary disposition to conserve the form of the pontificate is lost. For this reason, the papal office is lost by the pope alone

---

[233] Constitutio Apostolica «*Vacantis Apostolicæ Sedis*» Pius XII, 8 December 1945.

without the action of any external agent. John of St. Thomas himself, following Cajetan and Suárez, admits that in the case of permanent insanity a deposition is not necessary, but the see would be vacated just as if the pope had died, and the cardinals could then proceed to the election of a new pope just as if the see had been vacated by renunciation. (IX. p. 254) As with TACIT RENUNCIATION which takes place when an officeholder defects from the faith into public heresy, and is in the nature of an **abdication**, as Ballerini and Bellarmine explained in the cited passages, the papal office would be lost by a public act of formal heresy as soon as the pertinacity is manifested. As is the case with death and explicitly expressed abdication, likewise also in both cases in which the renunciation is not explicitly expressed, whether it be a case of permanent insanity or public defection from the faith, the **necessary disposition to conserve the form of the pontificate would be lost**, so that by the act of manifest heresy, the pope would "cease by himself to be pope",[234] as Bellarmine phrases it, *"sine alia vi externa"*. So just as a pope who becomes mentally incapacitated by irreparable brain damage would lose office by that fact, and not by the judgment of the cardinals, or the bishops in a council; so likewise, a pope who would defect publicly into heresy would cease by himself to be pope, because heresy destroys the necessary disposition by which the form of the pontificate can be conserved in the pope.

There are two reason why the form of the pontificate cannot remain in the pope without the necessary disposition, which is faith:

1) Because the form of the Church consists in the external profession of faith,[235] without which, one is not even united to the Church by the bond of faith, and therefore is incapable of representing the unity of faith, as Gregory XVI observed: «Now it is clear that if there were not in the Church and in the Pope the sameness of spirit, of feelings and of doctrines, there could not be in

---

[234] *De Romano Pontifice, lib. ii cap. xxx* — «per se desinere esse papam.»

[235] *De Ecclesia Militante cap. x* — «Formam Ecclesiae non esse fidem internam (nisi Ecclesiam invisibilem habere velimus) sed externam, idest, fidei confessionem. Id quod apertissime docet s. Augustinus lib. 19. contra Faustum, cap. 11. et experientia idem testatur; illi enim admittuntur ad Ecclesiam, qui profitentur fidem.»

the latter the true representation of the former. Therefore the Pontiff cannot represent the Church, who together does not necessarily represent its unity».[236] This was clearly explained by Bellarmine in his refutation of Cajetan's deposition theory in *De Romano Pontifice lib. ii. cap. xxx*, where he explained that faith is the necessary disposition to conserve the form of the pontificate in the person.[237] The reason why this is so is that "*a manifest heretic is in no manner a member of the Church, i.e., neither in mind, nor in body, as well as neither by internal union, nor external union.*"[238] A manifest heretic is intrinsically incapable of visibly representing the faith he publicly opposes. In *De Ecclesia Militante cap. iv*. Bellarmine refutes the error of those such as Alphonsus de Castro who taught that even those heretics and apostates who openly professed false doctrine are members and part of the Church,[239] proving from Scripture, from the Council of Nicea, from the Fathers, and finally from the consideration that, "since the Church is an united multitude, (for it is indeed a people, a kingdom, and one body) and this union consists principally in the profession of the one faith and the observance of the same laws and rites; no reason permits us to say that they are of the body of the Church, who have no conjunction

---

[236] Gregory XVI, *Il trionfo della santa sede*, Capo XXIII, p. 270 — «Or egli è chiaro che, qualora non vi fosse e nella Chiesa e nel Papa medesimità di spirito, di sentimenti e di dottrine, non vi potrebbe neppur essere in questo la vera rappresentanza di quello. Dunque il Pontefice non può rappresentare la Chiesa, che insieme non ne rappresenti necessariamente l'unità».

[237] *De Romano Pontifice lib. ii. cap. xxx* — «ista dispositione sublata per contrariam quæ est hæresis, mox papa desinit esse; neque enim potest forma conservari sine necessariis dispositionibus.»

[238] *Ibid*. — «haereticus manifestus, nullo modo est membrum Ecclesiae, id est, neque animo, neque corpore, sive neque unione interna, neque externa.»

[239] *De Ecclesia Militante cap. iv* — «Haereticos et apostatas baptizatos, Alphonsus de Castro lib. 2. de justa haereticorum punitione cap. 24. docet esse membra et partes Ecclesiae, etiam si palam falsam doctrinam profiteantur.»

at all with it."[240] Citing the authority of St. Paul to Titus,[241] even those who remain incorrigible and do not leave of their own volition are outside the Church, for which reason even a pope who would remain obstinate in heresy after correction would cease by himself to be pope and deposed *ipso facto*.[242] In *cap x* he treats on the question of occult heretics and infidels thoroughly, and examines several objections, and among them the objection that, "Often it happens, or certainly it can happen, that manifest heretics will simulate themselves as Catholics, also Jews, Turks, Pagans mix in with the faithful, and nevertheless they will not be of the Church, or else we will say the Church is the assembly of heretics, pagans, and hypocrites."[243] He then, before

---

[240] *Ibid.* — «Accedit postremo, quod cum Ecclesia sit multitudo unita et ista unio praecipue in professione unius fidei, et earndem legum ac rituum observatione consistat; nulla ratio permittit, ut eos de Ecclesiae corpore esse dicamus, qui cum eo nullam omnino conjunctionem habent.»

[241] *De Rom. Pont. lib. ii. cap. xxx* — «Praeterea ad Tit. 3. *Haereticum Hominem post unam et alteram correptionem devita, sciens quia subversus est, qui ejusmodi est, et delinquit, cum sit proprio judicio condemnatus.*»

[242] *De Romano Pontifice lib. ii. cap. xxx* — «Quarta opinio est Cajetani in tract. De auctor papae et conc. cap. 20. et 21. ubi docet, papam haereticum manifestum non esse ipso facto depositum sed posse, ac debere deponi ab Ecclesia: quae sententia meo judicio defendi non potest. Nam inprimis, quod haereticus manifestus ipso facto sit depositus, probatur auctoritate et ratione. Nam inprimis, quod haereticus manifestus ipso facto sit depositus, probatur auctoritate et ratione. Auctoritas est b. Pauli, qui in epist. ad Titum 3. jubet, postquam manifeste apparet pertinax, vitari, et intelligit ante omnem excommunicationem, et sententiam judicis: ut ibidem scribit Hieronymus, ubi dicit, alios peccatores per sententiam excommunicationis excludi ab Ecclesia; haereticos autem per se discedere et praecidi a corpore Christi: at non potest vitari papa manens papa; quomodo enim vitabimus capus nostrum? Quomodo recedemus a membro nobis conjuncto? Ratio vero et quidem certissima haec est. Non Christianus non potest ullo modo esse papa, et Cajetanus fatetur in eod. lib. cap. 26. et ratio est, quia non potest esse caput id quod non est membrum; et non est membrum Ecclesiae is qui non est Christianus: at haereticus manifestus non est Christianus, ut aperte docet Cyprianus lib. 4. epist. 2 Athanasius ser. 2. cont. Arian. Augustinus lib. De grat. Christ. cap. 20. Hieronymus cont. Lucifer. et alii; haereticus igitur manifestus papa esse non potest.»

[243] *De Ecclesia Militante cap. x* — «saepe accidit, aut certe accidere potest, ut haeretici manifesti alicubi simulent se catholicos, item Judaei, Turcae,

stating his own position, gives the answer of John Driedo (who believed not only the baptized, but all those who are believed to be baptized, are in the Church): "In the first place it is difficult for such as these to remain all the time undetected, but even if they would delude the Church for a long time; nothing troublesome would be able to result from that: for the Church does not number them among hers, but for the reason of the external profession (nor are men judged for internal things) that external profession is most holy, albeit they make evil use of it. Accordingly they are of the body of the Church while they are joined to the faithful by that bond of profession and obedience, which binds the universal Church, and reduces it into one body."[244] Bellarmine then explains against the opinion of John Driedo: "For according to the other opinion, which a little before we said was more true, it is to be responded, Jews, Turks, Pagans, and also manifest heretics, who simulate themselves to be Christians and Catholics, are not of the Church, except according to external appearance and supposedly, not truly."[245]

Only secret heretics would still belong to the body of the Church, but as putrid members, like a noxious body fluid, but for so long as the bond of faith is preserved by external profession, they remain members of the Church until the bond of profession is broken by openly asserting heresy in such a manner that exhibits a clear *indicium* of formal heresy, thereby severing themselves from the body and

---

Pagani miscent se fidelibus, et tamen aut ipsi de Ecclesia non erunt, aut Ecclesiam esse dicimus coetum haereticorum et paganorum hypocritarum.»

[244] *Ibid.* — «Ad quartum dico, in primis difficile esse, ut ejusmodi homines non continuo detegantur, sed tamen etiamsi longo tempore deludant Ecclesiam; nihil inde incommodi accidere posse: nam Ecclesia non eos numerat inter suos, nisi ratione professionis externae (nec enim de internis homines judicant) professio autem illa externa sanctissima est, licet ab illis male usurpetur, Itaque sunt illi de Ecclesiae corpore, dum fidelibus junguntur eo vinculo professionis et obedientiae, quod Ecclesiam universam ligat, et in unum corpus redigit.»

[245] *Ibid.* — «Nam secundum alteram sententiam, quam nos paulo ante veriorem esse diximus, respondendum erit, Judaeos, Turcas, Paganos, nec non manifestos Haereticos, qui simulant se esse Christianos et Catholicos non esse de Ecclesia, nisi secundum apparentiam exteriorem et putative, non vere.»

thereby ceasing to be members of the Church, but until that happens, *"occult heretics are united and are members only by external union"*.[246] Only secret heretics would remain in the Church. In this manner secret heretics would still be members of the Church, but manifest heretics masquerading as faithful Catholics would not, and this would certainly be true of unbaptized infidels in general, and even of manifest heretics posing as Catholics in places where it is not known that they are heretics, since as manifest heretics they are not members of the Church, and even in those situations where they feign themselves Catholics, they cannot be simultaneously both members and non-members. For the unbaptized who are not feigning, but mistakenly believe themselves to be baptized, the question is more complicated, and regarding this category of unbaptized, Bellarmine seems more to agree with Driedo:

> For this that someone be of the body of the Church, the character is not required, but external baptism; nor is external baptism required for one to be so assessed and be of the Church, but only to be admitted. If someone asks to be admitted into the Church, it is not done without baptism. However if someone says he is baptized and the contrary is not known, he will be admitted to the other sacraments, and by this he will be of the body of the Church. And the indication of this, is that if afterward it should be known that he was not baptized, if this happened by his own fault, he will be expelled from the congregation, nor will he be received unless he be baptized after doing penance. But if it is not his fault, he will not be driven away, but what was lacking will be completed in him, nor will he be judged to have not been in the Church, but will be judged to have entered from elsewhere than from the ordinary door. Whence Innocent III. Cap. *Apostolicam,* on the unbaptized priest, judged the unbaptized priest to have truly been in the Church, and ordered the sacrifice to be offered for his soul, as is done for the other faithful departed. And Dionysius of Alexandria,[247] as is stated in book 7 ch. 8 of

---

[246] *Ibid.* — «hæretici occulti sunt uniti & sunt membra, solum externa unione.»

[247] St. Dionysius the Great of Alexandria, fourteenth Pope and Patriarch of Alexandria from 8 December 248 until his death on 22 March, 264. *Wikipedia* notes he was, "Called "the Great" by Eusebius, Basil of Caesarea and others, he was characterized by the Catholic Encyclopedia as

Hist. Eccles.²⁴⁸ judged a certain individual to have been truly in the Church, who was discovered to not have been baptized, but only had received the other sacraments in the manner of the baptized.²⁴⁹

Thus, (he explains) the form of the Church is the external faith, i.e., the confession of faith, as St. Augustine most explicitly taught, and experience itself attests, they are admitted to the Church who profess the faith.²⁵⁰

2) Because it pertains to the nature of the pontificate that it is ordered to specific operations, and if those operations are rendered impossible, the form cannot be preserved in the person of the pope. St. Thomas explains, *"The mode of action follows the disposition of the agent, for each thing such as it is, such are its acts. And therefore, since virtue is the principle of some kind of operation, it must be that in the operator some conformed disposition pre-exist according to the virtue. Now virtue causes an ordered operation. And therefore virtue itself is an ordered disposition of the soul, namely*

"undoubtedly, after St. Cyprian, the most eminent bishop of the third century."'"

²⁴⁸ *Historia Ecclesiastica* of Eusebius of Caesarea.

²⁴⁹ *De Ecclesia Militante* cap. x — «Ad hoc, ut aliquis sit de corpore Ecclesiae, non requiri characterem, sed externum baptismum; nec externum baptismum requiri, ut quis censeatur et sit de Ecclesia, sed tantum ut admittatur. Si quis enim petit admitti ad Ecclesiam, id non fiet sine baptismo. Tamen si quis dicat se baptizatum, et non constet contrariuim, admittetur ad sacramenta caetera, et per hoc erit de corpore Ecclesiae. Et signum hujus est, quia si postea innotescat, illum non fuisse baptizatum, si quidem culpa ipsius id sit factum, expelletur de congregatione, nec recipietur, nisi post poenitentiam baptizetur. Unde Innocentius III. cap. *Apostolicam*, de presbytero non baptizato, judicavit, presbyterum non baptizatum vere fuisse in Ecclesia, et jussit pro ejus anima offerri sacrificium, ut pro aliis fidelibus. Et Dionysius alexandrinus, ut habemus lib. 7. cap. 8. Hist. Eccles. judicavit quemdam fuisse vere in Ecclesia, quem constabat non vere baptizatum, sed tantum percepisse alia sacramenta, ut baptizatum.»

²⁵⁰ *Ibid.* — «Formam Ecclesiae non esse fidem internam (nisi Ecclesiam invisibilem habere velimus) sed externam, idest, fidei confessionem. Id quod apertissime docet s. Augustinus lib. 19. contra Faustum, cap. 11. et experientia idem testatur; illi enim admittuntur ad Ecclesiam, qui profitentur fidem.»

insofar as that the powers of the soul are ordered in some way to one another, and to that which is outside."²⁵¹ The heretic lacking the virtue of faith, believes and professes one or more, but not all truths of faith by some other power than the virtue of faith, and therefore professes them by a mere natural power. The power of human reason is in its nature fallible and intrinsically subject to error. That which is professed by faith is professed infallibly *(IIᵃ IIᵃᵉ q. 1 a. 3)*, although without the fullness of the power of faith, one can err in reasoning with respect to the material object of faith, thinking something to be of faith when it is not. By means of the exercise of the charism of infallibility, by which is exercised the fullness of power of the virtue of faith, the pope by the exercise of this fullness of power is not subject to error in matters of faith. Hence, he cannot err in matters of faith as one can err in the exercise of the natural intellective power of the soul, mistakenly professing an error to be a dogma of faith; for which reason the pontiff, when exercising the charism of infallibility is not subject to any error in matters of faith. Therefore, while the external profession of faith alone is the necessary external disposition to visibly preserve the form of the pontificate in the person of the pope; the virtue of faith is necessary internally as a conforming disposition of soul by which a man is rendered capable of receiving the form of the pontificate which is the principle of operation for the infallible exercising of the function of the primacy, which, as Ballerini says, is the "proper power to bind together and guard Catholic unity"²⁵² — and thus, to secure and preserve the unity of faith by teaching infallibly in matters of faith and binding the whole Church to that teaching. A heretic, even if he is only a heretic internally, is capable only of fallibly teaching his opinions on matters of faith, but incapable of exercising the *munus* of teaching infallibly; because he lacks the necessary disposition of soul by which the pope is disposed and

---

²⁵¹ *Summa Theologiæ,* Iᵃ IIᵃᵉ q. 55. a. 2 ad 1 — «modus actionis sequitur dispositionem agentis, unumquodque enim quale est, talia operatur. Et ideo, cum virtus sit principium aliqualis operationis, oportet quod in operante præexistat secundum virtutem aliqua conformis dispositio. Facit autem virtus operationem ordinatam. Et ideo ipsa virtrus est quædam dispoitio ordinata in anima, secundum scilicet quod potentiæ animæ ordinantur aliqualiter ad invicem, et ad id quod est extra.»

²⁵² *De vi ac ratione primatus,* CAPUT IX. p. 41.

thereby rendered capable of actively exercising the *munus* of teaching infallibly. The heretic's natural capacities only furnish him with the capability to teach his own opinions in matters of faith, but his perverse habitual disposition of will against the teaching authority of the Church which he rejects, is a permanent contrary disposition which prevents him from intending to teach infallibly what the Church has received on the divine authority he rejects. A heretic pope would therefore be incapable of saying like the Apostle, *Ego enim accepi a Domino quod et tradidi vobis* (1 Cor. 11:23), because he cannot hand on that divine revelation which he refused to receive by rejecting the divine authority of the revealing God. Since sacramental power is exercised *ex opere operato*, the intention alone suffices even for an atheist to effect a valid sacrament; but the charism of infallibility does not operate like a sacrament; but in addition to the intention to teach the faith infallibly, it requires the power of the theological virtue of faith to unite the mind to the divine mysteries of faith as a necessary disposition in order to enable the pope to teach those divine mysteries with the fullness of the power of that virtue.

Unlike the charismatic graces which are transitory in nature, the *munus* of infallibility is not a fleeting grace which exists only in a passing manner such as the grace of prophecy, which is given only at those times when God wills, and cannot be summoned at will by the prophet.[253] Unlike prophecy, which transmits a revelation received by the prophet, the power of infallibility does not involve the receiving of any revelation, but of transmitting faithfully that which is believed on divine authority. Infallibility is a permanently abiding, and therefore *habitual* supernatural power existing in the soul as a power which the pope can exercise freely whenever he wills. Hence, the power of infallibility is a *habitus*, since "a *habitus* is that by which one acts when one wills" (*II^a II^æ q. 171 a. 2*).[254] Bernhard Blankenhorn O.P.

---

[253] *Summa Theologiæ*, II^a II^æ q. 171 a. 2 — «habitus est quo quis agit cum voluerit, ut dicit Commentator, in III de anima. Sed aliquis non potest uti prophetia cum voluerit, sicut patet IV Reg. III, de Eliseo, *quem cum Iosaphat de futuris requireret, et prophetiae spiritus ei deesset, psaltem fecit applicari, ut prophetiae ad hunc spiritus per laudem psalmodiae descenderet, atque eius animum de venturis repleret*, ut Gregorius dicit, super Ezech. Ergo prophetia non est habitus.»

[254] *Summa Theologiæ*, II^a II^æ q. 171 a. 2 — «habitus est quo quis agit cum voluerit.»

explains the difference between the two in the thinking of St. Thomas:

> Natural permanent forms like the agent intellect are an operational capacity or power of the soul whose actualization lies at the disposal of the human subject's free decision. Through the agent intellect, we abstract the intelligible species of whatever material being we decide to ponder through our senses. Thomas rightly argues that if the gift of prophecy were to involve an abiding active form (or an active *habitus*), then prophetic knowledge would lie at the disposal of the prophet's will. But Scripture shows that the actualization of prophecy is occasional, meaning, the act comes and goes. The biblical motive behind Thomas's choice of metaphysics for the gift of prophecy is evident. As Aquinas notes, various biblical texts make it clear that the prophets' extraordinary knowledge of God and his saving plan depends solely on the gracious divine will. Indeed, the saints continue to uphold the same biblical teaching. Aquinas's metaphysics partly proceeds from his firm adherence to the insistence of Scripture and Tradition that prophetic insight is only granted when and where the Holy Spirit wills it.
>
> Thomas explicitly limits himself to a discussion of two metaphysics, of which he rejects one. This becomes clear in the second half of the same article's *corpus*: "It follows therefore that the prophetic light is in the prophet's soul by way of a passion or transitory impression… But a *habitus* is an abiding form. Wherefore it is evident that, properly speaking, prophecy is not a *habitus*." Given the option between an active form and a "passion" or an actualization that is simply received from the outside, Aquinas understandably concludes that prophecy is a passing gift. Prophetic light is only present now and then, when the Spirit chooses to illumine the prophet. If the only alternative to an intrinsic, *active* form (i.e., an active *habitus*) is a momentary act triggered by God's gracious will and passively received by the beneficiary, then the choice seems obvious.
>
> Aquinas then quietly extends the metaphysics of prophecy to the other charisms. In question 171, article 2, he reflects on the metaphysical status of the prophetic gift, using biblical, patristic, philosophical and theological arguments. Later in questions 176-178, he quietly applies the conclusions about prophecy's metaphysical status to the other charisms.[255]

---

[255] *The Metaphysics of Charisms,* Bernhard Blankenhorn O.P., ANGELICUM, VOLUMEN 91, ANNUM 2014, FASCICULUS 3,

The charismatic graces, strictly speaking, do not require a conforming disposition to enable a person to exercise them, but they exercise them according to the transitory power that God confers on them to perform the operation. In *Traces of Otherness in St. Thomas Aquinas' Theology of Grace*,[256] Michael Luis Fagge explains:

> In the commentary on the first letter to the Corinthians we see the charismatic graces spoken of more thoroughly. [than in the commentary on Romans] In chapter 12 St. of the letter, St. Paul delineates the charismatic graces and St. Thomas will discuss them as he had in the *ST* only from a purely scriptural basis. In the twelfth lecture pertaining to I Cor. 12, 1-6, St. Thomas sees that the Apostle is trying to explain the gifts of the spirit or the charismatic gifts. [*C1Cor.* Cap. 12, lect. I, 710.] In this section he speaks of the gifts being given to those who do not possess God, those not in sanctifying grace, such as Balaam's ass or Caiphas... The charismatic graces are spoken of as giving strength to the Church but also being done by someone who may not be within the Church, a "sinner in whom the Holy Spirit does not dwell." [Cf. *C1Cor.* Cap. 12, lect 2, 725.]... The graces are not of wisdom or knowledge but the utterance of wisdom or knowledge. The utterances only benefit others since they are meant to be voiced for outside hearers. St. Paul also mentions faith as just the utterance of things of the faith.
>
> [T]he... The Apostle places in the charismatic graces not wisdom and knowledge, but the utterances of wisdom and knowledge, which pertains to the ability to persuade other by speech about matters pertaining to wisdom and knowledge.
>
> Now, the principle of the doctrine of salvation are the articles of faith, and in regard to this he adds: to another is given faith by the same Spirit. It is not taken there for the virtue of faith, because this is common to all members of Christ, according to Heb (11:6): "Without faith it is impossible to please God." But it is taken for the utterance of faith in the sense that a man is able rightly to propose manners of faith, or for the certainty of faith someone has in an excellent way.[257]

PONTIFICIA STUDIORUM UNIVERSITAS A SANCTO THOMA AQUINATE IN URBE, pp. 394-395.

[256] Michael Luis Fagge, *Traces of Otherness in St. Thomas Aquinas' Theology of Grace*, 2011, pp. 195-197.

[257] *Super I Cor.* Cap. 12 l. 2 — «Est tamen notandum quod sapientia et scientia inter septem dona spiritus sancti computantur, sicut habetur Is. XI, 2. Unde apostolus signanter inter gratias gratis datas non ponit sapientiam

The charism of infallibility is a habitual power proper to the person of the pope in virtue of his office, which he can operate at will. There is nothing externally extraordinary about its exercise that would perceptibly signify the supernatural character of its exercise. The pope merely needs to conform to the conditions necessary for the exercise of that power, making it clear that he is teaching infallibly. It is therefore not of the same nature as the charismatic gifts, such as prophecy and the other charismatic gifts, but it has in common with them only one characteristic, which is that it is not exercised for the spiritual benefit of the pontiff himself, but for others — for confirming the faith of the whole Church. On the other hand, that charismatic gift of faith which the Apostle mentions, is an *extraordinary* utterance of the matters of faith, which is a "freely given grace" (gratia gratis data) whose extraordinary charismatic character can be recognized as such, and can be exercised even by those without faith (such as when a pagan soothsayer confirms the truth of a Catholic's faith which is known to the soothsayer only by means of a special revelation). It is therefore of a distinctly different nature than the charism of infallibility, which, although not of the same nature as the gifts of the Holy Ghost, is of a nature that is more closely related to them insofar as both are of the nature of a habit. In *I^a II^{ae} q. 68 a. 1*, St. Thomas distinguishes between the gifts and the virtues: «Accordingly, in order to differentiate the gifts from the virtues, we must be guided by the way in which Scripture expresses itself, for we find there that the term employed is "spirit" rather than "gift." For thus it is written (Isaiah 11:2-3): "The spirit... of wisdom and of understanding... shall rest upon him," etc.: from which words we are clearly given to understand that these seven are there set down as being in us by Divine inspiration. Now inspiration denotes motion

---

et scientiam, sed sermonem sapientiae et scientiae, quae pertinent ad hoc ut homo aliis persuadere valeat per sermonem, ea quae sunt sapientiae et scientiae. Principia autem doctrinae salutis sunt articuli fidei et ideo quantum ad hoc subditur *alteri*, scilicet datur, *fides in eodem spiritu*. Non autem hic accipitur pro fidei virtute, quia hoc commune est omnibus membris Christi, secundum illud Hebr. XI, 6: *sine fide impossibile est placere Deo*. Sed accipitur pro sermone fidei, prout scilicet homo potest recte proponere ea quae fidei sunt, vel pro certitudine fidei quam aliquis habet excellenter, secundum illud Matth. XV, 28: *mulier, magna est fides tua.*»

from without.»[258] And then he applies this specifically in relation to teaching: «Now it is evident that whatever is moved must be proportionate to its mover: and the perfection of the mobile insofar as it is mobile, consists in a disposition whereby it is disposed to be well moved by its mover. Hence the more exalted the mover, the more perfect must be the disposition whereby the mobile is made proportionate to it; thus we see that a disciple needs a more perfect disposition in order to receive a higher teaching from his master. Now it is manifest that human virtues perfect man according as it is natural for him to be moved by his reason in his interior and exterior actions. Consequently man needs yet higher perfections, whereby to be disposed to be moved by God.»[259] Thus he explains that the gifts, which are habits, are more excellent than the virtues, but in *I^a II^{ae} q. 68 a. 4 ad 3* he explains that the theological virtues are more excellent than the gifts: «The mind of man is not moved by the Holy Ghost, unless in some way it be united to Him: even as the instrument is not moved by the craftsman, unless by contact or some other kind of union between them. Now the primal union of man with God is by faith, hope and charity: and, consequently, these virtues are

---

[258] *ST* I^aII^{ae} q. 68 a. 1 — «Et ideo ad distinguendum dona a virtutibus, debemus sequi modum loquendi Scripturae, in qua nobis traduntur non quidem sub nomine donorum, sed magis sub nomine spirituum, sic enim dicitur Isaiae XI, *requiescet super eum spiritus sapientiae et intellectus,* et cetera. Ex quibus verbis manifeste datur intelligi quod ista septem enumerantur ibi, secundum quod sunt in nobis ab inspiratione divina. Inspiratio autem significat quandam motionem ab exteriori.»

[259] *Ibid.* — «Manifestum est autem quod omne quod movetur, necesse est proportionatum esse motori, et haec est perfectio mobilis inquantum est mobile, dispositio qua disponitur ad hoc quod bene moveatur a suo motore. Quanto igitur movens est altior, tanto necesse est quod mobile perfectiori dispositione ei proportionetur, sicut videmus quod perfectius oportet esse discipulum dispositum, ad hoc quod altiorem doctrinam capiat a docente. Manifestum est autem quod virtutes humanae perficiunt hominem secundum quod homo natus est moveri per rationem in his quae interius vel exterius agit. Oportet igitur inesse homini altiores perfectiones, secundum quas sit dispositus ad hoc quod divinitus moveatur.»

presupposed to the gifts, as being their roots. Therefore all the gifts correspond to these three virtues, as being derived therefrom.»[260]

The Theological virtues are as the nature which is presupposed for the operation of the gifts. In *I^a II^{ae} q. 110 a. 3* St. Thomas explains, «infused virtues dispose man in a higher manner and towards a higher end, and consequently in relation to some higher nature, i.e. in relation to a participation of the Divine Nature... And thus, even as the natural light of reason is something besides the acquired virtues, which are ordained to this natural light, so also the light of grace which is a participation of the Divine Nature is something besides the infused virtues which are derived from and are ordained to this light, hence the Apostle says (Ephesians 5:8): "For you were heretofore darkness, but now light in the Lord. Walk then as children of the light." For as the acquired virtues enable a man to walk, in accordance with the natural light of reason, so do the infused virtues enable a man to walk as befits the light of grace.»[261]

In *I^a II^{ae} q. 49 a. 3* St. Thomas says, «Augustine says (De Bono Conjug. xxi) that "habit is that whereby something is done when

---

[260] *ST* I^aII^{ae} q. 68 a. 4 ad 3 — «Ad tertium dicendum quod animus hominis non movetur a spiritu sancto, nisi ei secundum aliquem modum uniatur, sicut instrumentum non movetur ab artifice nisi per contactum, aut per aliquam aliam unionem. Prima autem unio hominis est per fidem, spem et caritatem. Unde istae virtutes praesupponuntur ad dona, sicut radices quaedam donorum. Unde omnia dona pertinent ad has tres virtutes, sicut quaedam derivationes praedictarum virtutum.»

[261] *ST* I^a II^{ae} q. 110 a. 3 — «Virtutes autem infusae disponunt hominem altiori modo, et ad altiorem finem, unde etiam oportet quod in ordine ad aliquam altiorem naturam. Hoc autem est in ordine ad naturam divinam participatam [...] Sicut igitur lumen naturale rationis est aliquid praeter virtutes acquisitas, quae dicuntur in ordine ad ipsum lumen naturale; ita etiam ipsum lumen gratiae, quod est participatio divinae naturae, est aliquid praeter virtutes infusas, quae a lumine illo derivantur, et ad illud lumen ordinantur. Unde et apostolus dicit, ad Ephes. V, *eratis aliquando tenebrae, nunc autem lux in domino, ut filii lucis ambulate*. Sicut enim virtutes acquisitae perficiunt hominem ad ambulandum congruenter lumini naturali rationis; ita virtutes infusae perficiunt hominem ad ambulandum congruenter lumini gratiae.»

necessary." And the Commentator says (De Anima iii) that "habit is that whereby we act when we will."»²⁶² Then he explains it saying:

> In regard to the nature of habit, it belongs to every habit to have relation to an act. For it is essential to habit to imply some relation to a thing's nature, in so far as it is suitable or unsuitable thereto... Wherefore habit implies relation not only to the very nature of a thing, **but also, consequently, to operation, inasmuch as this is the end of nature, or conducive to the end**. Whence also it is stated (Metaph. v, text. 25) in the definition of habit, that it is a disposition whereby that which is disposed, is well or ill disposed either in regard to itself, that is to its nature, or in regard to something else, that is to the end... For, as we have said, habit primarily and of itself implies a relation to the thing's nature. If therefore the nature of a thing, in which the habit is, consists in this very relation to an act, it follows that the habit principally implies relation to an act. Now it is clear that the nature and the notion of power is that it should be a principle of act. Wherefore every habit which is as a subject of some power, principally imports order to an act... Habit is an act, in so far as it is a quality: and in this respect it can be a principle of operation. It is, however, in a state of potentiality in respect to operation.²⁶³

---

²⁶² «Augustinus dicit, in libro de bono coniugali, quod *habitus est quo aliquid agitur cum opus est*. Et Commentator dicit, in III de anima, quod *habitus est quo quis agit cum voluerit*.»

²⁶³ *ST* Iª IIæ q. 49 a. 3 — «Secundum quidem rationem habitus, convenit omni habitui aliquo modo habere ordinem ad actum. Est enim de ratione habitus ut importet habitudinem quandam in ordine ad naturam rei, secundum quod convenit vel non convenit. [...] Sed natura rei, quae est finis generationis, ulterius etiam ordinatur ad alium finem, qui vel est operatio, vel aliquod operatum, ad quod quis pervenit per operationem. Unde habitus non solum importat ordinem ad ipsam naturam rei, sed etiam consequenter ad operationem, inquantum est finis naturae, vel perducens ad finem. Unde et in V Metaphys. dicitur in definitione habitus, quod est dispositio secundum quam bene vel male disponitur dispositum aut secundum se, idest secundum suam naturam, aut ad aliud, idest in ordine ad finem. [...] Quia ut dictum est, habitus primo et per se importat habitudinem ad naturam rei. Si igitur natura rei in qua est habitus, consistat in ipso ordine ad actum, sequitur quod habitus principaliter importet ordinem ad actum. Manifestum est autem quod natura et ratio potentiae est ut sit principium actus. Unde omnis habitus qui est alicuius potentiae ut subiecti, principaliter importat ordinem ad actum.»

The habit of infallibility, therefore, is rooted in a power, which is the virtue of faith, so that just as the gifts are rooted in the theological virtues, likewise the habit of infallibility is rooted in the virtue of faith, and is operable in virtue of it. It is for this reason that the Lord rooted the infallibility of the Petrine *munus* in the personal virtue of faith of the one who exercises it; and therefore He prayed that Peter's faith, and in him the faith of his successors not fail, so that rooted in the virtue of faith, the exercise of the power infallibility would be rendered habitual and unfailing in the individual who exercises the Petrine *munus*.

As I explained in Volume One, a man is *metaphysically* an incapable subject of the papacy if he lacks the necessary disposition to receive the form of the pontificate in his person as a habit; and that *necessary disposition* is *the virtue of faith*. The virtue of faith is a necessary disposition because it conforms the matter as potentiality to its act, which is the form; which as the primary constitutive principle of being as *act*, constitutes the *nature* of a particular being as a *principium motus*. Since what first and foremost pertains properly to the nature of the pontificate is the *charism of infallibility*, which is the *power* to define infallibly in matters of faith, which in their substance are the *prima veritas* that remains inaccessible to the natural power of the human intellect; the fullness of the supernatural power of faith, unimpeded by its contrary disposition of infidelity, is required to exercise the power of the charism in order to attain to the *prima veritas*, which is God, the formal object of faith; because the virtue of faith is the necessary internal *dispositive habit* which enables the pope to profess the faith infallibly. The reason for this is that a *merely external and material profession of a faithless pope would not be a dispositive habit in the pope's soul, because it is not a virtue*; and therefore it would not enable a man to define the faith infallibly; because in whichever manner the motion of the human mind would reach God, that motion pertains to virtue: «*motus humanæ mentis qualitercumque Deum attingeret, ad virtutem pertinet.*» (*Quaestiones Disputatae de Virtutibus q. 4 a. 1 ad 6*)[264] The mind is first united to the revealed *prima veritas* by faith, so that its access to the truths of faith is by means of the virtue of faith whose object is God.

---

[264] *Quaestiones Disputatae de Virtutibus Q. 4 a 1 ad 6* — «The motion of the human mind howsoever it would reach God, pertains to virtue.»

Having received the truths of faith by means of the virtue of faith, the pope, by means of the charism of infallibility teaches those truths with the fullness of power of the virtue. Therefore, the *necessary disposition* to conserve the form of the pontificate in the person of the pope, most certainly is the *virtue* of faith acting internally in the soul as a **dispositio animæ**: «*Mode of action follows on the disposition of the agent: for such as a thing is, such is its operation. And therefore, since virtue is the principle of some kind of operation, there must needs pre-exist in the operator in respect of virtue some corresponding disposition. Now virtue causes an ordered operation. Therefore* **virtue itself is an ordered disposition of the soul,** *in so far as, to wit, the powers of the soul are in some way ordered to one another, and to that which is outside.*» ($I^a\ II^a$ q. 55 a. 2 ad 1)[265] While the *visible external aspect* of the form of the pontificate is visible insofar as the external profession of faith is a visible attribute of the external form; faith *simpliciter* as a virtue is the necessary ontological disposition for uniting the form of the pontificate as a qualitative habit to the person who is the matter, because internal faith as a virtue is the necessary disposition which conforms the matter to the form of the pontificate by ordering the matter to its end, which is the proper operation of the form considered in its nature as a *principium motus*. That operation proper to the habit of the pontificate which pertains essentially to the Petrine *munus* is the function of teaching the faith with the fullness of the power of faith, which is to teach the faith infallibly. Therefore, while the visible externality of the form of the pontificate is manifested in the *external* profession of faith, it does not suffice to dispose a man ontologically for the reception and conservation of the *form of the pontificate,* insofar as that form is for the habit its constitutive principle of being, which itself is ordered to the operation of the charism, for which operation the virtue of faith as a *dispositio animae* is the *necessary disposition,* and therefore, *the virtue of faith* is the necessary

---

[265] *ST* $I^a\text{-}II^a$ q. 55 a. 2 ad 1 — «modus actionis sequitur dispositionem agentis, unumquodque enim quale est, talia operatur. Et ideo, cum virtus sit principium aliqualis operationis, oportet quod in operante praeexistat secundum virtutem aliqua conformis dispositio. Facit autem virtus operationem ordinatam. Et ideo ipsa virtus est quaedam dispositio ordinata in anima, secundum scilicet quod potentiae animae ordinantur aliqualiter ad invicem, et ad id quod est extra.»

disposition for a man to receive the form of the pontificate as a qualitative habit of his *suppositum*.

Bellarmine in his doctrine on faith as the necessary disposition for the form of the pontificate to exist as a perfection in the pontiff as a subject perfectible by that form as a principle of operation, is following St. Thomas' doctrine on the nature of form as act of matter and principle of motion in natural bodies: "Every form of a natural body is the principle of motion proper to that body, as the form of fire is the principle of its motion."[266] [...] "That which is the first principle of living is the act and form of living bodies: but the soul is first principle of living things that live: therefore it is the act and form of a living body."[267] [...] "For the soul is in the body as the perfection in the perfectible. But the perfectible by a soul is an organic body: for the soul is the act of a physical organic body having life in potentiality, as is said in II *de anima*. Therefore, there is not a soul unless in an organic body."[268] Thus, the necessary dispositions for a soul to exist as the form and principle of motion in a living body are that the body be physical and organic, and as such, it is capable of the operations proper to its mode of being: "the soul is the principle of motion and cognition".[269] Just as a material body cannot receive or conserve a soul as its form without the necessary disposition of it being a physical and organic body; so Bellarmine teaches that a man cannot receive or conserve the form of the pontificate without the necessary disposition of faith. First, he explains, in order to become a pope, a

---

[266] *Sentencia De anima*, lib. 2 l. 7 n. 15 — «Omnis forma corporis naturalis est principium motus proprii illius corporis, sicut forma ignis est principium motus eius.»

[267] *Sentencia De anima*, lib. 2 l. 3 n. 9 — «Illud quod est primum principium vivendi est viventium corporum actus et forma: sed anima est primum principium vivendi his quae vivunt: ergo est corporis viventis actus et forma.»

[268] *Quaestio disputata de anima*, a. 10 arg. 1 — «Anima enim est in corpore sicut perfectio in perfectibili. Sed perfectibile ab anima est corpus organicum: est enim anima actus corporis physici organici potentia vitam habentis, ut dicitur in II de anima. Ergo anima non est nisi in corpore organico.»

[269] *Sentencia De anima*, lib. 1 l. 5 n. 1 — «anima est principium motus et cognitionis.»

man must receive the form of the pontificate; "Accordingly when the Cardinals create the Pontiff, they exercise their authority, not over the Pontiff because he as yet is not, but on the matter, i.e., on the person whom they dispose in some manner by the election, so that he receive from God the form of the Pontificate".[270] He then proves that faith is the necessary disposition for the reception of the form: "Either Faith is the necessary disposition *simpliciter* for this that someone be Pope, or only that he rightly be [pope]. If the first; then with this disposition removed by the contrary which is heresy, he straightaway ceases to be Pope: for neither can the form be conserved without the necessary dispositions."[271] Then he gives the reason why faith is absolutely necessary:

> Either the total disposition, which is the character and Faith, is necessary *simpliciter,* or not, but a partial disposition suffices. If the first; therefore with faith removed, the necessary disposition would simply not remain, because the total (disposition) was necessary *simpliciter,* and it is already no longer total. If the second, then faith is not required except to be rightly a pope, and consequently because of its defect, the Pope cannot be deposed. *Hence,* those which have the uttermost disposition to destruction thereafter cease to be, without any external power, as is evident; therefore a heretic pope without any other deposition would cease by himself to be Pope.[272]

---

[270] *De Romano Pontifice lib. ii cap. xxx* — «Itaque Cardinales dum Pontificem creant, exercent suam auctoritatem, non supra Pontificem quia nondum est, sed circa materiam, idest, circa personam quam per electionem quodammodo disponunt, ut a Deo Pontificatus formam recipiat»

[271] *Ibid* — «Vel Fides est dispositio necessaria simpliciter ad hoc ut aliquis sit Papa, vel tantum ad bene esse. Si primum; ergo ista dispositione sublata per contrariam quæ est hæresis, mox Papa desinit esse: neque enim potest forma conservari sine necessariis dispositionibus.»

[272] *Ibid.* — «Vel totalis dispositio, quae est character & Fides, est necessaria simpliciter, vel non, sed sufficit partialis. Si primum; ergo remota Fide, non amplius remanet dispositio necessaria simpliciter, quia totalis erat necessaria simpliciter, & jam non est amplius totalis. Si secundum; ergo Fides non requiritur nisi ad bene esse, & proinde propter ejus defectum Papa deponi non potest. Deinde quæ habent ultimam dispositionem ad interitum, paulo post desinunt esse sine alia vi externa, ut patet; igitur & Papa haereticus sine alia depositione per se desinit esse Papa.»

Thus, since faith *simpliciter* is the conforming disposition without which a man cannot be constituted as pope and function as pope, it was not without foundation that Innocent III said in the below cited passage that he would «not believe so easily that God would permit the Roman Pontiff to err against faith: for whom he prayed spiritually in Peter: <I have prayed for thee, Peter, etc (Luke 22)>» Innocent gives the reason why he believed that God would not permit the Roman Pontiff "to err against faith" by falling into the "spiritual fornication" of heresy, i.e. the "error of infidelity", and that reason is that without the virtue of faith, he would be incapable of fulfilling the duty of his office to strengthen the faith of others, and would therefore be liable to judgment by the Church for the sin against faith:

> Because I am a servant, I must be faithful and prudent, so that I may give the family nutriment at the right time. Three things especially God requires from me, which are distinguished by these three words, and these are, faith of heart, prudence of action, victual of mouth: this is, that I be faithful in heart, that I be prudent in action, and that I give nourishment in the mouth... Unless I be solid in faith, how can I strengthen others in faith? That it is recognized to pertain especially to my office the Lord testified: «I have prayed for thee, Peter, that thy faith not fail, and thou once being converted, confirm thy brethren» (*Luke* xxii)... For this reason the faith of the Apostolic See never failed in any disturbance, but remained always integral and unimpaired: so that the privilege of Peter would continue unshaken. Faith is so necessary for me that while for other sins I have only God for a judge, for only the sin committed against faith, I can be judged by the Church. For *he who does not believe, already has been judged.* (John 3: 18)[273]

---

[273] "Cum enim sim servus, debeo esse fidelis et prudens, ut dem familiæ cibum in tempore. Tria præcipue Deus requirit a me, quæ notant his verbis videlicet, fidem cordis, prudentiam operis, cibum oris: hoc est, ut sim fidelis in corde, ut sim prudens in opere, et dem cibum in ore... Nisi enim ego solidatus essem in fide, quomodo possem alios in fide firmare? Quod ad officium meum noscitur specialiter pertinere, Domino protestante: «Ego, inquit, pro te rogavi, Petre, ut non deficiat fides tua, et tu aliquando conversus, confirma fratres tuos (*Luc*.xxii).» Rogavit, et impetravit: quoniam exauditus est in omnibus pro sua reverentia. Et ideo fides apostolicae sedis in nulla nunquam turbatione defecit, sed integra semper et illibata permansit: ut Petri privilegium persisteret inconcussum. In tantum enim fides mihi

Since this charism is singular and personal, and is ordered to the *munus* of preserving the unity of the Church, only the Pontiff can exercise it alone; and the totality of the bishops without the pope, cannot exercise it while they are separated from unity with him, because they do not have the *munus* of unity, but to the pontiff alone was given the primacy with its singular and personal *munus* of binding the whole Church in the unity of faith. Hence, it is heresy to assert that a council can declare a certainly valid pope guilty of heresy with binding juridical force on the whole Church. For so long as a man is validly constituted as pope, that power to judge in a matter of faith and bind the whole Church pertains exclusively to his authority. The pope only loses that authority when he dies or abdicates. Permanent insanity is judged by theologians to be morally equivalent to death because by the loss of the intellective faculty, the capacity to exercise the *munus* is lost. Heresy, if it is public constitutes an act of abdication, as Ballerini and Gregory XVI explained; and is taught in the 1917 Code of Canon Law. (Can. 188.4°) Heresy, if it is not public, is also a moral death in relation to its incapacitating effect on the heretic's power to exercise the Petrine *munus*, as I have explained; so that a man reputed to be pope who exhibits the *indicia* of grave suspicion would not only create by those *indicia* a presumption of guilt, but also a presumption of vacancy of the Apostolic See.

If the pope would explicitly, immediately and directly express disbelief in a dogma with manifest *dolus* of heresy, the act would by its very nature sever him from the body of the Church and constitute an act of **TACIT ABDICATION**. If the profession of heresy is expressed directly and *implicitly*, the *dolus* would not be manifestly certain, but on the foundation of the *indicia* he would become a suspect of heresy, casting doubt on the validity of his pontificate, for which reason he could then be issued solemn corrections on the basis of that presumption, which if unheeded, would render his pertinacity plainly and certainly manifest, making it evident and certain that he is indeed a formal heretic and not a valid holder of the papal office.

---

necessaria est ut cum de cæteris peccatis solum Deum judicem habeam, propter solum peccatum quod in fide committitur possem ab Ecclesia judicari. Nam qui non credit, iam iudicatus est. (Joh.3 18)" (*Sermo II* «IN CONSACRATIONE PONTIFICIS MAXIMI»)

Now while it is plainly evident that one who is insane cannot function according to the nature of the papacy, so that a pope who would suffer severe brain damage would cease to be pope just as if he had died; similarly, the same is true for a heretic. A heretic cannot function according to the nature of the papacy, as I have explained, because faith is the necessary disposition to perform the duties of the office, which require him to teach only the true faith; and when necessary, to teach the faith infallibly. However, to teach the faith infallibly he must have the intention and the capacity to do so, and that capacity depends on the *necessary disposition of faith* by which the truths of faith are attainable. A heretical putative pope is an enemy of the faith for whom the integral truth of faith is not attainable, for which reason he lacks the *necessary disposition* to have the capacity to teach the true faith infallibly, because without faith his natural capacities only furnish him with the ability to teach his own opinions, and thereby wittingly or unwittingly he can only destroy the true faith with his false teachings, being incapable of exercising the *munus* of confirming the faith infallibly with the fullness of the power of faith. But this is within the power of a true pope, because to him is promised that his faith will not fail precisely so that he can be disposed by faith to exercise the power of faith to its fullness and thereby teach the faith infallibly. Innocent III taught, «I however would not believe so easily that God would permit the Roman Pontiff to err against faith: for whom he prayed spiritually in Peter: <I have prayed for thee, Peter, etc. (Luke 22)>»; and he believed this because to the pope has been given the "spiritual fullness" in such a manner that «the others are called into a share», but because Peter is the head; and the fullness, he says, is in the head, he explains, «but Peter alone is assumed into the fullness of power.»[274] It is for this reason that Innocent says he has rejoiced:

---

[274] «Ego tamen facile non crediderim, ut Deus permitteret Romanum pontificem contra fidem errare: pro quo spiritualiter oravit in Petro: <Ego, inquit, pro te rogavi, Petre, etc. (Luc.xxii),> Ergo *qui habet sponsam, sponsus est.* Haec autem sponsa non nupsit vacua, sed dotem mihi tribuit absque pretio pretiosam, **spirilualium videlicet plenitudinem** et latitudinem temporalium, magnitndinem et multiudinem utrorumque. Nam caeteri vocati sunt in partem sollicitudinis, solus autem Petrus assumptus est in **plenitudinem potesatis.**» (*Sermo III «IN CONSECRATIONE PONTIFICIS»*);

And because of what expression of speech it is for me to rejoice? For that one of course which the Lord spoke to the apostles: «I will be with you all days up to the end of the world (*Matth.* XXVIII).» And especially to Peter: «Simon, behold Satan has sought to sift you as wheat, etc. (*Luke* XXII).» This is the voice of the Spouse, for which I rejoice; for as He foretold Simon a battle, who promised victory, thus He enjoins the office, who expends for assistance. He foretells battle when He says: «Satan has sought to sift you as wheat.» He promises victory, when He adds: «I have prayed for thee, that thy faith not fail (*Ibid.*).» For: «this is the victory which conquers the world, our faith (*I John* V).» He enjoins the office, when He says: «Confirm thy brethren (*Luke* XXII).» He expends assistance, when He says: «I have prayed for thee, Peter (*ibid.*).» — «He is heard in all things because of his reverence (*Hebr.* V).» — «The Lord is my helper, I will not fear what man does to me (*Ps.* CXVII).»[275]

As is explained below, Innocent makes it clear that when he says he does not believe that God would permit the pope "to err against faith" (*contra fidem errare*),[276] he does not here speak so much of

---

«*Tu*, inquit, *vocaberis Cephas* (*Joan.* 1), quod exponitur caput; quia sicut in capite consistit **omnium sensuum plenitudo, in cæteris autem membris pars est aliqua plenitudinis: ita cæteri vocati sunt in partem sollicitudinis, solus autem Petrus assumptus est in plenitudinem potestatis.**» (*Sermo II* «IN CONSACRATIONE PONTIFICIS MAXIMI»)

[275] *Sermo III* «*IN CONSECRATIONE PONTIFICIS*» — Et propter quam vocem mihi gaudendum est? Propter illam utique, quam Dominus inquit apostolis: «Vobiscum ero omnibus diebusuaque ad consummationem sæculi (*Matth.* XXVIII)» Et specialiter Petro: «Simon, ecce Satanas expetivit ut cribraret vos sicut triticum, etc. (*Luc.* XXII).» Hæc est vox Sponsi, pro qua gaudeo; quia sicut prædicit Simoni pugnam, qui promitit victoriam, sic injungit officium, qui impendit auxilium. Pugnam prædicit, cum ait: «Satanas expetivit ut cribraret vos sicut triticum.» Victoriam promitit, cum addit: «Ego autem roavi pro te, ut non desinat fides tua (*ibid.*).» Nam: «Hæc est victoria quæ vincit mundum, fides nostra (*I Joan.* V).» Officium inJungit, cm dicit: «Confirma fratres tuos (*Luc.* XXII).» Auxilium impendit, cum ait: «Ego pro te rogavi, Petre (*ibid.*).» — «Exauditur enim in omnibus pro sua reverential (*Hebr.* V).» — «Dominus mihi adjutor, non timebo quid faciat mihi homo (*Psal.* CXVII).»

[276] *Sermo III* «*IN CONSECRATIONE PONTIFICIS*» — «Ego tamen facile non crediderim, ut Deus permitteret Romanum pontificem contra fidem errare.»

material error in the pope's teaching, but he speaks properly of formal heresy, because in these sermons he equates that *contra fidem errare* with the "error of infidelity," (*infidelitatis errorem*),[277] and "spiritual fornication" (*Fornicationem non dico carnalem, sed spiritualem*),[278] and the "sin committed against faith (*peccatum quod in fide committitur*),[279] in which the sin of formal heresy properly consists. Thus, the charism of infallibility which is included in the power of the primacy[280] can never be diminished or cancelled by heresy in the person of the pope, because the pope's faith, without which the charism of infallibility cannot operate, will not be permitted by God to fail. Without faith, the pope cannot confirm the faith of others, therefore Innocent asks, *"Unless I be solid in faith, how can I strengthen others in faith?"*[281] And likewise Bellarmine, *"How, I ask, will a heretic Pope confirm the brethren in faith and always preach the true faith?"*[282] And therefore Bellarmine argues and concludes: 1) "Faith is *simpliciter* a necessary disposition for someone to be Pope," 2) "then this disposition being removed by the contrary which is heresy, the Pope straightaway ceases to be Pope: nor can the form be conserved without the necessary dispositions," 3) "therefore a heretic pope without any other deposition would cease by himself to be Pope."[283] But, Bellarmine explains also why that

---

[277] *Sermo III. «IN CONSECRATIONE PONTIFICIS»*

[278] *Ibid.*

[279] *Sermo II «IN CONSACRATIONE PONTIFICIS MAXIMI»*

[280] *Pastor Æternus* — «*Ipso autem Apostolico primatu*, quem Romanus Pontifex tamquam Petri principis Apostolorum successor in universam Ecclesiam obtinet, *supremam quoque magisterii potestatem comprehendi*» — "That apostolic primacy which the Roman Pontiff possesses as successor of Peter, the prince of the apostles, includes also the supreme power of teaching."

[281] *Sermo II «IN CONSACRATIONE PONTIFICIS MAXIMI»*

[282] *De Rom. Pont. lib. iv cap. vi* — «At quomodo, quæso, confirmabit fratres in Fide, & veram Fidem semper prædicabit Pontifex hæreticus?»

[283] *De Rom. Pont. Lib. ii cap. xxx* — «Deinde. Vel Fides est dispositio necessaria simpliciter ad hoc ut aliquis sit Papa, vel tantum ad bene esse. Si primum; ergo ista dispositione sublata per contrariam quæ est hæresis, mox Papa desinit esse: neque enim potest forma conservari sine necessariis dispositionibus... *Deinde*, quae habent ultimam dispositionem ad interitum, paulo post desinit esse, sine alia vi externa, ut patet; igitur et Papa haereticus sine alia depositione *per se* desinit esse Papa.»

cannot ever really happen; because the pope's faith cannot fail, being that, *"the Pope by his own nature can fall into heresy, but not when there is posited the singular assistance of God which Christ obtained for him by his prayer: but Christ prayed that his faith not fail,"*[284] for which reason it is taught in *Pastor Æternus* that the operation of the charism has never failed precisely because Christ promised that the pope's faith will never fail: «Indeed, their apostolic teaching was embraced by all the venerable fathers and reverenced and followed by all the holy orthodox doctors, for they knew very well that **this See of St. Peter always remains unblemished by any error, in accordance with the divine promise of our Lord and Saviour to the prince of his disciples: "I HAVE PRAYED FOR THEE THAT THY FAITH MAY NOT FAIL**; and when thou hast turned again, strengthen thy brethren."»[285]

If the pope's faith could fail, so that the infallible power of the primacy could be mutated in the pope by the pope's heresy, and made in some manner inferior to the non-infallible collective power of the bishops in a council, as John of St. Thomas affirms would happen in a case of papal heresy, then, in direct contradiction to the dogma of the primacy, the occupant of the See of Peter would no longer be able to freely exercise the primacy by means of infallibly settling a dispute between himself and the bishops in a matter of faith. He would no longer be the *supreme judge in all cases*, which is contrary to the dogma of the primacy: «*Since the Roman Pontiff, by the divine right of the apostolic primacy, governs the whole Church, we likewise teach and declare that he is the* **supreme judge** *of the faithful* **in all cases that refer to ecclesiastical**

---

[284] St. Robert Bellarmine, *De Romano Pontifice, lib. iv, cap. vii* – «Respondeo ad primum argumentum: inde recte colligi, posse Papam ex natura sua incidere in haeresim, non tamen posita singulari Dei assistentia, quam Christus oratione sua illi impetravit: oravit autem Christus, ne deficeret Fides ejus.»

[285] *Pastor Æternus* — «Quorum quidem apostolicam doctrinam omnes venerabiles Patres amplexi et sancti Doctores orthodoxi venerati atque secuti sunt; plenissime scientes, hanc sancti Petri Sedem ab omni semper errore illibatam permanere, secundum Domini Salvatoris nostri divinam pollicitationem discipulorum suorum principi factam: Ego rogavi pro te, ut non deficiat fides tua, et tu aliquando conversus confirma fratres tuos.»

examination»[286] If the infallible power of the primacy could be altered by the pope's heresy, so that it would be for the council and not the pope to decide whether or not the pope's opinion is heresy, and for the council to settle the matter with the finality in the manner of a supreme authority superior to the altered power of the pope, whose primacy would no longer exist as a primacy that could be freely exercised over the whole Church, then the exercise of the primacy would effectively be transferred to the Council. This is quite impossible, and it is a heresy to assert it. *Pastor Æternus* declares: «"**The Holy Roman Church possesses the supreme and full primacy and principality over the whole Catholic Church**. She truly and humbly acknowledges that she received this from the Lord himself in blessed Peter, the prince and chief of the apostles, whose successor the Roman Pontiff is, together with the fullness of power; *and since before all others she has the duty of defending the truth of the faith, so if any questions arise concerning the faith, it is by her judgment that they must be settled.*"»[287] This primatial function can never be exercised by the collective episcopal power of the totality of the bishops of the world gathered together in a council, because, as *Pastor Æternus* teaches, this function is ordered to the unity of the Church and therefore it pertains exclusively by divine appointment to the successor of Peter alone, to whom the whole Church must remain in hierarchical subordination: «Wherefore we teach and declare that, by divine ordinance, the Roman Church possesses a pre-eminence of ordinary power over every other Church, and that **this jurisdictional power of the Roman Pontiff** is both episcopal and immediate. **Both**

---

[286] *Pastor Æternus* — «Et quoniam divino Apostolici primatus iure Romanus Pontifex universae Ecclesiae praeest, docemus etiam et declaramus, eum esse iudicem supremum fidelium (Pii PP. VI Breve, *Super soliditate* d. 28 Nov. 1786), et in omnibus causis ad examen ecclesiasticum.»

[287] *Pastor Æternus* — «Approbante vero Lugdunensi Concilio secundo, Graeci professi sunt: Sanctam Romanam Ecclesiam *summum et plenum primatum* et principatum super universam Ecclesiam catholicam obtinere, quem se ab ipso Domino in beato Petro Apostolorum principe sive vertice, cuius Romanus Pontifex est successor, *cum potestatis plenitudine recepisse* veraciter et humiliter recognoscit; et *sicut prae ceteris tenetur fidei veritatem defendere, sic et, si quae de fide subortae fuerint quaestiones, suo debent iudicio definiri.*»

clergy and faithful, of whatever rite and dignity, both singly and collectively, are bound to submit to this power by the duty of *hierarchical subordination* and true obedience**, and this not only in matters concerning faith and morals, but also in those which regard the discipline and government of the Church throughout the world.».[288] It is heresy to assert, on the false and heretical pretext, which claims that if the bishops judge that by heresy the pope's primacy has been altered and rendered somehow inferior to the power of the bishops, that the bishops could then summon an ecumenical council to judge against a pope on a matter of faith, rather than that they submit to the pope's judgment, to which all are bound in hierarchical subordination. The proposition is directly contrary to the solemn teaching of the First Vatican Council: «And so they stray from the genuine path of truth who maintain that it is lawful to appeal from the judgments of the Roman pontiffs to an ecumenical council as if this were an authority superior to the Roman Pontiff.»[289] The right to judge in matters of faith with finality pertains *exclusively* and *inalienably* to the authority of the Roman Pontiff. No council can on any pretext, least of all on the pretext that it has jurisdiction over the "conjunction", declare that *it* has by way of exception the jurisdiction to judge a true pope's opinions heretical, because such a jurisdiction is by divine right a *primatial jurisdiction* which pertains exclusively

---

[288] *Pastor Æternus* — «Docemus proinde et declaramus, Ecclesiam Romanam, disponente Domino, super omnes alias ordinariae potestatis obtinere principatum, et hanc Romani Pontificis iurisdictionis potestatem, quae vere episcopalis est, immediatam esse: **erga quam cuiuscumque ritus et dignitatis pastores atque fideles, tam seorsum singuli quam simul omnes, officio *hierarchicae subordinationis*, veraeque obedientiae obstringuntur,** non solum in rebus, quae ad fidem et mores, sed etiam in iis, quae ad disciplinam et regimen ecclesiae per totum orbem diffusae pertinent; ita ut custodita cum Romano Pontifice tam communionis, quam eiusdem fidei professionis unitate, Ecclesia Christi sit unus grex sub uno summo pastore. Haec est catholicae veritatis doctrina, a qua deviare salva fide atque salute nemo potest.»

[289] *Pastor Æternus* — «Quare a recto veritatis tramite aberrant, qui affirmant, licere ab iudiciis Romanorum Pontificum ad oecumenicum Concilium tamquam ad auctoritatem Romano Pontifice superiorem appellare.»

to the holder of the primacy. If the pope would become in some manner subject to that *conciliar jurisdiction,* and on the supposed authority of that **Ersatz Primacy** deprive him of the pontificate, that would make a council the holder of the supreme authority to judge the pope's opinions; to which authority the pope would be bound to defer whenever the council judges him to be in heresy. It is precisely because the pope's faith cannot fail that a council may never presume to judge that a valid pope's primacy has been mutated and in some manner rendered inferior to their **Ersatz Primacy**. If that were possible, the unity of the Church would be shattered, and the Church would break up into thousands of sects. Indeed, the council itself would likely break up into factions as history demonstrates. A council does not have the *munus,* and therefore does not the power to preserve the unity of the Church, since it does not even have the power to preserve the unity of itself with the Church if it separates from unity with the successor of Peter. Therefore Ballerini explains: «Against a certain Pontifical right there is actually no power of a general council: since on account of the same right, which is not from the electors, or from the Church, but is granted immediately by God, a true Pontiff, superior to the whole Church, and also to general synods (as we have proven), is removed from the jurisdiction of all the others inferior to him. Indeed for this reason the machinations and actions of the Baselensians against Eugene IV, the true and certain Pontiff, were able to accomplish nothing to depose him, and deflected them into open schism.»[290]

To exercise the *munus* to teach infallibly, that "spiritual fullness" of the power of faith is required, as Bellarmine explained, «because it seems to require the sweet disposition of the providence of God. For the Pope not only should not, but cannot preach heresy, but rather

---

[290] *De Potestate Ecclesiastica. De casu Schismatis, quo duo vel plures se se gerant tamquam Pontifices;* caput IX § III p. 130 — «... contra certum Pontificium jus nulla vel generalis concilii potestas est: cum ob idem jus non ab electoribus, nec ab Ecclesia, sed a Deo immediate tributum, verus Pontifex toti Ecclesiæ, & generalibus quoque synodis (ut probavimus) superior, ab aliorum omnium sibi inferiorum jurisdictione subtrahatur. Hac quidem de causa Basileensium molimina & gesta contra Eugenium IV. unicum certumque Pontificem illegitima & inania nihil potuerunt ad ipsum deponendum, & in apertum schisma deflexerunt.»

should always preach the truth. He will certainly do that, since the Lord commanded him to confirm his brethren, and for that reason added: "I have prayed for thee, that thy faith shall not fail," that is, that at least the preaching of the true faith shall not fail in thy throne. How, I ask, will a heretic Pope confirm the brethren in faith and always preach the true faith? Certainly God can wrench the confession of the true faith out of the heart of a heretic just as he placed the words in the mouth of Balaam's ass. Still, this will be a great violence, and not in keeping with the providence of God that sweetly disposes all things.»[291] As I explained in Volume One, this "great violence" in the case of a human person would be contrary to nature, and is therefore impossible. Thus, for these reasons a pope cannot even fall into formal heresy as a private person, and therefore, Bellarmine concludes, «It is proven». Yet while the moral death that would cause the cessation of the papacy in a lunatic or one severely brain damaged would be obvious to all; it would not be so obvious to perverse minded prelates in the case of a heretic who panders to their ambitions, so that the damage to the faith and morals of the faithful everywhere would be aggravated by unresolvable schisms and dissentions which could only be settled by an act of supreme authority — a supreme authority which would be lacking in the case of a pope who by his plainly recognizable heresy would lose the form of the pontificate, and with it its jurisdiction as well. If a pope were to fall from office by an act of tacit abdication by professing obstinate heresy, in losing office, he would lose the supreme authority of the office that he forfeited; and a suppletive supreme authority is not provided to a council or any other ecclesial body by divine law. With such an absence of supreme authority, the unity of the Church would

---

[291] *De Romano Pontifice lib. iv cap. vi* — «Nam Pontifex non solum non debet, nec potest hæresim prædicare, sed etiam debet veritatem semper docere, & sine dubio id faciet, cum Dominus illi jusserit confirmare fratres suos, & propterea addiderit, *Rogavi pro te, ut non deficiat fides tua,* idest, ut saltem non deficiat in throno tuo prædicatio veræ Fidei: at quomodo, quæso, confirmabit fratres in Fide, & veram Fidem semper prædicabit Pontifex hæreticus? Potest quidem Deus ex corde hæretico extorquere veræ Fidei confessionem, sicut verba posuit quondam in ore asinæ Balaam: at violentum erit, & non secundum morem providentiæ Dei suaviter disponentis omnia.»

suffer an incurable defect in that there would exist no remedy for the maximum necessity of such a catastrophe, which even John of St. Thomas, in the cited passage, admitted would threaten the Church with destruction of her faith and unity, for which reason he judged rightly that it would be absolutely necessary for the heretic to be deposed. Such a one, by the disposition of divine providence, would be able to be proven to have never been a valid pope, for which reason, an act of supreme authority would not be necessary, but the jurisdiction of the Church over the election of a pope would suffice to authoritatively remove the heretical intruder from the throne he usurps.

> 3. «Nor Jerome when he says a heretic leaves the body of Christ, does he exclude that judgment of the Church especially in such a grave matter such as the deposition of a pope, but she judges the quality of the crime, which by itself excludes from the Church without any other additional censure, provided however that it be declared by the Church; even though of himself he separates from the Church, however in respect to us the separation is not understood to have taken place without this declaration. And similarly to that reason given we respond, that the non-Christian, who in respect to himself and in respect to us is not a Christian, cannot be pope, if however in respect to himself he is not a Christian, because he has lost the faith, but in respect to us he has not yet been juridically declared to be an infidel or a heretic, no matter how manifestly he may be according to private judgment, yet in respect to us he is a member of the Church, and consequently the head. Therefore the judgment of the Church is required, by which he is proposed as a non-Christian, and to be avoided, and then he ceases to be pope in respect to us, and consequently he did not desist even in himself, because all which he did was valid in itself.»[292]

---

[292] John of St. Thomas, *Op. cit.* p. 263 — «XXVI. ... Nec Hieronymus quando dicit hæreticum per se discedere a corpore Christi, excludit ipsum Ecclesiæ judicium præsertim in re tam gravi, qualis est depositio papæ, sed criminis judicat qualitatem, quod per se sine alia censura superaddita excludit ab Ecclesia, dummodo tamen per Ecclesiam declaretur; licet enim ex se sepatet ab Ecclesia, tamen quoad nos non intelligitur facta separatio sine ista declaratione. Et similiter ad rationem respondetur, quod non Christianus, qui quoad se, et quoad nos Christianus non est, non potest esse papa, si tamen quoad se Christianus non sit, quia fidem amisit; quoad nos autem adhuc non fit juridice declaratus, ut infidelis, vel hæreticus,

Sed contra — The fundamental logical inconsistency in this passage consists in the assertion that one who is manifestly a heretic and therefore separated from the Church *quoad se*, and accordingly judged so by private judgment, would, still be a member of the Church and the head because he remains to be so *quoad nos*, and therefore would still actually be a member of the Church and its head. John of St. Thomas' distinction *quoad se/quoad nos* is not a Thomistic distinction, [293] and is a distinction only in the subjective order, and *not in the order*

---

quantumcumque manifestus sit secundum privatum judicium, adhuc quoad nos est membrum Ecclesiæ, et consequenter caput. Requiritur ergo judicium Ecclesiæ, quo proponatur, ut non Christianus, et evitandus, et tunc desinit quoad nos esse papa, et consequenter antea non desierat etiam in se, quia omnia quæ faciebat erat valida in se.»

[293] This distinction between what exists *quoad se* and *quoad nos* is not a Thomistic distinction as Siscoe claims in his e-mail message to me "I applied the Thomistic distinction of quoad se/quoad nos to show that, just because heresy *of its nature* severs a person from the Church (spiritually), does not mean heresy, *of its nature*, causes a person to cease being a *member* of the Church (legally). And I quoted the great John of St. Thomas **who explained it exactly the way I did.**" Siscoe elaborates: "Did you even read John Salza's recent article that prompted this e-mail exchange? John and I both contributed to that article so it represents both of our opinions. We both affirm that the sin of heresy, of its nature, separates a person from the Church quoad se (of itself), but the sin of heresy, of its nature, does not result in a separation from the Church quoad nos (according to us), nor does it result in the loss of office. [...] As long as a person remains a member of the Church quoad nos – even if he has committed the sin of heresy and has lost the faith – he remains a legal member of the Church; and if the person in question is a bishop or Pope, he retains his office until the crime has been legally established by the proper authorities." The distinction made by St. Thomas when referring to what is known, only makes the distinction between what is known *per se simpliciter* or *secundum se simpliciter*, and what is known *quoad nos per se notum*: "quod est notum per se simpliciter, et quod est quoad nos per se notum." (*Summa Contra Gentiles lib. I. cap. xi.*); and in Iª IIæ q. 94 a. 2: "Dicitur autem aliquid per se notum dupliciter, uno modo, secundum se; alio modo, quoad nos." He uses the term *quoad se* only once in the *Summa Theologiæ* in the question on simony (IIª IIæ q. 100 a. 6 ad 1) where he explains the distinction not as regarding what is known or true, but as relating to action, specifically concerning the applicability of a canonical suspension whether it is binding *quoad se* or *quoad alios*. The

of being, and is therefore founded on a fallacy which fails to distinguish between what exists in the order of being, and is therefore prior and better known *per se*, as opposed to what is better known *quoad nos*. Hence, if the defection into heresy is manifest, or is at least visible and recognizable as such, then it is evident and by nature better known *per se* that he is separated from the Church, and consequently the heretic's separation from the Church is true *pe se*, because it is **true in the order of being**, even if it is not always immediately or manifestly evident *quoad nos*. If the heretic's separation is actually known by us, he is separated *quoad nos*, and since it is known as an evident fact, it is known to exist *per se* because, "that which is non-existent cannot be known".[294] One who is publicly seen to visibly separate himself from the Church by an act of manifest heresy, is publicly seen by that act to sever directly and *per se* the external bond which united him to the body as a member, and therefore he ceases to be a member *simpliciter*, i.e. without qualification, and therefore it cannot be said that the separation exists only in a qualified manner, i.e. *quoad se*, but not *quoad nos*, as if the separation is merely *spiritual* in the manner of an internal separation. Thus, it truly can be said of him, "of himself (*quoad se*) he separates from the Church", by an actual visible severing of the external bond of union which effects a true and real *ontological* separation and exclusion from membership in the Church. It therefore does not follow, and is contradictory to say that the said separation which the heretic has accomplished *of himself*, being

---

proposition which logically involves the contradiction that something can be true in the order of being *quoad se*, but at the same time not be true in the order of being, because it is not true *quoad nos*, belongs properly to John of St. Thomas alone, and is not founded on any principle or distinction stated anywhere in the works of St. Thomas. St. Thomas follows Aristotle's doctrine exactly on knowledge that is prior and better known as elaborated in the *Posterior Analytics*, which, like all the works of Aristotle and every other book he ever read, he knew entirely by memory. This is evident, as Klemens Vansteenkiste O.P. explained in his Angelicum lectures, because he quoted verbatim the multitude of texts he cited, but often deviating slightly from the written text in the book, because he always quoted the passages from memory without looking them up.

[294] *The Works of Aristotle*, Translated Into English Under the Editorship of W. D. Ross, Oxford, *Posterior Analytics*, Book I No. 2, p. 224.

visibly a true and unqualified act of separation from external union and membership, is subject to the qualifying condition that the actual separation does not really take place unless, "it be declared by the Church; even though of himself he separates from the Church," for the reason that "in respect to us (*quoad nos*) the separation is not understood to have taken place without this declaration." John of St. Thomas' error on this point is rooted in his failure to take into account the ambiguity of the terms upon which is based the "*distinction between truths prior to us and truths without qualification prior*",[295] which terms properly distinguish between the nature of what exists *per se* and is better known and prior without qualification, and what is known *quoad nos*.[296] What is true *per se* is "*prior and better known in the order of being*"[297] and therefore **"without qualification prior"** — whereas what is true *quoad nos* is qualified as "*what is prior and better known to man*".[298] What John of St. Thomas says is only known *quoad se*, is actually known *per se*, and is *per se* prior and better known *in the order of being*. First of all, if the act of separation which has taken place is true in the order of being, then it is true *per se*. For that separation *per se* to be true in the order of being, it must be a *visible* act which directly and *per se* severs the external bond of union, and consequently it is necessarily a separation that is *knowable quoad nos*, even if it is not actually known to all. If the manifest act which necessarily causes separation from the Church is immediately seen and known, then it is known as evidently true to us (*quoad nos*), and therefore judged by us to have really taken place in the order of being, because the premises of that judgment,

---

[295] *Ibid. Posterior Analytics*, Book I No. 2, p. 227.

[296] *Ibid.* p. 224 — "Now 'prior' and 'better known' are ambiguous terms, for there is a difference between what is prior and better known in the order of being and what is prior and better known to man. I mean that objects nearer to sense are prior and better known to man; objects without qualification prior and better known are those further from sense. Now the most universal causes are furthest from sense and particular causes are nearest to sense, and they are thus exactly opposed to one another."

[297] *Ibid.* p. 224.

[298] *Ibid.*

being primary and therefore *basic truths*,[299] are manifestly true.[300] A separation that exists *per se* is therefore known to exist *quoad nos* if the act causing that separation from the Church is immediately seen by us as evidently true, and accordingly forms the basis of our judgment. Then accordingly, from the immediately evident premises of our judgment, the separation is judged to be evidently true, being seen to be true in its evident principles. If the premises are immediately *known* (such as the cause of separation which is the act of heresy), and certain (such as the definition of what specifies the act as heretical), then they are certainly true, and consequently the judgment affirming that the heretic has separated himself from the Church necessarily follows as a conclusion from those premises, and is therefore *known* to be necessarily and certainly true in the order of being, because, "*that which is non-existent cannot be known*". [301] The reason why this is true is that, "Nothing is intelligible according to that it is in potency, but according to that it is in act, as is said in *IX Metaph*. Whence, since the possible intellect is in potency only in relation to intelligible being, it cannot be understood unless through its form which becomes by act".[302] Nothing is simply nothing at all, so there is nothing in the non-existent that can be known. Whatever is known, is known insofar as it *is*, and it *is* in virtue of its being *in act* through its form, and therefore exists in some manner, and is some*thing*, some *being* that can be

---

[299] *Ibid.* — "In saying that the premisses of demonstrated knowledge must be primary, I mean that they must be the 'appropriate' basic truths, for I identify primary premiss and basic truth. A 'basic truth' in a demonstration is an immediate proposition. An immediate proposition is one which has no other proposition prior to it."

[300] *Ibid.* p. 224 — "The premisses must be the causes of the conclusion, better known than it, and prior to it; its causes, since we possess scientific knowledge of a thing only when we know its cause; prior, in order to be causes; antecedently known, this antecedent knowledge being not our mere understanding of the meaning, but knowledge of the fact as well. Now 'prior' and 'better known' are ambiguous terms…"

[301] Aristotle—Works, *Posterior Analytics*, Book I No. 2, p. 224.

[302] *Quaestiones disputatae De anima Quaestio sexta decima* — «Et hoc ideo est, quia nihil est intelligibile secundum quod est in potentia, sed secundum quod est actu, ut dicitur in IX Metaph. Unde, cum intellectus possibilis sit in potentia tantum in esse intelligibili, non potest intelligi nisi per formam suam per quam fit actu.»

known: "For that which first falls in the apprehension is *being*, the notion of which is included in whatsoever one apprehends."[303] Therefore, a separation whose existence *per se* is necessarily contingent on an act that is visible and knowable as a true and certain external fact, is by that very contingency necessarily also a separation *quoad nos*, but if due to weakness of mind, some of us have not yet arrived at the truth of the heretic's separation, then, for them only, it is not yet known *quoad nos* as a fact, since for them that knowledge is posterior and less known *quoad nos* than the fact which is prior and better known in the order of being *per se*. Yet since the one, who according to John of St. Thomas, is separated from the Church *of himself*, i.e. "*quoad se*" but not *quoad nos*, is evidently separated *per se* from the Church *in the order of being*, then even if due to weakness of mind some of us do not subjectively grasp the evident truth of the reality of this separation in the order of being in the apprehension of our intellect and judge accordingly, the manifest heretic, nevertheless, being visibly separated *per se* from the body of the Church *in the order of being*, is separated from membership in the Church independently of whether or not some of us, or even most of us, actually arrive at knowledge of that truth which is *per se* plain as the light of day: "For as the eyes of bats are to the blaze of day, so is the reason in our soul to the things which are by nature most evident of all."[304] Hence, Bellarmine says, "Often it happens, or certainly it can happen, that manifest heretics will simulate themselves as Catholics, likewise Jews, Turks, Pagans mix in with the faithful, and nevertheless they will not be of the Church". Accordingly, one who in the order of being is not a true pope *per se*, is likewise not a pope in the order of being *quoad nos*, but will only appear to be pope to the weak-minded or the wilfully blind, but will not be pope because he is not of the Church.

When a judgment is made, by which one assents to something that is *evidenter verum*, it is true *per se* even if it is judged privately. That judgment is not of something *believed*, but of what is *plainly visible* and therefore **known by us** to be true **in the order of being** *per se*. The

---

[303] *Summa Theol.* Iª IIæ q. 94 a. 2 — «Nam illud quod primo cadit in apprehensione, est ens, cuius intellectus includitur in omnibus quaecumque quis apprehendit.»

[304] Aristotle—Works, *Metaphysics*, Book α 1, p. 2238.

indefectibility of the Church is entirely dependent on the natural capacity of the human mind aided by grace to know and accordingly judge whether a man is a true Pope or a heretical intruder and impostor. The truths of faith are matters of divine revelation which are not visible to us because they transcend the natural power of the human intellect, and therefore must be assented to by an act of faith in the divine mysteries infallibly transmitted to us by the evidently credible testimony of the Church. For this reason we cannot have access to the divine mysteries by Private Judgment because the act of faith is a judgment by which one assents to the divine truths transmitted to us by the infallible testimony of the Church, guaranteed by the authority of the revealing God. In order to assent to the divine revelation by means of faith in the divine authority of the Church's testimony, the Church must be visible to us, so as to be recognizable by the use of our natural faculties in order to be judged thereby to be the bearer of the authentic and authoritative testimony of the truths of faith which we believe with an assent of faith; for which reason it lies within the capacity of private judgment to be able to recognize and acknowledge which witness bears the authentic and authoritative testimony to the divine truths. Since the faith of the Church is the faith of Peter, the members must be capable of distinguishing and judging which man is the successor of Peter in order to know who is the rock upon which the authority of Church rests, and whose testimony is therefore to be assented to by an act of faith — *Ubi Petrus, ibi Ecclesia*. Hence, the truths of faith must be believed on the divine authority of the Church's testimony, transmitted infallibly by the successor of Peter and the bishops in communion with him; while the successor of Peter and the ecclesiastical hierarchy in communion with him must be able to be recognized and known by the natural powers of the intellect aided by grace as the authentic bearers of the apostolic testimony. If the members of the Church cannot know by the power of their intellective faculty which man is the head of the Church and the bearer of the primacy and its charism of infallibility, it will be impossible for them to give their assent to his teaching on the basis of that infallible authority. Therefore, it is in virtue of the Church's visibility that the true pope can be recognized and known by the natural intellective faculty so that his authority can be acknowledged and his teaching accepted in faith. Thus, the truths of revelation are received on the basis of the Church's authority, but the pope and the Church hierarchy in communion with him which bear that authority can be recognized and known as such in virtue of the attribute of visibility, because what is visible can be known according to reason by one's own judgment, but what is of faith is not knowable by private judgment and needs be believed on authority of those who can be recognized and known to be authentic successors of the apostles and the authentic transmitters of the apostolic testimony.

The Church, therefore, is visible, because it is a visible body of visible members who are constituted as members by their visible profession of faith in the divinely revealed dogmas. Hence, if the head would cease to be a member, he would cease to be the head, because the head is in its nature the chief member of the body, so that by visibly corrupting the nature of the chief member the head is visibly destroyed. It is *de fide* that heresy visibly separates one from membership in the Church by its very nature, and this is so because one who is constituted as a member by his visible profession of faith in the dogmas of faith would sever himself from the body and therefore cease to be a member by a visible act of contumacious disbelief in a dogma; so if a pope would visibly disbelieve a dogma with the obvious *dolus* of pertinacity, he would visibly cease to be a member and the head of the Church. Since the cessation from membership, and consequently of headship would be plainly visible to the mind and therefore verifiable as certain by means of the natural intellective power of judgment, a declaration made by authority would not be required for one to assert what is already known by reason. Therefore it pertains to natural law that a private individual has the right to judge that a public defector from the faith has fallen from office, insofar as he has the natural capacity to mentally apprehend the visible act of defection and verify as certain that the act has taken place if the matter and the *dolus* of heresy are plainly visible. The fact that only the legitimate ecclesiastical authority has the power to juridically declare whether such a defection has taken place or not does not take away the natural right of the individual to judge privately according to right reason. Thus the assertion that the manifest heretic remains a member of the Church *quoad nos* until he has been declared a heretic by ecclesiastical authority is without any rational basis and plainly erroneous.

It is only when it is so plainly visible so as to be certain that the head and members are in communion with each other in the *unity of faith, of worship and governance* that the dogmatic fact of a pontificate can be infallibly asserted, because **it is by this means that the unity of the head with the members is seen.** If that visible unity is lacking, then the certitude regarding the actual existence in an individual of the supreme and infallible authority will be lacking until that visible unity is restored. Until that happens, the primacy of the individual conscience takes precedence over the uncertain authority of a doubtful head and consequently over the intermediate authority subordinate to the uncertain supreme authority, because no one has the right to bind the conscience of his subjects in a matter that cannot be certain until the lack of certitude regarding that supreme authority is rectified; and until the certainty of the actual existence in an individual of that infallible authority is restored, there can be no infallible dogmatic fact ascribed to any claim on the papacy which would bind the conscience of the members to accept that claim. Until that plainly visible unity is restored, there are only uncertain claims of doubtful popes, and no one can be bound by a superior to be subject to a doubtful pope: *Papa dubius, papa nullus.* In such a situation, the only thing that can be certain is the verifiable existence of positive doubt, which all moralists and canonists teach is a just reason to withdraw submission to a papal claimant. This is why I made a reply to Fr. David Hewko, who has characterized my position on the question of whether Francis or Benedict is the true pope without examining my arguments, but simply gratuitously labelled it as "absurd". In my reply I explained my position that a manifest heretic is not a member of the Church, and is therefore an incapable subject of the papacy. Even if a man who was elected pope should later be discovered to have been a heretic at the time of his election, he would not be a valid pope, but would simply need to be removed. That is the ruling of Pope Paul IV, confirmed by Pope St. Pius V. The proposition that a heretic pope would first need to be judged by the Church to lose office is logically incoherent and heretical. Fr. Hewko says, "The Pope is the highest authority on earth and no one can depose him. He must step down by his own volition, as Pope

Benedict did." Fr. Hewko assumes *a priori* that Benedict renounced his *munus*; yet a careful analysis of the act of renunciation proves that he did not unequivocally renounce his claim on the *munus,* as is necessary by law for the act to be valid. Fr. Hewko has failed to explain how we can know that Francis is the pope when there are two claimants to the *munus*, and many Catholics are not certain as to which claimant would possess the supreme authority to judge the question; and after they depart this world, which claimant's successor will possess the authority to judge these matters with finality. When it is said in response by others, "the Church" must judge, is it not understood that the definitive and final judgment can only consist of a judgment ratified by a certain pope, and not a doubtful one? And such a ratification of a judgment of "the Church" cannot be made unless the question would first be resolved? And how would it first be resolved, so that the judgment of "the Church" could be ratified by a certain pope, unless men first arrive at a private judgment through the use of the intellective faculty of judgment to arrive at a reasonable and certain conclusion; so that the private judgment becomes a general consensus, leading to a universal acceptance of one claimant over the other? This is how schisms caused by antipopes were historically resolved: Not by a definitive judgment of "the Church", which is quite impossible while the positive doubt persists over which man is the true pope representing the authority of the Church; but by private judgment which becomes the prevailing general consensus, and finally becomes a universal acceptance of one claimant over the other. Thus, the private judgment of St. Bernard of Clairvaux and Peter the Venerable, gained general ascendency, so that the whole Church eventually accorded universal acceptance and obedience to Innocent II, and abandoned Victor IV, who then submitted to Innocent II. This is how disputed papacies have nearly always been decided, when by means of private judgment a general consensus was reached in favour of one claimant; and the other claimant(s) either submitted to the universally accepted one (as eventually "Victor IV", and later "John XXIII" did); or the rival claimant lost the support of the whole Church, (as did Pedro de Luna, a.k.a. "Benedict XIII", who then lived in isolation in Paniscola, claiming until the bitter end to be the legitimate pope, even after the Council declared him a schismatic and heretic, and elected Pope

Martin V, whose election subsequently received universal acceptance by the whole Church after Benedict's successor, Clement VIII ceded his claim to Martin V). Thus it was not a decreed judgment of Church authority, but a universal consensus of private judgment which eventually accorded to Martin V the universal acceptance, which Bellarmine explains, sufficed to constitute him as the true pope.[305] Therefore, private judgment must come first, because it is by means of private judgment that universal acceptance is reached, which settles the dispute; and then, only afterwards, with the disputed papacy already resolved by general consensus and universal submission to one man, is a papal ratification by a certain pope even possible. St. Alphonsus explains how it works:

> It does not also matter that in the past centuries some pontiff was illegitimately elected, or fraudulently intruded into the pontificate; it is enough that he was accepted by the whole church as pope, since he already was made a legitimate and true pontiff by this acceptance. **But if for some time he had not been truly accepted universally by the church, in that case the papal see would have vacated for that time, as it is vacated during the death of the popes. Thus neither does it matter that in the event of a schism there was a long time in doubt who was the true pontiff; because then one would have been true, though not well known enough; and if none of the antipopes had been true, then the pontificate would finally be vacated.**[306]

---

[305] *De Conciliorum Auctoritate,* cap. xix. p. 71 — «Benedictus autem non cessit, sed post ejus obitum Clemens VIII. successor ipsius cessit Martino V, quem omnis Ecclesia ut verum pontificem, venerabatur, id quod sufficit, ut Martinus esse posset verus papa.»

[306] *Verità Della Fede,* Opera Del Beato Alfonso Maria de' Liguori, Tomo Secondo, Monza, 1823, pp. 156-157 — «Niente ancora importa che ne' secoli passati alcun Pontefice sia stato illegittimamente eletto, o fraudolentemente siasi intruso nel pontificato; basta che poi sia stato accettato da tutta la Chiesa come Papa, attesoché per tale accettazione già si è renduto legittimo e vero Pontefice. Ma se per qualche tempo non fosse stato veramente accettato universalmente dalla Chiesa, in tal caso per quel tempo sarebbe vacata la Sede Pontificia, come vaca nella morte de' Pontefici. Così neppure importa che in caso di scisma siasi stato molto tempo nel dubbio chi fosse il vero Pontefice; perché allora uno sarebbe stato

Thus, the opinion expressed by some, (such as The Catacombs Forum), which asserts the necessity of an authoritative "judgment of the Church" to resolve doubtful claims on the papacy, is quite absurd. Such a judgment of authority, in the absence of the authority of a certain pope, is a judgment that could not be made until a general consensus is first reached by means of private judgment which then becomes universal and thereby settles the doubt by reason of *universal and peaceful acceptance*. Without the doubt first being resolved in this manner, the doubt simply could not ever be resolved, since the judgment made by a doubtful authority would continue *ad infinitum*, unless there would already be a certain pope who can judge the question with authority and finality. It seems not to have occurred to those who posit the need for a judgment of authority to resolve the doubt, that if there exists a positive doubt about the validity of a putative pope's claim on the papacy, that claimant's jurisdiction is itself doubtful; and for so long as the doubt remains, there will be no certain authority on earth competent to rule on the question by an act of authority. Hence, in such cases when there is positive doubt about the validity of a claimant's pontificate, the validity of the claim itself is doubtful, and therefore his jurisdiction is doubtful, and therefore the authority of his doubtful pontificate cannot be presumed valid: *Papa dubius, Papa nullus*. (A doubtful pope is no pope). In such a case when it cannot be determined that there is a certain pope, it is the general consensus of theologians, including St. Alphonsus, Ballerini, Bordoni, Pope Gregory XVI and many others who explain that the Apostolic See would be presumed vacant, and the interim authority would pertain to a Council to elect a pope. In fact, in such a situation, it is thus pronounced in the fourteenth session of the Council of Constance.[307] The indefectibility of the Church guarantees that the

---

il vero, benché non abbastanza conosciuto; e se niuno degli antipapi fosse stato vero, allora il pontificato sarebbe vacato.»

[307] «The most holy general synod of Constance, etc., enacts, pronounces, ordains and decrees, in order that God's holy church may be provided for better, more genuinely and more securely, that the next election of the future Roman pontiff is to be made in the manner, form, place, time and way that shall be decided upon by the sacred council; that the same council can and may henceforth declare fit, accept and designate, in the manner and form that then seems suitable, any persons for the purposes of this election,

Church will never err by universally rejecting the claim of a true pope and uniting to a false head.

In the case of a manifestly pertinacious public heretic, the pertinacity itself is absolutely certain proof that the claimant is not a true pope even if he appears on the surface to have been validly elected and universally accepted. The opinion that such a one could validly occupy an ecclesiastical office directly opposes the Church's teaching on the nature of heresy, as I have amply demonstrated in Volume One. Christ prescribed no directives to be observed in order to deal with a case of papal heresy; neither is there given in scripture or anywhere in apostolic tradition some precept for prosecuting and deposing a suspected pope-heretic who would still validly occupy the papal office, nor is there any law prescribing a procedure for expelling a pope who has fallen from office already by his heresy having ceased by himself to be pope; for which reason it is absolutely certain that divine law makes no allowance for a heretic to ever validly ascend to the throne of Peter, or for a valid pope to fall from the papacy because of heresy.

> 4. XXIII. [...] therefore in no case can the Church have a superior power to that one [to the power of the pope] unless in the case that power is rendered dependent from the Church, and inferior to it, and because it is rendered inferior in that case already that power has been changed and does not remain the same as it was before, if indeed before it was superior to the whole Church and independent from her; but in that case it is made dependent and inferior; therefore never is it verified that the Church has a power over the power of the pope formally, because that it would have a power over that one in some case, that power must be formally different, and not so broad, and supreme as before. Nor from any authority is it verified that Christ the Lord gave in this manner power to the Church over the power of the pope, for the things spoken of in the case of heresy, do not indicate a superiority over the power of the pope formally, but only an avoidance, a separation, and a denying of communion, etc. Nor is there a foundation, that we should

---

whether by active or by passive voice, of whatever state or obedience they are or may have been, and any other ecclesiastical acts and all other suitable things, notwithstanding any proceedings, penalties or sentences; and that the sacred council shall not be dissolved until the said election has been held.» [Tanner Translation]

say Christ the Lord, who without any restriction gave the supreme and independent power to Peter, and to his see, determined that for the case of heresy it would be dependent and inferior to the power of the Church formally, in the nature of power, so that it would remain a subordinate power in respect to the Church, and not superior as before. [...] But when a case of heresy is spoken of superiority is not attributed in respect to the pope, the order is given to avoid, to separate, and not be in communion with the heretic, which does not at all indicate superiority, and without it they can be salvaged; therefore the power of the Church is not superior in respect to the power of the pope even in the case of heresy [...] For the Church can declare the crime of the pontiff, and propose him to the faithful as one to be avoided according to divine law, according to which a heretic is to be avoided. The pontiff to be avoided is necessarily rendered powerless by the force of such a disposition so that as the head of the Church who is a member to be avoided by her, and consequently he cannot have influence over her; therefore by the force of such a power the Church dissolves the conjunction of the pontificate with this person ministerially and dispositively. The consequence is evident, because the agent which can induce a disposition in the subject, to which is connected necessarily the separation of the form and with which the form cannot remain in the subject, having the power over the dissolution of the form, and mediately touches the form itself, so that it is to be separated from the subject, not to be destroyed in itself, as is clear in an agent corrupting a man, for neither does it destroy the form, it induces the dissolution of the form, putting the disposition in the matter with which the form cannot remain. Thus also when the Church can declare a pontiff to be avoided, it can induce a disposition in that person, with whom the pontificate cannot remain, and this it is dissolved ministerially, and dispositively by the Church, authoritatively by Christ, as in designating him by election she disposes him ultimately to receive the conferral of power by Christ the Lord: and ministerially creates the pope. And when Cajetan says the Church can act authoritatively in the conjoining or the separation of the pontificate from the person, ministerially in the pontificate itself it is to be understood in this manner, that the Church has the authority to declare the crime of the pontiff, as it does to designate him to be pope, and what is authoritative in respect to the declaration is dispositive, and ministerial in respect to the form, that it be conjoined or separated, for in the form itself absolutely, and in itself the Church can do nothing, since it is not a power subject to her.[308]

---

[308] «XXIII. ergo in nullo casu potest Ecclesia habere superiorem potestatem ad istam, (i.e. ad potestatem papæ) nisi pro illo casu reddatur illa potestas dependens ab Ecclesia, et inferior ad illam, et quod redditur inferior pro illo casu jam potestas illa mutata est et non manet eadem quæ ante, si quidem ante erat super ad totam Ecclesiam et independens ab illa; pro illo autem casu redditur dependens et inferior; ergo numquam verificatur quod Ecclesia habet potestatem supra potestatem papæ formaliter, quia ut habeat potestatem supra illam pro aliquo casu, debet illa potestas esse formaliter alia, et non ita ampla, et suprema sicut ante. Neque ex aliqua auctoritate constat Christum Dominum dedisse hoc modo potestatem Ecclesiæ supra potestatem papæ, ea enim quæ in casu hæresis loquuntur, non indicat superioritatem supra potestatem papæ formaliter, sed solum evitationem, separationem, negationem communicationis, etc. Quæ salvari potest sine potestate superiori formaliter supra potestatem papæ. Nec est fundaentum, ut dicamus Christum Dominum, qui sine ulla restrictione dedit supremam, et independentem potestatem Petro, ejusque sedi, determinasse, ut pro casu hæresis esset dependens et inferior ad potestatem Ecclesiæ formaliter in ratione potestatis, ita quod maneret subordinata potestas respectu Ecclesiæ, et non superior sicut ante. [...] Quando autem loquitur in casu hæresis non superioritatem attribuit respectu papæ, sed solum præcipit evitari, separari, et non communicare hæretico, quæ omnia superioritatem non indicant, et sine illa salvari possunt; ergo potestas Ecclesiæ non est superior respectu potestatis papæ etiam in casu hæresis. [...] XXIV. ... Nam Ecclesia potest declarare crimen pontificis, et ipsum ut evitandum proponere fidelibus secundum jus divinum, quo hæreticus evitandus est. Pontifex autem evitans ex vi talis dispositionis necessario redditur impotens, ut sicut caput Ecclesiæ, quia est membrum evitandum ab illa, et consequenter non potest in illam influere; ergo ex vi talis potestatis Ecclesia dissolvit conjunctionem pontificatus cum ista persona ministerialiter et dispositive. Patet consequentia, quia agens quod potest inducere dispositionem in subjecto, cui necessario annexa est separatio formæ et cum qua forma stare non potest in subjecto, potest supra dissolutionem formæ, et mediate tangit ipsam formam, ut separandam a subjecto, non ut in se destruendam, sicut patet in agente corrumpente hominem, nec enim formam destruit, dissolutionem formæ inducit, ponendo dispositionem in materia, cum qua forma non potest stare. Sic ergo cum Ecclesia potest ut evitandum pontificem declarare, potest inducere dispisitionem in illa persona, cum qua pontificatus stare non potest, et sic dissolvitur ministerialiter, et dispositive ab Ecclesia, auctoritative autem a Christo, sicut designando ipsum per electionem

Sed contra — The propositions, some considered singly and all of them together as a complete doctrine are entirely heretical: The propositions directly contradict and negate the *total fullness of supreme power of the Primacy*, which is a *"full and supreme power"* (*Pastor Æternus*), and therefore a *"full and absolute jurisdiction"* (*Vacantis Apostolicæ Sedis*). The Church has no power whatsoever — neither authoritative nor ministerial, to act dispositively or ministerially, as a formal or instrumental cause, directly or indirectly, on or against the holder of the *full and absolute power of the Primacy*, since if it did, that power of the primacy would not consist of a *total fullness*, and the jurisdiction would not be *full and absolute* — and that being the case, the primacy would no longer be the primacy.

Taken as a whole, the doctrine is heretical, but I here point out the most blatantly heretical passages in the text:

> 1. «in no case can the Church have a superior power to that one [to the power of the pope] **unless in the case that power is rendered dependent from the Church, and inferior to it, and because it is rendered inferior in that case already that power has been changed and does not remain the same as it was before, if indeed before it was superior to the whole Church and independent from her; but in that case it is made dependent and inferior... that power must be formally different, and not so broad, and supreme as before.**»

The proposition that the pope's **supreme** and **absolute** power can be altered in such a manner that it would become dependent and inferior in any respect whatsoever to the power of the rest of the Church directly denies the dogma of the primacy in that Vatican I solemnly defined the power of the primacy as **full, total, and supreme**, and therefore not subject to diminution or alteration of any

---

disponit ipsum ultimate, ut recipiat collationem potestatis a Christo Domino: et ministerialiter creat papam. Et quando dicit Cajetanus Ecclesiam posse auctoritative in conjunctionem, vel seprarationem pontificatus a persona, ministerialiter vero in ipsum pontificatum intellegendus est hoc modo, quod Ecclesia habet auctoritatem declarandi crimen papæ, sicut et designandi ipsum in papam, et quod auctoritativum est respectu declarationis est dispisitivum, et ministeriale respectu formæ, ut conjungendæ vel separandæ, nam in ipsam formam absolute, et in se nihil potest Ecclesia, cum non sit ei subordinata potestas.»

kind or in any degree. The **PRIMACY**, according to the solemn dogmatic definition, **is the full and supreme apostolic authority of the Roman Pontiff over the whole Church which consists in the *total*, *full* and *supreme power of jurisdiction* over every diocese, pastor and every individual member of the Church.** The proposition that the power of the primacy can be altered or mutated is absurd and heretical on its face, in view of the power of the primacy being solemnly defined as *total*, *full*, and *supreme*, and therefore in its very nature and in every respect is a superior power to every other ecclesiastical power. Indeed, who would have the authority to judge whether the primacy has been altered or not — the supreme and infallible judge, or his inferiors whose jurisdiction is hierarchically subordinate to his own? If it is judged by the council that the primacy has been altered and rendered dependent on its own power, how would the council explain that the solemn and definitive judgment of the pope in a matter of faith would not be infallible, and would be of less authority than their own fallible judgment? Since a validly reigning pope, whether he can be a heretic or not, cannot err in his definitions in matters of faith,[309] how can it be asserted that when the council fallibly judges the pope to be a heretic on some point of doctrine, that the pope, cannot exercise his prerogative as supreme judge to infallibly determine with irreformable finality the judgment of the Church on that point of doctrine? How can it be asserted that the council's fallible judgment can pre-empt the infallible authority of the supreme and final arbiter of all disputes in matters of faith? How can the council forbid the pope to judge infallibly? Will the council then declare the pope's solemn judgment to be heresy, and that the fallible judgment of the council is to be preferred? And if it is claimed that the pope's primacy has been altered by his heresy, so that being inferior, his definitions would no longer be infallible, then the Church would have erred in defining solemnly that whenever the pope

---

[309] Bellarminus, *De Rom. Pont. lib. iv cap. ii* — «Quarta sententia est quodammodo in medio. Pontificem, sive hæreticus esse possit, sive non, non posse ullo modo definire aliquid hæreticum a tota Ecclesia credendum: hæc est comunissima opinio fere omnium Catholicorum» This is the "fourth opinion" of Bellarmine solemnly dogmatized in 1870.

defines on matters of faith and morals, his judgments are infallible.[310] Thus it is plainly seen, that the thesis of John of St. Thomas which asserts that the primacy is altered by heresy, thereby rendering the pope inferior to the council and subject to its judgment is heretical.

It is manifestly evident that if the primacy could undergo any mutation or alteration, what would remain would not be the Roman Primacy, but something else which could not serve the purpose for which the Primacy was instituted by Christ, namely, **the unity of the Church**. The primacy therefore, being absolutely supreme and infallible in its nature, and uniquely ordered to the unity of the Church, is essentially a *different* power from that which is common to all bishops, and which is totally immune from any exercise of episcopal power which is absolutely subordinate to the primacy. It is different in its nature ultimately because of the different end, to wit, the **unity of the Church**, to which it is ordered. If the power of the primacy could be altered by its holder in such a manner that it could be rendered inferior to, and dependent in any manner on a subordinate power, then the unity of the Church could not be preserved; because the power of the primacy being absolutely supreme is the sole absolute principle of unity of faith and discipline for the whole Church. It is precisely for the reason that the subordinate power of the bishops not being supreme, would be incapable of maintaining the unity of the Church, that Christ instituted the papacy with its full and supreme power, which because of its absolute supremacy is an essentially different power, distinct and singular, which no subordinate power could touch in any way whatever without destroying it as the principle of unity, and thus destroying the primacy itself; since, at the very instant when the pope's supreme power would be mutated and thereby rendered

---

[310] *Pastor Æternus*. Caput IV — «docemus et divinitus revelatum dogma esse definimus: Romanum Pontificem, cum ex Cathedra loquitur, id est, cum omnium Christianorum Pastoris et Doctoris munere fungens, pro suprema sua Apostolica auctoritate doctrinam de fide vel moribus ab universa Ecclesia tenendam definit, per assistentiam divinam, ipsi in beato Petro promissam, ea infallibilitate pollere, qua divinus Redemptor Ecclesiam suam in definienda doctrina de fide vel moribus instructam esse voluit; ideoque eiusmodi Romani Pontificis definitiones ex sese, non autem ex consensu Ecclesiae irreformabiles esse.»

dependent and inferior; that *fullness of power*, in which the primacy essentially consists, would no longer exist in the pope as a supreme power, so that it could then no longer be said that the pope possesses a full and supreme jurisdiction — which is to say, that the pope would already be deprived of his jurisdiction and have already ceased to be pope.

Thus the coercive power of the pope, existing to constrain the members within the bonds of communion is **total, supreme, and unique to his office**; and therefore **absolute and unlimited in such a manner that it is *incapable of becoming dependent on the bishops who do not have that singular munus of preserving the unity of the whole Church pertaining to their office***. Furthermore, since the authority of the primacy infallibly binds the members of the universal Church absolutely to be in communion with the pontiff in the unity of faith, a heretic would be incapable of assuming this *munus* because heresy is directly opposed to the unity of faith — i.e. heresy directly opposes the principle bond of unity, which is faith. The members most certainly cannot be bound to communion with a heretic, because divine law binds them to shun the heretic; but if the pope were a heretic, the members would be bound to remain in communion with him because of his superior authority. It is evidently for this reason that Bellarmine, speaking of the form of the pontificate which is visible in the orthodox profession of faith, taught that a pope who falls into manifest heresy, by visibly professing against the faith, would visibly lose the necessary disposition to conserve in himself the form of the pontificate; and therefore, he would "cease by himself to be pope" entirely by himself, "without any external agent", acting as a dispositive cause provoking the disjunction of the form.[311]

Ballerini elaborates on this point of the essential difference between the common apostolic power of the bishops and that which distinguishes it from the nature of the unique, supreme, and total coercive power of the papal primacy to bring about and enforce ecclesial unity which Christ directly confers on the pope:

---

[311] *De Rom. Pont. Lib. ii cap. xxx* — «*Deinde*, quae habent ultimam dispositionem ad interitum, paulo post desinit esse, sine alia vi externa, ut patet; igitur et Papa haereticus sine alia depositione *per se* desinit esse Papa.»

The difference of power between Peter and the apostles, and also between the Roman Pontiffs, the successors of St. Peter and the other Bishops, the successors of the Apostles is of the maximum importance to be noted. St. Peter and all the other Apostles were equal in power except for only **the proper and personal right of the primacy.** [...] From this, **primacy of special jurisdiction,** which Christ gave to Peter alone among the Apostles, **to him some special corresponding right had to coincide, which was not to be had in common with the others**: otherwise, the primacy itself would have been an empty title of honour, not of right. Furthermore **this right of the primacy properly is gathered from the end for which the primacy itself was instituted** (See De vi ac ratione primatus c. 8 & 9.) which since it was instituted by Christ for forming and perpetually guarding unity in the whole Church, **the particular right to bind together and guard the unity of the Church to have been conferred on St. Peter, by which all Christians are compelled to unity is to be asserted.**[312]

And he elaborates further:

But this proper power to bind together and guard Catholic unity cannot be a mere faculty of representing unity, but of a proper coercive power of proper jurisdiction for forming and containing it is demanded. [...] For if one head was necessary to impede schisms and preserve the unity of the Church, and with that plan in mind Peter was constituted

---

[312] *De Potestate Ecclesiastica*, Caput I § III. p. 12 — «Discrimen potestatis inter Petrum & Apostolos, nec non inter Romanos Pontifices S. Petri successores & alios Episcopos successores Apostolorum notandum maxime est. S. Petrum & Apostolos omnes potestate pares fuisse excepto tantum jure proprio ac personali primatus, qui fuit non meri honoris & ordinis, fed præcipuæ jurisdictionis primatus, exploratum fecimus ex iis, quæ annuentibus quoque adversariis catholicis probavimus libro *De vi ac ratione primatus c.* 2. & 3. Ex hoc autem præcipuae jurisdictionis primatu, quem uni Petro inter Apostolos Christus tribuit, jus aliquod peculiare ipsi debuit competere, quod aliis commune nom fuerit: alias primatus ipsius inane nomen fuisset meri honoris, non juris. Hoc porro jus primatus proprium ex fine instituendi ipsius primatus est colligendum (Vid. lib. De vi ac ratione primatus c. 8 et 9.) qui cum ob formandam & perpetuo custodiendam in tota Ecclesia unitatem fuerit institutus a Christo, jus ad hanc totius Ecclesiæ unitatem compingendam atque tuendam præcipuum S. Petro collatum fuisse dicendum est, quo omnes Christiani ad unitatem cogantur.»

the head of the Church, so as to guard and defend that unity [...] it is beyond doubt that he had to receive a power to compel to unity: for if the primacy were constituted of only a representation of unity without a coercive right, a primacy of mere order and honour would result, which no Catholic admits.[313]

St Alphonsus elaborates this same point thusly:

It is the nature of unity that there is to be one Church from which all other churches depend on doctrine, so that one faith will be preserved in all of them. This one Church, from which arises ecclesiastical unity, of course is the Roman Church, as St. Cyprian writes: *To the cathedra of Peter, and to the* PRINCIPAL *Church, from where priestly unity has originated. Epist.* 4. Whence St. Irenæus, speaking of the same Roman Church, says, *With this Church, because of its greater* PRINCIPALITY, *every church must agree, that is those who are the faithful everywhere. Lib.* 3. *adv. hær. cap.* 3. *n.* 2. [...] For which reason the Roman Church is called the *centre of unity*. What does the *centre of unity* mean? It means that just as all the lines at the circumference are united at the centre, so in the judgment of the Roman Church all churches are united and come to rest [...] Therefore, for the preservation of the unity of doctrine and faith in the whole Church, the Lord constituted the one Roman Pontiff the *head of truth* (according to St. Cyprian), so that he rule the whole Church, and all the faithful and bishops depend on him, and come to rest in his judgments. [...] But Febronius insists: St. Cyprian says: *The one Episcopate, whose part is held in solidity by the single bishops*. What, he says, does that, '*is held in solidity*' mean, but that the single bishops have charge over the whole episcopate? This is how Febronius understands that text; but Cardinal Bellarmine and Fr.

---

[313] *De vi ac ratione primatus*, CAPUT IX p. 41 — «Hæc autem idonea unitatis catholicæ compingendæ atque custodiendæ potestas, non meram unitatis repraesentandæ facultatem, sed ejus formandæ & continendæ vim plane coactivam, jurisdictionis propriam efflagitat. [...] Si enim unum caput ad schismata impedienda unitatemque Ecclesiae servandam necessarium fuit, & eo quidem consilio Petrus a Christo caput Ecclesiæ constitutus est, ut unitatem eamdem custodiret & vindicaret, [...] vim proculdubio cogendi ad unitatem obtinere debuit: sola et enim unitatis figura atque repræsentatione schismata tolli vel impediri non possunt. Præterquam quod si sola unitatis repræsentatio absque coactivo jure Petri primatum constitueret; primatus meri ordinis & honoris inde oriretur, quem nemo catholicorum admittit.»

Mamachius do not understand it that way, and others commonly, indeed not even Fr. Natalis Alexander, *historia eccl. diss.* 4. *sec.* 1. §. 3. *object.* 7. Cyprian said *is held solid,* but he did not say by the single bishops equally *is held in solidity.* There the Holy Doctor did not mean to say anything other than that all the bishops make up one body, by which the whole Church is ruled; so that all rule the integral episcopate, but each one in his portion; for if St. Cyprian thought each bishop has charge of the whole Church, he would certainly have said: *The one Episcopate, which is all by the single bishops held in solidity:* but he said, *whose part is held solid by the single bishops.* All therefore hold the one episcopate in solidity, but each one rules it in his own portion; and all depend on one head, just as all the rays flow from the one sun, so that thus the unity of the Church and the faith will be preserved. [314]

---

[314] Alfonso Maria de' Liguori, *Vindiciae pro suprema pontificis potestate adversus Iustinum Febronium,* Torino, 1832, Cap. VII p. 110 - 112 — «Natura unitatis est, quod una adsit ecclesia, a qua omnes aliæ ecclesiæ circa doctrinam fidei pendere debeant, ut sic una fides in omnibus perpetuo servetur. Hæc una ecclesia, ex qua oritur unitas ecclesiastica, utique est romana, ut scribit s. Cyprianus: *Ad Petri cathedram, atque ad ecclesiam* PRINCIPALEM, *unde unitas sacerdotalis eaeorta est. Epist.* 4. Unde s. Irenæus, de eadem romana ecclesia loquens, dixit: *Ad hanc enim eccle siam, propter potentiorem* (legunt alii potiorem) PRINCIPALITATEM, *necesse est omnem con venire ecclesiam, hoc est eos, qui sunt undique fideles. Lib.* 3. *adv. hær. cap.* 3. *n.* 2. Quapropter ecclesia romana vocatur *centrum unitatis* Quid significat *centrum unitatis?* Significat, quod sicut omnes circumferentiæ lineæ in centro uniuntur, sic in judicio ecclesiæ romanæ omnes ecclesiæ uniuntur et quiescunt. [...] Ad unitatem igitur doctrinæ et fidei in tota ecclesia servandam, unum romanum pontificem *veritatis caput* (juxta s. Cyprianum) Dominus constituit, ut ipse universam regat ecclesiam, omnesque fideles, et episcopi ab ipso pendeant, ac in ejus judiciis quiescant. [...] Sed instat Febronius: s. Cyprianus ait: *Episcopatus unus, cujus a singulis in solidum pars tenetur.* Quid denotat, inquit, illud *in solidum tenetur,* nisi quod singuli totius episcopatus ecclesiæ curam habent? Sic intelligit Febronius textum illum; sed non sic intelligunt card. Bellarminus, p. Mamachius, et alii communiter, imo nec etiam p. Natalis Alexander, *historia eccl. diss.* 4. *sec.* 1. §. 3. *object.* 7. Dixit s. Cyprianus *in solidum teneri,* sed non dixit a singulis *in solidum teneri* æqualiter. S. Doctor ibi non aliud dicere voluit, quam omnes episcopos unum componere corpus, quo universa regitur ecclesia; ita ut omnes integrum episcopatum regunt, sed unusquisque pro sua parte; si enim s. Cyprianus sentiret quemque episcopum totius ecclesiæ curam habere, utique dixisset: *Episcopatus unus, qui totus a singulis in solidum tenetur:* sed dixit, *cujus a*

The reason why the Roman Pontiff is the *centre of unity*, St. Alphonsus explains, is because Peter is the rock upon which the Church was founded,[315] and therefore the head of the Church which cannot fail:

> Since therefore Peter is the rock, or is the foundation of the Church, he cannot fail; otherwise, if the foundation could fail, one day also the Church could fail; but this is impossible, for the promise already made in the same place: *Et portæ inferi non prævalebunt adversus eam*. And if Peter cannot fail, neither can his successors Pontiffs; since Jesus Christ having promised that hell will never prevail against the Church, the promise must necessarily be understood as made for always, as long as the Church lasts. Nor is it worth anything to say that the promise was not made directly to Peter, but to the Church, while it was made to Peter as representative of the Church. But if the Church is meant by rock, then must we say that the Church is the foundation of the Church? Or that there are two churches, one of which is the foundation, and the other is the building? The truth is that Peter was constituted by the Lord as the foundation of the Church for the good of the same, hence Peter was given to be *Saxum inmobile molem continens*, as wrote. S Augustine (*Serm. De Cath.*): Unmovable stone, not subject to wavering; for, as well warns Origen (*in Matth.* 16.): *Si prævalerent* (portæ inferi) *adversus petram, in qua fundata Ecclesia erat, contra Ecclesiam etiam prævalerent.* [If the gates of hell would prevail against the rock, on which the Church was founded, they would also prevail against the Church.] So that the firmness of foundation was directly given to Peter and indirectly to the Church, since it is true that the foundation supports the house, not the house that supports the foundation.[316]

---

singulis in solidum pars tenetur. Omnes igitur tenent unum episcopatum in solidum, sed unusquisque illum pro sua portione regit; et omnes ab uno capite pendent, sicut omnes radii ab uno sole manant, ut sic ecclesiæ et fidei unitas servetur.»

[315] Alfonso Maria de' Liguori, *Vindiciae pro suprema pontificis potestate adversus Iustinum Febronium*, Torino, 1832, p. 22 — «S. Hilarius: *O in nuncupatione novi nominis felix ecclesiæ fundamentum! O beatus cæli janitor!* S. Ambrosius; *Petra enim dicitur, quod primus in actionibus fidei fundamenta posuerit, et saxum immobile totius operis christiani molem contineat.* Serm. 47.»

[316] Alfonso Maria de' Liguori, *Verità Della Fede*, Tomo Secondo, Monza, 1823, pp. 161-163 — «Giacché dunque Pietro è la pietra, o sia il fondamento della Chiesa, egli non può mancare; altrimenti, se potesse mancare il

Thus, St. Alphonsus stated in the above cited passage, that because Christ founded the Church on Peter, who as the rock, neither he nor his successors can fail in defining and judging in matters of faith, He therefore entrusted to Peter alone the *power of the keys*: "We have already said above, the apostles received immediately from Christ a power indeed equal and which Peter received, as the first founders of the Gospel; but all of them were subject to Peter as the head, and chief, as all the Fathers proclaim."

Pope Pius VI taught that the doctrine of the singular, supreme and unique personal power of the pope given by Christ to him alone to safeguard the unity of the Church has always been a perpetual dogma of the universal magisterium of the Church:

> That the Church was founded by Christ on the solidity of the rock, and that by **the singular gift of Christ**, Peter was chosen to be Prince of the Apostolic Choir in preference to all the others with **the power to take his place**, and that as a consequence he took charge and **the supreme authority** to feed the whole flock, to confirm the brothers and **to dissolve and bind throughout the world, is a Catholic dogma which, received from the mouth of Christ, taught and defended with continuous preaching of the Fathers, has been held most holy**

---

fondamento, potrebbe un giorno, mancare anche la Chiesa; ma ciò è impossibile, per la promessa già fatta nello stesso luogo: *Et portæ inferi non prævalebunt adversus eam*. E se Pietro non può mancare, né anche possono mancare i Pontefici suoi successori; poiché avendo promesso Gesù Cristo che contro la Chiesa non prevarrà mai l'inferno, la promessa dee necessariamente intendersi fatta per sempre, finché durerà la Chiesa. Ne vale dire che la promessa non fu fatta direttamente a Pietro, ma alla Chiesa, mentre fu fatta a Pietro come rappresentante la Chiesa. Ma se per la pietra si dee intender la Chiesa, dunque dobbiam dire che la Chiesa è il fondamento della Chiesa? O che vi sono due Chiese, di cui una è il fondamento, e l'altra è l'edificio? La verità si è che Pietro fu costituito dal Signore fondamento della Chiesa per bene della medesima, onde a Pietro fu dato l'esser *Saxum inmobile molem continens,* come scrisse S. Agostino (Serm. de Cath.): pietra immobile, non soggetta a vacillare; poiché, come bene avverti Origene (*in Matth*. 16.): *Si prævalerent* (portæ inferi) *adversus petram, in qua fundata Ecclesia erat, contra Ecclesiam etiam prævalerent*. Sicchè la fermezza di fondamento direttamente fu data a Pietro e indirettamente alla Chiesa, essendo vero che il fondamento sostiene la casa, non la casa sostiene il fondamento.»

in every age by the universal Church, and often confirmed against the errors of the innovators with the decrees of the Supreme Pontiffs and the Councils.[317]

Considering the primacy as it is defined and is constituted in its nature, it is seen that the proposition which says that the pope's personal power of primacy, which is a full and supreme jurisdiction conferred upon him directly by God, can be altered by heresy in such a manner that this total fullness of supreme power is mutated and made in some manner inferior and subject to the dispositive action of the bishops exercising their merely episcopal power, so that the bishops united together in an ecumenical council could exercise a ministerial power and dispositively bring about the removal of the pope's absolute jurisdiction over them, is *heresy*. It pertains essentially to the nature of the primacy that it is *inseparable from the person of the pope*, and therefore, *only if the pope would first separate himself from the papacy would the primatial power of absolute jurisdiction cease to be operative in him*. Accordingly Pope Gregory XVI explains, «*Now the point of the question is not, whether the Church can take away from one the dignity and pontifical authority, but **whether in the primacy her representation is essentially included**; which can never be denied, when it is not shown before, that the Church has at some time suspended in the real and subsisting Pope the exercise of his primatial rights, and therefore also that of representing her; and that in spite of this he has enjoyed an active, functioning and effective primacy, with the essential right to make his authority felt.*»[318] On this

---

[317] Pius pp. VI. *Super soliditate*, Dat. Romæ 28. novembris 1786. Anno XII. — «Super soliditate petrae fundatam a Christo Ecclesiam, Petrumque singulari Christi munere prae caeteris electum, qui vicaria potestate apostolici chori princeps existeret, totiusque adeo gregis pascendi, fratres confirmandi, totoque orbe ligandi, ac solvendi summam curam, auctoritatemque in successores omni aevo prorogandam susciperet: dogma catholicum est, quod ore Christi acceptum, perenni patrum praedicatione traditum, ac defensum, Ecclesia universa omni aetate sanctissime retinuit, saepiusque adversus novatorum errores summorum pontificum, conciliorumque decretis confirmavit.»

[318] Gregory XVI, *Op. cit.* p. 270 — «Ora il punto della questione non è, se possa la Chiesa togliere ad uno la dignità ed autorità pontificia, ma se nel primato essenzialmente comprendasi la di lei rappresentanza; il che non si potrà giammai negare, quando prima non si dimostri, che abbia talvolta la

unshakable basis he concludes that «*we can always conclude that the current representation of the Church is inseparable from the pontifical primacy.*»[319] **The pope can separate himself from the papacy, but the absolute power of the primacy cannot be separated dispositively from the pope by the external agency of the bishops.**

> 2. «Nor from any authority is it verified that Christ the Lord gave in this manner power to the Church over the power of the pope, **for the things spoken of in the case of heresy, do not indicate a superiority over the power of the pope formally, but only an avoidance, a separation, and a denying of communion,** etc. ... For **the Church can declare the crime of the pontiff, and propose him to the faithful as one to be avoided** according to divine law, according to which a heretic is to be avoided.»

The issuance of a **juridical declaration of heresy by a council** against the pope that would **bind the whole Church**, and **an order of a council that would coercively bind the whole Church by decreeing that the pope be avoided, separated and denied communion**, being manifestly **contrary and directly opposed to the nature of the primacy** in view of it being a council's attempt to appropriate to itself and exercise the right of the primacy, and to impede its exercise by the pope, constitutes a clear usurpation of the **full and supreme power of jurisdiction over the whole Church** which the pope by divine right can always freely exercise for so long as he is validly constituted as the successor of Peter. The **declaration of the crime of heresy could only be made in hierarchical subordination to the pope's *full and supreme jurisdiction*.** By his full and supreme power of jurisdiction, the pope can nullify any declaration whatsoever issued by his subordinates and decree his own judgment. Therefore, **any council which would presume to subject the pope to a judgment on matters of faith or morals,**

Chiesa sospeso nel vero e sussistente Papa l'esercizio de' suoi primaziali diritti, e perciò di quello pure di rappresentarla; e che ciò non ostante abbia egli goduto di una primazia attiva, operosa, ed efficace, col diritto essenziale di farne sentire l'autorità.»

[319] *Ibid.* — «Finché adunque gli avversarii non ci adducano argomenti più convincenti, potremo sempre concludere, che l'attuale rappresentanza della Chiesa è inseparabile dal pontificio primato.»

thereby denying his right to determine with finality all judgments of the Church in matters of faith with an exercise of his primacy, would be guilty of schismatically refusing to be subject to the Roman Pontiff. Similarly, the act of a council to order that the Supreme Pontiff be avoided by the faithful and separated from the Church is directly opposed to the unity of the Church, and is totally schismatic in its nature.

3. «by the force of such a power the Church dissolves the conjunction of the pontificate with this person ministerially and dispositively.»

The nature of ecclesiastical power is such that the Church has absolutely no power whatsoever over the conjunction of the pontificate with the person of the pope, neither formally nor ministerially and dispositively. The pope, *according to the nature of the primacy*, possesses an **absolute power of jurisdiction over the whole Church and over the conjunction which joins him to the pontificate. The conjunction is dissolved only by death or abdication. It pertains to the pope's supreme authority to judge all questions of heresy WITH FINALITY. Therefore, by declaring an indubitable and actually reigning pope a heretic, a council usurps a power which it does not possess, because the power to judge with finality pertains exclusively to the supreme jurisdiction of the pontiff. The usurpatory exercise of such a non-existent power is utterly incapable of introducing a disposition into the matter that would dissolve the conjunction which joins the pope to the papacy. Such an act which attempts directly against the power of the primacy constitutes the crime of schism in its purest form and severs from the body of the Church all those who would presume to judge the pope and attempt to deprive him of the pontificate which no one on earth can cause to be removed from him, whether directly or indirectly, mediately or immediately; formally, ministerially, or dispositively.**

4. XIX. It is responded that this council can be brought together by the authority of the Church which is in the bishops themselves or the greater part of them; the Church has the right to segregate herself from

a heretic pope by divine law, and consequently to apply all means necessary *per se* for such a segregation; now a means necessary and *per se* is to juridically verify such a crime; but there cannot be a judgment in a matter so grave, except by a general Council, because it treats of the universal head of the Church, wherefore this pertains to the judgment of the universal Church, which is a general Council [...] For which reason the pontiff cannot annul or reject such a Council, because he is a party*, and the Church has from divine law that it can convene to this end, because she has the right to segregate herself from the heretic.320

[*A persons who is directly involved or interested in a legal proceeding involving opposing parties.]

5. But that we not speak of the authority itself in whose power the judgment is to be made, but of the convocation of the Council, by whom it is to be made, I consider it not to be committed to someone determinate; but this can be done either by the cardinals, who can relay this information to the bishops, or it can be passed on to the others by the neighbouring bishops, that they all convene; or it can be done even at the urging of the princes, not indeed so much as a coercive convocation, just as when a pontiff convokes a Council, but by a denunciative convocation, that denounces such a crime to the bishops, and manifests that they should assist.321

---

320 «XIX. Respondetur, quod illud Concilium congregari potest auctoritate Ecclesiæ, quæ est in ipsis episcopis, vel majore eorum parte; habet enim jus Ecclesia ad segregandum se a papa hæretico ex jure divino, et consequenter ad adhibendum omnia media ad talem segregationem per se necessaria; medium autem necessarium, et per se est ut juridice constet tale crimen; non potest autem in re tam gravi competens esse judicium, nisi per Concilium generale, quia tractatur de universali capite Ecclesiæ, unde pertinet hoc ad judicium universalis Ecclesiæ, quod est Concilium generale. [...] Quare pontifex non potest tale Concilium annulare, aut recusare, quia ipse est pars, et Ecclesia habet ex jure divino posse illud congregare ad hunc finem, quia habet jus ut segreget se ab hæretico.» [p. 259]

321 «XIX. ... Quod si non de ipsa auctoritate loquamur in cujus virtute judicandum est, sed de convocatione Concilii, a quo sit facienda, existimo id non esse alicui determinate commissum, sed posse hoc fieri vel a cardinalibus, qui hanc notitiam ad episcopos derivare possunt, vel a propinquioribus episcopis id posse denuntiari aliis, ut omnes conveniant; vel etiam ad instantiam principum id fieri posse, non quidem quantum ad convocationem coactivam, sicut quando pontifex convocat ad Concilium, sed convocatione denuntiativa, qui tale crimen episcopis denuntiatur, et manifestatur ut illi sucurrant.» [p. 259]

COMMENTARY ON TEXT

1. «[T]his council can be brought together by the authority of the Church which is in the bishops themselves or the greater part of them» — *sententia hæretica*

The proposition directly opposes the full and absolute power of jurisdiction of the pope over the whole Church. It is *de fide* that the summoning of a council is the exclusive right of the holder of the Petrine Primacy. That an authority of the Church to convoke a council against a certainly valid pope simply does not exist has been already proven, but there exists in the Church only the power to convene in a council to judge the question of a doubtful pope or popes when the see is presumed vacant. It was also the opinion of Febronius that the bishops have the power to convoke a council without the pope's authorization, to which St. Alphonsus replied: "But Pius II in his constitution, *In minoribus*, attests: *We have not found* (a council) *to have been ratified, which while there being an indubitable Roman bishop, that was convened without his authority.* Who is to be believed, the pontiff or Febronius."[322] Indeed, who is to be believed, John of St. Thomas and Cajetan, or the Popes and Doctors of the Church? Against the opinion that a pope can ever be bound to the decision of a council, St. Alphonsus in *cap. vii* of the same work says, "Indeed not at all, as the same [Pope] St. Gregory declared; for in cases of faith he said the pope is the supreme and infallible judge, who must determine them, with these words: *If it should happen that there arise a dispute in a case of faith, it is to be endeavoured that it be brought to our examination, insofar as by us it is to be brought to an end with a suitable judgment. Lib. 7. epist. 2.*"[323] Indeed, the sheer number

---

[322] Alfonso Maria de' Liguori, *Vindiciae pro suprema pontificis potestate adversus Iustinum Febronium*, Torino, 1832, Cap. IX p. 143 — «Sed Pius II. in sua constitut., *In minoribus*, testatur: *Nullum invenimus* (concilium) *fuisse ratum, quod, stante romano indubitato præsule, absque ipsius auctoritate convenerit.* Cuinam credendum: pontifici, an Febronio?»

[323] Alfonso Maria de' Liguori, *Vindiciae pro suprema pontificis potestate adversus Iustinum Febronium*, Torino, 1832, Cap. VIII. p. 137 — «Minime quidem, ut idem s. Gregorius declaravit; nam in fidei causis dixit, papam esse judicem supremum, et infallibilem, qui eas determinare debet, his verbis: *Siquam contentionem de fidei causa evenire contigerit, ad nostram studeat*

of citations of popes and Fathers enumerated by Bellarmine and de' Liguori to support this teaching is staggering. So, whether you believe like Febronius,[324] who held that the convocation of councils does not at all pertain to the pope,[325] or if you believe like Cajetan and John of St Thomas, that it pertains to the authority of the bishops to convene in a council against a validly reigning pope in a dispute in a matter of faith, you are a heretic either way — because it is solemnly defined that it pertains exclusively to the papal authority to settle disputes in matters of faith with finality; and it is solemnly taught by the supreme magisterium that episcopal authority, according to its very nature, is hierarchically subordinate to the primacy of the pope; whose jurisdiction is defined to be full and supreme; and his power, total and absolute; so that the primacy cannot be subject to mutation or alteration in such a manner as John of St. Thomas asserts, that having been so altered, "*that power must be formally different, and not so broad, and supreme as before,*" without that same primacy thereby ceasing to exist. Hence, as St. Alphonsus says in the cited passage, expressing the same judgment on this point as Bellarmine, Ballerini, Innocent III, and Gregory XVI: "If ever a pope as a private person would fall into heresy, then he would immediately fall from the papacy; for since he would be outside the Church, he could no longer be the head of the Church. Whence in that case the Church would have to not in fact depose him, because no one has power over the pope, but declare him to have fallen from the pontificate."

> 2. «[N]ow a means necessary and *per se* is to juridically verify such a crime; but there cannot be a judgment in a matter so grave, except by a general Council, because it treating of the universal head of the Church,

---

perducere notionem, quatenus a nobis valeat congrua sine dubio sententia terminari. Lib. 7. epist. 2.»

[324] "**Johann Nikolaus von Hontheim**, pseudonym Justinus Febronius, (born Jan. 27, 1701, Trier [Germany]—died Sept. 2, 1790, Montequentin, Luxembourg), historian and theologian who founded Febronianism, the German form of Gallicanism, which advocated the restriction of papal power." [*Encyclopædia Britannica*]

[325] *Ibid.* Cap. IX p. 143 — «Febronius asserit primo, quod convocatio conciliorum minime ad papam pertinet.»

wherefore this pertains to the judgment of the universal Church, which is a general Council» - *sententia hæretica*

The proposition directly opposes the very letter of the dogma of the full and supreme power of jurisdiction of the pope over a general council.

    3. «But that we not speak of the authority itself in whose power the judgment is to be made, but of the convocation of the Council, by whom it is to be made... either by the cardinals... by the neighbouring bishops, that they all convene... it can be done even at the urging of the princes, not indeed so much as a coercive convocation, just as when a pontiff convokes a Council, but by a denunciative convocation, that denounces such a crime to the bishops, and manifests that they should assist... this pertains to the judgment of the universal Church, which is a general Council [...] For which reason the pontiff cannot annul or reject such a Council, because he is a party, and the Church has from divine law that it can convene to this end, because she has the right to segregate herself from the heretic.» — *sententia hæretica*

So, the summons would have authority but no coercive force on the bishops (!), but its non-coercive force would be of an authority that binds the pope! What might be the nature of such an authority that has not the power to bind anyone except the pope? Since without the pope convoking the council, it is for good reason that neither John of St. Thomas nor anyone else has ever been able to provide a cogent argument demonstrating by whose authority such a council would be convoked, because no such authority exists, other than the PRIMACY. Without a single and indisputable coercive authority absolutely binding in conscience on the totality of bishops, such as that which exists only in the Primacy, there would be no power sufficient to convene a council and maintain it in ecclesial unity. There would be nothing to prevent the bishops from convoking multiple councils, nor to prevent a council from breaking up into several competing councils. Indeed, regional hierarchies who have their differences with hierarchies of other regions could convene as many councils as there are governing bodies in professional sports — and there could then be as many popes elected as there are champions named by the competing governing bodies. There already have been historical instances of such eventualities which resulted only in producing schisms and multiple popes. Even the Council of Constance, which did not depose any true pope, but only deposed antipopes and elected a true pope, only convened validly when it convened in the fourteenth session under the authority of Pope Gregory XII. The proposition therefore is patently nonsensical and directly opposes the dogma of the Primacy, solemnly defined as a "full and supreme power of **jurisdiction** over the whole Church, [...] the **total fullness**, of this supreme power; [...] **ordinary and immediate** both over all and each of the **churches** and over all and each of the **pastors** and **faithful**". [*Pastor Æternus*]

Therefore, John of St. Thomas was correct on one point in this matter, namely, "it does not appear by whom such a deposition is to be made", since such a deposition can be made by no one: He explicitly teaches that a "general council" can depose a pope, by an "***act of judgment***" and "***jurisdiction***", which directly opposes the dogma of the Primacy defined at the First Vatican Council, as well as the doctrine of the Fifth Lateran Council: "[I]t is clearly established that *the Roman Pontiff alone, possessing as it were authority over all Councils, has full right and power of proclaiming Councils, or transferring and dissolving them*, not only according to the testimony of Sacred Scripture, from the words of the holy Fathers and even of other Roman Pontiffs, of our predecessors, and from the decrees of the holy canons…" If the bishops would dare to challenge the pope's absolute authority over a council and presume to convene in a council to judge against the pope in a matter of faith, then who, other than the pope, would be the supreme arbiter to judge the dispute between the council and the pope? The Church has only ONE HEAD, from which the unity of the Church depends:

> St. Antoninus (part. 13. tit. 2. §. 3. cap. 3.) produces the reason why a council cannot be appealed to against a pope: *Because the Church has unity from the unity of the head; whence, Jn. 10., Christ says* Fiet unum ovile, et unus pastor. *If it would be licit to appeal from the pope, the pope would not be head, but there would be two heads.* Few words, but they wonderfully explain the substance of the matter. And accordingly the same St. Antoninus (part. 3. tit. 23. cap. 3. §. 3.) did not hesitate to write: *But neither can appeal be made to a general council against a pope, because the pope is superior to every council; nor does it have the power, whatever it does, unless by the authority of the Roman*

*Pontiff it be given force and confirmed. Therefore to think that a council can be appealed to against a pope is heretical.*³²⁶

SALZA & SISCOE DEFEND THE HERETICAL THESIS WITH SOPHISTRY AND SUBTERFUGE

Siscoe fraudulently cites examples of what he calls "dicretionary judgments" of the Church against popes in his articles, some of which I mention in Volume One — none of which ever resulted in a pope falling from office. Pope Gregory XVI, as I mentioned above, following the teaching of Bellarmine, Ballerini, and St. Alphonsus explains that the judgment would not be against a currently reigning pontiff, "but only against the person, who was **before** adorned with papal dignity."³²⁷ Thus, if a pope were to become a manifest heretic, he would cease by himself to be pope, and the Church in declaring him a heretic would not be subjecting the pope to a judgment, (which is a judgment that even an ecumenical council would lack the jurisdiction to make), but would merely declare that the *man*, being a manifest heretic, is manifestly not the pope — regardless of whether or not he ever was a valid pope.

Siscoe also claims that no bishop has ever fallen from office for heresy without first being judged by the Church; which is false. Pope St. Celestine I declared that Nestorius had already lost his jurisdiction from the moment he began to preach heresy. I explained the case in the first volume of this work and in my posts, but Salza & Siscoe neglect to mention that in their deceptive hit piece. Siscoe and Salza

---

³²⁶ Alfonso Maria de' Liguori, *Vindiciae pro suprema pontificis potestate adversus Iustinum Febronium*, Torino, 1832, p. 164 — «S. Antoninus (part. 13. tit. 2. §. 3. cap. 3.) affert rationem, propter quam nequit a papa ad concilium appellari: *Quia ecclesia habet unitatem ex unitate capitis; unde, Jo. 10., dicit Christus:* Fiet unum ovile, et unus pastor. *Si licitum esset appellare a papa, papa non esset caput, sed essent duo capita.* Pauca verba, sed rei substantiam mirabiliter explicant. Ac proinde idem s. Antoninus (part. 3. tit. 23. cap. 3. §. 3.) non dubitavit sic scribere: *Sed nec ad concilium generale a papa appellari potest, quia papa est omni concilio superior; nec robur habet, quidquid agitur, nisi auctoritate romani pontificis roboretur et confirmetur. Sentire ergo quod a papa ad concilium appellari possit, hæreticum est.*»

³²⁷ D. Mauro Cappellari ora Gregorio XVI, *Op. cit.*, Venezia, 1832, p. 270.

deny that Nestorius lost his jurisdiction in the manner declared by Pope St. Celestine (i.e. he was declared to have lost it before he was judged by the Church), but they obstinately claim that he was deprived of office afterwards by the pope — which directly contradicts what Pope Celestine actually declared in his judgment. Fr. Gerald McDevitt, in *The Renunciation of an Ecclesiastical Office* quotes St. Celestine: "And in a letter to the clergy of Constantinople, Pope St. Celestine I says: The authority of Our Apostolic See has determined that the bishop, cleric, or simple Christian who had been deposed or excommunicated by Nestorius or his followers, after the latter began to preach heresy shall not be considered deposed or excommunicated. For he who had defected from the faith with such preachings, cannot depose or remove anyone whatsoever."

St. Robert Bellarmine teaches most explicitly (*De Romano Pontifice, lib. ii. cap. xxx*) that it is **heresy by its very nature,** (***ex natura haeresis***), which **severs the heretic from the Church,** and **causes the immediate loss of ecclesiastical office**: «Thenceforth, **the Holy Fathers teach in unison, that not only are heretics outside the Church, but they even lack all Ecclesiastical jurisdiction and dignity *ipso facto*.**» In *De Ecclesia Militante* Bellarmine says it is demonstrated by the testimony of the Fathers who teach with a common consensus that those who are outside the Church have no authority or jurisdiction in the Church;[328] and quoting St. Augustine, Bellarmine declares that *all heretics* and *all schismatics* have departed from the Church.[329] Salza & Siscoe desperately attempt to interpret the Fathers as teaching that the heretic's severing himself from the Church and the subsequent loss of office does not take place by itself, but result from a judgment by ecclesiastical authority on the *crime of heresy*. Bellarmine, in his refutation of the Fourth Opinion utterly destroys that argument: «*Nor does the response which some make avail, that these Fathers speak according to ancient laws, but now since the decree of the*

---

[328] «Secundo demonstratur hoc idem ex testimoniis eorum Patrum, qui communi consensu docent, eos qui sunt extra Ecclesiam, nullam habere auctoritatem aut jurisdictionem in Ecclesiam.» [*De Controversiis Christianae Fidei Adversus Hujus Temporis Haereticos, Tomus Secundus, Liber Tertius, De Ecclesia Militante Toto Orbe Difusa, Cap. X,* Neapoli, 1837, p. 90.]

[329] «s. Augustinus… Sic enim ait… *Omnes hæretici, omnes schismatici ex nobis exierunt idest, ex Ecclesia exierunt*» [*Ibid.* p. 89.]

Council of Constance they do not lose jurisdiction, unless excommunicated by name, or if they strike clerics. I say this avails to nothing. **For those Fathers, when they say that heretics lose jurisdiction, do not allege any human laws which maybe did not exist then on this matter; rather, they argued from the nature of heresy (ex natura hæresis)**. *Moreover, the Council of Constance does not speak except on the excommunicates, that is, on these who lose jurisdiction through a judgment of the Church. Yet* **heretics are outside the Church, even before excommunication, and deprived of all jurisdiction, for they are condemned by their own judgment**, *as the Apostle teaches to Titus; that is,* **they are cut from the body of the Church without excommunication, as Jerome explains.**»[330] Thus, St. Robert Bellarmine proves that it is the teaching of scripture, interpreted unanimously by the Fathers, that heretics are outside the Church and lose all jurisdiction entirely by themselves — straightaway (*mox perdere omnem jurisdictionem*). On this point, he is also following St Thomas Aquinas: «The power of jurisdiction is that which is conferred by a mere human appointment. Such a power as this does not adhere to the recipient immovably: so that it does not remain in heretics and schismatics; and consequently they neither absolve nor excommunicate, nor grant indulgence, nor do anything of the kind, and if they do, it is invalid.» (*Summa Theol. II^a II^a q. 39 a. 3*)[331] In his argument Bellarmine cites this article of St. Thomas explicitly: «Finally

---

[330] *De Romano Pontifice lib. ii cap. xxx* — «Neque valet, quod quidam respondent, istos Patres loqui *secundum antiqua jura,* nunc autem ex decreto Concilii Constantiensis non amittere jurisdictionem, nisi nominatim excommunicatos, & percussores clericorum; hoc, inquam, nihil valet. Nam Patres illi cum dicunt haereticos amittere jurisdictionem, **non allegant ulla jura humana**, quae etiam forte tunc nulla extabant de hac re: **sed argumentantur** *ex natura haeresis*. Concilium autem Constantiense, non loquitur *nisi de excommunicatis,* id est, de his, qui per sententiam Ecclesiae amiserunt jurisdictionem. Haeretici autem etiam ante excummunicationem sunt extra Ecclesiam, & privati omni jurisdictione: sunt enim proprio judicio condemnati, ut docet Apostolus ad Titum3. V. II. Hoc est: praecisi a corpore Ecclesiae, sine excommunicatione, ut Hieronymus exponit.»

[331] «Potestas autem iurisdictionalis est quae ex simplici iniunctione hominis confertur. Et talis potestas non immobiliter adhaeret. Unde in schismaticis et haereticis non manet. Unde non possunt nec absolvere nec excommunicare nec indulgentias facere, aut aliquid huiusmodi, quod si fecerint, nihil est actum.»

even St. Thomas 2. 2. Q. 39. art. 3. teaches schismatics lose all jurisdiction straightaway, and anything they attempt to do from jurisdiction is invalid.»[332]

In this article, St. Thomas explains that the spiritual power is twofold (*duplex est spiritualis potestas*): sacramental and jurisdictional (*una quidem sacramentalis; alia iurisdictionalis*). The sacramental power remains even in those who fall into schism or heresy; and he explains why this is so; [333] but he also explains why schismatics and heretics lose the right to exercise the sacramental power.[334] Then, in the above cited passage, the Angelic Doctor explains why one who falls into schism or heresy (*in schisma sive in haeresim labatur*) simply loses the power of jurisdiction. In this teaching, St. Thomas provides the theological foundation for the teaching of Pope St. Celestine on a heretic's loss of jurisdiction: "For he who had defected from the faith with such preachings, cannot depose or remove anyone whatsoever."

The foundation of this doctrine of automatic loss of all jurisdiction by heretics and schismatics (and *a fortiori* apostates) is that *it pertains to the very nature of the sins of heresy, schism and apostasy* that they *per se* separate one from the unity of the Church. St. Thomas explains that *schism* is opposed to unity, whence it is said that the **sin** of schism is **directly** and ***per se*** opposed to unity; and he explains that the word

---

[332] *De Romano Pontifice lib. ii cap. xxx* — «Denique etiam D. *Thomas* 2. 2. Q. 39. art. 3. docet schismaticos mox perdere omnem jurisdictionem, et irrita esse, si quae ex jurisdictione agere conentur.»

[333] *II*ᵃ *II*ᵃ *q. 39 a. 3* — «Sacramentalis quidem potestas est quæ per aliquam consecrationem confertur. Omnes autem consecrationes Ecclesiæ sunt immobiles, manente re quæ consecratur, sicut patet etiam in rebus inanimatis, nam altare semel consecratum non consecratur iterum nisi fuerit dissipatum. Et ideo talis potestas secundum suam essentiam remanet in homine qui per consecrationem eam est adeptus quandiu vivit, sive in schisma sive in hæresim labatur, quod patet ex hoc quod rediens ad Ecclesiam non iterum consecratur.»

[334] *Ibid.* — «Sed quia potestas inferior non debet exire in actum nisi secundum quod movetur a potestate superiori, ut etiam in rebus naturalibus patet; inde est quod tales usum potestatis amittunt, ita scilicet quod non liceat eis sua potestate uti. Si tamen usi fuerint, eorum potestas effectum habet in sacramentalibus, quia in his homo non operatur nisi sicut instrumentum Dei; unde effectus sacramentales non excluduntur propter culpam quamcumque conferentis sacramentum.»

schism is derived from *scission* (Lat. scissio), which means, "the action or state of cutting or being cut; a cutting apart; a severing", because schism is a special sin which according to its nature severs one from the Church (*II*ᵃ *II*ᵃᵉ *q. 39 a. 1 co.*). Now **that which is intended *per se* constitutes the *species* of the act**; and thus ***schism is properly a special sin in that it intends directly to separate one from the unity of the Church.*** ³³⁵ **Both sins, *schism* and *heresy*, are *per se* opposed to the unity of the Church**, since **heresy is** *per se* **a schismatic act opposed to the unity of the one faith**; and schism is *per se* opposed to the unity of ecclesiastical charity; and for which reason, ***every heretic is a schismatic***, but not vice versa.³³⁶ **Thus, a schismatic act, whether it be an act of *pure schism*, or a simple act of *formal heresy*, is in its very nature a *sin* that *severs* the perpetrator from the body of the Church, because it separates one *per se* from the unity of the Church.** The Church is *One* in virtue of her unity: 1) unity of faith, 2) unity of cult, 3) unity under one visible head. Thus Canon Law states that "Those baptised are fully in communion with the Catholic Church on this earth who are joined with Christ in its visible structure by the bonds of profession of faith, of the sacraments and of ecclesiastical governance." (can. 205). When one commits a *sin* that *per se* visibly severs any one of those bonds of communion, one is separated by that act from the unity of the body of the Church. Thus, **schismatics, heretics and apostates** *miserably separate themselves* from the unity of the Church *by the very nature of their*

---

³³⁵ *II*ᵃ *II*ᵃᵉ *q. 39 a. 1 co.* — «Scissio autem unitati opponitur. Unde peccatum schismatis dicitur quod directe et per se opponitur unitati, sicut enim in rebus naturalibus id quod est per accidens non constituit speciem, ita etiam nec in rebus moralibus. In quibus id quod est intentum est per se, quod autem sequitur præter intentionem est quasi per accidens. Et ideo peccatum schismatis proprie est speciale peccatum ex eo quod intendit se ab unitate separare quam caritas facit.»

³³⁶ *II*ᵃ *II*ᵃᵉ *q. 39 a. 1 ad 3* — «hæresis et schisma distinguuntur secundum ea quibus utrumque per se et directe opponitur. Nam hæresis per se opponitur fidei, schisma autem per se opponitur unitati ecclesiasticæ caritatis. Et ideo sicut fides et caritas sunt diversæ virtutes, quamvis quicumque careat fide careat caritate; ita etiam schisma et hæresis sunt diversa vitia, quamvis quicumque est hæreticus sit etiam schismaticus, sed non convertitur.»

sin, and are **NOT** separated by the penalty attached to the crime **BY AUTHORITY**; whereas those who are separated for other crimes, are expelled *by legitimate authority*, as *Mystici Corporis* teaches. Referring specifically to the expulsion from the Church of heretics, schismatics, and apostates, the Canon Law Society Commentary explains, "The Church, does not expel persons from its midst. Essentially the apostate, heretic, or schismatic withdraws those bonds (of full communion) by a personal act. The Church recognises this in declaring the bonds severed..." [337]

In Canon Smith's *The teaching of the Catholic Church*, it is explained:

«Pius XII has reaffirmed in the clearest language what are the conditions for membership of the Church. "Only those are to be accounted really members of the Church who have been regenerated in the waters of Baptism and profess the true faith, and have not cut themselves from the structure of the Body by their own unhappy act or been severed there from, for very grave crimes, by the legitimate authority."»... [707] «Nevertheless the melancholy possibility must be envisaged of those who may have "cut themselves off from the structure of the Body by their own unhappy act or been severed there from, for very grave crimes, by the legitimate authority." In other words, the Church, as being a perfectly constituted society, has the right for grave reasons of excluding from membership. She may pass sentence of, or lay down conditions which involve excommunication.»... [708] «**Certain sins — viz., apostasy, heresy and schism** [Can. 1325, § 2.] **— of their nature cut off the guilty from the living Body of Christ**. [...] Heresy, objectively considered, is a doctrinal proposition which contradicts an article of faith; from the subjective point of view it may be defined as an error concerning the Catholic faith, freely and obstinately persisted in by a professing Christian.» [...] «It can hardly be denied that those who take up any of these positions — [i.e. heresy, schism, or apostasy]... sever themselves by their own act from membership of the Church.»[338]

---

[337] James A. Coriden, Thomas J. Green, Donald E. Heintschel; *THE CODE OF CANON LAW, A Text and Commentary*, Commissioned by THE CANON LAW SOCIETY OF AMERICA, et al., p. 128.

[338] Canon George F. Smith, D.D., Ph.D., *Op. cit.,* XX THE CHURCH ON EARTH, PART I, THE CATHOLIC CHURCH: THE SOCIETY OF THE REDEEMED — § VI: MEMBERSHIP p. 706.

The teaching is clear enough so that no one should have any difficulty understanding the Catholic magisterial doctrine on this point, namely, that heretics are separated from membership in the Church *by their own public act of heresy*, and *not by a judgment of ecclesiastical authority*. Nevertheless, in order to justify their heretical belief that a heretic pope must be judged *by the authority* of the Church before losing office, Salza & Siscoe deny the infallible doctrine of the universal magisterium which teaches that the heresy *by itself* separates the heretic from the body of the Church; and they concocted their own bizarre doctrine according to which it is only the *crime* of heresy, and not the *sin* of heresy that severs the heretic from membership. On that basis, they fallaciously claim that one guilty of public heresy remains a member of the Church until judged a heretic by Church authority unless the act is "public and notorious" — a *crime* that is canonically *notorious by fact*. Incredibly, they cite in support for their doctrine a quotation of Msgr. Van Noort, who explains that the *sin* of heresy severs a man automatically from the Body of the Church (!):

> "b. Public heretics (and a fortiori, apostates) are not members of the Church. They are not members because they separate themselves from the unity of Catholic faith and from the external profession of that faith. Obviously, therefore, they lack one of three factors—baptism, profession of the same faith, union with the hierarchy—pointed out by Pius XII as requisite for membership in the Church. The same pontiff has explicitly pointed out that, unlike other **sins**, heresy, schism, and apostasy automatically sever a man from the Church. 'For not every sin, however grave and enormous it be, is such as to sever a man automatically from the Body of the Church, as does schism or heresy or apostasy'." (Dogmatic Theology, Volume II, Christ's Church, p. 241-242.)

Now since that may not be enough to convince their readers that only the *crime* of heresy but not the *sin* of heresy severs one from membership in the Church, they also quote Msgr. Joseph Clifford Fenton on the same point, who speaks of the **sins** of schism, heresy, and apostasy which by their own nature separate a man from the Church (!):

«Fr. Fenton wrote: "In the encyclical, the Holy Father speaks of schism, heresy, and apostasy, as **sins** [admissum] which, of their own nature, separate a man from the Body of the Church. He thereby follows the traditional procedure adopted by St. Robert himself in his De Ecclesia Militante. The great Doctor of the Church devoted the fourth chapter of his book to a proof that [public] heretics and apostates are not members of the Church."» [339]

An act is a *sin* because it is a transgression against divine law. An act is a *crime* because it is listed as a *penal offense* in *ecclesiastical law*: «"*Nullum crimen, nulla poena sine lege poenali,*" [Eichmann, *l. c.*, p. 27.]»[340] According to the nature of a *crime*, a *crime* does not separate the offender from the body of the Church *by the nature of the act*, but the offender is separated *by authority*, i.e. by means of *excommunication*. Heresy, schism, and apostasy are the sole exceptions. Pius XII teaches that they sever one from membership in the body of the Church not "by authority", as in the manner of *crimes*; but "*suapte natura*": *by the very nature of the sinful act*:

«In Ecclesiae autem membris reapse ii soli annumerandi sunt, qui regenerationis lavacrum receperunt veramque fidem profitentur, neque a Corporis compage semet ipsos misere separarunt, vel ob gravissima admissa a legitima auctoritate seiuncti sunt [...] Siquidem non omne admissum, etsi grave scelus, eiusmodi est ut — sicut schisma, vel haeresis, vel apostasia faciunt — suapte natura hominem ab Ecclesiae Corpore separet.» [ACTA APOSTOLICAE SEDIS— Annus XXXV – Series II – Vol. XM – DCCCC – XLIII - ACTA PII PP. XII — LITTERAE ENCYCLICAE — Mystici Corporis Christi — Datum Romae, apud Sanctum Petrum, die xxix mensis Iunii, in festo Ss. Apostolorum Petri et Pauli, anno MDCCÇCXXXXIII, pp. 202 203]

«Actually only those are to be included as members of the Church who have been baptized and profess the true faith, and who have not been so unfortunate as to separate themselves from the unity of the Body, or been excluded by legitimate authority for grave faults committed. [...] For not every sin, however grave it may be, is such as of its own nature to sever a man from the Body of the Church, as does schism or heresy or apostasy.» [*MYSTICI CORPORIS CHRISTI* — ENCYCLICAL OF POPE PIUS XII][341]

---

[339] *True or False Pope?* p. 158

[340] The Rev. P. Chas. Augustine, O.S.B., D.D.; *A COMMENTAY ON THE NEW CODE OF CANON LAW.*, B. HERDER BOOK CO., St. Louis, London, 1922, Volume VIII, p. 12, footnote 4.

[341] http://www.vatican.va/content/pius-xii/en/encyclicals/documents/hf_p-xii_enc_29061943_mystici-corporis-christi.html

Only those who are counted as members in the Church (In Ecclesiae autem membris reapse ii soli annumerandi sunt), are those who have been baptized and have professed the faith (qui regenerationis lavacrum receperunt veramque fidem profitentur), and have not *separated themselves* from the unity of the body, or *have been separated for grave faults by legitimate authority*. Accordingly *not every sin*, even *a grave misdeed*, would *separate – as do schism, heresy or apostasy – a man from the body of the Church by its very nature*.

Thus, the definitive teaching of the Pacellian *ordinary magisterium* sets forth that the perpetrators of crimes, *"have been separated by legitimate authority"*; but *unlike all other grave sins*, the sins of *"schism, heresy, and apostasy by their very nature* separate a man from the body of the Church." **Thus, the encyclical explicitly distinguishes between "those who are counted as members in the Church" and those who are not members, because they have either, 1) "been excluded by legitimate authority for grave faults committed", or 2) have "miserably separated themselves" by committing acts of schism, heresy or apostasy.** According to this explicit teaching, those who have *miserably separated* themselves, are **excluded from membership, i.e. from "those who are counted as members of the Church".** Heretics are not merely separated from the Church by their own actions *quoad se*, but not *quoad nos*, as Salza & Siscoe heretically maintain, **but the encyclical states *simply* that *they have miserably separated themselves from the body of those who are counted as members in the Church*.** Those who visibly separate themselves by their own actions alone simply do not count as members in the Church. It is not a question of *quoad se* or *quoad nos*, but it is taught *simpliciter* that those who commit acts that *suapte natura* visibly separate them from the body of the Church, are excluded from *those who are counted as members*.

Hence, it is inescapable and undeniable that the doctrine set forth in *Mystici Corporis* teaches that the sin of heresy by itself, and by its very nature, considered *per se* in its nature as an ***act,*** and not because it *per accidens* happens to be a ***crime***, separates one from membership in the body of the Church — that is, *by its very nature* as a sinful public act of disbelief in an article of faith, **heresy severs the heretic from membership in the Church BY ITSELF, *without a judgment by Church authority*.** This is a doctrine that must be believed with *divine* *and Catholic faith,* because, as I have explained in Volume One, it was proven by St. Robert Bellarmine that this doctrine is taught *unanimously by the Fathers*; and it is taught repeatedly in papal *ordinary magisterium,* by St. Pius V in the *Roman Catechism* and by St. Pius X in his *Catechism* as well. Bellarmine also proved from St. Thomas and the *unanimity of the Fathers* that all jurisdiction and ecclesiastical dignity are lost *ipso facto* by public heresy, and not by any human law or judgment by any human authority, but *"by the nature of heresy".* That notwithstanding, Salza & Siscoe flatly deny these doctrines of the *universal magisterium* and assert categorically and heretically that even for a public act of manifest formal heresy, one is not separated from membership in the Church without the judgment of Church authority; and such a one who is guilty of a public act of formal heresy does not lose office automatically, *ipso jure,* but only when the crime is judged by the Church. On this point they follow the discredited and dissident opinion of John of St. Thomas, who gratuitously claimed, that the heresy must be *public and juridically notorious* ("publica et juridice notoria"), and who heretically elaborated, "The pope does not cease to be the pope **before any ecclesial trial sentence** by the fact itself of heresy, and before **he is proposed as to be avoided**. Neither is Jerome, when he says that the heretic exits by himself from the Body of Christ, excluding him from the judgment of the Church, especially in a thing so grave as the deposition of a pope, but she judges the quality of **the crime** [of heresy] **that excludes from the Church** without any over added censure, **as long as it is declared by the Church."**[342]

So where does that leave Siscoe's proposition that "no bishop has ever fallen from office for heresy without first being judged by the Church"? It leaves it resting on a contradiction: Against the above cited explicit ruling of Pope St. Celestine I, they argue saying we can see just how mistaken they are who,

> «claim that Nestorius was immediately deposed, *ipso facto,* the moment he began preaching heresy (in 428 A.D.), which was three years before he was deposed at the Council of Ephesus (in 431 A.D.) On the contrary, he was deposed *at the council,* as St. Bellarmine himself taught,

---

[342] *Cursus Theologicus II-II De Auctoritate Summi Pontificis,* Disp. II, Art. III, De Depositione Papae, XXVI.

when he wrote: "Certainly, Nestorius was deposed from the episcopacy of Constantinople by the Council of Ephesus [A.D. 431], from the mandate of Pope Celestine, as Evagrius witnessed." In *De Membris Ecclesia* (sic), St. Bellarmine further explained that heretical bishop are to be deposed by a council, or by the Pope Himself: "And it is certain that the practice of the Church has always been that heretical bishops be deposed by bishop's councils, or by the Sovereign Pontiff." Obviously, neither Pope Celestine, the Council of Ephesus, nor St. Robert Bellarmine say anything about a heretical bishop losing his office, *ipso facto*, simply because a layman in the street personally thinks he is a heretic, even if he is a bishop who is publicly preaching heresy.»

Thus, after creating a false paradigm,[343] they finish their argument by positing a contradictory notion of the term *"ipso facto"*, premising their absurdity on this point by obfuscating again on the distinction between *ipso jure* loss of office and *penal deprivation of office* (i.e. deposition), which they do by asserting the nonsensical proposition that those who subscribe to this supposedly «erroneous interpretation of Bellarmine, will never be able to understand how Bellarmine could say "the Holy Fathers teach unanimously not only that heretics are outside of the Church, but also that they are *'ipso facto'* deprived of all ecclesiastical jurisdiction and dignity," yet, in the very same book, explicitly state that Nestorius "was deposed from the episcopacy of Constantinople by the Council of Ephesus."» Now a deposition properly so-called is an act of penal deprivation inflicted by authority, whereas *ipso facto* deposition is not properly a penalty, but is a self-inflicted loss of office which occurs as a juridical consequence of defection from the faith, as has been explained; so it is easy enough for anyone to understand what Bellarmine meant in the cited passages — anyone, that is, except Salza & Siscoe. In the first passage Bellarmine explained that heretics lose office and jurisdiction *ipso facto*

---

[343] Salza & Siscoe deceptively create a false paradigm when they say, "Obviously, neither Pope Celestine, the Council of Ephesus, nor St. Robert Bellarmine say anything about a heretical bishop losing his office, *ipso facto*, simply because a layman in the street personally thinks he is a heretic, even if he is a bishop who is publicly preaching heresy." As has been explained, the *ipso facto* loss of office takes place because the heretic has committed a public act which *per se* separates him from the Church, and not because third parties judge that the person is a heretic.

by the act of manifest heresy, and in the second that the Council of Ephesus inflicted the penalty of deposition on Nestorius. Then they assert their contradictory notion of *ipso facto*: «The reason they will consider these two statements to be in direct contradiction to one another, is because they have failed to understand that the *ipso facto* loss of office for a manifest heretic occurs when the Church itself establishes "the fact" of manifest heresy, in the ecclesiastical forum, not simply when an individual Catholic personally "discerns" that the prelate is guilty of the sin of heresy.» The very notion of an act that produces an *ipso facto* effect that is contingent upon the judgment of another party is a contradiction in itself. It is a notion which confuses the application of the *ipso facto* provision itself and the application of its juridical effects in the external forum. This point of law is explained in the commentary of the Canon Law faculty of the University of Navarra on Canon 1363:

> **1363** ... The c. has deliberately silenced the declaratory sentence, because it was understood that, for *latae sententiae* penalties, no executorial decree is given (cf. *Communicationes* 9 [1977] 174). However, it should be clarified that one thing is the application of the *latae sententiae* penalty, which occurs *ipso facto* upon the commission of the crime; and another, the application in the external forum, especially of those effects more properly legal, such as, for example, the invalidity of acts of jurisdiction: these effects, which are born with the declaratory sentence, and the rest, which only from said sentence can be demanded in the external forum, they must require an executorial decree so that they can take effect.[344]

---

[344] *Código De Derecho Canónico Edición Bilingüe Y Anotada*, Universidad De Navarra, Facultad De Derecho Canónico, p. 849 — «**1363** ... El c. ha silenciado deliberadamente la sentencia declaratoria, porque se entendió que, para las penas *latae sententiae,* no se da decreto ejecutorio (cfr. *Communicationes* 9 [1977] 174). Sin embargo, conviene aclarar que una cosa es la aplicación de la pena *latae sententiae,* que se realiza *ipso facto* cometido el delito; y otra, la aplicación en el fuero externo, sobre todo de aquellos efectos más propiamente jurídicos, como, por ej., la invalidez de los actos de jurisdicción: estos efectos, que nacen con la sentencia declaratoria, y los demás, que sólo a partir de dicha sentencia pueden exigirse en el fuero externo, sí deben requerir decreto ejecutorio para que puedan tener vigencia. De ahí que también la acción penal para urgir la aplicación de la sentencia declaratoria deba estar sometida a prescripción.»

Furthermore, just as they previously argued on the provisions in the 1917 Code, their argument here rests also on a conflation of the administrative *ipso jure* **loss of office** incurred by the fact of defection from the Catholic faith decreed in Canon 194 § 2 with the *deprivation of office* mentioned in Canon 196 — § 2, prescribed as a **penalty for a crime** which is mandated to be carried out by legitimate authority *"secundum præscripta canonum de iure poenali"*.[345] The loss of office took place *ipso jure* at the time Nestorius began preaching heresy, as the pope stated in the declaration; while the formal act of *penal deprivation of office* was accomplished when Nestorius was deposed from the bishopric of Constantinople at the Council of Ephesus. So what is so difficult about that to understand, Mr. Siscoe?

It is precisely to provide a basis for asserting against the universal magisterium that ecclesiastical office is not lost *ipso facto* without the judgment of the Church, that they insist that only the *crime* of heresy and not the *sin* severs a heretic from membership in the Church — because according to them, that fact that heresy is a crime means that one does not lose office *ipso jure* without a judgment of the Church. Since it is infallibly taught *de fide* that heresy separates one from membership in the Church by its very nature, they have resorted to assert the patent absurdity that *heresy is in its nature a crime*, which in spite of being absurd on its face, I already devoted ample space in Volume One to thoroughly refute them on every point of their argument.

They also ineptly cite a passage of canonist Gianfranco Ghirlanda SJ in defence of their errant opinion that a heretic-pope's loss of office would not take place until his heresy has been declared by the Church. Now Fr. Ghirlanda, former rector of the Gregorian University, who studied the past millennia of canonical tradition concerning the loss of papal office; in an article entitled, *Cessazione dall'ufficio di Romano Pontefice*[346] published in 2013 in the *Civiltà Cattolica* wrote: «The vacancy of the Roman See occurs in case of the cessation of the office on the part of the Roman Pontiff, which happens for

---

[345] «**Can. 196** — § 1. Privatio ab officio, in poenam scilicet delicti, ad normam iuris tantummodo fieri potest.§ 2. Privatio effectum sortitur secundum praescripta canonum de iure poenali.»

[346] http://chiesa.espresso.repubblica.it/articolo/1350455.html.

four reasons: 1) Death, 2) Sure and perpetual insanity or complete mental infirmity; 3) Notorious apostasy, heresy, schism; 4) Resignation. In the first case, the Apostolic See is vacant from the moment of death of the Roman Pontiff; *in the second and in the third from the moment of the declaration on the part of the cardinals*; in the fourth from the moment of the renunciation.» What needs to be pointed out is that the vacancy actually takes place *ipso facto*, because the office is lost *ipso jure*. A little further down in the same article, Fr. Ghirlanda explains:

> «The criterion then is the protection of ecclesial communion itself. There where this no longer existed on the part of the Pope, he would no longer have any power, because ipso iure he would fall from his primatial office. This is the case, admitted in doctrine, of the notorious apostasy, heresy and schism, in which the Roman Pontiff could fall, but as a "private doctor", who does not commit the assent of the faithful, because by faith in the personal infallibility that the Roman Pontiff has in the performance of his office, and therefore in the assistance of the Holy Spirit, we must say that he cannot make heretical statements wanting to commit his primatial authority, because, if he did so, he would fall ipso jure from his office. However in such cases, since "the first seat is not judged by anyone" (c. 1404), no one could depose the Roman Pontiff, but there would only be a declaration of the fact, which should be on the part of the Cardinals, at least of those present in Rome. This eventuality, however, although foreseen in the doctrine, is considered totally improbable by intervention of the Divine Providence in favour of the Church (4).»

Fr. Ghirlanda has explained that the loss of office is automatic (*ipso jure*); but the fact of the vacancy gains juridical recognition upon the issuance of a declaratory sentence of the cardinals; much as when a pope who dies in his sleep vacates the office at the moment of his death, but the juridical vacancy occurs only upon the recognition of the fact of the pope's death by the cardinal *camerlengo*. Fr. Ghirlanda's usage of the term "notorious" does not imply that the *ipso jure* loss of office would only take place by an act of canonically notorious heresy, i.e. *nororious by fact*, since he is certainly aware of the canonical distinction between *notorious* and *public* acts, and the canon specifies that ecclesiastical office is lost *ipso jure* for **public** defection from the faith. The *Catholic Encyclopedia*, which I quoted in Volume One on the question of the distinction between notorious and public heresy, explains the entry "**Notorious**" saying,

> Ordinarily it is equivalent to public, manifest, evident, known; all these terms have something in common, they signify that a thing, far from being secret, may be easily known by many. Notoriety, in addition to this common idea, involves the idea of indisputable proof, so that what is notorious is held as proved and serves as a basis for the conclusions and acts of those in authority, especially judges. To be as precise as is possible, "public" means what any one may easily prove or ascertain, what is done openly; what many persons know and hold as certain, is "manifest"; what a greater or less number of persons have learnt, no matter how, is "known"; what is to be held as certain and may no longer be called in question is "notorious"... Whatever is easily shown and is known by a sufficient number of persons to be free from reasonable doubt is notorious in fact.

I have amply proven in Volume One that the proposition which says that a validly reigning pope could be subjected to a trial is heretical; and I have proven that the proposition which holds that *one who is guilty of manifestly formal public heresy is not excluded from membership in the Church until it has been declared by the Church,* is also heretical; and makes total nonsense of the teaching of *Mystici Corporis,* which says that heretics «***miserably separated themselves from the unity of the Body***»; and that the exclusion from membership in the Church due to heresy takes place **by the nature of heresy**, i.e. *suapte natura*, which means *directly* and *immediately* by the nature of the act itself, and therefore **neither directly, dispositively, nor in any manner** "*by legitimate authority*". Salza & Siscoe, who notwithstanding this *de fide* teaching that heretics, who are separated from membership in the Church **by the nature of heresy**, and thereby «***miserably separated themselves from the unity of the Body***», and are **NOT** separated "*by legitimate authority*", nevertheless maintain obstinately and irrationally that heretics, who are separated by the nature of heresy and **not by authority**, are still not separated without a judgment by Church authority (*except under circumstances specified according to their own private judgment*[347]), and therefore *by legitimate authority*. Thus, **their**

---

[347] As has been explained in Volume One, in order to twist the teaching of the Church to make it appear to fit into their own heretical framework,

entire doctrine that a manifest heretic pope would not fall from office without the judgment of the Church rests on a flat contradiction.

Undaunted by the fact that their entire doctrine on this point rests on a contradiction, Salza & Siscoe blindly adhere to this absurdity with a fanaticism that crosses the boundary of irrationality and enters the realm of lunacy. In Volume One I mentioned that, «Salza & Siscoe speak of my, "erroneous opinion", which according to them is based on, "a misreading/misapplication of Pope Pius XII's Mystici Corporis Christi [...] in which the Pope says 'For not every offense (admissum), although it may be a grave evil, is such as by its very own nature to sever a man from the Body of the Church, as does schism or heresy or apostasy.'"[6] According to them, the teaching in this passage is that "Pope Pius XII is referring to the *'offense' or CRIME (not SIN) of heresy, which severs one from the Body of the Church, after the formal and material elements have been proven by the Church.*"» So then, what was their response to this? In their *Formal Reply,* **Exposing the Errors of Fr. Paul Kramer on Mystici Corporis Christi**, Salza & Siscoe reply, «So, where did Fr. Kramer get the idea that we "insist" *admissum* must be translated as crime? You guessed it. He got it from a Sedevacantist website, and he even admits the same.» Actually, I got the idea from their own writings: In *John Salza Responds to Another Sedevacantist*, Salza insists on what he judges to be the proper understanding of Pius XII's usage of the term "admissum": «Again, Pope Pius XII is referring to the "offense" or CRIME (not SIN) of heresy, which severs one from the Body of the Church, after the formal and material elements have been proven by the Church.» It is on this false premise that Salza then fallaciously asserts his error which I have already exposed, «The sin of heresy alone does NOT "sever the person from the Body of the

---

Salza & Siscoe posit the exception of *notorious heresy* defined according their own arbitrarily crafted definition of *notorious by fact*, which restrictively specifies circumstances which they enumerate according to their own private judgment against the magisterium of the Church, which teaches that *public heresy*, which conforms to the canonical definition of "public", but not necessarily *notorious*, constitutes an act of defection from the faith, which by its own nature separates the heretic from membership in the body of the Church.

Church" because sin is a matter of the internal forum.» The proposition is contrary to the Church's perpetual teachings, 1) that the sin of heresy by its nature separates one from the Church, and, 2) that internal sins are a matter of the internal forum, and public sins are a matter of the external forum. If the sin is public and the moral imputability of the act is also manifestly evident, then the heretic by himself severs the juridical bond which united him to the Church as a member. Salza even goes so far as to say, «Further, in order to be guilty of the crime of heresy, the Church must prove the subjective element of the crime (pertinacity), in addition to the objective element.» The idiocy of this assertion is remarkable — what he is saying is that In order to *be guilty* of the crime, the Church must prove the guilt; but the Church cannot prove the guilt unless one is first actually guilty of the crime. One must *be guilty* of the crime before one can be proven guilty! Where does all this nonsense lead? It leads directly to heresy. On page 3 of their article, Salza & Siscoe declare: «The formal separation from the Body of the Church occurs when the juridical bond is severed by the public act (crime) of notorious heresy (notorious by fact), or when the crime has been judged and declared by the Church (notorious by law).» Thus **they heretically deny that the public sin of manifestly obstinate heresy by its own nature severs the heretic from the body of the Church, and by its own nature severs the juridical bond of membership *ipso jure*** — but it is all for naught that they assert this heresy, **because the rest of the Church in its entirety has *no power to judge a pope* and declare his crime juridically; being that the jurisdiction of the primacy is *total* and *absolute*,** so that all ecclesiastical power is subordinate to his jurisdiction.

I have amply demonstrated in Volume One that a manifest heretic by his own words and actions is not a member of the Church, and is therefore an incapable subject of the papacy, even before judgment by the Church; and furthermore that heresy *per se* renders a man incapable of assuming the form of the pontificate. Thus, even if a secret heretic elected to the papacy should later be discovered to have been a heretic at the time of his election, he would not be a valid pope, but would simply need to be removed. That, as I have explained and documented in Volume One, is the ruling of Pope Paul IV. It is declared by Paul IV in *Cum Ex Apostolatus Officio,* and confirmed by

St. Pius V in *Inter Multiplices,* that the election to the papacy of even an occult heretic who is discovered afterwards to be a heretic is invalid, even if he receives universal acceptance and obedience (*adorationem, seu ei praestitam ab omnibus obedientiam*) from the whole Church. That rule remains forever in force, even if the statute of human positive law, i.e. the "merely ecclesiastical law",[348] were to be abrogated, because it is easily shown to be a statutory application of a precept of divine law. The decree states that even if the heretic pope-elect not yet known to be a heretic would receive obedience from all, his election is null and void, and needs only to be declared so. The ruling is founded on the *doctrinal principle* that a heretic *per se* is an **incapable subject** of the papacy. Thus, not only would a public heretic be an incapable subject of the papacy for the reason that as a manifest heretic he would no longer be a member of the Church, but heresy *per se* and *simpliciter* renders a man *an illegitimate subject* of the papacy, so that a heretic is simply incapable of assuming the form of the papacy and thereby being conjoined to it. This is what Innocent III taught when he explained in *Sermo III* that the conjunction of a man to the papacy is a *spiritual matrimony between the Roman Pontiff and the Church*, which can only exist between legitimate persons (*solus consensus inter legitimas personas efficit matrimonium*), and that heretics and schismatics are aliens who are not to be recognized, but are simply to be hunted down and driven away.[349] In virtue of the pope's participation in Christ's headship over the Church as her Spouse (Eph. 5: 23), the Roman Pontiff, upon becoming *Vicar of Christ* on earth gains a participation in Christ's spousal relation to his Bride;[350]

---

[348] Canon 11— «Legibus mere ecclesiasticis tenentur baptizati in Eccelesia catholica vel in eandem recepti, quique sufficienti rationis usu gaudent et, nisi aliud iure, expresse caveatur, septimum aetatis annum expleverunt.»

[349] Innocentius III. *Sermo III.* «*IN CONSECRATIONE PONTIFICIS*» — "Veritas inquit in Evangelio: «Cognosco oves meas, et cognuscunt me meæ (*Joan.* X)»: alienum non sequuntur sed fugiunt, quia non noverunt vocen alienorum. Alieni autem sunt hæretici et schismatici, quos Ecclesia Romana non sequitur, sed persequitur et fugat."

[350] *Eph. 5: 23* — "Because the husband is the head of the wife, as Christ is the head of the church. He is the saviour of his body."; *2 Cor. 11: 2* —

for which reason he may not cede the papacy and resign without moral justification, hence, Innocent teaches, "*Vir autem iste alligatus uxori, solutionem non quærit, non cedit*". He is bound by divine law to remain united to his spouse. (1 Cor. 7: 11[351]) He cannot not be deposed, "*non deponitur*". However, by the sin of infidelity, the necessary disposition for the spiritual matrimonial union between the Roman Pontiff and the Church would cease to exist, being destroyed by its contrary disposition, which is heresy; and thus, one who becomes a heretic, becomes an *incapable subject* of the papacy, lacking the necessary disposition to be a *legitimate spouse*. Therefore, Innocent teaches in *Sermo III*:

> Propter causam vero fornicationis Ecclesia romana posset dimmitere Romanum pontificem. Fornicationem non dico carnalem, sed spiritualem; quia non est carnale, sed spirituale conjugium, id est propter infidelitatis errorem; quoniam «qui non credit, jam judicatus est *(Joan. iii)*»: et in hoc articulo intelligitur, quod legitur in Evangelio, quod audistis: «Vos estis sal terræ, quod sis al evanuerit in quo salietur? *(Matth. V.)*»[352]

That he speaks here only of a hypothesis is evident in his use of the verb *posset*[353] in the third-person singular imperfect active subjunctive, thus:

> For reason of fornication the Church *would be able* to dismiss the Roman Pontiff. I do not mean carnal fornication, but spiritual; because it is not carnal but a spiritual marriage, that is because of the error of infidelity; because «he who does not believe, has already been judged *(John* III)»: and it is understood in this clause, which is read in the Gospel, which you heard: «You are the salt of the earth, but if the salt would expire *(evanuerit)* in what would it be salted? *(Matth.* V.)»

"For I have espoused you to one husband that I may present you as a chaste virgin to Christ."

[351] *1 Cor. 7: 11* — "And let not the husband put away his wife."

[352] Innocentius III. *Sermo III.* «*IN CONSECRATIONE PONTIFICIS*»

[353] «Propter causam vero fornicationis Ecclesia romana **posset** dimmitere Romanum pontificem.»

Thus, if a pope *would* fall into heresy, having become an *incapable subject*, and therefore an *illegitimate spouse*, **the pontificate would expire in him**, and for that reason, the Church would be able to dismiss him as one who is already no longer pope, having already been condemned by God out of the words of his own mouth. (Luke 19:22) In the following sentence, Innocent provides the scriptural basis for why, in his judgment, such an eventuality as a pope falling into the sin of infidelity is impossible:

> I however would not believe so easily that God would permit the Roman Pontiff to err against faith: for whom spiritually he prayed in Peter: < Ego, inquit, pro te rogavi, Petre, etc. (Luc.xxii),> Therefore *He who has the bride, is the bridegroom etc.* This bride did not wed in vain, but bestowed upon me a precious and priceless dowry, namely the spiritual fullness and temporal latitude, and the magnitude and the multitude of both. For the others have been called in a part of the care, but only Peter has been assumed into the fullness of power.[354]

It is to be noted, that when he says "to err against faith", he is not speaking here properly of *papal infallibility*, which only prevents the pope from erring objectively in his definitions, but the point on which he is expressly expounding in this sermon is of an *error against faith*, intended properly to mean **a pope falling into personal heresy**, i.e. the *"error of infidelity"* as a form of *"spiritual fornication"*, by which one would *"wither away into heresy"* as one *"who does not believe"*. Thus clearly he employs the expression *"to err in faith"* to properly mean *"spiritual fornication"*, which is the personal sin of heresy that falls outside the scope of papal infallibility but fully within the *"fullness of power"* which includes the *"spiritual fullness"*. Thus, the *"spiritual fullness"* he speaks of here is not a fullness in a restricted sense that would be limited to the

---

[354] Innocentius III. *Sermo III.* «*IN CONSECRATIONE PONTIFICIS*» — «Ego tamen facile non crediderim, ut Deus permitteret Romanum pontificem contra fidem errare: pro quo spiritualiter oravit in Petro: <Ego, inquit, pro te rogavi, Petre, etc. (Luc.xxii),> Ergo *qui habet sponsam, sponsus est.* Haec autem sponsa non nupsit vacua, sed dotem mihi tribuit absque pretio pretiosam, spirilualium videlicet plenitudinem et latitudinem temporalium, magnitndinem et multiudinem utrorumque. Nam caeteri vocati sunt in partem sollicitudinis, solus autem Petrus assumptus est in plenitudinem potesatis.»

objective infallibility of solemn definitions pronounced within the scope of the primatial jurisdiction, but a **fullness of spiritual power** which includes what Bellarmine described as *the singular assistance of God which Christ obtained for him by his prayer that his faith not fail.* **This power has been given only to the head of the Church:**

> Thou shalt be called Cephas (*John* 1), which denotes the head, because in the head consists the fullness of all senses, but in the other members there is some part of the fullness: consequently the others are called in a part of the solicitude, but Peter alone has been assumed into the fullness of power.[355]

Thus on the foundation of Innocent III's teaching, Bellarmine concludes in *De Romano Pont. lib. iv. cap vii* on the question of whether a pope can become a heretic or not: "From there it is gathered correctly that the Pope by his own nature can fall into heresy, *but not when there is posited the singular assistance of God which Christ obtained for him by his prayer: but Christ prayed that his faith not fail.*" Thus it can be seen why no specific provision was enacted in *Cum ex apostolatus officio* to adjudicate the case of a true and valid pope who would fall into heresy, nor for that matter, in the entire history of the Church has there ever been decreed any papal legislation whatsoever to provide for such an eventuality, because such an eventuality was never believed by the popes to be a real possibility, and their belief on this point is confirmed by the teaching of Innocent III, St. Robert Bellarmine, and the perpetual papal pronouncements on the absolute injudicability of the pope. As I have said, if such a thing would be allowed by God — that a true pope could fall into heresy, then God would absolutely have had to provide a statutory remedy for the maximum necessity that such a catastrophe would generate. The fact that God did not provide such a remedy proves absolutely that divine providence makes no allowance for such an eventuality to ever take place.

---

[355] Innocentius III. *Sermo II.* «*IN CONSECRATIONE PONTIFICIS MAXIMI*» — «*Tu*, inquit, *vocaberis Cephas* (Joan. 1), quod exponitur caput; quia sicut in capite consistit omnium sensuum plenitudo, in cæteris autem membris pars est aliqua plenitudinis: ita cæteri vocati sunt in partem sollicitudinis, solus autem Petrus assumptus est in plenitudinem potestatis.»

Thus it can be seen that it is not merely a point of law but a *doctrine of divine revelation* that a heretic as such is intrinsically incapable of assuming or preserving in himself the form of the pontificate, and that a true and valid pope cannot defect into formal heresy. Consequently, as a strict corollary, it is according to divine law that universal acceptance effects a *sanatio in radice* for a canonically invalid election[356] **only** if the one who is elected is **not a heretic**, and therefore, is a *capable subject* and as such, *valid matter* for assuming the papacy; and for there to be a *sanatio in radice* by universal acceptance, that universal acceptance must be absolute, which is to say, *unconditional, unequivocal,* and *exclusive*; so if a heretic were capable of validly assuming the papacy and would be elected and universally accepted (which in reality would be impossible), he would be constituted a valid pope according to divine law, and therefore no merely human law would have the power to overrule divine law and deprive him of the papacy, for which reason it is evident that the above cited provision of *Cum Ex Apostolatus Officio* on the invalidity of the election of secret heretic to the papacy, even if he has been universally accepted, is not a merely human law, but pertains to divine law. Secondly, for the same reason that no merely human law could cause a pope to fall from office *ipso facto* by his heresy, but only one that is founded on divine law,[357] no pope who validly obtains the papacy by *sanatio in radice* according to divine law can be deprived of

---

[356] Alfonso Maria de' Liguori, *Verità Della Fede*, Tomo Secondo, Monza, 1823, p. 156 — «Niente ancora importa che ne' secoli passati alcun Pontefice sia stato illegittimamente eletto, o fraudolentemente siasi intruso nel pontificato; basta che poi sia stato accettato da tutta la Chiesa come Papa, attesochè per tale accettazione già si è renduto legittimo e vero Pontefice.» "It does not also matter that in the past centuries some pontiff was illegitimately elected, or fraudulently intruded into the pontificate; it is enough that he was accepted by the whole church as pope, since he already was made a legitimate and true pontiff by this acceptance."

[357] R. P. Francisci Suarez, *Opera Omnia*, Paris 1863 (Vivés), *Tomus Doudecimus, Tractatus Primus, De Fide Theologica. Disputatio X. De Summo Pontifice, Sect. VI.* p. 316: «...nec vere cadere potest Pontifex ipso facto a sua dignitate propter jus humanum, tum quia illud esset latum vel ab inferiori, scilicet concilio, vel ab æquali, nempe preedecessore Papa; at neuter horum habet vim coactivam, ut punire valeat Pontificem æqualem, vel superiorem.»

the papacy by papal decree of a previous pope, because: 1) *Par in parem non habet potestatem*, and more importantly, 2) No pope has the power to nullify the law of God. Yet it was decreed in that cited provision of *Cum Ex* that one who is elected pope and is later discovered to be a heretic is not a valid pope *even if he would have been universally accepted*, which can only be possible if that provision itself pertains to divine law, because it decrees an exception to the principle of universal acceptance, which itself pertains to divine law. Thus, it follows strictly that it is of divine law that a heretic is *simpliciter et absolute* an incapable subject of the papacy; and consequently, if a man exhibits the *dolus* of formal heresy, it is proven with absolute certitude by that fact alone that his election was invalid and he is not a valid pope even if he were to receive universal acceptance. Conversely, since it is by divine right that one who is truly accepted universally is the true pope, a heretic could not actually receive such *unconditional, unequivocal,* and *exclusive* universal acceptance, but the acceptance would be *defective,* and therefore would at best only exist according to appearance, as it indeed does, or at least did for some time in the case of Jorge Mario Bergoglio.

The proposition, however, that a heretic pope validly holding office would first need to be judged by the Church to lose office is heretical, because, if he were indeed a valid pope, it would violate the rights of the Primacy: *Pastor Æternus* defines the pope as the **supreme judge in all cases that refer to ecclesiastical examination**: «iudicem supremum... in omnibus causis ad examen ecclesiasticum spectantibus.» It pertains to the very nature of the ***judicial supremacy*** of the Roman Pontiff that his supremacy admits of no exception because the ***fullness of power*** of the Primacy has been solemnly defined to be **TOTAL**, and therefore, ***absolute***. According to the solemn definition of *Pastor Æternus*, a reigning pontiff possesses not just a share in the fullness, but the ***"total fulness of supreme power"***; and therefore is constituted as the ***"supreme judge"*** in **ALL CASES**: ***"if anyone says*** that the Roman pontiff has merely an office of supervision and guidance, and not *the full and supreme power of jurisdiction over the whole church*, and this *not only in matters of faith and morals, but also in those which concern the discipline and government of the church dispersed throughout the whole world*; or that he has **only the principal part,** but not *the total fullness, of this* *supreme power*, or that this power of his is not ordinary and immediate both over all and each of the churches and over all and each of the pastors and faithful: ***let him be anathema.***" Therefore, the proposition that "the Church", which is to say, *a council,* could, by way of exception, judge a valid pope it considers a heretic on a matter of faith, is heretical, because, 1) a council has no share in the pope's total fullness of supreme primatial power; and, 2) the Second Council of Lyon defined that definitive judgment in matters of faith is reserved to the pope: *"This Holy Roman Church possesses the supreme and full primacy and authority over the whole Catholic Church, which it recognizes in truth and humility to have received with the fullness of power from the Lord himself in St. Peter, chief of the Apostles. And just as more than the others it is bound to defend the truth of the faith, thus if there will have arisen questions of faith, by its judgment they must be defined etc."* On this basis, Vatican I defined: "*Since the Roman pontiff, by the divine right of the apostolic primacy, governs the whole church,* **we likewise teach and declare that he is the supreme judge of the faithful**' whose jurisdiction extends to "*all cases which fall under ecclesiastical examination*"; for which reason, "The **sentence of the apostolic see** (than which there is no higher authority) *is not subject to revision by anyone, nor may anyone lawfully pass judgment thereupon* [54]. And so *they stray from the genuine path of truth who maintain that it is lawful to appeal from the judgments of the Roman pontiffs to an ecumenical council as if this were an authority superior to the Roman pontiff.*" The "total fullness of supreme power" admits absolutely no exception, because it is an *absolute power* — "a full and absolute jurisdiction over the entire planet" (*plenam absolutamque iurisdictionem supra totum orbem*)[358] Hence, St. Thomas explains, "To his authority... it pertains to DETERMINE WITH FINALITY the matters of faith, so that they may be held by all with unshakable faith." (*Summa Theol. II^a II^a q. 1, art. 1*) **THE POPE CANNOT BE JUDGED IN MATTERS OF FAITH** BECAUSE HE IS THE SUPREME JUDGE TO WHOSE AUTHORITY IT PERTAINS TO JUDGE **ALL MATTERS OF FAITH**. If a man is manifestly a formal heretic it is of divine precept that he must be avoided and excluded from communion; but if he is a true pope, it is

---

[358] Constitutio Apostolica «*Vacantis Apostolicæ Sedis*» Pius XII, 8. December 1945.

of divine precept that all members of the Church must remain in communion with him, and no one on earth may judge otherwise than as he judges. **Therefore:** being that as a heretic, divine law decrees he must be judged and be declared a heretic to be avoided by the authority of the Church, the heretic absolutely falls under the jurisdiction of the Church — and because he falls under the jurisdiction of the Church, it is certain that he is not a true and valid pope in possession of the "*full and absolute jurisdiction*" of the Primacy.

Since the pope, while in office, is the supreme judge who in virtue of his universal primacy exercises "a *full and absolute jurisdiction*", **he alone is the final and infallible judge in all disputes concerning matters of faith, against whose judgment no one may appeal, not even to an ecumenical council.** Cardinal Manning observes, «Mauro Cappellari, afterwards Gregory XVI., affirms that the supreme judge of controversies is the Pontiff, "distinct and separate from all other Bishops; and that his decree in things of faith ought by them to be held without doubt."» Pope Gregory bases the doctrine expressed in this proposition on the teaching of St. Thomas:

> St. Thomas offers here a most minute prospectus of the privileges, which in the Roman Pontiff the lovers of truth glory to venerate. Speaking of the symbol of faith, he seeks after who is the supreme judge of disputes, to whom belongs the solemn edition of the symbol, that is, the norm of our belief, and concludes: 1. ° That it is the Pope: 2. ° distinct, and separate from all the other bishops, having to indeed be held by these, *inconcussa fide*, what he determines as the dogma of faith: 3. ° He proves it from Christ's Prayer and Precept: 4. ° from the unity of faith which is to be professed throughout the Church, which unity would be lacking, if the Pope were not the supreme judge of the disputes, and the only promulgator of the dogmatic definitions: 5., nor can it be said that he does it by usurpation and private authority, nor that this should be done only by the general councils independently of him: since all that is done by them has no force to oblige absolutely, without the involvement of the Pope, from whom depends the convocation and the authoritative confirmation of the councils themselves: *cuius auctoritate synodus congregatur, et eius sententia confirmatur.*[359]

---

[359] Gregory XVI, *Op. cit.*, p. 123 — «S. Tommaso per tanto offre quivi un prospetto il più minuto dei privilegi, che nel romano Pontefice si gloriano di venerare gli amanti della verità. Parlando egli del simbolo della fede, cerca

In virtue of his office as Vicar of Christ and pastor of the universal Church, the pope is always able to freely exercise supreme, full, immediate, and universal power in the Church (CIC 1983, Can. 331); and therefore he alone possesses the authority to preside over a council, and to designate and constitute the business to be transacted by the council; and to transfer, suspend or dissolve the council, and to confirm its decrees. (CIC 1917, Can. 222. §2) The powers specified in these canons were defined by the Fifth Lateran Council; and therefore, they are not the matter of merely ecclesiastical laws, but are powers inherent in the Primacy of the Roman Pontiff, solemnly defined to be absolutely supreme by the First Vatican Council. A council does not possess the authority to judge against the pope in a matter of faith or morals, but it is the pope alone, "to whose authority it pertains to DETERMINE WITH FINALITY the matters of faith, so that they may be held by all with unshakable faith." S. Thom. 2, 2, q. 1, art. 1 o.[360] Therefore, the pope, while in office, is the supreme judge in all cases with the total fullness of the supreme power of

---

chi sia il supremo giudice delle controversie, a cui appartenga la solenne *edizione* di esso simbolo, cioè della norma di nostra credenza, e conchiude: 1.° che è il Papa: 2.° distinto, e separato dagli altri Vescovi tutti, dovendo anzi da questi tenersi, *inconcussa fide*, quanto egli determina qual dogma di fede: 3.o lo prova dall'orazione e precetto di Cristo: 4.° dall'unità di fede che dee professarsi in tutta la Chiesa, la quale unità verrebbe a mancare, se il Papa non fosse il supremo giudice delle controversie, ed il solo promulgatore delle dogmatiche definizioni: 5., né può dirsi che facciolo per usurpazione e privata autorità, né che ciò convenga ai soli generali Concilii indipendentemente da lui: poiché tutto ciò che da essi si fa non ha forza di obbligare assolutamente, senza il concorso del Papa, da lui dipendendo e la convocazione e l'autorevole conferma degli stessi Concilii: *cuius auctoritate synodus congregatar, et eius sententia confirmatur.*»

[360] Quoted by Pope Gregory XVI in the cited work, p. 123 — «10. The holy doctor therefore sets forth the terms of the controversy, seeking to answer, *utrum ad summum Pontificem pertineat fidei symbolum ordinare* (3): and he replies, yes. *Dicendum quod nova editio symboli necessaria est ad vitandum insurgentes errores. Ad illius ergo auctoritatem pertinet editio symboli, ad cuius auctoritatem pertinet FINALITER DETERMINARE ea, quae sunt fidei, ut ab omnibus inconcussa fide teneantur. Hoc autem pertinet ad auctoritatem summi Pontificis, ad quem maiores et difficiliores Ecclesiae quaestiones referuntur, ut dicitur in Decretalibus extra, de Baptismo, cap. majores.*»

jurisdiction, and as such, he alone is the final and infallible judge in all cases of faith and morals, against whose judgment no one may appeal, not even to an ecumenical council.

Therefore, when they who have been led astray into heresy by Salza & Siscoe, assert of a pope who is said to be a true and valid pope, that, "the Church" must judge him a heretic before he can lose office; it must be understood that *according to the dogma of the Primacy, the definitive and final judgment objectively on the heretical opinion itself, as well on the pertinacity of the subject of the defection from the faith, fall exclusively within the jurisdiction of the holder of the Primacy for so long as he remains in office.* Thus, *it is only if a pope were to first pronounce the sentence of condemnation upon himself,* and **as an immediate and direct *ipso facto* consequence of his defection into heresy, he would fall from office *ipso jure***, would the Apostolic See then be vacant, and the judgment of the Church would not be pronounced against the pope, "but only against the person, who was *before* adorned with papal dignity."[361]

I have explained at some length in Volume One that the question of deposing a heretic pope who is a true and valid pope is a question on an impossible hypothesis that cannot ever be realized in the actual life of the Church, since it is impossible for a true and valid pope to be a heretic, because a heretic is an *incapable subject* of the papacy, or as Innocent III phrased it, an *alien*. This is proven quite easily: John of St. Thomas, in the above cited passage, following Cajetan rightly observes that it is absolutely a matter of divine precept that the heretic must be avoided. The argument is absolutely airtight in its logic, but it leads inexorably to a seemingly unresolvable paradox insofar as the absolutely unconditional precept of divine law to avoid a heretic strictly requires that if a pope were a heretic he would have to be separated from the Church by authoritative sentence; but also according to divine law, as pope, 1) being the head of the Church, the members of the Church would be required by divine law to remain united to him in ecclesial communion; and, 2) his primacy would make him *injudicable*, being absolutely above the jurisdiction of his inferiors, and therefore *totally immune from the juridical effects of any*

---

[361] D. Mauro Cappellari ora Gregorio XVI, *Op. cit.*, Venezia, 1832, p. 270.

judgment they might make. Consequently, for so long as he is pope he absolutely cannot be judged by the Church and separated from her as divine positive law absolutely requires to be done to heretics — *Ergo*: A pope cannot be a heretic or become a heretic; and as a strict corollary, a heretic is intrinsically incapable, and therefore is an *incapable subject* of assuming the habit of the papacy. What the argument of John of St. Thomas overlooks is that one who is manifestly a heretic having severed the principle bond of communion, which is faith, has already ceased to be in communion with the Church by the very fact of his heresy which directly and *per se* visibly severs his bond with the Church *ipso facto*, for which reason all offices and ecclesiastical dignity are lost, and he is separated from the body of the Church *ipso jure*, as the Council of Constance ruled in the case of Pedro de Luna. Therefore, by the very fact that the public heretic is no longer a member of the Church, he is rendered incapable of being the chief member, i.e. the head.

St. Robert Bellarmine affirms the same apostolic teaching on this point of the avoidance of heretics, and adds, saying that since it is of divine precept that after two warnings the obstinate heretic must be avoided, the prescribed avoidance must be observed *even before excommunication by the Church.*[362] However, he then points out that the pope cannot be avoided — it is impossible because, 1) as members of one body we are joined to the pope as the head;[363] and 2) because the pope cannot be judged by anyone.[364] The head possesses an absolute jurisdiction over all the members, who by divine precept are bound to remain subject to him (*Unam Sanctam*). The members cannot separate from the head without dissolving the divine constitution of the Church, as the earlier cited passages of both Bellarmine and Bordoni point out. Since it is commanded by God as absolutely to be observed, and it is defined *de fide,* that **every human being on earth**

---

[362] «Auctoritas est B. Pauli, qui in epist. ad Titum 3. Jubet, hæreticum post duas correptiones, idest, postquam manifeste apparet pertinax, vitari, & intelligit ante omnem excommunicationem, & sententiam judicis.»

[363] «at non potest vitari Papa manens Papa; quomodo enim vitabimus Caput nostrum? quomodo recedemus a membro nobis conjuncto?»

[364] *De Romano Pontifice, liber ii cap. xxvi* — «*Romanus Pontifex a nemine in terris judicari potest.*»; *liber iv cap. vii* — «non posse Pontificem judicari.».

must be subject to the Roman Pontiff[365]; and it is also absolutely commanded by God and perpetually taught by the Church that ***heretics are to be excluded from communion with the Church and must be avoided*** — it follows strictly from these premises that **there exists an absolute metaphysical incompatibility between the papacy and heresy because a pope who is a *heretic* absolutely must be avoided because he is a *heretic*, but at the same time the members of the body absolutely and unconditionally must remain united in communion with the *pope*. Since there exists an absolute incompatibility between the papacy and heresy, it is absolutely impossible for a heretic to be pope or for a pope to be a heretic.**

Ex supradictis it also follows strictly that to the extent that one is according to canonical criteria a suspected heretic, he is suspected not to be a valid pope but is a *papa dubius*; because *suspicion* founded on factual *indicia*, being not certain but only *probable*, is in the nature of a *presumption* and *doubt*, which constitutes a presumption of nullity, because a doubtful pope is no pope: **Papa dubius, Papa nullus.** It is for this reason that the Church, (as proven above in the cited passages of Gregory XVI and John of St. Thomas), possesses the infallible power to determine whether the *papa dubius* is a legitimate and valid pope or an invalid intruder, because the Church is divinely constituted as one body under one head and "one flock under one shepherd" (*Pastor Æternus*) — and that divine constitution would be destroyed if the Church would unite to a false head; or if the members would separate from the true head.

As I explained earlier, it is a point of doctrine, taught by Innocent III and unanimously by theologians that if a pope is a heretic, he can be judged; so that if the *indicia* of heresy are in evidence, it follows strictly that the case against him can be adjudicated. If the heretic pope is to be prosecuted and convicted, it can only be done if the right of injudicability inherent in the primacy is already not existing in him even before the judicial process begins, because he cannot be prosecuted or judged while in possession of the right of injudicability

---

[365] Bonifacius VIII, *Unam Sanctam,* 18 novembris 1302 — «Porro subesse Romano Pontifici omni humanae creaturae declaramus, dicimus, definimus et pronunciamus omnino esse de necessitate salutis.»

inherent in the primacy. Therefore, if a pope is a heretic, then by the very fact that he can be judged for heresy, it is proven that he is not a true and valid pope, because the habit of the pontificate which renders the pope injudicable would already necessarily be absent from him even before the judicial process begins, and before the conviction renders his heresy public and notorious. Since it is impossible for an occult heretic to invisibly cease to be pope even after the external *indicia* would necessarily render him judicable as a *papa dubius*; it follows strictly that a valid pope cannot fall into occult heresy; irrespective of whether or not the occult heresy is external or internal, because in either case, if and when the *indicia* of his formally occult but materially public heresy become known, then once they become known he necessarily becomes judicable, which would be impossible if he were to remain in possession of the papacy. **But if the pope were to fall into occult heresy as pope, an irresolvable paradox would result if afterward, the *indicia* sufficient to establish a presumption of nullity would become external and known, because he would then necessarily have to invisibly cease to be pope in order to become judicable and be judged; but since it is absolutely impossible for him to cease invisibly to be pope, then remaining in office as pope, he would necessarily remain absolutely injudicable as pope while at the same he would necessarily become judicable as a heretic; for which reason it is impossible *absolute et simpliciter* for a pope to fall into heresy.** And since, if it should occur that the pope's heresy would only be materially but not formally public, then, on the basis of the *indicia* of suspicion alone, it would not be able to be known whether or not he is a formal heretic, since those *indicia* would not suffice to determine whether he is still injudicable as a valid pope, or judicable as one who has fallen into formal heresy and ceased to be pope. Since the indefectibility of the Church renders her infallible in the power to recognize a false pope from a true pope, divine providence will necessarily dispose that one who exhibits the *indicia* of suspicion will be able to be recognized in either case: if he is a heretic, then God will provide sufficient evidence to prove he was never a true and certain pope (because as a heretic he could not invisibly fall from office). If his heresy is proven, it would thereby be proven that he was never a true pope, and the nullity of his pontificate would be confirmed by the lack of his unequivocal and exclusive acceptance as pope by the whole Church; but if his guilt cannot be proven sufficiently according to juridical standards, then divine providence would necessarily dispose that the invalidity of his claim would be manifested in some other way, such as from evidence of the invalidity of his election; or if in addition to the *indicia* of heresy, but with the canonical formalities of the heretic's election appearing to be validly fulfilled, then it could be gathered that the election was doubtful due to an uncertain or equivocal acceptance of his claim by the universal Church, since it is impossible for an *incapable subject* of the papacy to be canonically elected and receive exclusive and certain universal acceptance from the whole Church. If the irresolvable and founded positive doubt brought about by the *indicia* of heresy would remain, then the suspect would necessarily have to be judged to be a *papa dubius and therefore no pope*. What is certain is that God will not allow the whole Church to separate from a true pope or to unite to a false pope.

Citing the work of Da Silveira, Don Curzio Nitoglia explains that the opinion, which holds that a pope cannot be a heretic, is the one that is most commonly taught as the most probable by the majority of theologians and Doctors: Bellarmine, Francisco Suárez, Melchior Cano, Domingo Soto, John of St. Thomas, Juan de Torquemada, Louis Billot, Joachim Salaverri, A. Maria Vellico, Charles Journet (and Cajetan who is not cited by Da Silveira, but is demonstrated by Msgr. Vittorio Mondello in *La dottrina del Gaetano sul Romano Pontefice*, Messina, Istituto Arti Grafiche di Sicilia, 1965, cap. V, pp. 163-194 e cap. VI, pp. 195-224). According to this opinion, the pope as pope cannot fall into formal heresy, whereas he can favour heresy or fall into material heresy as a private doctor or also as pope, but only in the non-defining magisterium, which in neither infallible nor [absolutely] binding.[366] Bordoni, who held the opinion to be "very

---

[366] «la *prima opinione* o meglio l'antecedente, che è quella insegnata comunemente come la più probabile dalla maggior parte dei teologi e dei Dottori: S. Roberto Bellarmino, Francisco Suarez, Melchior Cano, Domingo Soto, Giovanni da San Tommaso, Juan de Torquemada, Louis Billot, Joachim Salaverri, A. Maria Vellico, Charles Journet (ed anche il Gaetano non citato dal Da Silveira, ma lo dimostra mons. Vittorio Mondello, ne *La dottrina del Gaetano sul Romano Pontefice*, Messina, Istituto Arti Grafiche di Sicilia, 1965, cap. V, pp. 163-194 e cap. VI, pp. 195-224) è che

probable", cites Suárez, Pedro de Simanca, Domingo Bañez, and Bellarmine to be of this opinion; and mentions that Bonacina,[367] cites others who were of the same opinion, explaining that they (as well as he) based their opinion on the belief that the words, *Ut non deficiat fides tua* were spoken *simpliciter*, and therefore without distinction between the public or the private person.[368] Bordoni also argued extensively on the notable disputed cases proving that none of those popes was a formal heretic. Bellarmine, before him, even in a more detailed manner, examined the disputed cases, proving that no pope had ever been a formal heretic in *De Romano Pontifice, lib. iv, cap. viii - xiv*. Bordoni says on this question, that it is more metaphysical than moral; and that until then, **in no pope has the pertinacity of heresy dominated, nor will it ever, because God would not permit it.**[369] Before him, St. Robert Bellarmine argued along the same lines in *De Romano Pontifice, lib. iv, cap. vii*, first citing the opinion, saying: "Many canons teach that the Pope cannot be judged unless he may be discovered to have deviated from the faith, therefore he can deviate from the faith. Otherwise these canons would be to no effect. It is clear from the preceding canon, *Si Papa*, dist. 40, from the 5th Council

---

il Papa come Papa non può cadere in eresia formale, mentre può favorire l'eresia o cadere in eresia materiale come dottore privato oppure come Papa, ma solo nel magistero non definitorio, non obbligante e quindi non infallibile (cfr. A. X. Da Silveira, p. 33, nota 1; cfr. B. Gherardini, *Concilio Ecumenico Vaticano II. Un discorso da fare*, Frigento, Casa Mariana Editrice, 2009; *Tradidi quod et accepi. La Tradizione, vita e giovinezza della Chiesa*, Frigento, Casa Mariana Editrice, 2010; *Concilio Vaticano II. Il discorso mancato*, Torino, Lindau, 2011; *Quaecumque dixero vobis. Parola di Dio e Tradizione a confronto con la storia e la teologia*, Torino, Lindau, 2011; *La Cattolica. Lineamenti d'ecclesiologia agostiniana*, Torino, Lindau, 2011).»

[367] Martino Bonacina (1585-1631) Italian bishop and jurist.

[368] Bordoni, *Sacrum Tribunal Iuducum*, cap. v. p. 131 – «Quartum quod multum probabile sit errare non posse ut privatum, docent Suar. *Disp.* 10 *sect sect.* 6 *dub.*4; Siman. Bannes, Bellarm. cum aliis quos pro se citat Bonacina in Bullam *disp.* 13 *q.*2*p.*1 *num.* 12 quia putant illa verba. *Ut non deficiat fides tua*. Dicta sunt simpliciter, ac proinde sine ulla distinctione personæ publicæ aut privatæ…»

[369] Bordoni, *Op. cit.* cap. vi. p. 149 – «Sed hæc quæstio magis Metaphysica est, quam moralis, & hactenus gratia Dei favente in nullo Pontifice dominata fuit pertinacia hæresis, nec dominabitur, quia id Deus non permitteret.»

under Symachus, from the Eighth general council, act 7, from the third epistle of Anacletus, the second epistle of Eusebius, and from Innocent III."[370] And then he argues that it cannot be concluded from those canons that a pope can in fact become a heretic: "I say those canons do not mean the Pope can err as a private person but only that **the Pope cannot be judged**; it is still not altogether certain whether the Pontiff could be a heretic or not. Thus, they add the condition 'if he might become a heretic' for greater caution."[371] He then gives the reason why a pope cannot become a heretic even as a private person: "From there it is gathered correctly that the Pope by his own nature can fall into heresy, *but not when there is posited the singular assistance of God which Christ obtained for him by his prayer*: but Christ prayed that his faith not fail, not lest he would fall into other vices."[372] His second point to prove the argument is *ab eventu*: "2) It is proven *ab eventu*. Since up until now none has been a heretic, or certainly it cannot be proven that any one has been one; therefore it is a sign that it cannot be."[373] Bordoni was even more blunt than Bellarmine on this point: "But how could a heretic pope be deposed?" and he replies with the words of Bonacina[374]: "This is an idle question, since it

---

[370] *De Romano Pontifice, lib. iv, cap. vii* – «Multi canones docent, Pontificem non posse judicari, nisi inveniatur a fide devius; ergo potest deviare a Fide: alioqui frustra essent illi canones. Antecedens patet ex can. Si Papa dist. 40. Ex Concilio V sub Symmacho, ex Concilioi VIII. Generali act. 7. Ex Anacleto epist. 3.Eusebio epist. 2. Ex Innocentio III. In serm. 2. De consecrate. Pontif.»

[371] *Ibid.* – «Canones autem citati loquuntur expresse de haeresi; igitur non loquuntur de errore judiciali, sed personali Pontificis. Secundo dico; canones illos non velle dicere, Pontificem etiam ut privatam personam posse errare, sed tantum non posse Pontificem judicari: quia tamen non est omnino certum, an possit necne esse haereticus Pontifex; ideo ad majorem cautelam, addunt conditionem, nisi fiat haereticus.»

[372] *Ibid.* – «Respondeo ad primum argumentum: inde recte colligi, posse Papam ex natura sua incidere in haeresim, non tamen posita singulari Dei assistentia, quam Christus oratione sua illi impetravit: oravit autem Christus, ne deficeret Fides ejus, non autem ne incideret in alia vitia.»

[373] *De Romano Pontifice, lib. ii cap. xxx* — «Secundo probatur ab eventu; nam hactenus nullus fuit hæreticus, vel certe de nullo probari potest, quod hæreticus fuerit; ergo signum est, non posse esse.»

[374] Martino Bonacina (1585-1631) Italian bishop and jurist.

supposes what is false, that a Pope, who cannot err, can fall into the error of heresy."*375* St. Alphonsus says on the same point, "That some Pontiffs have fallen into heresy, some have tried to prove it, but have never proven it, nor will they ever prove it; and we will clearly prove the opposite in the end of Chapter X... but we must rightly presume, as Cardinal Bellarmine says, that God will never allow any of the Roman Pontiffs, even as a private man, to become a heretic, notorious, or hidden."*376* Commenting on Ballerini, Don Curzio explains, "If one studies well the thought of don Pietro Ballerini, one sees that according to him, the pope is obligated to place himself under supernatural faith, and the natural moral law as well as the divine law; there is no human authority over him, but his power is limited to that which God has given to him who is his vicar on earth, which is only when he defines and infallibly binds; but when expressing opinions on matters not yet defined, he can err; and in an *eventual* and *possible* case of external heresy, Ballerini is not opposed to the *possibility* that the pope could fall, not dealing with definitions, but he maintains that *it has never happened in all the history of the Church and will never happen.*"*377* **It will never happen because it cannot ever**

---

375 Bordoni, *Sacrum Tribunal Iudicum,* cap. v. p. 131 – «*Quomodo autem deponatur Papa hæreticus? respondebit Bonacina… vanam esse hanc questionem, cum falsum supponat, Papam, qui nullatenus errare potest, incidere in errorem hæresis.*»

376 Alfonso Maria de' Liguori, *Verità Della Fede,* Tomo Secondo, Monza, 1823, Parte III. Capo. VIII. p. 157 – «Che poi alcuni Pontifici sieno caduti in eresia, taluni han cercato di provarlo, ma non mai l'han provato, né mai lo proveranno; e noi chiaramente proveremo il contrario nella fine del *Capo X.* … ma dobbiam giustamente presumere, come dice il Cardinal Bellarmino, che Iddio non mai permetterà che alcuno de' Pontefici Romani, anche come uomo private, diventi eretico né notorio, né occulto.»

377 «Se si studia bene il pensiero di don Pietro Ballerini si vede che secondo lui il Papa è obbligato a sottomettersi alla fede soprannaturale e alla morale naturale e divina; non ha nessuna autorità umano/ecclesiastica sopra di lui, ma il suo potere è limitato da quello di Dio di cui è il Vicario in terra; soltanto quando definisce e obbliga a credere è infallibile; come dottore privato opinando su questioni non ancora definite può errare; infine in caso di *eventuale e possibile* eresia esterna il Ballerini non si oppone alla *possibilità* che il Papa vi cada, non trattandosi di definizioni, ma ritiene che ciò *non si è mai verificato nella corso della storia della Chiesa e non si verificherà mai.*» Ballerini: «Sed haec hypothesis nullo facto comprobatur; siquidem nullus vel privatus error

happen, and it cannot ever happen because *the heresy of a pontiff would deprive the Church of her foundation; so the manifest heresy of a claimant would therefore be the ultimate and most certain proof that he is not a true pontiff but a false pope*; and therefore the church that would follow him into heresy would be a false church.

* * *

«For the Pontiff if he could be a heretic, it will be only by denying some truth defined beforehand; but he cannot be a heretic, while he defines something new; then he does not have an opinion against something defined by the Church.» — *De Rom. Pont. lib iv cap vii.*[378]

Q.—What if the pope does not deny something solemnly defined, but in the manner of Arius, teaches a new heresy not yet solemnly condemned, but nevertheless an error contrary to a truth of faith taught definitively by the ordinary and universal magisterium of the Church (i.e., what Ballerini refers to as an *"evident article of faith"*)?

Resp. — If his error does not oppose *"any defined or evident article of faith"* he cannot be judged, but his error can be opposed. An article of faith is *defined* if it has been solemnly defined by the pope or definitively taught universally by the ordinary magisterium either *explicitly*, or clearly seen to be contained in the principles of an explicit definitive teaching — such as the equality of the divine persons having been seen plainly and indisputably taught in the profession of the divinity of the individual divine persons of the Trinity. However, what is plainly evident in general may not be plainly and indisputably evident to all, such as In the case of John XXII: the article of faith may have been evident to nearly everyone in the Church except the pope himself, but it was not evident to *him,* and it had not been

---

cuipiam Pontifici adscriptus contra ullum dogma evidens aut definitum hactenus inventus est, aut futurus putatur.» [*De Potestate ecclesiastica Summorum Pontificum et Conciliorum generalium*; p. 129.]

[378] *De Rom. Pont. lib iv cap vii.* — «Nam Pontifex si possit esse haereticus, solum erit negando aliquam veritatem antea definitam; non autem potest esse hæreticus, dum ipse aliquid novi definit; tunc enim non sentit contra aliquid definitum ab Ecclesia.»

solemnly defined, so it could not be so easily proven to him that he was in heresy. If a reputed pope whose claim is doubtful would obstinately deny any of the principle dogmas, or an indisputably obvious truth of faith that is so universally known and has been clearly professed by the whole Church throughout the ages, the fact of his pertinacity in heresy would be seen manifestly as *evidenter verum*. Against such an evidently true fact of manifest heresy, there can be no legitimate dispute. It would be the duty of the bishops and cardinals to declare him a public heretic to be shunned, and to elect a legitimate pope in his place; so that anyone who would accept his claim on the papacy would know that they themselves fall into schism if they would continue to remain subject to his illegitimate claim on the papal throne. However, if he is not merely reputed to be pope, but is a true and indubitable pope who defines on a disputed point, his definition will be true and infallible. But if he only appears to be a true pope, but is in reality a false pope and a heretic, his definition might be heretical, *even on a point not yet solemnly defined*, for which reason, the falsity of his claim on the papacy would need to be established in order to safeguard the faith of all those who would be otherwise led into an error in faith by his false definition. It would then be of the gravest necessity that he be denounced to the whole Church as a heretic and intruder, and that his claimed pontificate be declared null and void. In the above cited passages, Ballerini explained, more precisely than Bellarmine on this point: 1) "The present question can only refer to that case in which the Pope, deceived by private judgment would believe, and pertinaciously contend something contrary to **any defined or *evident* article of faith**, which is properly heresy."[379] 2) "He undoubtedly, who having been once or twice corrected, does not repent, but **remains obstinate in a belief contrary to** *a manifest or defined dogma...* declares himself to be a heretic. [etc]"[380]

---

[379] Ballerini, *De Pot. Ecc.* pp. 127 — «Ad eum itaque casum tantummodo praesens quaestio referri potest, quo Papa privato judicio deceptus crederet, & pertinaciter propugnaret aliquid contrarium cuipiam articulo fidei evidenti, aut definito, quod haeresis proprium est.

[380] *Ibid.* p. 128 — «Qui nimirum semel & bis correctus non resipiscit, sed pertinax est in sententia dogmati manifesto aut definito contraria... tum vero semetipsum palam declarat haereticum [etc.]»

Q. Who is the judge? How do we judge if he is a false pope who is defining some new heresy as a dogma, or a true pope defining a dogma infallibly? *Resp.* If he is teaching a new heresy not yet formally condemned with an *anathema*, but still plainly against the belief universally professed and ordinarily taught, he can be judged doubtful or no pope either on the basis of an invalid election or a doubtfully valid election; or if the heresy is certain, even if logically but not explicitly contrary to a solemn dogma explicitly defined (as was the case with Arius even before the definition of Nicea, and with Nestorius even before the definition of Chalcedon), but can be seen in its principles to be manifestly against the universal faith of the Church evident in the unanimous consent of the Fathers, Doctors, or in the unanimity of theologians, he can be condemned as a heretic. Bellarmine's proposition on this point is valid for the merely hypothetical question he was addressing, on the impossible case of a true pope who would personally be a formal heretic in his private opinions, even expressing those opinions in his non definitive teachings, but not in his definitions, which would be protected by the grace of infallibility. The more important question would need to address the possible case which is not just a pure hypothesis, but which could actually happen if an invalidly, but apparently validly elected heretic, commonly reputed by a sizable majority to be a legitimate pope, would profess or teach — or even define against something that has been definitively taught by the Church. Then it would be most important to understand exactly what is properly meant by the term "definitively taught" in relation to a pope who would offend against a definitively held truth of faith not yet solemnly defined by a pope or council.

In his work, *The Earliest Development of Excommunication latae sententiae*, Peter Huizing S.J. pointed to a solution to this question when he addressed a particular point on a bishop's loss of jurisdiction for heresy and penned the words, "The decretists undoubtedly admitted that a heretic was «ipso facto» cut off from the Church as an excommunicated person. Some expressly state that even if there were no positive legislation of the Church on the point, the separation arose from the Natural Law."³⁸¹ St. Robert Bellarmine later pointed out the unanimous teachings of the Fathers on this point, and concluded that such a loss of office does not result from any human law but "from the nature of heresy." Huizing continued, "If he were excommunicate then he also lost his jurisdiction immediately, for an excommunicate cannot sit in judgment on the faithful. Gratian himself treats this matter. In C. 24 q. I, he deals with the question of whether a heretical bishop still has the power to excommunicate his subjects. The answer is relatively simple if the heresy which he maintains has already been condemned [...] An action against the heretic is unnecessary, the excommunication which has once and for all been settled takes effect. The heretical bishop is therefore excommunicated and has lost his power to condemn his subjects. This is therefore a clear case of excommunication latæ sententiæ". Huizing then asks, "But what is the position of the bishop who «ex corde suo» has thought out a new heresy? Gratian decides that as soon as he begins to proclaim a heresy he loses the power to excommunicate." And he answers, **"Gratian's opinion was already the common opinion in his day**, but there was a negligible one or two who held the opposing opinion."³⁸² In fact, on this point, Gratian was simply affirming the principle applied by Pope. St. Celestine in the case of the heretic Nestorius. For a dogma to be considered "definitively taught" it is not strictly required that it be solemnly defined by the extraordinary magisterium. It is not as though a solemnly defined dogma is somehow a *new* dogma, but it is only newly defined in a different way than it had been previously taught, or even definitively taught previously by the ordinary and universal magisterium of the Church. The dogma of the Primacy was already a dogma definitively taught by the universal and ordinary magisterium before it was solemnly defined by the First Vatican Council in 1870, as Pius VI pointed out already in 1786 in *Super Soliditate*, where he taught that the Primacy **"is a Catholic dogma which, received from the mouth of Christ, taught and defended with continuous**

---

[381] I have provided my own argument for this opinion in Volume One, pp. 174-176.

[382] Peter Huizing, *The Earliest Development of Excommunication latae sententiae*, Studia Gratiana 3 (1955), p. 286.

preaching of the Fathers, has been held most holy in every age by the universal Church, and often confirmed against the errors of the innovators with the decrees of the Supreme Pontiffs and the Councils." The solemn definitions give a greater precision to the meaning of a dogma in such a manner which ends the discussions between conflicting opinions on how the doctrine is to be interpreted. Thus, the dogma of the Immaculate Conception, which had already been commemorated in the liturgy of the Roman Patriarchate for many centuries, and had likewise been explicitly professed, but had been diversely interpreted by opposing schools of theologians, was solemnly defined 1854 by Pius IX in such a manner that ended the controversy forever. So, since a heretic is defined by the canons not only as one who disbelieves a solemnly defined revealed truth, but also one who disbelieves a truth that has been definitively proposed as a revealed truth by the ordinary and universal magisterium; that leaves the question: Who is the final judge to determine whether a doctrine not yet solemnly defined by the extraordinary magisterium has been already defined infallibly by the ordinary and universal magisterium — and who can then define its precise meaning? It is the pope, and only the pope who has the *munus* from Christ to judge such a question and bind the whole Church to his judgment with definitive finality. Since it is a matter of divine law that not only heretics who obstinately deny or doubt solemn definitions of faith, but **all heretics** — even those heretics who obstinately disbelieve those truths which must be believed with divine and Catholic faith, are to be excluded from communion with the Church; it is not within the competency of an imperfect council to determine with definitive finality whether or not a true and valid pope has fallen into heresy on such a point that has not yet been definitively settled. Only the pope is appointed by Christ to definitively determine with infallible finality what is or is not heresy in a matter not yet solemnly defined. The Church can judge the heretic intruder in such a matter only if the man is a *papa dubius*, and therefore presumed to be no pope, so that it would not be the pope who is judged a heretic, and who then falls from office and is deposed by the Church; but a heretic would be judged to have been invalidly elected, and to never have validly held office, and therefore would only be deposed *as a precautionary measure*, as the Council of Constance had deposed Antipope Benedict XIII *ad omnem cautelam*.

Only if a true pope would flatly express his open disbelief in a clearly defined or evident article of faith could he then be judged and deposed, as Innocent III taught, but as Dominic Prümmer OP observed, "The authors indeed commonly teach that a pope loses his power through certain and notorious heresy, *but whether this case is really possible is rightly doubted.*" [383]

Accordingly, my own answer to this question of a pope professing or teaching a heresy not yet solemnly defined was given in Volume One, and is as follows with only slight revision:

> But what if he were to profess a new heresy not yet condemned — something clearly against a doctrine of divine faith and the ordinary magisterium that has not yet been solemnly defined; or a doctrine not immediately and directly opposed to the letter of a solemn definition, but opposed to the unanimous opinion of theologians on the proper meaning of a defined dogma? If his heresy would be against a manifest dogma of divine faith as it is and has been unanimously, universally, and perpetually *professed* and understood by Catholics, which is manifestly contained by strict logical implication in a solemnly defined or universally professed article of faith; then, as was in the case of Arius,[384] it would be licit for him to be rejected by Catholics as a heretic and shunned as an infidel even on a point that had not yet been *explicitly*

---

[383] *Manuale Iuris Canonci*. Freiburg im Briesgau: Herder 1927. p. 95

[384] The *Catholic Encyclopedia* relates that Arius, "was made presbyter [...] in 313, and had the charge of a well-known district in Alexandria called Baucalis. This entitled Arius to expound the Scriptures officially, and he exercised much influence when, in 318, his quarrel with Bishop Alexander broke out over the fundamental truth of Our Lord's divine Sonship and substance. While many Syrian prelates followed the innovator, he was condemned at Alexandria in 321 by his diocesan [bishop] in a synod of nearly one hundred Egyptian and Libyan bishops. Deprived and excommunicated, the heresiarch fled to Palestine. He addressed a thoroughly unsound statement of principles to Eusebius of Nicomedia, who yet became his lifelong champion and who had won the esteem of Constantine by his worldly accomplishments. [...] In 321 was held the council that first condemned Arius, then parish priest of the section of Alexandria known as Baucalis. After his condemnation Arius withdrew to Palestine, where he secured the powerful support of Eusebius of Caesarea." Thus he was rightly condemned as a heretic on a point that the Church had not yet solemnly defined.

defined by the extraordinary magisterium; because such an *error against divine faith* on a point that is theologically certain and therefore *de fide divina*, and which is at the same time *strictly implied in a defined article of faith*, is essentially no different from, and is virtually identical to a defined article of faith; and would actually pertain to the universal and ordinary magisterium as a definitive truth of faith because it can be seen to be defined in principle and is generally held throughout the Church as a truth of faith. A clear example of this is the case of Arius: Since the full and equal divinity of Jesus Christ as the Son of the Eternal Father, was seen to be so clearly taught in scripture, and was universally *professed* in even the most primitive *credal formulæ* of the Church; the Bishop of Alexandria, St. Alexander, saw fit to condemn his error, and excommunicate Arius for heresy even before the Council of Ephesus infallibly professed against the Arian heresy with an explicit formulation. What is mainly the basis for justifying such a judgment of heresy on a doctrine not yet explicitly condemned by the magisterium but contrary to the faith of the Church, is expressed by St. Robert Bellarmine in his letter to Fr. Paolo Foscarini: "Nor may it be answered that this is not a matter of faith, for if it is not a matter of faith from the point of view of the subject matter, it is on the part of the ones who have spoken. It would be just as heretical to deny that Abraham had two sons and Jacob twelve, as it would be to deny the virgin birth of Christ, for both are declared by the Holy Ghost through the mouths of the prophets and apostles."

Indeed, Fr. Elbert Wilhelm Westhoff, Doctor of Sacred Theology, in the editor's preface of the 1845 edition of Ballerini's *De vi ac ratione primatus Romanorum Pontificum,* notes a passage of Cardinal Francesco Sforza Palavicino that is particularly relevant to this point:

> Appositely the learned Cardinal Sfortia Pallivicinus in *lib. 6 cap. 18.* expounding on the certitude of faith: "For the assent of faith it is not necessary, it is said, that the declaration of the Church always precede the single articles: otherwise for recognizing the dogmas of faith the reading of the divine scriptures would have no import, but the Church would have allowed everything else to be doubted except for the definition; and for several centuries the few things the Church defined. But to the contrary we read, the holy Fathers even before the definitions of the Church detested as heretics those who challenged some article, *drawn from the common understanding of the words of scripture:* and on that account the Church afterwards condemned them, even naming them as

impious and inflicting on them the anathema; which would have been iniquitous, unless they had been bound by faith to believe the article, before the Church had declared it. For which reason regarding matters of dogma and morals all of the Fathers could not have been deluded, indeed equally so the Church, which is forged from them and agrees with them." St. Augustine rightly explained the same thing with clear words in *lib. II. In Julian.*: "He who rejects the Saints, confesses himself to reject the Church of Christ" and the Fifteenth Synod of Toledo: "Whatever is believed against the Holy Fathers, is understood to be astray from the right rule of faith."[385]

What is certain, as Gregory XVI explained in the above cited passage,[386] is that the Church has the power to recognize a false pope, because that is necessary for her in order to remain united as one body to its true head, and constituted as the one true Church professing the true faith as "one flock under one shepherd". As, Innocent III taught, the sheep, *"do not follow the stranger but flee,*

---

[385] «Apposite doctissimus Cardinalis Sfortia Pallivicinus Trident. lib. 6 cap. 18. Nr. 5 de certitudine fidei argumentans: "Fidei assensui necesse non est, inquit, ut singulos articulos semper Ecclesiae declaratio antecedat: alioquin ad fidei dogmata cognoscenda nullam haberet vim divinae scripturae lectio, sed Ecclesia dumtaxat definitio; et per aliquot saecula, quibus paucula quaedam Ecclesia definivit, licuisset de reliquis omnibus dubitare. At contra legimus, sanctos Patres etiam ante definitions Ecclesiae detestatos fuisse tamquam haereticos eos, qui aliquem articulum refellabant, *de communi sententia e scripturae verbis deductum:* atque ea de causa Ecclesia postmodum in Conciliis eosdem execrate est, etiam impiorum nominee et anathemata inflicto; quod sane iniquum fuisset, nisi per fidem ad credendum articulum obstringerentur, antequam Ecclesia declarasset. Ea propter in rebus ad dogmata Moresque spectantibus Patres omnes hallucinari non posset, quin partier hallucinetur Ecclesia, quae tandem ex illis conflatur, et cum illis consentit. Hoc tamen intelligendum est, ut Paulo ante notavimus, cum Patres illam scripturae sententiam tamquam certam affirmant." Idem paucis aeque perspicuis verbis explicavit S. Augustinus lib. II. In Julian.: "Qui Sanctos rejicit, fatetur se universam Christi Ecclesiam rejicere" et Synuodus XV. Toletana: "Quidquid creditur contra Sanctos Patres, intelligitur aberrare a recta regula fidei."» [Pp. iv–v]

[386] D. Mauro Cappellari ora Gregorio XVI, p. 46 — «... it is clearly certain that Jesus Christ, wanting *immutable, visible and perpetual* government, founded for the safety of the faithful, must have provided the Church with all means, which are necessary in order not to be governed by an illegitimate leader.»

because they do not know the voice of strangers. The strangers are the heretics and schismatics, which the Roman Church does not follow, but pursues and drives away."[387] The heretic must not only be resisted, such as a valid pope who errs materially, and whose material heresy would destroy the Church if it would not be resisted; [388] but the formal heretic, as Innocent teaches, must be "cast out and trampled by men" (*Sermo IV. «IN CONSECRATIONE PONTIFICIS».*), otherwise his defection from the true Church of Christ will be replicated in his followers, who together with him will constitute a *false church*. Therefore it is necessary that a heretic "pope" be rejected by the Church, so that Catholics will not be induced into defecting with the false pastor and thereby be seduced into his false church. Since Christ's sheep only heed the voice of the true shepherd, and do not hearken to the voice of the stranger, it is imperative that the true shepherds denounce the heretic as an alien intruder and declare him deposed, so that the sheep may more easily recognize him as the false shepherd of a false church. It is necessary that the false pope be declared a heretic and deposed, because in order that Catholics not be led astray into defection from the true Church by the false shepherds, as happened during the time of the Protestant Reformation, it is absolutely necessary for Catholics to be able to clearly recognize which is the true Church: «For this it is necessary for us that it be verified with infallible certitude, which congregation of men is the true Church of Christ; for since the traditions of Scripture, and all dogmas plainly rest on the testimony of the Church, unless we are certain, which is the true Church,

---

[387] Innocentius III. *Sermo III. «IN CONSECRATIONE PONTIFICIS»*

[388] Cf. *De Romano Pontifice, lib. ii. cap. xxix* — «Refpondeo: negando confequentiam, quoniam ad refiftendum invafori & fe defendendum, non requiritur ulla auctoritas; neque eft opus ut qui invaditur fit judex & fuperior eo a quo invaditur; at ad judicandum & puniendum, requiritur auctoritas. Itaque ficut licet refiftere Pontifici invadenti corpus, ita licet refiftere invadenti animas, vel turbanti Rempublicam, & multo magis fi Ecclefiam deftruere niteretur: licet, inquam, ei refiftere, non faciendo quod jubet, & impediendo ne exequatur voluntatem fuam; non tamen licet eum judicare, vel punire, vel deponere, quod non eft nifi fuperioris. Vide de hac re Cajetanum tract. de auctor. Papæ & Conc. cap.27. Et Joan. de Turrecremata *lib.* 2. cap. 106.»

everything will be altogether uncertain.»³⁸⁹ *De Eccl. Mil. lib. III c. x* **That Church is the true Church, which is united in the profession of the true faith of Christ with the true pope, who is constituted as the one shepherd over the one flock of Christ.** That church is the false church which has a heretic for its head, and which professes the heresy of its false shepherd, no matter how universal and visible it might be. It is certain that if there are two claimants to the papal *munus*, that pontiff could only be the true pope who, even if he errs only materially in faith, is *not a contumacious heretic*; and he would certainly be the true pope if he has been universally and peacefully accepted by the faithful and hierarchy at least at some time before the manifestly formal heretic was elected. **If it were possible for a man to be constituted simultaneously as a valid pope and a heretic, he could not be deposed; and it would be impossible to distinguish between a true pope and a false pope according to the criterion of the orthodoxy or the heterodoxy of their faith, and consequently, between the true and false Church over which each one respectively presides.** Indeed, based on what Bellarmine says in the above cited passage on the Church, we can say the same of the pope: *Unless we are certain, which is the true Pope, everything will be altogether uncertain.* Thus, **the criterion of orthodoxy is the ultimate standard for judgment determining which is the true pope and the true Church**: A manifest heretic is not the pope, even if he appears to be universally and peacefully accepted. A manifest heretic's "church", by professing the heresy of the false pope, plainly lacks the form of the Church which consists in the orthodox profession of faith, and is therefore a false and counterfeit church which has evidently separated itself from communion with the true Church of Christ — from the Church of all time which professes the ancient apostolic faith in communion with the true successor of Peter. The true Church of Christ is not the one that professes heresy in communion with a false and heretical pope, but is only that Church

---

[389] *De Eccl. Mil. lib. III c. x* — «Ad haec, necesse est ut nobis certitudine infallibili constet, qui coetus hominum sit vera Christi Ecclesia; nam cum Scripturae traditiones, et omnia plane dogmata ex testimonio Ecclesiae pendeant, nisi certissimi simus, quae sit vera Ecclesia, incerta erunt prorsus omnia.»

which professes the faith taught by Christ: *Vera enim Ecclesia est, quae profitetur Christi fidem.*[390]

Thus, in deposing a heretical papal claimant, **once it is proven with certitude that the man is a formal heretic, it is therefore also proven that the man was never in fact a true and valid pope.** His deposition would not constitute a violation of the rights of the Primacy, because the heretic is an incapable subject of the papacy. It would simply be a judgment and removal of an intruding impostor who usurped the papal throne. Thus it is to no avail that Salza & Siscoe attempt to defend their heretical belief that a validly reigning pope can be judged by the Church by quoting a passage of *De Ecclesia Militante*[391] on the ***hypothesis*** of a secret heretic being discovered to be a heretic who is then judged guilty of heresy:

> «Bellarmine: "It is certain, whatever one or another might think, a secret heretic, if he might be a Bishop, **or even the Supreme Pontiff**, does not lose jurisdiction, nor dignity, or the name of the head in the Church, **until either he separates himself publicly from the Church (i.e., openly leaves the Church), or being convicted of heresy, is separated against his will**" (Bellarmine, On the Church Militant, ch X).»

Bellarmine had already proven with arguments presented in 1) *De Conciliorum Auctoritate cap. xvii*, and 2) *lib. ii cap. xxvi* of *De Romano Pontifice* that the pope, 1) "Being supreme head of the Church, he cannot be judged by any other ecclesiastical power", and 2) "does not recognize any judgment over him on earth." It is clear from Bellarmine's comment in *De Conciliorum Auctoritate cap. xviii*, cited above, which he made in reference to the apocryphal case of infidelity against St. Marcellinus, that the "separation" in question would not be in the nature of a deprivation of office following a judgment against an actually reigning pope; but the judgment would be an acknowledgment of the fact that being proven to be a heretic or an

---

[390] S. Robertus Bellarminus, *De Ecclesia Militante*, cap. xv.

[391] *De Ecclesia Militantis,* cap. x — «Certum est autem, quidquid unus, aut alter senserit, occultum haereticum, si Episcopus, aut etiam summus Pontifex esset, non ammitere jurisdictionem, nec dignitatem, aut nomen capitis in Ecclesia, donec aut ipse se ab Ecclesia publice separet, aut convictus haereseos invitus separetur.»

infidel, it would thereby be proven that he is not a member of the Church, and therefore, he is not the pope. In *caput xxi* of *De Concilliis et Ecclesia*, where he refutes the conditions demanded by the Protestants for holding a council (*Refutantur conditiones, quas Lutherani requirunt in concilio celebrando.*), Bellarmine refutes the objection, ["Thirdly, that the Roman Pontiff should not summon a council, nor preside over it, but that he should be one of the litigating parties, inasmuch as he is the one who is accused, and no one should be the judge and a party."] [392] saying, "The third condition is unjust; because the Roman Pontiff cannot be deprived of his right to summon councils, and presiding over them, in whose possession the right has been for 1500 years, unless beforehand he would be convicted by a legitimate judgment to not be the supreme pontiff."[393] It is precisely in this sense that he explains later in the paragraph, "It happens to be that the pontiff in a council is not the sole judge, but he has many colleagues, that is, all the bishops, who, if they could to convict him of heresy, they could even judge and depose him, albeit unwillingly."[394] Thus, it is proven absolutely that the judgment and conviction which Bellarmine speaks of would not be made on a reigning pontiff still validly holding office, but on one who is in reality not a true pope; or hypothetically, on a pope who already ceased by his heresy to be pope — a hypothesis which he proved can never happen in reality. As is defined in *Pastor Æternus*, so also, it is already set forth in the doctrine of Bellarmine: The pope's power of jurisdiction is absolute and universal; and the Church has no power of its own to wield against him, except to judge that he is not a valid pope, either due to an invalid election, or because of evident heresy

---

[392] *De Concilliis et Ecclesia, caput xxi*, p. 40 — «Tertio ut pontifex romanus non indicat concilium, nec ei praesit, sed sit altera pars litiganlium, quandoquidem ipse est qui accusatur, et nemo debet simul esse judex et pars.»

[393] *Ibid.* — «Tertia conditio iniqua est; quia romanus pontifex non potest privari jure suo indicendi concilia, et eis praesidendi, in cujus possessione jam fuit per 1500. annos, nisi prius in legitimo judicio convincatur, non esse summus pontifex.»

[394] *Ibid.* — «Accedit, quod pontifex in concilio non est solus judex, sed habet multos collegas, idest, omnes episcopos, qui si eum convincere possent de haeresi, possent etiam eum judicare et deponere, licet invitum.»

proves he was never a valid pope. If the fact of heresy is absolutely manifest and certain, such as a flat denial of the dogma of the Trinity or the divinity of Christ, then the pontificate can be annulled, i.e., judged null and void *ab initio*; but if in the course of investigation it does not emerge that the heresy is seen as a manifestly evident fact, then, in accordance with the judgment of the Fourth Roman Council under Pope St. Symmachus, the pope himself is the judge, even if he himself the one who is accused.[395] Since a judgment of papal heresy can only consist of a judgment of nullity of a man's pontificate, the power to make such a judgment is premised absolutely on the already existing nullity of the pontiff's claim on the papacy, which is presumed in the case of a doubtful pope — doubtfully valid due a doubtfully valid election, or due to positive doubt because of the very grave *indicia* of heresy against him. If the suspected heretic would still be a valid pope at the time of his trial, or any time before his conviction by the court, the proceedings would be absolutely null and void, since, as Bellarmine says, "Being supreme head of the Church, he cannot be judged by any other ecclesiastical power". The presumption of a real vacancy of the Apostolic See is the absolute prerequisite upon which the validity of a judgment against a pontiff is premised. The contrary assertion, namely, that a valid pope remains in office until he is convicted is heretical, because it attributes to the Church a power to be exercised against the absolute power of the Primacy. In the hypothetical case of an actually reigning pontiff validly holding office, who falls into formal heresy, Bellarmine says, "the Supreme Pontiff, does not lose jurisdiction, nor dignity, or the name of the head in the Church, *until either he separates himself publicly from the Church, or being convicted of heresy, is separated against his will.*" In such a hypothetical case, Bellarmine explains that as a *public heretic* he separates himself publicly from the body of the Church if he refuses to be corrected; and if his heresy is *occult*, upon being proven a heretic, it is thereby proven that he is not a true pope, or is no longer a valid pope, and he can therefore be judged — hence: *he is separated against his will* by means of a merely declaratory sentence.

---

[395] *Ibid.* p. 41 — «Denique in concilio IV. romano sub Symmacho legimus, episcopos omnes dixisse, concilium non potuisse jure indici, nisi a pontifice, etiamsi ipse esset, qui accusabatur.»

Bellarmine's refutation of the opinion that a secret heretic would fall from office at the instant he falls into heresy also proves that the judgment would not be made on a reigning pontiff still validly holding office. The argument: "Thus, the second opinion is that the Pope, in the very instant in which he falls into heresy, even if it is only interior, is outside the Church and deposed by God, for which reason he can be judged by the Church. That is, he is declared deposed by divine law, and deposed de facto, if he still refused to yield." The thesis sets forth that even if the heresy is only interior, the heretic is already deposed by God, *for which reason*, he can be judged by the Church. "That is, he is declared deposed by divine law, and deposed de facto, if he still refused to yield." Thus, according to the opinion, with the pope having already been deposed by God and no longer pope, the Church can judge him by declaring him deposed by divine law; and if he refuses to yield, the Church can actually depose him *de facto*. Thus, it is not even a question of judging or deposing an actual pope still holding office, but of judging and declaring deposed the man who was pope before he fell from office at the instant he fell into heresy.

Bellarmine counters by pointing out that "Jurisdiction is certainly given to the Pontiff by God, but with the cooperation of men, as is obvious; because this man, who beforehand was not Pope, has from men that he would begin to be Pope, therefore, it is not removed by God unless it is through men. But a secret heretic cannot be judged by men; [That is, he is declared deposed by divine law, and deposed de facto], nor is he willingly disposed to relinquish that power." Bellarmine then explains that God would not remove that power except by men. The reason why is that a secret heretic invisibly judged and deposed by God cannot be judged by men: The man who would be invisibly deposed by God, and no longer pope, cannot be judged by men to have been deposed by God because his heresy cannot be detected. But unless that judgment be made by men, God will not invisibly withdraw his jurisdiction, because it was given with the visible cooperation of men. Bellarmine concludes his refutation by pointing out that "the foundation of this opinion is that occult heretics are outside the Church," and, "that it is false we will copiously demonstrate in Book I *De Ecclesia*."[396] In *De Eccl. Mil. cap. x*,[397] after treating on public heretics and apostates earlier in the work, Bellarmine explains, "There remain finally the occult infidels, i.e. those, who have neither internal faith, nor any Christian virtue, and nevertheless they externally profess the Catholic faith for some temporal advantage, and by means of communion of sacraments mix in with the true faithful," and he quotes Augustine who describes them as being like noxious fluids in the body of Christ: *Sic sunt in corpore Christi, quomodo humores mali*. He then argues at length to prove that, "They, who are conjoined only by external profession to the other faithful are true exterior parts, precisely even members, although arid, and dead members of the Church."

Thus, in Bellarmine's refutation of the second opinion, there is absolutely not even the question an antecedent judgment against a still validly reigning pontiff as Salza & Siscoe falsely assert; but only that God will not invisibly depose the pope because the *ipso facto* fall from office cannot be judged by men to have taken place. The Salza-Siscoe argument which holds that Bellarmine's refutation of the second opinion proves that in the fifth opinion an antecedent judgment of a reigning pontiff is required for a manifest heretic to fall from office, is entirely without foundation.

The very idea itself of a pope falling into heresy, even heresy that is occult or not sufficiently manifest, so that it would need to be proven by a council before he can fall from office upon conviction is, as I have thoroughly proven in Volume One, a *pure hypothesis founded on an impossible premise*. Bellarmine himself gave the reason why it is impossible when he said in *De Romano Pontifice, lib. iv, cap. vii*, "it is gathered correctly that the Pope by his own nature can fall into heresy, *but not when we posit the singular assistance of God which Christ asked for him by his prayer*." After the First Vatican Council declared that this singular assistance promised to Peter that his faith may not fail has been given to all Peter's successors, it has become the generally

---

[396] *De Romano Pontifice lib. ii. cap. xxx* — «Adde, quod fundamentum hujus opinionis est, quod haeretici occulti sint extra Ecclesiam, quod esse falsum nos prolixe ostendimus in lib. 1. de Eccl.»

[397] *De Eccl. Mil. cap. x.* — «eos, qui sola externa professione conjuncti sunt fidelibus caeteris, esse veras partes exteriores, atque adeo etiam membra, licet arida, et mortua, corporis Ecclesiae.»

accepted opinion of theologians that the pope cannot become a heretic. Since the First Vatican Council the "First Opinion" has become the *opinio communissima*, as Don Curzio Nitoglia (quoted in Part III Section II of Volume One) points out; and is arguably (as I explained in Part III Section III) not merely probable, but *theologically certain* or at least *proximate to faith*. Fr Jean-Michel Gleize points out (in his article *The Question of Papal Heresy*) in reply to the question, "Can a pope fall into heresy?": "In fact, the negative answer to this question is the **common opinion** of theologians of the modern era." As I pointed out in Volume One, Moynihan proved the hypothesis of a pope falling into heresy originates not from any patristic tradition, but from an erroneous attribution of a Medieval canon (*Decretum Gratiani* [*Concordia discordantium canonum*], pars I, dist. 40, canon 6, *Si Papa*) based on a hypothesis formulated by Cardinal Umberto di Silva Candida († ca. 1061), to St. Boniface († 5 June 754).[398] And similarly Don Curzio points out, «Monsignor Vittorio Mondello (*La dottrina del Gaetano sul Romano Pontefice*, cit., pp. 163-194) explains that the hypothesis of the possibility of a heretic pope derives from the Decree of Gratian (dist. XL, cap. 6, col. 146) written between 1140 and 1150, in which is found a fragment erroneously believed to be of St. Boniface, († 5 June 754).»[399] In Part III of Volume One I provided the metaphysical foundation of this thesis which I have demonstrated above, but so far Salza & Siscoe have responded to all of my arguments only with contrived sophistry, crude fallacies, and gratuitous ridicule. So, when Bellarmine speaks of "a secret heretic, if he might be a Bishop, or even the Supreme Pontiff," and he explains that such a one "does not lose jurisdiction, nor dignity, or the name of the head in the Church, until either he separates himself publicly

---

[398] Cf. Moynihan, *Op. cit.* pp. 27-41.

[399] «Monsignor Vittorio Mondello (*La dottrina del Gaetano sul Romano Pontefice*, cit., pp. 163-194) spiega che l'ipotesi della possibilità del Papa eretico deriva dal Decreto di Graziano (dist. XL, cap. 6, col. 146) composto tra il 1140 e il 1150, in cui si trova riportato un frammento creduto erroneamente di S. Bonifacio († 5 giugno 754), un monaco benedettino dell'Exeter in Inghilterra inviato da papa Gregorio II ad evangelizzare la Germania, consacrato arcivescovo di Magonza e martirizzato dai Frisoni, che è considerato l'apostolo della Germania e il cui corpo riposa a Fulda.» [https://doncurzionitoglia.wordpress.com/2016/08/18/ipotesi-papa-eretico/]

from the Church, or being convicted of heresy, is separated against his will," he is clearly speaking only in the context of a pure hypothesis that is founded on the *impossible premise* that a pope can even become a heretic; and therefore, in view of his own doctrine of the *absolute injudicability of a reigning pontiff*, which he bases on the authority of solemn pronouncements of the popes and councils, and on the nature of the papacy as a divinely constituted monarchy, it is logically excluded in his doctrine that papal loss of office for heresy can be contingent in any way on the judgment of the pope's inferiors. Thus according to Bellarmine's opinion on such a hypothesis, either the pope is judged and deposed on the *founded presumption* subsequently proven that he is not a valid pope, and therefore on the certain knowledge that at the time he is judged he was already not the pope, or else he is still the supreme judge who simply cannot be judged by anyone on earth. This is evident from what he said in his refutation of Cajetan's *fourth opinion* — that faith is, 1) either a necessary disposition *simpliciter* for one to be pope, or is necessary only *ad bene esse*, i.e. to be a good pope:

> Either Faith is the necessary disposition *simpliciter* for this that someone be Pope, or only that he rightly be [pope]. If the first; then with this disposition removed by the contrary which is heresy, he straightaway ceases to be Pope... If the second, then faith is not required except to be rightly a pope, and consequently because of its defect, the Pope cannot be deposed."[400]

As I have explained, *the Church cannot err in any actual judgment on the validity of a claimant's pontificate, because to do so would constitute a defection of the Church from her divine constitution*. Such a judgment could only be confirmed as final and definitive upon the accession to the papacy of an indubitably valid pope, i.e. one who is not a heretic, and who has gained universal and peaceful acceptance of the whole Church. This is in fact how the doubt about the contested papacy was resolved by the Council of Constance. The Council, 1) condemned Antipope Benedict XIII as a heretic and schismatic, 2) declared that he had already fallen from any office he may have previously held, 3) elected

---

[400] *De Rom. Pont. lib. ii. cap. xxx.*

Martin V, who subsequently gained the universal acceptance of the whole Church.

As the supreme judge immune from all judgment by his inferiors, a valid pope suspected of heresy and subsequently convicted of heresy (according to juridical standards of proof which is not absolutely certain) would not be validly convicted, and the judgment would have no effect except in the pure hypothesis that he had already vacated the office by having become an incapable subject of the papacy. If he were to be considered a valid pope and already a secret heretic before the time he was judged, then even as a heretic validly holding office, he would necessarily have to be considered a capable subject of the pontificate, and therefore immune from the subsequent judgment by his inferiors after the discovery of his heresy; and he would remain a valid pope even after conviction and deposition by his inferiors, because as pope, he would remain the supreme, final, and infallible judge with the primatial power to overturn the judgment of his inferiors. Therefore, in the hypothetical case of a valid pope who falls into heresy, *only if the heresy already rendered him an incapable subject, even before judgment and conviction after the heresy is found out*, only then could he be validly judged, convicted and deposed, having already been a non-pope and *minor quolibet catholico* even before his heresy is discovered and judged.

Although it would be of metaphysical necessity for the heretic to desist from the papacy even if he were to lose only the necessary internal disposition to conserve the form of the pontificate, it would be impossible for the visible head of the Church to invisibly cease to be pope merely by losing the necessary internal disposition to conserve the form of the papacy, as Bellarmine proved in his refutation of the second opinion in *De Romano Pontifice lib. ii cap. xxx*. Furthermore, he also proves it impossible in the tenth chapter of *De Ecclesia Militante*, because if the heretic would invisibly cease to be pope, it would bring about the defection of the Church, as a result of the Church then being united to a false head. Therefore, since it is impossible for the pontificate to be lost invisibly, it is of strict necessity that there be included in the grace of office the efficacious grace to preserve the pontiff in the virtue of faith, lest by his defection from the faith, the Church would defect not only by being united to a false head, but also, with the pope having invisibly ceased to be pope, the fallen pope would also cease to be capable of infallibly confirming the faith, which would also bring about the defection of the Church from the true faith, since the unity of the faith would no longer be able to be preserved by an infallible pope. Thus, if it were possible for a secret heretic to validly hold the papal office, being that it would be impossible for a secret heretic to invisibly fall from the pontificate; it would therefore be impossible for a formally occult but materially public heretic to be judged and removed from the papal office upon conviction by his subordinates, because any judgment against him would be made while he would still enjoy the divine privilege of papal injudicability inherent in the absolute power of the primacy.

It is objected, however, that Bellarmine does in fact contradict the principle of absolute papal injudicability in his exposition on the supposed deposition of Pope Liberius. Bellarmine devoted an entire chapter (*De Romano Pontifice lib. iv. cap. ix*) to the case of Liberius, and he does indeed say Liberius did not teach heresy nor was he a heretic, but only sinned by external act (*non tamen Liberius aut hæresim docuit, aut hæreticus fuit, sed solum peccavit actu externo*), thus, he was not a heretic but was thought to be one (*tamen habebatur*); so the Roman clergy abrogated his pontificate and elected Felix, "and from that time Felix began to be the true Pontiff." He concludes by saying that, "Although Liberius was not a heretic, he was held to be a heretic, due to the peace made with the Arians, and on the basis of that presumption his pontificate could rightly be abrogated."[401] To this objection it can only be said that Bellarmine's conclusion, "on the basis of that presumption his pontificate could rightly be abrogated," does indeed flatly contradict his own doctrine as well as the teachings of the popes and councils he cited as the proof from authority that the pope absolutely cannot be judged by anyone. Indeed, after the definition of the Primacy in 1870, the proposition that a validly reigning pope

---

[401] *De Romano Pontifice, lib. iv. Cap. ix* — «Post biennium deinde successit lapsus Liberii, de quo fupra diximus; tunc vero Romanus Clerus, abrogata Liberio Pontificia dignitate, ad Felicem se contulit, quem Catholicum esse sciebat; & ex eo tempore cœpit Felix verus Pontifex esse. Tametsi enim Liberius hæreticus non erat, tamen habebatur, propter pacem cum Arianis factam, hæreticus; & ex ea praesumptione merito potuit ei Pontificatus abrogari.»

could have his pontificate abrogated by his inferiors for any reason can be seen to be heretical in that it directly opposes the "total fullness of supreme power" which that definition solemnly declared to pertain to the authority of the Roman Pontiff.

The reason for Bellarmine's contradicting his own doctrine was the erroneous belief commonly held at the time, that Felix II became the pope while Liberius was still living; and therefore he reasons that, "unless we admit that Liberius had failed in constancy in upholding the Faith, we are compelled to exclude Felix II, who bore the pontificate with Liberius still living, from the number of pontiffs, although the Catholic Church venerates this same Felix as a Pope and Martyr."[402] However, since the time of Pope John XXIII, the Church no longer venerates Felix II as a pope and martyr, because he was neither pope nor martyr; and the true, historical St. Felix the Martyr was never a pope.[403] Faced with what he believed to be an indisputable historical fact, he was forced to attempt to explain how that fact came

---

[402] *Ibid.* — «nisi fateamur, Liberium aliquo tempore dececiſſe à conſtantia in Fide tuenda; cogimur, Felicem II. qui Liberio vivente Pontificatum geſſit, a numero Pontificum excludere; cum tamen hunc ipsum Felicem ut Papam & Martyrem Ecclesia Catholica veneretur.»

[403] *Catholic Encyclopedia* — «When Constantius visited Rome in May, 357, the people demanded the recall of their rightful bishop Liberius who, in fact, returned soon after signing the third formula of Sirmium. The bishops, assembled in that city of Lower Pannonia, wrote to Felix and the Roman clergy advising there to receive Liberius in all charity and to put aside their dissensions; it was added that Liberius and Felix should together govern the Church of Rome. The people received their legitimate pope with great enthusiasm, but a great commotion rose against Felix, who was finally driven from the city. Soon after, he attempted, with the help of his adherents to occupy the Basilica Julii (Santa Maria in Trastevere), but was finally banished in perpetuity by unanimous vote of the Senate and the people. He retired to the neighbouring Porto, where he lived quietly till his death. Liberius permitted the members of the Roman clergy, including the adherents of Felix, to retain their positions. Later legend confound the relative positions of Felix and Liberius. In the apocryphal "Acta Felicis" and "Acta Liberii", as well as in the "Liber pontificalis", Felix was portrayed as a saint and confessor of the true Faith. This distortion of the true facts originated most probably through confusion of this Felix with another Felix, a Roman martyr of an earlier date.»

about; so he postulated that Liberius had been deposed, and was then replaced by "Felix II"; and in attempting this explanation, Bellarmine contradicted his own doctrine on the injudicability of the popes.

Bellarmine's exposition on this point reveals a logical inconsistency in his own thinking. In *liber i* and *liber ii* of *De Romano Pontifice* he demonstrates that the government of the Church is an absolute monarchy, and the greater part of *liber ii* is focused on proving the absolute supremacy of the papal monarchy by divine right; and in *liber iv* he elaborates the spiritual power of the Roman Pontiff. Among the many arguments set forth each in separate chapters of *liber ii*, from *cap. xii* to *cap. xxviii* of *liber ii*, proving that *The Roman Pontiff Succeeded Peter in the Ecclesiastical Monarchy*,[404] Bellarmine asserts the *absolute injudicability* of the pope by any human power in *cap. xxvi*; but in *liber iv. cap. ix*, in the above cited passage, he makes the contrary assertion, saying that although Liberius was not a heretic, since the pastors of the Church had sufficient evidence to establish a presumption amounting to juridical proof of heresy, "on the basis of that presumption his pontificate could rightly be abrogated". This proposition directly contradicts his own exhaustively elaborated doctrine of the pope's full, absolute, and supreme power upon which the Vatican I solemn definitions of papal primacy and infallibility were largely based.

In *lib i. cap. ix.* Bellarmine argues that ecclesiastical government is pre-eminently monarchical, and in *cap. x* he proves the Petrine monarchy from the Gospel passage of Matthew 16: *Thou art Peter and on this rock I will build my Church, and I will give thee the keys of the kingdom of heaven, and whatever thou shalt bind on earth will be bound in heaven, and whatever thou shalt loose on earth will be loosed in heaven*; simply commenting that, "The plain and obvious meaning of these words is that under the two metaphors is understood the promise to Peter of rulership of the whole Church."[405] In the following chapter he adds, "The

---

[404] «XII. *Romanum Pontificem Petro Succedere in Ecclesiastica Monarchia; provatur ex divino jure & ratione Successionis.*»

[405] «Ac ut a primo incipiamus, prior locus eft, Matth. 16. ubi sic legimus: *Tu es Petrus & super hanc petram edificabo Ecclesiam meam, & tibi dabo claves regni cælorum, & quodcumque ligaveris in terram, erit ligatum & in cœlis, & quodcumque folveris super terram, erit solutum & in cælis.* Quorum verborum planus & obvius

Catholics teach that what is meant by this metaphor (*on this rock I will build my Church*) is that to Peter was given the rulership of the whole Church, and particularly concerning Faith. Of a rock it is properly a fundamental characteristic to uphold and support. Also the Fathers explain it this way."[406] In *cap xiii* he explains what is meant by the keys in Matthew 16, saying, "We and all Catholics understand by the keys given to Peter, the supreme power in all the Church;" and in his third proof, which is from the Fathers, he says, "Chrysostom explaining this promise in Homily 55 in Matthew says, to Peter was committed the entire planet, and he was made the Pastor and Head of the whole Church."[407] In a fairly lengthy chapter of the same work, *lib. ii cap. xii*, Bellarmine presents multiple arguments which prove from divine law and reason that the Roman Pontiff succeeded Peter in the ecclesiastical monarchy. He begins, "Thus far we have demonstrated that the Roman Pontiff succeeds Peter in the Roman Bishopric, now we will set about to demonstrate the same regarding the succession in the primacy of the universal Church."[408] For the present purpose only the second and fifth arguments are of interest. In the second he argues from the unity of the Church, explaining that the Church is one and the same for all time, and therefore it must not change its form of government, so that if in the time of the Apostles there was one supreme ruler and head of the Church, then likewise in our time

---

sensus est, ut intelligamus, fub duabus metaphoris promissum Petro totius Ecclesiae principatum.»

[406] C A P U T XI. — «*Quid sit super petram edificari Ecclesiam, Matth. 16.* — Catholici autem docent, hac metaphora significari, Petro esse commissum regimen totius Ecclesiæ, & præcipue circa Fidem. Petrae enim fundamentali hoc est proprium, totum ædificium regere & sustentare. Atque hoc modo exponunt Patres.»

[407] C A P U T XIII. — «At nos & Catholici omnes per claves datas Petro, intelligimus summam potestatem in omnem Ecclesiam: … Tertio probatur ex Patribus: nam Chrysostomus hom. 55. in Matth. hanc promissionem exponens, dicit, Petro commissum universum Orbem terrarum, & ipsum factum Pastorem & Caput totius Ecclesiæ.»

[408] *Lib. II cap xii.* — «Demonstravimus hactenus, Romanum Pontificem Petro succedere in Episcopatu Romano: nunc id ipsum demonstrare aggredimur de successione in universae Ecclesiae primatu.»

also it must be so.[409] In the fifth he argues that the Church is a body, and besides Christ, he proves that the Church also has a head here on earth; and no other head can be assigned besides Peter, so that with the death of Peter, precisely because the Church is a body, it must not remain without a head, and so it was necessary for someone to succeed Peter.[410] Thus, the absolute rulership of Peter over the Apostles and the universal Church is passed on to his successors, so that the bishops could no more depose the Pontiff from his primatial office any more than the Apostles could have deposed Peter, the Prince of Apostles appointed by Christ, and replace him with someone else of their own choosing.

This is especially true, first, in consideration of Bellarmine's proof that the bishops have absolutely no share in the supreme rulership which pertains exclusively to the pope, but only a subordinate power that they can only exercise on an individual basis, and not collegially. In *lib. i cap. viii*, he shows that ecclesiastical governance does not primarily reside with the bishops: "First, never in the Scriptures does one read that the supreme power was given to a Council of priests: whatever authority was granted to the other Apostles and disciples by Christ, was not only given to all of them but even was even given to them singly; nor was it the task of a Council to exercise it: without doubt the single Apostles could, and also now the single bishops can teach, baptize, loose, bind, ordain Ministers etc. Matth. 18 is the only place where something is granted to a Council, when it is said: *Where two or three will be congregated in my name, there I am in their midst*. But neither here is it explained what is the power of the Council, highest,

---

[409] *Ibid.* — «Secundo ex unitate Ecclesiae. Nam Ecclesia est una & eadem omni tempore; non debet igitur mutari forma regiminis, quæ est forma etiam Reipublicæ & Civitatis. Quare si Apostolorum tempore, unus erat supremus Rector, & Caput Ecclesiae, hoc etiam tempore esse debet.»

[410] *Ibid.* — «Quinto, Ecclesia est unum corpus, & suum quoddam Caput hic in terris habet præter Christum, ut patet ex 1. Cor. 12. ubi posteaquam dixit Paulus Ecclesiam esse unum corpus, subject: *Non potest caput dicere pedibus» non estis mihi necessarii*, quod certe non convenit Christo; ipse enim potest dicere nobis omnibus, non estis mihi necessarii: nullum autem aliud Caput assignari potest præter Petrum, nec debet moriente Petro corpus Ecclesiae manere sine Capite; oportet igitur aliquem Petro succedere.»

mid-level, lowest..."[411] In the sixteenth and seventeenth chapters of *De Conciliorum Auctoritate* (cited above), Bellarmine proves there exists no supreme power in a council apart from the pope, neither formally nor suppletively; and the supreme Pontiff is absolutely over a council. Secondly and in particular, in view of the fact that, "to Peter was given the rulership of the whole Church, and particularly concerning Faith," (*De. Rom. Pont. lib. I cap. xi*) — enumerating and elaborating on the spiritual powers of the Roman primacy, Bellarmine explains in *lib. iv cap. i.* that **the pope is the supreme judge in settling controversies of faith and morals** (*quod Papa sit summus judex in controversis Fidei, & morum dijudicandis*).

On the spiritual powers of the supreme Pontiff, Bellarmine first sets forth the four main questions:

> Moreover, on the spiritual power of the Pontiff, although many points in particular could be dealt with, however there are four main questions. One on the power of judging controversies of Faith and morals; whether that power is located in the supreme Pontiff. The second concerning certitude; or, as we say, the infallibility of this judgment; whether the supreme Pontiff in judging controversies of Faith and morals can err. Third on the coercive power laws to be enacted; whether the supreme Pontiff not only can judge, and in judging not err; but also enact laws which bind men in conscience, and bind to believe or act as the supreme Pontiff has judged. Fourth on the imparting of this power, is the jurisdiction of all the other Ecclesiastical superiors undoubtedly transmitted to them by the supreme Pontiff, or is it received immediately from God.[412]

---

[411] C A P U T VIII. — «Primum nusquam in Scripturis legitur collata summa potestas Concilio sacerdotum: quæcumque enim auctoritas Apostolis cæterisque discipulis concessa a Christo est, non solum omnibus sed etiam singulis concessa est; neque ad eam exercendam erat opus Concilio: poterant enim sine dubio Apostoli singuli, & possunt etiam nunc singuli Episcopi, docere, baptizare, solvere, ligare, ordinare Ministros &c. solus est locus Matth. 18. ubi tribuitur aliquid Concilio, cum dicitur: *Ubi fuerint duo vel tres congregati in nomine meo, ibi sum in medio eorum.* At neque hic explicatur, quæ sit potestas Concilii, summane, an mediocris, an infima...»

[412] *Lib. iv cap. i* — «Porro de spirituali Pontificis potestate, etsi multa in particulari tractari possent, quatuor tamen sunt praecipue quaestiones. Una de potestate judicandi controversias Fidei, & morum; num videlicet ea

Before commenting any further, it can already be understood in virtue of the principles he already demonstrated, what will be his answers which logically follow from them by strict implication. Since Bellarmine himself uses the expression "fullness of power" to characterize the pontiff's supreme power which he proved is an authority which is *absolute et simpliciter* over the whole Church, it is almost superfluous to comment any further on the first question, as he admitted himself; but rather than say nothing further than to point out the evident truth that is already luminously clear in the principles alone, he proceeded to elaborate some proofs. So he continues:

> But neither will the first general question on the judge of disputes detain us in this place: for in the disputation *de verbo Dei* we already showed that the Judge of Controversies is not the Scripture, nor secular Princes, nor private men, although upright and learned, but Ecclesiastical Prelates. But in the disputation on Councils, it will be demonstrated that Councils, whether general or particular have judgment on controversies of religion, but that judgment then will finally be firm, and ratified when there will come the confirmation of the supreme Pontiff; consequently the final judgment is of the supreme Pontiff [...] Finally, this same point will also be made obvious in the following question. For if we will be able to demonstrate the judgment of the supreme Pontiff to be certain and infallible; it will also be evident that the same Pontiff is the supreme judge of the Church. For why would God bestow upon the Apostolic See the infallibility of judgment, unless He would grant to that same See **the supreme power in judgments**? But nevertheless, lest we say nothing in this place, we will, if you please, bring forth a few testimonies from the law, from the Gospel, and from the Fathers.[413]

---

potestas in summo Pontifice sita sit. Altera de certitudine; sive, ut sic loquamur, de infallibilitate hujus judicii; utrum summus Pontifex in judicandis controversiis Fidei & morum errare possit. Tertia de potestate coactiva legum ferendarum; an Pontifex summus non solum judicare possit, & in judicando non erret; sed etiam possit leges ferre, quæ homines in conscientia obligent, & cogant credere, aut, agere, prout summus Pontifex judicavit. Quarta de communicatione hujus potestatis, sitne videlicet omnium aliorum Ecclesiasticorum Præsulum jurisdictio a summo Pontifice illis communicata, an a Deo immediate accepta.»

[413] *Ibid.* — «Sed nec prima quastio generalis de judice controversiarum, hoc loco diutius nos detinebit: nam in disputatione de verbo Dei jam osendimus, Judicem Controversiarum non esse Scripturam, nec seculares

It is precisely this *supreme power in judgments* which the First Vatican Council defined as pertaining to the Roman Primacy in the above cited passage, where it is stated, that the Roman Church in the person of successor of Peter "possesses the supreme and full primacy and principality over the whole Catholic Church... together with the fullness of power;" for which reason it is by the judgment of this primacy that *all questions of faith must be decided:* ***si quae de fide subortae fuerint quaestiones, suo debent iudicio definiri.*** In a dispute over a matter of faith, a council cannot judge against a pope's judgment, because such a judgment requires a superior authority. St. Alphonsus, citing the Third Lateran Council (Cap. Licet. 6. de Elect. S. 3), explains, "the particular churches being spoken of, it is said that the questions can be defined with the judgment of the superior, but, speaking of the Roman Church, it is said: *In Romana vero Ecclesia aliquid speciale constituitur, quia non potest recursus ad superiorm haberi.* If there is no other superior from the Pontiff, he must necessarily be held to be infallible in his definitions. The same is said in the Roman Council under Pope Simmacus: *Papam esse summum pastorem, nullius, extra casum hæresis, judicio subjectum.* Tom. 2. Concilior."[414] So on the one hand, the

---

Principes, nec privatos homines, quamvis probos & doctos, sed Ecclesiasticos Praelatos. In disputatione vero de Conciliis, demonstrandum erit, habere quidem Concilia tam generalia, quam particularia judicium de controversiis religionis, sed illud judicium tum demum esse firmum, et ratum cum accesserit summi Pontifices confirmation; proinde ultimum judicium summi Pontificis esse. [...] Denique, idipsum in sequenti etiam quæstione planum fiet. Nam si demonstrare poterimus, judicium summi Pontificis certum ac infallibile esse; profecto constabit quoque eumdem Pontificem summum Ecclesiæ Judicem esse. Quorsum enim Deus attribuisset Apostolicae Sedi judicii infallibilitatem, nisi attribuisset eidem Sedi summam in judiciis potestatem? Nihilominus tamen, ne nihil omnino hoc loco dicamus, proferamus si placet pauca quædam testimonia ex lege, ex Evangelio, ex Patribus.»

[414] Alfonso Maria de' Liguori, *Verità Della Fede*, Tomo Secondo, Monza, 1823, Capo X. p. 283 — «parlandosi delle chiese particolari, si dice che i dubbj possono definirsi col giudizio del superiore, ma, parlandosi della Chiesa Romana, dicesi: *In Romana vero Ecclesia aliquid speciale constituitur, quia non potest recursus ad superiorem haberi*. Se dal Pontefice non v ' è ricorso ad altro superiore, necessariamente egli dee tenersi per infallibile nelle sue definizioni. Lo stesso si dice nel Concilio Romano sotto il Papa Simmaco:

pope is the supreme judge in all questions concerning matters of faith, with the exception that he can be judged for heresy. At first glance, one might be excused for easily being led to the conclusion on the basis of these rulings that the pope is the supreme judge over others in matters of faith, but where his own beliefs are concerned, the pope can be judged for heresy by the Church. Bellarmine himself admitted that the pope can be judged for heresy in *De Romano Pontifice lib. ii cap. xxx*:

> First, that a heretical pope can be judged, is expressly stated in can. *Si Papa* dist. 40. and in Innocent III's serm. 2. de consecr. Pontif. And what is more in the Eighth Synod act. 7 there is stated in the acts of the Roman Council under Hadrian, and in them it is contained that Pope Honorius was seen to be anathematized, because he was convicted of heresy, for which sole cause it is licit for inferiors to judge superiors. Here it is also to be noted, what even is probable that Honorius was not a heretic, and Pope Hadrian II, deceived from corrupted copies of the Sixth Synod falsely thought Honorius was a heretic: nevertheless we cannot deny that Hadrian with the Roman Council, indeed and the whole Eighth General Synod felt, in the case of heresy the Roman Pontiff can be judged.[415]

However, this simply cannot be that an indubitable and *validly reigning pontiff* can be judged for heresy while holding office as the successor of Peter, since it is precisely because it pertains to the pope's primatial authority, that in virtue of his full and absolute power of

---

Papam esse summum pastorem, nullius, extra casum hæresis, judicio subjectum. Tom. 2. Concilior.»

[415] «Primo, quoniam hæreticum Papam posse judicari, expresse habetur can. *Si Papa* dist. 40. & apud Innocentium serm. 2. de consecr. Pontif. Et quod majus est in VIII. Synodo act. 7 recitantur acta Concilii Romani sub Hadriano, & in iis continebatur, Honorium Papam jure videri anathematizatum, quia de haeresi fuerat convictus, ob quam solam caussam licet minoribus judicare majores. Ubi notandum est, quod etsi probabile sit, Honorium non fuisse hæreticum, & Hadrianum II. Papam deceptum ex corruptis exemplaribus VI. Synodi, falso putasse Honorium fuisse haereticum: tamen non possumus negare, quin Hadrianus cum Romano Concilio, immo & tota Synodus VIII. generalis senserit, in caussa haeresis posse Romanum Pontificem judicari.»

jurisdiction he is **absolutely** the supreme and final judge in **all cases under ecclesiastical jurisdiction** in matters of faith, and for precisely that reason, Bellarmine asserts in the above cited passage, that he enjoys the privilege of infallibility: "For why would God bestow upon the Apostolic See the infallibility of judgment, unless He would grant to that same See **the supreme power in judgments**?" Therefore, it is quite impossible that a Council, which is not infallible, would have the necessary jurisdiction to judge a pope, whose judgment is infallible, in the event that the pope himself would fall into heresy, unless the heretic pope would first cease by himself *ipso facto* to be pope, a Christian, and a member of the Church, without deposition or any other external agency; and for which reason, he, no longer superior but lower in rank than any Catholic, could be judged and punished by the Church. This is in fact Bellarmine's stated position on the question, as it must be and cannot be other, because Bellarmine's doctrine on the pope's absolute power over a council, dogmatized absolutely by the First Vatican Council, logically excludes that there could ever exist any exception to such a power for so long as that absolute primatial power exists in the pope. Therefore, it would only be possible for a pope to be subject to judgment for heresy if the validity of his pontificate were itself doubtful and presumed null, and the Apostolic See accordingly presumed vacant. It is only in this sense that the words of the above cited Roman Council (*"Papam esse summum pastorem, nullius, extra casum hæresis, judicio subjectum"*) can be understood in a manner consistent with the dogma of the primacy.

In the first chapter of the fourth book, where he outlined the four general questions to be treated, he mentioned also, "Besides these general questions there are other particular questions which are accustomed to be treated upon; such as whether the supreme Pontiff can convene, transfer, [and] dissolve general Councils... which we will treat upon in their proper place, God willing."[416] It was in the seventeenth chapter of *De Conciliorum Auctoritate* (quoted above) that

---

[416] *De Rom. Pont. lib. iv. cap. i* — «Præter has generales quaestiones tracari solent quædam aliæ particulares; ut, an possit summus Ponifex Concilia generalia congregare, transferre, dissolvere: ... In quibus locis eas, Deo volente, tractabimus.»

he answered that question in the affirmative, citing the Fifth Lateran Council.

Belarmine's doctrine on the simple and absolute superiority of the pope over a council is simply the strict logical corollary of his doctrine on the nature and power of the primacy and of ecclesiastical jurisdiction. In the twenty-second chapter of the fourth book (*De Rom. Pont.*), Bellarmine explained that it was only on the pontiff that Christ immediately conferred ecclesiastical jurisdiction. He begins saying, "There remains the final question of the derivation of Ecclesiastical power from the supreme Pontiff to the other bishops."[417] [exterior jurisdiction] He concedes that, "all agree on this that jurisdiction of the Bishops at least in general is of divine law: for Christ himself ordered the Church accordingly, that in her there be Pastors, Teachers, etc."[418] And he continues, "But the question is, whether canonically elected Bishops receive their jurisdiction from God, just as the supreme Pontiff receives it: or from the Pontiff. There are three opinions of Theologians about this."[419] "The first of them, who would have the Apostles and the other Bishops as well to have received and to receive jurisdiction immediately from God."[420] [Franciscus Victoria & Alphonsus a Castro] "The second is of them who would have the Apostles not from Christ but from Peter, and the Bishops not from Christ but from Peter's successor to have received, and receive jurisdiction."[421] [Joannes de Turrecremata &

---

[417] *De Rom. Pont. lib. iv. cap. xxii* — «Restat postrema quæstio de derivatione potestatis Ecclesiasticae a Pontifice summo ad Episcopos caeteros. [jurisdictionis exterioris].»

[418] *Ibid.* — «Et quidem omnes in eo conveniunt, jurisdictionem Episcoporum saltem in genere esse de jure divino: nam Christus ipse ita ordinavit Ecclesiam, ut in ea sint Pastores, Doctores &c.»

[419] *Ibid.* — «At quæstio est, an Episcopi canonice electi accipiant a Deo suam jurisdictionem, sicut eam accipit summus Pontifex: an vero a Pontifice. Sunt autem tres de hac re Theologorum sententiæ.»

[420] *Ibid.* — «Prima eorum, qui volunt, tam Apostolos, quam cæteros Episcopos immediate a Deo accepisse & accipere jurisdictionem.» [Franciscus Victoria & Alphonsus a Castro]

[421] *Ibid.* — «Altera est eorum, qui volunt, Apostolos non a Christo sed a Petro, & Episcopos non a Christo sed a Petri successore accepisse, vel accipere jurisdictionem.» [Joannes de Turrecremata & Dominicus Jacobatius]

Dominicus Jacobatius] "The third is the middle of them, who would have the Apostles to indeed have received from Christ immediately all their authority, but the Bishops not receiving it from Christ but from the supreme Pontiff. Thus Cajetan in tract. de auctorit. Papæ, & Concil. cap.3., Dominicus a Soto in 4. dist. 20. quaest. 1. art. 2., Franciscus Vargas in his book on this question, Hervæus in lib. de potest. Papæ, Gabriel in canonem Missae, lect. 3. And the same is seen to be the position of the old Scholastics, St, Bonaventure, (St.) Albert, Durandus, and others in 4. dist. 18. aut 20. aut 24., which sentence is most true; and therefore is briefly to be confirmed."[422] Then in the twenty-fourth chapter he asserts and proves that all bishops receive their jurisdiction from the pope[423]: "That all ordinary jurisdiction of the Bishops immediately comes down from the Pope is proven,"[424] eight proofs, the last of which: "Lastly the words of the Pontiff come into view, which are used in creating Bishops; for thus is said: *We provide to such Church such person, and place him in authority as Father and Pastor, and Bishop of the same Church, committing to him the administration in temporal and spiritual matters, in the name of the Father, and the Son, and the Holy Ghost, Amen.*"[425] Finally, in the seventeenth chapter of *De Conciliorum Auctoritate*, he cites the Fifth Lateran Council: "the Roman Pontiff alone, possessing as it were authority over all Councils, has full right and power of proclaiming Councils, or

---

[422] *Ibid.* — «Tertia est media eorum, qui volunt, Apostolos quidem accepisse a Christo immediate omnem suam auctoritatem, tamen Episcopos non a Christo sed a summo Pontifice eam accipere. Ita Cajetanus in tract. de auctorit. Papæ, & Concil. cap.3. Dominicus a Soto in 4. dist. 20. quaest. 1. art. 2. Franciscus Vargas in libello de hac ipsa quæstione, Hervæus in lib. de potest. Papæ, & Gabriel in canonem Missae, lect. 3. & eadem videtur sententia veterum Scholasticorum, B. Bonaventurae, Alberti, Durandi, atque aliorum in 4. dist. 18. aut 20. aut 24. quae sententia verissima est; & ideo breviter confirmanda.»

[423] *Ibid. cap. xxiv* — «*Episcopos omnes a Papa jurisdictionem accipere.*»

[424] *Ibid.* — «Quod vero omnis ordinaria jurisdictio Episcoporum a Papa immediate descendat, probatur...»

[425] *Ibid.* — «Accedant ultimo verba Pontificis, quibus utitur in creandis Episcopis; sic enim ait: *Providemus Ecclesiae tali de tali persona, & præficimur eum in Patrem & Pastorem, ac Episcopum ejusdem Ecclesiae, committentes ei administrationem in temporalibur, & spiritualibus, in nomine Patris, & Filii, & Spiritus sancti, Amen.*»

transferring and dissolving them"; and he also provides historical examples of the exercise that primatial power over councils, whether to approved confirm, or to condemn and quash.[426]

The reason why the bishops, who are successors of the apostles, do not receive their jurisdiction directly from God in the same manner that the pope as successor of Peter receives his jurisdiction directly from God, is the difference in the manner of succession, which Bellarmine explains:

> I answer: there is a great difference between the succession of Peter, and the other Apostles. For the Roman Pontiff properly succeeds Peter, not as an Apostle, but as the ordinary Pastor of the whole Church; and therefore the Roman Pontiff has jurisdiction from him, from whom Peter had it: but the Bishops do not properly succeed the Apostles, because the Apostles were not ordinaries, but extraordinaries, and as delegated Pastors, to which there is not succession. Nevertheless the Bishops are said to succeed the Apostles, not properly in that manner, where one bishop succeeds another, and one king another, but by another double manner. Firstly by reason of sacred episcopal orders. Secondly by a certain similitude and proportion: because undoubtedly as with Christ living on earth, the first ones under Christ were the twelve Apostles, then the 72 disciples; so now the first ones under the Roman Pontiff are the Bishops, after them the priests, then deacons etc.[427]

---

[426] *De Conciliorum Auctoritate,* cap. xviii, p. 69 — «Nam omnia revocantur tandem ad examen romani pontificis, et quae ille probat, recipiunlur, quae improbat rejiciuntur, ut testatur Gelasius in eadem epistola ad episcopos Dardaniae. Et quidem quod ad petitionem conciliorum approbaverit pontifex multa concilia, patet ex gestis jpsis conciliorum, praecipue I. II. III. IV. et VI. Quod autem pontifices aliquando conciliorum decreta reprobaverint, quod est apertum signum superioritatis, ex Basilio patet, qui in epistola ad Athanasium, quae est 52. scribit, videri sibi bonum, ut rogetur romanus episcopus, ut mittat aliquos in Graeciam, qui ejus nomine irritent concilium ariminense. Ipse etiam Damasus in epistola ad episcopos Illyrii reprobat concilium illud. Similiter Leo in epist. 55. ad Pulcheriam: *Consensiones,* inquit, *episcoporum, canonum apud Nicaeam conditorum regulis repugnantes, in irritum mittimus, et per auctoritatem b. Petri apostoli generali prorsus definitione cassamus. B. Gregorius lib. 4. epist. 34. Cuncta, inquit, acta illius synodi, sede contradicente apostolica, soluta, sunt.*»

[427] *De Romano Pontifice,* lib. iv. cap. xxv — «Respondeo: magnum esse discrimen inter successionem Petri, & aliorum Apostolorum. Nam

This follows from the fact that by reason of governance, the other apostles were not heads, rulers, and pastors in the same manner as Peter:

> The third way all the Apostles are said to be foundations is by reason of governance. They were all heads, rulers, and pastors of the universal Church, but not in the same way as Peter: they had the supreme and broadest power as Apostles or legates, but Peter as the ordinary Pastor: in the next place even so they had the fullness of power, comparatively however Peter would be their head, and they would depend on him, not the other way around.[428]

Salza & Siscoe make the absurd claim on page 300 of their magnum opus, "Bellarmine himself defended the opinion that a heretical Pope can be judged by a council"[429] — Bellarmine, as mentioned above, cites against this opinion the Fifth Lateran Council as *fere de fide*, which, he explained, explicitly and categorically declared that a pope *absolute et simpliciter* is over a council. He then quoted the verbatim text of the council in the same chapter: «Finally the last Lateran Council under Leo X in session. 11. expressly and ex professo

---

Romanus Pontifex proprie succedit Petro, non ut Apostolo, sed ut Pastori ordinario totius Ecclesiae; & ideo ab illo habet Romanus Pontifex jurisdictionem, a quo habuit Petrus: at Episcopi non succedunt proprie Apostolis, quoniam Apostoli non fuerunt ordinarii, sed extraordinarii, & quasi delegati Pastores, qualibus non succeditur. Dicuntur tamen Episcopi succedere Apostolis, non proprie eo modo, quo unus Episcopus alteri, & unus Rex alteri, sed duplici alia ratione. Primo ratione Ordinis sacri Episcopalis. Secundo per quamdam similitudinem & proportionem: quia nimirum sicut Christo in terris vivente, primi sub Christo erant Apostoli duodecim, deinde 72. discipuli; ita nunc primi sub Romano Pontifice sunt Episcopi, post eos Presbyteri, inde Diaconi &c.»

[428] *De Romano Pontifice*, lib. i. cap. xi — «Tertio modo dicuntur fundamenta omnes Apostoli, ratione gubernationis. Omnes enim fuerunt Capita, Rectores, & Pastores Ecclesiae universae, sed non eodem modo quo Petrus: illi enim habuerunt summam atque amplissimam potestatem ut Apostoli seu Legati, Petrus autem ut Pastor ordinarius: deinde ita habuerunt plenitudinem potestatis, ut tamen Petrus esset Caput eorum, & ab illo penderent, non e contrario.»

[429] *True or False Pope?* p. 300.

taught, the pope is above all councils, and condemned the contrary decree, published in the council of Basel: "it is clearly established that the Roman Pontiff alone, possessing as it were authority over all Councils, has full right and power of proclaiming Councils, or transferring and dissolving them, not only according to the testimony of Sacred Scripture, from the words of the holy Fathers and even of other Roman Pontiffs, of our predecessors, and from the decrees of the holy canons, but also from the particular acknowledgment of these same Councils."»[430] If Bellarmine had indeed held the position that a heretical Pope can be judged by a council, he would have pronounced a sentence of condemnation upon himself. St Alphonsus comments:

> Bellarmine writes that two things could oppose this council, regarding the declaration made of the Pope's superiority over the councils: the first, that it was not a general council, because the bishops did not reach the number of one hundred; but he replies that this cannot be said, while that was already legitimately summoned, was open to all, the Fathers were 107 and the true Pontiff presided there; and therefore this council commonly is held as legitimate, as Graveson, Baronio, Cabassuzio, Tomassino and innumerable others have it. The second thing, that it had not been received by everyone afterwards: but Bellarmine says that this is not very important; because the decrees of the council do not need (as is certain) the approval of the people, while they do not receive their authority from the people; and then he adds [in Chapter 17]: *Quod vero Concilium hoc rem istam non definivit proprie (by special canon) ut decretum catholica fide tenendum, dubium est; et ideo non sunt proprie hæretici qui contrarium tenent, sed a temeritate magna excusari non possunt.* Monsignor Bossuet said in his *Defense* etc. speaking of this council: *Pro certo œcumenicum haberi Bellarmini cunctatio et fluctuatio non sinit.* But Bellarmine does not doubt that the council was an ecumenical one, he

---

[430] *De Conciliorum Auctoritate,* cap. xvii. p. 68 – «Denique lateranense ultimum sub Leone X. sess. 11. diserte et ex professo docuit, pontificem esse supra omnia concilia, et reprobavit contrarium decretum, editum in concilio basileensi: *Solum:* inquit, *romanum pontificem, tamquam super onnmia comcilia auctoritatem habentem, comciliorum indicendorum, transferemdorum. ac dissolvendorum plenum jus, et potestatem habere, necdum ex sacrae Scripturae testimonio, dictis sanctorum Patrum ac aliorum romanorum pontificum, sed propriaetiam eorumdem conciliorum confessione, mamifeste constat.*»

only doubts if one can be said to be a heretic who holds a council to be above the Pope; **but he is certain that that one cannot excuse himself from the note of great temerity.**[431]

After Vatican I it is *de fide definita* that the totality of supreme power to judge lies exclusively within the jurisdiction of the holder of the primacy to exercise freely over the whole Church dispersed throughout the world or gathered together in an ecumenical council, and that his definitions are infallible and irreformable, and may not be appealed against, not even to an ecumenical council. The pope judges all and is judged by none.[432]

* * *

---

[431] *Verità Della Fede*, Opera Del Beato Alfonso Maria de' Liguori, Tomo Secondo, Monza, 1823, Capo IX. pp. 176-177: «Scrive il Bellarmino che due cose poteano opporsi a questo concilio, circa la dichiarazione fatta della superiorità del Papa sopra i concilj: la prima, che non fosse concilio generale, perché i vescovi non giunsero al numero di cento; ma risponde che ciò non può dirsi, mentre quello già fu legittimamente convocato, fu a tutti aperto, i Padri furono 107 e vi presedé il vero Pontefice; e perciò questo concilio comunemente si ha per legittimo, come lo hanno Graveson, Baronio, Cabassuzio, Tomassino ed altri innumerabili. La seconda cosa, che non fosse stato poi ricevuto da tutti: ma dice il Bellarmino che ciò poco in porta; perché i decreti de' concilj non abbisognano (come è certo) dell'approvazione del popolo, mentre non ricevono dal popolo la loro autorità; e poi soggiunge [in Chapter 17]: *Quod vero Concilium hoc rem istam non definivit proprie* (per Canone speciale) *ut decretum catholica fide tenendum, dubium est; et ideo non sunt proprie hæretici qui contrarium tenent, sed a temeritate magna excusari non possunt.* Disse monsignor Bossuet nella sua Difesa ec. parlando di questo concilio: *Pro certo œcumenicum haberi Bellarmini cunctatio et fluctuatio non sinit.* Ma Bellarmino non dubita che il concilio sia stato ecumenico, solo dubita se possa dirsi eretico chi tiene esser il concilio sovra del Papa; ma tiene per certo che costui non può scusarsi dalla nota di una gran temerità.»

[432] «[4] c. 16 (Gelasius I. a. 493) C. IX. qu. 3: *"Ipsi sunt canones qui appellationes totius ecclesiæ ad huius sedis examen voluere deferri. Ab ipsa vero nusquam prorsus appellari debere sanxerunt ac per hoc illam de tota ecclesia iudicare, ipsam ad nullius commeare iudicium nec de eius unquam præceperunt iudicio iudicari"*; c. 17 (idem a. 498) ead.: *"Cuncta per mundum novit ecclesia, quod sacrosancta Romana ecclesia fas de omnibus habet iudicandi neque cuiquam de eius liceat iudicare iudicio."*» [Hinschius, *Op. cit.* p. 297.]

John of St. Thomas held the opinion that juridical proof suffices to deprive the pope of the pontificate,[433] but unlike Bellarmine, who, contradicting his own doctrine, believed that in at least one instance, that of Liberius, that a pope not actually guilty of the crime of heresy had actually been validly deposed on the basis of juridical proof, John of St. Thomas, in the earlier cited passage, correctly held that such a conviction would appear to be impossible, because it would result in the defection of the Church. John of St. Thomas believed that Liberius was indeed guilty of the crime and was justly convicted, but not guilty of being a formal heretic himself, but of favouring heresy.[434] Both of them erred in their belief that a true pope could be deprived of the pontificate upon conviction, first, because the judgment would be made by an inferior power; and second, because the judgment would be based only on the standards of juridical proof, but without the fact of heresy being *evidenter verum*, which would be a condition *sine qua non* for a valid judgment of heresy against a pontiff. Since, as Ballerini proved, that no council can ever validly judge against a true and certain pope: such a conviction would be an invalid violation of

---

[433] *Cursus Theologicus II-II De Auctoritate Summi Pontificis, Disp. II, Art. III, De Depositione Papae*, p. 255-256: «XIII. Respondetur sine dubio Ecclesiam posse judicare et deponere pontificem, qui in re est innocens, probatur autem nocens, sicut si in re non esset hæreticus, exterius tamen probaretur juridice esse hæreticum, posset haberi pro non pontifice, quia sicut existente vera culpa amittere potest pontificatum, non quando illam commisit, et nondum ab Ecclesia judicata est, sed quando ab Eccesia declaratur, ita licet in re non habuerit illam culpam, si tamen ex declaratione Ecclesiæ illam habet, quia sic juridice probatur, amitit etiam pontificatum, quia sic expedit gubernationi Ecclesiæ, quæ humano modo fit, et secundum humanas probationes, quæ solum requirunt veritatem juridicam, non mathematicam, et quia pontificatus non consistit in charactere, qui nulla actione est delibilis, sed in jurisdictione, quæ ex moralibus conditionibus pendere potest, ideo ex culpa moraliter, et juridice notoria, tamquam ex conditione pendere potest potestas ista pontificia, licet in re innocens sit.»

[434] *Ibid.* p. 257 — «De fautore vero hæreticorum Azorius ubi supra capite septimo, tenet quod si papa fautor, aut defensor hæreticorum, et in hoc sit incorrigibilis poterit deponi, et capite tertio idem docet ex Turrecremata. Et favet exemplum Liberii, qui quando favit hæreticis, in ejus locum Felix suffectus est, quod non nisi abrogato eo fieri potuit juxta doctrinam communem.»

papal immunity inherent in the absolute jurisdiction of the primacy. In reality, such a conviction would simply be juridically impossible. However, if the Church were to judge in a case of uncertain popes, or if a pope considered doubtful because of *indicia* of heresy, would then be judged to be no pope on the basis of heresy subsequently demonstrated to be a certain fact proven to the degree of being *evidenter verum*, then the *exclusive, unconditional,* and *unequivocal* universal acceptance of the pope elected in his place would confirm infallibly that the one convicted and deposed was never a valid pope, and that the one elected in his place is the true pope.

Both John of St. Thomas and Bordoni[435] insist on the absolute necessity that proper juridical procedures be observed in the trial. **However such a trial can only be considered licit and valid if sufficient *indicia* have been verified to firmly establish a *presumption of vacancy* of the Apostolic See.** The reason for this,

---

[435] Bordoni, *Sacrum Tribunal Iudicum,* cap. vi. p. 158 — «In depositione Papæ Concilium formare debet iuridicum processum a principio vsque ad finem, consequenter omnes actus dependere habent a potestate legitima eiusdem Concilij, aliter nihil validi ageretur, processus enim fabricatus sine competenti iudice, aut ab eo, qui caret iurisditione, nullus est, & inualidus, doct.in tit. de foro compet. Maranta *part.6.§.* Et peruenitur aliquando *nu.* 102. & in hoc nulla difficultas, quia omnis actus vt sit iuridicus, & validus essentialiter dependet a iurisditione. Bald. in *l. omne verbum, C. com. de legat.* Alex. *lib.*4. *confil.* 52. *num.*30. ex Rota Roman. *vol.* 1. *decis.*451. *nu.* 2. Ex quo non placet, quod ait Caiet. *cap.*21. antequam sententia depositionis feratur in Papam, Concilium non procedere contra ipsum potestate coactiua, sed tantum reprehensiua, & intimatiua, iudicium, enim hoc non ex confessione sua extorta præceptis, censuris, aut tormentis, sed ex euidenti facto, aut verbo hæresis incorrigibiliter expectatur. Non placet inquam, quia etiam contra Papam formandus est processus a Concilio, & cum maiori diligentia, quam si fabricaretur contra quemcumque alium, agitur enim de supremo Principe, ex quo eius hæresis cum pertinacia luce meridiana clarior apparere debet, id autem euenire non potest, nisi formetur directe, & iuridice processus, nec quidquam prodest, quod eius factum, vel verbum sit euidenter hæresis, quia id non est iuridice manifestum, vt supponit sententia in reum ferenda, præterquamquod verba, & facta transeunt, & euanescunt, neque proinde corpus delicti permanens dicitur habere. Quod actus omnes sententiam depositionis Papæ præcedentes legitime fieri debeant potestate coactiua ex Turrecr.& alijs refert Cord.l.4.*q.* 11.ad finem.»

as explained above, is that while the Church possesses absolutely no jurisdiction whatsoever to judge a pope, **she has the jurisdiction to determine the legitimacy of claims on the papacy** — the reason being, as John of St Thomas himself explained, is that in every eventuality in which there exists a reasonable doubt that the man is a true pope, or that his election is valid, it pertains to the jurisdiction of the Church to decide the question.[436] Besides St. Robert Bellarmine, St. Alphonsus, and Pope Gregory XVI, whom I cited above, John of St. Thomas also elaborated this point, and cites Suárez to be of the same opinion.[437] In the above cited passage of *De Conciliorum Auctoritate*, Bellarmine explained, "For a doubtful pope is considered no pope, and thus, to have power over him is not to have power over the pope." It is for these reasons that, as I explained in Volume One, such a trial would more properly be an inquest, rather than a penal trial, because the purpose of the procedure would be to verify the vacancy of the Apostolic See. St. Alphonsus adds, "Thus neither does it matter that in the event of a schism there was a long time in doubt who was the true pontiff; because then one would have been true, though not well known enough; and if none of the antipopes had been true, then the pontificate would finally be vacated."[438] On this point, at least, John of St. Thomas was correct, and was in agreement with the Doctors of the Church; but he was not correct on the following point.

In the case of a heretic pope, John of St. Thomas says, «And neither because of heresy is the pope directly judged, but because from Scripture, and divine law the Church is bound to segregate herself, and not communicate with the heretic, therefore with the declaration having been made that he is a heretic the Church cannot regard him as the head, because it cannot communicate with him, but a head to which a body is not united, and with whom it does not

---

[436] *Ibid.* XI. p. 255.

[437] *Ibid.* XI. p. 255.

[438] *Verità Della Fede*, Opera Del Beato Alfonso Maria de' Liguori, Tomo Secondo, Monza, 1823, Capo VIII. p. 157 — «Cosi neppure importa che in caso di scisma siasi stato molto tempo nel dubbio chi fosse il vero Pontefice; perché allora uno sarebbe stato il vero, benché non abbastanza conosciuto; e se niuno degli antipapi fosse stato vero, allora il pontificato sarebbe vacato.»

communicate, is not a head.»[439] First of all, if he were still the pope, the rest of the Church would have no power to judge him, neither directly nor indirectly, because the pope alone possesses the supreme authority to judge whether or not his opinion is heretical. If he would indeed be a heretic, then, as Gregory XVI pointed out in the earlier cited passages, that a judgment in such an instance as this would not be a judgment against an actually reigning pontiff, but against the person who before was the pope, because by the very fact of his heresy, he would fall by himself from the pontificate, because "the Pontiff cannot represent the Church, who together does not necessarily represent its unity". As is explained above, according to Bellarmine, it was precisely because a heretic is incapable of representing the unity of faith, that the form of the pontificate cannot be conserved in him, and consequently, he would cease by himself to be pope without any deposition and without any other external agency. The cited passage of John of St. Thomas is a prime example of proof of what I mentioned earlier, that all the theories of papal deposition which claim for the Church a power to depose a validly reigning pope for heresy are founded on logically incoherent premises that violate the principle of the excluded middle insofar as a judgment that is not a direct judgment has not the nature of a judgment — it is not *juridical*, but is *something else*. It cannot be legitimately argued that since a heretic must be avoided and separated from communion with the Church, a heretic pope is therefore to be deposed by the Church. Divine law makes no allowance for such an eventuality, because it confers an absolute totality of ecclesiastical power on the pope, which would not be a *total fullness of supreme power* if, in the exceptional case of a heretic pope, God had granted some share of that power to the Church to judge a validly reigning pope. If God had so willed it, he would have granted a share in the supreme power by means of an exceptional provision that would have been prescribed in a judicial precept of divine positive law, but this He did not do, but on the contrary, He bestowed upon the pope a *total fullness of supreme power*. Thus, the remedy of an *indirect*

---

[439] «Et neque propter hæresim directe judicatur papa, sed quia ex Scriptura, et jure divino Ecclesiæ tenetur segregare se, et non communicare hæretico, ideo facta declaratione quod sit hæreticus Ecclesia non potest ipsum respicere ut caput, quia non potest ei communicare, caput autem cui corpus non est unitum, et cui non communicat, non est caput.»

judgment is no remedy at all because it is devoid of any jurisdiction — it is simply not a *judgment* in the juridical sense. If the man is a heretic, then he is not a true pope, but as a manifest heretic, he is *minor quolibet catholico*, and therefore **he can be judged directly by the Church with a proper act of jurisdiction** as is so clearly expressed in the sermons of Innocent III and in the doctrine of St. Robert Bellarmine. But if he is a valid pope, then, as the popes have repeatedly taught, he simply cannot be judged by men. This is the solution to the dilemma of judging a heretic pope, first conceptualized by the French School of the Early Decretists, ennunciated by Huguccio of Pisa, and taught by Innocent III; then systematically formulated afterward by St. Robert Bellarmine, refined by Ballerini and St. Alphonsus, and then taught by Pope Gregory XVI as a private doctor.

Bordoni also understood perfectly the logical incoherence of the Cajetanian-John of St. Thomas position on this point, for which reason his critique of Cajetan's conjunction theory totally demolishes Cajetan's doctrine on the deposition of a heretic pope. Since John of St. Thomas based his own doctrine of deposition on the same fallacious foundation as Cajetan, Bordoni does not even consider John of St. Thomas's arguments to be worthy of mention, because his critique of Cajetan destroys both of their errant theories on this point. Bordoni argues, «But is not this power of a Council to depose a Pope greater than the papacy? Absolutely, otherwise a Council could not act in the deposition of a Pontiff, if in this case it were not of a greater power, that which acts in the destruction of another is always of a greater strength and power in order to overcome the one being acted upon, thus a Council, if it is to destroy the Pontiff, must have a greater power than the Pope.»[440]

On this point he is absolutely correct: a Council's power to depose a valid pope could only exist if it is a greater power than that of the papacy; which means that for such a greater authority to exist, God would have had to expressly provide a precept in divine positive law

---

[440] Bordoni, *Sacrum Tribunal Iudicum*, cap. vi. p. 156 — «Sed numquid hæc potestas Concilij Papam deponedi est maior Papatu? Vtique, alioquin Concilium non posset agere in depositionem Pontificis, si in hoc casu non esset maioris potestatis, id enim quod agit in alterius destructionem maioris semper est virtutis, & potentiæ, vt passum superare possit, sic Concilium si habet destruere Pontificem maiorem Papa in hoc debet habere potestatem.»

granting the exceptional power to the Church to judge the supreme judge. Therefore, if God would allow such an eventuality to actually take place in which a pope would fall into formal heresy, it would have been necessary for Him to legislate an exceptional judicial remedy, whether that be for a trial of a suspected heretic pope, the deposition of a pope judged guilty of heresy, or even for the removal of a valid pope who lost office *ipso jure* for having publicly defected into heresy or schism. There exists no such exceptional remedy in divine positive law. God has not decreed any provision as a remedy for such an eventuality. Therefore it is impossible in reality, but only hypothetically possible for a pope to become a heretic. That a public heretic would fall from the pontificate *ipso facto* is *theologically certain*; and if it were not, it would not have been taught by Pope Innocent III, nor would it eventually have been taught with virtual unanimity by theologians who admit at least the hypothetical possibility of an occurrence of papal heresy. But, since God does not legislate provisions for what is only hypothetical but will never actually take place, the mere lack of any revealed divine precept for such a case does not imply that an automatic fall would not happen if a pope were to fall into public heresy, but it only proves that divine providence will not allow such a fall to take place, because without a divinely prescribed remedy, it would be left to private judgment to decide which of the opposing judgments is correct, the judgment of the imperfect council or the judgment of the fallen pope, thereby irremediably destroying the unity of the Church, since there would exist no certain and infallible supreme authority which could decide the dispute between them with finality. **This point above all must be emphasized:** If a man ceases by himself to be pope, he loses the primacy and its infallibility. None of his judgments or definitions will be infallible because he is no longer pope. This is evidently clear and indisputable. However, **the opinion that by heresy the primacy is mutated in one who remains pope in such a manner that he can no longer exercise it, and he can therefore be judged by a council, can be plainly seen to be heretical, because then, in that case, the pope could no longer freely exercise his primatial jurisdiction as supreme judge, and his definitions issuing from a mutated primacy would no longer be *ex sese* infallible and irreformable.** The reason for this is that if as a result of his personal heresy expressed only as a private doctor, his primacy would be mutated, so that he would lose the capacity to exercise the primacy and it would become inferior to a council and therefore subject to its judgment; his solemn definitions would no longer be infallible, nor would his papal judgments have any jurisdictional force. However, since the *supreme magisterium* pertains to the primacy itself,[441] if the power to exercise the primacy could be altered or mutated by personal heresy in a man who remains pope even as a heretic, then that pope who falls into heresy as a private person would no longer be capable of exercising his infallible magisterium. **Papal infallibility would thereby cease to exist in a heretic pope**. The very purpose for which the primacy was instituted would be subverted, thus destroying the divine constitution of the Church, since the pope upon falling into heresy but still remaining pope, would no longer be able to function as the final and infallible judge of disputes in matters of faith and morals, but would be bound to submit to the judgment of a council. This is exactly what John of St. Thomas heretically proposes as a remedy In the above cited passages, namely, **the convening of a council against the will of a validly reigning supreme pontiff**, saying, "It is responded that this council can be brought together by the authority of the Church which is in the bishops themselves or the greater part of them;" and then he proposes Luther's heretical argument which Bellarmine refuted, claiming, "the pontiff cannot annul or reject such a Council, because he is a party". As I pointed out in Volume One in my brief critique of Cajetan's deposition theory and have explained in this volume: The *munus* of preserving the unity of the Church in the purity of the Catholic faith was singularly entrusted by Christ to Peter and his successors, and not to the bishops. It cannot be accomplished by a council, even an ecumenical council comprised of all the bishops of the world, because, *the strength and validity of a council is begotten out of the consent and conjunction of the body*

---

[441] *Pastor Æternus* — «**Ipso autem Apostolico primatu,** quem Romanus Pontifex tamquam Petri principis Apostolorum successor in universam Ecclesiam obtinet, **supremam quoque magisterii potestatem comprehendi,** haec Sancta Sedes semper tenuit, perpetuus Ecclesiae usus comprobat, ipsaque oecumenica Concilia, ea imprimis, in quibus Oriens cum Occidente in fidei charitatisque unionem conveniebat, declaraverunt.»

with the head: «**Firmitas concilii nascitur ex consensione et conjunctione corporis cum capite.**» *De Conciliorum Auctoritate,* **Caput X.**

Accordingly, *Pastor Æternus* declares: «Therefore whoever succeeds to the chair of Peter obtains by the institution of Christ himself, the primacy of Peter over the whole Church... For this reason because of its greater pre-eminence, it has always been necessary for every Church, that is, the faithful everywhere, to be in agreement with that See, from which the rights of venerable communion flow to all as members joined to the head, they will coalesce into one structural framework (S. Iren. Adv. haer. I. III c. 3, et Conc. Aquiiei. a. 381 inter opp. S. Ambr. ep. XL).»[442]

The power of primacy, which consists in the *plenitudo potestatis,* is an essential attribute proper to the habit of the papacy, so that if the necessary habitual disposition for the operation of the power by which the exercise of the *full and supreme jurisdiction* is accomplished would be removed by some contrary disposition, then that which pertains to the essential nature of the papacy itself would be removed, thereby evacuating the habit of the papacy from the person. Thus, the primacy would not be altered or mutated, as John of St. Thomas maintained, but the habit of the papacy itself would be evacuated from the pope, as Bellarmine explained in *De Romano Pont. lib. ii. cap. xxx* — «Thereupon, those things which have the final disposition to ruin, shortly thereafter cease to exist, without another external force, as is patent; therefore, also a heretical Pope, without another deposition ceases by himself to be Pope.»

The repeated papal condemnation against judgment and deposition by any human power of a validly constituted and actually reigning Pontiff remains an article of faith:

«St. Anacletus said in relatus cap. *Eiectionem fin. dist. 79.* The Lord has reserved for himself the casting out of Supreme Pontiffs, in that

---

[442] «Unde quicumque in hac Cathedra Petro succedit, is secundum Christi ipsius institutionem primatum Petri in universam Ecclesiam obtinet. ... Hac de causa ad Romanam Ecclesiam propter potentiorem principalitatem necesse semper fuit omnem convenire Ecclesiam, hoc est, eos, qui sunt undique fideles, ut in **ea Sede, e qua venerandae communionis iura in omnes dimanant**, tamquam membra in capite consociata, in unam corporis compagem coalesceret (S. Iren. Adv. haer. I. III c. 3, et Conc. Aquiiei. a. 381 inter opp. S. Ambr. ep. XL).»

by no human power; but by divine power only can the Pope be deposed.»[443]

Therefore: An indubitable, true and valid pope may simply not be tried or deposed, but only one who is at least doubtful — a *papa dubius*, and therefore one who on the basis of the firmest of evidence is *presumed to be a false and invalid pope*. If it would be possible for a true and indubitable pope to fall into heresy and to manifest pertinacity, it would only be that by manifesting his public pertinacity in a crime which consists in a sin that by its nature separates a man from the Church by itself, that he would be plainly admitting in the presence of the divine tribunal and the representatives of the Church that his crime against the unity of the Church has indeed separated him from the body of the Church and consequently from the office he held. With that open admission of crime against divine law, he would be condemned by his own judgment like any other criminal offender who openly admits his crime; for which there is no need for the Supreme Judge to pronounce the sentence which the heretic has already pronounced against himself,[444] but, as Bellarmine phrased it, "the Pope who is manifestly a heretic ceases by himself to be Pope and head, in the same way as he ceases to be a Christian and a member of the body of the Church; and for this reason he can be judged and punished by the Church."[445] Without the pertinacity of heresy manifested plainly before the divine Tribunal and witnessed by men, no mere human court whether secular or ecclesiastical would have the power to subject a validly reigning pope to a judgment for the crime of heresy or any other crime; but if the pontiff were to plainly manifest the pertinacity of heresy, then being "already judged", he

---

[443] Bordoni, *Sacrum Tribunal Iudicum*, cap. vi. p. 158 — «dixit S. Anaclctus relatus cap. *Eiectionem fin. dist.79*. Eiectionem Summorum Pontificum sibi Dominum reseruasse, in quantum nullus humana potestate; sed tantum diuina Papam deponere potest.»

[444] *De Rom. Pont. lib. ii. cap. xxx* — «Yet heretics are outside the Church, even before excommunication, and deprived of all jurisdiction, for they are condemned by their own judgment, as the Apostle teaches to Titus; that is, they are cut from the body of the Church without excommunication, as Jerome expresses it.»

[445] *Ibid.*

would cease by himself to be pope, and need only to be "cast out", as Innocent III teaches, "and trampled by men."

Bordoni proves from the canonical tradition and jurisprudence of the Church exactly why the half-baked theory of Cajetan, and consequently that also of John of St. Thomas, simply does not hold together:

> «In the deposition of a pope the Council must frame a juridical process from the beginning to the end, consequently all acts have to depend on a legitimate power of the same Council, otherwise it will act validly in nothing, a process carried out without a competent judge, or from one who lacks jurisdiction, is null and invalid, doct.in tit. de foro compet. Maranta *part.6.§. Et peruenitur aliquando nu.* 102. and in this there is no difficulty, for every act in order that it be juridical and valid, essentially depends on jurisdiction Bald. in *l. omne verbum, C. com. de legat.* Alex. *lib.*4. *confil.* 52. *num.*30. ex Rota Roman. *vol.* 1. *decis.*451. *nu.* 2. From which it is not acceptable what Cajetan says *cap.* 21. Before the sentence of deposition is delivered against the Pope the Council does not proceed against him with coercive power, but only reprehensively and accusingly, for the judgment is expected, not from a confession extorted by commands, punishments or torture, but from evident incorrigible deeds or words of heresy. I say it is not acceptable, for even against the Pope the process is to be organized by the Council, and with greater diligence than if it would be framed against anyone else, the action is dealing with the foremost Chief, from whom his heresy with pertinacity must appear more clearly than the light of midday, and that cannot happen unless the process is framed directly and juridically, Nor does it profit, that his deeds or words be evidently of heresy, because it is not juridically manifest, as a sentence to be delivered against an offender supposes, besides which actions and words pass by and vanish, and from that a lasting corpus delicti cannot be had. That all the acts preceding the sentence of deposition of the Pope must be legitimately carried out with coercive power, from Torquemada... [ex Turrecr.& alijs refert Cord.l.4.*q.* 11.ad finem.]»[446]

---

[446] Bordoni, *Sacrum Tribunal Iudicum*, cap. vi. p. 158 — «In depositione Papæ Concilium formare debet iuridicum processum a principio vsque ad finem, consequenter omnes actus dependere habent a potestate legitima eiusdem Concilij, aliter nihil validi ageretur, processus enim fabricatus sine competenti iudice, aut ab eo, qui caret iurisditione, nullus est, & inualidus, doct.in tit. de foro compet. Maranta *part.6.§. Et peruenitur aliquando nu.*

Therefore, in order for the deposition of a heretic to be valid, the process must begin not with the trial of a certain pope which could not be juridically carried out from beginning to end, but with a proper juridical inquest of a *papa dubius* who is presumed to be a *papa nullus*; and therefore, the deposition process could legitimately begin with evidence constituting positive doubt regarding the validity of the accused's claim on the pontifical *munus* thereby establishing a presumption of nullity, or if the heresy is both materially and formally *manifestly evident,* the deposition could be carried out straightaway by means of a declaration. For there to be any presumption of nullity at all there must be juridical *indicia* of heresy sufficient to establish probable cause of heresy according to juridical standards, together with evidence sufficient to establish positive doubt of a valid election; unless the *indicia* of heresy establish pertinacity in *violent suspicion,* or by themselves positively demonstrate the certain and evident *fact* of formal heresy, which would constitute absolute proof of nullity and dispense *per se* with any further need of examination. The inquest in the matter of a suspected heretic that does not begin on the basis of jurisdiction is not a juridical process and has no juridical force; but it would be like a police investigation — no matter how convinced the police may be that a suspect is guilty, that opinion does not constitute

---

102. & in hoc nulla difficultas, quia omnis actus vt sit iuridicus, & validus essentialiter dependet a iurisditione. Bald. in *l. omne verbum, C. com. de legat.* Alex. *lib.*4. *confil.* 52. *num.*30. ex Rota Roman. *vol.* 1. *decis.*451. *nu.* 2. Ex quo non placet, quod ait Caiet. *cap.*21. antequam sententia depositionis feratur in Papam, Concilium non procedere contra ipsum potestate coactiua, sed tantum reprehensiua, & intimatiua, iudicium, enim hoc non ex confessione sua extorta præceptis, censuris, aut tormentis, sed ex euidenti facto, aut verbo hæresis incorrigibiliter expectatur. Non placet inquam, quia etiam contra Papam formandus est processus a Concilio, & cum maiori diligentia, quam si fabricaretur contra quemcumque alium, agitur enim de supremo Principe, ex quo eius hæresis cum pertinacia luce meridiana clarior apparere debet, id autem euenire non potest, nisi formetur directe, & iuridice processus, nec quidquam prodest, quod eius factum, vel verbum sit euidenter hæresis, quia id non est iuridice manifestum, vt supponit sententia in reum ferenda, præterquamquod verba, & facta transeunt, & euanescunt, neque proinde corpus delicti permanens dictitur habere. Quod actus omnes sententiam depositionis Papæ præcedentes legitime fieri debeant potestate coactiua ex Turrecr.& alijs refert Cord.l.4.*q.* 11.ad finem.»

a juridical sentence. The sentence must come from someone with the necessary jurisdiction to pronounce it — i.e. from the cardinals if possible, or a council if necessary. No matter how greatly a council may believe a man is an illegitimate pontiff and heretic, there is no jurisdiction to try him in the absence of *evidently credible and founded positive doubt* regarding the legitimacy of his claim; and without such evidence sufficient to establishing a *founded positive doubt*, the council would have no more jurisdiction to convict a suspected heretic than the police would have to convict a criminal suspect they believe to be guilty on the basis of an insufficiently substantiated suspicion. Furthermore, if "before the sentence of deposition is delivered against the Pope" the council "does not proceed against him with coercive power, but only reprehensively and accusingly," then the entire proceeding is invalid; because **a council that lacks the jurisdiction to conduct a trial with judicial authority lacks also the authority to pronounce a sentence, even a merely declarative sentence.** That being said, **since the Church certainly possesses the jurisdiction to judge doubtful popes, the process of judging and deposing them must be carried out authoritatively with coercive force.**

It is precisely the *declarative sentence*, which according to John of St. Thomas, introduces the disposition that ministerially and dispositively causes the dissolving of the conjunction of the papacy with the pope thereby separating them. Since the supreme power for the totality of the members of the Church to juridically issue a declarative judgment of heresy against their head, who is the supreme judge (whose power is total and whose jurisdiction is absolute) is utterly absent in the totality of the members of the Church, even in virtue of their totality, (which without the head is no totality at all), there exists no power whatsoever in the pope's subordinates to dissolve the conjunction. Ballerini therefore rightly judged that no council possesses any power whatsoever over a valid pope, saying: «undoubtedly the right of the primacy always remains in reality with a true and legitimate Pontiff, who always, being superior to the whole Church and whatever council by this right of the primacy, is removed from the jurisdiction of those others.» It is not within the power of the pope's subordinates to judge that a true and certain pope is to be deposed for heresy, but only to judge whether or not a man is a true and valid pope or no pope at all.

What John of St. Thomas also failed to understand is that by the very fact that the pope would visibly defect into heresy, the head would no longer be in communion with the members, having severed the bond of faith, and, being therefore no longer united to the body as a member, he would already no longer be the head, even before the declaration, which, if made against a true pope, would be null and void for lack of jurisdiction. Since to be juridical, the declaration of heresy requires jurisdiction over *the person* who is declared a heretic, which jurisdiction is lacking in a valid pope's inferiors; even a so-called "indirect judgment" made against the pope would be a juridical nonentity (in canonical language, *habetur pro infecto*), which therefore, being juridically non-existent (*tamquam non existens*), would be incapable of acting as a dispositive cause to effect his fall from office, which therefore would necessarily have to take place *ipso facto*, before all judgment, or not at all. It is for this reason that Bellarmine, who taught explicitly and demonstrated indisputably that the pope is an absolute monarch, who by divine right cannot be judged by any human power, and could only be judged if he were to have ceased by himself to be pope, explained: "Therefore, the true opinion is the fifth, according to which the Pope who is manifestly a heretic ceases by himself to be Pope and head, in the same way as he ceases to be a Christian and a member of the body of the Church; and for this reason he can be judged and punished by the Church."

Salza & Siscoe concoct a grotesquely twisted interpretation of Bellarmine's "fifth opinion", arguing that:

> What Bellarmine means is that the ipso facto loss of office occurs when the Church judges him to be a heretic, and before the vitandus declaration. This is evident from the fact that he is attempting to refute Cajetan's opinion, which maintains that the fall is not ipso facto after he is judged by the Church, but only follows the juridical sentence of the vitandus declaration (which, again, directly separates the Church from the Pope, not the Pope from the Church). The reason Kramer and the Sedes have misunderstood Bellarmine is because they have misunderstood Cajetan's opinion, and therefore did not know what Bellarmine was trying to refute.

This interpretation is manifestly nonsensical, firstly, in view of the fact that its conclusion, namely, that Salza & Siscoe understand Bellarmine correctly, and that that, "Kramer misunderstood Bellarmine", is founded on the gratuitously asserted premise that "Kramer misunderstood Cajetan's opinion"; and secondly, in view of the fact that in refuting Cajetan, Bellarmine says nothing about the thesis "which maintains that the fall is not ipso facto after he is judged by the Church, but only follows the juridical sentence of the vitandus declaration"; but *he argues expressly that the pope simply cannot be deposed by the Church,* and says it is proven that the manifest heretic pope is *ipso facto* deposed;[447] and, as I have explained in Volume One, he refutes Cajetan by demonstrating and explaining why **neither the bishops nor the cardinals can depose a pope.** He begins his refutation of the opinion by addressing the thesis of Cajetan: "The fourth opinion is of Cajetan," and he cites the source in Cajetan's writings, "in tract. de auctor. Papæ & Conc. cap. 20. & 21."; and then he states Cajetan's thesis: "a manifest heretic pope is not deposed ipso facto but can, and must be deposed by the Church" — and he judges the opinion to be indefensible: "which sentence in my judgment cannot be defended."[448] That Bellarmine most certainly does not mean, as Salza & Siscoe claim, "that the ipso facto loss of office occurs when the Church judges him to be a heretic, and before the vitandus declaration," can be plainly seen in the above cited passage, in his own positing the reason why the heretic would fall from office *ipso facto*, to wit, that with the necessary disposition which is Faith, "being removed by the contrary which is heresy, the Pope straightaway ceases to be Pope," and "therefore a heretic pope without another deposition would cease by himself to be Pope." This is patently not the doctrine of Suárez, who said in the above cited passage, "when the Church would depose a Pope, she would not do it as a superior, but by the consent of Christ the Lord she would juridically declare him to be a heretic," and then, "if the Pope is heretical and

---

[447] *De Rom. Pont. ii. xxx.* — «Nam *in primis,* quod hæreticus manifestus *ipso facto* sit depositus, probatur auctoritate & ratione.»

[448] *De Rom. Pont. ii. xxx.* — «Quarta opinio est Cajetani in tract. de auctor. Papæ & Conc. cap. 20. & 21. ubi docet, Papam hæreticum manifestum non esse ipso facto depositum sed posse, ac debere deponi ab Ecclesia: quæ sententia meo judicio defendi non potest.»

incorrigible, as soon as a declaratory sentence is pronounced by the legitimate jurisdiction of the Church, he ceases to be Pope." Incredibly, Salza and Siscoe adamantly still continue to maintain the absurdity that Bellarmine and Suárez were of the identical opinion on this question.

Having given the reason why a heretic would fall from the pontificate *ipso facto,* Bellarmine then proceeds to directly refute Cajetan's deposition theory by dismantling its foundation; firstly, as explained above, by proving that to conserve the form of the pontificate, the character alone does not suffice, but, "the total disposition, which is the character and Faith, is necessary *simpliciter,*" so that "faith is the necessary disposition *simpliciter* for this that someone be pope"; secondly, by proving that "the Fathers teach in unison that heretics are not only outside the Church; but also they are deprived ipso facto of all jurisdiction and ecclesiastical dignity."[449] Bellarmine continues, "Then what Cajetan says secondly, that the Pope can be deposed by the Church truly and by authority, is seen to be no less false than the first;" and he exposes the fatal defect in Cajetan's conjunction theory by pointing out that if the Church deposes an unwilling pope, she is certainly above the pope. He then refutes Cajetan's objection, which says that this would not be so, because, "the Church in deposing the pope, does not have authority over the pope, but over the conjunction of the person with the pontificate." With multiple arguments Bellarmine exposes the fallacy of Cajetan's assertion, namely, "That the Church can conjoin the pontificate to such a person, and nevertheless for that it is not said to be above the Pontiff; thus she can separate the pontificate from such a person in the case of heresy, and yet it will not be said she is above the pontiff." The foundation of Bellarmine's arguments against this thesis are that the bishops cannot depose the pope, because even though the pope deposes bishops, and in doing so does not destroy the Episcopacy but only separates its jurisdiction from that person, it does not follow that they possess power over the conjunction so as to separate the papacy from the pope; nor do they have the power to

---

[449] *De Rom. Pont. ii. xxx.* — «Denique SS. Patres concorditer docent, non solum hæreticos esse extra Ecclesiam; sed etiam ipso facto carere omni jurisdictione & dignitate Ecclesiastica.»

exercise the authority of a judge in deposing the pope; and that the whole Church is not simply the sum of its parts, so that the pope's authority over the whole being such that he can separate them, somehow arises out of the totality of those parts together, so that consequently the Church from which would arise the supreme authority over the whole, would have the power over the whole, and therefore over conjunction to separate the pope from the papacy.[450] Bellarmine proved that the primacy over the whole Church is conferred directly by Christ on the pontiff, and does not derive in any way from the Church; whereas the jurisdiction of the bishops is conferred upon them by the pope. Thus, the pope possesses supreme power over the whole Church *simpliciter et absolute*.

Bellarmine finishes with Cajetan, explaining why the cardinals have absolutely no power to depose a pope:

> Nor is Cajetan's example of the electors valid, who have the power of applying the Pontificate to a certain person, and yet they have no power over the Pope. For while a thing is being made, the action is exerted on the matter of the thing that will be, not on the composite which as yet is not: but while a thing is being destroyed, the action is exerted over the composite, as is clear in natural things. Accordingly when the Cardinals create the Pontiff, they exercise their authority, not over the Pontiff because he as yet is not, but on the matter, i.e., on the person whom they dispose in some manner by the election, so that he receive from God the form of the Pontificate; but if they would depose the Pontiff, they would necessarily exercise authority over the composite, i.e., over the person endowed with the pontifical dignity, i.e. over the Pope.[451]

---

[450] *De Rom. Pont. ii. xxx.* — «At contra. Nam primo, ex eo quod Papa deponit Episcopos, deducunt, Papam esse supra Episcopos omnes, & tamen Papa deponens Episcopum non destruit Episcopatum, sed solum separat ab illa persona. Secundo deponi invitum a Pontificatu sine dubio est poena; igitur Ecclesia invitum Papam deponens, sine dubio ipsum punit: at punire est superioris & judicis. Tertio, quia secundum Cajetanum & cæteros Thomistas, re idem sunt totum & partes simul sumptae; igitur qui habet auctoritatem in partes simul sumptas, ita ut eas separare possit, habet etiam in ipsum totum, quod ex partibus illis consurgit.»

[451] *De Rom. Pont. ii. xxx.* — «Neque valet Cajetani exemplum de electoribus, qui habent potestatem applicandi Pontificatum certae personae,

Hence, Bellarmine concludes, **"*Therefore*, the true opinion is the fifth, according to which the Pope who is manifestly a heretic *ceases by himself* to be Pope and head, *in the same way as he ceases to be a Christian and a member of the body of the Church*; and *for this reason* he *can be judged and punished by the Church*."** Bellarmine devotes an entire chapter (*lib. ii cap. xxvi*) to prove the thesis that, "The supreme Pontiff is judged by no one" — and he categorically states that, "the Roman Pontiff cannot be judged by anyone on earth."[452] According to Bellarmine, a pope could lose office only by

---

& tamen non habent potestatem in Papam. Nam dum res fit, actio exercetur circa materiam rei futurae, non circa compositum quod nondum est: at dum res destruitur, exercetur circa compositum, ut patet in rebus naturalibus. Itaque Cardinales dum Pontificem creant, exercent suam auctoritatem, non supra Pontificem quia nondum est, sed circa materiam, idest, circa personam quam per electionem quodammodo disponunt, ut a Deo Pontificatus formam recipiat; at si Pontificem deponerent, necessario exercerent auctoritatem supra compositum, idest, supra personam Pontificia dignitate præditam, idest, supra Pontificem.»

[452] «Argumentum decimum sumitur ex eo quod Romanus Pontifex a nemine in terris judicari potest. Non enim potest evidentius ostendi principatus ejus, quam si ostendatur ita omnibus prelatus, ut nemini sit subjectus... Loquimur ergo de Pontifice ratione solius pontificatus; ac dicimus eum, etiam si ditionem temporalem nullam haberet, non posse ullo modo judicari in terris ab ullo Principe christiano, sive saeculari, sive ecclesiastico; neque ab omnibus simul in Concilio congregatis... Observandum est tertio, rationem praecipuam, cur Papa judicari non possit, esse, quia Princeps est Ecclesiae totius, et proinde superiorem in terris non habet, nam quia summus Princeps est Ecclesiae, non potest judicari ab ullo Ecclesiastico Antistite, et rursum, quia respublica Ecclesiastica spiritualis est, ac proinde major, ac sublimior quavis republica temporali, propterea summus Princeps Ecclesiae dirigere et judicare summum Principem reipublicae temporalis; non autem ab eo dirigi, aut judicari debet, nisi rectus ordo, et ipsa rerum natura pervertatur. Haec, inquam, est ratio primaria; et, ut Scholae loquuntur, a priori: tamen, quia haec ratio assumit id, quod in tota haec disputatione probare nitimur; videlicet Romanum Pontificem Principem esse totius Ecclesiae: idcirco hac, et similibus rationibus praetermissis, ex testimoniis Conciliorum, Pontificum, Imperatorum, ac Doctorum Ecclesiae demonstrabimus, Romanum Praesulem judicari non posse: ut inde confirmemus primariam nostrum thesim; quae est, Romanum Pontificem caput et principem esse Ecclesiae universae.»

separating himself from the pontificate entirely "by himself", i.e. by his own act of removing the necessary disposition to conserve the form of the pontificate. In Bellarmine's doctrine, it is only the Pope himself who could introduce the disposition incompatible with the papacy, which is heresy: "this disposition being removed by the contrary which is heresy, the Pope straightaway ceases to be Pope." (*ista dispositione sublata per contrariam quæ est hæresis, mox Papa desinit esse*) Salsa & Siscoe have absurdly inverted Bellarmine's meaning by saying, "What Bellarmine means is that the ipso facto loss of office occurs when the Church judges him to be a heretic, and before the vitandus declaration." In their *magnum opus* they equated the plainly different opinions of Bellarmine and Suárez, claiming, "Bellarmine and Suarez held that upon the Church's adjudication of the crime, a heretical Pope loses his office *ipso facto* as a matter of Divine law, without the Church having to, technically, depose him (this is the "Fifth Opinion" of Bellarmine)."[453] Nor do they stop there, but as we have seen, they also attribute the Suarezian variation of the fourth opinion to Ballerini as well; but strangely (or perhaps not really so strangely at all), the teaching of St. Alphonsus on this point is totally absent from their book, because the Holy Doctor explicitly stated that, "if ever a pope as a private person would fall into heresy, then he would immediately fall from the papacy," — which is the opinion Salza & Siscoe contemptuously dismiss as "sedevacantist theology," and a "sedevacantist misinterpretation of Bellarmine".

As on so many other points, Salza & Siscoe have completely inverted the teaching of Bellarmine, as they have also done with the teachings of the popes, Doctors, and Fathers of the Church. The "fifth opinion" which holds that a public heretic automatically falls from office entirely by himself *ipso facto* was not an original opinion formulated by Bellarmine, but was already a well-known opinion in his day, which had first appeared in the late twelfth century among the Early Decretists. That opinion was already expressed in the *Summa Et est sciendum*,[454] which explained, "But why is heresy special? Because

---

[453] *True or False Pope?* p. 332.

[454] Moynihan, *Op. cit.* p. 64, footnote 67 — «Also known as the *Glossae Stuttgardiensis*. The work was written under the pontificate of Pope Lucius III, between the years 1181-1185, in the French province of Sens. — Kuttner, *Repertorium*, pp. 195-196.»

other sins do not rupture the unity of the Church. Whereas in other instances a man can be a member of the Church, although a putrid member; but heresy or schism violate the unity itself and defiles the foundation of faith and corrupts it, so that when one is a heretic, he is less than any Catholic."[455] Moynihan cites in Chapter Three of the cited work quotations of other Early Decretists' *Summae* in which the same opinion was expressed. It simply beggars belief that Salza & Siscoe would attribute to Bellarmine such a crudely ignorant misinterpretation of that opinion which had already been widely known among theologians and canonists for more than four centuries before him. Paul Hinschius, in his monumental work on Canon Law explained in 1869 that, a number of Catholic writers, (mentioning by name **Innocent III** and **St. Robert Bellarmine**), taught that **since a pope who falls into heresy would already leave the Church and forfeit the Pontificate**, his removal would not constitute an exception to the rule, *Apostolica Sedes a nemine judicatur,* since a council could no longer depose him in the proper sense of a juridical deposition of a reigning Pontiff, but could only declare that the loss of office had already taken place:

> «A number of Catholic writers, however, do not want to find any exception to this rule because the pope, who has fallen into heresy, thereby leaves the Church himself, so that he forfeits the pontificate and thus the Council can no longer impose a deposition, but only verify the fact of the loss of papal dignity. [3] (This idea already occurs in Innocent III. (In Sermo IV. In consecrat. Pontiff. Opp. Colon. 1575. 1. 197)): «Potest (pontifex) from hominibus iudicari vel potius iudicatus ostendi, si videlicet evanescat in haeresim, quoniam qui non credit, iam iudicatus est») See also Bellarmine, Christ. fidei controv. III. De Romano pontifice II. 30. (ed. Ingolstadt. 1605. 1083): «Est ergo opinionio quinta vera, papa haereticum manifestum per se desinere esse christianus et membrum corporis ecclesiae, quare ab ecclesia posse eum iudicari et puniri. Haec est sententia omnium veterum patrum qui docent haereticos manifestos mox amittere omnem jurisdictionem»; Fagnan. comm. Ad c. 4. X. de

---

[455] «Sed quare est in haeresi speciale? Quia caetera peccata unitatem ecclesiae non rumpunt. Cum caeteris enim uicis potest esse homo membrum ecclesiae licet putridum. Haeresis uero uel scisma ipsam uiololant (sic) unitatem et fundamentum fidei maculant et corrumpunt, unde cum sit haereticus est quolibet catholico minor».

elect. I. 6.n. 70 ff; Fragosi, regime reipubl. Christianae lib. II. C. I. §. 2.n.21 (Lugduni. 1648, 2, 11); Kober, deposition. P. 585.»[456]

In the above cited passage of *De Potestate Ecclesiastica,* Don Pietro Ballerini, who famously followed the fifth opinion of Bellarmine, stated that those who follow this opinion, "assert the right of a general council over a Pope deviating from the faith, but whom they propound to be a heretic; because they believe such a Pontiff by the heresy itself to be severed and cut off from the foundation of the Church which is faith, and consequently from the Church itself, and to have utterly fallen from the Pontificate, and in this hypothesis it will be the right of the general council over him, who is no longer the Pontiff, nor does he possess the primacy."[457] Ballerini adds that this was already the doctrine of Pope Innocent III, whom he cited in a footnote, saying: "(1) Innocent III favours this opinion, in his third sermon writing on the day of his consecration; *To such an extent faith is necessary for me, that, while for other sins I have God for a judge, because of the sin which is committed against faith, I could be judged by the Church.* See Sylvium in 2. 2. S. Thomæ tom. 3. q. 39. art. 3. conclus. 2."[458] Likewise St. Alphonsus, as quoted above, said on this question, "We answer, that if ever a pope as a private person would fall into heresy, then he would immediately fall from the papacy; for since he would be outside the Church, he could no longer be the head of the Church. Whence in that case the Church would have to not in fact depose him, because

---

[456] Paul Hinschius, *System des katholischen Kirchenrechts mit besonderer Rücksicht auf Deutschland,* Erster Band, Berlin, 1869, p. 307 – «Eine Reihe katholischer Schriftsteller wollen aber darin keine Ausnahme von der gedachten Regel finden, weil der in Ketzerei verfallene Papst sich dadurch selbst von der Kirche ausscheide, damit weiter den Pontifikat verwirke und also das Konzil keine Deposition mehr verhängen könne, sondern nur die Thatsache des erfolgten Verlustes der Päpstlichen Würde zu konstatiren habe.«

[457] Ballerini, *Op. cit.* pp. 127-128.

[458] *De Pot. Ecc.* p. 127 footnote 1: «(1) Favet huic sententiæ Innocentius III. sermone tertio habito die suæ conscerationis scribens; *In tantum fides mihi necessaria est, ut, cum in cæteris peccatis Deum judicem habeam, propter peccatum, quod in fide committitur, possim ab Ecclesia judicari.* Vide Sylvium in 2. 2. S. Thomæ tom. 3. q. 39. art. 3. conclus. 2.»

no one has power over the pope, but declare him to have fallen from the pontificate."[459]

The fact that by divine decree the pope possesses the unmitigated absolute power of the supreme judge, which excludes that he may ever be judged by anyone for so long as he validly holds office, proves absolutely that if the pontiff were to become a manifest heretic he would no longer legitimately hold office as a valid pope, since the Church in judging the heretic, would not be judging the pope, but, as Gregory XVI expressed it, the Church would only be judging "the person who was before adorned with the papal dignity". It was the same Gregory XVI who wrote, «it is clearly certain that Jesus Christ, wanting *immutable, visible and perpetual* government, founded for the safety of the faithful, **must have provided the Church with all means, which are necessary in order not to be governed by an illegitimate leader,**» Now it is clear that if God would allow a pope to fall pertinaciously into an obvious heresy, so that the fact of his heresy and his pertinacity would be manifestly evident to all who hold the Catholic faith, the Church, under normal circumstances, would likely be able to remedy the situation, since general agreement could be reasonably expected *under normal circumstances*. However, in this hypothesis, in a Church torn apart by factions and heresies, it is difficult to envisage how even a council as a last resort would be able to remedy such a situation, but given that even under such dire and challenging circumstances there would be no other remedy available than that one which is the last resort, it is theorized that a council would have to be convoked, and the outcome would have to be left to the provident wisdom of God, under whose omnipotent governance all creatures are subject. However, since this remedy is nowhere prescribed in the deposit of revelation, it remains only a hypothetical solution. No such remedy has been prescribed by God because God will never permit that the situation will arise in which the Church will be faced with having to deal with a true pope who falls into heresy, because the gift of unfailing faith has been given to Peter's successor, constituting him, and not a council, as the *Saxum inmobile molem continens*.

---

[459] Alfonso Maria de' Liguori, *Vindiciae pro suprema pontificis potestate adversus Iustinum Febronium*, Torino, 1832, p. 142.

Similarly also, *no clearly indicated means has been found to be provided in the deposit of revelation to judge between an imperfect council and a canonically elected true pope who would then become a doubtful pope, after falling under grave suspicion of heresy for having exhibited indicia of heresy on a point definitively taught by the universal magisterium, but not yet solemnly defined by a pope or council.* It is overly simplistic to say that a council could simply resolve the dilemma, because there is no guarantee of infallibility, nor of unanimity, especially if the council would consist of competing factions holding opposing doctrinal positions. *Only the act of a supreme and infallible power would be able to render a definitive judgment in such a situation as this, which of its very nature would require an infallible act of supreme authority in order for it to be settled definitively.* This *supreme and infallible power* exists only in the holder of the **Primacy**, so if there would be positive doubt as to whether or not the power of the primacy would still exist in the person of the true pope who then becomes a doubtful pope due to suspicion of heresy, there would be no available means to reach a definitive judgment of his case, unless his pertinacity in heresy, or his doctrinal orthodoxy could be clearly established and unanimously agreed — but unless the fact could be seen by all as *evidenter verum,* there would exist no conceivable means by which a definitive judgment could be reached. The Church would be reduced to a condition of having two, or even multiple entities competing for headship if unanimity could not be achieved in a council, as St. Alphonsus observed:

> St. Antoninus (part. 13. tit. 2. §. 3. cap. 3.) produces the reason why a council cannot be appealed to against a pope: *Because the Church has unity from the unity of the head; whence, Jn. 10., Christ says* Fiet unum ovile, et unus pastor. *If it would be licit to appeal from the pope, the pope would not be head, but there would be two heads.* Few words, but they wonderfully explain the substance of the matter.[460]

Hence, it lies within the Church's power only to judge whether or not a claimant was validly elected, and for that, the Church would have to judge whether or not the claimant was a capable subject of assuming the papacy. Therefore, **TWO CORROLARIES**

---

[460] Alfonso Maria de' Liguori, *Vindiciae pro suprema pontificis potestate adversus Iustinum Febronium,* Torino, 1832, p. 164.

FOLLOW BY STRICT LOGICAL NECESSITY: 1) *that it is impossible for a true pope to fall into formal heresy*, and; **2)** *a manifest heretic pope is one who can be shown by the fact alone of manifest heresy to have never validly assumed the papacy, nor to have ever legitimately occupied the pontifical office.*

I explained earlier that the ruling of Paul IV mentioned above [that the election of a heretic is invalid] is founded on the *doctrinal principle* that a heretic *per se* is an **incapable subject** of the papacy; and since no specific divine precept prescribing a remedy for the case of papal heresy can be found in divine revelation, we have what is a certain proof from reason that a pope cannot fall into formal heresy: It would contradict the divine wisdom if God were to permit that the Church should be ruled and governed by an illegitimate pastor and heretical destroyer of the Church, without prescribing any clear and infallible remedy for what Bordoni rightly calls the *necessitas maxima* of such a catastrophe of there being a pope, who exhibits the *indicia* of pertinacity in formal heresy, or in his words and actions exhibits the *indicia* of the gravest suspicion of heresy, without there being in place by divine institution an infallible juridical remedy to prevent the heretic from destroying the Church. The only remedy that does exist is the one prescribed by Paul IV — which is the same as what the medieval canonists referred to as an *exceptio*. This remedy could be practically applied to ferret out the heretic and expose his pertinacity by means of *dubia, formal correction*; and finally a *declaratory sentence* of heresy, nullity, and vacancy. By this means it would be proven that the "pope" in question from the time he was elected was never a valid holder of the Petrine office.

The absolute power of the primacy by its very nature excludes the possibility that a true and valid pope could ever be judged a heretic, because in virtue of that absolute power, a valid pope judges all and cannot be judged by anyone, and it is in his exclusive power to make the final determination of all judgments in matters of faith as the supreme judge of all disputes. It is precisely because, 1) the jurisdiction of the pope, in virtue of his primacy, is *full and absolute*, and, 2) in the exercise of that jurisdiction his faith cannot fail, that the solemn papal definitions are absolutely to be followed. *Thus, the theories of ministerial deposition of a heretic pope formulated by Cajetan and John of St. Thomas are ultimately reducible to the heresy of Conciliarism, because they ascribe to a council, against the "full and supreme jurisdiction" of the primacy, a power to deprive the pope of his right to exercise his own primatial authority as supreme judge, and to appropriate to itself that authority to judge a dispute in a matter of faith with finality against the pope, thereby nullifying his "full and supreme jurisdiction".* Nowhere in the deposit of revelation can it be found that God granted such an exceptional *supreme power* to an imperfect ecumenical council, but the sole and exclusive supreme ecumenical power in the Church is the *full and supreme jurisdiction* of the UNIVERSAL PRIMACY OF JURISDICTION which Christ bestowed exclusively and personally upon Peter and his successors to exercise over the whole Church as *"supreme judge of the faithful"*. Since God did not provide any specific remedy in the deposit of revelation for a heretic pope to be judged and deposed by the Church, it proves that God will never allow a heretic to become a valid pope or a valid pope to become a heretic; because if a pope could be a heretic while holding office, there would exist no prescribed means to remove him, nor would there be any means by which formal heresy could always be proven with infallible certitude, and therefore, there would exist no power to prevent the heretic from destroying the Church and causing her defection, *because a valid pope remains the supreme judge of whether or not his own opinion is heretical.* But if a council were juridically capable of deciding that a pope, has altered and mutated his primacy by heresy, judging him to have rendered himself incapable of exercising his *munus* of infallibility, so that his definitions would no longer be infallible, then the pope would no longer be the *supreme* and *infallible judge*, nor could his definitions be followed absolutely, but the council would function as the supreme judge with neither the authority of the primacy, nor the charism of infallibility, thereby nullifying the primacy and its *munus* to preserve the unity of the Church by means of absolutely infallible judgments. Accordingly, the Cajetan-John of St. Thomas conjunction theory is logically reducible to pure and unmitigated Conciliarism.

More simply stated: If John of St. Thomas' thesis were true, namely, that heresy alters the primacy in such a manner that it is *mutated*, rendering the pope incapable of exercising the powers of the primacy, which are the 1) the full and supreme jurisdiction to govern, to judge, to legislate, and 2) the power to teach infallibly with binding authority; then it would lie within the jurisdiction of the council to judge if the pope's primacy has been thusly altered, rendering the pope incapable of defining infallibly; with the result that the authority to judge in matters of faith would ultimately not pertain to papal jurisdiction, but it would be transferred to the Council. The exception would become the rule, because it would pertain to the authority of the Council to judge the quality of the pope's definitions — whether they are fallible definitions proceeding from an altered primacy of a heretic or from a properly functioning primacy of an infallible Catholic pope. Such a judgment requires the supreme jurisdiction which has been solemnly defined to exist only in the primacy of the Roman Pontiff. But if the pope's primacy could be mutated by heresy, it would fall within the *Ersatz Primacy* of the Council to judge whether the pope's opinion falls under a previous anathema or not; or whether it is contrary to a previous definition, or contrary to a dogma of the universal magisterium not yet solemnly defined, but infallibly taught definitively by the ordinary and universal magisterium. Thus it would ultimately lie within the *Ersatz Primacy* of the Council to judge in each instance whether the pope is capable of exercising the power to teach infallibly, or if he is a heretic incapable of teaching infallibly; and papal definitions would not be absolutely and certainly infallible, because definitions of a pope whose primacy is mutated, thereby rendering him incapable of exercising the primacy, would not be infallible, because papal infallibility depends essentially on the exercise of the primacy. Thus, the *Ersatz Primacy* of the Council would not exist by way of exception, but the Council would ultimately possess the full and supreme jurisdiction to decide questions and disputes in matters of faith. It would therefore not even be an *Ersatz Primacy,* but would be a primacy pure and simple. Therefore, if it were possible for the primacy to be altered and mutated by heresy, infallibility would only exist if the Council were to ratify all papal definitions as being made by a pope who has not altered his primacy by heresy; and it would also lie within the supreme jurisdiction of the council to judge that pope who made the definition is a heretic, who having altered his primacy by heresy, is no longer capable of exercising his primacy to teach infallibly. Therefore, if the pope is judged by the Council to be a heretic whose primacy has been mutated by heresy, his definitions would not be infallibly and irreformable *ex sese*, but would be subject to the judgment of the Council. The pope would not be the supreme judge, nor would his definitions be infallible *per se*. The pope would not possess the *total fullness of supreme power*, but that power would ultimately lie within the jurisdiction of the Council. Hence, the doctrine of Cajetan-John of St. Thomas is ultimately reducible to Conciliarism in its purest form, even if on the surface it appears at first to be opposed to Conciliarism. Thus, the divinely instituted monarchical authority of the Church would ultimately be subject to the aristocratic authority of a Council — an aristocratic authority which would be the worst possible for the Church, as St. Robert Bellarmine explained in the above quoted passage (*De Romano Pontifice, lib. i. cap. viii*).

Therefore, there exists only one doctrinally orthodox solution to the question of papal heresy and the deposition of a heretic pope: If a man exhibits the manifestly certain matter and *dolus* of heresy, he thereby manifests himself to be an *incapable subject* of the papacy — a *papa nullus* who never was a true pope, and whose claimed jurisdiction need not be recognized by anyone at any time; and who can be judged, set aside, and punished by the Church. Thus, the ultimate criterion as to whether a man is a valid pope or not is the criterion of orthodoxy, so that (hypothetically) even if he, as a proven heretic, would nevertheless be accorded universal and peaceful acceptance, which due to various factors can be almost impossible at times to determine, he would be judged to have never validly occupied the office. But a true universal and peaceful acceptance of a heretic is impossible, because Christ's sheep *"do not follow the stranger but flee, because they do not know the voice of strangers. The strangers are the heretics and schismatics"* (Innocent III *Sermo III*). The judgment against the heretic would become binding on the whole Church after being confirmed by the subsequent election of an indubitably true and certain pope. But if a *valid pope* could at the same time be a heretic, there would be no one who could judge him — yet, as a heretic, it is of divine precept that he must be judged — but there would be no supreme judge to act with jurisdiction as an infallible final arbiter in the dispute between the pope and the council, and consequently, there could be no final determination of the Church's judgment in the dispute, because without the Pope acting as the *supreme judge* exercising his primatial jurisdiction to *infallibly* bind the whole Church to his decision, there can be no final decision of an infallible judge. Without the pope exercising the primatial power of the keys, the Church would be left with no other means but Private Judgment to decide between the two, resulting in the shattering of the Church's unity, because the keys were given to Peter alone, and to none of the other Apostles, and therefore an imperfect council is incapable of rendering such a judgment which of its nature requires the exercise of the supreme primatial authority. This is in fact the judgment of St. Alphonsus on this point, that heresy can only be ultimately determined by the infallible judgment of the pope; and he explains why it cannot be otherwise: "It is so true; for, if the infallibility in matters of faith are removed from the supreme pontiff, no other means suffices (as we will see below) to convict heretics."[461] And, citing a multiplicity of Fathers in the first chapter of the work, he explains the reason why no other means suffices to judge heretics, which is namely, that the Pope, as successor of Peter, stands alone as the solid rock upon which the faith is founded, and upon which everything else in the Church is built and depends; and therefore, if hell would prevail against the faith of the pope, upon which the infallibility of the Church rests and depends, then it would prevail against the Church itself. In this vein he quotes Origen, "And elsewhere the same Origen (In Ch. 16. Matthew) uttered that thought full of juice: *If hell would prevail against the rock on which the Church was founded, it would even prevail against the Church.*"[462] Therefore, he explains, the principal point in this matter is that, given that the papal authority is the supreme and infallible foundation upon which the Church is built, all questions and disputes must end with the pope's judgment; and that the unity of faith cannot be preserved unless his sentence will be held by the whole Church.[463] There is only one priest who is the one judge acting in the place of Christ, and all heresy arises out of refusal to adhere to his judgments.

---

[461] Alfonso Maria de' Liguori, *Vindiciae pro suprema pontificis potestate adversus Iustinum Febronium*, Torino, 1832, p. 13 — «Idque nimis verum est; nam, sublata infallibilitate circa res fidei a pontifice romano, nullum suppetit medium (ut infra videbimus) ad hæreticos convincendos.»

[462] *Ibid.* p. 12 — «Et alibi idemque Origenes (In cap. 16. Matthæi) protulit illam succi plenam sententiam: *Si prævalerent inferi adversus petram in qua ecclesia fundata est, etiam adversus ecclesiam prævalerent.*»

[463] Cf. *Ibid.* p. 14-31.

«We repeat here that memorable judgment of Cyprian: *For neither from anywhere else have heresies arisen, or have schisms been born, than from there that the Priest of God is not obeyed, and besides one is considered in the Church at the same time priest and judge in the place of Christ. Lib. 1. ep. ad Corn. papam.* Note, *one priest the judge in the place of Christ.*»[464] — St. Alphonsus de Liguori

* * *

ST. ALPHONSUS PROVES THAT THE CHURCH CAN NEVER JUDGE A TRUE POPE

9. Since therefore in the body the head governs and rules over all the members; thus the Pope governs and rules the whole Church. ... [Ed - *But if the pope does not govern the members united in a council:*] So the mystical body of the Church will be a monster, while it has two heads. But the limbs without a head are nothing but a severed body; how then can the council be a whole body and represent the Church without its head the Roman Pontiff? And how can it be called a general council without the head, when in the same First Council of Nicea it was said: *Councils must not be celebrated without the judgment of the Roman Pontiff?* Whence then wrote Pope St. Damasus (Epist. 2. Ad Steph. Et Conc. African.): *By none of the bishops are the decrees to be given force, to which the Roman Pontiff has not granted approval, and before all his judgment is awaited: nor are any councils considered to be brought together, which are not supported by the Apostolic authority.* And St. Athanasius (Epist. Ad Felic. II.) *It is sanctioned by the canons, that without the Roman Pontiff nothing in major cases ought to be determined.* And in fact in the Nicene II Council under Hadrian I. in the year 781 with the concurrence of 350 bishops, the preceding Constantinopolitan Synod was censured, and for what reason? *Because it did not have the Roman Pontiff cooperating... in the manner that must be done in synods. Act.* 6. The same happened to the Ariminensian Council, although it had 400 Fathers. The same happened for the Ephesian Council II. in the case of Eutyches, because Pope St. Leo did not accept it. [...] [p. 180] 14. But let us see the intrinsic reason for this, why the Pope is superior to the councils. The reason is, because

---

[464] *Ibid.* p. 31 — «Repetamus hic memorabilem illam Cypriani sententiam: *Neque enim aliunde hæreses obortæ sunt, aut nata schismata, quam inde quod sacerdoti Dei non obtemperatur; nec unus in ecclesia ad tempus sacerdos, et ad tempus judex vice Christi cogitatur. Lib.* 1. *ep. ad Corn. papam.* Nota, *sacerdos unus judex vice Christi.*»

the government of the Church is purely monarchical, so the head of the Church has no other superior or equal. It is already known that there are three kinds of government: *democratic*, in which the supreme power is in the people; *aristocratic*, in which the power is in the elected ministers; *monarchical*, in which full power is all in the head alone. Everyone agrees that the monarchical government is the most perfect: *The optimal rulership*, wrote S. Thomas, *of the multitude, is that it be ruled by one: for the peace and unity of the subjects is the end of rulership: the more apt cause of unity is one, than many. And then he concludes: It occurs that questions are brought up concerning matters of faith: but the Church would be divided by the diversity of opinions, unless it would be conserved in unity by the judgment of one.* […] [p. 181] 15. Catholics on the other hand uniformly say that Jesus Christ, leaving this world, left the supreme power of the Church to St. Peter and through him to all his successors; so taught St. Thomas in the aforementioned passage, where, after saying that the monarchical government is the best of all, he adds: Whence Christ said: *And there shall be one fold and one shepherd.* St. Antoninus writes the same (p. 3. Tit. 22. Chap. 2. §. 3.) saying that Christ, having constituted the Pontiff his vicar, established the monarchical power in the Church. And so everyone says; and Jean Gerson writes that he is a heretic who would pertinaciously deny to the Pope the monarchical state: *The Papal state supernaturally and immediately instituted by Christ, as having the monarchical and regal primacy in the ecclesiastical hierarchy, according to which unique supreme state the Church militant is said to be one under Christ: which state anyone presumes to contest, or diminish, or equate with some other particular Ecclesiastical state, if he does this pertinaciously, he is a heretic, a schismatic, impious, and sacrilegious. He falls into heresy so many times expressly condemned from the beginning of the Church until today; both by Christ's institution of the pre-eminence of Peter over the other Apostles, and by the tradition of all the Church in its sacred utterances and general councils.* Gers. Tract. de Statib. Eccl. Cons. 1. [p. 186] But here is the clear reason given by S. Antoninus (part. 13. Tit. 2. S. 3. Chap. 3.) For which it cannot be appealed from the Pope to a council: Because the Church has unity from the unity of the head; *whence (John 10.) Christ says: there shall be one fold and one shepherd. If it would be licit to appeal from the Pope, the Pope would not be the head, but there would be two heads.* [p. 189] Furthermore, the Fathers of the Roman Council under Pope Symmachus said: *The Pope is the supreme pastor, subject to no judgment except in the case of heresy.* Tom. 2. Concilior. More St. Thomas in de Pot. q. 1st. to. 4. ad 13. Writes thus: *From the actions of the Council of Chalcedon it is deemed first, that the judgment of the synod is confirmed by the Pope: secondly that from a synod appeal is made to the Pope: thirdly, that from the Pope no appeal is made to a synod, as is had from the actions of the Council of Ephesus.* […] [p. 193] But they cannot deny that this council, so that it has supreme authority, and is infallible by itself, independently of the Pope, it must be legitimate. And in order for it to be legitimate, it is not enough for it to be numerous of many bishops congregated together, since there have been numerous councils, such as the Milanese Council II. under Pope Liberius of 300 Fathers, the Ariminese under S. Damasus of 600 Fathers, the Ephesian II. under St. Leo of 280 Fathers, but with all that they have been censured by the Church; so in order that the council be ecumenical it must have all the necessary conditions, that is to say that it be uniform to the divine Scriptures, to the tradition of the Fathers, that it be convened by those who have authority over it, and that there be freedom in giving votes. Now, as doubt arises as to whether or not these conditions coincided together in a council, there must necessarily be a judge who decides it; and this cannot be other than the Pope: otherwise if anyone says that this judgment should be made by another council, the same doubt can occur in this second council, and so it could go on infinitely. [p. 194] This judge must therefore necessarily be the Pope, who is the head of the Church. [p. 195] 23. I also ask: is the Pope in making this declaration and judgment, fallible or infallible? If it is fallible, this declaration of his is of little or no use; because, since his judgment is fallible, the doubt remains standing as before. If then we say that the Pope is infallible in this, then there is an eternal and irremediable schism [196]. For in this case there would be two heads in the Church, both supreme, without there being a judge who can decide the doubts, given that the Pope and the council disagree between them. And how can it be said that by doing so God would have provided for his Church ...? [...] the Church will become a reduction of contrasts and schisms, without any way of ever sedating them. For this reason St. Jerome said: *For this reason one is elected among the twelve, so that being constituted as head, the occasion for schism will be removed. Lib. de Unit. Eccl.* And saying that, it cannot be doubted that S. Jerome felt that the authority of this head was supreme and infallible; otherwise dissensions could never have been avoided, as writes St. Thomas ... speaking of the Pope's authority: [p. 197] *but the Church would be divided by the diversity of opinions, unless it would be conserved in unity by the judgment of one. St. Thom. contra Gentes lib.* 4. *cap.* 76. [...] otherwise as for the revealed truths we would have nothing firm, but the whole thing would be in contrast and confusion. [...] And here be it allowed me to repeat the passage of S. Cyprian, who wrote: *For neither from anywhere else have heresies arisen, or have schisms been born, than from there that the Priest of God is not obeyed, and besides one is considered in the Church at the same time priest and judge in the place of Christ. Lib.* 1. *Epist. ad Cornel.* [p. 201] Furthermore, let us not doubt that when the bishops together with the Pope define some point of faith, then certainly the Holy Spirit assists everyone; but this does not take away that in such a council the Pope is the head, who defines the dogma that must be held, since all the authority of the council is already in the Pope. [...] It is therefore not denied that the Fathers of the general council are infallibly directed by [p. 202] the Holy Spirit, as the Pope is directed; but when? When they are united with the Pope in judgment, since in the Council of Jerusalem the Apostles were united with St. Peter. But when they are discordant and divided, then that council is no longer legitimate, nor can it be said to be anymore ecumenical; it is a severed body; they are limbs without a head, they no longer represent the Church; for the Church must have its head. [...] It is answered that since the supreme power in the Church is one, and not two, if we do not want to give the Church two supreme heads, when the bishops in the council participate in a common action with the Pope, it is not that their greater number becomes higher in authority to the Pope, and it does not even happen that then there are two distinct powers; but it is that then the same supreme power, which already before all resided in the Pope, extends to them, and becomes common;[465]...[i]

From this explanation of St. Alphonsus it becomes clear what the Roman Council under Pope Symmachus meant when it taught, *"The Pope is the supreme pastor, subject to no judgment except in the case of heresy."* It cannot mean that a true and valid pope can be judged by his inferiors in the case of heresy, because then the supreme and infallible judge would be judged by an inferior and fallible judge. There would either be two heads judging against each other; or, if the council were to be considered supreme in such a case by way of exception, then the dogma which defines that the judgment of all disputes in matters of faith is reserved exclusively to the pope would be erroneous. Thus, in accordance with the teaching of Bellarmine, Ballerini, St. Alphonsus and Gregory XVI — all of whom based their teaching on the doctrine of Innocent III — it would not be a true pope who would be judged a heretic and deposed by his inferiors; but it would be a doubtful pope, presumed to be no pope, who then for reason of his evident heresy would be judged by the Church to be no pope, because the Church infallibly recognizes the heretic for what he is: an alien, an outsider, an impostor, who is not their shepherd but a heretic: *"For*

---

[465] *Verità Della Fede*, Opera Del Beato Alfonso Maria de' Liguori, Tomo Secondo, Monza, 1823, Capo IX. pp. 169-170, 180-181, 186, 189, 193, 194-197, 201-202.

such faith the Roman Pontiff and the Roman Church have kept for each other, that they suitably are able to fit together, which the Truth says in the Gospel: «I know my sheep, and mine know me (John X)»: they do not follow the stranger but flee, because they do not know the voice of strangers. The strangers are the heretics and schismatics, which the Roman Church does not follow, but pursues and drives away. They recognize and hear their own, not apostate but apostolic: not Cathar but Catholic, receiving and rendering the conjugal debt, receiving from him the debt of providence, and rendering the debt of reverence." — Innocent III

Tantam enim fidem Romanus pontifex et Romana Ecclesia sibi semper invicem servaverunt, ut eis congrue valeat coaptari, quod Veritas inquit in Evangelio: «Cognosco oves meas, et cognuscunt me meæ (*Joan.* X)»: alienum non sequuntur sed fugiunt, quia non noverunt vocen alienorum. Alieni autem sunt hæretici et schismatici, quos Ecclesia Romana non sequitur, sed persequitur et fugat. Suum autem cognuscunt et audiunt, non apostaticum, sed apostolicum: non Catarum sed catholicum, recipiens et reddens debitum conjugale, recipiens ab eo debitum providentiæ, et reddens debitum reverentiæ.

Innocentius III. *Sermo III.* «*IN CONSECRATIONE PONTIFICIS*»

JOHN SALZA AND ROBERT SISCOE REMAIN OBSTINATE IN THEIR CONCILIARIST HERESY

Robert J. Siscoe says, «*We did not falsify the teaching of Ballerini. In the book [True or False Pope?], we state over and over again that the pope will not lose his jurisdiction until the Church establishes the crime (that is the phrase we use). The Church "establishes the crime" by judging that the doctrine he professes is qualified as heretical (not a lesser error), and then issuing one or more ecclesiastical warnings. If the pope remains hardened in heresy in the face of these warnings, he publicly* **reveals his pertinacity and thereby manifests his heresy** *(since heresy requires pertinacity). This is an indirect judgment of the Pope which reveals that "he is already judged" (by God). All of this precedes the loss of papal jurisdiction for an heretical Pope. That is how we explain it in the book, and it is exactly how Ballerini explains it.*» In the earlier quoted Ballerini passage cited by Siscoe, Siscoe asserts the heretical proposition that a pope will "*lose his jurisdiction*" when the Church judges "*the doctrine he* *professes is qualified as heretical'*. As I have shown in these first two volumes, Salza & Siscoe have drawn this heresy of *Mitigated Conciliarism* directly from the writings of Cajetan and John of St. Thomas, which were written centuries before the solemn definitions on papal primacy and infallibility of Vatican I anathematized all such opinions which assert any power whatsoever of a council to judge in matters of faith against a validly reigning Roman Pontiff. To date, John Salza and Robert Siscoe remain obstinate in their Conciliarist heresy. Their contumacy in heresy is plainly evident in their explicitly stated heresy which they assert even after five years of correction, in their most recent replies to my objections on their website:

Objection 1: «An imperfect council is incapable of judging on a matter of faith infallibly, and therefore cannot definitively judge with finality whether a pope's opinion is heresy, and from there determine that the pope is indeed a contumacious heretic."»

Salza & Siscoe Reply to Objection 1: «That is why theologians and canonists distinguish between a "new heresy," and one that has already been the subject of an infallibly judgment by a Pope or council, and teach that a Pope can only be declared a heretic for contumaciously denying the latter. Once the Church has defined a dogma, everyone — including future Popes — are bound to believe it; and anyone who denies a defined dogma — including a future Pope — will be a heretic.»

Commentary: Salza & Siscoe heretically claim that an IMPERFECT ECUMENICAL COUNCIL is the FINAL AND SUPREME JUDGE in the matter of judging whether or not a validly reigning pope's opinion is heretical, and that a self-appointed "council" has the necessary jurisdiction to decide in a matter of faith against a validly reigning pope; and that a validly reigning Pontiff can be declared a heretic for contumaciously asserting a doctrine that the council judges to have already been infallibly condemned by a previous Pope or council. However, it has been repeatedly taught solemnly and definitively by the supreme magisterium that the final judgment in ALL matters of faith is reserved to the authority of the pope. I have already cited verbatim the texts of the relevant decrees in Volume One and in subsequent posts, but Salza & Siscoe shove them aside and deliberately ignore them, and continue to insolently assert their position which directly contradicts those solemn pronouncements. It is SOLEMNLY DEFINED in *Pastor Æternus* that the authority to decide all questions on matters of faith pertains absolutely to the FULL AND SUPREME JURISDICTION of the POPE, which Pastor *Æternus* defines as a "**total fullness of supreme power**". Therefore it pertains to the exclusive jurisdiction of the Roman Pontiff to judge whether an opinion is a *new heresy*, or one that has already been the subject of an infallible judgment by a Pope or council. Such decisions are reserved in the final instance to the pope, to whose authority it pertains to DETERMINE THE CHURCH'S JUDGMENT WITH FINALITY.

Objection 2: «If an 'imperfect council' presumes to judge a true and validly reigning pope guilty of heresy, the pope as supreme judge possesses the right and the power to overrule the council and judge the matter with infallibility and finality.»

Salza & Siscoe Reply to Objection 2: «Not if his jurisdiction were "removed by God" (i.e. he is ipso facto deposed), the moment the council convicted him of heresy. At that point, he would no longer be Pope, and hence would no longer be the "supreme judge" with "the right and power to overrule the council."»

Commentary: Not only is falsehood of this proposition already evident not only from what has been said in my comment on the previous reply, but its absurd silliness is seen in the consideration that if the proposition were true, then the supreme and final authority to judge such a question would not necessarily reside with either the pope or the council, but with whichever of the two would be the first to judge. If the pope would define, then his judgment is final and infallible. If the council would judge first, then upon the fallible judgment of the council, the pope would be invisibly stripped of the papacy by God the moment the council convicted him of heresy. And if the council's judgment would be erroneous, how could it be that God would still remove the pope's jurisdiction, so that the pope would then no longer have the authority to infallibly condemn the council's error? Yet this is exactly what Pope St. Gregory VII and did when a group of German bishops attempted to convoke a council to against him. He condemned and excommunicated them all. And Eugenius IV remained with his jurisdiction intact when the rebellious council fathers of Basel who had refused to obey the papal command to desist from the council previously convoked by Martin V, then fell into open schism and proceeded to condemn the pope for his alleged heresy and schism. As has been pointed out, it is SOLEMNLY DEFINED in *Pastor Æternus* that the authority of the bishops exists in HIERARCHICAL SUBORDINATION to the FULL AND SUPREME JURISDICTION of the POPE. A self-appointed "council" lacks all authority to "convict" a valid pope of heresy, because it pertains to the FULL AND SUPREME JURISDICTION of the pope that he can overrule the judgment of his subjects by an act of his FULLNESS OF POWER. By his TOTAL FULLNESS OF SUPREME POWER, the pope possesses the FULL AND ABSOLUTE JURISDICTION OVER ALL COUNCILS as was defined by the Fifth Lateran Council. A self-appointed "council" has no legitimate power to "convict" a true pope, because the "council's" judgment is null and void without the pope's confirmation: IT LIES WITHIN THE POPE'S FULL AND ABSOLUTE JURISDICTION TO QUASH AND INFALLIBLY CONDEMN THE FALLIBLE JUDGMENT OF ANY SELF-APPOINTED "IMPERFECT COUNCIL". If a fallible council of bishops really possessed the authority to convict a validly reigning pope of heresy, then the Church could not avoid defecting from the faith, because, as St. Alphonsus explained, "as for the revealed truths we would have nothing firm, but the whole thing would be in contrast and confusion." And he explains, citing St. Thomas, that this would be so, because, "*the Church would be divided by the diversity of opinions, unless it would be conserved in unity by the judgment of one. St. Thom. contra Gentes lib. 4. cap. 76.*" That ONE, says Ballerini, **«*is the Roman Bishop, the one high priest, to whom the whole Church, and the unity of the whole Church is committed.*»**[466]

Objection 3: «No council can arrogate the power to itself (1) to nullify or suppress the pope's right of primacy to judge the case as the supreme, final, and infallible judge, and then (2) presume to arrogate to itself the supreme power to judge the pope's opinion heretical with finality, and (3) command the pope with coercive juridical force to submit to the judgment of the Council.»

---

[466] Ballerini, *De Vi Ac Ratione Primatus Romanorum Pontificum Et De Ipsorum Infallibilitate Iin Definiendis Controversiis Fidei*, Monasterii Westphalorum 1845, c. 13. §. 3., num. 13, p. 116.

Salza & Siscoe Reply: «In reply to (1), the council does not suppress the Pope's right to judge matters of faith; it "convicts him of heresy" for denying an already defined dogma, and Christ strips him of his supreme jurisdiction.»

Commentary: It lies EXCLUSIVELY within the FULL AND ABSOLUTE JURISDICTION of the PRIMCAY TO JUDGE WHETHER OR NOT AN OPINION OPPOSES AN ALREADY DEFINED DOGMA. The proposition that asserts the right of a self-appointed "council" to "convict" a valid pope of heresy DIRECTLY OPPOSES THE DOGMA WHICH DEFINES THAT THE FINAL JUDGMENT IN SUCH MATTERS IS RESERVED TO THE POPE'S AUTHORITY.

* * *

So the question needs to be asked, how is it that Salza & Siscoe have been able to gain such a following among Catholic readers, and even among members of the clergy who ought to know better? How have they succeeded in seducing so many from the most staunchly orthodox sector of Catholicism away from orthodoxy and dragging them into heresy? The answer to this question can be found in a little book which is so great a spiritual treasure, that St. Francis de Sales carried it on his person and read a page of it each day for eighteen years. That book is *The Spiritual Combat* by Don Lorenzo Scupoli. Although it has been decades since I read it, there is one point the author explains that has remained indelibly fixed in my memory, and it is this: *The devil succeeds in drawing souls into evil by presenting evil under the appearance of good.* This favourite artifice of the devil is the chosen means employed by Salza & Siscoe to lead souls into heresy; and the artifice succeeds by the applying the methods of *propaganda*.

Salza & Siscoe draw unwary souls into heresy by leading them to believe that reading their book, (*True or False Pope?*), will protect them from falling into the error of *Sedevacantism*. The poisoned bait is presented to the readers and dangled before their eyes in the subtitle of the book — *Refuting* **Sedevacantism** *and other Modern Errors*. The book is not so much about refuting Sedevacantism than it is about leading souls away from the Catholic Church by drawing them into the Temple of the new religion by means of the heresy of *Mitigated*

Conciliarism; so that they will remain within the body of the *Conciliar Church* even after the *Conciliar Church* will have formalized its defection from Catholicism by departing from the unity of true apostolic Church as divinely constituted while retaining the *name* of "Catholic Church" – even after the conciliar *Reformation* will have consummated the construction of the *counterfeit church* built on the foundation of the false religion of **Freemasonry**. The poisonous thesis of the book is the proposition that no matter how manifestly heretical the *Conciliar* bishops and pope may become, ***they remain the true hierarchy of the Catholic Church until the public judgment of the Church condemns them as heretics***. What this means is that (according to them) the *Sankt Gallen Mafia* Pope will remain in office as the valid pope of the Catholic Church until he is judged a heretic by the *Sankt Gallen Mafia!* This is demonstrated by Salza's own words, where he says in his e-mail of Sept. 13, 2016, "Show us where the CHURCH teaches that individual Catholics can judge that public pertinacity has been established in the external forum, WHEN THAT JUDGMENT IS CONTRARY TO THE PUBLIC JUDGMENT OF THE CHURCH." As I have explained, when there exists a solid evidentiary basis for positive and probable doubt about the validity of a reputed holder of the Petrine office, his status is *doubtful*, and, as the most eminent authorities affirm, the see is presumed vacant for so long as the doubt persists. In such cases it is unanimously taught by canonists and theologians that one is not bound to accept such a "doubtful pope". One is permitted to judge privately under such circumstances, because there can exist no public judgment binding upon the whole Church if it is not made in conjunction with the primacy of jurisdiction existing in a true and indubitable pope. Such a primacy cannot be verified as certainly existing in a particular claimant until the doubt is resolved, which can only happen when certitude regarding the identity of the rightful holder of the primatial authority is restored. The reason why Salza so adamantly advocates the idea that if a pope would publicly and manifestly defect from the faith into formal heresy, no private individual would have any right to assert that the fact of defection and loss of office has taken place without there first having been made a public judgment of the Church, is that Salza professes the heretical doctrine that the Church must first judge a heretic pope before he would lose office, and consequently, by asserting that Bergoglio is a valid holder of the papal office, it is thereby asserted that he cannot lose the papal office unless he would first be judged guilty of heresy by the Church. This is plainly evident from his own words in an e-mail addressed to me: «Your statement "the Church plays no role in the loss of office" truly shows how unread you are on these issues. John of St. Thomas and others teach that the Church is the dispositive cause of the loss of office for a reigning Pope (when she makes a judgment of public pertinacity), after which Christ severs the bond between the heretic (matter) and papacy (form), as efficient cause. But you wouldn't know this because you evidently haven't studied these issues in depth.» Salza's verdict: "it is difficult to believe that Fr. Kramer has done any real study of St. Bellarmine." Salza, as has been explained earlier, believes that St. Robert Bellarmine is also of the opinion that the Church must first judge the heretic pope for the loss of office to take place: «Our interpretation of Bellarmine is exactly how all the classical theologians have interpreted him, namely, that the "fact" of public pertinacity must be established by the Church, not individual Catholics.» As I have amply demonstrated, according to Bellarmine's own words, the office would be lost *ipso facto* and without any external agency (such as a judgment of the Church) for the reason that the public act of formal heresy would destroy by itself the necessary disposition (which is faith) for the pope to retain the form of the pontificate, so that he would cease *by himself* to be pope without another deposition (*sine alia depositione*). The visible loss of faith, according to Bellarmine, renders the conservation of the form of the pontificate in the person impossible, so that the pope would cease by himself to be pope without any external agency (*sine alia vi externa*). Salza's reply: "Siscoe and I can assure you, you don't know this material like you think you do".

Then, what does Salza mean by the *public judgment of the Church?* He means this: "your anticipated response that Bergoglio has publicly departed (with pertinacity) from the Magisterium as the rule of faith is, AGAIN, contrary to the judgment of the Cardinals and bishops, and also contrary to Bergoglio's own public statements, **which are only materially heretical**". Salza, the *Sankt Gallen Mafia* advocate, has already pronounced his own judgment of acquittal on his *Sankt Gallen Mafia* client, by declaring the *indicia* against Bergoglio to amount to no more than evidence of mere material heresy, and therefore innocent of formal heresy. Furthermore, *he equates his own private judgment of the case with a public judgment of the Church*, merely on the basis of the false claim that there has been issued a "judgment of the Cardinals and bishops" declaring "Bergoglio's own public statements" to be orthodox, and therefore, in Salza's opinion, "only materially heretical". This proposition itself heretically presupposes the premise that the cardinals and bishops possess the ecclesiastical power to judge the doctrinal orthodoxy of an actually reigning pontiff, which Salza alleges Bergoglio to actually be. Not only has no definitive judgment ever been pronounced by the cardinals and bishops on Bergoglio's orthodoxy, but such an ambiguous and merely implicit judgment as is alleged to have been made by the hierarchy in favour of Bergoglio is in reality no judgment at all, first, because they have made no claim of jurisdiction to judge the man they consider to be the pope; second, because a merely implicit judgment would not fulfil even the minimum requirements for a valid juridical act; and third, because in order for such an implicit judgment as that to be juridical, and binding upon the whole Church, it would need to eventually be formalized and ratified by an indubitably valid pope. For so long as the *indicia* remain, the positive doubt persists, and no binding judgment is possible until the doubt will have been definitively resolved. As I have amply proven, the power of the cardinals and bishops to judge a pope is conditioned upon the invalidity of that pope's pontificate. If he is a true pope, he simply cannot be judged by anyone else's attempt at a juridical act. This is a dogma of faith. If he exhibits the evidently true fact of the *dolus* of formal heresy, he manifests that he is a false pope, and can be judged and deposed. This is a truth of the universal magisterium as I have amply proven. If it can be shown that there are *indicia* of vehement or violent suspicion amounting to a high probability of formal heresy, then one may judge accordingly that the putative pope is a *papa dubius*. In such a case the see would be presumed vacant, and it would be the duty of the pastors of the Church to resolve the doubt by means of a process leading to a proper judgment — the process the medieval canonists called an *accusatio*. The presentation of the *dubia* is part of this process. If the *indicia* constitute manifestly evident proof of formal heresy, then the pastors must depose the intruder straightaway without a trial. This kind of procedure is what the medieval canonists referred to as an *exceptio*. The *indicia* against Bergoglio are manifestly evident, but the spineless pastors of the Church maintain themselves in a blatant state of supine ignorance of this glaring reality, and accordingly, they avoid fulfilling their duty to judge at all cost, contriving every possible excuse to justify their inexcusable inaction; while Salza & Siscoe effectively cheer them on in their reprehensible negligence, justifying their failure to judge as their duty of office requires by falsely asserting that they have *already judged!* In reality, the process of rendering judgment against the counterfeit Argentinian usurper was stalled when it stopped after the presentation of the *dubia*.

Salza then resorts to another artifice of sophistry, clearly implying in principle but not stating explicitly that a higher level of *indicia* exist against Ratzinger than exist against Bergoglio: "You are desperate to make Bergoglio worse than his predecessors, but just read Ratzinger's books. Ratzinger proves that he KNOWS what the Church teaches, and yet departs from it in his writings, unlike Bergoglio."[467] According to Salza's own private opinion (or more correctly, according to one of his four contradictory opinions[468]), based upon his own criteria for

---

[467] Subject: Re: Salza's Colossal Blunder - 13/09/2016 16:13 (GMT+00:00).

[468] 1) A declaration is not required, 2) A declaration is required, 3) A declaration might be required, 4) Whether a declarartion is requireds or not is irrelevant: 1) "WE DO NOT HOLD THAT A DECLARATORY SENTENCE IS REQUIRED FOR LOSS OF OFFICE!" 2) "The loss of office for a cleric is a vindictive penalty, and there is a process in Church law which must precede vindictive penalties" (*True or False Pope?* p. 260), and in their *Formal Reply* they quote Benedict XIV, "a sentence declaratory of the offence is always necessary in the external forum"; "For a Pope to publicly defect from the Church, he would have to publicly renounce the Magisterium as the infallible rule of faith (and choose another rule, i.e., joining another religion). None of the conciliar Popes have done this, and thus they have not publicly defected from the Church according to the Church's judgment. Their material heresies, false worship and even public sins against the Faith do not constitute public defection from the Church. Indeed, the conciliar Popes may have spiritually severed themselves from the Church by the sin of heresy (which happens by the very nature of heresy), but they are not legally severed from the Church until the Church either (1) declares them guilty of heresy, or (2) they publicly defect from the Church (and note well that the 1983 Code of **Canon law requires a**

judging one a pertinacious heretic, ***Salza states that Joseph Ratzinger fulfils the criteria which he judges sufficient for Ratzinger being judged a formal heretic***, while he pronounces Bergoglio innocent of the charge of formal heresy. In an e-mail message to me,[469] Salza explained, «WE DO NOT HOLD THAT A DECLARATORY SENTENCE IS REQUIRED FOR LOSS OF OFFICE!» — and he elaborates further, "As I said in the last email, whether a declaratory sentence is required after the Church establishes the fact of public pertinacity is irrelevant." Salza then explains how pertinacity is established, saying, "Public formal heresy" requires "public pertinacity": «**This is your key error**, because pertinacity will be considered public *only* if the person **publicly renounced the Church as the infallible RULE of faith** – either by publicly defecting from the Catholic religion, *or* **publicly admitting that he knowingly and willfully rejects a dogma of Faith**."»[470] So, very clearly Salza has stated that what suffices for a pope to lose office is that public pertinacity be established by the judgment of the Church; and that pertinacity will be considered so established by the fact of the heretic "***publicly admitting that he knowingly and willfully rejects a dogma of Faith***," and he adds, "Pope Francis has done neither". Thus, for Salza, the heretic's public admission of disbelief suffices to constitute the Church's judgment of pertinacity, since no declaratory sentence is

---

canonical warning and a declaration by the Church externally recognizing the public defection has taken place)." 3) «a reigning Pope will not lose his office before the Church has established the crime, and most probably not before the Church issues a declaratory sentence. However, we do concede that if a Pope were to openly and publicly *leave the Church* of his own will, as opposed to simply professing heresy, a case could be made that God would sever the bond that united the man to the pontificate at the moment his public defection was acknowledged by the Church, even without a declaratory sentence of the crime (for example, if the Pope publicly declared he was no longer Catholic and then joined and became a pastor of the Lutheran sect).» (*True or False Pope?* pp. 280-281)] 4) "As I said in the last email, whether a declaratory sentence is required after the Church establishes the fact of public pertinacity is irrelevant." (John Salza — Date: 14/09/2016 — 03:22)

[469] From: John Salza — Date:14/09/2016 — 03:22.
[470] John Salza: Thu, Jun 22, 2017, 5:12 PM

required: «WE DO NOT HOLD THAT A DECLARATORY SENTENCE IS REQUIRED FOR LOSS OF OFFICE!» The absurdity of Salza's opinion is patent in that the heretic's public admission of disbelief is his own judgment which he pronounces upon himself, and is in no manner whatsoever a judgment made by the Church. Nevertheless, on one point only we do agree, namely, that such an admission would indubitably establish the fact of a pope's formal heresy. So, while Salza says (without presenting any evidence) that Francis has not publicly admitted, "that he knowingly and willfully rejects a dogma of faith;" he asserts (again without producing any evidence), **"Ratzinger proves that he KNOWS what the Church teaches, and yet departs from it in his writings, unlike Bergoglio."** Thus, according to John Salza, Jorge Mario "Francis" Bergoglio is not established as a formal heretic by the public judgment of the Church, but he judges that Pope Benedict XVI fulfils what are in fact the Church's criteria for a public judgment of pertinacity, namely, **"that he KNOWS what the Church teaches, and yet departs from it in his writings,"** — and Salza in this context makes it absolutely clear (or at least he deceptively attempts to make it *appear* to be absolutely clear[471]) that he does not speak of some lesser offense than heresy, but he clearly intends to convey the idea that if one says that Bergoglio can be judged guilty of

---

[471] Salza habitually resorts to this very devious sort of verbal sleight of hand in order to leave himself the defence of saying something like, "I never said he heretically denies dogma, but only departs from Church teaching to a degree less than heresy." But in this instance such an objection intended in the latter sense would be silly and meaningless because his objection would not constitute a valid refutation of my proposition that Bergoglio is a heretic, unless he intends the objection to mean that Ratzinger knowingly departs from *de fide* dogma, and not merely from *Catholic Doctrine*; because only then would it follow logically that if Bergoglio is a heretic, then Ratzinger is also a heretic; but it would not follow from that premise, that Ratzinger is also a heretic, if the objection intended to mean only that Ratzinger departs from *Catholic Doctrine*, but not from the dogma of faith. Understood in the latter sense, Salza's objection would confirm my position rather than refute it, so it is patent that he did not intend the objection to be understood in the latter sense, namely, that *Ratzinger only departs from Church teaching to a degree less than heresy.*

heresy, then Ratzinger must likewise also be judged guilty of the same. Thus, according to Salza's argument, if the *indicia* of heresy against Bergoglio constitute proof of formal heresy, then on the evidence of Ratzinger's own admission, it must also be necessarily concluded that the *indicia* of heresy against Ratzinger also constitute proof of formal heresy — and he evidently intends this conclusion without citing any of Ratzinger's propositions as evidence, and without there ever having been any formal corrections, nor the Church having ever issued any declaration! According to the patently irrational outbursts of John Salza, public judgment of pertinacity is made by establishing the crime, without the need for a declaratory sentence, because, "*A merely declaratory sentence of the crime is not a juridical act.*"[472] Therefore, he says, "You confuse the public judgment of pertinacity with a declaratory sentence of the crime, which shows you don't know the material."[473] And so, after stating the logically incoherent argument that the Church renders a public judgment by somehow establishing the crime without pronouncing any judgment, nor indeed declaring anything at all; and stating moreover the patent falsehood that a declaratory sentence is not a juridical act, (and consequently not a public judgment), Salza makes the insane observation, "You are not making even the most basic, elementary distinctions. You are not capable of discussing the finer points of this theology because you don't even know the basics."[474]

Thus, Salza shamelessly defends the indefensible, falsely accusing (or deliberately making it appear that he is accusing) Pope Benedict of the *dolus* of formal heresy while exonerating the heretic Bergoglio, who says Christ's command to teach and convert the whole world to the true faith is *venom*. For two thousand years the Church infallibly teaches as a dogma of the universal magisterium that she has received the mission from Christ to convert all nations on earth to the Gospel of Christ — to convert them to "this true Catholic faith, outside of which no one can be saved,"[475] and Bergoglio, with persistent

---

[472] *True or False Pope?* p. 275.
[473] From: John Salza — Date:14/09/2016 — 03:22.
[474] From: John Salza — Date:14/09/2016 — 03:22.
[475] «Hanc **veram Catholicam Fidem, extra quam nemo salvus esse potest**, quam in praesenti sponte profiteor et veraciter teneo, eandem integram, et immaculatam usque ad extremum vitae spiritum,

obstinacy flatly denies and explicitly rejects this universally professed dogma of faith. It is quite impossible for Bergoglio to be ignorant of the fact that this teaching is a dogma of faith, since it is one of the most universally known dogmas taught to Catholic children at the very beginning of their religious education in the decades and centuries before Vatican II, but Salza says Bergoglio is not a formal heretic, and that his heresy is only *material*: "he in fact has publicly stated that he is not departing, and does not intend to depart, from the Church as the rule of faith" — "Bergoglio's own public statements," says Salza, "are only materially heretical". Salza did not provide any reference to any of "Bergoglio's own public statements," but he expects us to blindly accept his gratuitous assertions. However, that Bergoglio's heresy on this point is only material is quite impossible, given the fact that invincible ignorance in this case is inconceivable. I have already sufficiently explained also in Volume One why Bergoglio's crime of heresy against the faith of the Church is absolutely inexcusable and beyond legitimate dispute — and in this case, is in no manner whatsoever subject to any mitigating factors. On the other hand, I have read the relevant Ratzinger writings, most of them even in the original German. In Volume One I, explained what are the *indicia* of formal heresy, and briefly enumerated the principal *indicia* of formal heresy against Bergoglio; and I mentioned that no such clear cut *indicia* are to be found in the writings of Ratzinger. Certainly no one has succeeded in pointing out any such certain *indicia* of manifestly evident formal heresy. Salza has not even attempted to do so but only asserts it gratuitously with an utterly unsubstantiated *ipse dixit*. The foundation of Salza's deceitful sophistry on this point is the fallacy of the unstated but implicit premise that in order to prove Bergoglio guilty of heresy, it is also necessary to prove the innocence of Benedict XVI and all the Conciliar Popes. In any case, Salza stops short of explicitly accusing Pope Benedict XVI of formal heresy, or that he has cut himself off from membership in the Church. Salza reserves that explicit

---

constantissime, Deo adiuvante, retinere et confiteri, atque a meis subditis, vel5 illis, quorum cura ad me in munere meo spectabit, teneri, doceri et praedicari, quantum in me erit, curaturum, ego idem N. spondeo, voveo ac iuro. Sic me Deus adiuvet et haec sancta Dei Evangelia.» [*Profession of Faith*, First Vatican Council, Session 2: 6 January 1870]

anathema for Fr. Kramer alone, whom he declares guilty of formal heresy for allegedly having asserted a heretical proposition: a heretical proposition which I have never asserted, but which Salza himself deceptively constructed from a logically incoherent misrepresentation of my words — thus, a deliberate fraud based on a twisted *non sequitur* which does not follow from anything this author has ever written. Thus, the ultimate reason for Salza stating the opinion that "*Ratzinger proves that he KNOWS what the Church teaches, and yet departs from it in his writings, unlike Bergoglio,*" is plainly apparent, and is best described in the words of St. Thomas Aquinas: "For there are some who have such a presumptuous opinion of their own ability that they deem themselves able to measure the nature of everything; I mean to say that, in their estimation, everything is true that seems to them so, and everything is false that does not."[476]

In the second part of this volume I will examine some of the more problematic doctrinal formulations in Ratzinger's writings, and will show that while there exist *indicia* of heresy in his writings, these *indicia* do not constitute clear-cut evidence of formal heresy, but only amount to material heresy. Indeed, there have been shown to be *indicia* amounting to evidence of material heresy even in the writings of the saints, such as expressions suggestive of Subordinationism in the Christology of St. Justin Martyr, and traces of the heretical teachings of Gioacchino da Fiore in the thinking of Pope St. Celestine V. Such *indicia* do not prove that the one who asserts the proposition is a heretic. Such *indicia* can be easily found in the discourses and writings of the Conciliar popes from John XXIII to Benedict XVI, as they can, albeit much less frequently, be found in the expressions of popes of earlier ages, such as in the sermons of John XXII. Salza knows this perfectly well, as he and Siscoe have stated plainly in their writings that the mere expression of heretical propositions do not constitute proof of formal heresy (except in the case of Fr. Kramer to whom they fraudulently attribute a heretical proposition), yet they deceitfully resort to a more subtle form of this crude Sedevacantist

---

[476] *Summa Contra Gentiles* 1 Cap. 5 — «Sunt enim quidam tantum de suo ingenio praesumentes ut totam rerum naturam se reputent suo intellectu posse metiri, aestimantes scilicet totum esse verum quod eis videtur et falsum quod eis non videtur. CG Book 1.»

objection in their attack against the personal orthodoxy of Pope Benedict XVI, in order to defend their man Bergoglio against the proven accusation of formal heresy which disqualifies him from holding the papal office — all for the purpose of upholding the bogus pontificate of the usurper who seeks to destroy the Catholic religion and replace it with an ecumenical cult of Masonic stripe — what Masons call a "dogma-free Christianity", founded on a neo-pagan notion of God and revelation. That neo-pagan cult is what Freemasons call the "Ancient Mysteries", which are the foundation of their abominable pagan religion. As a holder of the Proficiency Card which authorized him to teach Masons how to perform the rituals of Freemasonry, Salza is certainly aware of the religious significance of the *Ancient Mysteries* in the abominable sect of Masonry. It is the stated goal of Freemasonry, documented by Abbé Henri Delassus (1836-1921) in his monumental three volume exposition on Freemasonry, *Le problème de l'heure présente*, that the agenda of Masonry is to replace Catholic worship with the Luciferian rites of Freemasonry. Somehow, Salza has failed to mention this in any of his works which purport to expose the secrets of Freemasonry. When the visible form of the Church will be seen to be destroyed from even the vastly greater portion of the ecclesial *œcumene*, by its profession of false Masonic dogmas, by the institution of heretical and invalid Masonic inspired ecumenical rites, and by its being governed by a manifestly heretical "pope", then that portion of the Church will have defected from the true Church, even if it will be constituted of what had previously been the vastly greater and more visible portion of the Church. That is Bergoglio's stated agenda: to institute IRREVERSIBLE reforms which will bring about the defection of the Catholic Church by bringing the Church into communion with the Protestant sects (and ultimately with non-Christian religions). It is manifestly evident that such heretical reforms as these, by their very nature, will, by themselves consummate the defection of the Conciliar Church from the One Holy Catholic and Apostolic Church, even without any juridical declaration from the hierarchy. Yet, according to the skewed Masonizing thinking of John Salza and Robert Siscoe, when that defection happens, if anyone then will dare to assert the truth and judge in conscience according to the plainly evident and undeniable evidence that a defection from the Catholic Church spearheaded by Bergoglian Rome has taken place, that judgment of conscience by which the faithful refuse to defect with the defectors will constitute a schismatic act of Private Judgment. According to their skewed Masonizing theology which inverts the visible truth, the false new church of Bergoglian apostate Rome — the Masonic monstrosity which is already emerging as a distinct body from its previous existence as a Modernist cancer within the body of the Catholic Church, even after its manifestly visible defection from the true faith and its separation from the body of orthodox believers will still have to be considered the true Church. According to Salza & Siscoe, this new sect already emerging as a deformed caricature of Catholicism will still have to be considered as the crucified Catholic Church infiltrated and occupied by internal enemies. It will then be declared by the defecting heretical-schismatic pastors of the Masonic *antichurch*, that those who refuse to follow them out of the true Church and into the new *Sect* are heretical and schismatic — as if no true Catholic has the right to reject the false new religion of a manifestly evident public defector from the faith and to refuse to hear the voice of that heretic antipope stranger, and to follow only the true Vicar of Christ and remain in communion with the true pope of the true Church, because "the sheep follow him, because they know his voice. But a stranger they follow not, but fly from him, because they know not the voice of strangers." (John 10: 4-5)

As I proved from many authorities, as well as from Scripture, and from Catholic prophecy, a false Church will indeed usurp the place of the true Catholic Church for a time. It was even related by Padre Gabriele Amorth that he was told by St. Pio of Pietrelcina that the Secret of Fatima foretells of the false church (which was also prophesied by others whom I quoted in the first volume of this work). Padre Amorth related to José María Zavala what Padre Pio told him is in the Third Secret of Fatima concerning the false church:

> —Excuse me for insisting on the Third Secret of Fatima: Did Padre Pio then relate it to the loss of faith in the Church? Don Gabriele furrows his eyebrows and puts his chin forward. He seems very affected. "Indeed," he agrees. One day, Padre Pio told me very saddened: «You know, Gabriele? It is Satan who has entered the bosom of the Church and within a short time will come to rule a false Church. My God! Some

kind of Antichrist! When did he prophesy that to you? —I inquire. "It must have been around 1960, since I was already a priest then." —That's why John XXIII was so panicky about publishing the Third Secret of Fatima, wouldn't people think that the anti-Pope or whatever was him...? A slight complicit smile curves Father Amorth's lips.[477]

In a truly Conciliaristic spirit, Salza & Siscoe oppose the right of the faithful to any legitimate judgment of conscience against the heresy of the defecting Conciliar Church, which they deceptively insist is the infiltrated Catholic Church. However, the Conciliar Church ultimately does not intend to exercise power by a divinely instituted monarchical authority, but by an essentially anti-papal and anti-monarchical *Conciliar,* Soviet style authority, in which a mere figurehead, chairman-of-the-board-like "pope" will be answerable to an ecclesiastical *Presidium* (Президиум) under which the Roman Curia will function like a *Soviet of Ministers* (совет министров), which in turn will preside over a loose confederation of regional *Soviets* (советы), which already exist in the form of *Episcopal Conferences,* which were granted official canonical status by Paul VI in his 1968 *Motu Proprio, «Ecclesiae Sanctae».* I don't remember the author's name, but in 2009 while in Baguio City, I read a well-documented book published in 1963, which I borrowed from Mr. William L., and in the book there were revealed many not publicly well-known background historical facts about the Second Vatican Council. What was very solidly proven was that the power that hijacked the council, the so-called "Rhein Group" consisting mainly of prelates from German and Dutch speaking countries of Northern Europe, and some modernist leaning

---

[477] Zavala, José María, *El secreto mejor guardado de Fátima,* Grupo Planeta, Kindle Edition, p. 179: «—Disculpe que insista sobre el Tercer Secreto de Fátima: ¿El Padre Pío lo relacionaba entonces con la pérdida de fe en la Iglesia? Don Gabriele frunce las cejas y adelanta el mentón. Parece muy afectado. —En efecto —asiente—. Cierto día, el Padre Pío me dijo muy compungido: «¿Sabes, Gabriele? Es Satanás quien se ha introducido en el seno de la Iglesia y dentro de no mucho tiempo llegará a gobernar una falsa Iglesia». —¡Dios mío! ¡Una especie de Anticristo! ¿Cuándo le profetizó eso? —inquiero. —Debió de ser hacia 1960, pues yo entonces ya era sacerdote. —¿Por eso tenía tanto pánico Juan XXIII a publicar el Tercer Secreto de Fátima, no fuera a pensar la gente que el antiPapa o lo que fuese era él...? Una ligera sonrisa de complicidad curva los labios del padre Amorth.»

French bishops as well, was led and directed behind the scenes from inside the Vatican by none other than Cardinal Giovanni Battista Montini. Montini was a Master of Hegelian dialectic, which in practical terms amounted to Orwellian *doublespeak*. As Paul VI, he wanted to horizontally exalt the council according to a communistic, masonizing egalitatisnism, and minimize the vertical papal monarchistic exercise of authority, as is so vulgarly expressed in the well-known Marxist slogan, "Power to the people!" To this end, he could not enforce his communistic agenda with a monarchical edict, because that would violate his own Masonic ideal of *Liberté, Egalité, Fraternité*. So he resorted to a devious Hegelian dialectical application of a self-negating assertion of authority which proclaimed the authority of the council without a definitive act of primatial authority: On Jan. 12, 1966, Pope Paul VI declared: "In view of the pastoral character of the Council, it has avoided pronouncing in an extraordinary way dogmas carrying the note of infallibility." But in his closing discourse to the Second Vatican Council, a document which pertains to the official acts of the Council, Pope Paul VI while categorically declaring that the Council did not define any doctrine, nevertheless asserted its conciliar magisterial authority — "*Nunc vero animadvertere iuvat, Ecclesiam per suum magisterium, quamvis nullum doctrinæ caput sententiis dogmaticis extraordinariis definire voluerit, nihilominus circa plurimas questiones cum auctoritate doctrinam proposuisse suam ...*"[478] By papal act he declares the magisterial authority of the council as such, but not by an authority based on an infallible exercise of the papal primacy. Hence, it is clear why Jorge "Francis" Bergoglio exalts Montini above all the other popes: Montini institutionalized Conciliarism: Montini was the founder of the new *Soviet* Church — the *Conciliar* Church, ruled according to the principle proposed by Lenin on 2 May 1917,[479] "All power to the Soviets." (Вся власть Советам) Thus, it is only logical that Bergoglio is a self-declared enemy of this divinely instituted monarchy which constitutes the government of the Church. Indeed, he is condemned by the words of

---

[478] *Sacrosanctum Oecumenicum Concilium Vaticanum II Constitutiones, Decreta, Declarationes; Documenta*, p. 1072.

[479] John Riddell, *'All Power to the Soviets' — A slogan that launched a revolution*, in Marxist Essays and Commentary, https://johnriddell.com/category/communist-international/

his own mouth, having declared in May of 2019 his agenda to utterly demolish the monarchical government of the Church: "The Vatican City State as a form of government, the Curia, whatever it is, is the last European court of an **absolute monarchy**. The last. The others are now constitutional monarchies, the court is diluted. **Here there are still court structures that must fall.**"[480] That is Bergoglio's agenda: **Down with the Monarchy! All power to the Soviets!**

I have met the burden of proof against Bergoglio. The burden of proof is on Salza and not me. Salza alleges that not just the same but an even greater degree of more incriminating evidence exists against Ratzinger than does against Bergoglio, but makes no attempt to prove it; but he nevertheless deceitfully replies, "the burden is on you to prove otherwise." How the writings of such an author as this hack, whose expositions are chronically replete with sophistry founded on crude fallacies and saturated with theological and doctrinal errors, as well as factual and historical falsehoods, could seduce so many souls into heresy can only be understood by considering the methods of propaganda that he and Siscoe employ to achieve the aims of their diabolical agenda.

In methods and practice, Salza & Siscoe reveal themselves to be not so much as pious disciples of Our Lord Jesus Christ, but show themselves rather as devilish disciples of Edward Louis Bernays, the *'Father of Propaganda'* and the nephew of Sigmund Freud. In his 1947 essay *The Engineering of Consent*, Bernays explained: "This phrase quite simply means the use of an engineering approach—that is, action based only on thorough knowledge of the situation and on the application of scientific principles and tried practices to the task of getting people to support ideas and programs." Bernays explained how getting people to support a hidden agenda is accomplished by making use of what modern education has achieved by transforming the mind of the common man into a 'rubber stamp'; and by manipulating that 'rubber stamp' to get people to support ideas and agendas. "But instead of a mind," Bernays explained, "universal literacy has given a rubber stamp, a rubber stamp". And then he elaborates, "Each man's rubber stamp is the twin of millions of

---

[480] https://www.catholicnewsagency.com/news/pope-francis-responds-to-heresy-accusation-china-concerns-16641.

others, so that when these millions are exposed to the same stimuli, all receive identical imprints." And he observes:

> The amazing readiness with which large masses accept this process is probably accounted for by the fact that no attempt is made to convince them that black is white. Instead, their preconceived hazy ideas that a certain grey is almost black or almost white are brought into sharper focus. Their prejudices, notions, and convictions are used as a starting point, with the result that they are drawn by a thread into passionate adherence to a given mental picture.

In what is perhaps his most famous work, *Propaganda*, Bernays explains that the propagandist "has to have some vital seed to sow," because "a mutual need has to exist before either can become positively effective. Propaganda is of no use," he explains, "unless he has something to say which the public, consciously or unconsciously, wants to hear."

Salza & Siscoe play on the fears of ordinary Catholics by conjuring up the spectre of *Sedevacantism*, presenting any opinion that opposes their own heresy as an heretical expression of *Sedevacantism*; so that they can then demonize any argument, idea, or person that is an obstacle to the success of their heretical agenda by labelling them as *Sedevacantists*. In this manner they poison the well against anyone who would expose their heresy and the foul purpose they seek to accomplish by labelling their opponents as **heretics**. As a high-degree Mason, Salza learned the devilish art of presenting evil under the guise of good — an art at which he is a consummate master: He and Siscoe strive to create the appearance that they are defending the Catholic Church against the schismatic errors of *Sedevacantism*; but in reality, under the smokescreen of opposing *Sedevacantism*, they are attempting to create the appearance of legitimacy for the counterfeit Conciliar *Sect* which is at present occupying the Vatican and driving the true Church underground.

To further their diabolical ends, Salza & Siscoe rigorously follow Saul Alinsky's *Rules for Radicals*. Rule 13 is, «*Pick the target, freeze it, personalize it, and polarize it." Cut off the support network and isolate the target from sympathy. Go after people and not institutions; people hurt faster than institutions.*» Their principal weapon to accomplish this is the ruthless use of ridicule, which is Rule 5: «*"Ridicule is man's most potent weapon."*

There is no defense. It's irrational.» In all their screeds and diatribes they have published against me, they have followed these rules unswervingly, but they have done so with such fanatical zealotry, that they make themselves ridiculous, so that the predictable result of their efforts will be in the end to neutralize themselves. Their obsessive practice of replying to my theology by denigrating me with demeaning personal *ad hominem* abuse and outright calumny has created such a grotesque caricature of myself — a caricature which depicts an image of a man who is so ignorant of theology and of such diminished mental capacity, that anyone inclined to listen to their propaganda would be led to believe it would have to be nothing short of a miracle for me to not only be able to compose a serious theological work, but even to be able to complete a coherent sentence. Thus have their efforts amounted to nothing but clownish buffoonery; but their malicious buffoonery still achieves some degree of success among their followers by means of their most lethal weapon – the LIE. Here is just one example of their mindless ridicule: «More contradictions from Fr Kramer, who just said a heretic can also be an infidel. We make all the proper distinctions in our book, approved by scholars who forgot more theology than Fr Kramer ever knew.» Since Salza clearly indicated that in his opinion I did not make a proper distinction between heretics and infidels, I pointed out in my reply that heresy, as St. Thomas explains, is a species of infidelity, and that the term "infidelity" is used in this generic, all-encompassing sense which includes heresy and all other species of unbelief. Even St. Paul in his Epistle to the Romans used the term in this sense: «ἵνα ῥυσθῶ ἀπο των **ἀπειθούντων** εν τῃ ιουδαια.»[481] The word **ἀπειθούντων** (nom. pl. — **ἀπειθούντες**) is a broad term which comprises all species of infidelity, and indiscriminately denotes in a general sense, all sorts of *disbelievers, unbelievers,* and *infidels.*[482] I have enumerated some of the

---

[481] Romans, 15: 31 – "That I may be delivered from the **unbelievers** that are in Judea, and that the oblation of my service may be acceptable in Jerusalem to the saints."

[482] 1 Pet. 2:8 "οἳ προσκόπτουσιν τῷ λόγῳ **ἀπειθοῦντες** εἰς ὃ καὶ ἐτέθησαν." = "who stumble at the word, **neither do believe**, whereunto also they are set." Full verse: "And a stone of stumbling, and a rock of scandal, to them who stumble at the word, neither do believe, whereunto

more egregious examples of their vulgar and entirely gratuitous ridicule they have inveighed against me in Volume One.

Salza & Siscoe adamantly refuse to admit they have made even the slightest error — even after I exposed the absurdity of their doctrines and the sophistry behind their crudes lies; yet they obstinately persist in them as if they had not already been thoroughly debunked, so they are left with no other weapon in their arsenal but to mindlessly repeat their lies. These thoroughly rabid heretics continue to follow the dictum of Voltaire, which is to make the lie stick by constantly repeating it: *"Mentez, mentez, il en restera toujours quelque chose."* **Their lie is that it is I and not they who are the heretics.** By engaging in this practice, they make use of what is perhaps the most notorious weapons used by Freemasons to discredit their critics: *"Accuse the other side of that which you are guilty."* The late Cardinal Eduard Gagnon, who was a personal friend during the years when I lived in Rome, explained this to me — how the Masons' tactic is to accuse their opponents of exactly that which they are guilty. His Eminence even related to me a recent historical example of this sort of devilry which was employed against faithful Catholics who opposed the agenda of the Sect. This is exactly the Masonic tactic that Salza & Siscoe use against me in their endeavour to discredit the voice that exposes their heretical propaganda which promotes the agenda of *Ecclesiastical Freemasonry*.

It was Siscoe who wrote, "for the sin [of heresy] to be judged, it must be public; and needless to say the judgment of the public sin must proceed from the proper authorities, not from the individual Catholic in the pew". He states most explicitly, "All throughout our book, we make the distinction between a Catholic who merely professes a heretical doctrine and someone who has openly left the Church." However, with the most insolent hypocrisy, this is what he had the audacity to reply to me on 14 October 2016: "Due to your heretical ecclesiology, you are now a sworn enemy of the Church, and that is how you will be treated." In his hypocrisy, *Siscoe has repeatedly accused me of openly leaving the Church for merely professing propositions that he as a private layman believes are*

---

also they are set." (καὶ λίθος προσκόμματος καὶ πέτρα σκανδάλου· οἳ προσκόπτουσιν τῷ λόγῳ **ἀπειθοῦντες**· εἰς ὃ καὶ ἐτέθησαν.)

heretical, but which the Church has never condemned, and which many approved authors have professed; yet, he is the one who insists that one cannot judge another to be a heretic simply for having uttered propositions privately judged to be heretical[483] — but that is exactly the reason why he judges me to have left the Church: **«Your false understanding of the Conciliar Church is what has led you into your heresy.»** Merely on the basis of what he considers to be my "false understanding of the Conciliar Church"; and in explicit contradiction to his and Salza's stated principle that one is not a heretic merely for professing heretical propositions, Siscoe had the audacity to declare in above cited message: «WE [i.e. Siscoe & Salza] recognize you as being outside of the Church due to your public sin of heresy, even though the Church has not yet declared you to be a heretic» — «Here's what you don't understand: You have publicly defected from the faith by leaving the Church. You are now a public heretic. Period. You are no longer a Catholic priest (since you are no longer a member of the Catholic Church).» Thus, Salza & Siscoe teach that for all other cases "judgment of the public sin must proceed from the proper authorities" – but in my case, they themselves possess the supreme authority to pre-empt the authority of the Church, and as laymen lacking formal training in Theology, to privately judge a Rome educated Catholic priest in matters of faith.

It is at this point that the question begs to be asked: *What is it about my ecclesiology that makes them feel so threatened that they are driven to declare me a heretic?* The answer, of course, is that my ecclesiology, which I learned from my Thomist professors in Rome, exposes their own weirdly concocted Masonic inspired ecclesiology to be heretical. The foundation of their heretical ecclesiology is founded on a radically heterodox notion of sin. According to Salza & Siscoe, "Sin is

---

[483] Salza & Siscoe were compelled to be less vitriolic in expressing their public condemnations posted on their website, due to the glaring self-contradiction that the more explicit expression of their judgments against me would create; since it remains their stated opinion that only the Church can judge in cases of heresy, except (of course) for heresy that Salza & Siscoe judge to be "public and notorious" — and that means any publicly expressed opinion that conflicts with their own bizarre dogmatic beliefs. Nevertheless, their less explicit but still clearly expressed judgments of heresy against me remain posted on their website.

internal." Salza & Siscoe fail to understand the basic distinction between an internal sin and an external sin. An internal sin is a sin of thought, as opposed to an external sin which is a sin of words or deeds. An external sin is occult if the sin is not known by anyone, or only by very few individuals. An external sin is public if was done in public, and is sufficiently widely known so that it is considered to be a public sin. Salza & Siscoe manifest a profound but crassly affected confusion throughout their writings in their contrived expositions on the distinctions between internal and external sin, sin and crime; and the manner in which these things relate to the Church's doctrine on defection from the Church and the loss of papal office resulting from such a defection. Their heretical proposition that «*the sin of heresy alone does not sever one from the Church*», is founded on the heterodox belief that it pertains to the distinction between *sin* and *crime* that *sin is a matter of the internal forum*. They attempt to justify their indefensible position by appealing to the canonical distinction between an act that is materially and formally public, and an act that is materially public but formally occult. On the basis of this distinction, they errantly judge that a sin which is *materially* public, but *formally occult*, is an *internal sin*; and therefore beyond the scope of Canon Law, because "the Church does not judge internals". On this utterly spurious foundation, Salza & Siscoe errantly declare that one who flagrantly and publicly professes even the most blatant and inexcusably heretical proposition with plainly obvious canonical *dolus,* cannot be considered to have *ipso facto* defected from the faith, or fallen from office, or ceased to be a member of the Church, without there having been pronounced a judgment by Church authority. Accordingly, only if the heretic explicitly admits that his doctrine is heretical, or explicitly rejects the Church as the rule of faith, or obstinately persists in heresy after ecclesiastical warnings, would he then be separated from the body of the Church *ipso facto*, otherwise he remains in the Church as a visible member in such a manner that even the public sin of manifestly formal heresy would not constitute a defection from the faith which would provoke an *ipso jure* loss of ecclesiastical office – and even then, the loss of office would only occur upon the issuance of at least a declaratory sentence. Their crude obfuscation on the distinction between internal and external sin becomes manifestly apparent when one considers the manner in which it is explained and applied in the canons of the Church. Canon 1321 § 1 of the 1983 Code describes a canonical crime as an *"externa legis vel præcepti violatio"*, which is *"graviter imputabilis ex dolo vel ex culpa"*; and the 1917 Code likewise defines a canonical delict: «*Can. 2195. §1. Nomine delicti, iure ecclesiastico, intelligitur externa et moraliter imputabilis legis violatio cui addita sit sanctio canonica saltem indeterminata.*» An *"externa legis vel præcepti violatio"*, which is *"graviter imputabilis ex dolo vel ex culpa"* is an **external mortal sin** — it is not an "externalized internal sin" as Salza & Siscoe maintain.

The reason why Salza & Siscoe remain so blindly entrenched in this error, is that it is the foundation of their bizarre doctrine, which holds that the *sin of heresy* and the *crime of heresy* are acts of **two different species** — which means that the **sin of heresy is internal**, but the **external act of heresy is a crime according to its very nature** — and **a crime falls within the jurisdiction of the Church, and must be judged by the Church before one can be separated from membership in the Church**. Salza & Siscoe fallaciously argue that since external heresy falls within the parameters of the definition of a crime in canon law (i.e. an external violation of a law or precept, etc.), external heresy is therefore by definition a crime, and for this reason heresy is in its intrinsic nature a crime. The argument leading to the false conclusion is a crude fallacy based on an elementary error in logic: External heresy is indeed a crime because it falls within the parameters of the canonical definition of a delict; but that only *accidently qualifies* external heresy as a crime. Heresy is not a crime according to its nature, because what specifies the nature of a crime, as crime is defined in law, ***does not fall within the definition of heresy***. Their incoherent argument self-destructs in a mass of contradictions: Since *notorious heresy* is just as much a crime as *public heresy;* if public heresy requires a judgment of the Church before a heretic is separated from the body of the Church because it is a *crime*, then for the same reason, the *crime* of *notorious heresy* would also require a judgment of the Church to be pronounced before a notorious heretic would cease to be a member. Furthermore, the *final and most glaring contradiction lies at the end of their argument*, which asserts that on the one hand, one who "openly leaves the Church" by an act of "public and notorious" heresy, ceases *ipso facto* to be a member of the Church, even without any judgment from Church authority; but at the same time, if a *pope* were to openly defect from the Church in this manner and thereby cease automatically to be a member of the Church, he would still remain in office as pope until a sentence, (or a judgment of some sort) is passed against him for the crime of heresy. This is the final product of "genius" which these two heretical verbal con-artists have served up to their unsuspecting Catholic readers: an argument which ends by asserting that a pope who would openly defect from the Church and cease to be a member of the Church, would still continue to be the *head,* while already no longer a *member!* The utter silliness of their claim that external heresy is a crime in its nature becomes especially obvious when one considers that according to the 1983 *Code of Canon Law,* the mere externality of the act of heresy does not constitute external heresy as a crime, unless in addition to the element of *externality* the act is also committed with *alterity.* Thus it is written in the Code: "1330 The crime that consists of a declaration or another manifestation of the will, doctrine or knowledge is not considered consummated, if no one perceives such declaration or manifestation."[484] The Canon Law Faculty of the University of Navarra comments on this point in its exposition on Canon 1364: "**1364** *Crime.* In c. 751 are the definitions of heresy, apostasy and schism. As long as the requirements established there are met the sins of heresy, apostasy and schism exist; now, for there to be a crime, it is also required that such action is not only external but also has direct social impact through alterity, that is, that such action must be received by third parties (c. 1330): With this explanation, the doctrinal discussion on the sufficiency or not of the pure external nature of the action is resolved so that it can be classified as criminal."[485]

---

[484] «Canon 1330 — Delictum quod in declaration consistat vel in alia voluntatis vel doctrinae vel scientiae manifestatione, tamquam non consummatum censendum est, si nemo eam declarationem vel manifestationem percipiat.»

[485] *Código De Derecho Canónico Edición Bilingüe Y Anotada,* Universidad De Navarra, Facultad De Derecho Canónico, p. 849 — «**1364** *Delito.* En el c. 751 se encuentran las definiciones de herejía, apostasía y cisma. Siempre que se den los requisitos allí establecidos existen los pecados de herejía, apostasía y cisma; ahora bien, para que haya delito se requiere, además, que tal acción no sea sólo externa sino que también tenga incidencia social directa a través de la alteridad, es decir, que tal acción ha de ser recibida por terceros (c.

Undaunted by the clear and unambiguous teaching of *Mystici Corporis*, Salza & Siscoe manifest their obstinate persistence in blind opposition to the divinely revealed truth, by deceitfully posting a craftily worded objection on their website supposedly written by a priest (who remains anonymous[486]), which attempts to uphold their absurd distortion of the doctrine of faith by arguing from the premise that the teaching of *Mystici Corporis* "seems to be of a comparative nature," and "specifies by what means one is separated from the Body of the Church," and teaches that sins such as abortion do not of their own nature "sever the sinner from the Body of the Church; it is the law that does." However, the letter fails to mention that the encyclical explicitly teaches that *unlike all other grave sins*, the sins of "schism, heresy, and apostasy *by their very nature* separate a man from the body of the Church." *It is precisely this truth of faith which Salza & Siscoe deny* — so in order to deflect attention away from this truth of faith and obscure it, the heresy promoting letter introduces an off-point argument on a different but related matter, namely, on the undisputed truth that it pertains exclusively to the Church's authority to juridically determine and pronounce a sentence on apostasy, heresy, and schism.

1330): con esta explicitación se resuelve la discusión doctrinal sobre la suficiencia o no del puro carácter externo de la acción para que ésta pueda ser calificada de delictuosa.»

[486] The key excerpt: «Since paragraphs 21 (22) specifies by what means one is separated from the Body of the Church, what is said in paragraphs 22 (23) seems to be of a comparative nature, indicating, for example that the sin of abortion (grave scelus)—although one incurs excommunication by murdering her baby—is a sin that "of its nature" does not sever the sinner from the Body of the Church; it is the law that does. Likewise an attack on the Pope. However, since the most serious sins of apostasy, heresy and schism, sins directly against God and the unity of the Mystical Body of Christ are such that the Church, the Mystical Body of Christ, must determine the "dolus", the malice involved, which the Church does by Its Canon Law when She says that "Where there has been an external violation, imputability is presumed, unless it appears otherwise" [c. 1321 §3] (consider so called schism of the SSPX in 1988). When it comes to apostasy, heresy and schism, the means of establishing the malice of these crimes are not only complex but even disputed, and it is solely the responsibility of the Church in making a judgment; individuals of their own accord cannot arrogate to themselves the rendering of a judgment.»

The author states that, "When it comes to apostasy, heresy and schism, the means of establishing the malice of these crimes are not only complex but even disputed, and it is solely the responsibility of the Church in making a judgment; individuals of their own accord cannot arrogate to themselves the rendering of a judgment." But the deceitful sophistry of the argument consists in the apparently deliberate failure to mention that establishing the malice of *manifest heresy*, is not complex or difficult, because, as I have already explained, it is of such a nature that it "cannot be concealed by any subterfuge, nor excused by any excuse admitted in laws (*in talibus adiunctis commissum, ut nulla tergiversatione celari nulloque iuris suffragio excusari possit*)". Hence, *manifest heresy* is something that can plainly be seen and known by anyone who is possessed of the mental capacity and the honesty to do so, and therefore it is one's right in natural law to judge accordingly **in a private capacity**, which is entirely different than *arrogating to oneself the rendering of a juridical judgment*, which would only take place if one were to usurp the judicial function by presuming some force of law in one's private judgments. Thus it is as Christopher Ferrara explains in *Fatima Perspectives*, "It is an axiom of our religion that no person on earth can judge the Pope in the sense of a penal sentence with juridical effect."[487] So, the fact that it pertains solely to the authority of the Church to render a judgment with juridical effect does not in any way negate or impede the right of the individual to assent to and affirm an immediately evident and certain fact such as the evidently certain fact of manifest heresy. Nevertheless, Salza & Siscoe deliberately attempt to deceive their readers to believe their false doctrine by claiming that the Church's teaching forbids the individual to exercise the natural right to privately assent to and acknowledge the evidently true fact of manifest heresy. What this means ultimately, according to the perverse Salza-Siscoe doctrine, is that once the much greater and more visible portion of the Church visibly defects with its perfidious infidel "pope" and its Modernist hierarchy from the true faith, and constitutes **a new ecclesial body in which the form of the Church is not visible**, that heretical entity will still be the Catholic Church until it is juridically declared to be a false church by legitimate ecclesiastical authority (i.e.

---

[487] http://archive.fatima.org/perspectives/fe/perspective1068.asp

by itself); and consequently, all Catholics would be morally bound to be members of that counterfeit "church" and be subject to its supposed authority.

*Thus, the ultimate purpose of their lengthy and logically incoherent pseudo-theological convolutions on this point is to justify their heretical conciliaristic belief that no matter how manifestly formally heretical a pope might be, he would not lose office unless he would first be judged guilty of the crime of heresy by the Church, i.e., by a **COUNCIL**.* In practical terms what that means (according to the Salza-Siscoe doctrine), is that once *Ecclesiastical Masonry*, through the agency of the *Sankt Gallen Mafia* gained control of the Vatican, with *their man*, the heretic Bergoglio having intruded onto the papal throne; *that heretical usurper, no matter how manifestly evident his defection into heresy, must be considered a true and valid pope for so long as he is not judged guilty of heresy by a hierarchy that remains firmly under the control of the same Ecclesiastical Masonry.* What this would ultimately mean (if it were true) is that the members of the true Church will be morally bound to remain subject to a manifestly heretical Mason-dominated hierarchy under a manifestly heretical Masonizing "pope", who will all be considered to remain as the canonically valid officeholders of the Catholic Church, even after they will have all publicly defected into formal heresy, and will have institutionalized heretical reforms in the vast portion of the ecclesial body they control, which reforms would then actually formally constitute of the body of defectors a *counterfeit church* in that the form of the true Church will be visibly absent from it; and having a visible heretical form, will be seen to have visibly defected from the body of the true Church, which will be reduced greatly in numerical membership and geographical extension throughout the world. Thus, the Salza-Siscoe doctrine would make of the false church the true Church, and the true Church would be considered a sect.

It is precisely on this point, to wit, the proposition asserting the possibility of a sizable reduction in numbers and geographical extension of the Catholic Church, that Salza & Siscoe declare their judgment of heresy upon me; maintaining that an overtly heretical organization under the governance of a raving heretic "pope" would still be the One, Holy, Catholic and Apostolic Church — as if it would suffice for that organization to still be part of the Catholic Church, provided only that it be visible and universal, even after it would have departed from the Apostolic faith and sacraments, but would not have been judged heretical by the "ecclesiastical authority" [i.e. *by itself*]; while the much smaller and geographically limited remnant of orthodox Catholic laity and hierarchy, perhaps even for some time without a visible head, and still adhering to the dogma of faith, but so reduced in numbers and visibility so as to appear to have been "swept, as it were from the face of the earth,"[488] would not be the true Church, but according to them, it would only amount to no more than a schismatic *sect*.

I have elaborated with precision in what qualified sense it can be asserted that the Church will eventually be reduced in visibility and numbers. In order to maintain the semblance of credibility for their heretical ecclesiology, Salza & Siscoe resort to the lie, saying, "Fr. Kramer errs by confusing the predictions of an underground Church during the end times, with a farcical reduction of the number of faithful **to only a handful**, and ends by denying the mark of catholicity." As I have already stated time and again, I have **never** said that the number of faithful will ever actually be reduced to a handful — **this claim is a malicious invention of Salza & Siscoe**. To justify their false accusation, they quote Msgr. Van Noort out of context: «… As Van Noort explained above, the mark of catholicity (i.e., universality) requires "moral catholicity" (i.e., large numbers of people) which is a perpetual quality of the true Church.» Salza & Siscoe have grossly misrepresented the doctrine of Msgr. Van Noort on the *moral catholicity* of the Church. In *De Ecclesia Christi, Art. IV De Ecclesiæ Catholicitate*, Van Noort explains the distinction between *absolute* and *moral* catholicity, and the diffusion of the Church's members throughout the world which is necessary for there to be that *moral catholicity*: "Catholicitas facti consistit in lata diffusione actuali per orbem; quæ si revera ad omnes et singulas gentes pertingit, vocatur catholicitas *absoluta;* si ad multas tantum gentes se extendit, dicitur catholicitas *moralis*. Jam ecclesiæ Christi necessarium est, ut post prima exordia *semper gaudeat diffusione moraliter universali et*

---

[488] Henry Edward Cardinal Manning, *The Present Crisis of the Holy See*, 1861, London: Burns and Lambert, pp. 88-90.

progressiva, donec tandem aliquando ad omnes omnino gentes perveniat."[489] Salza & Siscoe quoted an English version of Van Noort on these points, but what they deliberately left out in their quotations of the passages of Van Noort's exposition are the texts in which Van Noort qualifies his statements on the diffusion and number of the faithful throughout the world: "*Ecclesia post prima exordia semper conspicua esse debet diffusione moraliter universali,* hoc scil. sensu, quod semper gremio suo comprehendere debet *ingentem numerum hominum de multitudine gentium.* [...] Jam qualitas, quæ absque ulla temporis limitatione exhibetur veluti character proprius ecclesiæ, ei semper convenire debet, **saltem aliquo gradu**. [...] Ex *verbis Christi et testimonio apostoli.* Christus absolute voluit, ut ecclesia inter omnes gentes diffunderetur et ad hunc effectum auxilium perenne promisit. Necesse igitur est, ut ecclesia huic suæ destinationi semper actu respondeat, **saltem aliqua mensura**."[490] The passages in which he qualifies his statements with the words, **saltem aliquo gradu**, and, **saltem aliqua mensura**, are conspicuously absent in the Salza-Siscoe article. It is precisely by means of these qualifications that Msgr. Van Noort makes allowance for the massive reductions in numbers and geographical diffusion of the faithful throughout the world in times of schism and heresy, and especially during the defection at the time of the great apostasy towards the end of the world.[491] Concerning that great defection of the end time, Van Noort points out that it is *only the* **more common opinion** *of theologians* that rejects the hypothesis that the Church could be so overwhelmed by heresies that it would be restricted for a brief time to one region; and he says only that (in his opinion) it does not seem that the predictions of the Sacred Scriptures on the great

---

[489] G. Van Noort; *De Ecclesia Christi, Art. IV De Ecclesiæ Catholicitate,* Hilversum in Hollandia, 1932, N. 116 II. p. 126.

[490] *Ibid.* N. 117 2°. p. 128

[491]*Ibid.* p. 129, 3° «*Diffusio moraliter universalis, quæ ecclesiæ semper competit, debet esse progressiva.* [...] (p. 130) Observa tamen, *continuitatem* progressivæ expansionis nimis urgendam non esse; nam loci citati non videntur excludere, quominus ecclesia aliquando notabiliter decrescere queat per schismata aut hæreses, (quarum ortum Scriptura prædixit) quin perdita *statim* resarciantur.»

defection at the end of the world are to be interpreted in this sense.[492] Thus, Msgr. Van Noort's exposition on the *moral catholicity* of the Church does not entirely rule out that the Church during the great tribulation of the end time could even possibly result in the Church being largely, or even almost completely limited to one geographical area; and even makes complete allowance for the possibility, and even the overwhelming likelihood that the Church, during that great apostasy and persecution, *may result in the reduction of the number of the Church's members to a relatively **small number*** in comparison to the vastly greater number of members of the immediately preceding period. This last proposition, for which Van Noort makes explicit allowance, coincides exactly with my own opinion on the question, but according to the fundamentalism of Salza & Siscoe, that opinion denies the Church's *note of catholicity*. Yet, in spite of the fact that my own exposition on this question, as I ***repeatedly pointed out to them***, is plainly in full agreement with that expressed by many eminent theologians and approved ecclesiastical writers, Salza & Siscoe continue to obstinately assert that ***when I give voice to that opinion***, it is, *according to them*, heretical: "Fr. Kramer not only denies the doctrine of moral catholicity but has embraced the heretical Protestant definition of the Church (i.e., "an invisible Church of true believers"). It is quite sad to see Fr. Kramer now publicly professing Protestant errors in the name of Catholicism."

I have explained at some length the Church's doctrine of moral catholicity in Volume One, quoting eminent ecclesiastical and approved authors. I have explained precisely in what manner the Church will be reduced to a relatively small number compared to its previously much larger number. In Chapter 7 of *De Notis Ecclesiæ*, St. Robert Bellarmine teaches on the note, "Amplitudo", explaining in what sense the universal geographical extension of the Church is to be understood: It is does not mean that the Church must be simultaneously present in all regions of the οἰκουμένη; and, (such as during the great tribulation of the end times), Bellarmine concurs with

---

[492] *Ibid.* p. 129, 3° – «Nihilominus theologi communius rejiciunt hypothesim ecclesia ita hæresibus obrutæ, ut saltem pro brevi tempore ad unam regionem coarcteretur. Neque in hunc sensum interpretandæ videntur prædictiones Scripturæ de magna defectione in fine mundi.»

the opinion of Driedo, explaining that the Church could eventually become so small as to be restricted to only one province, and be absent from the rest of the world.[493]

What I have said is that the Church will be reduced to a small number during the great persecution foretold in the book of the Apocalypse; and not only does this opinion not deny the dogma of the indefectibility of the Church by destroying its catholicity or its visibility, but is in fact the doctrine of scripture as interpreted by the ancient Fathers, and is therefore at the very least *proxima fidei*.

In a portion of a passage of Cardinal Manning I cited in Volume One,[494] it is stated that, "The writers of the Church tell us that in the latter days the City of Rome will probably become apostate from the Church and the Vicar of Jesus Christ; and that Rome will again be punished, for he will depart from it, and the judgment of God will fall on the place from which he once ruled over the nations of the world." (p. 87) Fr. E. Sylvester Berry, in his work on The Apocalypse of St. John says, "After the destruction of Rome in the days of Antichrist, it shall forever remain a heap of ruins and the haunt of filthy animals; "that great city shall be found no more at all." (p.193)

At the beginning of Chapter XX, Fr. Berry explains, "[P]ractically all interpreters who accept these conclusions (that Antichrist must be a definite individual and... that he has not yet made his appearance in the world) take the reign of Antichrist as a prelude to the last judgment and the end of the world. Then contrary to the plain sense of Holy Scripture, they place the universal reign of Christ before the reign of Antichrist." (p. 189)

"A careful reading of the Apocalypse," Fr. Berry explains, "shows clearly that Antichrist will appear long centuries before the last

---

[493] *De Notis Ecclesiae*, Caput VII — «nota, non requiri, ut hoc fiat simul, ila ut uno tempore in omnibus provinciis necessario esse oporteat aliquos fideles: satis enim est, si fiat successive. Ex quo id sequitur, quod si sola una provincia retineret veram fidem, adhuc vere et proprie diceretur Ecclesia catholica, dummodo clare ostenderetur, eam esse unam et eandem cum illa, quae fuit aliquo tempore, vel diversis in toto mundo, quemadmodum nunc quaelibet dioecesis dicitur catholica, quia est continuata cum aliis, quae faciunt unam Ecclesiam catholicam.»

[494] Henry Edward Cardinal Manning, *The Present Crisis of the Holy See*, 1861, London: Burns and Lambert, pp. 88-90.

judgment and the end of the world. In fact his reign will be but the final attempt of Satan to prevent the universal reign of Christ in the world." (p. 189-90) This opinion that the universal reign of Christ in the world will follow the reign of Antichrist is supported by the prophecy of St. John Eudes (which I read about 25 years ago), who foretold that the triumph of the Heart of Mary will be a triumph over the Antichrist. I mention this here only in order to dispel the false interpretations that conclude that the great tribulation of the time of Antichrist cannot happen in the very near future; and also to provide a general context for the events that are foretold in scripture and by ecclesiastical writers, when the Church will be persecuted to near extinction, but will, by divine intervention, rise in triumph from her apparent defeat. While it is not altogether certain that the reign of Antichrist will precede the second coming of Christ by many centuries, it is certain that the defeat of the Antichrist will not take place at the very end after the universal reign of Christ in the world. It is certain firstly because another period after Antichrist's reign is foretold in Scripture. Thus is it written in Isaiah 56:7 — "I will bring them into my holy mount, and will make them joyful in my house of prayer: their holocausts, and their victims shall please me upon my altar: for my house shall be called the house of prayer, for all nations."; and Micah 4:1 — "But it shall come to pass in the end of days that the mountain of the Lord's house shall be established on the top of the mountains, and shall be lifted up above the hills; and the peoples shall flow unto it."; and Isaiah 2:2 — "And in the last days the mountain of the house of the Lord shall be prepared on the top of mountains, and it shall be exalted above the hills, and all nations shall flow unto it"; and Daniel 12: 10-12 — "Many shall be chosen, and made white, and shall be tried as fire: and the wicked shall deal wickedly, and none of the wicked shall understand, but the learned shall understand. And from the time when the continual sacrifice shall be taken away, and the abomination unto desolation shall be set up, there shall be a thousand two hundred ninety days, Blessed is he that waiteth and cometh unto a thousand three hundred thirty-five days." Secondly, there is not agreement on how long will be the succeeding period, but it is inconceivable that Christ would come to judge the world with his own kingdom on earth in ruins, since it was He who said, "I have overcome the world," which would not be true if He were to have established his kingdom on earth, only for it to be overcome and destroyed by his adversary, at which time he would then return to the scene of his defeated kingdom only to destroy his adversary, but not to restore his own kingdom in a triumph whose glory must necessarily exceed all the glories of his kingdom throughout the ages. St. John Eudes says in *The Admirable Heart of Mary*, "All the holy Fathers (16) agree that after the death of antichrist the whole world will be converted, and although some of them assert that the world will last but a few days after his death, while others say a few months, some authorities insist that it will continue to exist many years after. St. Catherine of Siena, St. Vincent Ferrer, St. Francis of Paula and a number of other saints have predicted this ultimate universal conversion." [(16). Dionysius the Carthusian in cap. 3, Epist. 1 ad Ther.; Cornelius a Lapide in cap. 2, Epist. ad Rom. vers. 15.]

In this context one can place the future events spoken of by Cardinal Manning, who wrote, "And therefore the writers of the Church tell us that the City of Rome has no prerogative except only that the Vicar of Christ is there; and if it become unfaithful, the same judgments which fell on Jerusalem, hallowed though it was by the presence of the Son of God, of the Master, and not the disciple only, shall fall likewise upon Rome." (p.88) Manning cites multiple authorities, including St. Robert Bellarmine: "In the time of Antichrist, Rome shall be desolated and burnt, as we shall learn from the sixteenth verse of the seventeenth chapter of the Apocalypse." (p. 89)

Manning continues, "Finally, Cornelius à Lapide sums up what may be said to be the common interpretation of theologians… 'These things are to be understood of the city of Rome, not that which is, nor that which was, but that which shall be at the end of the world… For from Christian it shall again become heathen. It shall cast out the Christian Pontiff, and the faithful who adhere to him. It shall persecute and slay them…'". (p. 90)

Thus we have the context of Cardinal Manning's words:

"The apostasy of the city of Rome from the vicar of Christ and its destruction by Antichrist may be thoughts very new to many Catholics, that I think it well to recite the text of theologians of greatest repute. First Malvenda, who writes expressly on the subject, states as the opinion of Ribera, Gaspar Melus, Biegas, Suarez, Bellarmine and Bosius that Rome shall apostatize from the Faith, drive away the Vicar of Christ and return to its ancient paganism. ...Then the Church shall be scattered, driven into the wilderness, and shall be for a time, as it was in the beginning, invisible; hidden in catacombs, in dens, in mountains, in lurking places; for a time it shall be swept, as it were from the face of the earth. Such is the universal testimony of the Fathers of the early Church."[495]

"Such is the universal testimony of the Fathers," says Manning, the Church "will be as it was in in the beginning" — "invisible, hidden… swept, as it were from the face of the earth"; and this is "the universal testimony of the Fathers"; but according to Salza & Siscoe, this is an opinion that denies the essential mark of the catholicity of the Church.

In the great commentary of Cornelius à Lapide, explanation is given of the meaning of the words spoken by Christ in the 12th chapter of the Gospel of St. Luke, where the Lord describes His Church as a "pusillus grex", a "little flock". And the first reason given why the Lord refers to the Church as a "little flock" is: "PUSILLUS GREX, id est parvus, Primo, quia tum pauci erant fideles" — at the beginning the number of faithful was small; and also is small in comparison with the great number of the infidels and the wicked (pusillus est grex fidelium si comparatur cum maxima multitudine infidelium, & impiorum); and he cites the opinion of Bede, according to whom the flock is small in comparison to the number of reprobates (ad comparationem majoris numeri reproborum).

The Church will be comprised of a small number of faithful especially during the persecution of Antichrist for all the reasons given above, because, as ecclesiastical writers explain, that during that exceptional persecution, by the disposition of the divine will, the Church will revert for a time to the state it was in during the early persecutions. This is explained by Cardinal Manning not as merely his own personal opinion, but, as he says in his own words, "In treating of this subject, I shall not venture upon any conjectures of my own, but shall deliver simply what I find either in the Fathers of the

---

[495] Henry Edward Cardinal Manning, *The Present Crisis of the Holy See*, 1861, London: Burns and Lambert, pp. 88-90.

Church, or in such theologians as the Church has recognised, namely, Bellarmine, Lessius, Malvenda, Viegas, Suarez, Ribera, and others".

"The history of the Church," says Cardinal Manning, "and the history of our Lord on earth, run as it were in parallel. For three-and-thirty years the Son of God incarnate was in the world, and no man could lay hand upon Him. No man could take Him, because His "hour was not yet come." There was an hour foreordained when the Son of God would be delivered into the hand of sinners. He foreknew it; He foretold it."

"In like manner with His Church. Until the hour is come when the barrier shall, by the Divine will, be taken out of the way, no one has power to lay a hand upon it. The gates of hell may war against it; they may strive and wrestle, as they struggle now with the Vicar of our Lord; but no one has the power to move Him one step, until the hour shall come when the Son of God shall permit, for a time, the powers of evil to prevail. That He will permit it for a time stands in the book of prophecy. When the hindrance is taken away, the man of sin will be revealed; then will come the persecution of three years and a half, short, but terrible, during which the Church of God will return into its state of suffering, as in the beginning; and the imperishable Church of God, by its inextinguishable life derived from the pierced side of Jesus, which for three hundred years lived on through blood, will live on still through the fires of the times of Antichrist." (pp. 55-56)

"THE CHURCH OF GOD WILL RETURN INTO ITS STATE OF SUFFERING, AS IN THE BEGINNING" – when it was a "*pusillus grex*" (Luke 12:32); a "little flock", small in number.

Cardinal Louis Edouard Pie, a contemporary of Cardinal Manning, wrote, "The Church, though still a visible society, will be increasingly reduced to individual and domestic proportions." ... "Surrounded on all sides, as the other centuries have made her great, so the last will strive to crush her. And finally the Church on earth will undergo a true defeat... 'and it was given unto him [the Antichrist] to make war with the saints and to overcome them.'" (Apocalypse 13:7)

Hillaire Belloc, honoured by Pius XI with the title, "Defender of the Faith", expresses the same opinion, (which Salza & Siscoe claim to be heretical), namely, that the Church during the great tribulation will be severely reduced in numbers. In *The Great Heresies*, (which I read multiple times and of which I have multiple copies, including an original edition), Belloc says, "The Church will not disappear, for the Church is not made of mortal stuff; it is the only institution among men not subject to the universal law of mortality. Therefore we say, that the Church may not be wiped out, but that it may be reduced to a small band almost forgotten amid the vast numbers of its opponents and their contempt of the defeated thing."

This opinion, which Salza & Siscoe say is heretical, has been voiced also by the future Pope Benedict XVI in a radio address on Hessischer Rundfunk in Germany in 1969:

"It [the Church] will become small and will have to start pretty much all over again. It will no longer have use of the structures it built in its years of prosperity. The reduction in the number of faithful will lead to it losing an important part of its social privileges."[496]

Salza even consulted with me on doctrinal points while he was writing his book, *True or False Pope?*, and we remained on friendly terms. It was only when I publicly differed with him on a point of doctrine, that he furiously turned against me and started accusing me of heresy. This is what I wrote, and to which he and Siscoe responded with a four part series of articles accusing me of heresy, and heaping contempt on me with denigrating and demeaning attributions:

«Salza thinks it is a heresy to hold that the Church will be reduced to a small number, and revert to the catacombs, and for a short time become invisible. If Salza's doctrine were right, then the ancient Fathers, and all the eminent authorities cited by Cardinal Manning were wrong. Cardinal Manning's position is supported by the unanimous consent of the Fathers.»

That was all I said — a mild criticism of his opinion, and he replied by directing sacrilegious contempt against a Catholic priest, and accusing me of heresy as well. I wrote and propagated my article in defence of my doctrinal position. Salza & Siscoe have responded by setting themselves up as a self-appointed vigilante Inquisition — acting like a tribunal which pronounces its verdict of Private Judgment against me for heresy; declaring me to be a public enemy of the Church! And THEY are the ones who falsely accuse me in their

---

[496] That radio address, *What Will the Church Look Like in 2000*, was reproduced in full in a book entitled *Faith and the Future*, published in 2009 by Ignatius Press.

website article of adhering to the Protestant doctrine of Private Judgement against the public judgment of the Church!

The Catholic Bishops Conference of the Philippines (CBCP) sent my writings to Rome to be examined by the Sacred Congregation for the Doctrine of the Faith (CDF), and the Pontifical Commission for the Authentic Interpretation of the Code of Canon Law. This was announced in a notification by the Secretary of the CBCP, Bishop Nestor Cariño, which appeared in one of the nation's most widely distributed daily newspaper, the *Manila Bulletin* on 1 August, 1995.

Since 1995 - 1996, my doctrinal writings have been examined by the competent authorities of the Holy See. Salza is an attorney. He knows what that means. I mentioned the fact that my writings had been sent to Rome for examination on page 117 of my above mentioned book. He read my book. He cannot be ignorant of the fact that my case was sent to Rome for examination two decades ago.

In 1996, I personally went to Rome to enquire about the status of the official inquiry being conducted about my writings. An official at the CDF, a priest named Fr. -----, met with me and discussed my case with me. I handed over to him some further writings of mine that I had published some months after the inquiry had begun. In the course of the discussion, the CDF official stated categorically that the dicastery had made no judgment against me.

As an attorney, John Salza knows perfectly well that he has absolutely no right to pronounce a private judgment on a doctrinal matter in which he is not only academically not competent, but was actually sent to Rome to be judged by the competent dicastery. That Salza & Siscoe pronounce me to be a heretic on a matter that was submitted by the Philippine bishops to Rome for judgment, is a gravely sinful act of usurpation of ecclesiastical function; and is a punishable crime according to the Code of Canon Law:

«Can. 1389 §1. A person who abuses an ecclesiastical power or function is to be punished according to the gravity of the act or omission, not excluding privation of office, unless a law or precept has already established the penalty for this abuse.»

«§2. A person who through culpable negligence illegitimately places or omits an act of ecclesiastical power, ministry, or function with harm to another is to be punished with a just penalty.»

Salza & Siscoe are fully aware that they are gravely culpable of committing the crime of usurpation of ecclesiastical function when they pronounce their solemn judgment against me: This is what they posted on their website:

> «we can cite St. Thomas who explains that just as it pertains to the proper authorities to write the law, so too does it pertain to them to interpret it and apply it to individual cases. The following is from the Summa:
> "Since judgment should be pronounced according to the written law, as stated above, he that pronounces judgment, interprets, in a way, the letter of the law, by applying it to some particular case. Now since it belongs to the same authority to interpret and to make a law, just as a law cannot be made except by public authority, so neither can a judgment be pronounced except by public authority, which extends over those who are subject to the community." [3]
> Furthermore, the Angelic Doctor goes on to explain that it is unlawful for a person to render a judgment he has no authority to make, noting that those who do such a thing are guilty of the unjust act of "judgment by usurpation."
> "Judgment is lawful in so far as it is an act of justice. Now it follows from what has been stated above (1, ad 1,3) that three conditions are requisite for a judgment to be an act of justice: first, that it proceed from the inclination of justice; secondly, that it come from one who is in authority; thirdly, that it be pronounced according to the right ruling of prudence. If any one of these be lacking, the judgment will be faulty and unlawful. First, when it is contrary to the rectitude of justice, and then it is called 'perverted' or 'unjust': secondly, when a man judges about matters wherein he has no authority, and this is called judgment 'by usurpation'...."»

They demonstrate that they know perfectly well that it is a crime for them to usurp the ecclesiastical function of judgment in doctrinal matters, but do not hesitate to commit the crime in a highly visible, public manner. The fraud which is the basis of the calumnious verdict of heresy which the Salza-Siscoe vigilante tribunal solemnly pronounces against me consists not only in their false assertion which claims I say the Church will be reduced to a handful, but more importantly, it is their basing of their judgment of heresy on their understanding of a doctrine that has not been defined by the Church.

How great must be the number of Catholics in the world for the Church to be truly catholic (universal)? How small can that number be reduced to, and to what degree can the visibility of the Church be diminished during the exceptional time of the Great Tribulation foretold by Christ and the Apostles? ***The Church has not dogmatically defined on these points***, so Salza and Siscoe have absolutely no basis to justify their hypocritical accusation of heresy against me. They base their judgments on the opinions of the authors of theological works, and they treat these opinions as if they were solemn dogmatic definitions that are definitive, infallible, *ex sese* irreformable, and not subject to any qualification or revision. Their hypocrisy is patent due to the fact that Archbishop Lefebvre, Fr. Gregor Hesse S.T.D. ,[497] Christopher A. Ferrara, Mgr. Tissier de Mallerais, and many other Catholic authors (some of whom I have quoted), have expressed the same opinions as I have expressed, which Salza & Co. declare to be heretical when I pronounce them; while they remains silent on the others expressing the same opinions, and even recognizes them as orthodox in their doctrine and worthy of

---

[497] Salza & Co. fraudulently quote Fr. Gregor Hesse against me on the point of defection from the faith and the Church. In order to deceive their readers into believing that Fr. Hesse was of the same opinion as Salza-Siscoe, who maintain that heretics are not severed from the Church without a judgment from Church authority, they quote Dr. Hesse's words which explain that "there is no formal schism unless it is declared schism". Salza & Siscoe oafishly interpret the theologian's words to mean that there is no schism unless the Church authority declares it! Long before the days of YouTube, by which Salza & Siscoe access the words of Fr. Gregory, I lived in Rome and earned my degrees at the same Pontifical University where he earned his theological degrees. We spent many evenings together in Rome discussing Philosophy, Theology, and ecclesiastical issues. We met many times afterward in Canada, USA, Vienna, Rome, Los Angeles, Belize, etc. – we were the closest of friends from 1975 to 2006. (We first met on the assembly line at the Mercedes-Benz factory in Germany while working at our summer jobs in 1975) No one on earth knows the theological mind of Fr. Gregor Hesse as well as I do. It was I who suggested and convinced him to write his doctoral thesis on the Theology of Chesterton. What Fr. Gregor was saying (and any academically qualified theologian knows this), is that for someone to be a schismatic, that one must declare himself to be separated, either by words or actions, and ***not the other way around***.

respect. When I pointed out this glaring double standard employed by Salza & Co. in their private vigilante condemnation of me as a heretic, ***their reply was to accuse me of trying to create division in the traditional movement!*** I need not say that such blatant obfuscation is tantamount to a manifest admission of guilt on their part.

Salza and Siscoe declare me to be a heretic, because I declare the Conciliar Church to be a heretical entity. Salza & Co. explicitly declare the Conciliar Church to be the Catholic Church, and adamantly insist that those who refuse to be in communion with the Conciliar Church are outside of the Church. They say my position that the Conciliar Church is not the Catholic Church is a heresy that denies the indefectibility of the Church. They claim that in order to remain in communion with the Church, it is necessary to be in communion with the Conciliar hierarchy, and be subject to the Conciliar pope (no matter how manifestly heretical he may be). Fr. Gregor Hesse, in his homily in Woonsocket RI, in 1997 declared the Conciliar Church to be, "that counterfeit church out there". There are others still living who are witnesses, and who vividly remember Fr. Hesse speaking those words in that sermon. Archbishop Lefebvre was, to my knowledge, the first one to point out the essential difference between the "Conciliar Church" and the Catholic Church. The bishop he consecrated, Mgr. Bernard Tissier de Mallerais, in his article, *Is There A Conciliar Church*,[498] theologically elaborates the essential differences between the conciliar Church and the Catholic Church. In defining the Conciliar Church, Mgr. Tissier sets forth the material cause, efficient cause, final cause, and formal cause that constitute the Conciliar church as a an entity distinct and different from the Catholic Church – "two Churches that have the same heads and most of the same members", a "counterfeit Church", "although we can reduce the belonging to it of most of its members to a simple material belonging, from the simple fact that most of the members follow the movement by conformity, without knowing or sharing the goals of the Conciliar Church". He quotes the author, Julio Meinvielle, who describes the Conciliar Church as a "Church of publicity magnified in propaganda, with bishops, priests, and theologians publicised,

---

[498] L'Eglise conciliare existe-t-elle? - http://www.dominicainsavrille.fr/leglise-conciliaire-existe-t-elle/.

perhaps won over to the enemy and changing from the Catholic Church to the gnostic Church, (as against) the other, Church of silence, with Pope faithful to Jesus Christ in its teaching and with some priests, bishops and faithful who are attached to it, scattered like the *pusillus grex* over all the earth."

Mgr. Tissier further explains that, "Formally considered the conciliar church is a sect which occupies the Catholic Church"; and "the establishment of the Conciliar Church is the fruit of a plan plotted by Freemasonry". Mgr. Tissier quotes Archbishop Lefebvre, "Which Church are we talking about? Are we talking about the Catholic Church, or another Church, a Counter Church, a counterfeit of the Catholic Church?" – "The Church of today is only the true Church in the measure that it continues exclusively, and makes itself one with exclusively the Church of yesterday and of all time." Mgr Tissier finally asks, "And besides this vulgar conciliar Church, what remains of the Catholic Church? We respond that, even reduced to a modest number, the sane faithful and perhaps only one faithful bishop, as perhaps will be according to Father Emmanuel, the Church at the end of time, the Catholic Church remains the Catholic Church." While **I have never maintained that the Church will be reduced to such dire circumstances** as hypothesized by Mgr. Tissier, It needs to be borne in mind that **the magisterium of the Church has not defined on this point**; and **therefore, Salza & Siscoe act with criminal malice to declare me to be a heretic for allegedly having professed such a doctrine as this, which in fact I have never professed**; and they manifest their premeditated hypocrisy and malice in declaring me to be a heretic for allegedly professing this doctrine which I do not profess, while feigning reverence and respect for Mgr. Tissier who does profess it as a hypothetical possibility — and they yet have the sacrilegious and demonic audacity to declare the calumny that it is I, and not they, who am without personal integrity.

By propagating their fundamentalist error on the visibility of the Church, which denies that the Church will undergo a temporary defeat, in which it will appear to have been "swept, as it were from the face of the earth," Salza & Siscoe aid and abet the Masonic agenda which aims to replace the Catholic Church with an ecumenical, dogma free "church", against which St. Pius X warned, and Pope Leo XIII foresaw in his vision and foretold in his prayer. St. Pius X warned in *Notre charge apostolique* (1904), where he spoke of "the great movement of apostasy being organized in every country for the establishment of a One-World Church which shall have neither dogmas nor hierarchy, neither discipline for the mind nor curb for the passions, and which under the pretext of freedom and human dignity, would bring back to the world the reign of legalized cunning and force, and the oppression of the weak, and all those who toil and suffer." (para. 44) When that is achieved then there will only be one great obstacle left on earth that will oppose that godless ecumenical unity of the entity which the same St. Pius X describes as "a Democracy which will be neither Catholic, nor Protestant nor Jewish" (para. 43) — that great obstacle will be the true and unreformed Catholic Church which will continue to 'hold fast to the Catholic Faith, integral and undefiled' (Athanasian Creed). Then there will be unleashed the most ferocious, intense and universal persecution of the Church that there has ever been and ever will be: the attempt to exterminate the Catholic Faith and Tradition from the face of the earth — and this bloody campaign to exterminate Catholics, depicted in the vision of the Third Secret of Fatima, will be carried out in the name of Vatican II and Ecumenism! Thus, we finally grasp what Pius XII was referring to when he said shortly after the end of World War II: "Mankind must prepare itself for sufferings such as it has never before experienced."[499] It will be then that the Crucifixion of Christ will be renewed in his bride and Mystical Body with the consummation of the Mystery of Iniquity (2 Thess. 2: 15), described by Pope Leo XIII:

> «*Behold the Church, the Spouse of the Immaculate Lamb, filled with bitterness and inebriated with gall by the most crafty enemies; who have laid impious hands on all that is most sacred. Where the See of the most blessed Peter and the Chair of the truth, was constituted as the light of the nations, there they have set up the throne of their abominable impiety, so that the shepherd being struck, the sheep may be dispersed.*»[500]

---

[499] Quoted by Desmond Birch in *Trial, Tribulation and Triumph*.

[500] From the 1930 Raccolta: «Questi sì astuti nemici hanno riempito ed inebriato con impudenza ed amarezza la Chiesa, la Sposa dell'immacolato Agnello, ed hanno posto empie mani sui suoi più sacri possedimenti. Nel luogo santo medesimo, nel quale è stata stabilita la Sede del beatissimo

¹ 9. Siccome dunque nel corpo il capo governa ed impera a tutte le membra; così il Papa governa e regge tutta la Chiesa. [But if the pope does not govern the members united in a council] Dunque il corpo mistico della Chiesa sarà un mostro, mentre ha due capi. Ma le membra senza capo non sono altro che un corpo monco; come dunque il concilio può esser corpo intiero, e rappresentar la Chiesa senza il suo capo il Pontefice Romano? E come può chiamarsi concilio generale senza il capo, quando nello stesso Concilio Niceno I. si disse: *Non debent præter sententiam Romani Pontificis concilia celebrari* Onde scrisse poi S. Damaso Papa (Epist. 2. ad Steph. et Conc. African.): *Nullo episcoporum numero decreta firmari, quibus Romanus Pontifex assensum non præbuit, et hujus ante omnia expectandam sententiam esse: nec ulla unquam rata concilia legi, quæ non sunt fulta Apostolica auctoritate.* E S. Atanasio (Epist. ad Felic. II): *Canonibus quippe sancitum est, ut absque Romano Pontifice in majoribus causis decerni nihil debeat.* Ed in fatti nel Concilio Niceno II. sotto Adriano I. nell'an no 781 col concorso di 350 vescovi fu riprovato il Sinodo antecedente Costantinopolitano, e per qual ragione? *Quia non habuit cooperarium Romanum Pontificem... quemadmodum fieri in synodis debet. Act. 6.* Lo stesse avvenne per il Concilio Ariminense, quantunque fosse stato di 400 Padri. Lo stesso avvenne per il Concilio Efesino II nella causa di Eutichete, perché S. Leone Papa non l'accetto. [...] [p. 180] 14. Ma vediamo di ciò la ragione intrinseca, perché il Papa è superiore ai concilj. La ragione si è, perché il governo della Chiesa è puro monarchico, onde il capo della Chiesa non ha altri né superiore, né eguale. E noto già che vi sono tre sorte di governo: *democratico*, in cui la podestà suprema è nel popolo; *aristocratico*, in cui la podestà è ne' ministri eletti; *monarchico*, in cui la piena podestà è tutta nel solo capo. Tutti convengono che il governo monarchico sia il più perfetto: *Optimum regimen*, scrisse S. Tommaso, *multitudinis est, ut regatur per unum: pax enim et unitas subditorum finis est regiminis: unitatis autem congruentior causa est unus, quam multi*. E poi conclude: *Circa ea quæ fidei sunt, contingit quæstiones moveri: per diversitatem autem sententiarum divideretur Ecclesia, nisi in unitate per unius sententiam conservaretur.* [...] [p. 181] 15. I cattolici all'incontro uniformemente dicono che Gesù Cristo, partendo da questo mondo, lasciò la podestà suprema della Chiesa a S. Pietro e per lui a tutti i suoi successori; così insegnò S. Tommaso nel luogo citato, ove, dopo aver detto che il governo monarchico è fra tutti l'ottimo, soggiunge: *Unde Christus dixit: Et fiet unum ovile et, unus pastor*. Lo stesso scrive S. Antonino (p. 3. tit. 22. cap. 2.§ .3) dicendo che Cristo, avendo costituito il Pontefice suo vicario, ha istituita

Pietro e la sedia della Verità per la luce del mondo, essi hanno innalzato il trono della loro abominevole empietà, con l'iniquo piano per il quale allorché il Pastore viene colpito le pecore siano disperse.»

la podestà monarchica nella Chiesa. E così dicono tutti; e Giovan Gersone scrive esser eretico chi pertinacemente negasse al Papa lo stato monarchico:

Status Papalis institutus a Christo supernaturaliter et inmediate, tamquam primatum habens monarchicum et regalem in ecclesiastica hierarchia, secundum quem statum unicum supremum Ecclesia militans dicitur una sub Christo: quem statum quisquis contestare, vel diminuere, vel alicui Ecclesiastico statui particulari coæquare præsumit, si hoc pertinaciter faciat, hæreticus est, schismaticus, impius, atque sacrilegus. Cadit enim in hæresim toties expresse damnatam a principio nascentis Ecclesiæ usque hodie; tam per institutionem Christi de principatu Petri super alios Apostolos, quam per traditionem totius Ecclesiæ in sacris eloquiis suis et generalibus conciliis. Gers. Tract. de Statib. Eccl. Cons. 1. [p. 186] Ma ecco la ragione chiara addotta da S. Antonino (part. 13. tit. 2. S. 3. cap. 3.) per cui non può appellarsi dal Papa al concilio: *Quia Ecclesia habet unitatem ex unitate capitis; unde (Joan. 10.) dicit Christus: Fiet unum ovile et unus pastor. Si licitum esset to appellare a Papa, Papa non esset caput, sed essent duo capita.* [p. 189] Di più i Padri del Concilio Romano sotto Simmaco Papa dissero: *Papam esse summum pastorem, nullius, extra casum hæresis, judicio subjectum.* Tom. 2. Concilior. Di più S. Tommaso de Pot. q. 1o. a. 4. ad 13. scrive così:

Ex gestis Chalcedonensis Concilii habetur primo, quod sententia synodi a Papa confirmatur: secundo quod a synodo appellatur ad Papam: tertio, quod a Papa ad synodum non appellatur, ut habetur ex gestis Concilii Ephesini. […] [p. 193] Ma non possono negare che questo concilio, acciocchè abbia l'autorità suprema, e sia da sé infallibile, indipendentemente dal Papa, egli debba esser legittimo. Ed acciocché sia legittimo, non basta che sia numeroso di molti vescovi insieme congregati, giacché più concilj sono stati numerosi, come il concilio Milanese II. sotto Liberio Papa di 300 Padri, l'Ariminese sotto S. Damaso di 600 Padri, l'Efesino II. sotto San Leone di 280 Padri, ma con tutto ciò sono stati riprovati dalla Chiesa; onde affinché il concilio sia ecumenico e legittimo dee avere tutte le condizioni necessarie, cioè che sia uniforme alle divine Scritture, alla tradizione de' Padri, che sia convocato da chi ne ha l'autorità, e che vi sia libertà nel dare i voti. Or, accadendo il dubbio se in un concilio sian concorse o no, queste condizioni, vi ha da esser necessariamente un giudice che lo decida; e questi non può esser altri che il Papa: altrimenti se alcuno dicesse che tal giudizio debba farsi da un altro concilio, in questo secondo concilio può accadere lo stesso dubbio, e così potrebbe andarsi in infinito. [p. 194] Questo giudice dunque necessariamente dee essere il Papa, ch' è il capo della Chiesa. [p. 195] 23. Inoltre dimando: il Papa in fare tal dichiarazione e giudizio, è fallibile o infallibile? Se è fallibile, questa sua dichiarazione poco o niente serve; perché, essendo fallibile il suo giudizio, resta in piedi il dubbio come prima. Se poi dicesi che in ciò il Papa è infallibile, ecco allora uno [196] scisma eterno ed irremediabile. Poiché vi sarebbero in tal caso due capi nella Chiesa, ambedue supremi, senza che vi sia giudice che possa decidere i dubbj, dato che il Papa ed il concilio tra di loro discordino. E come può dirsi che Iddio facendo così avrebbe ben provveduto alla sua Chiesa…? [...] la Chiesa diverrà un ridotto di contrasti e scismi, senza che vi sia maniera di mai sedarli. Perciò dicea S. Girolamo: *Propterea inter duodecim unus eligitur, ut, capite constituto, schismatis tollatur occasio. Lib. de Unit. Eccl.* E dicendo ciò, non può dubitarsi che S. Girolamo sentiva che l'autorità di questo capo fosse suprema ed infallibile; altrimenti non mai avrebbero potuto evitarsi le dissensioni, come appunto scrive S. Tommaso… parlando dell'autorità del Papa: *Per diversitatem autem sententiarum* [p. 197] *divideretur Ecclesia, nisi in unitate per unius sententiam conservaretur. S. Thom. contra Gentes lib. 4. cap. 76.* [...] (and he adds) altrimenti in quanto alle verità rivelate noi non avremmo niente di fermo, ma il tutto sarebbe in contrasto e confusione. [...] E qui mi sia permesso di ripetere il passo di S. Cipriano, che scrisse: *Neque enim aliunde hæreses obortæ sunt, aut nata schismata, quam inde quod Sacerdoti Dei non obtemperatur, nec unus in Ecclesia ad tempus sacerdos et ad tempus judex vice Christi cogitatur. Lib. 1. Epist. ad Cornel.* [p. 201] Inoltre diciamo non mettersi in dubbio che quando i vescovi nel concilio unitamente col Papa definiscono qualche punto di fede, allora certamente assiste a tutti lo Spirito Santo; ma ciò non toglie che in un tal concilio il Papa sia il capo, il quale definisce il dogma che dee tenersi, poiché tutta l'autorità del concilio sta già nel Papa. [...] Non si nega dunque che i Padri del concilio generale son diretti infallibilmente dallo [p. 202] Spirito Santo, com'è diretto il Papa; ma quando? Quando essi son uniti col Papa di sentenza, siccome nel Concilio Gerosolimitano gli Apostoli erano uniti con S. Pietro. Ma quando son discordi e divisi, allora quel concilio non è più legittimo, né può dirsi più ecumenico; è un corpo monco; sono membra senza capo, né più rappresentano la Chiesa; poiché la Chiesa dee avere il suo capo. [...] Si risponde che essendo la podestà suprema nella Chiesa una sola, e non due, se non vogliamo dare alla Chiesa due capi supremi, quando i vescovi nel concilio concorrono col Papa, non è che il loro maggior numero divenga superiore nell'autorità al Papa, e neppur avviene che allora sieno due podestà distinte; ma è che allora la stessa podestà suprema, che già prima tutta risiedea nel Papa, si estende ad essi, e si fa comune.

PART TWO

THE CASE AGAINST BERGOGLIO

SECTION I

The Invalid Resignation of Benedict XVI
"The Church will be eclipsed. At first, we will not know which is the true pope."[501]

Melanie Calvat

> «The resignation was theologically not properly carried out. In principle, the Pope is the foundation of unity, an everlasting principle. A bishop resigns and is then a simple member. But a Pope is installed by Christ.» — Cardinal Gerhard Ludwig Müller[502]

In Volume One I explained in the *Introduction* exactly why Pope Benedict's act of renunciation was null and void, basing my argument largely on the expert analysis of Canon Law professor Stefano Violi, in his article, «*La rinuncia di Benedetto XVI. Tra storia, diritto e coscienza*»; which appeared in the *Rivista Teologica di Lugano* in February 2013. Fr. Violi's position expressed in that article can be summed up in his own words, "Benedict XVI declared his renunciation of the Petrine ministry. Concerning the dictate of the canon, however, he declared his renunciation not of the office but of its administration." In his more recent article, «*Officium* e *munus* tra ordinamento canonico e comunione ecclesiale» which appeared in the journal, *Stato, Chiese e pluralismo confessionale* in November, 2019, Violi concluded with the

---

[501] Abbot Paul Combe: *The Secret of Melanie and the Actual Crisis*, 1906, Rome, p.137.

[502] «Der Rücktritt war theologisch nicht richtig verarbeitet. Der Papst ist im Prinzip das Fundament der Einheit, ein immerwährendes Prinzip. Ein Bischof tritt ab und ist dann einfaches Mitglied. Ein Papst aber ist von Christus eingesetzt.» [Seewald, Peter. Benedikt XVI.: Ein Leben. Kapitel 74: Der Beginn einer neuen Ära Droemer eBook. Kindle Edition]

opposite opinion, saying: "Aware that the ontological participation in the sacred *munera* determines an existential link with the mission entrusted to him, Benedict XVI, in his formal act of renunciation, did not use the ambiguous codicial formula *renuntiatio muneri* of can. 332 § 2 CJC 1983. He declared instead of renouncing the *ministerium*. At this point, the considerations made so far in relation to the distinction between *munus* and office, re-read in the light of the practice adopted by Benedict XVI after the renunciation, seem to me to attest to the persistence of the hypostatic and irrevocable connection with the *munus* of bishop of Rome in the person of the resignant pope also following the loss of the office of Roman Pontiff."[503] I don't think it needs to be pointed out that the observation made by the young man in *Fiddler on the Roof*, about one man's logically impossible affirmation of two mutually opposed statements, equally applies to these two propositions: *They both can't be right*. When an expert canonist presents a penetrating analysis of well researched relevant material on the complex question of Benedict XVI renunciation in two different articles, and comes up with two opposite conclusions, it is safe to say at the very least, that one can legitimately assert the existence of positive doubt about the validity of the act of renunciation, and the consequent positive doubt concerning the legitimacy of Jorge Bergoglio's claim on the Petrine *munus*. Indeed, there exists so much doubt and confusion in the minds of many Catholics which is only increasing with time, as it becomes more and more apparent each day that the visible form of the pontificate seems to be not only absent, but positively incapable of existing in the man from Argentina who calls himself "Bishop of Rome", that it can now be safely judged that the foretold eclipse of the Church has begun, when, "*At first, we will*

---

[503] «Consapevole che l'*ontologica* partecipazione ai sacri *munera*, determina un legame esistenziale con la missione affidatagli, Benedetto XVI, nel suo atto formale di rinuncia, non ha utilizzato l'ambigua formula codiciale *renuntiatio muneri* del can. 332 § 2 CJC 1983106. Ha dichiarato invece di rinunciare al *ministerium*[107]. A questo punto le considerazioni fin qui fatte relativamente alla distinzione tra *munus* e ufficio, rilette alla luce della prassi adottata da Benedetto XVI successivamente alla rinuncia, mi sembra attestino la persistenza del nesso ipostatico e irrevocabile con il *munus* di vescovo di Roma nella persona del papa resignante anche in seguito alla perdita dell'ufficio di Romano Pontefice.»

not know which is the true pope." The extreme necessity for the Church to resolve all doubts and uncertainties about the legitimate occupant of the See of Rome can be gathered from the second part of the prophecy which foretells the dire persecution of the Church that will follow immediately after the fulfilment of the first part: "Then secondly, *the Holy Sacrifice of the Mass will cease to be offered in churches and houses*; it will be such that, *for a time, there will not be public services any more*. But I see that the Holy Sacrifice has not really ceased: *it will be offered in barns, in alcoves, in caves, and underground.*" That is already the situation at present in some countries, (such as here in Ireland) where public Masses have been outlawed. The pastors of the Church can ill afford to think a wait-and-see approach to the present crisis in the papacy is prudent, because time is running out. In his enumeration of the principle parts of prudence, St. Thomas lists *solertia* as one of the eight principle parts of the virtue. Thus, in order to act prudently, the hierarchy needs to act quickly and with adroit resourcefulness in order to avert the direst consequences for the unity of the Church. There is certainly doubt and disagreement in the minds of many concerning the legitimacy of Jorge Bergoglio's claim on the papal *munus*. In order to resolve the crisis, all doubt regarding the validity of the claims on the Petrine *munus* must be definitively settled. If this is not done straightaway in a timely manner, then what can be expected to result from such negligent inaction will be a most ruinous schism such as has never existed in all the history of the Church. A proper judgment must be made to resolve all doubts about who holds the totality of the Petrine *munus*.

The utterly fallacious objection has been stridently and repeatedly proposed by Salza & Siscoe, asserting that anyone who questions the legitimacy of Bergoglio's claim on the papacy is guilty of *private judgment against the public judgment of the Church*. The objection is fallacious because it presumes something that is not been demonstrated: that an act of supreme ecclesiastical authority has unequivocally determined that Jorge Bergoglio is the exclusive holder of the Petrine *munus*. An ambiguous judgment of the cardinals and bishops which accepts in some manner both mens' claims on the *munus* cannot be legitimately construed as a judgment which binds the whole Church to unequivocal and exclusive acceptance of only one of the two ambiguous claims on the Petrine *munus*. Such a judgment by itself is neither *supreme* nor *absolute*, because it lacks the exercise of the supreme authority which exists in the primacy of an indubitably certain pope. It is not supreme because a judgment of the bishops and cardinals by itself is not an act of primacy; and it is not absolute because it is conditional when their judgment is premised on the acceptance of the conditions of the renunciation by which the resignant pope expresses his will to retain some aspect of his *munus*. Under such circumstances, acceptance of the subsequent papal election is *conditional* if the acceptance itself is conditioned on the limiting stipulations made in the act of resignation of the holder of the primacy, whose conditions can neither be overruled nor convalidated by his subordinates, because he is the holder of the *munus* with its *fullness of supreme power*, and his act of resignation therefore, is either valid or invalid entirely by itself. If the resignation is *unconditional* then the successor's election can be validly accepted unconditionally. If the resignation is *conditional*, and not absolute and unequivocal, the subsequent election of a successor is invalid, and is incapable of a valid acceptance because the resignation itself is invalid. An acceptance of a pope elected after a conditional, and therefore invalid resignation would be founded on an error, and would therefore be necessarily conditional, for which reason, such an acceptance, not being univocal and absolute, would be null and void even if made universally and peacefully.

The incontestable fact that Pope Benedict XVI has maintained some claim on his papal *munus* proves absolutely, that he remains in full possession of the primacy as a result of the conditionality of his renunciation of the *munus*. The reason for this is that the nature of the papacy is such, that the actual holder of the office possesses the primacy in virtue of the Petrine *munus* which he possesses in its absolute and indivisible fullness, so that a pope who would attempt to renounce the papal office by an act that lacks a total and unconditional renunciation of the *munus*, by the very act of his stipulating a qualifying condition of the renunciation, whereby the intention is asserted in the act, to retain anything whatsoever of the *munus* he received from Christ upon his election, albeit only "spiritual" and not jurisdictional, nullifies the act in virtue of the fatal equivocation brought about by the logical opposition of contradictory assertions made in the act. However, such an equivocation as was made in Pope Benedict's act of renunciation has created an ambiguous situation in the Church, in which, in spite of all the qualifications and equivocations made in his and Bergoglio's claims on the *munus,* there remain in the last analysis, two claims on the Petrine *munus.* This situation at the very least creates a founded *positive doubt* about the validity of Bergoglio's claim on the pontificate, so that it cannot be maintained that one who doubts or contests the doubtful claim makes a judgment against the public judgment of the Church, because a public judgment of the Church that would bind the whole Church cannot be made by the bishops and cardinals by themselves, but a judgment can only be binding on the whole Church when it is unequivocally determined with finality by the exercise of the primacy of a pope who is a true and certain pope. A doubtful pope who asserts an ambiguous claim on the papacy is presumed to be no pope, for which reason his judgments would not constitute a juridical act that would determine with finality the judgment of the bishops and cardinals, making it binding upon the whole Church. Without the primacy certainly existing in virtue of ONE man's unequivocal and exclusive claim on the *munus,* the doubt remains unresolved, and consequently, there cannot be said to exist a judgment binding on the whole Church. The ambiguous acceptance of both claims is such that it is not an unconditional and unequivocal acceptance of one by the whole Church. Thus, the fulfilment of the criterion of universal and peaceful acceptance for establishing the infallible dogmatic fact of a certain pontificate existing in Jorge Bergoglio is lacking.

Lastly, the power to bind the whole Church with a judgment pertains exclusively to the supreme authority of the individual holder of the Petrine *munus,* and does not exist suppletively even in the totality of the rest of the hierarchy. The entire hierarchy is incapable of making a judgment binding upon the whole Church if a true and certain pope is not himself also making that judgment with them in a clear manner that eliminates all doubt. Until Benedict XVI unequivocally relinquishes all claim on the Petrine *munus,* unconditionally and absolutely, he remains the sole holder of the Petrine *munus.* And if he were indeed to do that, then unless the formal heresy established by certain *indicia* incriminating Jorge Bergoglio would be be purged, there could exist no act of primacy of a certain pope to ratify and thereby confer a final determination of the Church's judgment alleged to have been made on the question in favour of Jorge Bergoglio's claim on the pontificate. Without such a final determination being made by which the judgment of the cardinals and bishops would be confirmed by a certain pope, the doubt would persists, and for so long as the doubt persists, it cannot be asserted that a binding act of ecclesiastical authority has been exercised from which there arises the obligation of the members of the Church to be subject to a particular claimant of the *munus*. Under the present circumstances, for so long as the claimants themselves assert an uncertain claim on the papacy, no definitive judgment in favour of one or the other is possible, unless it be made by the one whose resignation is doubtfully valid by reasserting his claim in an unequivocal manner. A full and unequivocal renunciation of the *munus* by Pope Benedict would not suffice to legitimize Bergoglio's claim, because there would remain for Bergoglio the disqualifying *indicia* of heresy which render him an incapable subject of the papacy. For so long as a founded positive doubt persists, there can exist no certain authoritative judgment to which the members of the Church are bound to an uncertain claimant. Under such circumstances, the members of the Church have the right to judge according to their informed conscience in this question for so long as the matter remains in doubt, because no authority is required to exercise a simple right of conscience to resolve a doubt that the Church authority fails to definitively resolve in the external forum, and which can only be definitively resolved by the pontiff's own unequivocal and formal clarification on what he intended to renounce and what he intended to retain when he renounced his exercise of the *ministerium* on 11 Feb. 2013. The pastors of the Church steadfastly ignore, and refuse to even acknowledge the presence of this elephant in the basilica. There exists as yet no definitive ruling on who possesses the totality of the Petrine *munus*. Meanwhile, the clergy and faithful are left to fend for themselves with their own conscience. Authority is required only to exercise power over others, so no authority is required for a Catholic to judge for himself according to his conscience which man is the true pope for so long as the matter has not been settled with a clear-cut assertion of authority emanating from the true pope himself. Since all Catholics are bound by divine law to be subject to the Roman Pontiff, every individual Catholic must attempt as best as he can to ascertain which claimant is the true pope. At present, we still await a final and definitive judgment, but we continue to be given only equivocations. Benedict renounced the active exercise of the ministry but until now in some manner he still explicitly retains his claim on the *munus* he received from Christ upon being elected pope. From there, it simply does not follow that Bergoglio's claim on the pontificate has been judged valid by ecclesiastical authority. Confusion reigns because the whole Church awaits a clear clarion call from on high while from the commanding heights there is only heard the muffled sound of an "uncertain bugle" (1 Cor. 14:8)

KEY PASSAGES FROM FR. VIOLI'S LATEST ARTICLE ON POPE BENEDICT'S RESIGNATION WITH COMMENTARY

«Pope Benedict's renunciation brought the issue of the relationship between *munus* and *officium* back to the attention of canonists and theologians, increasing the complexity of the issue due to the intertwining with the theological — canonical problems inherent in the genesis of the primacy of Peter and in the not always linear history of its theological — juridical configuration.»[504]

One generally looks to the definitions provided in the Code of Canon Law and in the authoritative commentaries on it in order to gain a precise understanding of the relationship between the two terms, but the issue is much deeper and far more complex that what is summarily stated in the Code, or even than what can be found in commentaries on the Code. It should come as no surprise that Joseph Ratzinger had a far more complete grasp of the matter than what can be gained from reading the commentaries on Canon Law.

«It will be the Second Vatican Council to lay the foundations for fully defining the relationship of hyperonymity of *munus* with respect to *officium*, adding to the usual meanings of *munus* a new theological

---

[504] La rinuncia di papa Benedetto ha riproposto all'attenzione di canonisti e teologi il tema della relazione tra *munus* e *officium,* accrescendo la complessità della questione a motivo dell'intreccio con le problematiche teologico-canonistiche inerenti alla genesi del primato di Pietro e alla storia non sempre lineare della sua configurazione teologico-giuridica.

meaning already implicitly present in the Vulgate, characterized by a semantic surplus compared to the eponymous *officium*.»[505]

The usual meanings of *munus* are those found in the better Latin dictionaries and in the commentaries on Canon Law. Fr. Violi carefully examined Jerome's usage of the term in his Vulgate translation in order to excavate the meanings of biblical terms which are translated as *munus,* and from there explained how the term in its biblical connotations became the basis for the theological meaning of *munus* fully defined in the Second Vatican Council.

«Precisely the theological concept of *munus,* — at the same time a gift of grace and commitment — fits in well with the two distinct but non-separable orders of the one ecclesial reality.»[506]

«Compared to the interpretation that sees the meanings of *gift, assignment and office* as alternatives, the proposed exegesis considers them as interdependent. The gift becomes an assignment at the same time, just as the office presupposes, before an assignment conferred by legitimate authority, a gift of grace. Therefore, whenever *munus* assumes the meaning of *obligation, function, assignment,* it nevertheless presupposes the meaning of *gift*.»[507]

«Precisely the *baptismal munus,* in the mutual immanence of the meanings of gift, task and mission, founds and structures ecclesial communion, according to can. 204 §1 CJC 1983:

"The faithful of Christ are those who, having been incorporated into Christ through baptism, are constituted the people of God and

---

[505] Sarà il Concilio Vaticano II a porre le basi per definire compiutamente la relazione di *iperonimia* di *munus* rispetto a *officium*, affiancando ai significati consueti di *munus* una nuova accezione teologica, già implicitamente presente nella *Vulgata,* caratterizzata da una eccedenza semantica rispetto all'iponimo *officium*.

[506] «Proprio il concetto teologico di *munus,* - a un tempo dono di grazia e impegno - ben si accorda con i due ordini distinti ma non separabili dell'unica realtà ecclesiale.»

[507] «Rispetto all'interpretazione che vede tra loro alternativi i significati di *dono, incarico* e *ufficio,* l'esegesi proposta li considera come interdipendenti. Il dono diventa al contempo incarico, così come l'ufficio presuppone, prima di un incarico conferito dalla legittima autorità, un dono di grazia. Pertanto, ogni volta che *munus* assume il significato di *obbligazione, funzione, incarico,* presuppone comunque il significato di *dono*.»

therefore, made partakers in their own way of the priestly, prophetic and royal function (*munus*) of Christ, are called to carry out, according to each one's condition, the mission that God has entrusted to the Church to be accomplished in the world ".»[508]

Violi notes that here in the canon the term *munus* is used to denote a function in the more general sense which does not involve the exercise of a *sacra potestas*. Thus:

«At the origin of the *munera fidelium* there is not the ecclesiastical authority that confers an ecclesiastical office, but the Holy Spirit, defined by Augustine as the *Ditator fidelium*, that is, the one who enriches the faithful.»[509]

Ultimately it is by the ordering of divine providence that all *munera* are given.

«The office of diocesan bishop, like other ecclesiastical offices, is subject to "loss" 103. As can. 184 §1, "The ecclesiastical office is lost with the expiration of the pre-established time, having reached the age limits defined by law, by renunciation, transfer, removal and also by deprivation". With reference to the renunciation of the diocesan bishop, can. 401, § 1, rightly speaks of "*renuntiatio ab officio*", not of *renuntiatio muneri*.»[510]

---

[508] «Proprio il *munus battesimale*, nella reciproca immanenza dei significati di dono, compito e missione, fonda e struttura la comunione ecclesiale, secondo il can. 204 §1 CJC 1983: "i fedeli di Cristo sono coloro che, essendo stati incorporati a Cristo mediante il battesimo, sono costituiti popolo di Dio e perciò, resi partecipi nel modo loro proprio della funzione (*munus*) sacerdotale, profetica e regale di Cristo, sono chiamati ad attuare, secondo la condizione propria di ciascuno, la missione che Dio ha affidato alla Chiesa da compiere nel mondo"[89]. "Christifideles sunt qui, utpote per baptismum Christo incorporati, in populum Dei sunt constituti, atque hac ratione muneris Christi sacerdotalis, prophetici et regalis suo modo participes facti, secundum propriam cuiusque condicionem, admissionem exercendam vocantur, quam Deus Ecclesiae in mundo adimplendam concredidit".»

[509] «All'origine dei *munera fidelium* non c'è l'autorità ecclesiastica che conferisce un ufficio ecclesiastico, ma lo Spirito Santo, definito da Agostino come il *Ditator fidelium*, Colui cioè che arricchisce i fedeli.»

[510] «L'Ufficio di Vescovo diocesano, al pari degli altri uffici ecclesiastici, è soggetto alla "perdita"[103]. Come statuisce il can. 184 §1, "L'ufficio ecclesiastico si perde con lo scadere del tempo prestabilito, raggiunti i limiti d'età definiti dal diritto, per rinuncia, trasferimento, rimozione e anche per

Here it is necessary to point out that a bishop needs only to renounce his **office** of diocesan ordinary in order to relinquish his jurisdiction over his diocese and thereby cease to be the diocesan *ordinary*, without renouncing his episcopal *munus* altogether; but for the pope, that does not suffice: The pope must entirely renounce his papal *munus* without retaining anything of it in order to cease to hold office as pope, because unlike a bishop, who does not need to entirely renounce his episcopal *munus*, but only his *munus* as diocesan ordinary — intending not to cease being a bishop, but only to cease being the ordinary over his diocese — the pope, in order to relinquish the papacy, must not merely intend to relinquish his *power* of ordinary jurisdiction over the universal Church, but he must intend altogether to cease being the *pope* in order to relinquish his office. The reason for this is that a Bishop Emeritus is still a bishop, but a retired bishop, but a pope who renounces his *munus* ceases to be pope, and as a former pope, he is only a retired bishop. Accordingly, a pope must renounce entirely the Petrine *munus* in order to cease to be pope, and if he expresses an intention to retain anything whatever of the papal *munus* in his act of renunciation, the act is **null and void**.

«The *missio canonica* entrusted to a bishop does not in fact involve identification between the sacramental ontological *munus* and the office conferred on it. If in the diocesan bishop "*munus*" and "office" coincide *manente officio*, at the moment of renunciation, the episcopal see becomes vacant (Can. 416 CJC 1983). The renunciate loses his office and the attached powers. However, the sacramental ontological participation of the resignant bishop to the *munera* deriving from the consecration that does not involve the exercise of the powers attached to the office does not fail. The Council itself mentions, for example, a "*sollicitudo*" which, although not exercised by acts of jurisdiction, contributes greatly to the good of the universal Church" (LG 23).»[511]

---

privazione". Con riferimento alla rinuncia del Vescovo diocesano, il can. 401, § 1, parla giustamente di "*renuntiatio ab officio*", non di *renuntiatio muneri*.»

[511] «La *missio canonica* affidata a un vescovo non comporta infatti l'identificazione tra il *munus* ontologico sacramentale e l'ufficio conferitogli. Se nel Vescovo diocesano "*munus*" e "ufficio" coincidono *manente officio*, nel momento della rinuncia la sede episcopale diventa vacante (Can. 416 CJC 1983). Il rinunciante perde l'ufficio e le potestà annesse. Non viene meno

Upon resignation of his office, a diocesan ordinary does not lose the *munus* which pertains to his episcopal state as a consecrated bishop, but loses only the *munus* to exercise jurisdiction to teach, govern, and rule his subjects. Similarly the pope who resigns, retains the *munus* of his episcopal state as a consecrated bishop, but to validly resign the papacy, he must totally renounce the **papal** *munus*, because while not intending to cease to be a bishop, he must absolutely intend to relinquish his **Petrine** *munus* in order to relinquish the Petrine office and cease to be pope. The Petrine *munus* is absolutely singular, and therefore exclusive to the individual who as holder of the office of Supreme Pontiff, possesses in his person the primacy, so that for the Petrine office to be validly renounced, the *munus*, which is essentially and entirely connected with that office, must be entirely renounced and voluntarily forfeited to effect the person's separation from the office and its primacy. Whatever *munus* the former pope retains is spiritual and episcopal, but is of a different nature than the Petrine *munus*, which is absolutely singular, and therefore pertains totally and exclusively to the papacy existing as a habit in the actually reigning Pontiff. Pope Benedict XVI, by expressly elaborating the meaning of what he declared in his act of renunciation, that the assignment he had received from the Lord upon his election as pope was "for always," and is not revoked by his renunciation of the active exercise of his ministry as Bishop of Rome, manifested his intention already expressed in the *Declaratio* to retain some essential aspect of the *Petrine munus*; and thus, having expressed his intention to retain something essentially and inextricably bound to the papal office, nullified the act of renunciation of the office. Seven years later he reiterated in his interview with Peter Seewald that he retains that "mandate" (*Auftrag*). The seemingly irreconcilable contradictions are all resolved if one understands the Hegelian dialectic that consciously or unconsciously underlies his renunciation of the papal ministry. When his logically opposing statements (thesis-antithesis) accomplish a negation of the negation, which is built into the antithesis by its

---

però la partecipazione ontologica sacramentale del vescovo resignante ai *munera* derivanti dalla consacrazione che non comportano l'esercizio dei poteri annessi con l'ufficio. Il Concilio stesso menziona per esempio una *sollicitudo* "che, sebbene non sia esercitata con atti di giurisdizione, contribuisce sommamente al bene della Chiesa universale" (LG 23).»

qualifications, a synthesis results with a qualified reaffirmation of the original thesis. Benedict's resignation was invalid because he qualified it by expressly intending to retain some aspect of the Petrine *munus* which he received upon his accepting the papal election. Unless the pope renounces the entire *munus simpliciter et absolute*, it is not validly renounced at all. He does not understand that the indivisible *munus* he received from God upon his election was received whole and indivisible, so that by not renouncing the entire *munus* he received upon accepting his election to the papacy, in order to retain what he perceived to be the separable spiritual aspect of the papal *munus*, he necessarily retains the integral *munus* in its entirety. There is only one pope, and it is he who possesses the entire *munus*, and he does not lose or relinquish anything of the Petrine *munus* unless he renounces the *munus* completely and absolutely. A true "Pope Emeritus" cannot exist: he can only be a former pope who totally relinquishes the Petrine *munus*, and reverts to being a **bishop** — one who fully intended to relinquish every aspect of the Petrine *munus*, thus, a Bishop Emeritus of Rome, retaining the basic episcopal *munus*, but nothing of the papal *munus*. If he, intending to keep something of the Petrine *munus*, did not renounce it entirely, then the entire *munus* remained with him and continues to remain with him to the present day. Benedict XVI stated clearly enough on Feb. 27, 2013 that his commitment (i.e. the Petrine *munus*) which he received from Christ on 19 April 2005 is "for always", and his decision to renounce the active exercise of the ministry "does not revoke this". His latest equivocations in this regard which appeared in Seewald's biography, have no juridical effect of *sanatio in radice* on his invalid renunciation, because he has equivocated again, saying that while he renounced the office he retains some spiritual aspect of the Petrine *munus* as a "mandate" (*Auftrag*), which, as he explained earlier, was received from Christ when the cardinals elected him. The Petrine *Auftrag* or *munus* is absolutely indivisible and unique to the one man who possesses the habit of the supreme pontificate as the successor of Peter. One who expresses the intention to retain any aspect of it retains the entire *munus petrinum*, and remains in office as pope and successor of Peter, even if he has contradictorily expressed the intention to renounce the office, because such a flat contradiction constitutes a nullifying equivocation which is contrary to the nature of a juridical act, as I explained in Volume One. Nevertheless, the contradictory idea that the pope can renounce his office and jurisdiction without entirely renouncing the *munus* he received upon accepting his election to the papacy is the erroneous substrate upon which the invalid formulation of his renunciation is founded.

«Precisely the possibility of distinguishing between the office of diocesan Bishop with the attached powers and the *munus* of diocesan Bishop emeritus, allows to hypothesize the co-presence in the same diocese of the diocesan Bishop, holder of the office, with the emeritus bishop, without configuring in any way the hypothesis of a "diarchy".»[512]

This is possible because both the diocesan ordinary and the emeritus bishop are bishops. Their *munus* is not identical, but in both cases, the *munus* is **episcopal**; but only the ordinary occupies the office of diocesan bishop with its corresponding power of governance. The emeritus bishop is one who has been discharged from his service and *munus* as ordinary, as is clear from the meaning of the word "emeritus": From Oxford: "mid 18th century: from Latin, past participle of *emereri* 'earn one's discharge by service', from *e-* (variant of *ex-*) 'out of, from' + *mereri* 'earn'." As an *emeritus*, a bishop is relieved of his *munus gubernandi et docendi* — but he remains a bishop and successor of the Apostles, so his *munus episcopale* remains with him as an *emeritus*. A former pope — a pontiff who has validly renounced the *munus petrinum*, ceases altogether to be pope, and having renounced his *munus*, he is no longer the successor of Peter but only a bishop and successor of the Apostles, retaining nothing of the papacy or of the Petrine *munus*. The only thing a former pope retains is his *munus episcopale* as a successor of the Apostles, and nothing of the *munus petrinum* which pertains uniquely and exclusively to the individual who is the successor of **Peter**. If a former pope were capable of retaining a passive aspect of the Petrine *munus* even after his renunciation of the office, that would create a dual papacy with both men possessing some aspect of the *munus* — in Pope Benedict's

---

[512] «Proprio la possibilità di distinguere tra l'ufficio di Vescovo diocesano con le potestà annesse e il *munus* di Vescovo diocesano emerito, consente di ipotizzare la copresenza nella stessa diocesi del Vescovo diocesano titolare dell'ufficio con il vescovo emerito, senza configurare in alcun modo l'ipotesi di una "diarchia".»

own words, "the pope of action" and "the pope of prayer"⁵¹³: One pope, the *Bishop of Rome*, holding the active aspect of the *munus* with its power of governance, and the other pope, the *Pope Emeritus*, no longer in possession of the *munus gubernandi* with its ordinary jurisdiction over the diocese of Rome and whole Church, **but still somehow a pope, and in some manner a successor of Peter**, who would "remain in the enclosure of Saint Peter"⁵¹⁴ in virtue of his continuing passive role in exercising the Petrine *munus*.

«According to the magisterium of Pope Benedict, the *munus* of the Bishop of Rome, obtained with the legitimate election accepted by him together with the episcopal consecration, like the *munus* of the other bishops, implies "an always and for always".»⁵¹⁵

Except for the claim that these words were spoken magisterially, the proposition is entirely correct if it is understood in the properly qualified sense that the essential distinction between the Petrine *munus* and the episcopal *munus* demands. The words, "an always and for always" were not spoken magisterially, as if he intended to teach on some point of doctrine, but in pronouncing these words, he intended only to clarify his meaning on precisely what was juridically intended in the act. Thus, the pronouncement does not pertain to the magisterium of Pope Benedict, but only expressed his opinion. The essential qualification which must be intended in the proposition is

---

⁵¹³ These are in fact the exact words which Pope Benedict uses to describe the *de facto* Benedict-Bergoglio dual papacy: "Jorge Mario Bergoglio sarebbe stato «il Papa dell'azione», Ratzinger «il Papa della preghiera», come ripete spesso Benedetto." — *L'uomo che veglia sul Vaticano. Su 7 il dialogo con Benedetto XVI* di Massimo Franco: Benedetto XVI, l'uomo che veglia sul Vaticano - Corriere.it

⁵¹⁴ Benedict XVI General Audience Saint Peter's Square Wednesday, 27 February 2013: "I no longer bear the power of office for the governance of the Church, but in the service of prayer I remain, so to speak, in the enclosure of Saint Peter." — «Non porto più la potestà dell'officio per il governo della Chiesa, ma nel servizio della preghiera resto, per così dire, nel recinto di san Pietro.»

⁵¹⁵ «Stando al magistero di papa Benedetto, il *munus* del Vescovo di Roma, ottenuto con l'elezione legittima da lui accettata insieme con la consacrazione episcopale, al pari del *munus* degli altri vescovi, comporta "un sempre e un per sempre".»

this: Unlike the episcopal *munus* of all bishops as successors of the apostles, the acceptance of the Petrine *munus* by the successor of Peter in the Primacy does not imply "an always and for always", but according to its nature, the duration of the Petrine *munus* expires upon the cessation of the papacy in the person of the pope when he renounces the papacy. When a pope validly renounces the papacy, he ceases entirely to be pope and successor of Peter in the Primacy, and with the cessation of his papacy by his act of renunciation, his *munus petrinum* ceases entirely by that act, and he reverts to being only a successor of the apostles in the episcopacy, retaining only his *munus episcopale*. Any equivocation or expression of conditionality which would contradict or oppose the total and unconditional intention to renounce the *munus petrinum* would constitute a fatal defect of intention that renders the act juridically null and void, with the consequence that he would remain in office as pope even after the invalid act.

> «Aware that the ontological participation in the sacred *munera* determines an existential link with the mission entrusted to him, Benedict XVI, in his formal act of renunciation, did not use the ambiguous codicial formula *renuntiatio muneri* of can. 332 § 2 CJC 1983. He declared instead of renouncing the *ministerium*. At this point, the considerations made so far in relation to the distinction between *munus* and office, re-read in the light of the practice adopted by Benedict XVI after the renunciation, seem to me to attest to the persistence of the hypostatic and irrevocable connection with the *munus* of bishop of Rome in the person of the resignant pope also following the loss of the office of Roman Pontiff.»[516]

---

[516] «Consapevole che l'*ontologica* partecipazione ai sacri *munera*, determina un legame esistenziale con la missione affidatagli, Benedetto XVI, nel suo atto formale di rinuncia, non ha utilizzato l'ambigua formula codiciale *renuntiatio muneri* del can. 332 § 2 CJC 1983106. Ha dichiarato invece di rinunciare al *ministerium*107. A questo punto le considerazioni fin qui fatte relativamente alla distinzione tra *munus* e ufficio, rilette alla luce della prassi adottata da Benedetto XVI successivamente alla rinuncia, mi sembra attestino la persistenza del nesso ipostatico e irrevocabile con il *munus* di vescovo di Roma nella persona del papa resignante anche in seguito alla perdita dell'ufficio di Romano Pontefice.»

As has been explained, the "persistence of the hypostatic and irrevocable connection with the *munus* of bishop of Rome in the person of the resignant pope also following the loss of the office of Roman Pontiff," is not a magisterial teaching of Benedict XVI, but is only an opinion, and is a *non sequitur* that exists in the mind of Joseph Ratzinger, and is not consistent with Catholic teaching on the nature of the Petrine *munus*.

> «I therefore believe that the term "*ministerium*" used by the *Declaratio* is to be understood in this case as a synonym of *officium*, according to a possible meaning already identified by Peter Erdö in the different uses of *ministerium* in the Council. This reading is confirmed by the words spoken by Benedict XVI in his last audience: "I no longer carry the power of the office for the government of the Church". The object of the renunciation, or "the ministry of the Bishop of Rome", not only suggests, but also imposes this interpretation.»[517]

I disagree entirely with Fr. Violi that that «the term "*ministerium*" used by the *Declaratio* is to be understood in this case as a synonym of *officium*,» even if it were subjectively intended by Pope Benedict to convey that meaning. Nevertheless, even if it were to be understood that way, that would not remedy the nullity of the act; because what is ultimately essential to the question of validity or nullity is not whether Benedict XVI subjectively intended to renounce the *officium* rather than the *ministerium*. What nullified the act was his failure to formally express the intention to renounce simply and absolutely his *munus*; since by expressing his intention to maintain in himself an *irrevocable connection* with the *munus* he received upon his election by the cardinals even *after the loss of the office of Roman Pontiff*, he thereby expressed his intention to irrevocably retain an essential aspect of the *officium* which cannot be relinquished except by renouncing the *munus*

---

[517] «Ritengo pertanto che il termine "*ministerium*" utilizzato dalla *Declaratio* sia da intendersi in questo caso come sinonimo di *officium,* secondo un possibile significato già individuato da Peter Erdö nei diversi utilizzi di *ministerium* nel Concilio[109]. Tale lettura trova conferma nelle parole pronunciate da Benedetto XVI nella sua ultima udienza: "Non porto più la potestà dell'officio per il governo della Chiesa"[110]. L'oggetto della rinuncia, ovvero "il ministero del Vescovo di Roma", non solo suggerisce, ma anche impone questa interpretazione.»

absolutely. As is explained below in Section II, in a juridical act the terms employed must properly be understood as they are defined and understood in law. Therefore, the way that Pope Benedict may have personally intended his words to be understood does not remedy the fatal nullifying defect that the improper use of terms in a juridical act creates.

> «Acceptance of the legitimate election does not only imply the conferral of a mere ecclesiastical office; it places the seal on the *Petrine charism*, also an irrevocable gift of God, which configures the bishop of Rome, successor of Peter, in a singular way compared to the other bishops. This singularity appears to persist also in the emeritus bishop of Rome, at least according to the evocative reference of the Roman see: "I remain somehow in the enclosure of Peter". Here Benedict seems to interpret the perpetuity of the spiritual bond suggested by Innocent III between the Roman Pontiff and the See of Rome, not in the office or in the *potestates*, but in the *munus*.»[518]

The *Petrine charism*, as has been explained, is not in a proper personal and unconditional sense "an irrevocable gift of God". According to Innocent III (*Sermo III* — IN CONSECRATIONE PONTIFICIS), the permanent spiritual bond exists only between the Church and the current **officeholder** who is the **actually reigning pontiff**: "But the sacrament between the Roman Pontiff and the Roman Church remains so firm and stable, that only by death are they separated from each other... This man [the Roman Pontiff] is bound to the wife, [the Roman Church] he does not seek an unbinding, he does not yield, he is not deposed; for «*he stands or falls by his master*»

---

[518] «L'accettazione della legittima elezione non comporta soltanto il conferimento di un mero ufficio ecclesiastico; pone il sigillo al *carisma petrino*, anch'esso dono irrevocabile di Dio, che configura il vescovo di Roma, successore di Pietro, in modo singolare rispetto agli altri vescovi. Tale singolarità appare permanere anche nel vescovo emerito di Roma, almeno stando al richiamo evocativo della sede romana: "rimango in qualche modo nel recinto di Pietro". Qui Benedetto sembra interpretare la perpetuità del legame spirituale suggerito da Innocenzo III tra il Romano Pontefice e la sede di Roma, non nell'ufficio o nelle *potestates,* ma nel *munus.*»

(Rom. XIV)."⁵¹⁹ Benedict interprets Innocent III incorrectly if he thinks that Innocent implies a perpetuity of the *munus petrinum* persisting, even after the bond between the pontiff and the office ceases. Any alluding to the teaching of Innocent III on the indissolubility of the bond is to no avail. In the text of Innocent's sermon, he is clearly speaking strictly of the indissoluble bond between the pope and the Church which exists in virtue of his office, which is so stable and firm that the two, are only separated by death. Since *he stands or falls by his master*, he cannot be deposed, but would only become incapable of remaining in the union if he would be guilty of spiritual fornication, which is heresy, for which he would be cast out, i.e. deposed, and separated from the Church.⁵²⁰ The doctrine of

---

⁵¹⁹ "Sacramentum autem inter Romanum pontificem et Romanam Ecclesiam tam firmum et stabile perseverat, ut non nisi per mortem umquam ab invicem separentur ... Vir autem iste [Romanus Pontifex] alligatus uxori, [Ecclesiæ Romanæ] solutionem non quærit, non cedit, **non deponitur; nam «suo domino aut stat, aut cadit»** (Rom. XIV)." [*Sermo III De Diversis* — IN CONSECRATIONE PONTIFICIS]

⁵²⁰ The reason he gives for this, quoting St. John, is that as a heretic, the pope would be already judged, (quoniam *«qui non credit, jam judicatus est»* (*Joan.* iii).), and therefore, for reason of fornication, not carnal but the error of infidelity, the Roman Church can dismiss the Roman Pontiff; since the matrimony can only exist between legitimate persons (*solus consensus inter legitimas personas efficit matrimonium*): «Propter causam vero fornicationis Ecclesia romana posset dimmitere Romanum pontificem. Fornicationem non dico carnalem, sed spiritualem; quia non est carnale, sed spiritual conjugium, id est propter infidelitatis errorem; quoniam «qui non credit, jam judicatus est (*Joan.* iii)»: et in hoc articulo intelligitur, quod legitur in Evangelio, quod audistis: «Vos estis sal terræ, quod sis al evanuerit in quo salietur? (*Matth.* V.)» Ego tamen facile non crediderim, ut Deus permitteret Romanum pontificem contra fidem errare: pro quo spiritualiter oravit in Petro: <Ego, inquit, pro te rogavi, Petre, etc. (Luc.xxii),> Ergo *qui habet sponsam, sponsus est*. Haec autem sponsa non nupsit vacua, sed dotem mihi tribuit absque pretio pretiosam, spirilualium videlicet plenitudinem et latitudinem temporalium, magnitndinem et multiudinem utrorumque. Nam caeteri vocati sunt in partem sollicitudinis, solus autem Petrus assumptus est in plenitudinem potesatis.» By the sin of infidelity, the necessary disposition for the spiritual matrimonial union between the Roman Pontiff and the Church would cease to exist; and thus the heretic, no longer a legitimate

Innocent III is based on the belief of the early Church which held that a bishop was bound to his diocese for life, and could not transfer to another diocese. Indeed, this belief was reflected in the early discipline of the first centuries which did not allow transfers of an ordinary from one diocese to another. Even the pope was not elected by poaching a bishop from a neighbouring diocese,[521] but the popes were first chosen from the local clergy, and only later were outside bishops elected to the papacy. Even then, the spiritual bond between a bishop and his diocese was believed to be so strong that it was considered indissoluble; and on the basis of this indissolubility, he remained in office until death. Even when he became old and feeble, and required assistance to carry out his duties, he did not resign and retain some spiritual aspect of his *munus,* but precisely because the *munus* was for life, he and his office were considered inseparable until death. It was only with Paul VI's break with tradition in *Christus Dominus* that some legal fiction was needed to perpetuate the bond between the bishop and his diocese after his compulsory resignation perversely mandated at age 75 in the decree. Indeed, no one has explained how it is that the *munus* remains "for always" for an emeritus bishop in relation to his last diocese over which he held office, but does not remain "for always" in relation to the previous diocese or dioceses where he may have held office before being transferred to his last diocese before resigning: Joseph Ratzinger was the Archbishop of Munich and Freising from 1977 to 1982, but he is not listed as "Bishop Emeritus" of that archdiocese, but the emeritus

---

spouse, would cease to be pope, and could therefore be deposed: "In such a case it should be said of him: *If salt should lose its savour, it is good for nothing but to be cast out and trampled under-foot by men.*" [*Sermo IV De Diversis*] By "cast out", Innocent means "deposed", and by "trampled underfoot by men, "despised by the people": (*mittatur foras,* id est ab officio deponatur: *et conculcetur ab hominibus,* id est a populo contemnatur). Innocent states explicitly that he does not believe God would permit this to happen: *Ego tamen facile non crediderim, ut Deus permitteret Romanum pontificem contra fidem errare: pro quo spiritualiter oravit in Petro:* <*Ego, inquit, pro te rogavi, Petre, etc.* (*Luc.xxii*)>

[521] The first pope that I am aware of who had previously been the bishop of another diocese before his election to the papacy in 882 was Marinus I, who had been the bishop of Caere.

bishops of that archdiocese are Friedrich Wetter and Franz Dietl. Thus, the idea of a *Pope Emeritus* who retains some spiritual aspect of the Petrine *munus* has no basis in Catholic Doctrine or tradition. The Petrine *munus* is exclusive to one man, the reigning Pontiff. A former pope is an emeritus bishop of the diocese of Rome and nothing more. He is a *Bishop Emeritus* because he is still a bishop, but he cannot be a *Pope Emeritus* because a former pope is no longer a pope, but is only a bishop. His *munus* as an emeritus bishop is strictly episcopal because he is still a bishop. It is not *Petrine* because a former pope is no longer the pope, and is therefore incapable of holding anything of the *munus petrinum*. Consequently, **he retains absolutely nothing of the Petrine *munus*,** which is passed on to his successor, integral and indivisible. Thus, if a pope does not totally and simply renounce his *munus,* he remains in office as pope, no matter how much he might intend the *effect* of vacating the office by his act of renouncing only the ministry while retaining some aspect of the *munus*, because only a juridical act which renounces the *munus* can have the effect of vacating the office. To vacate the papal office, the object of a valid resignation must be the renouncing of the *munus*, as is stated in Canon 332 § 2. This act has the *effect* of vacating the office. If the act renounces only the *ministry* but **with the intention to retain some aspect of the *munus*,** then the *munus* is not renounced and the office is not vacated. This is the nullifying *defect* in Benedict XVI's act of renunciation; founded on the invalidating *substantial error* (Canon 188) which is patent in the act of renunciation. This is what I explained briefly in my recent interview on rivelazione.net to Samuel Colombo:

> The head of the Church, and representative of Christ on earth remains until now Pope Benedict XVI. As recently as last year, he speaks of still having the spiritual function of his *munus* (Auftrag) which he received from Christ when he was elected to the papacy. He has referred to himself as the pope of prayer, and Bergoglio as the pope of action. There can be only one pope who possesses the entire Petrine *munus* exclusively, because there can be only one pope, and the whole *munus* is his, with the primacy that is included in it. A diocesan bishop can become a Bishop Emeritus because even after he relinquishes his power of governance, he is still a bishop, so he still has the general episcopal *munus* of a successor of the apostles. A former pope is no longer a successor of Peter as head of the Church. He cannot be a Pope Emeritus because

his *munus* is no longer Petrine, but after his renunciation, his *munus* is not Petrine but only episcopal, like all other bishops. So, a pope who renounces his *munus* cannot be a Pope Emeritus. If he did not renounce his papal *munus* entirely and unconditionally, then he retains the entire *munus* and continues in his office with the universal primacy over the whole Church. The fact that Benedict expressly stated his intention to renounce the ministry but retain the spiritual aspect of the papal *munus* proves that he did not renounce the *munus* unconditionally and totally. Such a qualified renunciation is invalid, because the renunciation of an office does not admit of any degree, but is all or nothing. The Petrine *munus* does not in any way admit a reduced form or a lower degree. Like marriage: You cannot be married to a degree but not totally. It's all or nothing. The one individual who is the pope is the sole and exclusive holder of the Petrine *munus*. Benedict XVI did not totally renounce it, but made a qualified and therefore invalid renunciation of the Petrine *munus*. He still thinks it was valid. His thinking it valid does not make it valid. Only a total and unconditional renunciation would be valid. A conditional renunciation cannot effect the vacating of the office, even if Benedict thinks it does. That is a nullifying *substantial error* (canon 188).

* * *

The defective nature of Pope Benedict's act of renunciation was already evident in his mode of expressing his decision to renounce his exercise of his active ministry as pope, clearly distinguishing between the *ministerium* and the *munus*. This distinction was already clearly expressed in his *Declaratio* of renunciation in which he declared, "*Conscientia mea iterum atque iterum coram Deo explorata ad cognitionem certam perveni vires meas ingravescente aetate non iam aptas esse ad munus Petrinum aeque administrandum.*" [I have come to the certainty that my strengths, due to an advanced age, are no longer suited to an adequate exercise of the Petrine **munus**.] He clearly states here that the aging process has rendered him unfit to **administer** the duties of his *munus*. Since he is here referring to duties of administration, it is patent that he employs here the term *munus* according to its strict sense in canon law which defines an **office** as a stable *munus*.[522] He speaks of official administrative duties, and mentions specifically **his incapacity to exercise the active ministry to govern and teach**: *"Attamen in mundo nostri temporis rapidis mutationibus subiecto et quaestionibus magni ponderis pro vita fidei perturbato ad navem Sancti Petri gubernandam et ad annuntiandum Evangelium etiam vigor quidam corporis et animae necessarius est, qui ultimis mensibus in me modo tali minuitur, ut incapacitatem meam ad ministerium mihi commissum bene administrandum agnoscere debeam."* [However, in today's world, subject to so many rapid changes and shaken by questions of deep relevance for the life of faith, in order to govern the barque of Saint Peter and proclaim the Gospel, both strength of mind and body are necessary, strength which in the last few months, has deteriorated in me to the extent that I have had to recognize my incapacity to adequately fulfill the ***ministry*** entrusted to me.] However, he explains that the nature of the papal *munus* is **essentially spiritual**, and therefore is not exercised only by the administrative duties of words and actions, but no less by prayer and suffering: *"Bene conscius sum hoc munus secundum suam essentiam spiritualem non solum agendo et loquendo exsequi debere, sed non minus patiendo et orando."* [I am well aware that this ***munus***, due to its essential spiritual nature, must be ***carried out not only with words and deeds, but no less with prayer and suffering***.] But since Benedict considers this passive aspect of the Petrine *munus* **irrevocable**, he prefaced his renunciation by carefully distinguishing between the *munus* and the *ministerium*. And, in the next sentence he declares his intention to renounce not the *munus* but the *ministerium*: *"Quapropter bene conscius ponderis huius actus plena libertate declaro me ministerio Episcopi Romae, Successoris Sancti Petri, mihi per manus Cardinalium die 19 aprilis MMV commisso renuntiare ita ut a die 28 februarii MMXIII, hora 20, sedes Romae, sedes Sancti Petri vacet et Conclave ad eligendum novum Summum Pontificem ab his quibus competit convocandum esse."* [For this reason, and well aware of the seriousness of this act, with full freedom I declare that I renounce the ***ministry*** of Bishop of Rome, Successor of Saint Peter, entrusted to me by the Cardinals on 19 April 2005, in such a way, that as from 28 February

---

[522] «**Can. 145** — § 1. Officium ecclesiasticum est quodlibet munus ordinatione sive divina sive ecclesiastica stabiliter constitutum in finem spiritualem exercendum.»

2013, at 20:00 hours, the See of Rome, the See of Saint Peter, will be vacant and a Conclave to elect the new Supreme Pontiff will have to be convoked by those whose competence it is.] Prof. Violi explains the rationale for Benedict's renunciation of the **ministry** but not of the *munus*: "Benedict XVI declared his renunciation of the Petrine ministry. Concerning the dictate of the canon, however, he declared his renunciation not of the office but of its administration. A renunciation limited to the active exercise of the *munus* constitutes the absolute novelty of the resignation of Benedict XVI [...] Benedict XVI exercised the fullness of power by depriving himself of all the power inherent to his office... without however abandoning his service to the Church; this continues through the exercise of the most eminently spiritual dimension inherent to the *munus* entrusted to him, which he did not intend to renounce."[523] Thus the intention he expressed in his *Declaratio* to renounce the **ministry** but not the *munus* becomes clearly intelligible, and if there were any doubt about his meaning, he expressed again that intention fifteen days later in his final public audience on 27 February 2013: «Here allow me to return once again to April 19, 2005. The seriousness of the decision was also in the fact that from that moment on I was always and forever committed by the Lord. Always [...] The "always" is also a "forever" – there is no longer a return to the private. My decision to renounce the active exercise of the ministry does not revoke this.» Since a precise understanding of his meaning requires a careful consideration of the words he used to express his intention, we must look to the words in the original language he spoke to express that intention:

---

[523] Stefano Violi, *Facoltà Teologica dell'Emilia Romagna — Facoltà di Teologia (Lugano)*; **La rinuncia di Bernedetto XVI. Tra storia, diritto e coscienza**; in *Rivista Teologica di Lugano* (2/2013) — «Benedetto XVI dichiarava la sua rinuncia al ministero petrino. Rispetto al dettato del canone però dichiarava di rinunciare non già all'ufficio ma alla sua amministrazione. La rinuncia limitata all'esercizio attivo del munus costituisce la novità assoluta della rinuncia di Benedetto XVI. [...] Benedetto XVI ha esercitato la pienezza del potere privandosi di tutte le potestà inerenti il suo ufficio, per il bene della Chiesa, senza però abbandonare il servizio alla Chiesa; questo continua mediante l'esercizio della dimensione più eminentemente spirituale inerente al *munus* affidatogli, al quale non ha inteso rinunciare.» [http://chiesa.espresso.repubblica.it/articolo/1350913]

«Qui permettetemi di tornare ancora una volta al 19 aprile 2005. La gravità della decisione è stata proprio anche nel fatto che da quel momento in poi ero *impegnato* sempre e per sempre dal Signore. Sempre [...] Il "sempre" è anche un "per sempre" – non c'è più un ritornare nel privato. La mia decisione di rinunciare all'esercizio attivo del ministero, non revoca questo.» He says from the moment he made the decision to accept the papal *munus* on April 19, 2005, "I was always and forever committed by the Lord." His words, spoken in Italian were, "da quel momento in poi ero *impegnato* sempre e per sempre dal Signore." So, he says, by accepting his election to the papacy, he was **committed** (impegnato); and this **commitment** he received upon his election to the papacy is for **always**, and is **not revoked by his decision to renounce the active ministry**: "The "always" is also a "forever" — there is no longer a return to the private. My decision to renounce the active exercise of the ministry does not revoke this."

One is **committed** (impegnato) in virtue of having received a **commitment** (impegno), which in Latin is expressed by the word *munus*. In German, the precise equivalent for *munus* as it is used in this context is is *Auftrag*. He stated that his *munus* was "for always", and his decision to renounce the active ministry does not revoke his *munus*. His most recent affirmation of this position, was published in his new biography *Benedikt XVI — Ein Leben,* by Peter Seewald. He was asked to respond to the question, «Cardinal Raymond Burke, one of the four "Dubia" authors who formulated doubts about the papal text "Amoris laetitia", said in November 2016 that "Amoris laetita" had created confusion: "There has been a terrible split in the Church, and that is not the way of the Church." Pope Francis did not answer the "Dubia". Should he have done it better?»[524] Benedict's very revealing answer to the question was, "I do not want to take a direct position on the last questions, because this would lead too much into the specifics of the Church government and would therefore leave the spiritual dimension, which alone is still my mandate. (*Auftrag*)" In

---

[524] "Kardinal Raymond Burke, einer der vier »Dubia«-Autoren, die Zweifel am päpstlichen Lehrschreiben »Amoris laetitia« formulierten, erklärte im November 2016, dass »Amoris laetita« Verwirrung geschaffen habe: »Da ist eine fürchterliche Spaltung in die Kirche geraten, und das ist nicht der Weg der Kirche.« Papst Franziskus hat auf die »Dubia« nicht geantwortet. Hätte er das besser tun sollen?"

his own words spoken in German, «Zu den letzten Fragen möchte ich nicht direkt Stellung nehmen, weil dies zu sehr ins Konkrete der Kirchenregierung hineinführt und damit die spirituelle Dimension verlassen würde, die allein noch mein Auftrag ist.» The German word he used is *Auftrag*, which means, assignment, mandate, duty — and in Latin it is expressed by the word *munus*. So in May of 2020 he speaks of still having this *munus* which he received at the moment he became pope, as he had explained on 27 February 2013; and he leaves absolutely no doubt as to his meaning, because he explicitly referred back to that very statement he made in his last public audience: "I can therefore only refer to what I said in my last general audience on February 27, 2013."[525] As noted above, it was in that last general audience that he spoke of having been "committed by the Lord" upon being elected pope. Now to express "committed" in Italian, he used the word "impegnato", which in German is *beauftragt* or *verpflichtet*. The *commitment* itself with which one is committed is in Italian, *impegno,* and in German is *Pflicht* or *Auftrag*, which in Latin is expressed by the word *munus*. Benedict XVI has reiterated in Peter Seewald's biography published a few weeks ago (as of this writing) in the clearest and unequivocal terms, that the *munus* he received from the Lord upon his election to the papacy has not been revoked by his renunciation of his active exercise of the ministry and still remains with him; and clearly it was for this reason that he carefully distinguished between *munus* and *ministerium* at the beginning of his *Declaratio* of renunciation, and then declared his renunciation not of his Petrine *munus* but of the *ministerium*. If he had renounced his Petrine *munus* he would have vacated the Chair of Peter — vacating the papal **office** while retaining his episcopal *munus*; thus he would be an emeritus bishop. Expressly renouncing not his Petrine *munus,* but only the exercise of the power of governance he says, "I no longer bear the power of office for the governance of the Church, but in the service of prayer I remain, so to speak, in the enclosure of Saint Peter".[526] The act expressly intended to renounce the power of

---

[525] «Ich kann daher nur auf das verweisen, was ich in meiner letzten öffentlichen Generalaudienz am 27. Februar 2013 gesagt habe.»

[526] «Non porto più la potestà dell'officio per il governo della Chiesa, ma nel servizio della preghiera resto, per così dire, nel recinto di san Pietro.»

governance only, but not the *munus* he received upon his election. Since the expressed **object** of the act of renunciation was not the *munus* itself, but only the activity connected with it, namely, the *ministerium,* i.e. the *exercise* of "power of governance", the subjectively intended *effect* of the act to vacate the office, and to thereby vacate the Chair of Peter and forfeit the power of governance is not brought about.[527] That can only be validly brought about by renouncing the *munus* itself. The object of a valid papal renunciation must be the *munus* itself, and not merely the ministerial activity connected with it. The act of renunciation was **null and void**, so that Benedict XVI remains in office the only legitimate pope of the Catholic Church. Benedict remains in office in spite of the defectively expressed intention to **effect** the vacating the office by his renunciation of his ministry but not his office. Only by expressly and unconditionally renouncing the *munus* he received from Christ upon his acceptance of his papal election, would the act have the effect of vacating the office and the forfeiture of the *full and supreme jurisdiction* of that office. What Prof. Violi's analysis of the term *munus* and of Pope Benedict's use of that term in his act of renunciation actually proves is that by renouncing his ministry, even if by renouncing the ministry he intended to renounce the office, the office is not vacated, because Benedict clearly expressed his intention to retain in some manner his *munus* while intending by that qualified act the forfeiture of the office and its jurisdiction. By qualifying the act in this manner, he nullified the act and thereby rendered it incapable of any valid juridical effect. The *sine qua non* condition for a valid resignation of the papal office is a rightly expressed intention to renounce the *munus*: "Canon 332 § 2 — Si contingat ut Romanus Pontifex **muneri suo** renuntiet, **ad validitatem** requiritur ut renuntiatio libere fiat et **rite manifestetur,**

---

[527] The distinction between intending the **object**, as opposed to intending the **effect** of an act is most clearly illustrated in the administration of the sacraments. A person who has the intention of baptising might even be an atheist, who has no intention to effect the forgiveness of sins by the sacrament he administers, but because he intends to baptise, the effect of the sacrament is the remission of sins, even if the minister does not intend this effect.

non vero ut a quopiam acceptetur."⁵²⁸ "**Canon 126 — Actus positus ex ignorantia aut ex errore, qui versetur circa id quod eius substantiam constituit, aut qui recidit in condicionem *sine qua non*, irritus est...**".⁵²⁹

It must also be asked, "Why did Pope Benedict renounce his office in such an unorthodox manner that rendered his act invalid?" Benedict provides us with some insight on this question in his reply to Seewald's question: «One sentence from the sermon on your inauguration was particularly remembered: "Pray for me that I will not flee fearfully from the wolves." Did you foresee what else would happen to you?» Benedict replied, «But the real threat to the Church and thus to the Petrine service lies not in these things, but in the worldwide dictatorship of apparently humanistic ideologies, which contradicting means exclusion from the basic social consensus. A hundred years ago, anyone would have thought it absurd to speak of homosexual marriage. Today, anyone who opposes this is socially excommunicated. The same applies to abortion and the production of people in the laboratory. Modern society is in the process of formulating an anti-Christian creed, which to resist against is punished with social excommunication. **The fear of this spiritual power of the Antichrist is then all too natural and it really takes the prayer help of an entire diocese and the world Church to resist it.**»⁵³⁰ Pope Benedict is no coward, and it was not out of

---

⁵²⁸ »§ 2. If it should happen that the Roman Pontiff renounces his *munus*, it is required for validity that the resignation be freely made and rightly manifested, but not that it is accepted by anyone.»

⁵²⁹ «Canon 126 — The act done by ignorance is null or by mistake when it affects what constitutes its substance or falls on a sine qua non condition...»

⁵³⁰ «Aber die eigentliche Bedrohung der Kirche und somit des Petrusdienstes liegt nicht in diesen Dingen, sondern in der weltweiten Diktatur von scheinbar humanistischen Ideologien, denen zu widersprechen den Ausschluss aus dem gesellschaftlichen Grundkonsens bedeutet. Vor hundert Jahren hätte es noch jedermann für absurd gehalten, von homosexueller Ehe zu sprechen. Heute ist gesellschaftlich exkommuniziert, wer sich dem entgegenstellt. Ähnliches gilt bei Abtreibung und für die Herstellung von Menschen im Labor. Die moderne Gesellschaft ist dabei, ein antichristliches Credo zu formulieren, dem sich zu widersetzen

cowardly fear that he fled from the wolves. Although he was not forced to resign, he was in a real sense of the word, **driven out by the wolves.** In October 2008 I related to the late Mons. Mario Marini, Secretary of the Pontifical Commission «*Ecclesia Dei*», that a priest who personally knew Pope Benedict explained to me that Benedict faced a formidable resistance from within the Church and the Curia to his efforts to govern the Church according to the law of God. In the spring of 1996 Don Marini had already told me, "Our hands are tied. We can do nothing, because it is the Masons who occupy the key positions." In my last meeting with him in October 2008, Don Mario said, "We are under Masonic occupation." He added that the strong resistance was not only within the Curia but was especially fierce in the French hierarchy, and he showed me a book in French which contained some relevant documentation concerning that matter. Subsequently the revelations of Cardinal Daneels made it quite clear that the resistance was not limited to the French hierarchy, but included the hierarchies of the Low Countries and German speaking hierarchies as well. Pope Benedict was not forced to resign, but was worn down by the constant collective resistance of prelates who owed him obedience and loyalty. In this context it is not difficult to grasp his meaning when he said, "But I knew I had to do it and that this was the right moment. Without this, I would also die and my pontificate would end."[531] So it seems clear enough that he was worn down by the resistance of faithless traitors until he finally gave up the ghost and resigned — but he resigned invalidly. By providential design, Benedict XVI remains to this day as the true pope. Jorge Bergoglio is an invalid intruder — an antipope — Antipope Francis.

---

mit gesellschaftlicher Exkommunikation bestraft wird. Die Furcht vor dieser geistigen Macht des Antichrist ist dann nur allzu natürlich, und es braucht wirklich der Gebetshilfe eines ganzen Bistums und der Weltkirche, um ihr zu widerstehen.»

[531] «Aber mir war klar, dass ich es tun musste und dass dies der richtige Augenblick war. Ohnedies würde ich auch sterben und mein Pontifikat enden.»

JUDGMENT

JORGE MARIO BERGOGLIO: HERETIC — INCAPABLE SUBJECT OF THE PAPACY

— WHO AM I TO JUDGE —

Many times in the last eight years I have expressed my own personal opinion that Jorge Mario Bergoglio is not and has never been the pope of the Roman Catholic Church on the basis that as a heretic, Bergoglio is an *incapable subject of the papacy*. The most commonly voiced objection to this personal belief (usually pronounced in an indignant tone) is, "You don't have the authority to judge!" The hugeness of the number of theologically semi-literate Catholics who make this objection confirm the truth of the scriptural proverb: "*Stultorum infinitus est numerus*." (Ecc. 1:15) I have explained in the first part to this volume what constitutes the essence of a proper *judicial* judgment, as opposed to the *mere* judgment of the mind. I speak tongue-in-cheek of the *mere* judgment of the mind, because without the judgment of the mind as the foundation of judicial judgment, there cannot even exist a true *judicial judgment*. In the judicial forum a pronounced *sententia* or verdict of the court is a **judgment.** Before the *sententia* is pronounced, it is an *opinion*. As an opinion it lacks juridical force. To be properly a *judgment* it must, 1) be pronounced by one who has judicial authority, and, 2) it must proceed from **knowledge of the cause** (as Ballerini pointed out in the cited passage), for which reason the *sententia* must proceed from factual evidence which establishes probable cause, and from there one arrives at a *judgment* of guilt beyond reasonable doubt. Without this **knowledge of the cause**, there cannot exist a true judgment in the judicial forum, because the purpose of the judicial process is to begin from what is suspected, and therefore merely believed or presumed, and to arrive at the truth by the process of reason, by which knowledge of the truth is reached through the discursive process of inquiry and discovery. Hence, the truth is arrived at by the process of reason which is terminated by an act of judgment, because judgment is an act of reason by which the mind arrives at an affirmation of the truth, and therefore judgment is properly a conclusion based on that which is known and not merely believed without factual evidence. It is for this reason that a judge (or a jury) who pronounces a judgment of guilt solely on the basis of *belief* in the presumed *credibility* of an accuser, but without any factual evidence constituting *knowledge of the cause*, without which a judicial judgment cannot consist, commits an act of perjury (as is explained below) and not an act of judgment or justice, because the judicial process is ordered to the end of rendering justice by a judgment of truth based on certain facts. It is patent therefore that judgment of truth can only be reached if it is founded on certain knowledge of facts, and not by judgment of mere *opinion* based not on knowledge of facts but on human faith alone.

The object of judicial judgment is the **truth** understood by the intellect moved to assent by grasping the causal relation between evidence and crime, and thus *judged to be true*, for which reason mere *belief*, (i.e. belief in the sense of an act of human faith not founded on factual evidence), that something is true does not constitute judicial judgment, since belief is a matter of *opinion* of things which are *believed* to be true, but not *understood* to be true on the basis of known facts, and therefore judged to be true. When the judgment proceeds from knowledge of the cause, there is **judgment** properly so called because it is founded knowledge of what is prior and certain. When the object of judgment is not certain as proceeding from knowledge of the cause, then what properly is judgment is lacking, and there is only unsubstantiated **opinion**. In the section on faith in *Secunda Secundæ* St. Thomas elaborates the distinctions between intellection and reasoning, knowledge and opinion; and what is believed by the virtue of faith:

> Faith imports assent of the intellect to that which is believed. Now the intellect assents to a thing in two ways. In one way, through being moved to assent by the object itself, which is known either by itself, as it is with the first principles, which are known by intellective understanding; or through something else already known, as it is with conclusions of which are knowledge. In the other way the intellect assents to something, not through being sufficiently moved to this assent by its proper object, but through a voluntary selection, whereby it turns to one side rather than to the other: and at any rate if this be done with doubt or fear of the other side, there will be opinion, while, if it be done with certitude without such fear, there will be faith. But those things are said to be seen which, by themselves, move our intellect or senses to

knowledge of them. Wherefore it is manifest that neither faith nor opinion can be of things seen either by the senses or by the intellect.[532]

Since the end itself of the judicial process is to begin from what is suspected, and is as yet a matter of opinion which is merely believed or presumed; and to arrive at the truth by the process of reason — judges, jurors, witnesses, and officers of the court are sworn under oath to fulfil their designated functions to this end which is truth and justice obtained through judgment. It is according to the very nature of the oath that it is ordered to this end: "What pertains to the end, the oath reaches for and entirely endeavours only to prove human justice and innocence, to close disputes and controversies, as the Apostle teaches in his letter to the Hebrews (Heb 6:16)."[533] This end is not achieved by terminating the process where it started — with mere belief, opinion, and presumption of credibility; but by arriving at justice through true judgment, for which purpose the oath is made:

> With certainty, for an oath to be made it is enough to call God as a witness, but in order for it to be just and holy, several other things are required which must be carefully explained. As Saint Jerome attests, Jeremiah briefly enumerates them, when he says: "I will swear, as the Lord lives, in truth, in judgment, and in justice "(Jer. 4:2). With these

---

[532] *II*ᵃ*II*ᵃ q. 1 a. 4 s. c. — «Respondeo dicendum quod fides importat assensum intellectus ad id quod creditur. Assentit autem alicui intellectus dupliciter. Uno modo, quia ad hoc movetur ab ipso obiecto, quod est vel per seipsum cognitum, sicut patet in principiis primis, quorum est intellectus; vel est per aliud cognitum, sicut patet de conclusionibus, quarum est scientia. Alio modo intellectus assentit alicui non quia sufficienter moveatur ab obiecto proprio, sed per quandam electionem voluntarie declinans in unam partem magis quam in aliam. Et si quidem hoc fit cum dubitatione et formidine alterius partis, erit opinio, si autem fit cum certitudine absque tali formidine, erit fides. Illa autem videri dicuntur quae per seipsa movent intellectum nostrum vel sensum ad sui cognitionem. Unde manifestum est quod nec fides nec opinio potest esse de visis aut secundum sensum aut secundum intellectum.»

[533] *Catechismus Romanus ex decreto concilii tridentini* — «Quod vero ad finem attinet, eo tendit iusiurandum atque id omnino spectat, ut hominis iustitiam et innocentiam probet, finemque litibus et controversiis imponat; quod etiam Apostolus in epistola ad Hebraeos docet.»

very words he summarized the components of which the complete perfection of an oath is comprised, truth, judgment, and justice.[534]

Justice therefore requires that whoever takes the oath, whether to give testimony as a witness or to render a judgment, may not offer a mere opinion, no matter how firmly believed, but must judge justly according to what is known to be true: "Indisputably the truth has the first place in an oath, insofar as the sworn assertion must itself be true, and who states it must judge it to be such, not by a light or rash conjecture, but by the force of the most certain proofs."[535] Unless judgment is reached *by the force of the most certain proofs*, the entire judicial process is subverted, and the judges and jurors who judge not on the basis of certain proofs, but on the basis of a mere belief in the credibility of an accusation, pervert the course of justice, and in so doing, perjure themselves:

> **Similarly one perjures himself who affirms with an oath something that he considers true, but which is false; unless to the extent that he is able, has applied all solicitude and diligence necessary for the entire matter to be verified and found out. For however much there is agreement between word and thought, he is guilty against this precept nevertheless.**[536]

---

[534] *Catechismus Romanus ex decreto concilii tridentini* — «Verum enimvero, licet ad iusiurandum satis sit Deum testem adhibere, tamen, ut rectum sanctumque sit, multo plura requiruntur, quae sunt diligenter explicanda. Ea vero breviter, teste divo Hieronymo, Ieremias enumerat, dum inquit: Iurabis, vivit Dominus, in veritate, et in iudicio, et in iustitia. Quibus sane verbis illa breviter summatimque complexus est, quibus omnis iurisiurandi perfectio continetur, veritatem, inquam, iudicium et iustitiam.»

[535] *Catechismus Romanus ex decreto concilii tridentini* – «Primum itaque in iureiurando locum veritas habet, nimirum ut quod asseritur, et ipsum verum sit, et qui iurat id ita esse arbitretur, non quidem temere aut levi coniectura adductus, sed certissimis argumentis.»

[536] *Catechismus Romanus ex decreto concilii tridentini* – «Simili quoque ratione peierat qui id iurat quod verum existimat, et tamen re vera falsum est; nisi, quantum potuit, curam et diligentiam adhibuerit, ut totam rem compertam atque exploratam haberet. Quamvis enim ipsius oratio menti consentiat, tamen huius praecepti reus est.»

It is therefore contrary to the very nature of judgment that a mere belief be offered in place of proper judgment, but as justice requires, judgment must be rendered accordingly as judgment is defined: "Judgment properly so called is delivered when one pronounces a sentence based on knowledge of the cause". It was to this end that the most basic rules of law regarding judgments of guilt or innocence were formulated. The sixth-century Digest of Justinian (22.3.2) provided the general rule of evidence which was introduced in Roman criminal law by emperor Antoninus Pius: "Ei incumbit probatio qui dicit, non qui negat" (Proof is incumbent upon him who asserts, not on him who denies). On this principle of natural justice is based the rule of the presumption of innocence, originally formulated in the early fourteenth century by the French cardinal and jurist Jean Lemoine: "item quilbet presumitur innocens nisi probetur nocens" (a person is presumed innocent until proven guilty)". Only then is the divine commandment fulfilled: "Judge not according to the appearance, but judge just judgment." (John 7:4)

Judicial judgment can only be pronounced in the judicial forum by one who possesses jurisdiction, but since it is itself founded upon and is preceded by the rational judgment which proceeds from the natural power of the intellect, there cannot even exist judicial judgment without the exercise of the natural power of reason common to all men by which judicial judgment is reached. St. Thomas explains:

> For to understand is simply to apprehend intelligible truth: and to reason is to proceed from one thing understood to another, so as to know an intelligible truth… But man arrives at the knowledge of intelligible truth by proceeding from one thing to another; and therefore he is called rational. It is evident therefore that reasoning is compared to understanding, as movement is to rest, or acquisition to possession; of which one belongs to the perfect, the other to the imperfect. And since motion always proceeds from something immovable, and ends in something at rest; hence it is that human reasoning, by way of inquiry and discovery, proceeds from certain things simply understood, which are the first principles; and, again, by way of judgment, returns by means

of resolving, to the first principles, in the light of which it examines what it has found."[537]

Thus it is, that judicial judgment depends entirely upon the rational power to arrive at the truth and grasp it with the understanding of the intellect. The judicial power requires authority. The power to reason and understand is a natural power of the intellective faculty to assent to what is known or seen by an act of **judgment**. The absurdity of the objection of those who say, "You have no authority to judge," is patent insofar as they are in effect saying, "You have no authority to understand," — as if one were in need of permission from someone in authority to assent to a truth that is known by the natural power of the intellective faculty. This is precisely the absurdity of Salza and Siscoe who scream in reply to my position on this point, which is that it is a right in natural law to assent to the known truth, by making me out to be some sort of reincarnation of Martin Luther, who pronounces "private judgment against the public judgment of the Church". The irony of their position is that it is precisely a definitive public judgment of the supreme authority of the Church to settle this specific question once and for all which is lacking at the present time. For now there is confusion in the minds of many, since there is one claimant of the Petrine *munus* who calls himself "Pope Emeritus" and another claimant of the Petrine *munus* who calls himself "Bishop of Rome". The present situation has created doubt in the minds of many, and is for a great number of confused Catholics exactly as Melanie of La Salette foretold, so that it can be said by them, that until the

---

[537] *Summa Theol.* Iª q. 79 a. 8 — «Intelligere enim est simpliciter veritatem intelligibilem apprehendere. Ratiocinari autem est procedere de uno intellecto ad aliud, ad veritatem intelligibilem cognoscendam... Homines autem ad intelligibilem veritatem cognoscendam perveniunt, procedendo de uno ad aliud, ut ibidem dicitur, et ideo rationales dicuntur. Patet ergo quod ratiocinari comparatur ad intelligere sicut moveri ad quiescere, vel acquirere ad habere, quorum unum est perfecti, aliud autem imperfecti. Et quia motus semper ab immobili procedit, et ad aliquid quietum terminatur; inde est quod ratiocinatio humana, secundum viam inquisitionis vel inventionis, procedit a quibusdam simpliciter intellectis, quae sunt prima principia; et rursus, in via iudicii, resolvendo redit ad prima principia, ad quae inventa examinat.»

question of which single individual of the claimants holds the Petrine *munus* will be authoritatively judged with finality, "*we will not know which is the true pope.*"

THE COUNTERFEIT POPE

> "In principle, the Pope is the foundation of unity, an everlasting principle."
> — Cardinal Gerhard Ludwig Müller —

For a man to be capable of receiving the form of the pontificate, he must himself visibly represent in his person the form of the Church, which is the orthodox profession of the Catholic faith. In one respect, a man is constituted as a pope in a similar manner as is a secular head of state. A secular president becomes the head of state when the legal requirements of his election or appointment are fulfilled. Even if they appear to have been fulfilled, if it is later found out that he was ineligible for the office, his administration can simply be annulled by the nation's supreme court. Even if the man would be elected in conformity with all the election laws, if he were later found out to be an foreign citizen of a hostile power, his election would simply be quashed, because he would be an *incapable subject*. It would not matter if his citizenship papers had been issued in good faith by the authorities: if the application for citizenship was invalid, then he was never a citizen in the first place; and as an alien, he would be incapable of assuming the office. A man cannot represent a nation as its head if he is a non-citizen, who is not a member of that nation but an alien citizen of an enemy nation. Likewise, a baptized and validly ordained bishop is incapable of representing the Church and her unity as pope and head, if by his public heresy, he represents that which opposes the faith of the Church. Such a one lacks the necessary disposition to receive the form of the pontificate since the unity of the Church is founded principally on the unity of faith. This is why Pope Gregory XVI, in the earlier cited passage explained the reason why a heretic cannot validly be pope, saying: «Now it is clear that if there were not in the Church and in the Pope the sameness of spirit, of feelings and of doctrines, there could not be in the latter the true representation of the former. Therefore the Pontiff cannot represent the Church, who together does not necessarily represent her unity.»

Unlike a secular head of state who becomes the head of state merely by compliance with applicable laws, what makes a man a pope is the metaphysical conjunction of the *form* with the matter, in a manner like that of a man, who is constituted of matter and form: the matter is the body; and the *form* is the rational soul. The pope is the composite of matter and form: the man is the matter conjoined to the papacy which is the form. It is in virtue of the form that a man is constituted and recognizable as a man, and is able to function accordingly; and similarly, it is in virtue of the form of the pontificate that a man is constituted and recognizable as the pope, and can validly perform the operations proper to the papacy. If there is not the same faith in the pope as in the Church, the man is an incapable subject of the papacy, because he cannot represent the unity of faith in the Church if he professes himself opposed to any article of faith. Just as the matter must have the necessary disposition of a physical-organic body to be united to the form for a man to come into being, similarly; the man who is the matter of the papacy must have the necessary disposition which is faith, to receive and conserve the form of the pontificate and thereby be constituted as a pope. Faith is the necessary disposition for a man to be pope, as Bellarmine explained, because the form of the Church consists and is seen in the profession of faith, and the form of the pontificate is recognizable in the pope's functional representation of safeguarding and confirming the Church's unity in his profession of the integral Catholic faith. It is for this reason, that the papacy differs from a secular headship of state, insofar as a citizen who is a Communist, who represents all that opposes the interests and values of the republic, if he would be lawfully elected president, he would be legally constituted as the president of the republic. There is no conjunction of matter and form required for a man to be constituted as president of a republic, but the only requirement would be that the letter of the law be observed — it is a purely legal matter for a man to be the president of a republic, because it is entirely by the formalities of law that he is constituted as president. On the other hand, if a heretic would even be otherwise canonically elected pope according to all the formalities of law, he would not be a valid pope, because he would lack the necessary disposition of being united to the Church by the bond of faith, which is necessary for the reception of the form of the pontificate in his person. This is the principle that underlies the earlier mentioned ruling of Paul IV on the invalidity of a heretic's election, and it is the reason why God would not permit a heretic to be canonically elevated to the papacy. Therefore, just as a man dies by the separation of the form from the matter when the matter lacks the disposition to preserve the union of body and soul; so likewise the pope, independently of anyone else's judgment, would cease by himself to be pope straightaway if the necessary disposition to maintain his conjunction with the form of the pontificate, would be removed. That necessary disposition for the matter and form of the papacy to be united, so that a man becomes pope; and for the union of the matter and form to be conserved in him so that he remains pope, is faith. Without faith, it is also impossible for a man to function infallibly as pope with the grace of office, because "each thing acts through its form, from which the thing has a certain being".[538] This is why Bellarmine said that faith is necessary *simpliciter*, for one to be pope, and not merely *ad bene esse*. It is by means of the specific operations acting through the form of the pontificate, visible in the person of the pope, that the pope is seen, in the words of Cardinal Müller, as "the foundation of unity, an everlasting principle". It is through the form that the papacy becomes intelligible in the person of the pope: "Nothing is intelligible according to that it is in potency, but according to that it is in act, as is said in IX Metaph. Whence, since the possible intellect is in potency only in relation to intelligible being, it cannot be understood unless through its form which becomes by act, which is the species abstracted from phantasms; *and every other thing is understood by its form*."[539]

---

[538] *Summa Contra Gentiles*, lib. 1 cap. 68 n. 3 — «cum **res quaelibet operetur per suam formam**, a qua est aliquod esse rei, oportet… etc.»

[539] *Quaestiones disputatae, De anima, Quaestio sexta decima* — «Ad octavum dicendum quod intellectus possibilis noster intelligit seipsum non directe apprehendendo essentiam suam, sed per speciem a phantasmatibus acceptam. Unde philosophus dicit in III de anima quod intellectus possibilis est intelligibilis sicut et alia. Et hoc ideo est, quia **nihil est intelligibile secundum quod est in potentia, sed secundum quod est actu, ut dicitur in IX Metaph. Unde, cum intellectus possibilis sit in potentia tantum in esse intelligibili, non potest intelligi nisi per formam suam per quam fit actu, quae est species a phantasmatibus abstracta; sicut *et quaelibet alia res intelligitur per formam suam*.»

Faith is the foundational principle, and therefore the necessary disposition for those operations specific to the papacy brought about by acts through its form, as is evident from the very nature of the papacy as it is accordingly ordered to its end: 1) "The Catholics teach that what is meant by this metaphor (*on this rock I will build my Church*) is that to Peter was given the rulership of the whole Church, and particularly concerning Faith." (Bellarm. *De Rom. Pont. lib. i cap. xi*); 2) "to the supreme Pontiff, to whom Christ granted the proper authority for the purpose of guarding unity especially in faith," (Ballerini *De Pot. Ecc.* p. 29); 3) "this primacy of special jurisdiction… was instituted by Christ for forming and perpetually guarding unity in the whole Church, the particular right to bind together and guard the unity of the Church" (*De Potestate Ecclesiastica*, Caput I § III. p. 12) Therefore, faith is the necessary disposition for the form of the pontificate to exist in the person who is its matter; for which reason Bellarmine says, "this disposition being removed by the contrary which is heresy, the Pope straightaway ceases to be Pope."[540]

It is ultimately in virtue of the conforming necessary disposition of faith, without which the form of the pontificate cannot exist in the person and constitute him as pope, nor operate in him to bind together the members, and infallibly guard the unity of the Church especially in matters of faith, that the existence of form of the papacy is confirmed to exist in the pope through its operation, as a habit inhering in the pope, who can thus be known with certitude and

---

[540] *De Rom. Pont. Lib. ii cap. xxx* — «*ista dispositione sublata per contrariam quæ est hæresis, mox Papa desinit esse.*» For nearly five years I have explained to Salza & Siscoe, that it is not a matter of law but of the nature of heresy; referring them to the passages where Bellarmine says it is not by any human law, but *ex natura hæresis* that the office is lost; and that the pope would cease by himself to be pope, without the agency of anyone else (*sine alia vi externa*), so I explained to them, "With or without the law, the heretic by the very nature of the sin of heresy ceases to be a Catholic and is incapable of holding office. Bellarmine explains this in De Romano Pontifice." Salza and Siscoe replied: "With this utterly erroneous assertion it does not seem possible that he has even read Bellarmine's De Romano Pontifice." Salza adds, "Fr. Kramer's analysis is one of the more shallow and superficial interpretations of Bellarmine that we have seen… it is difficult to believe that Fr. Kramer has done any real study of St. Bellarmine."

acknowledged by the whole Church to be the successor of Peter, whose faith, in virtue of the promise of Christ, can never fail. Conversely, when the public sin of infidelity is manifestly evident in the heresy of a papal claimant, then it can be seen and recognized as an evident fact that the heretic is **not a true pope, but a counterfeit pope** — and this is so because heresy is directly opposed to the necessary conforming disposition of faith, without which the form of the pontificate cannot exist in the man; so that his obstinate heresy is as unmistakable a sign as a pirate's ensign — signalling not the presence of the successor of Peter on the throne with the crossed keys of the Apostolic See, but manifesting the intruding imposture of the Destroyer of faith with the Skull and Crossbones of treasonous piracy. Jorge Bergoglio is the traitorous bearer of the pirate's ensign of heresy, who would hand over the Mystical Body of Christ to the enemy just as Judas Iscariot physically handed Christ over to His enemies. There cannot be any doubt in this regard, because unlike so many other cases in which there are verified the *indicia* establishing *suspicion of heresy*; in Bergoglio's case, we have before us the plainly manifest *indicia* of formal heresy — *indicia* which plainly exhibit the evident fact of Bergoglio's contumacy in heresy — plainly evident formal heresy which of its very nature renders a man incapable of receiving or conserving the form of the pontificate as a habit united to his person. Thus, it is an evident fact that because of his manifest heresy, Jorge Bergoglio is an *incapable subject of the papacy*.

The necessary disposition, namely faith, which is absolutely necessary for a man to be constituted as pope, is visibly and manifestly absent in the person of Jorge Mario Bergoglio. The man who calls himself Francis is evidently no more capable of functioning as the rock of Catholic unity than was Arius or Nestorius. Bergoglio is no more capable of representing the faith of the Catholic Church than was Martin Luther, who called the Holy Mass an **abomination** — and who Bergoglio singularly admires so much that he has held up Luther as one to be venerated by Christians on 13 October 2016, when he set up the statue of Luther in St. Peter's Square. Factual evidence constituting certain *indicia* of formal heresy have already been presented in Volume One of this work, but for the fact of Bergoglio's proven formal heresy to be recognized as such, it is necessary above all to be cognizant of there being no need for a juridical declaration by the Church for the fact of formal heresy to be recognized as certain, since the fact itself of the formal heresy can be plainly seen immediately as *evidenter verum* in virtue of his stark and explicit denial of the most primary truths of our religion; and from this fact alone it can be concluded with absolute certitude that Bergoglio is not the pope of the Catholic Church, because he is clearly an **infidel**, and therefore an *incapable subject of the papacy*. I will therefore present only a summation of the evidence already presented in Volume One with little addition — evidence which already by itself constitutes clear-cut proof that Bergoglio is an infidel intruder and a usurper who is utterly incapable of occupying the papal office, or any other office of the Catholic Church. To demonstrate this, it is not necessary to show that his magisterial teaching is heretical, or that something he stated in an official document or decree is heretical; but it suffices to show that Bergoglio, as a private person has publicly defected from the Catholic faith into formal heresy:

> "If ever a pope as a **private person** would fall into heresy, then he would immediately fall from the papacy; for since he would be outside the Church, he could no longer be the head of the Church." — St. Alphonsus de' Liguori

As I explained in Volume One, according to the canonical doctrine and universal practice of the Roman Church, heresy is established by the *indicia* of heresy, which are the words and deeds that constitute the evidence of heresy,[541] and according to the *indicia* of heresy, one is either a *formal* heretic, or a *suspected heretic*.[542] A *formal heretic* is one who firmly asserts his disbelief in a certain and defined article of faith, which has been proposed to be believed by all, and which he knows to be such.[543] To be judged a heretic it is not necessary for one to

---

[541] P. Francesco Bordoni, *Sacrum Tribunal Iudicum In Causis Sanctæ Fidei Contra Hæreticos Et Hæresi Suspectos*, p. 223 — «Indicium est signum probativum inducens iudicem in cognitionem delicti… [idest] ex verbis, vel factis.»

[542] *Ibid.* p. 221 — «Hæretici quatum facit ad explicationen huius capitis, sunt in duplici differentia, alii vocantur Formales, alii tantum Suspecti.»

[543] *Ibid.* p. 221 — «Formalis autem hæreticus dicitur ille, qui negavit firmiter, & ex corde aliquem articulum de fide certum, & expresse

explicitly admit to knowing that his opinion is heretical (since heretics usually refuse to admit they are in heresy), but, Fr. Charles Augustine explains, «Obstinacy may be assumed when a revealed truth has been proposed with sufficient clearness and force to convince a reasonable man.»[544] On this point he follows the teaching of the greatest authority in Moral Theology, St. Alphonsus de' Liguori.[545] Such a one is manifestly a formal heretic, and no previous warnings or admonitions are necessary to judge such a one to be guilty of formal heresy once the *indicia* of formal heresy are shown to have been exhibited.[546] They simply fall under the penalty set forth in canon 1364. Heresy is defined in Canon 751 as the "pertinacious post-baptismal denial or pertinacious doubt of some truth which must be believed with divine and Catholic faith".[547] Accordingly, the 1917 code of Canon Law defined what a heretic is in precisely the same terms in Canon 1325 §2 — "After the reception of baptism if one who retains the name of Christian pertinaciously denies or doubts some truth to be believed

---

definitum, quem scit esse talem, ab ecclesia propositum ab omnibus credendum, exprimendum se illum non credere.»

[544] The Rev. P, Chas. Augustine, O.S.B., D.D.; *A COMMENTAY ON THE NEW CODE OF CANON LAW.*, Vol. VI, St. Louis and London, 1921, p. 335.

[545] S. Alphonsus M. De Ligorio, *Theologia Moralis, Lib. II. Tract. I. De præcepto Fidei. Dubium III.* — «pertinaciter errare... est eum [errorem] retinere, postquam contrarium est sufficienter propositum: sive quando scit contrarium teneri a reliqua universali Christi in terris Ecclesia, cui suum iudicium præferat»

[546] P. Francesco Bordoni, *Manuale Consultorum*, p. 35 — «Quaeritur 6. An ad Pertinaciam requiratur praevia monitio... & nihilominus in sua Opinione persistens incipiat tunc esse pertinax, & formalis Haereticus? R. Nullam require monitionem, sed esse Haereticum formaliter hoc ipso, quod aserit aliquo pro vero, quod scit esse contra Fidem, in hoc enim formaliter consistit Pertinacia, quae non datur sine Scientia illius obiecti, contra quod est ipsa Pertinacia, quae includit Scientiam, ergo frustra praemonetur, qui scit se scire illud, cui adversatur; monitio enim fit ignorantibus, non scientibus.»

[547] «Can. 751 — Dicitur hæresis, pertinax, post receptum baptismum, alicuius veritatis divina et catholica credendæ denegatio, aut de eadem pertinax dubitatio.»

with divine and Catholic faith... he is a heretic"[548] The canon makes it clear that even those who still claim to be Catholic, but who pertinaciously deny or doubt any truth which must be believed with divine and Catholic faith are *heretics* who incur the penalty of excommunication. Thus, it will fully suffice to demonstrate that Jorge Bergoglio as a private person has fallen into formal heresy in order to prove that he is not the Pope of Rome and successor of Peter, but a withered and severed member cut off from communion with the Church by his own public acts of defection from the Catholic faith.

In so doing, what is necessary is to simply establish the certain fact of defection from the faith into heresy by showing that the *fact* can be seen as *evidenter verum* — not just a *presumed fact* reasonably believed with a high degree of probability to be a *true fact*, but a *known fact*, known with certitude to be true as something seen and perfectly understood, or so morally certain that there can be no reasonable argument stated in opposition to the fact. It is on the basis of this certain knowledge that the Church can judge that the man, being a heretic, is not the pope — he is not the legitimate spouse of the Roman Church, and for this reason, the Church can then pronounce the union null and void. In making this judgment, the Church is not judging the pope, because the Church cannot judge a validly reigning pope — it does not lie within the power of the pope's inferiors to judge an indubitable pope; and such a judgment, as has been amply proven, would be contrary to the nature of ecclesiastical power as divinely constituted in the Church: The pope judges all and is judged by none, but the Church can judge whether or not a man is truly her legitimate head by discerning whether he is a true pope or not. If he is plainly seen to be a heretic, he is simply not a valid pope. The Church can make this judgment because it is known and recognized that faith pertains essentially to the papal office (Innocent III. *Sermo II, De Diversis*[549]); so that if a man visibly embodies formal *disbelief* in

---

[548] «Can. 1325 §2 — Post receptum baptismum si quis, nomen retinens christianum, pertinaciter aliquam ex veritatibus fide divina et catholica credendis denegat aut de ea dubitat, hæreticus... est.»

[549] Innocentius III, *Sermo II De Diversis* «IN CONSACRATIONE PONTIFICIS MAXIMI» — "Nisi enim ego solidaltus essem in fide, quomodo possem alios in fide firmare? Quod ad officium meum noscitur specialiter pertinere, Domino protestante: «Ego, inquit, pro te rogavi, Petre,

the material object of faith definitively proposed by the ecclesiastical magisterium, the privation of the form of the pontificate will be visible in him; since the form of the pontificate visibly constitutes the pope as the unshakable foundation and centre of unity of the Catholic faith, which is the form of the Church itself, visible in the integral profession of the Catholic faith.

With respect to a pope, the Church can do no more than to judge whether a man is a true and certain pope or an impostor reputed to be pope (even by a vast number), and needs to do no more than that, as the historical actions of the Council of Constance proved. The council did not presume to judge or depose any validly elected pontiff, nor declare that such a one had fallen from the pontificate, but declared deposed the ones who were judged to be illegitimate claimants. So, while the Church has absolutely no power to judge a validly constituted pope for the crime of heresy, the Church can, nevertheless, judge that the *man* is no pope, because of manifestly evident formal heresy; or the Church can judge that he is no pope, according to the dictum, *Papa dubius, papa nullus*; if the positive doubt about his validity cannot be resolved due to his incorrigible persistence in *violent suspicion of heresy*, which renders it morally certain that he is a *formal heretic*. So, 1) he is judged to be no pope if he is manifestly and evidently a formal heretic, according to the definition: *A formal heretic is one who disbelieves expressly and explicitly something which he knows to be against Faith declared by the Church.*[550] And, 2) he is judged to be no pope if he remains incorrigible in *violent suspicion of heresy*. The first, i.e., manifestly evident formal heresy, can be seen by anyone mentally capable of such a judgment, and therefore can be judged accordingly by anyone with that capability. The second, to the extent that the incorrigibility of pertinacity is not always verifiable by all, must await the sentence of the competent ecclesiastical authority — but if it is plainly evident, then it too can be judged by anyone with the mental

---

ut non deficiat fides tua, et tu aliquando conversus, confirma fratres tuos (*Luc*.xxii).»"

[550] Bordoni, *MANUALE CONSULTORUM In Causis S. Officii contra Hæreticum pravitatem*, pp. 34-35: "Formalis Hæreticus est ille, qui discredit aliquid, quod expresse, & explicite scit esse contra Fidem ab Ecclesia declaratum. In hac enim Scientia consistit Pertinacia constituens Hæreticum formalem. Et in hoc omnes convenient nullo contradicente."

capacity to do so, but the private judgment of individuals, as important as it is in regard to universal acceptance or universal rejection, has no juridical force of its own. The vacancy must be juridically declared by the competent authority in order that conclave be lawfully convened to elect a new pope. The declaration does not cause the vacancy any more than a coroner causes a death when he pronounces a person dead. In the case of Jorge Bergoglio it can be seen to be manifestly evident on some points of dogma that he is a formal heretic, and on a multitude of others, he is incorrigibly *violently suspect of heresy*. It is certain, therefore, that Jorge Mario Bergoglio is not the Pope of the Catholic Church, nor the Bishop of Rome, nor the holder of any ecclesiastical office; but he is very much like Pedro de Luna before him, «*a cause of scandal to the universal church, a promoter and breeder of the ancient schism,*[551] *that long established fission and division in God's holy church, an obstructer of the peace and unity of the said church, a schismatic disturber and a heretic, a deviator from the faith, a persistent violator of the article of the faith One holy catholic church, incorrigible, notorious and manifest in his scandal to God's church, and that he has rendered himself unworthy of every title, rank, honour and dignity, rejected and cut off by God, deprived by the law itself of every right in any way belonging to him in the papacy or pertaining to the Roman pontiff and the Roman church, and cut off from the catholic church like a withered member.*» Thus pronounced the Council of Constance against Antipope Benedict XIII, and just such a pronouncement is all that remains to be done by the pastors of the Church against the infidel intruder Jorge Bergoglio, a.k.a. Antipope Francis.

THE FORMAL HERESY OF
JORGE MARIO "FRANCIS" BERGOGLIO

In presenting the evidence of formal heresy against Jorge Bergoglio, it must be borne in mind that the same criteria are uniformly applicable in all cases of heresy: one is judged a heretic according to the *indicia* of heresy as established by canonical tradition and the jurisprudence of the Roman Church, regardless of whether

---

[551] Inevitably Bergoglio, by means of the heretical reforms he is introducing and intends to consummate and make "irreversible," is breeding an even greater schism than the one that existed at the time of the Council of Constance.

the offender is a reputed pope or a mere pauper. It is on this point that there has been a major failing on the part of the cardinals who presented Bergoglio with the *Dubia*,[552] as well as the authors of the *Correctio filialis de haeresibus propagatis*.[553] While it is understood as given that **all** the writings and discourses of suspect theologians are to be examined for heretical content and submitted for judgment, in Bergoglio's case, the vastly greater portion of his writings and discourses have been summarily shoved aside and ignored, while all examination has been almost exclusively focused on his official documents and pronouncement; with the result that the most conclusive evidence has been excluded for no explicable reason. Just as one cannot assume from the onset that a suspected heretic is a valid pope, and consequently, that his definitions are infallible, and therefore only his private utterances are to be examined, because the object of the inquest must not be to determine if the pope is a heretic, but to determine, whether or not the man is truly the pope; conversely, for the same reason, namely, that the object of the heresy inquest is to ascertain whether or not the man is a true and valid pope, the suspect's private opinions are not to be summarily excluded from examination, as if only his official magisterium need be examined to determine whether he is a true and valid pope or a heretical usurper. Since the object of the inquest would be to ascertain whether the putative pope is a true and valid pope or a heretica intruder, all of his writings and discourses containing evidence of heresy must be examined, regardless of whether they are solemn official acts or mere private utterances and writings. Unfortunately, the *Dubia* cardinals, and the signatories of the *Correctio Filialis* have conducted their heresy examination by assuming as a premise that Bergoglio is a valid pope, thereby logically eliminating the possibility that any conclusion can be reached other than that Bergoglio is a true and valid pope; and above all, they have not properly attempted to determine whether or not he has fallen into formal heresy as a *private person*. At the very least, on the basis of his publicly expressed heretical personal opinions, their

---

[552] https://www.ncregister.com/blog/edward-pentin/full-text-and-explanatory-notes-of-cardinals-questions-on-amoris-laetitia.

[553] http://www.correctiofilialis.org/wp-content/uploads/2017/08/Correctio-filialis_English_1.pdf.

starting point should have been to consider him a *papa dubius*, since the *indicia* of heresy more than adequately justify placing him in that category — indeed, his evident pertinacity in professing 1) that even those who are without faith, and reject God are without sin if they follow their conscience; and 2) that it is morally illicit to attempt to convince others to abandon their false religion and embrace the true faith, both prove beyond all shadow of doubt that Bergoglio is not even a *suspected heretic* and *papa dubius*, but he is visibly and manifestly a *formal heretic* and no pope — one who is incapable of holding any ecclesiastical office, and therefore an impostor and intruder onto the papal throne. In these two brazenly and obstinately professed heretical beliefs, the **fact** of Bergoglio's formal heresy is plainly visible to the extent that no further argumentation is necessary to prove the charge than has already been presented in this work; but lest I say nothing more and thus deprive the readers of the treatise I have promised to deliver on this matter, I will present even more evidence, which will serve to confirm and underscore what has already been proven with absolute certitude earlier in this work; and I will not waste time arguing with the legion of Bergoglio's desperate defenders, who resort to crude sophistry in their attempts to make it appear that the charge of formal heresy does not hold up; but it is sufficient to point out that Bergoglio has summarily rejected all attempts at correction, thereby manifesting himself *incorrigible,* and that the *indicia* presented in the *Dubia* and the *correctio filialis,* while taken individually are at least to be considered to constitute *vehement suspicion of heresy* and *violent suspicion of heresy*; but combined, and in view of his obstinacy in the face of correction, they indubitably constitute *moral certitude of formal heresy.* Moreover, that moral certitude is only something added on to the already *plainly visible and certain formal heresy* manifested in Bergoglio's direct, explicit, immediate, and evidently conscious expression of disbelief in 1) the necessity of faith for salvation, and 2) the mission of the Church to make disciples of all nations by convincing them of the truth of the Catholic faith, and to abandon their adherence to false religions and convert them to Catholicism.

On these two points alone, Bergoglio demonstrates that he is not in communion with those who profess the historic, apostolic faith of the Catholic Church, which is visibly absent in him (placing him visibly outside of the Catholic Church), and therefore, the form of the pontificate is likewise visibly absent in him. Bergoglio not only denies dogma — he denies dogma as such — he denies dogma as the ***rule of faith*** which must be adhered to in order to be saved. He does this by denying the morally binding dogmatic force of the first and most fundamental dogmas of faith set forth in the Creed: ***Credo in uunum Deum***. Thus, he denies that there is even such a thing as a ***rule of faith***, because it pertains to the nature of a dogma that it is a binding rule on the conscience to be professed and believed as a condition for salvation. Consequently, by depriving dogma of its binding force on the conscience, Bergoglio denies the First Commandment, which commands all men as a condition for salvation to believe in God and to believe everything He has revealed; and to obey all of his commandments. By denying the morally binding force of the first article of the Creed, he denies the force and validity of dogma as such. By denying the necessity to believe in God, he denies the necessity to believe in any of the commandments of God. Thus, for Bergoglio, salvation depends not on faith in God and obedience to his commandments, but that one follow one's own conscience by doing what one thinks is right and avoiding what one thinks is wrong. Thus, Bergoglio's creed is a profession of religious indifferentism and a naturalistic moral relativism which forbids the teaching of mandatory belief in dogmas and compulsory obedience to divine precepts. The logical consequence which follows from his religion of radical Naturalism is expressed in his latest Encyclical, *Fratelli Tutti:* «281. A journey of peace is possible between religions. Its point of departure must be God's way of seeing things. "God does not see with his eyes, God sees with his heart. And God's love is the same for everyone, regardless of religion. Even if they are atheists, his love is the same. When the last day comes, and there is sufficient light to see things as they really are, we are going to find ourselves quite surprised". [278]»[554]

---

[554] «281. Tra le religioni è possibile un cammino di pace. Il punto di partenza dev'essere lo sguardo di Dio. Perché «Dio non guarda con gli occhi, Dio guarda con il cuore. E l'amore di Dio è lo stesso per ogni persona, di qualunque religione sia. E se è ateo, è lo stesso amore. Quando arriverà l'ultimo giorno e ci sarà sulla terra la luce sufficiente per poter vedere le cose come sono, avremo parecchie sorprese!».[278]» *LETTERA ENCICLICA FRATELLI TUTTI SULLA FRATERNITÀ E L'AMICIZIA SOCIALE* 3 October 2020.

Of course, we already know what he means by *we are going to find ourselves quite surprised* — Bergoglio has already said in his previous outbursts (quoted below) that **we are all going to meet in heaven!** The fruits of redemption are gained by the exercise of our natural faculties, without any need for supernatural faith or sacraments — even if we are atheists! This is Pelagianism with a vengeance. So, while it is rightly said that in many cases formal heresy can be difficult to determine, in such cases as Bergoglio's, in which the formal heresy can be plainly seen as the obvious and evident fact of obstinate denial of the most primary truths of faith, one may judge him a heretic straightaway, with the absolute certitude of a judgment based on the visible fact of heresy which is immediately seen as *evidenter verum*.

THE DUBIA

First, let us consider, The *Dubia*:

1. It is asked whether, following the affirmations of *Amoris Laetitia* (300-305), it has now become possible to grant absolution in the sacrament of penance and thus to admit to holy Communion a person who, while bound by a valid marital bond, lives together with a different person *more uxorio* without fulfilling the conditions provided for by *Familiaris Consortio,* 84, and subsequently reaffirmed by *Reconciliatio et Paenitentia,* 34, and *Sacramentum Caritatis,* 29. Can the expression "in certain cases" found in Note 351 (305) of the exhortation *Amoris Laetitia* be applied to divorced persons who are in a new union and who continue to live *more uxorio*?

2. After the publication of the post-synodal exhortation *Amoris Laetitia* (304), does one still need to regard as valid the teaching of St. John Paul II's encyclical *Veritatis Splendor,* 79, based on sacred Scripture and on the Tradition of the Church, on the existence of absolute moral norms that prohibit intrinsically evil acts and that are binding without exceptions?

3. After *Amoris Laetitia* (301) is it still possible to affirm that a person who habitually lives in contradiction to a commandment of God's law, as for instance the one that prohibits adultery (Matthew 19:3-9), finds him or herself in an objective situation of grave habitual sin (Pontifical Council for Legislative Texts, "Declaration," June 24, 2000)?

4. After the affirmations of *Amoris Laetitia* (302) on "circumstances which mitigate moral responsibility," does one still need to regard as

valid the teaching of St. John Paul II's encyclical *Veritatis Splendor*, 81, based on sacred Scripture and on the Tradition of the Church, according to which "circumstances or intentions can never transform an act intrinsically evil by virtue of its object into an act 'subjectively' good or defensible as a choice"?

5. After *Amoris Laetitia* (303) does one still need to regard as valid the teaching of St. John Paul II's encyclical *Veritatis Splendor*, 56, based on sacred Scripture and on the Tradition of the Church, that excludes a creative interpretation of the role of conscience and that emphasizes that conscience can never be authorized to legitimate exceptions to absolute moral norms that prohibit intrinsically evil acts by virtue of their object?

It is only too well known that Bergoglio chose not to respond to the questions. The authors of the *Correctio Filialis* called particular attention to this fact, when they wrote, "Your Holiness has refused to give a positive answer to the *dubia* submitted to you by Cardinals Burke, Caffarra, Brandmüller, and Meisner, in which you were respectfully requested to confirm that the Apostolic Exhortation *Amoris laetitia* does not abolish five teachings of the Catholic faith." As Edward Pentin pointed out, "Each of the *dubia* is aimed at eliciting from the Apostolic See clarification on key parts of the document, most notably whether it is admissible to allow any remarried divorcees without an annulment holy Communion." The *Dubia* are aimed principally at addressing the question of admitting to Holy Communion any who are still validly married but civilly remarried or cohabiting with a different partner. If Bergoglio were to answer in the affirmative to the first question, he would heretically deny a revealed moral truth infallibly taught and universally known as such. One may not be absolved and admitted to Holy Communion, «who, while bound by a valid marital bond, lives together with a different person *more uxorio* without fulfilling the conditions, etc.» He chose not to answer; and in doing so, he has manifested his *mens rea* on this point. His silence is morally equivalent to an obstinate affirmative admission of guilt, and therefore an admission of formal heresy. In fact, he already answered the question before it was asked. These were his words when previously asked for a clarification by Eugenio Scalfari: "This is the bottom line result, the de facto appraisals are entrusted to the confessors, but at the end of faster or slower paths, all the divorced who ask will be admitted."⁵⁵⁵ He has never denied saying these words after they were published, nor did he deny what he was reported to have said to the Argentinian woman who had married a divorced man: «An Argentine news agency reported that Pope Francis contacted Jacqui Lisbona after receiving a letter from her in which she said her local priest had refused her Communion on the grounds she was married to a divorced man. It was reported that Pope Francis told Ms Lisbona: "A divorcee who takes Communion is not doing anything wrong."»⁵⁵⁶ Regarding the second question, namely, «does one still need to regard as valid the teaching of St. John Paul II's encyclical *Veritatis Splendor,* 79, based on sacred Scripture and on the Tradition of the Church, on the existence of absolute moral norms that prohibit intrinsically evil acts and that are binding without exceptions?" By remaining silent, Bergoglio openly admits to professing the heresy denying, "the existence of absolute moral norms that prohibit intrinsically evil acts and that are binding without exceptions». The third question, «is it still possible to affirm that a person who habitually lives in contradiction to a commandment of God's law, as for instance the one that prohibits adultery (Matthew 19:3-9), finds him or herself in an objective situation of grave habitual sin»? Bergoglio's silence proves that according to him, it is not possible to affirm that a person who habitually and knowingly offends against a divine commandment lives in the state of mortal sin. His refusal to respond to the fourth question proves that he denies the revealed truth «based on sacred Scripture and on the Tradition of the Church, according to which "circumstances or intentions can never transform an act intrinsically evil by virtue of its object into an act 'subjectively' good or defensible as a choice"» Bergoglio's refusal to answer the fifth question proves that he heretically holds that there are "legitimate exceptions to absolute moral norms that prohibit intrinsically evil acts by virtue of their object". Bergoglio's refusal to respond to these *Dubia* by itself amply justifies the position of the

---

⁵⁵⁵ *Pope vs Church*, Thompson, Damien, https://www.questia.com/magazine/1P3-3858361431/pope-vs-church; http://fatima.org/perspectives/sd/perspective798.asp.

⁵⁵⁶ *Divorcee 'not wrong' to take Holy communion says Pope*, Maeve Connolly, in *The Irish News*, 25 April, 2014, http://www.irishnews.com/news/2014/04/25/news/divorcee-not-wrong-to-take-holy-communion-says-pope-89990/.

signatories of the *Open Letter to the bishops of the Catholic Church*,[557] which is, "to accuse Pope Francis of the canonical delict of heresy".

Why did Bergoglio refuse to answer the *Dubia*? These are serious questions concerning the gravest matters of revealed truths taught by the Church. Then he was corrected, but he contemptuously dismissed the *Filial Correction* as if it were the product of misguided minds — but it could not be considered the product of misguided minds unless one is to judge the *Dubia* themselves, presented by *four Cardinals of the Roman Church* to be also the product of misguided minds. The gravity of the subject matter in the *Dubia* and the dignity of the authors make it self-evident that the questions were not out of place; but being that they are questions on matters of faith and morals, it is morally *"sub gravi"* that they demand a response, with the consequence that (as I have already explained in Volume One), if left unanswered the *dolus* of heresy is tacitly but evidently manifested in Bergoglio's refusal to answer. In such a case as this the maxim applies: *Qui tacit consentire videtur ubi loqui debuit ac potuit.* ("Silence gives consent when one ought to have spoken or was able to.") From that maxim, as I explained in Volume One, flows the widely applied legal principle in criminal law: **the rule of tacit admission**. In this case Bergoglio's silence amounts to an admission of guilt.[558] There exists a strict moral obligation for a

---

[557] https://assets.documentcloud.org/documents/5983408/Open-Letter-to-the-Bishops-of-the-Catholic.pdf.

[558] Ferdinand Mackeldey explains in, *Compendium of Modern Civil Law*, New York 1845, pp. 162-163: «The declaration of one's will is made, 1. either *explicitly*, when expressed orally or in writing, by words or intelligible signs used instead of words;[a] 2. or *tacitly*,* which is the case where a person's actions admit of no other reasonable explanation than that he freely consented... *It is surprising that, in treating of the doctrine of tacit consent, there should be such a general confounding of the two legal principles, *"qui tacet consentit,"* and *"qui tacet non utique fatetur."* ... The canon law contains the same views as those which the Editor here advances, as will be seen on a reference to reg. 43 and 44 de reg. jur. in 6to., where Bonifacius first sets up the rule (43), "qui tacet consentire videtur;" and then says further (44), "is qui tacet non fatetur; sed nec utique negare videtur." Were both these rules to be applied to one and the same object, a direct contradiction would ensue; a supposition which is here wholly inadmissible, where the two rules follow the one immediately after the other. The fact that silence does not in every case imply consent, doubtless misled the jurists

man to straightforwardly profess one's faith when there is sufficient reason to doubt the orthodoxy of that one's faith; so that if the *Dubia* questions are not answered, the refusal to answer itself would be equivalent to a confession of guilt, having the effect of rendering the suspect, who, because of the *indicia* of heresy, would already have been a **doubtful pope**, *incorrigible* and *violenter suspectus de hæresi*, and a therefore *papa nullus*. As a *papa dubius* he would already have been presumed to be no pope, and therefore would already have fallen under the jurisdiction of the Church to be judged on whether his claim on the papacy is valid or not. After Bergoglio's refusal to respond to the *Dubia*, he must be considered to be certainly under the jurisdiction of the Church as one who is *minor quolibet catholico*. Therefore, (as the factual evidence of the case indicates), the Church has the gravest obligation to declare his claim on the pontificate null and void. Against such an illegitimate usurper, the legitimate pope (and the remaining faithful bishops) must resist with all their might, as Father Bordoni taught, "even unto death, rather than allow a schism to be brought about by ceding the rights of the papacy to a demonstrably illegitimate intruder."[559]

I have sufficiently explained in Volume One that when seriously questioned in matters of faith, there exists a grave obligation to respond, and if the questions given as a correction are left unanswered, then the *dolus* of heresy is plainly evident in the refusal to heed the correction and resolve the doubt with unequivocal responses. By refusing to respond to the *Dubia*, Bergoglio has indicated his assent to the heresy expressed in his own heretical propositions. In addition to what I have already explained in Volume One on the **Law of Tacit Admission**, it is also noteworthy to point out here that the maxim, "Silence Implies Consent" is affirmed in the *Torah*: «If a woman vows a vow to the Lord, and binds herself by an oath, being in her father's house in her youth; And her father hears her vow, and her oath with which she has bound her soul, and her

---

into regarding the rule, "qui tacet consentit," as of too sweeping a nature… consequently, when Bonifacius omitted to say in full, "qui tacet ubi voluntatem exprimere potuit et debuit, consentit," common sense dictates, that the limitation must be understood, as being implied in the rule itself.»

[559] P. Francesco Bordoni, *Sacrum Tribunal Iudicum In Causis Sanctæ Fidei Contra Hæreticos Et Hæresi Suspectos*, Romæ, 1648, p. 150.

father remains silent, then all her vows shall stand, and every oath with which she has bound her soul shall stand. But if her father disallows her in the day that he hears; not one of her vows, or of her oaths with which she has bound her soul, shall stand; and the Lord shall forgive her, because her father disallowed her.» (*Mattot* 5765) In *No Neutrality: Silence is Assent*,[560] Rabbi Bradley Artson explains, «Parashat Matot addresses the legal issue of the nullification of vows. It records the ancient law that a woman's vows can be nullified by her husband, provided that he cancels her vows immediately upon hearing them. If he delays in silence, her vow becomes irrevocably binding.» Then he provides the principle on which this prescription is founded: "Silence is assent." Then he elaborates, «The answer given by the Talmud is that "silence is like assent." Once the husband knows what his wife has sworn, he becomes a participant in her oath. At that point, he can either object immediately—disassociating himself from her words and thereby nullifying them—or he can remain silent, which effectively links the husband and the vow.» Thus, Rabbi Artson concludes, "There is no neutrality. Silence is assent." Bergoglio's silence effectively links him to the crime of heresy, because his silence is not merely a tacit assent to someone else's heresy, as appeared to be the case with Pope Honorius, but it is evidently a *tacit admission* of guilt for the crime of heresy verbally expressed in his own official acts. By refusing to respond, and thus manifesting himself to be incorrigible, Bergoglio has by that very fact of his silence plainly manifested his pertinacity in heresy, for which reason the authors of the *Open Letter to the bishops of the Catholic World* were amply justified in directing their accusation of *formal heresy* at Jorge Mario Bergoglio:

> «We accuse Pope Francis of having, through his words and actions, publicly and pertinaciously demonstrated his belief in the following propositions that contradict divinely revealed truth (for each proposition we provide a selection of Scriptural and magisterial teachings that condemn them as contrary to divine revelation; these references are conclusive but are not intended to be exhaustive.)»

---

[560] https://www.myjewishlearning.com/article/no-neutrality-silence-is-assent/.

Those "following propositions" are:

«I. A justified person has not the strength with God's grace to carry out the objective demands of the divine law, as though any of the commandments of God are impossible for the justified; or as meaning that God's grace, when it produces justification in an individual, does not invariably and of its nature produce conversion from all serious sin, or is not sufficient for conversion from all serious sin.»[561]

«II. A Christian believer can have full knowledge of a divine law and voluntarily choose to break it in a serious matter, but not be in a state of mortal sin as a result of this action.»[562]

«III. A person is able, while he obeys a divine prohibition, to sin against God by that very act of obedience.»[563]

---

[561] [Council of Trent, session 6, canon 18: "If anyone says that the commandments of God are impossible to observe even for a man who is justified and established in grace, let him be anathema" (DH 1568). See also: Gen. 4:7; Deut. 30:11-19; Ecclesiasticus 15: 11-22; Mk. 8:38; Lk. 9:26; Heb. 10:26-29; 1 Jn. 5:17; Zosimus, 15th (or 16th) Synod of Carthage, canon 3 on grace, DH 225; Felix III, 2nd Synod of Orange, DH 397; Council of Trent, Session 5, canon 5; Session 6, canons 18-20, 22, 27 and 29; Pius V, Bull Ex omnibus afflictionibus, On the errors of Michael du Bay, 54, DH 1954; Innocent X, Constitution Cum occasione, On the errors of Cornelius Jansen, 1, DH 2001; Clement XI, Constitution Unigenitus, On the errors of Pasquier Quesnel, 71, DH 2471; John Paul II, Apostolic Exhortation Reconciliatio et paenitentia 17: AAS 77 (1985): 222; Veritatis splendor 65-70: AAS 85 (1993): 1185- 89, DH 4964-67.]

[562] [Council of Trent, session 6, canon 20: "If anyone says that a justified man, however perfect he may be, is not bound to observe the commandments of God and of the Church but is bound only to believe, as if the Gospel were merely an absolute promise of eternal life without the condition that the commandments be observed, let him be anathema" (DH 1570). See also: Mk. 8:38; Lk. 9:26; Heb. 10:26-29; 1 Jn. 5:17; Council of Trent, session 6, canons 19 and 27; Clement XI, Constitution Unigenitus, On the errors of Pasquier Quesnel, 71, DH 2471; John Paul II, Apostolic Exhortation Reconciliatio et paenitentia 17: AAS 77 (1985): 222; Veritatis splendor, 65-70: AAS 85 (1993): 1185-89, DH 4964-67.]

[563] [Ps. 18:8: "The law of the Lord is unspotted, converting souls." See also: Ecclesiasticus 15:21; Council of Trent, session 6, canon 20; Clement XI, Constitution Unigenitus, On the errors of Pasquier Quesnel, 71, DH

«IV. Conscience can truly and rightly judge that sexual acts between persons who have contracted a civil marriage with each other, although one or both of them is sacramentally married to another person, can sometimes be morally right, or requested or even commanded by God.»[564]

«V. It is false that the only sexual acts that are good of their kind and morally licit are acts between husband and wife.»[565]

2471; Leo XIII, Libertas praestantissimum, ASS 20 (1887-88): 598 (DH 3248); John Paul II, Veritatis splendor, 40: AAS 85 (1993): 1165 (DH 4953).]

[564] [Council of Trent, session 6, canon 21: "If anyone says that Jesus Christ was given by God to men as a redeemer in whom they are to trust but not also as a lawgiver whom they are bound to obey, let him be anathema", DH 1571. Council of Trent, session 24, canon 2: "If anyone says that it is lawful for Christians to have several wives at the same time, and that this is not forbidden by any divine law, let him be anathema", DH 1802. Council of Trent, session 24, canon 5: "If anyone says that the marriage bond can be dissolved because of heresy or difficulties in cohabitation or because of the wilful absence of one of the spouses, let him be anathema", DH 1805. Council of Trent, session 24, canon 7: "If anyone says that the Church is in error for having taught and for still teaching that in accordance with the evangelical and apostolic doctrine, the marriage bond cannot be dissolved because of adultery on the part of one of the spouses and that neither of the two, not even the innocent one who has given no cause for infidelity, can contract another marriage during the lifetime of the other, and that the husband who dismisses an adulterous wife and marries again and the wife who dismisses an adulterous husband and marries again are both guilty of adultery, let him be anathema", DH 1807. See also: Ps. 5:5; Ps. 18:8-9; Ecclesiasticus 15:21; Heb. 10:26-29; Jas. 1:13; 1 Jn. 3:7; Innocent XI, Condemned propositions of the 'Laxists', 62-63, DH 2162-63; Clement XI, Constitution Unigenitus, On the errors of Pasquier Quesnel, 71, DH 2471; Leo XIII, encyclical letter Libertas praestantissimum, ASS 20 (1887-88): 598, DH 3248; Pius XII, Decree of the Holy Office on situation ethics, DH 3918; 2 nd Vatican Council, Pastoral Constitution Gaudium et spes, 16; John Paul II, Veritatis splendor, 54: AAS 85 (1993): 1177; Catechism of the Catholic Church, 1786-87.]

[565] [I Corinthians 6:9-10; "Do not err: neither fornicators, nor idolaters, nor adulterers, nor the effeminate, nor liers with mankind, nor thieves, nor covetous, nor drunkards, nor railers, nor extortioners, shall possess the kingdom of God." Jude 1:7; "As Sodom and Gomorrha, and the neighbouring cities, in like manner, having given themselves to fornication, and going after other flesh, were made an example, suffering the

«VI. Moral principles and moral truths contained in divine revelation and in the natural law do not include negative prohibitions that absolutely forbid particular kinds of action, inasmuch as these are always gravely unlawful on account of their object.»[566]

«VII. God not only permits, but positively wills, the pluralism and diversity of religions, both Christian and non-Christian.»[567]

Six of these seven heretical propositions are evidently strict logical corollaries of the above cited propositions enumerated in the *Dubia*, and the seventh from other of Bergoglio's public statements, insofar as all of these propositions are the foundational principles upon which the statements logically hinge; for which reason they can all be plainly and evidently seen to be heretical. In Volume One I called attention to the fact that, « He [Jorge Bergoglio] said on the one hand that the "great majority" of Catholic marriages are "null", and that

punishment of eternal fire." See also: Romans 1:26-32; Ephesians 5:3-5; Galatians 5;19-21; Pius IX, Casti connubii, 10, 19-21, 73; Paul VI, Humanae vitae, 11-14; John Paul II, Evangelium vitae, 13-14.]

[566] [John Paul II, Veritatis splendor 115: "Each of us knows how important is the teaching which represents the central theme of this Encyclical and which is today being restated with the authority of the Successor of Peter. Each of us can see the seriousness of what is involved, not only for individuals but also for the whole of society, with the reaffirmation of the universality and immutability of the moral commandments, particularly those which prohibit always and without exception intrinsically evil acts", DH 4971. See also: Rom. 3:8; 1 Cor. 6: 9-10; Gal. 5: 19-21; Apoc. 22:15; 4th Lateran Council, chapter 22, DH 815; Council of Constance, Bull Inter cunctas, 14, DH 1254; Paul VI, Humanae vitae, 14: AAS 60 (1968) 490-91; John Paul II, Veritatis splendor, 83: AAS 85 (1993): 1199, DH 4970.]

[567] [John 14:6; "I am the way, and the truth, and the life. No man cometh to the Father, but by me." Acts 4:11-12; "This is the stone which was rejected by you the builders, which is become the head of the corner. Neither is there salvation in any other. For there is no other name under heaven given to men, whereby we must be saved." See also Exodus 22:20; Exodus 23:24; 2 Chronicles 34:25; Psalm 95:5; Jeremiah 10:11; 1 Corinthians 8:5-6; Gregory XVI, Mirari vos, 13-14; Pius XI, Qui pluribus, 15; Singulari quidem, 3-5; First Vatican Council, Profession of Faith: Leo XIII, Immortale dei, 31; Satis cognitum, 3-9; Pius XI, Mortalium Animos, 1-2, 6].

some cohabiting relationships "have the grace of a real marriage because of their fidelity" and in fact may be "real marriages" because of this."[568] Now let us consider his exact words in their full context:

«**In the Argentine countryside, in the Northeastern region, there is a superstition: that couples have a child, they live together. In the countryside this happens. Then, when the child must go to school, they have a civil marriage. And then, as grandparents, they have a religious marriage. It is a superstition, because they say that having a religious wedding straight away scares the husband! We must also fight against these superstitions. Yet really, I say that I have seen a great deal of fidelity in these cohabiting couples, a great deal of fidelity; and I am certain that this is a true marriage, they have the grace of matrimony, precisely because of the fidelity that they have.**»[569]

The key proposition to consider is this: «*I am certain that this is a true marriage, they have the grace of matrimony, precisely because of the fidelity that they have.*» The proposition is plainly heretical, even considered solely by itself, but what is worse (as I explained in Volume One); the heretical belief itself is founded on a pantheistic notion of God which is essentially opposed to the monotheistic notion of the God of Catholicism and, as Cornelio Fabro explained in his *Introduzione all'ateismo moderno*, is logically reducible to philosophic atheism. I already pointed out that his statement asserting

---

[568] The Irish Catholic: http://irishcatholic.ie/article/understanding-pope%E2%80%99s-remarks-about-marriage.

[569] «Nella campagna argentina, nella zona del Nordest, c'è una superstizione: che i fidanzati hanno il figlio, convivono. In campagna succede questo. Poi, quando il figlio deve andare a scuola, fanno il matrimonio civile. E poi, da nonni, fanno il matrimonio religioso. È una superstizione, perché dicono che farlo subito religioso spaventa il marito! Dobbiamo lottare anche contro queste superstizioni. Eppure davvero dico che ho visto tanta fedeltà in queste convivenze, tanta fedeltà; e sono sicuro che questo è un matrimonio vero, hanno la grazia del matrimonio, proprio per la fedeltà che hanno. Ma ci sono superstizioni locali. È la pastorale più difficile, quella del matrimonio.» http://w2.vatican.va/content/francesco/en/speeches/2016/june/documents/papa-francesco_20160616_convegno-diocesi-roma.html

that monogamous cohabitation between baptized persons constitutes a valid marriage opposes the supernatural sacramentality of Holy Matrimony and manifests the anti-supernaturalism of the radical Naturalism of his belief system. If cohabitation were to be considered a valid marriage, then there would be no need for sacramental marriage, since the merely natural union of cohabitation would suffice for the grace of matrimony, and would fulfil the law of God — now that is indisputable heresy. Not only is there no need for sacramental marriage and its supernatural grace in Bergoglio's religion, but, as has been explained, there is no need for anything supernatural or absolute in his pseudo-religion; and therefore, according to the Bergoglian pseudo-Christianity: 1) «VI. Moral principles and moral truths contained in divine revelation and in the natural law do not include negative prohibitions that absolutely forbid particular kinds of action, inasmuch as these are always gravely unlawful on account of their object.», and 2) «V. It is false that the only sexual acts that are good of their kind and morally licit are acts between husband and wife.».

But, leaving aside for a moment the particular questions and amply documented propositions enumerated in the above cited letters, what is the most damning evidence of all, is the plainly visible reason why Bergoglio has adamantly and obstinately refused to respond to the *Dubia* and the *Correctio Filialis*, and that is because he has already publicly manifested in his private opinions that he is indubitably a pertinacious formal heretic incapable of holding any ecclesiastical office. His blatant disdain for dogma is rooted in a belief system in which supernaturally revealed dogmas can have no place. Bergoglio's "god", as I explained in Volume One, is not the God professed in Catholic dogma, but the *deus sive natura* of Spinoza and all of the modern philosophers whose systematic beliefs are founded on *immanentism*. This is why Bergoglio professed that his "god" is not the Catholic God of revelation whom we profess to be our Lord and God: "I believe in God, not in a Catholic God, there is no Catholic God, there is God and I believe in Jesus Christ, his incarnation. Jesus is my teacher and my pastor, but God, the Father, Abba, is the light and the Creator."[570]

---

[570] «E io credo in Dio. Non in un Dio cattolico, non esiste un Dio cattolico, esiste Dio. E credo in Gesù Cristo, sua incarnazione. Gesù è il

Notice how Bergoglio distinguishes between God and Jesus Christ in a Gnostic and Arian manner which reserves the divine attributes of being the "Creator" and "Light" to the Father; while Jesus Christ is only a "teacher" and "pastor" — because "his incarnation", according to the Bergoglian *incarnational sense* of "incarnation", is not in the nature of the *hypostatic union* understood in the orthodox sense that Jesus Christ in his earthly flesh was and is and remains forever the incarnate divine Person consubstantial with the Father (ὁμοούσιον τῷ Πατρί) who *descended from heaven and was incarnated by the Holy Ghost from the Virgin Mary* (κατελθόντα ἐκ τῶν οὐρανῶν καὶ σαρκωθέντα ἐκ Πνεύματος Ἁγίου καὶ Μαρίας τῆς Παρθένου) *and became man* (καὶ ἐνανθρωπήσαντα), with his human nature remaining hypostatically united to his divine nature, so that for the entire period while incarnate in his earthly flesh in this world, Our Lord Jesus Christ remained fully, *the onlybegotten Son of God, born of the Father before all ages, God from God, Light from Light, True God from True God, begotten not made, consubstantial with the Father, through whom all things were made* (φῶς ἐκ φωτός, Θεὸν ἀληθινὸν ἐκ Θεοῦ ἀληθινοῦ, γεννηθέντα οὐ ποιηθέντα, ὁμοούσιον τῷ Πατρί, δι' οὗ τὰ πάντα ἐγένετο). So while *Jesus Christ* is Bergoglio's *teacher and pastor*, He was no more than that — only a man during his life, but not God. Thus it can be seen that only God the Father is *Creator* and *Light* according to the Bergoglian *Gnosis*.

For Bergoglio, the "Catholic God" who is eternally perfect and who freely created us out of nothing; and who in his infinite beatitude has absolutely no need for us, ***does not exist:*** "'But what is God for you?'; 'God, God!'. But God does not exist: do not be scandalized! God does not exist like this! There is the Father, the Son and the Holy Spirit: they are persons, they are not an idea in the air ... This God spray does not exist!"[571] What does he mean when he says, "God does

---

mio maestro e il mio pastore, ma Dio, il Padre, Abbà, è la luce e il Creatore.» (https://www.repubblica.it/cultura/2013/10/01/news/papa_francesco_a_scalfari_cos_cambier_la_chiesa-67630792/)

[571] Homily in the Santa Marta chapel, 9 October, 2014. — «'Ma cosa è Dio per lei?'; 'Dio, Dio!'. Ma Dio non esiste: non scandalizzatevi! Dio così non esiste! Esiste il Padre, il Figlio e lo Spirito Santo: sono persone, non sono un'idea sull'aria... Questo Dio spray non esiste!»

not exist like this!" He explained this point two-and-a-half years later on June 7, 2017, when he stated in his General Audience, "God cannot be God without man."⁵⁷² Bergoglio explained, "But the Gospel of Jesus Christ reveals to us that God who cannot be without us: He will never be a God "without man"; it is He who cannot be without us, and this is a great mystery! God cannot be God without man: this is a great mystery."⁵⁷³ Such a "god" as this, which Bergoglio professes — a *God who cannot be God without man*, is **a "god" who cannot exist independently from the universe** — a mere demiurgic *anima mundi*, which is the *foundational belief of pagan religion*.

Thus, it is no mystery why Bergoglio introduced **pagan worship** into the Vatican on October 4, 2019. On November 8, 2019, it was reported by LifeSite News, «The female indigenous leader who planted a tree alongside Pope Francis in the Vatican Gardens ahead of the Amazon Synod was clear from the beginning about the syncretistic and pagan meaning of the act which, she explains, was intended to "satisfy the hunger of Mother Earth" and reconnect with "the divinity present in the Amazonian soil."»⁵⁷⁴ That Amazonian priestess, Ednamar de Oliveira Viana said in her statement of October 4, "The Synod is to plant this tree, water and cultivate, so that the Amazonian peoples are heard and respected in their customs and traditions experiencing the mystery of the divinity present in the

---

https://cosarestadelgiorno.wordpress.com/2014/10/09/il-dio-spray-non-esiste-esistono-persone-il-padre-il-figlio-e-lo-spirito-santo-omelia-di-papa-francesco-del-9-ottobre-2014/.

⁵⁷² "Dio non può essere Dio senza l'uomo." https://www.youtube.com/watch?v=St5M9pvQd7I.

⁵⁷³ "Ma il Vangelo di Gesù Cristo ci rivela che Dio che non può stare senza di noi: Lui non sarà mai un Dio "senza l'uomo"; è Lui che non può stare senza di noi, e questo è un mistero grande! Dio non può essere Dio senza l'uomo: grande mistero è." http://www.vatican.va/content/francesco/it/audiences/2017/documents/papa-francesco_20170607_udienza-generale.html

⁵⁷⁴ https://www-lifesitenews-com.cdn.ampproject.org/v/s/www.lifesitenews.com/mobile/news/female-indigenous-leader-reveals-pagan-significance-of-tree-planting-ceremony-in-vatican-gardens?usqp=mq331AQCKAE%3D&amp_js_v=0.1#aoh=15787609535315&referrer=https%3A%2F%2Fwww.google.com&amp_tf=From%20%251%24s&ampshare=https%3A%2F%2Fwww.lifesitenews.com%2Fnews%2Ffemale-indigenous-leader-reveals-pagan-significance-of-tree-planting-ceremony-in-vatican-gardens.

Amazonian ground."⁵⁷⁵ Since the mentioned "customs and traditions" of the Amazonian peoples are specifically **pagan**, understandably a clarification was sought regarding the identity of who is represented in the pagan statue used in the ceremony. The report continued, «Midway through the Amazon Synod, as the identity of the Pachamama statue was being sought, LifeSite asked Vatican media officials if they could provide an "authoritative text from the Vatican or REPAM so that the question of what happened in the Vatican Gardens [could] be resolved."» It then mentioned that «Paolo Ruffini, prefect of Vatican communications and president of the Amazon Synod's information commission, described the tree as "sacred",» and that «Two days later, at an October 21 press conference, Vatican spokesman Matteo Bruni asked Mauricio López Oropeza, executive secretary of REPAM, to comment on the [Pachamama] statue's meaning — thus offering him the opportunity to comment also on the ceremony — but López declined to comment, shrugging off the question.» On October 25, Bergoglio himself ended all speculation regarding the significance and identity of the statue when he said, "I would like to say a word about the *pachamama* statues that were removed from the Church at Traspontina," and he added that the Incan fertility goddess idols "were there without idolatrous intentions".⁵⁷⁶ So, a pagan fertility rite of nature worship took place in the Vatican by the invitation of Jorge Bergoglio, and in this rite prayers were offered, according to the Vatican News commentator, "in direct communion with Mother Earth". The rite was offered before a pagan idol, and Bergoglio actively participated in the rite (as can be seen in the video⁵⁷⁷), but it was later claimed by a Vatican functionary that the rite was performed "without idolatrous intentions"! The claim is simply not credible: It was, after all, a pagan ritual ceremony (*el pago a la tierra*⁵⁷⁸) offered to a

---

⁵⁷⁵ https://docs.google.com/document/d/1OUVKTMjh4TPA057aPU0i4FMhW4SHwD619W09OsxZOew/mobilebasic?urp=gmail_link.

⁵⁷⁶ https://www.lifesitenews.com/news/full-transcript-of-the-popes-comments-on-pagan-pachamama-statues.

⁵⁷⁷ https://www.youtube.com/watch?v=H6P39XswlzI&feature=youtu.be&t=421

⁵⁷⁸ The Amazon Synod and the Pachamama - Home of the Mother

pagan deity in a rite of nature worship.[579] According to the mentioned *customs and traditions of the Amazonian peoples*, the fertility goddess *Pachamama* holds a higher place than Jesus Christ and his Most Holy Mother, who have only been syncretistically absorbed into the pagan cult of the *Pachamama* worshippers. *Pachamama*, in the nature worship of the Amazon, is subordinate only to the "gods of the mountains," whose rites traditionally included human sacrifice in past centuries. In the same article it was mentioned that, «Cardinal Gerhard Müller commented on the incident Thursday night on EWTN's The World Over with Raymond Arroyo. He said: "The great mistake was to bring the idols into the Church, not to put them out, because according to the Law of God Himself – the First Commandment – idolism [idolatry] is a grave sin and not to mix them with the Christian liturgy." "To put it out," Müller added, "to throw it out, can be against human law, but to bring the idols into the Church was a grave sin, a crime against the Divine Law."»

For Bergoglio, however, it was no mistake — he is a self-confessed Mother Earth worshipper, who admitted to the representatives of the pagan Jains sect on June 1, 2016: "We all like mother Earth, because it is she who gave us life and protects us."[580] This statement is an absolutely heretical and blasphemous abomination. It is GOD — **God, the Father Almighty, Creator of heaven and earth**, who gave us life — not *"Mother Earth"*, as Bergoglio professes. I repeat here that it is because GOD created us and gave life to us, that we profess Him *Dominum* et *Vivificantem* — *"The Lord and Giver of Life"*. "Mother Earth" does not give us life, but it is GOD, who created the earth and everything in it, and who gives life to all living things, and who became hypostatically incarnate in the womb of the Virgin Mary and died on the Cross, so that we may "have life, and have it more abundantly" (John 10:10), who gave us life. It was GOD who formed man from the lifeless slime of the earth, and breathed into him the breath of life, and man became a living soul: «*formavit igitur Dominus*

---

[579] El pago a la tierra en los Andes (boletomachupicchu.com)

[580] "A noi, a tutti, piace la madre Terra, perché è quella che ci ha dato la vita e ci custodisce; direi anche la sorella Terra, che ci accompagna nel nostro cammino dell'esistenza." http://m.vatican.va/content/francescomobile/it/speeches/2016/june/documents/papa-francesco_20160601_institute-of-jainology.html; https://youtu.be/EOnH-NmkMv0.

Deus hominem de limo terræ et inspiravit in faciem eius spiraculum vitæ et factus est homo in animam viventem» — (Gen. 2:7) *It is precisely our profession of the one true God, Creator of heaven and earth, and of all things animate and inanimate, that distinguishes us from the pagans*; and it was Melchisedech's profession of God Almighty that distinguished his religion from that of his pagan Caananite countrymen: "But Melchisedech the king of Salem, bringing forth bread and wine, for he was the priest of the most high God, blessed him, and said: Blessed be Abram by the most high God, who created heaven and earth." (Genesis 14:18 - 19) It is precisely the notion of the **EARTH** as the giver of life and provident protector of life, and which conceives of "God" not as a transcendent, infinitely and eternally perfect Supreme Being; but merely as an immanent demiurge; a "divine" life giving principle which constitutes the world as the divine womb that gives life and a share of divinity to all things in nature (such as the Amazonian soil), that distinguishes a specifically pagan religion from Christianity. The Word made flesh is replaced with the pantheistic *Incarnationalism* of "God" as "the living soul of the world", which culminates in the deification of man and nature. Yet man is deified only insofar as he is a part of nature. Contrary to the perpetual faith of the Church and the explicit teaching of scripture (Genesis 1: 26-28[581]) Bergoglio declared in his tweet of September 3, 2020, "Today we hear the voice of creation admonishing us to return to our rightful place in the natural created order – to remember that we are part of this interconnected web of life, not its masters." The "natural created order" for Bergoglio conceives of creation in a deifying pantheistic sense which deifies man to the extent that he condemns capital punishment apparently

---

[581] *Genesis 1:26-28:* "And God said, Let us make man in our image, after our likeness: and let them have dominion over the fish of the sea, and over the fowl of the air, and over the cattle, and over all the earth, and over every creeping thing that creepeth upon the earth. So God created man in his own image, in the image of God created he him; male and female created he them. And God blessed them, and God said unto them, Be fruitful, and multiply, and replenish the earth, and subdue it: and have dominion over the fish of the sea, and over the fowl of the air, and over every living thing that moveth upon the earth."

according to the Marcionist belief[582] professed by Freemasonry, i.e. in the "The rude conception of sternness predominating over mercy in the Deity,"[583] — professing this Old Testament precept of divine law to be morally wrong — against the perpetual faith of the Church and the explicit teaching of scripture.[584] It is this pantheistic *Incarnationalism* which conceives of "God" as an immanent *divine principle* — as "Mother Earth" — as the world-soul and womb which generates all life. It is this pagan and pantheistic religion, which conceives of God as "the living soul of the world", and which Cardinal Manning explained in the passages I cited in Volume One, is the embodiment of the spirit of Antichrist, which Jorge Bergoglio professed on June 1, 2016 when he confessed his faith in Mother Earth, and whom he authorized to be worshipped in a pagan rite on October 4, 2019 in the Vatican Gardens.

The absolute proof that Bergoglio does not worship the Christian God, but is manifestly a pagan masquerading as a Christian is evident in his own words, "God cannot be God without man." By what we can know with certitude about God by the natural power of the intellect, it is most easily demonstrated that this proposition is evidently false; and that it opposes the nature of God in such a manner that it is reducible to pantheistic immanentism, and ultimately to philosophic atheism. All knowledge to be acquired begins from what is already known and proceeds to knowledge of what was unknown, and what is known is seen through the application of the

---

[582] Benedict XVI, «GRACE AND VOCATION WITHOUT REMORSE: COMMENTS ON THE TREATISE *DE JUDAEIS*» — "Marcion created a canon of the New Testament that stands in stark contrast to the Bible of Israel. The God of Israel (Old Testament) and the God of Jesus Christ (New Testament) are conceived as two different and opposing deities. For Marcion, the God of the Old Testament is a God of merciless justice; the God of Jesus Christ is the God of mercy and love."

[583] Albert Pike, *Morals and Dogma of the Ancient and Accepted Scottish Rite of Freemasonry*, p.321.

[584] Benedict XVI, «GRACE AND VOCATION WITHOUT REMORSE: COMMENTS ON THE TREATISE *DE JUDAEIS*» — "Of course, the Marcionite temptation persists and reappears in certain situations in the history of the Church." It has reappeared in Jorge Bergoglio condemnation of the divine precept of capital punishment.

first principles, which are immediately evident. As Gallus Manser O.P. explained in his classic exposition of Thomism, *Das Wesen des Thomismus*, the first principles are reducible to one foundational principle (the principle of non-contradiction), which is founded on the transcendental notion of being as ontologically distinct from non-being, and related as act and potentiality. All being apprehended immediately by the mind can be understood to be constituted of potentiality and act, as non-being brought into being as potentiality reduced to actuality necessarily by what is already in act; since, as Manser expressed it, "*Aus Nichtsein kann nichts entstehen.*" Thus, all that exists in the universe depends on a first mover in which there is no composition of potentiality and act, but the pure act of the totality of essential being, which as essential being contains within itself the totality of all perfection of being *simpliciter*. Hence it follows strictly that God, who is essential being — and therefore the fullness of being in its absolute and eternal perfection, is **pure act** (*actus purus*), in whom there cannot exist potentiality or motion; for which reason the divine essence is God's being, which is indistinguishable from his operation; and therefore his infinite and eternal perfection is self-contained, so that He cannot possibly stand in need of any perfection to be gained from his creation. Any proposition about God which professes, «He will never be a God 'without man',» is a profession of *pagan belief*. It is from this poisoned well of disbelief in the Christian God, that all of Bergoglio's heretical doctrines are drawn — the disbelief he expressed when he said, "I believe in God, not in a Catholic God, there is no Catholic God."

I have already explained in Volume One how Bergoglio's notion of the Blessed Trinity denies the infinite and eternal perfection of God by denying the infinitely perfect and eternal unity of the Divine Persons; and that Bergoglio's "Blessed Trinity" is not the same Trinity as the One theologically elaborated by St. Hilary, St. Augustine, and St. Thomas, but the occult "Trinity" of the esoteric *Gnosticism* of Freemasonry; and that Bergoglio's belief system, being based on a *Gnostic* incarnational immanentism, logically excludes the ontological possibility of the Hypostatic Union in the mystery of the Incarnation of the Son of God professed in Catholicism, since the Christian dogma of this revealed mystery presupposes the existence of an infinitely perfect and *transcendent*, Triune God, whose eternally begotten λογος became uniquely incarnate; thus Bergoglio's notion of God reduces the Deity we profess to be the One God (ἕνα Θεόν) who is *Almighty* (Παντοκράτορα) and the *Creator of heaven and earth, of all things visible and invisible* (ποιητὴν οὐρανοῦ καὶ γῆς, ὁρατῶν τε πάντων καὶ ἀοράτων), to a mere demiurgic *deus sive natura* in a properly pandeistic Spinozan sense, according to which it could be said, as in the words of Meister Eckhart, in a manner applicable in a radical ontological sense to all things equally, including the Incarnate Word Himself, that "All things are words of God." This heretical *Incarnationalism* is blatantly evident in the passages of Bergoglio's discourses which I cited in Volume One. Bergoglio's disbelief in the Christian God of the deposit of revelation set forth in all the credal formulae and dogmatic pronouncements of the Catholic Church, and his profession of a false and pagan notion of God are the plainly evident principles of his belief system — a religion without the need nor even the metaphysical possibility for the theological virtue of faith in the absolutely supreme and perfect Triune God, nor for belief in the full divinity of Jesus Christ as the Eternal Word of the Father hypostatically united throughout his entire earthly life to the human nature virginally conceived supernaturally by the Holy Ghost in the womb of the Virgin Mary. Thus it is easily understood why Bergoglio did not deny having said, nor did he make any comment or clarification after he was quoted by his friend, Scalfari, as having stated that, "Jesus of Nazareth, once he became a man, although he was a man of exceptional virtue, was not a god at all." Scalfari wrote in La Repubblica, "Anyone who has had the good fortune to meet with him and speak with him in utmost confidence – as I have done several times – knows that Pope Francis conceives of Christ as Jesus of Nazareth: a man, not an incarnate god. Once incarnate, Jesus ceases to be a god and become a man, until his death on the cross."

It is scarcely conceivable that Scalfari has quoted Bergoglio inaccurately when one considers that they have been meeting with each other periodically throughout the duration of the Bergoglian "pontificate"; and on numerous occasions, Scalfari has reported direct quotations of Bergoglio's assertions which are directly opposed to several of the most universally known dogmas of the Catholic faith. Has Bergoglio even once denied having made these statements? No, not only has he not denied making the heretical statements, but he has even included the content of one of their conversations published by Scalfari in his own book, *Interviste e conversazioni con giornalisti*.⁵⁸⁵ He certainly would not have done that if Scalfari had been guilty of defaming him with fabricated heretical quotations. Indeed, he would have denounced Scalfari for publishing lies if indeed the quoted passages of the conversations had been fabricated. On October 10, 2019, Antonio Socci commented on Scalfari's bombshell revelation of Bergoglio's reported denial of the divinity of Christ, saying, "Such an affirmation is totally incompatible with Catholicism: he who pronounces it not only cannot any longer be pope, but **cannot even be said anymore to be Catholic**. He is outside the Church."⁵⁸⁶ This is absolutely correct. What he said after that is also entirely correct — that Bergoglio must either depart immediately or issue an unequivocal denial of the words attributed to him by Scalfari. He has done neither. While there has only been a weakly worded disclaimer questioning the accuracy of the quoted words issued by the director of the Vatican *Sala Stampa*, **without any clear or explicit denial**, Bergoglio has again met with Scalfari as recently as August 2, of this year (2020) — eleven days ago from the time of this writing, with Scalfari again reporting the words of Bergoglio spoken in conversation between them, without so much as a whimper of protest from Bergoglio or the Vatican. If Scalfari had really published grave falsehoods against Bergoglio, he would certainly have never have provided Scalfari with yet another opportunity to slander him by meeting with him again. These facts constitute a clear *indicium* of formal heresy spoken in private in previous conversations with the knowledge that the heretical statements would be published, but that they were clearly made under such circumstances which would provide the heretic with the opportunity to express his heresy with at least some minimal degree of plausible deniability; whereas in his public appearances, Bergoglio maintains a mere pro forma semblance of orthodoxy on this dogma, as well as on other points of dogma which he denies

---

⁵⁸⁵ Jorge Mario Bergoglio Papa Francesco, *INTERVISTE E CONVERSAZIONI CON I GIORNALISTI*; Libreria Editrice Vaticana, Città del Vaticano, 2017; La Repubblica, **Abbattere I muri**, Eugenio Scalfari, *Lunedì 7 novembre 2016*, p. 341.

⁵⁸⁶ https://www.antoniosocci.com/gesu-non-era-dio-lo-avrebbe-detto-bergoglio-a-scalfari-riferisce-scalfari-e-il-vaticano-invece-di-smentire-categoricamente/.

openly in these clearly orchestrated private conversations with Scalfari, as well as in other informal statements made both in private and in public. Thus, when his orthodoxy was called into question some years ago, his reported reply was, "I can recite the Creed." Indeed, any heretic can recite the Creed and profess the faith externally as a mere formality when it suits him, but does he **believe**? The *indicia* established by canonical tradition clearly demonstrate that he does not.

I already explained in Volume One that Jorge Bergoglio is a manifest formal heretic, and that this is plainly demonstrated in his outright and explicit rejection of some of the most basic dogmas of Christian belief — notably, 1) his rejection of the mission of the Church based on Christ's explicit teaching on evangelizing and converting all nations; 2) his rejection of the dogma of absolute necessity of faith for justification and redemption; 3) his rejection of the Catholic doctrine on marriage; 4) his rejection of the dogma of hell; 5) his rejection of the Church's teaching on capital punishment; and 6) his pagan notion of "God" which logically denies the dogmatic Christian doctrine of God as distinct from and infinitely transcending the created universe; which he contemptuously dismisses as a vague "idea in the air" (un'idea sull'aria)[587], a "god spray"[588], and a "Catholic God"; and 7) his radical rejection of the dogma of the cessation of the Mosaic Covenant and its supersession by the New Covenant of Jesus Christ.

Regarding the first point, it was reported by ANSA and by *Avvenire* that Bergoglio, on 13 October 2016 declared: "it is not licit to convince someone of your faith," [...] "Proselytism is the strongest venom against the path of ecumenism."[589] If that were still not clear enough, there is also his elucidation of this point to Eugenio Scalfari:

---

[587] Homily in the Santa Marta chapel, 9 October, 2014. https://www.lastampa.it/vatican-insider/it/2014/10/09/news/il-papa-dio-non-e-uno-spray-un-idea-nell-aria-1.35600232; https://www.youtube.com/watch?v=M9t9pWeBRFw.

[588] *Ibid.*

[589] «"Non è lecito convincere della tua fede: il proselitismo è il veleno più forte contro il cammino ecumenico". A lanciare il grido d'allarme è stato il Papa, rivolgendosi a braccio ai luterani ricevuti in udienza oggi nell'Aula Paolo VI.» — ANSA; https://www.avvenire.it/chiesa/pagine/papa-

«Proselytism is a solemn nonsense, it makes no sense. We must know ourselves, listen to ourselves, make grow the awareness of the world that surrounds us. This happens to me after a meeting, I look forward to another because new ideas are born and new needs are discovered. This is important: know, listen and widen the circle of thoughts. The world is crossed by paths that zoom in and out, but the important thing is that they take us to what is good.»[590]

Now the universally accepted and commonly understood dictionary definition of the word "proselytize" given by Merriam-Webster is "to induce someone to convert to one's faith".[591] What Bergoglio has said in these passages is that the solemn commission Christ gave to the apostles to **make disciples of all nations**, to **teach them to observe all He commanded**, and to **baptize them and bring them into the Church**, is **"illicit"**, **"solemn nonsense"**, and **"venom"**. Whoever would think this plainly heretical sense is not what Bergoglio intended needs to think again after reading this: "Are you going to convince someone else to become a Catholic? No, no, no! Go meet him, he's your brother! And that's enough." (Message for the feast of St. Cajetan in Argentina, 7 August 2013)[592] Bergoglio's words are as heretical as they are blasphemous — and totally inexcusable. Our Lord Jesus Christ solemnly sent the apostles on a mission which the Church has always understood and taught to mean that they, as preachers of the faith, are *to convert the nations to the Catholic*

---

luterani-rifugiati; https://it.zenit.org/2016/10/13/francesco-ai-luterani-il-proselitismo-il-veleno-piu-forte-contro-lecumenismo/.

[590] «Il proselitismo è una solenne sciocchezza, non ha senso. Bisogna conoscersi, ascoltarsi e far crescere la conoscenza del mondo che ci circonda. A me capita che dopo un incontro ho voglia di farne un altro perché nascono nuove idee e si scoprono nuovi bisogni. Questo è importante: conoscersi, ascoltarsi, ampliare la cerchia dei pensieri. Il mondo è percorso da strade che riavvicinano e allontanano, ma l'importante è che portino verso il Bene». www.repubblica.it/cultura/2013/10/01/news/papa_francesco_a_scalfari_cos_cambier_la_chiesa-67630792/.

[591] https://www.merriam-webster.com/dictionary/proselytizing.

[592] *Messaggio per la festa di S. Gaetano in Argentina*, 7 agosto 2013 — «Vai a convincere un altro che si faccia cattolico? No, no, no! Vai ad incontrarlo, è tuo fratello! E questo basta» [Socci, Antonio. *Non è Francesco: La Chiesa nella grande tempesta*, Milano, 2014, p. 165.]

faith and baptize them into the Church, saying literally, "Therefore go and make disciples of all nations, baptizing them in the name of the Father, and of the Son, and of the Holy Spirit" (Matthew 28: 19). «πορευθεντες ουν μαθητευσατε παντα τα εθνη βαπτιζοντες αυτους εις το ονομα του πατρος και του υιου και του αγιου πνευματος» He used the word μαθητευσατε, which means "make disciples" (μαθητής = disciple). It does not mean to go and meet with them and have friendly dialogues with them on equal footing, but to "**preach the Gospel**" v. 15 (κηρυξατε το ευαγγελιον), *"teaching them to obey everything I have commanded you"* — **"teaching them"**(διδασκοντες αυτους); and then He declared, "He who believes and is baptized will be saved; and he who does not believe will be condemned." (Mark 16:16) «ο πιστευσας και βαπτισθεις σωθησεται ο δε απιστησας κατακριθησεται» Literally, "The one believing and being baptized will be saved but the one disbelieving will be condemned." (κατακριθησεται = "judged against") This is the teaching of Jesus Christ, but Bergoglio teaches the exact opposite: "But listen, never does one bring the gospel with proselytism. If someone claims to be a disciple of Jesus and comes to you with proselytism, this is not a disciple of Jesus."[593] In his prayer intention video of Jan. 2016[594], Bergoglio declared:

> Most of the inhabitants of the planet declare themselves believers, this should provoke a dialogue between the religions. Only with dialogue, we will eliminate intolerance and discrimination. Interreligious dialogue is a necessary condition for peace in the world. We must not stop praying for it and collaborating with those who think differently. Do you want to propose something? I trust you to spread my request for this month: May the sincere dialogue between men and women of different religions bear fruits of peace and justice. Many think differently, they feel differently. They seek God or find God in different ways. Some even call themselves agnostics, who do not know if God exists or not. And others declare themselves atheists. In this multitude, in this range

---

[593] VISITA AL LICEO CLASSICO "PILO ALBERTELLI" DI ROMA - *DIALOGO DEL SANTO PADRE FRANCESCO CON GLI STUDENTI - Venerdì, 20 dicembre 2019* — «Ma senti, mai, mai si porta il vangelo con proselitismo. Se qualcuno dice di essere discepolo di Gesù e ti viene col proselitismo, questo non è discepolo di Gesù.»

[594] https://www.youtube.com/watch?v=-6FfTxwTX34&feature=youtu.be.

of religions and the absence of religions, there is only one certainty that we have for everything: We are all children of God.[595]

Any mitigating factor that might excuse Bergoglio is quite inconceivable, given that he cannot possibly be ignorant of the words spoken by the Lord himself, which the magisterium of the Church has always taught to be understood in their plain literal sense; meaning that *the Gospel is to be preached to all nations for the purpose of making converts of them*, with the proviso that if they refuse to convert, they will be damned for eternity. Upon this solemn Gospel teaching is founded the solemn dogma of faith defined multiple times by the extraordinary magisterium, and perpetually taught by the ordinary and universal magisterium, that **Outside the Church there is no salvation.** This formula was first pronounced by St. Cyprian of Carthage (*extra ecclesiam nulla salus*[596]), and has been so unanimously taught throughout the ages, that no further comment is necessary except to point out

---

[595] «La mayor parte de los habitantes del planeta se declaran creyentes, esto debería provocar un diálogo entre las religiones. Sólo con el diálogo, eliminaremos la intolerancia y la discriminación. El diálogo interreligioso es una condición necesaria para la paz en el mundo. No debemos dejar de orar por él y colaborar con quienes piensan distinto. ¿Querés proponer algo? Confío en vos para difundir mi petición de este mes: Que el diálogo sincero entre hombres y mujeres de diversas religiones, conlleve frutos de paz y justicia. Muchos piensan distinto, sienten distinto. Buscan a Dios o encuentran a Dios de diversa manera. Incluso algunos se dicen agnósticos, que no saben si existe Dios o no. Y otros, se declaran ateos. En esta multitud, en este abanico de religiones y de ausencia de religiones hay una sola certeza que tenemos para todo: Todos somos hijos de Dios.» https://opusdei.org/es-es/article/el-papa-explica-en-video-su-intencion-mensual-de-enero-de-2016/.

[596] St. Cyprian of Carthage, *Letter to Jubaianus* — «If the Baptism of public witness and of blood cannot profit a heretic unto salvation, because there is no salvation outside the Church, ("extra ecclesiam nulla salus") how much the more worthless is it for him, in secret places in the caves of robbers, dipped in the contagion of adulterous water, not merely not to have put off his former sins, but even to have added new and greater ones!» [William A. Jurgens, *The Faith of the Early Fathers*, vol. 1, Collegeville, MN: The Liturgical Press, 1970, p. 238]

that it was solemnly professed by the Fourth Lateran Council,[597] and as recently as the First Vatican Council it was again solemnly professed.[598] It is inconceivable that Bergoglio, formerly a professor of Theology, could be ignorant of this teaching, yet he remains obstinate in professing that all will be saved, even those outside the Church who reject Christ and his Church.

From the principles *Indifferentism* inherent in the Spinozan Naturalism of Bergoglio's faithless religion of *Pandeism*, (which is logically reducible to *pantheism*), it necessarily follows by way of strict logical implication that: «VII. God not only permits, but positively wills, the pluralism and diversity of religions, both Christian and non-Christian.» For Bergoglio, in direct contradiction to the dogma of Trent, we are all equally children of God, regardless of whether we are Jewish, Christian or Muslim: "This one was Mohammedan, this one was Jewish… we are all the same, all children of God and this purifies your gaze, it makes it human."[599] The dogmatic teaching of the Council of Trent, the explicit teaching of Scripture, and the universal and perpetual magisterium all teach the diametrical opposite. St. Alphonsus de Liguori in his exposition on the dogmatic teachings of the Council of Trent explained, "When we say that faith is necessary for the remission of sins, we mean to speak of the Catholic faith, not heretical faith. Without the habit of this faith, no man is justified."[600] The reason for this is explained in the teaching of Pope St. Pius V in the *Roman Catechism*: "And just as this one Church

---

[597] Innocentius III. in concilio generali, cap. I. — «Una vero est fidelium universalis ecclesia, extra quam nullus omnino salvatur.»

[598] «Hanc veram Catholicam Fidem, extra quam nemo salvus esse potest, quam in praesenti sponte profiteor et veraciter teneo, eandem integram, et immaculatam usque ad extremum vitae spiritum, constantissime, Deo adiuvante, retinere et confiteri, atque a meis subditis, vel illis, quorum cura ad me in munere meo spectabit, teneri, doceri et praedicari, quantum in me erit, curaturum, ego idem N. spondeo, voveo ac iuro. Sic me Deus adiuvet et haec sancta Dei Evangelia.»

[599] *Venerdì, 20 dicembre 2019* — «Questo era maomettano, questo era ebreo… siamo tutti uguali, tutti figli di Dio e questo ti purifica lo sguardo, te lo fa umano.»

[600] St. Alphonsus Liguori, *An Exposition and Defense of All the Points of Faith Discussed and Defined by the Council of Trent.*

cannot err in faith or morals, since it is guided by the Holy Ghost; so, on the contrary, all other societies arrogating to themselves the name of church, must necessarily, because guided by the spirit of the devil, be sunk in the most pernicious errors, both doctrinal and moral."[601] Heresy cannot unite us to God, because "Man is more than ever separated from God by infidelity, because he has not even true knowledge of God: and by false knowledge of God, man does not approach Him, but is distanced from Him."[602] The dogma on these points has been so clearly and solemnly defined, that it is absolutely inexcusable for anyone to profess that one can be saved without faith, which is to say, outside the Catholic faith — without entering the Catholic Church as a formally incorporated member, or at least implicitly *in voto*, as the cited passages of St. Robert Bellarmine and St. Alphonsus de Liguori have explained the dogma of Trent. Whoever would presume to teach or profess otherwise, departs from the body of the Catholic Church. That dogmatic teaching is clearly set forth in the canons and decrees of the Council of Trent[603]:

---

[601] «Sed quemadmodum haec una Ecclesia errare non potest in fidei ac morum disciplina tradenda, cum a Spiritu Sancto gubernetur; ita ceteras omnes, quae sibi Ecclesiae nomen arrogant, ut quae diaboli spiritu ducantur, in doctrinae et morum perniciosissimis erroribus versari necesse est.» [*CATECHISMUS ROMANUS* - Ex Decreto Concilii Tridentini Ad Parochos, Capitulum X, 18 *Ecclesia in fidei, aut morum dogmatibus errare non potest.*]

[602] *I*ᵃ *II*ᵃ *q. 10 a.1* — «... Unde tanto aliquod peccatum est gravius quanto per ipsum homo magis a Deo separatur. Per infidelitatem autem maxime homo a Deo elongatur, quia nec veram Dei cognitionem habet; per falsam autem cognitionem ipsius non appropinquat ei, sed magis ab eo elongatur.»

[603] **SESSIO VI - 13 ian. 1547 - [Decretum de iustificatione]-Caput I.: De naturae et legis ad iustificandos homines imbecilitate** — Primum declarat sancta Synodus ad iustificationis doctrinam probe et sincere intelligendam oportere ut unusquisque agnoscat et fateatur quod cum omnes homines in praevaricatione Adae innocentiam perdidissent facti immundi et (ut apostolus inquit) natura filii irae quemadmodum in decreto de peccato originali exposuit usque adeo servi erant peccati et sub potestate diaboli ac mortis... **[Caput III.: Qui per Christum iustificantur]** Verum etsi ille pro omnibus mortuus est non omnes tamen mortis eius beneficium recipiunt sed ii dumtaxat quibus meritum passionis eius communicatur. Nam sicut revera homines nisi ex semine Adae propagati nascerentur non

nascerentur iniusti cum ea propagatione per ipsum dum concipiuntur propriam iniustitiam contrahant: ita nisi in Christo renascerentur numquam iustificarentur cum ea renascentia per meritum passionis eius gratia qua iusti fiunt illis tribuatur... **[Caput IV.: Insinuatur descriptio iustificationis]** Quibus verbis iustificationis impii descriptio insinuatur ut sit translatio ab eo statu in quo homo nascitur filius primi Adae in statum gratiae et adoptionis filiorum Dei per secundum Adam Iesum Christum salvatorem nostrum; quae quidem translatio post Evangelium promulgatum sine lavacro regenerationis aut eius voto fieri non potest sicut scriptum est: nisi quis renatus fuerit ex aqua et Spiritu Sancto non potest introire in regnum Dei. **[Caput VI.: Modus praeparationis]** Disponuntur autem ad ipsam iustitiam dum excitati divina gratia et adiuti fidem ex auditu concipientes libere moventur in Deum credentes vera esse quae divinitus revelata et promissa sunt atque illud in primis a Deo iustificari impium per gratiam eius per redemptionem quae est in Christo Iesu et dum peccatores se esse intelligentes a divinae iustitiae timore quo utiliter concutiuntur ad considerandam Dei misericordiam se convertendo in spem eriguntur fidentes Deum sibi propter Christum propitium fore illum que tamquam omnis iustitiae fontem diligere incipiunt ac propterea moventur adversus peccata per odium aliquod et detestationem hoc est per eam poenitentiam quam ante baptismum agi oportet; denique dum proponunt suscipere baptismum, inchoare novam vitam et servare divina mandata. De hac dispositione scriptum est: accedentem ad Deum oportet credere quia est et quod inquirentibus se remunerator sit et: confide fili remittuntur tibi peccata tua et: timor Domini expellit peccatum et: poenitentiam agite et baptizetur unusquisque vestrum in nomine Iesu Christi in remissionem peccatorum vestrorum et accipietis donum Spiritus Sancti et: euntes ergo docete omnes gentes baptizantes eos in nominee Patris et Filii et Spiritus Sancti docentes eos servare quaecumque mandavi vobis denique: praeparate corda vestra Domino... **[Caput VIII.: Quo modo intelligatur, impium per fidem, et gratis iustificari]** Cum vero apostolus dicit iustificari hominem per fidem et gratis ea verba in eo sensu intelligenda sunt quem perpetuus Ecclesiae catholicae consensus tenuit et expressit, ut scilicet per fidem ideo iustificari dicamur quia fides est humanae salutis initium fundamentum et radix omnis iustificationis sine qua impossibile est placere Deo et ad filiorum eius consortium pervenire; gratis autem iustificari ideo dicamur quia nihil eorum quae iustificationem praecedunt sive fides sive opera ipsam iustificationis gratiam promeretur; si enim gratia est iam non ex operibus; alioquin (ut idem apostolus inquit) gratia iam non est gratia.

The Council of Trent The Fifth Session

Celebrated on the seventeenth day of the month of June, in the year MDXLVI.

DECREE CONCERNING ORIGINAL SIN

That our Catholic faith, without which it is impossible to please God, may, errors being purged away, continue in its own perfect and spotless integrity, and that the Christian people may not be carried about with every wind of doctrine... the sacred and holy, ecumenical and general Synod of Trent, — lawfully assembled in the Holy Ghost, the three same legates of the Apostolic See presiding therein,--wishing now to come to the reclaiming of the erring, and the confirming of the wavering, — following the testimonies of the sacred Scriptures, of the holy Fathers, of the most approved councils, and the judgment and consent of the Church itself, ordains, confesses, and declares these things touching the said original sin:

1. If any one does not confess that the first man, Adam, when he had transgressed the commandment of God in Paradise, immediately lost the holiness and justice wherein he had been constituted; and that he incurred, through the offence of that prevarication, the wrath and indignation of God, and consequently death, with which God had previously threatened him, and, together with death, captivity under his power who thenceforth had the empire of death, that is to say, the devil, and that the entire Adam, through that offence of prevarication, was changed, in body and soul, for the worse; let him be anathema.

2. If anyone asserts, that the prevarication of Adam injured himself alone, and not his posterity; and that the holiness and justice, received of God, which he lost, he lost for himself alone, and not for us also; or that he, being defiled by the sin of disobedience, has only transfused death, and pains of the body, into the whole human race, but not sin also, which is the death of the soul; let him be anathema: — whereas he contradicts the apostle who says; By one man sin entered into the world, and by sin death, and so death passed upon all men, in whom all have sinned.

3. If any one asserts, that this sin of Adam, — which in its origin is one, and being transfused into all by propogation, not by imitation, is in each one as his own, — is taken away either by the powers of human nature, or by any other remedy than the merit of the one mediator, our Lord Jesus Christ, who hath reconciled us to God in his own blood, made unto us justice, santification, and redemption; or if he denies that the said merit of Jesus Christ is applied, both to adults and to infants, by the sacrament of baptism rightly administered in the form of the Church;

let him be anathema: For there is no other name under heaven given to men, whereby we must be saved. Whence that voice; Behold the lamb of God behold him who taketh away the sins of the world; and that other; As many as have been baptized, have put on Christ.

4. If any one denies, that infants, newly born from their mothers' wombs, even though they be sprung from baptized parents, are to be baptized; or says that they are baptized indeed for the remission of sins, but that they derive nothing of original sin from Adam, which has need of being expiated by the laver of regeneration for the obtaining life everlasting, — whence it follows as a consequence, that in them the form of baptism, for the remission of sins, is understood to be not true, but false, — let him be anathema. For that which the apostle has said, By one man sin entered into the world, and by sin death, and so death passed upon all men in whom all have sinned, is not to be understood otherwise than as the Catholic Church spread everywhere hath always understood it. For, by reason of this rule of faith, from a tradition of the apostles, even infants, who could not as yet commit any sin of themselves, are for this cause truly baptized for the remission of sins, that in them that may be cleansed away by regeneration, which they have contracted by generation. For, unless a man be born again of water and the Holy Ghost, he cannot enter into the kingdom of God.

5. If any one denies, that, by the grace of our Lord Jesus Christ, which is conferred in baptism, the guilt of original sin is remitted; or even asserts that the whole of that which has the true and proper nature of sin is not taken away; but says that it is only rased, or not imputed; let him be anathema.[604]

The Council of Trent The Sixth Session

Celebrated on the thirteenth day of the month of January, 1547.

DECREE ON JUSTIFICATION

CHAPTER I.
On the Inability of Nature and of the Law to justify man.

The holy Synod declares first, that, for the correct and sound understanding of the doctrine of Justification, it is necessary that each one recognise and confess, that, whereas all men had lost their innocence

---

[604] **The Council of Trent,** *The canons and decrees of the sacred and oecumenical Council of Trent,* Ed. and trans. J. Waterworth, London: Dolman, 1848, pp. 21-23.

in the prevarication of Adam-having become unclean, and, as the apostle says, by nature children of wrath, as (this Synod) has set forth in the decree on original sin,-they were so far the servants of sin, and under the power of the devil and of death…

CHAPTER III.
Who are justified through Christ.

But, though He died for all, yet do not all receive the benefit of His death, but those only unto whom the merit of His passion is communicated. For as in truth men, if they were not born propagated of the seed of Adam, would not be born unjust,-seeing that, by that propagation, they contract through him, when they are conceived, injustice as their own,-so, if they were not born again in Christ, they never would be justified; seeing that, in that new birth, there is bestowed upon them, through the merit of His passion, the grace whereby they are made just…

CHAPTER IV.
A description is introduced of the Justification of the impious, and of the Manner thereof under the law of grace.

By which words, a description of the Justification of the impious is indicated,-as being a translation, from that state wherein man is born a child of the first Adam, to the state of grace, and of the adoption of the sons of God, through the second Adam, Jesus Christ, our Saviour. And this translation, since the promulgation of the Gospel, cannot be effected, without the laver of regeneration, or the desire thereof, as it is written; unless a man be born again of water and the Holy Ghost, he cannot enter into the Kingdom of God.

CHAPTER VI.
The manner of Preparation.

Now they (adults) are disposed unto the said justice, when, excited and assisted by divine grace, conceiving faith by hearing, they are freely moved towards God, believing those things to be true which God has revealed and promised,-and this especially, that God justifies the impious by His grace, through the redemption that is in Christ Jesus; and when, understanding themselves to be sinners, they, by turning themselves, from the fear of divine justice whereby they are profitably agitated, to consider the mercy of God, are raised unto hope, confiding that God will be propitious to them for Christ's sake; and they begin to love Him as the fountain of all justice; and are therefore moved against sins by a certain hatred and detestation, to wit, by that penitence which must be performed before baptism: lastly, when they purpose to receive baptism, to begin a new life, and to keep the commandments of God. Concerning this disposition it is written; He that cometh to God, must believe that he is, and is a rewarder to them that seek him; and, Be of good faith, son, thy sins are forgiven thee; and, The fear of the Lord driveth out sin; and, Do penance, and be baptized every one of you in the name of Jesus Christ, for the remission of your sins, and you shall receive the gift of the Holy Ghost; and, Going, therefore, teach ye all nations, baptizing them in the name of the Father, and of the Son, and of the Holy Ghost; finally, Prepare your hearts unto the Lord.

CHAPTER VIII.
In what manner it is to be understood, that the impious is justified by faith, and gratuitously.

And whereas the Apostle saith, that man is justified by faith and freely, those words are to be understood in that sense which the perpetual consent of the Catholic Church hath held and expressed; to wit, that we are therefore said to be justified by faith, because faith is the beginning of human salvation, the foundation, and the root of all Justification; without which it is impossible to please God, and to come unto the fellowship of His sons: but we are therefore said to be justified freely, because that none of those things which precede justification-whether faith or works-merit the grace itself of justification. For, if it be a grace, it is not now by works, otherwise, as the same Apostle says, grace is no more grace.[605]

Finally the entire doctrine on justification in the decree is declared to have full dogmatic force under penalty of anathema:

«CANON XXXIII. — If any one saith, that, by the Catholic doctrine touching Justification, by this holy Synod inset forth in this present decree, the glory of God, or the merits of our Lord Jesus Christ are in any way derogated from, and not rather that the truth of our faith, and

---

[605] **The Council of Trent**, *The canons and decrees of the sacred and oecumenical Council of Trent*, Ed. and trans. J. Waterworth, London: Dolman, 1848, pp. 31, 32, 34.

the glory in fine of God and of Jesus Christ are rendered (more) illustrious; let him be anathema.»[606]

* * *

"Man is more than ever separated from God by infidelity, because he has not even true knowledge of God: and by false knowledge of God, man does not approach Him, but is distanced from Him." (*Summa Theologiæ - I^a II^æ q. 10 a.1*)

God is essential being ("I Am Who Am" [יהוה] – Exodus 3:14) and therefore the fullness of being, and consequently, nothing outside of God can exist except what is created by Him. Therefore God is One, and there exists no other god beside Him. ("I am the Lord, and there is none else: there is no God, besides me" – Isaiah 45:5) The essential being of God in which consists the divine substance is therefore known *per se* as the Primary Truth and the principle of all truth: ("**principium verborum tuorum veritas**" Ps. 118:160 [LXX – "ἀρχὴ τῶν λόγων σου ἀλήθεια"] – Ps. 118; 160; "**In principio erat Verbum**, et Verbum erat apud Deum, et **Deus erat Verbum**" Ioannes 1:1 ["Ἐν ἀρχῇ ἦν ὁ λόγος, καὶ ὁ λόγος ἦν πρὸς τὸν θεόν, καὶ θεὸς ἦν ὁ λόγος."]) Therefore the principle of all truth exists in God and is God, and is in its nature essentially One. It is for this reason that, "There is only one truth and in consequence there can be only one true religion." — St. Maximillian Kolbe [607]

Bergoglio's heresy asserts that different religions, Christianity, Judaism, and Islam, which teach irreconcilably opposed doctrines, have "a common father in faith", and that it was God's work to give birth to these religions which exist in essential opposition to each other: "This blessed place brings us back to our origins, to the sources of God's work, to the birth of our religions."[608] Since, according to

---

[606] «33. Si quis dixerit per hanc doctrinam catholicam de iustificatione a sancta Synodo hoc praesenti decreto expressam aliqua ex parte gloriae Dei vel meritis Iesu Christi Domini nostri derogari et non potius veritatem fidei nostrae Dei denique ac Christi Iesu gloriam illustrari: a[nathema] s[it].]»

[607] André Fossard, *Forget Not Love: The Passion of Maximillian Kolbe*, p. 119.

[608] **INCONTRO INTERRELIGIOSO** - *Piana di Ur, Sabato, 6 marzo 2021*: "Questo luogo benedetto ci riporta alle origini, alle sorgenti dell'opera di Dio, alla nascita delle nostre religioni. Qui, dove visse Abramo nostro

Bergoglio, it was God's work to give birth to these opposing religions, it is therefore Abraham as a prophet of God who brings us together in unity: "The Patriarch Abraham, who today brings us together in unity, was a prophet of the Most High."[609] The unity he speaks of is not limited to the three monotheistic religions which claim their origin from Abraham, but those to be brought into unity include also "other religions". Bergoglio is openly preaching a ***new religion*** which consists in the **unity of religions**: "Today we, Jews, Christians and Muslims, together with our brothers and sisters of other religions, honour our father Abraham by doing as he did: *we look up to heaven and we journey on earth.* [...] *We look up to heaven.* Thousands of years later, as we look up to the same sky, those same stars appear. They illumine the darkest nights because they shine *together.* [...] if we want to preserve fraternity, we must not lose sight of heaven." Bergoglio's religion is the *dogma free* Masonic *brotherhood of men under the fatherhood of God*: "**This is true religiosity: to worship God and to love our neighbour.** In today's world, which often forgets or presents distorted images of the Most High, believers are called to bear witness to his goodness, **to show his paternity through our fraternity.**"[610] Dogmas must be discarded because they are professed to be ***absolute truths***, and according to Jorge "Francis" Bergoglio, belief in "absolute Truth" is a "disease", it is "evil": One must not forget what he said in 2015: "Fundamentalism is a sickness that is in all religions... We Catholics have some — and not some, many — who believe they possess the absolute truth," For Bergoglio, to profess that the dogmas of faith are absolute truth is evil: "They do evil. I say this because it is my Church."[611]

---

padre... Dio chiese ad Abramo di alzare lo sguardo al cielo e di contarvi le stelle (cfr *Gen* 15,5). In quelle stelle vide la promessa della sua discendenza, vide noi."

[609] *Ibid.* — "Il patriarca Abramo, che oggi ci raduna in unità, fu profeta dell'Altissimo."

[610] *Ibid.* — "Ecco la vera religiosità: adorare Dio e amare il prossimo. Nel mondo d'oggi, che spesso dimentica l'Altissimo o ne offre un'immagine distorta, i credenti sono chiamati a testimoniare la sua bontà, a mostrare la sua paternità mediante la loro fraternità."

[611] http://www.catholicherald.co.uk/news/2015/11/30/pope-francis-says-he-is-not-losing-any-sleep-over-vatican-leaks-trial/;

It is a principal axiom of Masonic religion that dogmatic differences between peoples of different religions are ultimately the cause of the enmity and hatred that leads to conflicts and wars between nations. It is precisely for this reason that they seek to establish in their *New World Order*, a **UNIVERSAL DOGMA FREE RELIGION**. Thus, it is the Masonic opposition to Catholic dogmatic belief that is at the root of Bergoglio's disdain for strict adherence to tradition and the rule of faith of the Catholic religion. To abolish dogma is to abolish enmity and war, according to the diabolical creed of Freemasonry. So also for Bergoglio: If we are willing to abandon our belief in the absolute truth of dogma, which he says is a form of "fundamentalism" which leaves us "enclosed in one fragment of reality",[612] we will eliminate enmity. This is the perverse *gnostic* principle which underlies his childishly simplistic recipe for peace:

> From where, then, can the journey of peace begin? From the decision not to have enemies. Anyone with the courage to look at the stars, anyone who believes in God, has no enemies to fight. He or she has only one enemy to face, an enemy that stands at the door of the heart and knocks to enter. That enemy is *enmity*.[613]

Bergoglio's proposition, "Anyone who believes in God, has no enemies to fight," is a Masonic belief that is directly opposed to the divinely revealed truth of Scripture: "*And all that will live godly in Christ Jesus, shall suffer persecution.*" (Tim. 3:12) "*And you shall be hated by all men for my name's sake.*" (Luke 21:17) "*If the world hate you, know ye, that it hath hated me before you.*" (John 15:18) "*Think ye, that I am come to give peace on earth? I tell you, no; but separation.*" (Luke 12:51) "*The Lord said to my Lord: Sit thou at my right hand: Until I make thy enemies thy*

---

https://www.christianheadlines.com/blog/pope-francis-criticizes-fundamentalists-who-believe-they-possess-absolute-truth.html.

[612] This is the idea he expressed in *Fratelli Tutti*, as is explained below.

[613] **INCONTRO INTERRELIGIOSO** - *Piana di Ur, Sabato, 6 marzo 2021*: "Da dove può cominciare allora il cammino della pace? Dalla rinuncia ad avere nemici. Chi ha il coraggio di guardare le stelle, chi crede in Dio, non ha nemici da combattere. Ha un solo nemico da affrontare, che sta alla porta del cuore e bussa per entrare: è *l'inimicizia.*"

footstool. The Lord will send forth the sceptre of thy power out of Sion: rule thou in the midst of thy enemies." (Psalm 109) *"Why have the Gentiles raged, and the people devised vain things? The kings of the earth stood up, and the princes met together, against the Lord and against his Christ."* (Psalm 2) *"I will put enmities between thee and the woman, and thy seed and her seed: she shall crush thy head, and thou shalt lie in wait for her heel."* (Genesis 3:15) Therefore, the only way we as Christians can make the decision to not have enemies, is by joining the ranks of the enemies of Christ, i.e. to abandon our faith in Christ and embrace the ecumenical devilry of Freemasonry, which professes respect for all religions except one — the unreformed Catholic religion which it declares **infamous**. *"Ecrasez l'infâme!"* ("Crush the Infamous Thing!") was Voltaire's notorious battle cry against "clericalism", "intolerance", and "superstition" — all Masonic code-words which camouflage their true meaning, words which for Freemasons signify only *Catholicism*. Freemasonry is the implacable self-declared enemy of the Catholic Church against which it has declared eternal enmity in its war to the death against God and religion, but Bergoglio's response to the attacks against God and his Church is a conscious defeatism which exhorts Christians to surrender, and to abandon their profession in the absolute truth of the infallible dogmas of faith. Thus, Bergoglio has invoked the wrath of God upon himself and all who follow his impious directives to make peace with the enemies of Christ: "O Lord my God, if I have done this thing, if there be iniquity in my hands: If I have rendered to them that repaid me evils, let me deservedly fall empty before my enemies." (Psalm 7:4-5)

There is only one Abrahamic religion, and, as is explained below at length, that one is the religion of Jesus Christ, signified in the Old Testament and revealed in the New Testament, founded by the divine Saviour Jesus Christ, and built on the testimony of the Apostles and Prophets. Our Lord Jesus Christ declared to those Jews who rejected Him: "Abraham your father rejoiced that he might see my day: he saw it, and was glad." (John 8:56) The Covenant between God and men is established through ISRAEL, and not through any other Semitic tribes that claim descent from ISHMAEL: "O ye seed of Abraham his servant; ye sons of Jacob his chosen… He hath remembered his covenant for ever: the word which he commanded to a thousand generations. Which he made to Abraham; and his oath to Isaac: And he appointed the same to Jacob for a law, and to Israel for an everlasting testament." (Psalm 104:6-10)

The doctrine of the Quran is self-negating. It says the scriptures of the Apostles, Prophets have authority, and that Jesus Christ is a Prophet. The divine promise to bless all nations was made to Abraham. (Gen. 22:18) God made an irrevocable covenant with Abraham. Abraham had two sons, Ishmael and Isaac, but it was the younger son, Isaac, and not Ishmael, who would inherit the divine promises of the Abrahamic covenant. Isaac had two sons Essau and Jacob, and it was through Jacob that the covenant was renewed, and to Jacob's descendants that the covenantal promises were perpetuated. God renamed Jacob ISRAEL. The ISRAELITES are the foundation of the covenant between God and men. Therefore Our Lord Jesus Christ declared: *"Salvation is from the Jews."* (John 4:22) The true religion was not revealed to any non-Jewish Ishmaelite. There is no covenant between God and man mediated by Muhammad, but only by the Jewish Messiah, Jesus Christ, *"For there is one God, and one mediator between God and men, the man Christ Jesus."* (1 Tim. 2:5) Salvation is not through the seed of Ishmael but of Jacob: Luke chapter 1: "[26] *And in the sixth month, the angel Gabriel was sent from God into a city of Galilee, called Nazareth,* [27] *To a virgin espoused to a man whose name was Joseph, of the house of David; and the virgin's name was Mary.* [28] *And the angel being come in, said unto her: Hail, full of grace, the Lord is with thee: blessed art thou among women.* [29] *Who having heard, was troubled at his saying, and thought with herself what manner of salutation this should be.* [30] *And the angel said to her: Fear not, Mary, for thou hast found grace with God.* [31] *Behold thou shalt conceive in thy womb, and shalt bring forth a son; and thou shalt call his name Jesus.* [32] *He shall be great, and shall be called the Son of the most High; and the Lord God shall give unto him the throne of David his father; and he shall reign in the house of Jacob for ever.*"

The Israelite kingdom is the foundation of the Kingdom of God, as is evident in the Old Testament; and the totality of the Old Testament, founded on the Messianic promise, consists in its Messianic signification of its fulfilment by Jesus Christ. In the Old Testament Israel is signified by the images of the vine and the olive tree. In Jeramiah 11: 16-17 Israel is called a "green olive tree", and in Romans 11:17-27 St. Paul gives us the image of the wild olive branches grafted onto the tree; signifying the Gentiles being incorporated into the Kingdom of Israel. The Church does not replace Israel, because the New Testament of Jesus Christ is signified and foretold in the Old Testament as the fulfilment of the Messianic promises in Christ the King of the Jews. (John 19:19) The divine promises to the Israelite nation recorded in the scriptures are unconditional and therefore **irrevocable**. The kingdom that was taken from them was taken from the unfaithful Israelites as a punishment for their having been unfaithful to the Covenant, and finally for having rejected Jesus Christ, who was signified throughout the Old Testament as the fulfilment of all the Messianic prophecies. Therefore it is written in the Gospel (Matt. 21: 42 - 44) «*Jesus said unto them, "Did ye never read in the Scriptures: The stone which the builders rejected, the same is become the head of the corner. This is the Lord's doing, and it is marvelous in our eyes'?* [43] *Therefore say I unto you, the Kingdom of God shall be taken from you and given to a nation bringing forth the fruits thereof.*» The kingdom that was taken from them as a divine punishment for having rejected Christ was not taken away forever, but it will indeed be restored to the Jewish nation (Acts 1:6), but not before the time when they will finally submit to the rule of Christ, who in fulfilment of the Messianic prophecies is the King of the Jews: "*And Pilate asked him, saying: Art thou the king of the Jews? But he answering, said: Thou sayest it.*" (Luke 23:3) For so long as they resist the rule of Jesus Christ, they will be ground to powder: "And whosoever shall fall on this stone, shall be broken: but on whomsoever it shall fall, it shall grind him to powder." (Matthew 21:44) And of the Christ, whom David called his Lord (Matt. 22:24, Mark 12:36, Luke 20:41-43) it is written: "[1] *The Lord said to my Lord: Sit thou at my right hand: Until I make thy enemies thy footstool.* [2] *The Lord will send forth the sceptre of thy power out of Sion: rule thou in the midst of thy enemies.* [3] *With thee is the principality in the day of thy strength: in the brightness of the saints: from the womb before the day star I begot thee.* [4] *The Lord hath sworn, and he will not repent: Thou art a priest forever according to the order of Melchisedech.* [5] *The Lord at thy right hand hath broken kings in the day of his wrath.* [6] *He shall judge among nations, he shall fill ruins: he shall crush the heads in the land of the many*". (Psalm 109)

Thus, the restoration of the Israelite kingdom can only take place after the Jews will have placed themselves under the rulership of Christ, and then the time of the Gentiles will be completed, as Christ explained in His own words: «And they shall fall by the edge of the sword, and shall be led away captive into all nations: and Jerusalem shall be trodden down of the Gentiles, until the times of the Gentiles be fulfilled.» (Luke 21: 24) It is for this reason that He who is the Prince of Peace, said "Do not think that I came to send peace upon earth: I came not to send peace, but the sword." (Matt. 10:34) There cannot be peace on earth until the time of the Gentiles ends and Kingdom of Israel is restored, and this can only take place when the Jews will finally accept Jesus Christ as the Messiah, and be received into the Catholic Church. This will is the absolute prerequisite for the definitive establishment in the world the universal peace of the Kingdom of God which will be brought about by the restoration of the Israelite kingdom. This restoration of Israel will be brought about by the intercession of Mary, and is mysteriously signified in the Book of Esther. By defecting from their divine calling and rejecting Christ their King, they "Who both killed the Lord Jesus, and the prophets, and have persecuted us, and please not God, and are adversaries to all men" (1 Thessalonians 2:15); but they have not been cast off forever. Their election is irrevocable, and their self-imposed exile from the Kingdom of God will end: Romans 11 - "[11] *I say then, have they so stumbled, that they should fall? God forbid. But by their offence, salvation is come to the Gentiles, that they may be emulous of them.* [12] *Now if the offence of them be the riches of the world, and the diminution of them, the riches of the Gentiles; how much more the fulness of them?* [13] *For I say to you, Gentiles: as long indeed as I am the apostle of the Gentiles, I will honour my ministry,* [14] *If, by any means, I may provoke to emulation them who are my flesh, and may save some of them.* [15] *For if the loss of them be the reconciliation of the world, what shall the receiving of them be, but life from the dead?* [16] *For if the firstfruit be holy, so is the lump also: and if the root be holy, so are the branches.* [17] *And if some of the branches be broken, and thou, being a wild olive, art ingrafted in them, and art made partaker of the root, and of the fatness of the olive tree,* [18] *Boast not against the branches. But if thou boast, thou bearest not the root, but the root thee.* [19] *Thou wilt say then: The branches were broken off, that I might be grafted in.* [20] *Well: because of unbelief they were broken off. But thou standest by faith: be not highminded, but fear.* [21] *For if God hath not spared the natural branches, fear lest perhaps he also spare not thee.* [22] *See then the goodness and the severity of God: towards them indeed that are fallen, the severity; but towards thee, the goodness of God, if thou abide in goodness, otherwise thou also shalt be cut off.* [23] *And they also, if they abide not still in unbelief, shall be grafted in: for God is able to graft them in again.* ²⁴ *For if thou wert cut out of the wild olive tree, which is natural to thee; and, contrary to nature, were grafted into the good olive tree; how much more shall they that are the natural branches, be grafted into their own olive tree?* ²⁵ *For I would not have you ignorant, brethren, of this mystery, (lest you should be wise in your own conceits), that blindness in part has happened in Israel, until the fulness of the Gentiles should come in.* ²⁶ *And so all Israel should be saved, as it is written: There shall come out of Sion, he that shall deliver, and shall turn away ungodliness from Jacob.* ²⁷ *And this is to them my covenant: when I shall take away their sins.* ²⁸ *As concerning the gospel, indeed, they are enemies for your sake: but as touching the election, they are most dear for the sake of the fathers.* ²⁹ *For the gifts and the calling of God are without repentance."*

God has not rejected the Jewish people, but it is they who exiled themselves from their own kingdom when they rejected their own King. St. Alphonsus explains: *"The punishment which the poor Jews have suffered for so long for their obstinacy; while the poor see the dominion of Judea lost, the city destroyed, the temple burned, the sacrifices abandoned, and they scattered throughout the earth, without kings, without priests and without altar; all of which was foretold by the prophets: and they see it thus done completely accomplished, and yet obstinate they continue to deny their Saviour."*[614]

THE ENDURING JEWISH REJECTION OF CHRIST WILL USHER IN THE REIGN OF ANTICHRIST

It was foretold not only by Moses and the prophets, but most clearly by Jesus Christ Himself:

> *"²⁹ Woe to you scribes and Pharisees, hypocrites; that build the sepulchres of the prophets, and adorn the monuments of the just,* ³⁰ *And say: If we had been in the days of our Fathers, we would not have been partakers with them in the blood of the prophets.* ³¹ *Wherefore you are witnesses against yourselves, that you are the sons of them that killed the prophets.* ³² *Fill ye up then the measure of your fathers.* ³³ *You serpents, generation of vipers, how will you flee from the judgment of hell?* ³⁴ *Therefore behold I send to you prophets, and wise men, and scribes: and some of them you will put to death and crucify, and some you will scourge in your synagogues, and persecute from city to city:* ³⁵ *That upon you may come all the just blood that hath been shed upon the earth, from the blood of Abel the just, even unto the blood of Zacharias the*

---

[614] *Verità Della Fede*, Opera Del Beato Alfonso Maria de' Liguori, Tomo Secondo, Parte Terza, Monza, 1823, p. 64.

son of Barachias, whom you killed between the temple and the altar. ³⁶ *Amen I say to you, all these things shall come upon this generation.* ³⁷ *Jerusalem, Jerusalem, thou that killest the prophets, and stonest them that are sent unto thee, how often would I have gathered together thy children, as the hen doth gather her chickens under her wings, and thou wouldest not?* ³⁸ *Behold, your house shall be left to you, desolate.* ³⁹ *For I say to you, you shall not see me henceforth till you say: Blessed is he that cometh in the name of the Lord."* (Matthew 23:29-39)

The first commandment of the Covenant mandated the exclusive worship of the One God: "I am the Lord thy God who brought thee out of the land of Egypt, out of the house of bondage. Thou shalt not have strange gods before me." (Ex. 20:1) God warned them through Moses to beware of the pagan cult which is still practiced today by Masonry and Cabalism: "Keep your souls carefully...lest perhaps lifting up thy eyes to heaven, thou see the sun and the moon and all the stars...being deceived by error thou adore and serve them." (Deut. 4:15,19) God promised that His blessing would remain with them on the condition that they observe the Covenant that He established with them: "If thou wilt hear the voice of the Lord... and keep all his commandments... God will make thee higher than all the nations that are on the earth... if thou hear his precepts...the Lord shall cause thy enemies, that rise up against thee, to fall down before thy face... thou shalt be always above, and not beneath... if thou wilt hear the commandments of the Lord thy God." (Deut. 28:1-13) God warned the Israelites through Moses that the pagans would be a snare for them: "if thou serve their gods it will surely be a snare unto thee." (Ex. 23:33) He warned them that His curse will come upon them if they stray from the Covenant: The Lord shall send upon you curses: ... confusion and frustration in all that you undertake to do, until you are destroyed and perish quickly... until He has consumed you off the land which you are entering... (Palestine)... The Lord will make the rain of your land powder and dust... the Lord will cause you to be defeated by your enemies... the Lord will smite you with madness, and blindness and confusion of mind... you shall build a house and you shall not dwell in it... a nation which you have not known shall eat up the fruit of your ground and of all your labours... you shall be oppressed and crushed continually; so that you shall be driven mad by the sight which your eyes shall see... Because you did not serve the Lord your God... you shall serve your enemies whom the Lord will send against you… and He will put a yoke of iron upon your neck until He has destroyed you… the Lord will bring upon you afflictions, afflictions severe and lasting… you shall be left few in number…the Lord will take delight in bringing ruin upon you and destroying you…and you shall be plucked off the land… and the Lord will scatter you among all the peoples, from one end of the earth to the other…and among these nations you shall find no ease, and there shall be no rest for the sole of your foot…your life shall hang in doubt before you…you shall be in dread and have no assurance of your life. I will appoint over you sudden terror… you shall be smitten before your enemies, those who hate you shall rule over you… I will break the back of your power…I Myself will smite you sevenfold for your sins and I will bring a sword upon you that shall exact vengeance… and if in spite of this you will not hearken to me… then I will walk contrary to you in fury… I will scatter you among the nations and I will unsheathe the sword after you… those of you that are left shall pine away in your enemies' lands… (Deut. 28; Lev. 26)[615] The history of the Israelites chronicled in their own sacred books is a witness against them for their continual infidelity to the Covenant and their worship of the false gods of the pagans. When Moses descended from the mountain with the tablets of the Law, he found the Israelites practicing the Canaanite idol worship — they were worshiping the golden calf. God sent them prophets who threatened divine chastisement, but they persecuted the prophets, killed them, and declared them to be mad. This is all written in the books of the prophets. Finally the prophet Daniel announced: "… the malediction, and the curse, which is written in the book of Moses… is fallen upon us, because we have sinned against him… and we entreated not thy face, O Lord our God, that we might turn from our iniquities, and think on thy truth." (Daniel 9:11, 13) God warned the Jews that they would be blinded if they strayed from the Covenant, and Isaiah and David declared that this indeed would take place. (Isaiah 6:10; Psalms 68:24) Therefore, when Jesus Christ came, in fulfillment of the Scriptures, they did not recognize Him for what He was: the promised Messiah — foretold by Moses and the prophets. Rejected by the Jews, Jesus wept over Jerusalem, saying: *"If thou hadst known, and that in this*

---

[615] Revised Standard Version

thy day, the things that are to thy peace, but now they are hidden from thy eyes. For the days shall come upon thee, and thy enemies shall cast a trench about thee, and compass thee round, and straighten thee on every side, and beat thee flat to the ground, and thy children who are in thee: and they shall not leave in thee a stone upon a stone: because thou hast not known the time of thy visitation." (Luke 19:42-44) The Jews have not recognized the punishing hand of God at work in all that they have suffered. God had said to Moses: *"I will raise them up a prophet out of the midst of their brethren like to thee: and I will put my words in his mouth, and he shall speak to them all that I shall command him. And he that will not hear his words which he shall speak in my name, I will be the revenger."* (Deut. 18:18-19) That prophet was Jesus Christ, but they did not hear the words which He spoke in the name of the Eternal Father — and therefore the curse of Moses was poured out upon them, but their leaders still lead the people astray: They do not seek the Kingdom of God, by which God promised through the seed of Abraham to bless all the nations of the earth. (Gen. 18:18) They seek a messiah to their own liking, one who will serve their father, the devil and annihilate the nations: "⁴²Jesus therefore said to them: If God were your Father, you would indeed love me. For from God I proceeded, and came; for I came not of myself, but he sent me: ⁴⁴You are of your father the devil, and the desires of your father you will do. He was a murderer from the beginning, and he stood not in the truth; because truth is not in him. When he speaketh a lie, he speaketh of his own: for he is a liar, and the father thereof." (John 8:42,44)That is why Jesus said to them: "Search the scriptures...the same are they that give testimony of me. And you will not come to me that you may have life...Think not that I will accuse you to the Father. There is one that accuseth you, Moses, in whom you trust. For if you did believe Moses, you would believe me also; for he wrote of me. But if you do not believe his writings, how will you believe my words?" (John 5:39-40, 45-47) "I am come in the name of my Father, and you receive me not: if another shall come in his own name, him you will receive." (John 5:43) **The one who will come in his own name will be the Antichrist, who will seek mainly to exterminate first Christians and then also Jews, and ultimately he will attempt to implement the devil's plan to the annihilate the human race.** The global reign of the Antichrist "whose coming is according to the operation of Satan in all power and false signs and wonders" (2 Thess. 2:9) will bring about the consummation of the *Mystery of Iniquity* (2 Thess. 2:7) 325 which will be "revealed in its time" (v. 6), and will be utterly destroyed by the almighty Hand of God: "the Lord Jesus Christ will kill him by the breath of his mouth and destroy him by his appearing and his coming" (v. 8). The entire history of the world has been principally and ultimately a war waged between the *sons of light* (בְּנֵי אוֹר, *benei or*) and the *sons of darkness* (בְּנֵי חֹשֶׁךְ, *benei ḥoshekh*) between the Kingdom of God, the "children of light, and children of the day" and them who are "of the night" (1 Thess. 5:5) — a perpetual *"War of the Sons of Light Against the Sons of Darkness"*. (*Megillat Milḥamat B'ne*) So, enough said on Bergoglio's insanely vapid, and consciously defeatist outburst: "Anyone who believes in God, has no enemies to fight." If that were true, Jesus would never have said: "*But now if you have a purse, take it, and also a bag; and if you don't have a sword, sell your cloak and buy one.*" (Luke 22:35-36)

> ⁷ *And there was a great battle in heaven, Michael and his angels fought with the dragon, and the dragon fought and his angels:* ⁸ *And they prevailed not, neither was their place found any more in heaven.* ⁹ *And that great dragon was cast out, that old serpent, who is called the devil and Satan, who seduceth the whole world; and he was cast unto the earth, and his angels were thrown down with him.* ¹⁰ *And I heard a loud voice in heaven, saying: Now is come salvation, and strength, and the kingdom of our God, and the power of his Christ: because the accuser of our brethren is cast forth, who accused them before our God day and night.* ¹¹ *And they overcame him by the blood of the Lamb, and by the word of the testimony, and they loved not their lives unto death.* ¹² *Therefore rejoice, O heavens, and you that dwell therein. Woe to the earth, and to the sea, because the devil is come down unto you, having great wrath, knowing that he hath but a short time.*
>
> **APOCALYPSE 12:7-12**

* * *

Absolutely no one can be justified and redeemed from the state of damnation outside the Catholic Church without the Catholic faith, because the justified state exists in virtue of one's union with God in Theological Charity, which cannot exist without the theological virtues of faith and hope; but Bergoglio doesn't stop at saying that all religions lead to God, and that one can be saved in any religion — he says **no faith at all is necessary — one can gain the reward of eternal redemption without any faith in God whatsoever.** Incredibly, this man who is reputed by so many to be the pope of the Catholic Church and *Vicar of Christ* so totally rejects Christ's teaching and the entire doctrinal tradition of divine revelation founded on both Testaments on the necessity of faith in the One true God for salvation, as well as rejecting the divinely instituted authority of the testimony of the apostles and prophets on the necessity to observe the one, true religion, which has existed in various forms revealed in Scripture since the times of the most ancient patriarchs down to our own day; that it is quite inconceivable for him, who so utterly rejects the perpetual divinely revealed tradition of the ages, and even the very foundation of revelation, and the supernatural authority of that divine revelation, to be capable of being God's representative on earth. Bergoglio is condemned by the words of his own mouth. While speaking to a group of students at the Liceo Classico "Pilo Albertelli" in Rome,[616] on December 20, 2019, Bergoglio was asked, "If an atheist came to you and asked you a fundamental reason for starting to believe what would you answer?" In direct opposition to Jesus Christ's command to preach and teach, Bergoglio, who supposedly represents Christ on earth, replied, "In front of an unbeliever, the last thing I have to do is try to convince him. Never. The last thing I have to do is talk."[617] And the reason, he explains, why we need not convince them of our faith, or even of the existence of God, is that, "We are all equal, all children of God"![618]

Thus, for Bergoglio, the Gospel of Christ is ultimately superfluous, and one need not believe in Christ nor even in God to gain salvation. That Bergoglio is as explicit as he is obstinate in heresy on this point

---

[616] VISITA AL LICEO CLASSICO "PILO ALBERTELLI" DI ROMA - *DIALOGO DEL SANTO PADRE FRANCESCO CON GLI STUDENTI* - *Venerdì, 20 dicembre 2019.* http://www.vatican.va/content/francesco/it/speeches/2019/december/documents/papa-francesco_20191220_visita-liceo-albertelli.html

[617] «Davanti a un non credente l'ultima cosa che devo fare è cercare di convincerlo. Mai. L'ultima cosa che devo fare è parlare.»

[618] «siamo tutti uguali, tutti figli di Dio.»

is plainly evident in his *Letter to Those who do not Believe*[619], in which he writes: "*First of all, you ask me if the God of Christians forgives those who do not believe and do not seek faith. Given that — and this is the fundamental thing — God's mercy has no limits if one turns to him with a sincere and contrite heart, the question for those who do not believe in God is to obey their conscience. Sin, even for those who do not have faith, exists when one goes against conscience. Listening to and obeying it means, in fact, deciding in the face of what is perceived as good or evil. And on this decision the goodness or the wickedness of our actions is at stake.*"[620] In May 2013 he declared in a homily, «*The Lord created us in His image and likeness, and we are the image of the Lord, and He does good and we all have this commandment in our hearts: do good and do not do evil. All of us. 'But, Father, this is not Catholic! He cannot do good.' Yes, he can do it.... 'The Lord has redeemed all of us, all of us, with the Blood of Christ: all of us, not just Catholics. All! 'Father, and the atheists?' Also the atheists. All!'... We must meet by doing good. 'But, Father, I don't think so, I'm an atheist!' But do good: we will meet there.*»[621] When he says, "We will meet there, by "there" he means **heaven**, as is clear from his words in his General Audience

---

[619] http://www.vatican.va/content/francesco/it/letters/2013/documents/papa-francesco_20130911_eugenio-scalfari.html

[620] «Innanzi tutto, mi chiede se il Dio dei cristiani perdona chi non crede e non cerca la fede. Premesso che — ed è la cosa fondamentale — la misericordia di Dio non ha limiti se ci si rivolge a lui con cuore sincero e contrito, la questione per chi non crede in Dio sta nell'obbedire alla propria coscienza. Il peccato, anche per chi non ha la fede, c'è quando si va contro la coscienza. Ascoltare e obbedire ad essa significa, infatti, decidersi di fronte a ciò che viene percepito come bene o come male. E su questa decisione si gioca la bontà o la malvagità del nostro agire.»

[621] «'Il Signore ci ha creati a Sua immagine e somiglianza, e noi siamo l'immagine del Signore, ed Egli fa del bene e tutti noi abbiamo questo comandamento nel cuore: fai il bene e non fare il male. Tutti noi. 'Ma, Padre, questo non è Cattolico! Non può fare il bene'. Sì, può farlo.... 'Il Signore ha redento tutti noi, tutti noi, con il Sangue di Cristo: tutti noi, non solo Cattolici. Tutti! 'Padre, e gli atei?' Anche gli atei. Tutti!'... Dobbiamo incontrarci facendo il bene. 'Ma, Padre, io non credo, sono un ateo!' Ma fai il bene: noi ci incontreremo là'» http://giacintobutindaro.org/2013/05/26/secondo-papa-francesco-anche-gli-atei-vanno-in-paradiso/.

of November 26, 2014[622]: *"It's nice to think this, to think of heaven. All of us will meet up there, everybody. It is beautiful, it gives strength to the soul."*[623]

In these texts, Bergoglio has professed that *for those who do not have faith*, and, *for those who do not believe in God, sin exists when one goes against one's conscience.* So, if you do not believe in God, that's no problem: *"But do good: we will meet there. It is nice to think this, to think of Heaven. We will all be up there, all of us. It is beautiful, it gives strength to the soul."* This is Bergoglio in his own words: *"We are all children of God — Also the atheists. All! But do good: we will meet there."* **Even atheists who follow their conscience and do what they think is right are not guilty of sin, because** *"we all have this commandment in our hearts: do good and do not do evil. Sin, even for those who do not have faith, exists when one goes against conscience."* **In Bergoglio's religion, the first great commandment,** "Thou shalt love the Lord thy God with thy whole heart, and with thy whole soul, and with thy whole mind." (Mt.22:37), has been abolished, and has been replaced with the simple naturalistic dictum of morality acknowledged by Freemasonry as the sole foundation of religion: *"do good and do not do evil"*. Bergoglio's denial that the existence of God is a dogma that absolutely must be believed, and that the commandment to love God above all things must be obeyed in order to be saved; and that even the atheist who follows his conscience is without sin, is founded on Rousseau's principles,[624] but Bergoglio astutely doesn't say it in order

---

[622] http://w2.vatican.va/content/francesco/it/audiences/2014/documents/papa-francesco_20141126_udienza-generale.html; Il Vaticano corregge il Papa: "Gli atei vanno sempre all'inferno" — di Simona Vitale 28 maggio 2013 11:32 https://attualissimo.it/il-vaticano-corregge-il-papa-gli-atei-vanno-sempre-allinferno/. Note that the report on homily in question has been expunged from the Vatican Radio website, where one reads only the notification: "Sorry, the page is currently not available."

[623] «È bello pensare questo, pensare al Cielo. Tutti noi ci troveremo lassù, tutti. È bello, dà forza all'anima.»

[624] «In a letter he wrote to Cristopher de Beaumont, archbishop of Paris, J. J. Rousseau said: "The fundamental principle of every morality, on which I have reasoned in all my writings ..., is that man is naturally good, lover of justice and order; that there is no original perversity in the human heart, and that the first movements of nature are always right".» — Vide: Henri

to maintain the appearance of being a Christian (which he is not). According to Bergoglio's dogma-free Christianity, man is not born in a state of sin from which he stands in need of redemption by Christ through grace — through the first grace, which is *justification*, which is not obtained without the theological virtues of faith, hope and charity. This tenet of the Bergoglian creed denies by strict implication the Catholic dogma of Original Sin. Mgr. Henri Delassus notes that, "Of all Christian dogmas, the one that Freemasonry attacks most stubbornly is that of original sin, because it knows that with this it overturns the basis of Christianity and of the whole social state."[625] According to Bergoglio, we are all born into this world as children of God, and even if we don't believe in God or love God, all we need to do to be saved is to do what we believe is good and avoid what we believe is evil. Dogma as such is thereby abolished, as is dogmatic religion founded on authoritative divine revelation. Religion as such — as a divine institution, commanded to be observed according to divine law is abolished. You may believe the dogmas if you wish, and you may *privately* feel bound in conscience to obey the commandments, but according to the dogma-free Christianity of Bergoglio and Freemasonry, it is an abominable intolerance to profess that all men are bound by divine law to believe the dogmas and obey the supernaturally revealed commandments taught by the Catholic Church, and therefore it is wrong to convince others to abandon their errors and false beliefs and embrace the one true faith of Christ taught in the Catholic Church, outside of which no one can be saved. Bergoglio is the founder of a new and totally secular religion without faith, dogmas, or divinely revealed commandments. Religion is reduced to the observance of the Natural Law as understood according to the sovereign dictates of one's own conscience. Bergoglio has brought Luther's revolution to completion — a revolution which began with the secularization of charity by the

---

Delassus, *IL PROBLEMA DELL'ORA PRESENTE — ANTAGONISMO TRA DUE CIVILTA'*, SECONDA PARTE, Roma, 1907, p. 157.

[625] Vide: Henri Delassus, *IL PROBLEMA DELL'ORA PRESENTE — ANTAGONISMO TRA DUE CIVILTA'*, SECONDA PARTE, Roma, 1907, p. 154.

elimination of any need for good works for one to be saved,[626] and the elimination of ecclesiastical authority's binding power to teach dogmas and dictate morals, by making only fiducial faith in God necessary for salvation, and eliminating the need for virtuous works performed in charity and founded on love of God. Luther's revolution abolished dogma by replacing magisterial authority with the principle of Private Judgment. By denying the Church's infallible magisterial authority and replacing it with private judgment of the individual conscience in all matters of faith and morals, Luther abolished the entire substance of the material object of faith, thus negating the absolute value of objective truth from all magisterial dogmatic and moral teachings, reducing religious belief to the subjective tyranny of relativism — a relativism founded on Private Judgment — which is the basis for Bergoglio's relativism, which brands any claim on absolute objective truth as *intolerance*. Thus, not surprisingly, Bergoglio brands all claim on the possession of absolute truth as *fundamentalism*. On 30 Nov 2015, Bergoglio fanatically

---

[626] **cf. Ratzinger,** *Einführung in das Christentum*, pp. 167-168: «Because this hyphen [between Jesus and Christ] — let's say it again — is at the same time the hyphen between faith and love. Therefore, it is now also true that faith that is not love is not really Christian faith, but only appears as such — a fact that must be filed against a doctrinalistic misunderstanding of the Catholic concept of faith as well as against the secularization of love that emerges with Luther from the exclusivity of the justification of faith[12]. [12 Cf. *P. Hacker*, Das Ich im Glauben bei Martin Luther, Graz 1966, especially the section "Secularization of Love", 166-174. Using extensive textual evidence, *Hacker* shows that the reformational Luther (from around 1520 onwards) assigns to love the "external life", to the "use of the second tablet", life not towards God, but "towards men" and thus to the realm of the profane, to what is today called pure worldliness, that is, the "righteousness of the law", and thus secularly excludes it from the realm of grace and salvation. *Hacker* can thus convincingly make it clear that *Gagarten's* program of secularization can rightly refer back to Luther. It is clear that at this point Trent had to draw a decisive dividing line and that where the secularization of love is held, the dividing line still runs. Regarding *Gagarten*, attention should be drawn to the summarizing presentation and evaluation of his work by *A. v. Bauer*: Freiheit zur Welt (Säkularisation), Paderborn 1967.]

declared in a press conference:[627] «Fundamentalism is a disease that exists in all religions. In the Catholic Church we have some – many – and they go on sullying others through slander and defamation and this is wrong. I say this because it is my Church. Religious fundamentalism must be combatted. It is not religious, God is lacking, it is idolatrous.» Thus, according to Bergoglio, it is the members of the Church who constitute the body of faithful in the Church, who have been established by God on the authority of the Gospel truth preached by Jesus Christ, "according to the precept of the eternal God, for the obedience of faith" (Rom. 16: 25-26), whose obedient assent and strict adherence to the eternal truths of faith constitute them as *fundamentalists* — and therefore it is they who slander and defame others by professing the dogma that only the Catholic Church is the repository of absolute infallible truth, and that all other religions are *false*. Consequently, it follows strictly as a corollary of Bergoglio's proposition, that it is *that Church itself* which professes itself to have received from God, as the sole repository, the absolutely infallible truths of faith, which is fundamentalist and must be combatted, because, "It is not religious, God is lacking, it is idolatrous." Thus, Bergoglio follows exactly the example of Luther in attacking one of the most primary and foundational dogmas of our religion which binds the conscience absolutely, which is that there is only one true faith and one true Church — the Catholic Church, outside of which there is no salvation.

In *Luther and Lutherdom*, Fr. Heinrich Denifle O.P. observed what Luther said before he became a heretic: «Luther himself, some years earlier, had already said: "Heretics cannot themselves appear good unless they depict the Church as evil, false, and mendacious. They alone wish to be esteemed as the good, but the Church must be made to appear evil in every respect."»[628] As a heretic, Luther later

---

[627] *Pope Francis criticises 'fundamentalist' Catholics* – by Catholic News Service; http://www.catholicherald.co.uk/news/2015/11/30/pope-francis-says-he-is-not-losing-any-sleep-over-vatican-leaks-trial/; https://www.episcopalcafe.com/the-pope-fundamentalism-is-a-disease-in-all-religions/.

[628] Heinrich Denifle, *Luther and Lutherdom*, Translated from the Second Revised Edition of the German by Raymund Volz, Vol. I. Part I. Introduction, p. 15; *Luther und Luthertum in der ersten Entwickelung*, Zweite

incorporated this same perverse principle into his own agenda just as his Argentinian disciple does today by defaming the Church as *fundamentalist* and *idolatrous*. According to Bergoglio, anyone who professes the Catholic teaching that the Church's infallible magisterium constitutes the Church as the repository of *absolute truth* is an irreligious fundamentalist, and a practitioner of godless idolatry. Such a one, according to Bergoglio is anyone who believes in the absolute truth of the dogmas of faith and moral precepts revealed by God and infallibly taught by the Catholic Church. According to Bergoglio, such a one is a fundamentalist *whose fundamentalism must be combatted*. In his unholy crusade for reform (a reform which he expressly intends to be irreversible), Bergoglio follows the depraved Reformation perversion of Martin Luther, who by Private Judgment attempted to abolish both the dogmas of faith and the commandments of God.

It is no understatement to say that Luther attempted the abolition of the commandments of God in his perverse reform which created a new religion. Heinrich Denifle demonstrated this with his impeccable scholarship in his, *Luther and Lutherdom*. In that work he provides the verbatim passages of Luther which condemn the reformer with the words of his own mouth. In order to show just where Bergoglio's Luther inspired "reform" is leading, and to amply illustrate this point, I will quote some passages from Denifle's work. First, Denifle explains what is one of the most primary and universally known of all truths of our religion, namely, that whoever would be saved must fulfil the commandment to love God above all things. On page 160 of the cited work, he explains:

> The preceptor of St. Thomas Aquinas, Albert the Great, wrote his treatise "De adhaerendo Deo," after the death of his great disciple. He begins it with the words: "The end of Christian perfection is charity, by means of which one is attached to God. And to this attachment by means of charity, every one, if he desires to attain salvation, is in duty bound. It is effected by keeping the commandments and by union with the will of God. Thus is everything excluded that is contrary to the essence and the habit of charity, namely mortal sin."

---

durchgearbeitete Auflage, Erster Band, I. Abteilung, Mainz 1904, Einleitung, S. 13.

Note, "everything is excluded that is contrary to the essence and the habit of charity, namely mortal sin." According to Bergoglio, the commandments are merely ideals that one must strive to fulfil, but one can still be saved if one finds that obedience to the commandments proves too difficult or even seems to be impossible. Accordingly, one who finds it too difficult or impossible to observe the Sixth Commandment prohibition of adultery, may still receive the sacraments and remain in good standing with the Church as one who is unconditionally loved by God, who in his mercy will overlook the transgression — as if the commandment were merely a counsel, but not a **precept of divine law**. Denifle explains on page 155 the difference between the two: «For that, as St. Thomas teaches, is just the difference between counsel and commandment—the commandments must necessarily be kept whilst the observance of the counsels is left to the free discretion of each one. The former are indispensably necessary to the attainment of our last end, the latter serve for its better and easier attainment. 1. 2. qu. 108, a. 4.»[629] And on page 184, the most basic of divinely revealed truths which every Catholic child was taught upon reaching the age of reason, but which, following Luther's principles, Bergoglio denies: «Charles Fernand, monk of St. Vincent du Mans: "It is necessary to every Christian to believe in God, to hope for eternal life from Him, and to be of good

---

[629] *Iª IIæ Q. 108. a. 4.* — «Respondeo dicendum quod haec est differentia inter consilium et praeceptum, quod praeceptum importat necessitatem, consilium autem in optione ponitur eius cui datur. Et ideo convenienter in lege nova, quae est lex libertatis, supra praecepta sunt addita consilia, non autem in veteri lege, quae erat lex servitutis. Oportet igitur quod praecepta novae legis intelligantur esse data de his quae sunt necessaria ad consequendum finem aeternae beatitudinis, in quem lex nova immediate introducit. Consilia vero oportet esse de illis per quae melius et expeditius potest homo consequi finem praedictum. Est autem homo constitutus inter res mundi huius et spiritualia bona, in quibus beatitudo aeterna consistit, ita quod quanto plus inhaeret uni eorum, tanto plus recedit ab altero, et e converso. Qui ergo totaliter inhaeret rebus huius mundi, ut in eis finem constituat, habens eas quasi rationes et regulas suorum operum, totaliter excidit a spiritualibus bonis. Et ideo huiusmodi inordinatio tollitur per praecepta.»

life in the ordinary way, that is, to love and fear God and to keep His commandments."» Speaking of the disciples of Luther, "the apostles of the flesh", Denifle comments, «They had found a simpler means of seeing clearly through every obstacle—simple fiducial reliance upon Christ. "Is that not good tidings," their father taught, "if one is full of sins and the gospel comes and says: *'only have confidence and believe,'* and thy sins are then all forgiven thee? With this stop pulled out, the sins are already forgiven, there is no longer need of waiting."[55]»[630] Denifle then points out the inevitable consequences that his perverse teaching led to:

> The concubinaries of the fifteenth century had not pulled out this stop. The word of that same man had not yet forced its way to them: "Be a sinner and sin stoutly, but trust in Christ much more firmly, and rejoice in Him who is a conqueror of sin, of death, and of the world. Do not by any means imagine that this life is an abode of justice; sin must and will be. Let it suffice thee that thou acknowledgest the Lamb which bears the sins of the world; then can sin not tear thee from Him, even shouldst thou practice whoredom a thousand times a day or deal just as many death blows."[56] Had the concubinaries of the fifteenth century heard this utterance, I believe that their iniquity would have reached its full measure then instead of in the sixteenth century. If religion dwindles down to mere trust, and if the ethical task, the moral striving, of the individual is neglected, or rather forbidden, the result can be only the ruin of all morality.
>
> What, indeed, could give greater encouragement to one to sin stoutly, to persevere unscrupulously in concubinage, that is, in wild wedlock, and thus finally to go down into the abyss beyond redemption, than the teaching: Why seekest thou to exert thyself? It is not in thy power to fulfil the command: thou shalt not covet; in thy stead Christ has already fulfilled it as He has the rest of the commandments. If thou place thy trust in Him, all thy sins pass over upon Him. He is then truly the Lamb which beareth the sins of the world. Thou bearest them no longer. "Christ became the cover-shame of us all."[57] "The game is already won; Christ, the victor, has achieved all, so that it is not for us to add anything thereto, either to blot out sin, or to smite the devil, or to vanquish death; all these have already been brought under;"[58] for, "who believes that Christ has taken away sin, he is without sin like Christ.[59] "[631]

---

[630] Denifle, *Op. cit.* pp. 18-19.
[631] *Ibid.* pp. 19-20.

The encouragement to sin is found most explicitly stated in Luther's letters to Melanchton: 1) "If you are a preacher of grace, then preach a true and not a fictitious grace; if grace is true, you must bear a true and not a fictitious sin. God does not save people who are only fictitious sinners. *Be a sinner and sin boldly, but believe and rejoice in Christ even more boldly.... as long as we are here we have to sin.... No sin will separate us from the Lamb, even though we commit fornication and murder a thousand times a day.*" [632] 2) Letter 501 to Melanchthon: "*Pecca fortiter, sed crede fortius.*" i.e. "Sin boldly but believe more boldly." Denifle comments, "Luther was the author of the above assembled texts," and he points out (p. 22) the underlying principle of Luther's teaching, which also underlies the teaching of Luther's Argentinian disciple: "**He set up the principle that God imposed an impossible thing upon us, that the (sexual) instinct of nature cannot be resisted, that it must be satisfied.**" On page sixteen Denifle makes the observation which is particularly relevant to the present situation in the Church under the Bergoglian usurpation: "If, for the sake of carnal lust, the monastic vows were thus treated, and the violation of them was set forth as a work pleasing to God, it is evident that the storm would also put the indissolubility of marriage to the test and that adultery would no longer be considered a sin and a shame. And so it proved." Indeed it did. Denifle relates further:

> The new teachers likewise carried on as madly as possible—did it in their very sermons. In one of these, the spokesman [Luther] instructs his hearers on the married life as follows: "One easily finds a stiff-necked woman, who carries her head high, and though her husband should ten times fall into unchastity, she raises no question about it. Then it is time for the husband to say to her: 'If you don't want to, another does;' if the wife is unwilling, let the servant-girl come. If the wife is then still unwilling, have done with her; let an Esther be given you and Vashti go her way."[52] Quite logical: marriage under some conditions demands continency no less than does the religious state. The underlying Epicurean principle of this tendency was, that continency was an impossible requirement, that there is no resisting the instinct of passion,

---

[632] *Letter to Melanchthon*, August 1,1521, *American Edition, Luther's Works*, vol. 48, pp. 281-82, edited by H. Lehmann, Fortress, 1963, pp. 281-282.

and that resistance is even a kind of revolt against the disposition of God.⁶³³

In footnote 53 on the same page, Denifle provides the full text of the cited passage which he thought too offensive to give in German, but which I believe needs to be given here in English:

> ⁵³ The passage is offensive and therefore, in the German, I do not give it in full. It is to be found in Opp. Eseg. lat, I, 212, in Genes, c. 3, 7. In 1536, the Reformer taught the following: "But do we not feel at last, how filthy and horrible a thing sin is? If indeed lust alone cannot be cured by any remedy, indeed not even by marriage, which has been divinely ordained as a remedy for our weak nature. The greater part of married people live in adultery, and sing the familiar verse about the spouse: I can live neither with thee nor without thee. This horrible turpitude arises from the most honourable and excellent part of our body. I call it the most excellent because of the work of generation, which is the most excellent, since indeed it conserves the species. Through sin therefore the most useful members have become the most shameful. "With this cf. out of the year 1535, in c. 5 ad Gal III, 11 (Ed. Irmischer): "Whoever diligently examines himself (here I should speak presently with the pious spouses of both sexes) on this point then undoubtedly will find himself to be more pleased with the beauty or the manner of another's wife than his own (and vice versa). One loathes the lawful woman, but loves the forbidden one." Therefore even the "Pii"?⁶³⁴

---

⁶³³ Denifle, p. 17.

⁶³⁴ «⁵³ The passage is offensive and therefore, in tlie German, I do not give it in full. It is to be found in Opp. Eseg. lat, I, 212, in Genes, c. 3, 7. In 1536, the Reformer taught the following: "An non sentiemus tandem, quam foeda et horribilis res sit peccatum? Si quidem sola libido nullo remedio potest curari, ne quidem conjugio, quod divinitus inflrmae naturae pro remedio ordinatum est. Major enim pars conjugatorum vivit in adulteriis, et canit de conjuge notum versiculum: nee tecum possum vivere, nec sine te. Haec horribilis turpltudo oritur ex honestissima et praestantissima parte corporis nostri. Praestantissimam appello propter opus generationis, quod praestantissimum est, si quidem conservat speciem. Per peccatum itaque utilissima membra turpissima facta sunt." With this cf. out of the year 153.5, in c. 5 ad Gal III, 11 (Ed. Irmischer): "Quisquis hie (loquar jam cum piis conjugibus utriusque sesus) diligenter exploret seipsum, tum proculdubio

Denifle then notes on page 18, «From such a state of affairs, it was only a step farther to polygamy. Several of these apostles of the flesh did go to that length, inasmuch as, faithful to their principles, they allowed, at times, two and three wives. Some, indeed, of these fallen priests and monks themselves had several women at the same time. Later it was their own leader who accounted polygamy among the ultimate and highest things of Christian liberty; he would not forbid "that one take more wives than one, for," he says, "it is not contrary to Holy Writ." "Only to avoid scandal and for the sake of decency one should not do it."[54]»[635] What is most concerning today and should make us shudder, (since Bergoglio is determined to inflict Luther's reform on the Catholic Church in our time), is the consideration of the utter spiritual, moral and social ruin that the perverse and hellish doctrine of Luther brought about for the Church and society in general:

> As his teachings were depopulating the monasteries, so he himself furnished the incentive to the abduction of the consecrated virgins, the perpetrator being called by him a "blessed robber," and compared with Christ, who robbed the prince of the world of what was his." He took one of the abducted nuns, put up for sale, as a witness of his gospel, as his concubine, and called her his wife. He severed the bonds of marriage and destroyed its indissolubility by his theory, which in practice found expression in the whoredoms and adulteries so bitterly complained of. He did not forbid the taking of several wives and declared that polygamy was not strictly opposed to the word of God.[77] As a panacea for all sin, he prescribed only trust in Christ's forgiveness, without requiring love. He condemned the contrition, confession, and penance of the Catholic Church, reviled the Pope as Anti-christ, rejected the priesthood, the Mass, the religious state and every good work. It was his teaching that good works, even at their best, are sins, and even that a just man sins in all good works. As he had imposed sin upon Christ, so also did he put the fulfillment of our prayers upon Him. And with all of that, he extols himself as a saint, and presumes, if he did not do so, he would be

---

inveniet sibi magis placere formam seu mores alterius uxoris quam suae (et econtra). Concessam mulierem fastidit, negatam amat." Therefore even the "Pii"?»

[635] Denifle's footnote: «[54]M. Lenz. Briefwechsel Landgraf Philipp's des Groszmütigen von Hessen mit Bucer, I, 342. sq.»

blaspheming Christ. If ever a doctrine had to lead to the acme of wickedness, it was such a one as this.[636]

It is precisely the doctrine of his heresiarch master, Martin Luther, a doctrine "which had to lead to the acme of wickedness," which Bergoglio promotes relentlessly as a devoted disciple — a disciple so entrenched in his master's wickedness, that he pulls out the stop that even Luther himself dared not pull out: the prohibition against **Sodomy**. After more than seven years of devious and dishonest dissimulation; with Bergoglio constantly equivocating, one day claiming to uphold the teaching of the Church, and another day saying of sodomite priests, "Who am I to judge?" — the false pope of perfidy has finally come clean and declared in a documentary that premiered on October 21 (2020) in Rome: "Homosexuals have a right to be a part of the family. They're children of God and have a right to a family. Nobody should be thrown out, or be made miserable because of it."[637] With his customary and chronic deviousness, Bergoglio attempts to make it superficially appear that it is only a question of compassionately allowing homosexuals to live together with their family members, and not be thrown out of the house onto the street — but that is not what he is promoting here — that is not what he means when he says "They're children of God and have a right to a family." What Bergoglio is advocating is legal recognition for perverted unnatural unions which in their very nature constitute a threat to the divinely instituted social order founded on the family, consisting of a father, a mother, and their children. Bergoglio is proposing legal recognition of sterile sodomite unions which would create the parody of the natural family by a parallel institution to marriage: "What we have to create is a civil union law. That way they are legally covered," and he added, "I stood up for that." Yes indeed, in spite of his habitual mendacious posturing in the past years, when he consistently dissimulated in order to make it appear that he was upholding Catholic teaching on the issue, the sordid truth has now come out in the open. The Catholic News Agency reported, "In 2014, Fr. Thomas Rosica, who was then working in the Holy See's press

---

[636] Denifle, pp. 23-24.

[637] https://www.catholicnewsagency.com/news/pope-francis-calls-for-civil-union-law-for-same-sex-couples-in-shift-from-vatican-stance-12462.

office told CNA that Pope Francis had not expressed support for same-sex civil unions, after some journalists reported that he had done so in an interview that year. While a civil unions proposal was debated in Italy Rosica emphasized that Francis would not weigh in on the debate, but would emphasize Catholic teaching on marriage." Needless to say, homosexuals living together as couples and raising their children (whether adopted or procreated in previous natural unions) is utterly contrary to the Catholic teaching on marriage. The CNA report also called attention to the "story of the pontiff encouraging two Italian men in a same-sex relationship to raise their children in their parish church, which, one of the men said, was greatly beneficial to his children."

Bergoglio's advocacy of civil recognition of sodomite unions is a direct attack against the law of God which decrees: "Thou shalt not lie with mankind as with womankind, because it is an abomination." (Leviticus 18:22) Bergoglio's endorsement of this deviant abomination constitutes a direct break with the perpetual moral doctrine infallibly taught by the Catholic Church for two millennia, and explicitly by the Church of the Old Covenant since the Law was given by Moses. Echoing that constant teaching, in 2003, under the leadership of Cardinal Joseph Ratzinger, and at the direction of Pope John Paul II, the Sacred Congregation for the Doctrine of the Faith declared: "Respect for homosexual persons cannot lead in any way to approval of homosexual behaviour or to legal recognition of homosexual unions. The common good requires that laws recognize, promote and protect marriage as the basis of the family, the primary unit of society." The document clearly taught that support for such immoral unions is "gravely immoral", and it elaborated the point explaining that: "Legal recognition of homosexual unions or placing them on the same level as marriage would mean not only the approval of deviant behaviour, with the consequence of making it a model in present-day society, but would also obscure basic values which belong to the common inheritance of humanity. The Church cannot fail to defend these values, for the good of men and women and for the good of society itself."

Particularly enlightening is the recent observation of Archbishop Carlo Maria Viganò, who explains what can clearly be seen to be the underlying motive for the crescendo of Bergoglio's heretical provocations:

> It is not necessary to be a theologian or moralist to know that such statements are totally heterodox and constitute a very serious cause of scandal for the faithful. Attention, however: these words constitute the umpteenth provocation with which the ultra-progressive part of the Hierarchy tries to artfully arouse a schism, as it has already attempted to do with the Post-Synodal Exhortation *Amoris Laetitia*, the modification of the doctrine on punishment capital, the Pan-Amazon Synod and the filthy Pachamama, the Abu Dhabi Declaration then reaffirmed and aggravated by the Encyclical *Fratelli Tutti*. It seems that Bergoglio is boldly trying to "up the ante" in a crescendo of heretical statements, in order to force the healthy part of the Church — episcopate, clergy and faithful — to accuse him of heresy, and then declare it schismatic and "enemy of the pope". Jorge Mario Bergoglio tries to force some cardinals and bishops to separate from communion with him, resulting in not his own deposition for heresy, but the ouster of Catholics who want to remain faithful to the perennial Magisterium of the Church. This trap would have — in the presumed intentions of Bergoglio and his "magic circle" — the purpose of consolidating its power within a church that would only be nominally "Catholic" but in reality heretical and schismatic. This deception benefits from the support of the globalist elite, the mainstream media and the LGBT lobby, to which many clerics, bishops and cardinals are no strangers. Let us not forget that in many nations there are laws in force which punish as a crime those who, even on the basis of their Creed, consider sodomy reprehensible and sinful or who do not approve the legitimation of homosexual "marriage". A pronouncement by the bishops against Bergoglio on an issue such as that of homosexuality could authorize the civil authority to prosecute them criminally with the approval of the Vatican.[638]

---

[638] «Non occorre essere teologi o moralisti per sapere che tali affermazioni sono totalmente eterodosse e costituiscono un gravissimo motivo di scandalo per i fedeli. Attenzione, però: queste parole costituiscono l'ennesima provocazione con cui la parte ultra-progressista della Gerarchia cerca di suscitare ad arte uno scisma, come già ha tentato di fare con l'Esortazione Post-sinodale *Amoris laetitia*, la modifica della dottrina sulla pena capitale, il Sinodo pan-amazzonico e l'immonda Pachamama, la Dichiarazione di Abu Dhabi poi ribadita e aggravata dall'Enciclica *Fratelli tutti*. Pare che Bergoglio cerchi sfrontatamente di "alzare la posta" in un

In reality, it is Bergoglio himself who has separated himself from the Catholic Church by eliminating the most foundational principles of religion, the **absolute authority** of divinely revealed dogmas and of the moral precepts set forth in the Commandments of God. Bergoglio has thereby effectively abolished the law of God from religion and has made man a law unto himself and the measure of all things, so that it is man who dictates and defines his duties of conscience, and the terms of his relationship with God. Fr. Denifle said of Luther's doctrine, "If ever a doctrine had to lead to the acme of wickedness, it was such a one as this," and it was by means of Private Judgment that Luther, under the pretext of abolishing papal tyranny, attempted to abolish the law of God and banish the authority of Jesus Christ from religion and from the affairs of men. He did not accomplish that end in his day, but he left that task to be continued in the following centuries, and finally to be completed by Bergoglio some four centuries later. Bergoglio has unswervingly pursued this same agenda which in Luther's day had already let loose near-apocalyptic scenes of disorder and lawlessness which even shocked Luther himself. On this point, Denifle relates:

---

crescendo di affermazioni eretiche, in modo da costringere la parte sana della Chiesa – episcopato, clero e fedeli – ad accusarlo di eresia, per poi dichiararla scismatica e "nemica del papa". Jorge Mario Bergoglio cerca di costringere alcuni Cardinali e Vescovi a separarsi dalla comunione con lui, ottenendo come risultato non la propria deposizione per eresia, ma l'estromissione dei Cattolici che vogliono restare fedeli al Magistero perenne della Chiesa. Questo tranello avrebbe – nelle presumibili intenzioni di Bergoglio e del suo "cerchio magico" – lo scopo di consolidare il proprio potere all'interno di una chiesa che sarebbe solo nominalmente "cattolica" ma in realtà eretica e scismatica. Questo inganno si avvale dell'appoggio dell'élite globalista, dei media *mainstream* e della lobby LGBT, alla quale non sono estranei molti chierici, vescovi e cardinali. Non dimentichiamo poi che in molte nazioni sono in vigore leggi che puniscono come reato quanti, anche sulla base del proprio Credo, considerano riprovevole e peccaminosa la sodomia o che non approvano la legittimazione del "matrimonio" omosessuale. Un pronunciamento dei vescovi contro Bergoglio su una questione come quella dell'omosessualità potrebbe autorizzare l'autorità civile a perseguirli penalmente con l'approvazione del Vaticano.»

In a word, the entire concubinage of the fifteenth century and its congeneric continuation in the sixteenth, with all its abominations, pale before the doings and the teachings of the fallen priests and monks who, in the third decade of the sixteenth century, had branched off from the old movement. "Monasticism now truly lies stretched out on the ground" writes Erasmus, who certainly was not less than edified by the earlier condition, "but if the monks had only put off their vices with their cowls * * * "it seems to me there is a new kind of monks arising, much more wicked than the former, bad as these were. It is folly to substitute evil for evil, but it is madness to exchange the bad for even worse."[67] This, according to Luther, is what heretics do generally. "They exchange the evils in the Church for others greater. Often we are unwilling to tolerate a trivial evil and we provoke a greater one."[68] Like many others, Pirkheimer, who once had even joined the movement, wrote shortly before his death: "We hoped that Romish knavery, the same as the rascality of the monks and priests, would be corrected; but, as is to be perceived, the matter has become worse to such a degree that the Evangelical knaves make the other knaves pious,"[69] that is, the others still appear pious in comparison with the new unbridled preachers of liberty. But did not the father of the new movement himself acknowledge that "our (people) are now seven times worse than they ever were before. We steal, lie, cheat, cram, and swill and commit all manner of vices."[70] "We Germans are now the laughing-stock and the shame of all the countries, they hold us as shameful, nasty swine."[71] The same one that said this regrets to have been born a German, to have written and spoken German, and longs to fly from there, that he may not witness God's judgment breaking over Germany."[72] [639]

It was men like Cardinals Michele Ghislieri and Carlo Borromeo, who used the Holy Inquisition to erect, as it were, a barrier to defend Italy and Rome from the lawless rebellion against Christ and his Church, which the heretics waged north of the Alps. There were still Catholic lands where persecuted Catholics could flee to during the time of the Reformation, but now that a disciple of Luther sits upon the usurped throne of Peter, the lawlessness of that forerunner of Antichrist is beginning to erupt and overflow over the entire world, and thus pave the way for the reign of Antichrist, who will seek to accomplish, not just in one region, but throughout the whole world the total eradication of faith in Christ and obedience to the law of

---

[639] Denifle, p. 21.

God. The religion of Bergoglio's reform is the negation of religion as such — it is the abolition of God's rulership which is to be substituted not by mere anarchy, but by godless tyranny founded on the principle of **lawlessness** — the lawless revolt against divine authority enshrined in the principle of Private Judgment. It is that principle which Bergoglio has inherited from the Gnosticism of his spiritual master, Martin Luther. In *Martin Luther and the Gnostics*[640] it is stated:

«We cannot ignore what has been discovered in the thousands of notes written by Luther himself on the margins of books written by reputed theologians such as Augustine and Peter Lombard. The notes were written within the time periods of 1506 to 1516, and 1535 to 1545. But, they were much overlooked until the 20th century when the German scholar Theobald Beer enduringly read through the notes, studying the patriarch of Protestantism for thirty five years. Beer's research on Luther was eventually published in his 1980, 584 page publication, *Der fröhliche Wechsel und Streit,* in which he exposed and discoursed on the heretical gnostic beliefs and teachings of Luther. In fact, Melanchthon, a very close colleague of Luther and one of the head figures of the Protestant Reformation, criticized the German reformer as having "Manichean delirium".»

It was in those notes written by Luther's hand that were penned the reformer's expressions of utter contempt for the Person of Our Lord Jesus Christ — written in the spirit of **lawlessness** — the same spirit of lawless revolt against God which is foretold in Scripture will be the spirit of Antichrist, that will provoke the great apostasy foretold by the Apostle in 2 Thess. 2:3: "Don't let anyone deceive you in any way, for that day will not come until the apostasy (ἀποστασία) occurs and the man of lawlessness (ὁ ἄνθρωπος τῆς ἀνομίας) is revealed, the son of perdition (ὁ υἱὸς τῆς ἀπωλείας)." (**ἀνομίας** = lawlessness, iniquity; **απώλεια** = loss, perdition, wastage) If he is not prevented, Bergoglio, by means of his lawless rebellion against the

---

[640] https://oblongmedia-net.cdn.ampproject.org/v/s/oblongmedia.net/2017/01/30/martin-luther-and-the-gnostics/amp/?amp_js_v=a2&amp_gsa=1&usqp=mq331AQCCAE%3D#referrer=https%3A%2F%2Fwww.google.com&amp_tf=From%20,%251%24s&ampshare=https%3A%2F%2Foblongmedia.net%2F2017%2F01%2F30%2Fmartin-lutherdivinelyinstituted-and-the-gnostics%2F.

authority of the revealing God, will unleash the universal revolt against God's rulership on the whole world as is foretold in Scripture:

> Why do the nations rage and the peoples utter folly? The kings of the earth rise up and the rulers band together against the LORD and against his Christ, saying, "Let us break their chains and throw off their shackles." (Ps. 2)

The revolt against the authority of God and Christ is the very essence of heresy, which is evident in the very word itself, αἱρεσῖς, **which is defined as a choice, or a selection; and therefore a heresy; and is derived from the verb** αἱρέω – to take for oneself, choose, select; to prefer. Thus, heresy finds its embodiment in the principle of Private Judgment, by which one revolts against the authority of God whose incarnate Word instituted the Church to infallibly teach what we must believe and what we must do to be saved; and asserts that every individual man is free to reject that divine authority and judge privately for himself what (if anything), God has revealed, and what (if anything) we must believe and do to be saved — or indeed, if there is even such a thing as God, heaven, hell, or salvation. In *The Present Crisis of the Holy See*, Cardinal Henry Edward Manning explained, «Every age has its heresy, as every article of faith by denial receives its definition; and the course of heresy is measured and periodical; various materially, but formally one, both in principle and action; so that all the heresies from the beginning are no more than the continuous development and expansion of "the mystery of iniquity," which was already at work.»[641] That principle, of course, is *revolt* against divine authority. Accordingly, he explains, "All that I wish to point out is, to use a modern phrase, that the movement of heresy is one and the same from the beginning: that the Gnostics were the Protestants of their day, and the Protestants the Gnostics of ours; that *the principle is identical*, and the bulk of the movement unfolded to greater proportions; and its successes accumulated, and its antagonism to the Catholic Church changeless and essential."[642] Because *the principle is identical*, Manning explains, *there is a perfect ultimate*

---

[641] Henry Edwaed Manning, D.D., *The Present Crisis of the Holy See Tested by Prophecy*, London, 1861, p. 7.
[642] *Ibid.* pp. 9-10.

*unity in the history and development of heresy.*⁶⁴³ However, in Protestantism, that lawless principle of revolt inherent in the act of preferring one's own private opinion to what is taught by divinely instituted magisterial authority, was explicitly set forth by Luther as the foundational principle of religious belief, namely the principle of Private Judgment. Accordingly Manning says in the next sentence, "To name no more than these, Gnosticism, Arianism, and, above all, Protestantism, have generated each a multitude of subordinate and affiliated heresies. *But it is Protestantism which, above all others, bears the three notes of the inspired writers in the greatest breadth and evidence.*" These *three notes* he speaks of in this passage are, 1) schism, 2) heresy, 3) the denial of the Incarnation.

Manning elaborates on the three notes:

> The first is, schism, as given by St. John: "It is the last hour: and as you have heard that Antichrist cometh: even now there are become many Antichrists: whereby we know that it is the last hour. They went out from us; but they were not of us. For if they had been of us, they would no doubt have remained with us."
>
> The second note is, the rejection of the office and presence of the Holy Ghost. St. Jude says, "These are they, who separate themselves, sensual men" (i. e. ψυχικοί, animal or merely rational and natural men) "having not the spirit."† This necessarily involves the heretical principle of human opinion as opposed to Divine faith; of the private spirit as opposed to the infallible voice of the Holy Spirit, speaking through the Church of God.
>
> The third note is, the denial of the Incarnation. St. John writes, "Every spirit, which confesseth that Jesus Christ is come in the flesh is of God: and every spirit that dissolveth Jesus" (that is, by denying the mystery of the Incarnation, either the true Godhead, or the true manhood, or the unity or divinity of the person of the Incarnate Son) "is not of God, and this is Antichrist, of whom you have heard that he cometh, and he is now already in the world." Again he says, "Many

---

⁶⁴³ *Ibid.* p. 8 — «Physiologists tell us that *there is a perfect ultimate unity even in the countless diseases which devour the body*; nevertheless, each disease seems to throw out its progeny by a corruption and reproduction. *So in the history and development of heresy.* To name no more than these, Gnosticism, Arianism, and, above all, Protestantism, have generated each a multitude of subordinate and affiliated heresies.»

seducers are gone out into the world, who confess not that Jesus Christ is come in the flesh: this is a seducer and an Antichrist."[644]

† St. Jude 19.

The revolt against divine authority inherent in Luther's principle of Private Judgment led directly to the denial of the divinity of Jesus Christ. The erosion of the dogma of the Incarnation, of the full divinity of Jesus Christ, was brought about by the Protestant principle of Private Judgment, which eliminated the Church's magisterial authority to infallibly teach and interpret the revealed mysteries, thereby reducing the mystery of the Incarnation from the status of an infallible dogma of faith in the *hypostatic union* of the divine and human natures in Christ, to a mere matter of opinion, to be interpreted and understood as one chooses. Thus, there took place a progressive erosion of the dogma from the semi-Nestorianism of Calvin to the outright denial of the dogma by the "Father of Liberal Theology", Friedrich Schleiermacher, who wrote to his father, "I cannot believe that he who called himself the Son of Man was the true, eternal God; I cannot believe that his death was a vicarious atonement."[645] Thus it can be seen that in the foundational principle of Lutheranism there is the very embodiment of the revolt against Christ and its inevitable denial of Christ's divinity. As it was with Luther, it is likewise that self-same principle of *revolt against divine authority* — Private Judgment, which is the foundational principle of Bergoglio's belief system — Private Judgment which replaces the authoritative apostolic testimony perpetuated in the dogmas of the ecclesiastical magisterium with a mere "discernment" of the sovereign conscience made by the private individual. Luther eliminated the institutional magisterium as

---

[644] *Ibid.* pp. 5-6.

[645] Vide: B. A. Gerrish, *A Prince of the Church: Schleiermacher and the Beginnings of Modern Theology* (Philadelphia, 1984), p. 25. — "Faith is the regalia of the Godhead, you say. Alas! dearest father, if you believe that without this faith no one can attain to salvation in the next world, nor to tranquility in this—and such, I know, is your belief—oh! then pray to God to grant it to me, for to me it is now lost. I cannot believe that he who called himself the Son of Man was the true, eternal God; I cannot believe that his death was a vicarious atonement."

the dogmatic authority from the constitution of his "reformed" counter-church, thereby inaugurating in principle the "Dogma-Free Christianity" which led to the "Death of God" theology of secular post-Christian religion, which places the individual conscience on the seat of judgment even over God himself, and abolishes the Law of God by reducing the Commandments, as Bergoglio teaches, to mere *"ideals"* to be aimed for, and which one must strive to observe, but it not necessary for them to be observed absolutely as a condition for salvation. This is precisely the creed professed by Jorge Bergoglio, so publicly and so explicitly that it is only denied by those in a deep state of denial — a group which unfortunately comprises the vast majority of prelates in the Catholic Church. And one who might still be so clueless to ask, "What will all this lead to?" needs only consider what it has already wrought. Montini's humanist antiphon, *"Honour to man, king of the earth and today, prince of the heavens"*[646] has morphed into Bergoglio's profession of secular pseudo-Christianity, and has brought us to this consummation point of Luther revolt against divine law, so that now it is **man**, (supposedly redeemed by Christ and set free by the liberating truth of Enlightenment "Dogma-Free Christianity"), "Who opposes, and is lifted up above all that is called God, or that is worshipped, so that he sits in the temple of God, shewing himself as if he were God." (2 Thess. 2:4) This *cult of man* is the mortal threat to the faith of the Church — the threat to the Church which the true Pope, Benedict XVI warns of in the above cited passage: «But the real threat to the Church and thus to the Petrine service... the worldwide dictatorship of apparently humanistic ideologies, which contradicting means exclusion from the basic social consensus. A hundred years ago, anyone would have thought it absurd to speak of homosexual marriage. Today, anyone who opposes this is socially excommunicated. The same applies to abortion and the production of people in the laboratory. Modern society is in the process of formulating an anti-Christian creed, which to resist against is punished with social excommunication.»

Lutheran Private Judgment is the mortal enemy of the Catholic faith and is totally opposed in its very nature to the Gospel of Christ,

---

[646] *Documentation Catholique*(no.1580); *New York Times* 8 Feb 1971 - https://www.nytimes.com/1971/02/08/archives/pope-hailing-flight-calls...

yet Bergoglio has repeatedly stated his intention to bring about communion between the Catholic Church and the communities of Luther's Reformation. Four years ago (13 October 2016) Bergoglio declared, "We give thanks to God because today we, Lutherans and Catholics, are walking on the road that leads from conflict to communion… by virtue of our baptism, we all form the one Body of Christ. [*sententia hæretica*] The different members, in fact, form one body." In that same discourse he said, "We give thanks to God because today we, Lutherans and Catholics, are walking on the road that leads from conflict to communion." What he means by the "communion" and "common Christian witness" he mentioned to the Lutherans becomes clear from his own words to the Protestant pastor Brian Stiller: "I'm not interested in converting Evangelicals to Catholicism. I want people to find Jesus in their own community. There are so many doctrines we will never agree on. Let's be about showing the love of Jesus."

We do not form one body with the heretics, and there can never be communion between the members of Catholic Church and the Protestant sects, because any Catholic who would enter into a "communion" or "common Christian witness" with the Protestants in matters of faith, would defect from the Catholic faith and enter into communion with the revolt against the faith taught by Christ. This is so because there is only one God and therefore only one formal object of faith and only one Truth and one true religion — "one Lord, one faith, one baptism" (Eph. 4:5); for which reason the bonds of communion exist only within the Church of that true religion which professes the true faith of Christ. Communion with any other religious entity outside of the Catholic Church is therefore in the nature of a defection from the faith and communion of the Church. The very idea that there can exist "communion" — a union of oneness between 'communions' — between various denominations and "communions" professing different and opposing beliefs, all of which comprise one "Christian Church" is a heretical tenet of Protestant ecclesiology which holds that, "It is a mistake to refer, as many people do, to the various branches of the Church as 'religions'. If a church is a Christian church, it is part of the Christian religion. There is one Christian religion but there are many ways of expressing it, the ways of the various branches or 'communions' or denominations of the Christian church."⁶⁴⁷ This heresy is founded on the absurd notion that there can exist "communion,"⁶⁴⁸ i.e., a unity of oneness in Christian belief and Christian life, between communities which profess diverse and opposing beliefs and moral codes, practice essentially different rites of worship, and are governed by different rulers according to different constitutional structure and different laws. Thus it is Bergoglio who openly professes the same principles of revolt against the revealing authority of God as did Martin Luther and the Protestants, and all the heretics before them since Apostolic times. It is he who is in schism and heresy, and not the faithful Catholics who refuse to be in communion with him.

Since there exist only "one Lord, one faith, one baptism" (Eph. 4:5), there can exist only one true Church founded by Christ on the apostolic testimony to teach all nations the saving truths of divine revelation. It is that apostolic testimony which constitutes the Sacred Tradition of the Church. The First Vatican Council affirmed this point, "renewing the same decree" of the Council of Trent which declared:

> Furthermore, this supernatural revelation, according to the faith of the universal Church, as declared by the holy synod of Trent, is contained "in the written books and in the unwritten traditions which have been received by the apostles from the mouth of Christ Himself; or, through the inspiration of the Holy Spirit have been handed down by the apostles themselves, and have thus come to us".⁶⁴⁹

The one Sacred Tradition is therefore comprised of the body of revealed doctrine which exists both in written and oral form, as St. Paul teaches, "Stand fast and hold the traditions which ye have been taught, whether by word or by our epistle." (2 Thess. 2:15) Tradition, in the narrower sense as distinguished from Scripture, is understood

---

⁶⁴⁷ Charles W. F. Smith, *Discovering the Episcopal Church,* Forward Movement Publications, Cincinnati, 1989, p. 10.

⁶⁴⁸ «Used by Augustine, in belief that the word was derived from com- "with, together" + unus "oneness, union."» [https://www.etymonline.com/word/communion].

⁶⁴⁹ DS 3006.

as "the unwritten traditions", "received by the apostles from the Mouth of Christ", "or from the apostles themselves, at the dictation of the Holy Spirit". (Council of Trent) Together the written and unwritten tradition form one "divine deposit" (Vatican I), and thus form what St. Athanasius called the "actual original tradition, teaching and faith of the Catholic Church, which the Lord bestowed, the apostles proclaimed and the Fathers safeguarded."[650] The Sacred Doctrine contained in the Church's tradition being **one**, is therefore of its very nature *unchangeable:*

> For the doctrine of the faith which God has revealed ... has been entrusted as a divine deposit to the spouse of Christ, to be faithfully guarded and infallibly interpreted. Hence, also, that understanding of its sacred dogmas must be perpetually retained, which Holy Mother Church has once declared; and there must never be a recession from that meaning under the specious name of a deeper understanding. Therefore ... let the understanding, the knowledge, and wisdom of individuals as of all, of one man as of the whole Church, grow and progress strongly with the passage of the ages and the centuries; but let it be solely in its own genus, namely in the same dogma, with the same sense and the same understanding (St. Vincent of Lérins).[651]

The absolute immutability of the doctrine of the **one faith** was emphasized in the teaching of Pope Gregory XVI:

> This you will do perfectly if you watch over yourselves and your doctrine, as your office makes it your duty, repeating incessantly to yourselves that every novelty attempts to undermine the Universal Church and that, according to the *warning of the holy Pope Agatho, "nothing that has been regularly defined can bear diminution, or change,* or *addition, and repels every alteration of sense, or even of words."*[652]

It is because there is one God who is himself the ETERNAL SUBSISTENT TRUTH, and the AUTHOR OF ALL TRUTH, that the PRIMARY TRUTH can only be ONE, the *prima veritas* which is

---

[650] Athanasius, *ad Serapion,* 1:28.

[651] DS 3020, *Dogmatic Constitution Dei Filius* Vatican Council I. The Constitution quotes St. Vincent of Lérins, *Commonitorium primum* 23, n. 3.

[652] Pope Gregory XVI, *Mirari vos,* August 15, 1832.

the formal object of faith, for which reason it is irrational to maintain that opposing doctrines of different religions can all at the same time be true, or that the divinely revealed truth can undergo modification or alteration: *veritas Domini manet in aeternum*. (Ps. 116. v. 2) Likewise, the truths of reason cannot contradict the revealed truths of faith as Freemasonry maintains, because both are necessarily true, since if they were not true, truth would be both true and false, and would therefore be nothing. It is Freemasonry, following the esoteric tradition of *Hermetic Gnosticism* which professes the doctrine that the primordial revelation was given to mankind, and then was diffused throughout the whole world among all the tribes and nations, and therefore all ancient religions are true and of equal value.

Thus it is to Bergoglio that the words of Pope Gregory XVI most aptly apply: «Now it is clear that if there were not in the Church and in the Pope the sameness of spirit, of feelings and of doctrines, there could not be in the latter the true representation of the former. Therefore the Pontiff cannot represent the Church, who together does not necessarily represent its unity».[653] Bergoglio, in his public profession of revolt against the Catholic faith, exhibits that disposition which is contrary to the *'form of the pontificate'*, which represents the *'form of the Church"*, namely, the orthodox external profession of the Catholic faith.[654] Bergoglio cannot be a valid and legitimate pope, because, "one is incapable of this dignity and a decayed member cut off from the Church if he is a heretic,"[655] and

---

[653] Gregory XVI, *Il trionfo della santa sede*, Capo XXIII, p. 270 — «Or egli è chiaro che, qualora non vi fosse e nella Chiesa e nel Papa medesimità di spirito, di sentimenti e di dottrine, non vi potrebbe neppur essere in questo la vera rappresentanza di quello. Dunque il Pontefice non può rappresentare la Chiesa, che insieme non ne rappresenti necessariamente l'unità.»

[654] *De Ecclesia Militante* cap. x — «Formam Ecclesiae non esse fidem internam (nisi Ecclesiam invisibilem habere velimus) sed externam, idest, fidei confessionem. Id quod apertissime docet s. Augustinus lib. 19. contra Faustum, cap. 11.»

[655] Francesco Bordoni, *Sacrum Tribunal Iudicum In Causis Sanctæ Fidei Contra Hæreticos Et Hæresi Suspectos*, p. 137 — «Deus non permitteret Ecclesiam suam regi, & gubernari ab eo, qui incapax est huius dignitatis, & membrum putridum ab Ecclesia præcisum, si sit hæreticus; aut persona, quæ

therefore St. Alphonsus says,[656] a heretic is an *incapable subject* (*soggetto inabile*) of the Catholic papacy — incapable because he publicly represents a different faith from that of the Catholic Church, and is therefore *incapable of the office*.[657] One who openly opposes the faith of Christ is incapable of representing Christ as his Vicar on earth. Accordingly, as a public heretic, he represents a different church, a *parallel church*, which is not the Church of Christ, because, as Bellarmine teaches, "The true Church of Christ is that which professes the faith of Christ."[658]

Bergoglio represents "the other church", as Freemasons refer to their organization: "The Church of Heresy", which opposes the divinely revealed mysteries of Catholicism, and demeans belief in them as "superstition", and offensively denigrates its divinely instituted magisterial and governing authority and priestly ministry and power of orders as "clericalism". What is precisely denoted by the Masonic term "clericalism" is that aspect of the Catholic religion in which there exists the priestly order, with its sacramental *power of orders*, and its *magisterial authority*. In his interviews with the atheist Eugenio Scalfari, Bergoglio has explicitly stated his opposition to "Clericalism". "Clericalism" is a Masonic code-word that simply means "Catholicism" but it is employed in order to conceal Masonry's total opposition to the Catholic religion. "To better combat Catholicism," Cardinal Caro y Rodriguez explains, "Masonry invented a distinction between Clericalism and Catholicism, boasting of respect for Catholicism and of combating only clericalism, that is the intervention of the clergy into politics. ... Worthy of notice is the declaration made in this respect by Masonic Brother Courdavana, Professor of Letters at Douai, who in 1888 and 1889 gave conferences in the lodges of the province and of Paris. In one of the conferences the following was read: 'The distinction between

---

nunquam fuit in Ecclesia, ideo neuter potest esse legitimus sponsus, & caput Ecclesiæ.»

[656] Alfonso Maria de' Liguori, *Verità Della Fede*, Tomo Secondo, Monza, 1823, Capo IX. p. 159.

[657] *Ibid.* p. 207 — «Ma si risponde che la sola eresia, non già gli altri delitti rendono il Papa inabile al suo officio»

[658] *De Ecclesia Militante*, cap. xv — «*Vera enim Ecclesia est, quae profitetur Christi fidem.*»

Catholicism and clericalism is purely official, subtly adapted for the need of the public. But here in the lodge let us say it aloud, for the sake of truth: Catholicism and clericalism are one and the same thing."[659] Bergoglio denigrates the supernatural sacramental *power of orders* when he says, "Clericalism arises from an elitist and exclusivist vision of vocation, *that interprets the ministry received as a power to be exercised.*"[660] In the same discourse he attacked the Church's infallible magisterial authority by reducing it to *clericalism*: "This [*clericalism*] leads us to believe that we belong to a group that has all the answers" — as if the Church's faith in a priesthood endowed with a divinely instituted power to teach infallible truths in God's name were nothing but the arrogant pretext of *clericalism*.

Bergoglio's promotion of Masonic beliefs through the employment of Masonic terms is not limited to *clericalism*, but how often we hear him also speak of *solidarity*, *brotherhood*, *science*, *democracy*, in a context that patently spins the meaning of these words to denote exactly what Masonry intends to convey by them. In this modality of expression, Bergoglio follows a long established Masonic usage of these terms. Mgr. Delassaus explained in 1907: «How many perfidious formulas were created for two centuries! Under the reign of Philosophism it was "tolerance" and "superstition" which passed from mouth to mouth; under that Reign of Terror, "fanaticism" and "reason"»; And then he says of his own day, more than a century ago:

> Today the most popular words are "clericalism", "science", "democracy" and "solidarity"; science against faith, democracy against any religious, social and family hierarchy, the solidarity of the plebeians against all those who prevent the free enjoyment of the goods of this world, the rich who possess them and priests who forbid their unjust greed; solidarity therefore of all peoples who, from one point of the

---

[659] Cardinal Caro y Rodriguez, *The Mystery of Freemasonry Unveiled*, p. 75.
[660] *Address to the Synod Fathers at Opening of Synod 2018 on Young People, the Faith and Vocational Discernment* - https://zenit.org/2018/10/03/pope-francis-address-to-the-synod-fathers-at-opening-of-synod2018-on-young-people-the-faith-and-vocational-discernment/

world to the other, must help each other to break the triple yoke of property, authority and religion.[661]

St. Pius X warned in *Notre charge apostolique* (1904), of "the great movement of apostasy being organized in every country for the establishment of a One-World Church which shall have neither dogmas nor hierarchy, neither discipline for the mind nor curb for the passions, and which under the pretext of freedom and human dignity, would bring back to the world the reign of legalized cunning and force, and the oppression of the weak, and all those who toil and suffer." (para. 44) When that is achieved then there will only be one great obstacle left on earth that will oppose that godless ecumenical unity of the entity which the same St. Pius X describes as "a Democracy which will be neither Catholic, nor Protestant nor Jewish" (para. 43) On this One World Church being prepared by Freemasonry, Mgr. Delassus relates:

> In the second session of the assembly of 1883, Monday, September 19, M. Bro. ∴ Blaton was elected speaker. In the eighth session, Saturday 15 September, he was given the floor for the closing speech. This speech ended with the following: "... Then we can march to the definitive conquest of the profane world, and let me say it at the end, even if you should call my hopes fanciful - our growing minority will perhaps soon

---

[661] Henri Delassus, IL PROBLEMA DELL'ORA PRESENTE — ANTAGONISMO TRA DUE CIVILTA', SECONDA PARTE, Roma, 1907, p. 137 — «Quante perfide formole furono create da due secoli! Sotto il regno del Filosofismo furono "tolleranza" e "superstizione" che passarono di bocca in bocca; sotto quello del Terrore "fanatismo" e "ragione"; sotto la Restaurazione "antico regime", "decima", "privilegi"; sotto il secondo impero "il progresso"; al tempo della recente persecuzione in Germania il "Kulturkampf"; in Francia nel 16 maggio "il governo dei parroci". Oggi le parole più in voga sono col "clericalismo", la "scienza", la "democrazia" e la "solidarietà"; la scienza contro la fede, la democrazia contro ogni gerarchia religiosa, sociale e familiare, la solidarietà dei plebei contro tutti coloro che impediscono il libero godimento dei beni di questo mondo, ricchi che li possedono e preti che ne interdiscono l'ingiusta cupidigia; solidarietà quindi di tutti i popoli che, da un punto all'altro del mondo, devono vicendevolmente aiutarsi per rompere il triplice giogo della proprietà, dell'autorità e della religione.»

become the majority of the nation. On that day, M. F ∴ our work will have truly reached its destiny. In those buildings raised in all parts for centuries to religious superstitions and priestly supremacies, we will perhaps in turn be called to preach our doctrines; and in place of the clerical chants that still resound, it will be the hammers, the batteries and the acclamations of our order that will make the large vaults and vast pillars echo.[662]

Even more clearly Mgr. Delassus quotes the Masons themselves on the new religion of brotherhood, equality and solidarity they intend to impose on the whole world:

In 1900, on the occasion of the Universal Exposition, an international Masonic congress was held in Paris. It was the fourth time that all the Orients and all the lodges were invited to an international congress. The first took place in 1889, the second in Antwerp in 1894, the third in The Hague in 1896. In Paris, it was a question of studying the means to establish "continued relations between the various Masonic powers of the globe, regardless of any obedience and every rite, with the aim of mutual support for the search for scientific, philosophical and sociological truths ". The president Bro. Lucipia, ex-Communard, in his opening address, made this exhortation: "Let us work, my brothers, we bring our stone for the construction of the Temple of humanity, on the facade of which, when it is finished, it will be written: Solidarity rules the world ". Bro. Blatin, in his report, said that these relationships already existed. "Don't all Masons have the honor of bringing to the profane world the great moral idea, solidarity, based, abstraction made of every

---

[662] *Ibid.* p. 290 — «Nella seconda seduta dell'assemblea del 1883, lunedì 19 settembre, il F Blaton fu eletto oratore. Nell'ottava tornata, sabato 15 settembre, gli fu data la parola pel discorso di chiusa. Questo discorso si conchiuse con ciò che segue: "... Allora potremo marciare alla conquista definitiva del mondo profano, e permettetemi di dirlo sul finire, anche se doveste chiamare chimeriche le mie speranze - la nostra minoranza crescendo diventerà forse presto la maggioranza della nazione. In quel giorno, M.F∴ la nostra opera avrà veramente raggiunto i suoi destini. In quegli edifici innalzati in tutte le parti da secoli alle superstizioni religiose ed alle supremazie sacerdotali, noi saremo forse chiamati a nostra volta a predicare le nostre dottrine; ed in luogo delle salmodie clericali che risuonano ancora, saranno I martelli, le batterie e le acclamazioni del nostro ordine che ne faranno echeggiare le larghe volte e i vasti pilastri".»

religious formula, on a considered altruism?" Nevertheless, it was concluded that this agreement was not enough, but effective and continuous relations were necessary between the Orients. A few days later, the annual Convent met in the Grand Orient, and the speaker, making this decision known, motivated it thus: "The Vatican is the seat of an evil international, and it is absolutely necessary for a federation of all Masonic obediences to oppose it ". Having thus resolved to restrict all over the world the bonds which unite all secret societies against the Church, the international congress dealt with the "profane". Bro. Blatin asked that Masonic teaching be spread to the "profane masses, who gradually abandon the religions of the past" and that they give themselves the "satisfactions they require". Brother Cocq was more explicit: "It is religion itself that must be destroyed, it is the belief in superstitions and the supernatural, it is dogma".[663]

---

[663] *Ibid.* p. 25 — «Nel 1900, nell'occasione dell'Esposizione universale, si tenne a Parigi un congress massonico internazionale. Era la quarta volta che tutti gli Orienti e tutte le logge venivano invitate ad un congresso internazionale. Il primo ebbe luogo nel 1889, il secondo ad Anversa nel 1894, il terzo all'Aja nel 1896. A Parigi, trattavasi di studiare i mezzi onde stabilire "delle relazioni continuate tra le diverse potenze massoniche del globo, prescindendo da ogni obbedienza e da ogni rito, col fine di un reciproco appoggio per la ricerca delle verità scientifiche, filosofiche e sociologiche". Il presidente Fr. Lucipia, ex-comunardo, nel suo discorso d'apertura, fece questa esortazione: "Lavoriamo, miei fr., portiamo la nostra pietra per la costruzione del Tempio dell'umanità, sulla facciata del quale, quando sarà terminato, si scriverà: La solidarietà governa il mondo". Il Fr. Blatin, nel suo rapporto, disse che queste relazioni già esistevano. "Non hanno tutti i massoni l'onore di portare al mondo profano la grande idea morale, solidarista, basata, astrazion fatta d'ogni formula religiosa, sopra un altruismo ponderato?" Nondimeno si conchiuse che quest'accordo non bastava, ma erano necessarie tra gli Orienti relazioni effettive e continue. Alcuni giorni dopo, il Convento annuale si riunì al Grand'Oriente, e l'oratore, facendo conoscere questa decisione, la motivò così: "Il Vaticano è la sede d'una internazionale malefica, ed è assolutamente necessario opporle una federazione di tutte le obbedienze massoniche". Dopo aver in tal guisa risoluto di restringere in tutto il mondo i vincoli che uniscono tutte le società segrete contro la Chiesa, il congresso internazionale si occupò dei "profani". Il Fr. Blatin chiese che si diffondesse l'insegnamento massonico nelle "masse profane, che abbandonano a poco a poco le religioni del passato" e che loro si dessero le "soddisfazioni che richiedono". Il Fr. Cocq fu più

On page 312 of the same work, Mgr. Delassus quotes another speaker at the Masonic Congress of 1900:

> Pastor Beverluis told the Congress in 1900, "Christianity will be perfected by spiritualism, but not the Christianity of churches, dogmas, and rites... Then no more priests, no more anxieties of conscience! Then no more blind zealots, no more worship of the authority of a book; no more confessionalism, no more dogmatic system, no more infallibility of a man or a book. Then no longer fear of a cruel God, no longer mediation of Saints between God and man". The pastor calls this "a purified and simplified Christianity".[664]

It is precisely this "purified and simplified Christianity" without the belief in the supernatural[665] and dogma of the *religion of the past*, that Bergoglio promotes in the name of *reform* — reform which he told Fr. Adolfo Nicholas will be *irreversible*.[666] He states quite explicitly

---

esplicito: "È la religione stessa che bisogna distruggere, è la credenza alle superstizioni e al soprannaturale, è il dogma".»

[664] *Ibid.* p. 312 — «Il pastore Beverluis disse al Congresso del 1900, "Il cristianesimo sarà perfezionato dallo spiritismo, ma non il cristianesimo delle chiese, dei dogmi e dei riti ... Allora non più preti, non più angustie di coscienza! Allora non più zelatori ciechi, non più adorazione dell'autorità di un libro; non più confessionalismo, non più Sistema dogmatico, non più infallibilità di un uomo o di un libro. Allora non più timore di un Dio crudele, non più mediazione di Santi fra Dio e l'uomo". Il pastore chiama questo "un cristianesimo purificato e semplificato".»

[665] Bergoglio's frequently expressed utter disdain for dogma and contempt of the supernatural is the pure embodiment of the Masonic agenda summed up in the cited passage of Brother Cocq: "It is religion itself that must be destroyed, it is the belief in superstitions and the supernatural, it is dogma". Bergoglio's contempt for the supernatural aspect of religion is evident in his own words: "***Surprisingly, the account of the multiplication of the loaves does not mention the multiplication itself.*** *On the contrary, the words that stand out are: "break", "give" and "distribute" (cf. Lk 9:16). In effect, the emphasis is not on the multiplication but the act of sharing. This is important.* ***Jesus does not perform a magic trick; he does not change five loaves into five thousand*** *and then to announce: 'There! Distribute them!'* — Homily on Corpus Christi, Rome, June 23, 2019.

[666] Austen Ivereigh reported in *Crux* on May 13, 2017: «The Spaniard who was until earlier this year Superior General of the Jesuits has written a

his agenda for reform, which, coincidently, happens to be the reform agenda of Freemasonry:

> The church's pastoral ministry cannot be obsessed with the transmission of a disjointed multitude of doctrines to be imposed insistently. [...] The proposal of the Gospel must be more simple, profound, radiant. [...] the proclamation of the saving love of God comes before moral and religious imperatives. [...] Tradition and memory of the past must help us to have the courage to open up new areas to God. Those who today always look for disciplinarian solutions, those who long for an exaggerated doctrinal 'security,' those who stubbornly try to recover a past that no longer exists — they have a static and inward-directed view of things. [...] I have a dogmatic certainty: God is in every person's life. God is in everyone's life. [...] Religion has the right to express its opinion in the service of the people, but God in creation has set us free: it is not possible to interfere spiritually in the life of a person.[667]

Two ideas dominated the Masonic agenda which was announced at the congresses: "two ideas: 1° that an absolutely universal religion must be established on the ruins of all religions, through the lowering of barriers and the abolition of dogmas; 2° that this universal religion must be a social religion, a humanitarian religion, a religion of human progress, which goes so far as to provide man with paradise on earth."[668] It is easily recognized by anyone who has been paying

---

series of reminiscences about his conversations with Pope Francis, published in two parts in the Spanish Jesuit publication *Mensajero*. Father Adolfo Nicolás, SJ, wrote them while spending some weeks in his native country before heading for the Philippines capital, Manila, where he now lives. When Nicolás - who is the same age as Francis - spoke to him of his resignation as Superior General, Francis told him: "I myself am thinking of taking seriously Benedict's challenge." But then, some months later - faced, presumably, with some resistance to his reforms - Francis told him: "I ask the good Lord to take me once the changes are irreversible."»

[667] **INTERVIEW WITH POPE FRANCIS** by Fr Antonio Spadaro, Sept. 2013. http://www.vatican.va/content/francesco/en/speeches/2013/september/documents/papa-francesco_20130921_intervista-spadaro.html

[668] Henri Delassus, *Op. cit.* p. 283 — «due idee: 1° che una religione assolutamente universale deve stabilirsi sulle rovine di tutte le religioni, e ciò mediante l'abbassamento delle barriere e l'abolizione dei dogmi; 2° che

attention to Bergoglio's discourses and declarations that these words describe most aptly the reform agenda which he has constantly been promoting since his election in 2013. In the just published *Dio e il mondo che verrà — Una conversazione con Domenico Agasso*, Bergoglio declares: «It is time to remove social injustice and marginalization. We can no longer blithely accept inequalities... If we seize the current trial as an opportunity, we can prepare for tomorrow under the banner of **human fraternity**... we can heal injustice by building a **new world order** based on **solidarity**» In *Fratelli Tutti*, Bergoglio asserts the proposition, "From our faith experience and from the wisdom accumulated over centuries, but also from lessons learned from our many weaknesses and failures, we, the believers of the different religions, know that our witness to God benefits our societies." His own words betray the meaning in the strict sense that the "faith experiences" of the practitioners of all religions with equal right bear "witness to God," and to the divine truths. That the heresies of Religious Liberty and Indifferentism which assert the right to practice all religions with equal right by all is here intended by Bergoglio is manifested in his own words cited above, where he said, "Many think differently, feel differently, seeking God or meeting God in different ways. In this crowd, in this range of religions, *there is only one certainty that we have for all:* ***we are all children of God***". Even more explicitly in the Abu Dhabi «*Document on Human Fraternity for World Peace and Living Together*» Bergoglio asserted the heresies of Religious Liberty and Indifferentism[669] condemned by Pius IX: "Freedom is a right of every person: each individual enjoys the freedom of belief, thought, expression and action. The pluralism and the diversity of religions, colour, sex, race and language are willed by God in His wisdom, through which He created human beings. This divine wisdom is the source from which the right to freedom of belief and

---

questa religione universale dev'essere una religione sociale, una religione umanitaria, una religione di progresso umano, che giunge sino a procurare all'uomo il paradiso sulla terra.»

[669] That Religious Liberty and Ecumenism are properly heresies founded on the heresy of Indifferentism is explained briefly in my earlier work, *The Suicide of Altering the Faith in the Liturgy*, Ch. IV: Doctrinal Novelties of the Post-Conciliar Church, pp. 51-65.

the freedom to be different derives."⁶⁷⁰ It is in this context of *equality of rights* **to *publicly practice* and *express the beliefs* of different religions** that Bergoglio states the urgency to implement what coincidently happens to be the Masonic agenda of *solidarity, fraternity,* and *tolerance* — yes, the agenda consisting of the *liberty, equality, fraternity, solidarity,* and *tolerance* which are all of dogmas of Freemasonry. Thus, he says accordingly in *Fratelli Tutti:* «Issues of human fraternity and social friendship have always been a concern of mine. [...] In this case, I have felt particularly encouraged by the Grand Imam Ahmad Al-Tayyeb, with whom I met in Abu Dhabi, where we declared that "God has created all human beings equal in rights, duties and dignity, and has called them to live together as brothers and sisters".» To achieve this end, Bergoglio makes the ominous and sinister disclosure that, «In this regard, Grand Imam Ahmad Al-Tayyeb and I have called upon "the architects of international policy and world economy to work strenuously to spread the culture of tolerance and of living together in peace;» which is a thinly veiled formula for promoting the repression and persecution by state and international law enforcement of any religion which practices what Bergoglio calls *fundamentalism,* which (as noted above) he says is the **disease** of those in the Catholic Church "who believe they possess the absolute truth" (i.e. that their Church alone possess supernaturally revealed infallible dogmas to the exclusion of all other religions), and who (according to the conception of Hermetic Gnosticism) are "content with being enclosed in one fragment of reality." Bergoglio therefore expressly endorses the Masonic **political agenda** for the suppression of *"fundamentalist intolerance," "fanaticism,"* and *"closedmindedness"* — which all mean the same thing inside the Masonic Lodge, namely the agenda to suppress and outlaw the public practice and preaching of the orthodox and

---

⁶⁷⁰ Archbishop Carlo Maria Viganò has said that this idea is a "blatant heresy" and a "terrible blasphemy": "Saying that God wants to be worshipped as something other than how He revealed Himself means that the Incarnation, Passion, Death and Resurrection of our Savior are completely meaningless," and he rightly added, "It means that the reason for founding the Church, the reason for which millions of holy Martyrs gave their lives, for which the Sacraments were instituted, along with the priesthood and the papacy itself, are all meaningless."

traditional religion of **Catholicism**, which they impiously categorize in their writings as *intolerant fanaticism*, rigid and closedminded *clericalism*, and *superstition*. Accordingly Bergoglio says in *Fratelli Tutti:*

> At a time when various forms of fundamentalist intolerance are damaging relationships between individuals, groups and peoples, let us be committed to living and teaching the value of respect for others, a love capable of welcoming differences, and the priority of the dignity of every human being over his or her ideas, opinions, practices and even sins. Even as forms of fanaticism, closedmindedness and social and cultural fragmentation proliferate in present-day society, a good politician will take the first step and insist that different voices be heard.

Against Bergoglio's impious heretical ravings, we have the testimony of one of the most ancient Fathers, St. Irenæus of Lyons, who explained in Book Three, Chapter Four of his *Adversus Hæreses*, which begins with the heading, «Chapter IV.—The truth is to be found nowhere else but in the Catholic Church, the sole depository of apostolical doctrine. Heresies are of recent formation, and cannot trace their origin up to the apostles»:

> Since therefore we have such proofs, it is not necessary to seek the truth among others which it is easy to obtain from the Church; since the apostles, like a rich man [depositing his money] in a bank, lodged in her hands most copiously all things pertaining to the truth: so that every man, whosoever will, can draw from her the water of life. For she is the entrance to life; all others are thieves and robbers. On this account are we bound to avoid them, but to make choice of the thing pertaining to the Church with the utmost diligence, and to lay hold of the tradition of the truth.

I say that Bergoglio's heretical ravings, which are founded on the *Gnostic* belief that all religions are good and true, because each contains a "fragment of reality", is absurd, because the unstated foundational premise of his heresy rests on a **contradiction**. The contradiction consists in this, that while Catholicism professes itself to be the sole true religion to the exclusion of all others as false; the other religions also profess themselves to be the true religions; and therefore: If it is true that the Catholic religion is the only true religion, then it is true that all others are necessarily false religions; but if they are false religions, then they cannot also be at the same time true religions. As I have amply proven, the Catholic religion professes itself to be divinely instituted as the exclusive repository of the one and only, absolutely true faith, and that all the others are therefore necessarily false religions because they profess beliefs which stand in contradiction to the one true faith of the Catholic Church. From the time of the earliest Fathers, and then by St. Augustine (*City of God* Book XV), and again unanimously by countless doctors and theologians — it has been taught by the Church and explained again and again down through the ages that there has always existed in some form since Abel, and will exist until the end of the world, and as yet there exists **now,** only **one true religion**: *"The truth is to be found nowhere else but in the Catholic Church"*. (St. Irenæus) **If only one is true, then ALL the others are FALSE.** It cannot be said that it was true in the past, but now we have a deeper understanding of the Church and from that understanding we can see that is no longer true (since that proposition would only be true if the nature of the Church as instituted by Christ had been substantially altered into something else), because if it is no longer true that the Catholic religion is the only true one, then the perpetual Catholic dogma which professes that it is perpetually true is false, which, if the first proposition is also true, then it would necessarily result that the dogma is both false and true. Furthermore, if it can now be seen to be not true, then, being false, it is essentially and entirely false *per se*, and therefore it was necessarily also false in the past, because the proposition of its very nature is stated as an absolute truth without qualification, and therefore is universally applicable in a manner that absolutely transcends space and time, so that if it no longer applies with equal validity to our time, then it is and always has been false. The divine truths of our religion are eternal truths (Ps. 116), and are therefore immutable (Matt. 24:35), being that they are, "coming down from the Father of lights, with whom there is no change (παραλλαγὴ)[671], nor shadow of alteration (τροπῆς ἀποσκίασμα)[672]." (James 1:17) This is necessarily so, since the divine nature is eternal, and human nature,

---

[671] παραλλαγὴ = change, variation, mutation.

[672] τροπῆς ἀποσκίασμα.

: τροπῆς = change, alteration; ἀποσκίασμα = shadow.

created by God remains what it is as created by God.[673] What's more, if one would say that both propositions are true, (i.e. the Catholic dogma and Bergoglio's contrary belief), then that proposition actually says nothing and destroys itself because such things as those affirmed are actually nothing, because the proposition includes within itself a contradiction. Similarly, if one holds that the Catholic faith is true, but with the exception that it is not the *only* true faith, and that other faiths are also true, then that proposition also destroys itself because then the Catholic faith's profession that it is the only true faith would be both true and false. In the passage cited below, St. Thomas disposes of this silliness, explaining, *And because someone could say that he who claims that everything is true makes an exception of the one contrary to his own statement, or bars it from what holds universally, it follows that they will be able "to consider," or bring forward an infinite number of false statements against those who hold that all are true.* (Nevertheless, if it were true that the Catholic faith is not the *only* true faith, then the Catholic faith, by professing itself to be the only true faith would necessarily be false, and this is indubitably Bergoglio's belief.) Therefore, whoever would make such contradictory affirmations about what is true and false, as St. Augustine explains [PL 42, 481.], "does not realize that he is saying, 'If God is omnipotent, let him make true things false insofar as they are true.' "[674] There cannot exist two contradictory truths. Ralph McInerny summed up St. Thomas' position on this point saying, «Thomas replied by arguing that the two-truth theory violated

---

[673] *S.C.G* 1. Cap. 7 — «Ea quae sunt naturalia mutari non possunt, natura manente.»

[674] St. Thomas Aquinas, *De Æternitate Mundi* — «Secundo modo dicitur propter repugnantiam intellectuum aliquid non posse fieri, sicut quod non potest fieri ut affirmatio et negatio sint simul vera; quamvis Deus hoc possit facere, ut quidam dicunt. Quidam vero dicunt, quod nec Deus hoc posset facere, quia hoc nihil est. Tamen manifestum est quod non potest facere ut hoc fiat, quia positio qua ponitur esse, destruit se ipsam. Si tamen ponatur quod Deus huiusmodi potest facere ut fiant, positio non est haeretica, quamvis, ut credo, sit falsa; sicut quod praeteritum non fuerit, includit in se contradictionem. Unde Augustinus in libro contra faustum: quisquis ita dicit: si omnipotens est Deus, faciat ut ea quae facta sunt, facta non fuerint: non videt hoc se dicere: si omnipotens est Deus, faciat ut ea quae vera sunt, eo ipso quo vera sunt, falsa sint.»

the "fundamental law of thinking, the principle of contradiction".»[675] I will let Aristotle and St. Thomas speak for themselves on this point, which proves the absolute absurdity and falsehood of the heretical foundation of Bergoglio's essentially Masonic religion of the *universal brotherhood of man under the fatherhood of God*, which is yet again being promoted in *Fratelli Tutti*.

Concerning the principle of non-contradiction, our knowledge of its truth is founded on our knowledge of the nature of being as distinct from non-being. As mentioned earlier, St. Thomas explains, "that which first falls in the apprehension is *being*, the notion of which is included in whatsoever one apprehends." And then he elaborates: «Wherefore the first indemonstrable principle is that "the same thing cannot be affirmed and denied at the same time," which is based on the notion of "being" and "not-being": and on this principle all others are based, as is stated in Metaph. iv, text. 9.»[676] In Book Γ, Aristotle explains:

> For 'that which is' has two meanings, so that in some sense a thing can come to be out of that which is not, while in some sense it cannot, and the same thing can at the same time be in being and not in being – but not in the same respect. For the same thing can be potentially at the same time two contraries, but it cannot actually.[677] [...] Again, when a man, on being asked whether a thing is white, says 'no', he has denied nothing except that it is; and its not being is a negation.[678]

The foundation:

> Let this, then, suffice to show (1) that the most indisputable of all beliefs is that contradictory statements are not at the same time true, and (2) what consequences follow from the assertion that they are, and (3) why people do assert this. Now since it is impossible that contradictories should be at the same time true of the same thing, obviously contraries also cannot belong at the same time to the same thing. For of contraries,

---

[675] Ralph McInerny, *Aquinas* p. 21

[676] *Summa Theol.* Iᵃ IIᵃ Q. 94 a. 2 — «Et ideo primum principium indemonstrabile est quod non est simul affirmare et negare, quod fundatur supra rationem entis et non entis, et super hoc principio omnia alia fundantur, ut dicitur in IV Metaphys.»

[677] Aristotle—Works, *Metaphysics*, Book Γ, p. 2281.

[678] *Ibid.* p. 2289.

one is a privation no less than it is a contrary – and a privation of the essential nature; and privation is the denial of a predicate to a determinate genus. If, then, it is impossible to affirm and deny truly at the same time, it is also impossible that contraries should belong to a subject at the same time, unless both belong to it in particular relations, or one in a particular relation and one without qualification.[679] [...]

But on the other hand there cannot be an intermediate between contradictories, but of one subject we must either affirm or deny any one predicate. This is clear, in the first place, if we define what the true and the false are. To say of what is that it is not, or of what is not that it is, is false, while to say of what is that it is, and of what is not that it is not, is true; so that he who says of anything that it is, or that it is not, will say either what is true or what is false; but neither what is nor what is not is said to be or not to be.[680]

He also explains what he means by an 'intermediate', because there can be intermediates, for example, between white and black there is grey; but that is not properly an intermediate in the sense here specified ("of one subject we must either affirm or deny any one predicate"), because the contraries in a motion which involves a change, such as from black to white, does not involve grey as an intermediate, since the contrary to white would be non-white, and the motion from black to white would be a motion from the contrary of white, which is non-white: "But if it is really intermediate, in this way too there would have to be a change to white, which was not from not-white; but as it is, this is never seen."[681]

St. Thomas comments on the Stagirite's teaching:

> For first philosophy should argue dialectically against those who deny the principles of the particular sciences, because all principles are based on the principle that an affirmation and a negation are not true at the same time, and that there is no intermediate between them. Now these principles are the most specific principles of this science, since they depend on the concept of being, which is the primary subject of this branch of philosophy. But the true and the false belong specifically to

---

[679] *Ibid.* p. 2287, no. 6.
[680] *Ibid.* p. 2288, no. 7.
[681] *Ibid.* pp. 2288-2289.

the study of logic; for they depend on the kind of being which is found in the mind, with which logic deals; for truth and falsity exist in the mind, as is stated in Book VI of this work. Motion and rest, on the other hand, belong properly to the study of natural philosophy, because nature is defined as a principle of motion and of rest. Now the error made about truth and falsity is a result of the error made about being and nonbeing, for truth and falsity are defined by means of being and non-being, as has been said above. For there is truth when one says that what is, is, or that what is not, is not; and falsity is defined in the opposite way. And similarly the error made about rest and motion is a result of the error made about being and nonbeing; for what is in motion as such does not yet exist, whereas what is at rest already is. Hence, when the errors made about being and non-being have been removed, the errors made about truth and falsity and rest and motion will then also be removed.[682]
Aristotle then refutes the false opinions:

> Again, every object of understanding or reason the understanding either affirms or denies – this is obvious from the definition – whenever it says what is true or false.[683]

---

[682] *In Duodecim Libros Metaphysicorum Aristotelis Expositio*, lib. 4, l. 17 n. 1 — «Philosophus enim primus debet disputare contra negantes principia singularium scientiarum, quia omnia principia firmantur super hoc principium, quod affirmatio et negatio non sunt simul vera, et quod nihil est medium inter ea. Illa autem sunt propriissima huius scientiae, cum sequantur rationem entis, quod est huius philosophiae primum subiectum. Verum autem et falsum pertinent proprie ad considerationem logici; consequuntur enim ens in ratione de quo considerat logicus: nam verum et falsum sunt in mente, ut in sexto huius habetur. Motus autem et quies sunt proprie de consideratione naturalis, per hoc quod natura definitur quod est principium motus et quietis. Ad errorem autem qui accidit circa esse et non esse, sequitur error circa verum et falsum: nam per esse et non esse verum et falsum definitur, ut supra habitum est. Nam verum est cum dicitur esse quod est, vel non esse quod non est. Falsum autem, e converso. Similiter autem ex errore, qui est circa esse vel non esse, sequitur error qui est circa moveri et quiescere. Nam quod movetur, inquantum huiusmodi, nondum est. Quod autem quiescit, est. Et ideo destructis erroribus circa esse et non esse, ex consequenti destruuntur errores circa verum et falsum, quietem et motum.»

[683] Aristotle—Works, *Metaphysics*, Book Γ, p. 2289 no. 7.

While the doctrine of Heraclitus, that all things are and are not, seems to make everything true, that of Anaxagoras, that there is an intermediate between the terms of a contradiction, seems to make everything false; for when things are mixed, the mixture is neither good nor not-good, so that one cannot say anything that is true.[684]

In view of these distinctions it is obvious that the one-sided theories which some people express about all things cannot be valid – on the one hand the theory that nothing is true (for, say they, there is nothing to prevent every statement from being like the statement 'the diagonal of a square is commensurate with the side'), on the other hand the theory that everything is true. These views are practically the same as that of Heraclitus; for he who says that all things are true and all are false also makes each of these statements separately, so that since they are impossible, the double statement must be impossible too. – Again, there are obviously contradictories which cannot be at the same time true – nor on the other hand can all statements be false; yet this would seem more possible in the light of what has been said. – But against all such views we must postulate, as we said above,' not that something is or is not, but that something has a meaning, so that we must argue from a definition, viz. by assuming what falsity or truth means. If that which it is true to affirm is nothing other than that which it is false to deny, it is impossible that all statements should be false; for one side of the contradiction must be true. Again, if it is necessary with regard to everything either to assert or to deny it, it is impossible that both should be false; for it is one side of the contradiction that is false. – Therefore all such views are also exposed to the often expressed objection, that they destroy themselves. For he who says that everything is true makes even the statement contrary to his own true, and therefore his own not true (for the contrary statement denies that it is true), while he who says everything is false makes himself also false.[685]

And if the former person excepts the contrary statement, saying it alone is not true, while the latter excepts his own as being not false, none the less they are driven to postulate the truth or falsity of an infinite number of statements; for that which says the true statement is true is true, and this process will go on to infinity.[686]

---

[684] *Ibid.* pp. 2289-2290 no. 7.
[685] *Ibid.* pp. 2290-2291 no. 8.
[686] *Ibid.* p. 2291 no. 8.

St. Thomas then comments on the Stagirite's text:

> Thus he says that, "with these points settled," i.e., with the foregoing points established which have to be used against the paradoxical positions mentioned above, it is obviously impossible that the views of some men should be true, namely, that we must form an opinion "univocally," i.e., think in the same way, about all things, so that we should say that all things are equally true or equally false. For some thinkers said that nothing is true but everything false, and that there is nothing to prevent us from saying that all statements are just as false as the statement (which is false) that the diameter of a square is commensurate with one of its sides. But others have said that all things are true. Statements of the latter kind are a result of the opinion of Heraclitus, as has been pointed out; for he said that a thing is and is not at the same time, and from this it follows that everything is true.[687]
>
> And lest perhaps someone might say that besides these opinions there is also a third one, which states that everything is both true and false at the same time, he replies, as though meeting a tacit objection, that anyone who maintains this opinion also maintains both of the foregoing ones. Hence, if the first two opinions are impossible, the third must also be impossible.[688]

Then he presents arguments against the foregoing opinions, and the first of these is as follows: it is evident that there are certain

---

[687] *In Duodecim Libros Metaphysicorum Aristotelis Expositio*, lib. 4 l. 17 n. 2 — «Primo ponit opiniones falsas circa verum et falsum. Secundo reprobat eas, ibi, amplius autem palam etc. Dicit ergo, quod definitis, idest determinatis praedictis quae erant dicenda contra praedictas inopinabiles opiniones, manifestum est quod impossibile est quod quidam dixerunt quod univoce, idest uno modo sententiandum est de omnibus, ut dicamus omnia similiter esse falsa vel similiter esse vera. Quidam enim dixerunt nihil esse verum, sed omnia esse falsa, et quod nihil prohibet quin dicamus omnia sic esse falsa, sicut illa est falsa, diameter est commensurabilis lateri quadrati, quod est falsum. Alii vero dixerunt quod omnia sunt vera. Et huiusmodi orationes consequuntur ad opinionem Heracliti, sicut dictum est. Ipse enim dixit simul esse et non esse, ex quo sequitur omnia esse vera.»

[688] *Ibid.* lib. 4 l. 17 n. 3 — «Et ne forte aliquis diceret quod praeter has opiniones est etiam tertia, quae dicit quod omnia simul sunt vera et falsa, quasi tacitae obiectioni respondens dicit, quod qui hoc ponit, utrumque praedictorum ponit. Unde si duae primae opiniones sunt impossibiles, illam tertiam oportet esse impossibilem.»

contradictories which cannot be true at the same time or false at the same time, for example, the true and not-true, being and non-being. This can be better understood from what has been said. Therefore, if one of these two contradictories must be false and the other true, not all things can be true or all false.[689]

He gives the second argument. He says that in opposing "these views," or positions, "it is necessary to postulate," or request, not that someone should admit that something either is or is not in reality, as has been stated above, because this seems to be begging the question, but that he should admit that a word signifies something. Now if this is not granted, the dispute comes to an end; but if it is granted, it is then necessary to give definitions, as has already been stated above. Hence we must argue against these thinkers by proceeding from definitions, and in the case of the present thesis we must do this especially by considering the definition of falsity. Now if truth consists merely in affirming what it is false to deny, and vice versa, it follows that not all statements can be false, because either the affirmation or the negation of something must be true. For obviously truth consists simply in saying that what is, is, or in saying that what is not, is not; and falsity consists in saying that what is, is not, or in saying that what is not, is. Hence it is clear that it is true to say that that is of which it is false that it is not, or to say that that is not of which it is false that it is; and it is false to say that that is of which it is true that it is not, or to say that that is not of which it is true that it is. Thus from the definition of truth and falsity it is clear that not all things are false. And for the same reason it is clear that not all things are true.[690]

---

[689] *Ibid.* lib. 4 l. 17 n. 4 — «Deinde cum dicit amplius autem ponit rationes contra praedictas opiniones; quarum prima talis. Constat quasdam esse contradictiones quas impossibile est simul esse veras nec simul falsas, sicut verum et non verum, ens et non ens. Et hoc magis potest sciri ex dictis. Si igitur harum contradictionum necesse est alteram esse veram et alteram falsam, non omnia sunt vera nec omnia sunt falsa.»

[690] *Ibid.* lib. 4 l. 17 n. 5 — «Deinde cum dicit sed ad omnes secundam rationem ponit, dicens, quod ad istas orationes, idest positiones, non oportet quaerere, idest petere concedendum aliquid esse vel non esse in rebus, quemadmodum supra dictum est; quia hoc videtur petere principium. Sed hoc petendum est, quod detur nomina aliquid significare; quo non dato, disputatio tollitur. Hoc autem dato, oportet ponere definitiones, sicut iam supra dictum est. Et ideo ex definitionibus contra eos disputare oportet, et praecipue in proposito, accipiendo definitionem falsi. Si autem non est aliud

Here he gives the third argument, which runs thus: it is clear from what has been said above that we must either affirm or deny something of each thing since there is no intermediate between contradictories. It is impossible, then, for everything to be false. And by the same reasoning it is proved that it is impossible for everything to be true, i.e., by reason of the fact that it is impossible both to affirm and to deny something at the same time.[691]

He gives the fourth argument: all of the foregoing statements, or opinions, face this unreasonable result — they destroy themselves. This is "the view commonly expressed," i.e., a frequently heard statement made by all; and thus another text says, "It happens that it is commonly held." He proves this view as follows: anyone who says that everything is true makes the contrary of his own opinion true. But the contrary of his own opinion is that his own opinion is not true. Therefore he who says that everything is true says that his own opinion is not true; and thus he destroys his own opinion. Similarly it is evident that he who says that everything is false also says that his own opinion is false.[692]

---

verum, quam illud affirmare, quod falsum est negare, et e converso: et similiter falsum non aliud est quam affirmare id quod negare est verum, et e converso: sequitur quod impossibile sit omnia esse falsa; quia necesse erit vel affirmationem vel negationem esse veram. Patet enim, quod verum nihil est aliud quam dicere esse quod est, vel non esse quod non est. Falsum autem, dicere non esse quod est, vel esse quod non est. Et ideo patet, quod verum est dicere illud esse, quod falsum est non esse; vel non esse, quod falsum est esse. Et falsum est dicere id esse, quod verum est non esse; vel non esse quod verum est esse. Et ita, ex definitione veri vel falsi, patet quod non sunt omnia falsa. Et ratione eadem patet quod non omnia sunt vera.»

[691] *Ibid.* lib. 4 l. 17 n. 6 — «Deinde cum dicit amplius si tertiam rationem ponit, quae talis est. Constat ex praedictis, quod necesse est de quolibet aut affirmare aut negare, cum nihil sit medium in contradictione. Igitur impossibile est omnia falsa esse. Et eadem ratione probatur quod impossibile est omnia esse vera, per hoc quod ostensum est, quod non est simul affirmare et negare.»

[692] *Ibid.* lib. 4 l. 13 n. 5 — «Deinde cum dicit contingit autem quartam rationem ponit, quae talis est. Ad omnes praedictas orationes, idest positiones, contingit hoc inconveniens quod seipsas destruunt. Et hoc est famatum, idest famosum ab omnibus dictum. Unde alius textus habet, accidit autem et id vulgare. Quod sic probat. Ille enim, qui dicit omnia esse vera, facit opinionem contrariam suae opinioni esse veram; sed contraria suae opinionis est quod sua opinio non sit vera: ergo qui dicit omnia esse vera, dicit suam opinionem non esse veram, et ita destruit suam opinionem.

A qnd because someone could say that he who claims that everything is true makes an exception of the one contrary to his own statement, or bars it from what holds universally (and the same thing applies to one who says that everything is false), he therefore rejects this answer. He says that, if the one who says that everything is true makes his own contrary opinion an exception, saying that it alone is not true, and if the one who says that everything is false makes his own opinion an exception, saying that it alone is not false, none the less it follows that they will be able "to consider," or bring forward, an infinite number of true statements against those who hold that all are false, and an infinite number of false statements against those who hold that all are true. For granted that one opinion is true, it follows that an infinite number are true. And granted that one opinion is false, it follows that an infinite number are false. For if the position, or opinion, that Socrates is sitting is true, then the opinion that it is true that Socrates is sitting will also be true, and so on to infinity. For he who says that a true statement is true is always right; and he who says that a false statement is true is always wrong; and this can proceed to infinity.[693]

In capsulized form:

«Thus from the definition of truth and falsity it is clear that not all things are false. And for the same reason it is clear that not all things are true. [...] It is impossible, then, for everything to be false. **And by the same reasoning it is**

Et similiter manifestum est quod ille, qui dicit omnia esse falsa, dicit etiam seipsum dicere falsum.»

[693] *Ibid.* lib. 4 l. 17 n. 8 — «Et quia posset aliquis dicere quod dicens omnia vera excipit aut aufert ab universalitate suam contrariam, et similiter, qui dicit omnia esse falsa excipit suam opinionem: ideo hanc responsionem excludit; et dicit, quod si ille qui dicit omnia esse vera, excipiat suam contrariam, dicens solam eam esse non veram, et dicens omnia esse falsa excipiat suam opinionem dicens quod ipsa sola non est falsa, nihilominus sequitur quod contingat eis quaerere, idest repetere infinitas esse orationes veras contra ponentes omnia esse falsa, et infinitas falsas contra ponentes omnia vera esse. Si enim detur una opinio vera, sequetur infinitas esse veras. Et si detur una opinio falsa, sequetur infinitas esse falsas. Si enim haec positio vel opinio est vera: socrates sedet, ergo et haec erit vera: socratem sedere est verum. Et si illa est vera, ulterius haec erit vera, socratem sedere esse verum est verum, et sic in infinitum. Semper enim qui dicit de oratione vera quod sit vera, verus est. Et qui dicit de oratione falsa quod sit vera, falsus est. Et hoc potest procedere in infinitum.»

proved that it is impossible for everything to be true, i.e., by reason of the fact that it is impossible both to affirm and to deny something at the same time. [...] **all of the foregoing statements, or opinions, face this unreasonable result — they destroy themselves. [...] anyone who says that everything is true makes the contrary of his own opinion true. But the contrary of his own opinion is that his own opinion is not true. Therefore he who says that everything is true says that his own opinion is not true; and thus he destroys his own opinion.**»

In view of the aforesaid, it is plainly absurd and irrational for someone to say, "All religions are true. All religions are good. All religions are holy and lead to God," because, to be good a religion must be true, and to be true it must be in possession of the divinely revealed truth without the defect of any admixture of falsehood, but false religions, being the fabrication of men and not revealed by God, are deprived of the divine truth which unites us to God, and teach many falsehoods, and are therefore evil, because evil is in the nature of a privation,[694] and privation is contrary to good because the good is what nature desires, and the rational nature desires the perfection of what is true and good, rather than be deprived of it.[695] The privation of truth is the privation of the good insofar as the true and the good are included in each other,[696] and divine truth is supremely

---

[694] I*a* II*ae* q. 25 a. 2 co. — «malum est privatio boni.»

[695] *De malo*, q. 1 a. 1 co. — «alio modo potest intelligi ipsum malum, et hoc non est aliquid, sed est ipsa privatio alicuius particularis boni. Ad cuius evidentiam sciendum est, quod bonum proprie est aliquid in quantum est appetibile, nam, secundum philosophum in I Ethic., optime definierunt bonum dicentes, quod bonum est quod omnia appetunt; malum autem dicitur id quod opponitur bono. Unde oportet malum esse id quod opponitur appetibili in quantum huiusmodi.»

[696] *Summa Theol.* I*a* q. 79, a. 11 ad 2 — «verum et bonum se invicem includunt, nam verum est quoddam bonum, alioquin non esset appetibile; et bonum est quoddam verum, alioquin non esset intelligibile. Sicut igitur obiectum appetitus potest esse verum, inquantum habet rationem boni, sicut cum aliquis appetit veritatem cognoscere; ita obiectum intellectus practici est bonum ordinabile ad opus, sub ratione veri.» [The true and the good include one another, since the true is a certain good, otherwise it would not be desirable; and the good is in a certain sense true, otherwise it would not be intelligible. Therefore, just as the true can be an object of desire

desirable because it is the *summum bonum* — the supreme good and eternal Truth in which our beatitude consists. *Being and the good are convertible*,[697] — they are the same thing[698] since the good is what nature desires insofar as it *actually exists*,[699] and is *true* — because a

---

insofar as it has the nature of a good, as when someone desires to have cognition of the truth, so the object of the practical intellect is a good that can be ordered toward action, under the concept of the true.]

[697] *De veritate*, q. 1 a. 1 s. c. 2 — «ens et bonum convertuuntur.»

[698] *Summa Theol.* Iᵃ q. 79 a. 11 ad 2 — «Respondeo dicendum quod bonum et ens sunt idem secundum rem, sed differunt secundum rationem tantum. Quod sic patet. Ratio enim boni in hoc consistit, quod aliquid sit appetibile, unde philosophus, in I Ethic., dicit quod bonum est quod omnia appetunt. Manifestum est autem quod unumquodque est appetibile secundum quod est perfectum, nam omnia appetunt suam perfectionem. Intantum est autem perfectum unumquodque, inquantum est actu, unde manifestum est quod intantum est aliquid bonum, inquantum est ens, esse enim est actualitas omnis rei, ut ex superioribus patet. Unde manifestum est quod bonum et ens sunt idem secundum rem, sed bonum dicit rationem appetibilis, quam non dicit ens.» [Goodness and being are really the same, and differ only in idea; which is clear from the following argument. The essence of goodness consists in this, that it is in some way desirable. Hence the Philosopher says (Ethic. i): "Goodness is what all desire." Now it is clear that a thing is desirable only in so far as it is perfect; for all desire their own perfection. But everything is perfect so far as it is actual. Therefore it is clear that a thing is perfect so far as it exists; for it is existence that makes all things actual, as is clear from the foregoing. Hence it is clear that goodness and being are the same really. But goodness presents the aspect of desirableness, which being does not present.] NB — When he says "a thing is desirable only insofar as it is perfect," and, "all desire their own perfection," what is signified by the term *perfect* is, "whatever is not wanting in actuality" — «transumitur hoc nomen perfectum ad significandum omne illud cui non deest esse in actu.» (Iᵃ q.4 a. 1)

[699] *Summa Contra Gentiles* 1. Cap. 37 — «Bonum est quod omnia appetunt: ut philosophus optime dictum introducit, I Ethicorum. Omnia autem appetunt esse actu secundum suum modum: quod patet ex hoc quod unumquodque secundum naturam suam repugnat corruptioni. Esse igitur actu boni rationem constituit: unde et per privationem actus a potentia consequitur malum, quod est bono oppositum, ut per philosophum patet, in IX metaphysicae.» - [Furthermore, "the good is that which all things desire." The Philosopher introduces this remark as a "felicitous saying"

thing is good only insofar as it is true, *"for those which are the cause of the existence of other things are themselves beings most completely, and those which are the cause of the truth of other things are themselves true most completely. It is for this reason that the Philosopher concludes that the rank of a thing in its existence corresponds to its rank in truth, so that when one finds that which is most fully being, he finds there also that which is most fully true."*⁷⁰⁰ God is essential being — *ipsum esse subsistens*, which is manifested in the Name he revealed to Moses: יהוה (YHWH = I AM WHO AM), and therefore He is *subsistent truth*.⁷⁰¹ God is the primary and ***first truth***⁷⁰² and the ***formal object of faith*** (*I^a II^a q. 1 a. 1*), to Whom we are united, not by human faith, but by Catholic faith, the theological virtue faith, which is not found in any other religion, and without which there is neither

---

in *Ethics* I. But all things, each according to its mode, desire to be in act; this is clear from the fact that each thing according to its nature resists corruption. To be in act, therefore, constitutes the nature of the good. Hence it is that evil, which is opposed to the good, follows when potency is deprived of act, as is clear from the Philosopher in *Metaphysics* IX [9].]

⁷⁰⁰ *De veritate*, q. 1 a. 1 ad 5 — «cum enim illa quae sunt causa aliorum essendi sint maxime entia, et illa quae sunt causa veritatis sint maxime vera; concludit philosophus, quod idem est ordo alicui rei in esse et veritate; ita, scilicet, quod ubi invenitur quod est maxime ens, est maxime verum.»

⁷⁰¹ *Summa Theol.* I^a q. 3. a. 4 — «Hilarius dicit in VII de Trin., esse non est accidens in Deo, sed subsistens veritas.»

⁷⁰² *Summa Theol.* I^a q. 16 a. 5 co. — «Respondeo dicendum quod, sicut dictum est, veritas invenitur in intellectu secundum quod apprehendit rem ut est, et in re secundum quod habet esse conformabile intellectui. Hoc autem maxime invenitur in Deo. Nam esse suum non solum est conforme suo intellectui, sed etiam est ipsum suum intelligere; et suum intelligere est mensura et causa omnis alterius esse, et omnis alterius intellectus; et ipse est suum esse et intelligere. Unde sequitur quod non solum in ipso sit veritas, sed quod ipse sit ipsa summa et **prima veritas**.» [truth is found in the intellect according as it apprehends a thing as it is; and in things according as they have being conformable to an intellect. This is to the greatest degree found in God. For His being is not only conformed to His intellect, but it is the very act of His intellect; and His act of understanding is the measure and cause of every other being and of every other intellect, and He Himself is His own existence and act of understanding. Whence it follows not only that truth is in Him, but that He is truth itself, and the sovereign and **first truth**.]

justification nor forgiveness of sins. This is not a matter of opinion, but the dogma of Trent set forth in the *Decree on Justification*, and summed up by St. Alphonsus de' Liguori "When we say that faith is necessary for the remission of sins, we mean to speak of the Catholic faith, not heretical faith. Without the habit of this faith, no man is justified."[703] The Bergoglian proposition, that adherents of other religions are all children of God, and can be justified and redeemed without the Catholic faith directly opposes this dogma of Trent, and strictly implies that other religions are good, true and salvific — and it logically presupposes as its foundation the denial of the dogma of Original Sin, "the one that freemasonry attacks most stubbornly," the denial of which, "overturns the basis of Christianity".[704] This opinion, therefore, is not only false, but it is absurd because in teaching this heresy, Bergoglio, (in the words of St. Thomas), *"makes the contrary of his own opinion true. But the contrary of his own opinion is that his own opinion is not true. Therefore he who says that everything is true says that his own opinion is not true; and thus he destroys his own opinion."*

BERGOGLIO'S MASONIZED RELIGION AIMS TO DESTROY CATHOLICISM

Freemasonry seeks the total destruction of the Catholic Church. Masonry proclaims this to be its proper task. Cardinal Caro cited further Masonic testimony regarding their agenda to destroy Catholicism and replace it with a universal secular religion: In the Masonic review, *Acacia*, 1902,[705] one reads the following: "Freemasonry is the counter-church, the counter-Catholicism, the Church of Heresy", and in the Bulletin of the Grand Orient of France: "As to Catholicism...we Masons must pursue its utter demolition." A memorandum from the supreme Council confirmed these declarations: "The struggle being waged between Catholicism

---

[703] St. Alphonsus Liguori, An Exposition and Defense of All the Points of Faith Discussed and Defined by the Council of Trent.

[704] Henri Delassus, *IL PROBLEMA DELL'ORA PRESENTE — ANTAGONISMO TRA DUE CIVILTA'*, SECONDA PARTE, Roma, 1907, p. 154.

[705] Cardinal Caro y Rodriguez, *The Mystery of Freemasonry Unveiled*, p. 10.

and Masonry is a war to the death, without truce or quarter." The official Masonic journal, *Acacia*, stated in its Oct. 1902 issue: "Freemasonry is a church, the anti-church, the anti-Catholicism, the other church of free-thought." In 1961, Grandmaster F. A. Pinkerneil categorically stated that it is impossible for Masonry to lessen its opposition to the Catholic Church, and that in the last two centuries, Freemasonry has not changed.[706] Grandmaster J. Böni, in 1973, explained at length why Masonry and Catholicism remain, and must remain, eternally in enmity toward each other.[707]

Masonry seeks more than the destruction of the Catholic Church and every trace of Christianity. Masonry declares itself to be at war against God Himself. Cardinal Caro noted on page 106 of the cited work that at the International Congress of Brussels, Lafargue exclaimed: "War on God! Hatred to God! In this is progress! It is necessary to crush Heaven as if it were a piece of paper." And Masonic Brother Lanesan, in the solstitial festival of the Clement Friendship Lodge on March 13, 1880: "We must crush the infamous one, but that infamous one is not clericalism, that infamous one is God!"[708] In *Morals and Dogma of the Ancient and Accepted Scottish Rite of Freemasonry*, Albert Pike blasphemously comments on what Masonry considers to be the cruel God of the Sacred Scriptures whose **sternness predominates over *mercy*** [i.e. the "author of Evil" who sternly prescribed *capital punishment* in the Old Testament], saying:

> The Deity of the Old Testament is everywhere represented as the direct author of Evil, commissioning evil and lying spirits to men, hardening the heart of Pharaoh, and visiting the iniquity of the individual sinner on the whole people. The rude conception of sternness

---

[706] «Es erscheint unmöglich, die gegnerschaft der Katholischen Kirche auch nur zu mildern.wir können nichts mehr tun — und das werden wir tun — als eine bedauerliche Wandlung der Katholischen Kirche seit der Zeit, wo Bischöffe und Prälaten führende und angesehene Freimaurer waren, festzustellen und den Gründen nachzugehen. Jedenfalls haben wir Freimaurer uns in den beiden Jahrhunderten nicht gewandelt.» [Quoted by Manfred Adler, *Die Antichristliche Revolution der Freimaurerei*, p. 96.]

[707] J. Böni, *Kirche heute und Morgen, Quo vadis Ecclesia?* Verlag Fritz Meili, Trogen a Rh., 1973. [Quoted by Adler in the same work.]

[708] Cardinal Caro y Rodriguez, *The Mystery of Freemasonry Unveiled*, p. 106.

predominating over mercy in the Deity, can alone account for the human sacrifices, purposed, if not executed, by Abraham and Jephtah...

And he then proclaims the "deity" that Masons worship:

> "Lucifer the Light-bearer!"
> "Lucifer the Son of the Morning!"
> "Is it he who bears the Light...?"
> "Doubt it not" [709]

The official Masonic journal, *Acacia*, stated in its Oct. 1902 issue: **"Freemasonry is a church, the anti-church, the anti-Catholicism, the other church of free-thought."**[710] Pike explains what is the nature of the religion of that *other church*, the *anti-church* of "free thought": "In the ancient Orient all religion was more or less a mystery[711] ...Masonry is identical with the ancient Mysteries[712] [i.e. **Paganism**]... successor of the Mysteries". Masonry "still follows the ancient manner of teaching...Her symbols are the instruction she gives."[713] The Official Acts of the International Masonic Congress of Paris of 1889 sets forth a program for "the definite establishment of the *universal Social republic.*"[714] In the Masonic World Republic, there will be *"a new morality"* and *"a new religion."*[715] The *Bulletin of the Grand Lodge of the Scottish Rite* (*Bolletino della grande Loggia simbolica scozzese*) published on the day following Pope Leo XIII's condemnation of Masonry its own sarcastic commentary:

> Freemasonry cannot but thank the Supreme Pontiff for his latest encyclical. Leo XIII, with incontestable authority and a vast array of proofs, has demonstrated one more time that there exists an insuperable abyss between the Church of which he is the representative, and the

---

[709] Albert Pike, *Morals and Dogma of the Ancient and Accepted Scottish Rite of Freemasonry*, p.321.

[710] *Acacia, Revue des etudes maconiques*, Oct. 1902, pp. 3, 4.

[711] *Morals and Dogma of the Ancient and Accepted Scottish Rite of Freemasonry*, p. 22.

[712] *Ibid.*, p. 23.

[713] *Ibid.*, p. 22.

[714] Cardinal Caro y Rodriguez, *The Mystery of Freemasonry Unveiled*, pp. 96-97.

[715] *Rivista Massonica*, 1911, p. 347.

revolution, whose right hand is Freemasonry. All must accustom themselves to understand that the hour has come to choose between the old order, established on Revelation, and the new order, which does not recognize any other basis than human science and reason.[716]

In his encyclical, *Humanum Genus*, Pope Leo XIII stated that "the Freemasons":

> No longer making any secret of their purposes, they are now boldly rising up against God Himself. They are planning the destruction of holy Church publicly and openly, and this with the set purpose of utterly despoiling the nations of Christendom, if it were possible, of the blessings obtained for us through Jesus Christ our Saviour [...] There are several organized bodies which, though differing in name, in ceremonial, in form and origin, are nevertheless so bound together by community of purpose and by the similarity of their main opinions, as to make in fact one thing with the sect of Freemasons, which is a kind of centre whence they all go forth, and whither they all return. [...] There are many things like mysteries which it is the fixed rule to hide with extreme care, not only from strangers, but from very many members also; such as their secret and final designs, the names of the chief leaders, and certain secret and inner meetings, as well as their decisions, and the ways and means of carrying them out. [...] that which is their ultimate purpose forces itself into view — namely, the utter overthrow of that whole religious and political order of the world which the Christian teaching has produced, and the substitution of a new state of things in accordance with their ideas, of which the foundations and laws shall be drawn from mere "Naturalism."[717]

Pike explains exactly what is the Freemasonic religion of **Naturalism**: "God is the absolute of Faith; but the absolute of Reason is BEING."[718] Hence, the god of Masonry is the Pantheistic ALL of the Gnostics, Cabalists, and Manicheans — the *Deus sive Natura* of Spinoza's Pantheism, the Absolute of Hegel's dialectic, the "Omega-Point" of the pseudo-philosophical mystical pantheism

---

[716] Mgr. Henri Delassus, *Il problema dell'ora presente*, Vol. 2, p. 39. The complete reference is provided in the footnote on that page.

[717] Leo XIII, Encyclical, *Humanum Genus*, April 20, 1884.

[718] *Morals and Dogma of the Ancient and Accepted Scottish Rite of Freemasonry*, p. 97.

elaborated in the counterfeit theology of the French Jesuit, Pierre Teilhard de Chardin, and the nebulous "God" in the impenetrably convoluted musings of Jorge Bergoglio whom he heretically asserts cannot exist without us. Masonic Pantheism leads to the deification of Man: "MAN IS SUPREME OVER INSTITUTIONS AND NOT THEY OVER HIM. Man has natural empire over all institutions."[719] "In the vast cosmical changes the universal life comes and goes in unknown quantities, enveloping all in the invisible mystery of the emanations...making a force of Light, and an element of Thought... dissolving all save that point without length, breadth, or thickness, The MYSELF; reducing everything to the Soul atom; making everything blossom into God..."[720] Accordingly, the very earthy religion (if indeed it may be called a *religion*) of Jorge Bergoglio is so earth centred (that it deifies the Amazonian soil), and man centred (that it is entirely preoccupied with the concerns of this life in this world), that it has practically no concern for man's last end in the next world — for eternity and the last things: **Death, Judgment, Heaven**, and **HELL** (*hell* — which Bergoglio says doesn't exist). Why should we worry about **Judgment** and **HELL** if we all are going to meet there in heaven anyway?

Bergoglio attempts to secularize religion by eliminating from it not only the need for belief in Christ, but even the need for any belief in God at all, which makes him the greatest heresiarch of all time — a greater heresiarch than Simon Magus, Marcion, Mani (founder of Manichaeism), Arius, Pelagius, Nestorius, Jan Huss, Giordano Bruno, Cornelius Jansen,[721] John Calvin, and Martin Luther all combined. Bergoglio's explicit and unequivocal denial of the necessity of faith for salvation directly, explicitly, and immediately opposes the First Commandment, and rejects one of the most primary of all truths of faith set forth by the Council of Trent (cited above) and the first Vatican council: «And whereas the Apostle saith, that man is justified

---

[719] *Ibid.* p. 23.

[720] *Ibid.* p. 42.

[721] At least Jansen wrote in the Epilogue of his *Augustinus*, "I leave my work to the judgment of the Roman Church... I retract all that she will decide that I must retract." Bergoglio remains incorrigible and blindly obstinate in his heresy.

by faith and freely, *those words are to be understood in that sense which the perpetual consent of the Catholic Church hath held and expressed*; to wit, that *we are therefore said to be justified by faith, because faith is the beginning of human salvation, the foundation, and the root of all Justification; without which it is impossible to please God, and to come unto the fellowship of His sons*» (Council of Trent, Session 6); «[*The necessity of embracing faith and retaining it*]. *But, since "WITHOUT FAITH IT IS IMPOSSIBLE TO PLEASE GOD" [Heb. I 1 :6] and to attain to the fellowship of His sons, hence, NO ONE IS JUSTIFIED WITHOUT IT; NOR WILL ANYONE ATTAIN ETERNAL LIFE EXCEPT "HE SHALL PERSEVERE UNTO THE END ON IT"* [Matt. 10:22; 24:13].»[722] (First Vatican Council, Dogmatic Constitution *Dei Filius*)

In an article entitled, *The Vatican Corrects the Pope* by Simona Vitale[723], on May 28, 2013, it was reported, «However, in an "explanatory note on the meaning of 'salvation'", the Reverend Thomas Rosica, spokesman for the Vatican, stressed that being "good" alone is not enough to be saved. People who know the Catholic Church, he explained, "cannot be saved" if they "refuse to enter her or remain in her."»[724] Indeed, Fr. Rosica is entirely correct on that point, **but that is not what Bergoglio believes.** The article cited Bergoglio's entire heretical passage verbatim[725], and

---

[722] «Quoniam vero sine fide impossibile est placere deo et ad filiorum eius consortium pervenire ideo nemini unquam sine illa contigit iustificatio nec ullus nisi in ea perseveraverit usque in finem vitam aeternam assequetur.» — [*ASS*, vol. V (1869-1870), pp. 481- 493.]

[723] https://attualissimo.it/il-vaticano-corregge-il-papa-gli-atei-vanno-sempre-allinferno/

[724] «Tuttavia, in una *"nota esplicativa sul significato di 'salvezza'"*, il reverendo **Thomas Rosica,** portavoce del Vaticano, ha sottolineato che essere *"buoni"* da solo non è sufficiente per essere salvati. Le persone che conoscono la Chiesa cattolica, ha spiegato, *"non possono essere salvate"* se *"si rifiutano di entrare in lei o di rimanere in lei."*»

[725] «... *Il Signore ha redento tutti noi, tutti noi, con il Sangue di Cristo: tutti noi, non solo i cattolici. Tutti! 'Padre, gli atei?' Anche gli atei. Tutti! Siamo stati creati da bambini a somiglianza di Dio e il Sangue di Cristo ha redento tutti noi! E tutti noi abbiamo il dovere di fare del bene. E questo comandamento per tutti di fare del bene, penso, è un bel sentiero verso la pace. Se ognuno di noi fa la sua parte, se facciamo del bene agli altri, se ci incontriamo lì, facendo del bene, e noi andiamo lentamente, con*

commented, «Rosica also added that Pope Francis had "no intention of provoking a theological debate on the nature of salvation" in the course of his homily. The current theological confusion that began after the leader of 1.2 billion Catholics expressed his thoughts during the homily of his morning Mass on Wednesday, May 22, indicates that atheists should enjoy the fruits of eternal salvation if they were good.»[726] Bergoglio has stated categorically that belief in God is not necessary for salvation, which means that for him, the theological virtues are entirely superfluous. Sanctifying Grace is superfluous. We are just in the sight of God even if we have no faith at all and do not even believe in God, provided that we humanly strive to **do good and avoid evil**. Bergoglio's doctrine is radical Pelagianism in its starkest form, and it is pure *Masonism*. Against Bergoglio's perverted belief, St. Thomas teaches, "Every sin consists formally in aversion from God, as stated above (*I^a II^{ae} q. 71 a. 6; q. 73 a. 3*). Hence the more a sin separates a man from God, the graver it is. Now man is more than ever separated from God by unbelief, because he has not even true knowledge of God: and by false knowledge of God, man does not approach Him, but is distanced from Him."[727]

So on the one hand Bergoglio professes that we will all be saved — "Everybody". But what about those who do not even fulfil the minimum requirement of following one's own conscience and doing what one thinks is right? Bergoglio stated in a March 2018

---

dolcezza, a poco a poco, faremo quella cultura dell'incontro: abbiamo bisogno di quel tanto. Dobbiamo incontrarci per fare il bene. 'Ma io non ci credo, padre, io sono un ateo! ' Ma facciamo del bene: ci incontreremo là.»

[726] «Rosica anche aggiunto che Papa Francesco non aveva *"alcuna intenzione di provocare un dibattito teologico sulla natura della salvezza"*, nel corso della sua omelia. L'attuale confusione teologica iniziata dopo che il leader di 1,2 miliardi di **cattolici** ha espresso il suo pensiero durante l'omelia della sua messa mattutina di mercoledì, 22 maggio, indica che gli atei dovrebbero godere i frutti della salvezza eterna se fossero buoni.»

[727] «Respondeo dicendum quod omne peccatum formaliter consistit in aversione a Deo, ut supra dictum est. (I^a II^{ae} Q. 71 a. 6; Q. 73 a. 3) Unde tanto aliquod peccatum est gravius quanto per ipsum homo magis a Deo separatur. Per infidelitatem autem maxime homo a Deo elongatur, quia nec veram Dei cognitionem habet; per falsam autem cognitionem ipsius non appropinquat ei, sed magis ab eo elongatur.»

conversation with Eugenio Scalfari[728]: «"They are not punished, those who repent obtain the forgiveness of God and enter the rank of souls who contemplate him, but those who do not repent and cannot therefore be forgiven disappear. There is no hell, there is the disappearance of sinful souls."» Vatican spokesmen attempted to cast doubt on Bergoglio's profession of heresy; but it is well known that Bergoglio has been spouting this heresy for a long time. Three years earlier he said exactly the same thing, as Scalfari related: «What happens to that lost soul? Will it be punished? And how? The response of Francis is distinct and clear: there is no punishment, but the annihilation of that soul. All the others will participate in the beatitude of living in the presence of the Father. The souls that are annihilated will not take part in that banquet; with the death of the body their journey is finished.»[729] (So maybe we won't all meet "there" after all?) Leaving aside the glaring logical inconsistencies of the Bergoglian belief system — I say "belief system" because in reality it cannot even be properly called a religion — the one thing that emerges as foundational for that belief system is that it has no need for any religion at all. We can live and die without God, and even oppose religion if we think that is the morally right thing to do. We can even set ourselves in opposition to the very idea of God and combat religion if we think religion is an evil and God non-existent — and that notwithstanding, "We will all meet there" — i.e. **in heaven:** *"The Lord has redeemed all of us, all of us, with the Blood of Christ: all of us, not just Catholics. All! 'Father, and the atheists?' Also the atheists. All!'…. We must meet by doing good. 'But, Father, I don't think so, I'm an atheist!' But do good: we will meet there."* […] *"It is nice to think this, to think of Heaven. We will all be up there"* […] *"We are all children of God — Also the atheists. All! But do good: we will meet there."* Needless to say, this essentially Masonic profession of belief is hardly even a false religion, but a silly superstition at best — in reality, a faithless and perfidious **godlessness**. The dogma of faith solemnly taught by Trent is that ***"faith is the beginning of human salvation"***. The reason for this is

---

[728] https://rep.repubblica.it/pwa/esclusiva/2018/03/28/news/il_papa_e_un_onore_essere_chiamato_rivoluzionario_-192479298/?ref=RHPPRB-BH-I0-C4-P1-S1.4-T1.

[729] http://www.repubblica.it/politica/2015/03/15/news/quel_che_francesco_puo_dire_all_europa_dei_non_credenti-109542750/.

that union with God can only be brought about by faith: "Faith brings about four good effects. The first is that through faith the soul is united to God, and by it there is between the soul and God a union akin to marriage."[730] Without faith the soul is separated from God, and cannot be saved, and there cannot exist any reason that could morally justify a soul who faithlessly rejects God. In a person possessed of the use of reason, there cannot exist a legitimate excuse for rejecting God or disbelieving in Him. It is one thing for a feral heathen to be ignorant of the divine attributes that can be known by demonstration, and therefore, not having clear knowledge of God, he would be excused to some degree for such ignorance; but an atheist — one who rejects God and opposes belief in God as something evil or useless, is in no way excused for rejecting God as would be a feral human for simply not clearly knowing much of anything about the divine attributes. St. Thomas explains, «But the fact that a person lacks the aforesaid knowledge of God [i.e. a vague and imperfect knowledge of God] makes him appear very blameworthy. Indeed, a man's dullness is chiefly indicated by this: he fails to perceive such evident signs of God, just as a person is judged to be dull who, while observing a man, does not grasp the fact that he has a soul. That is why it is said in the Psalms (13:1, 52:1): *"The fool hath said in his heart: There is no God."*»[731] St. Thomas explains further in the *Summa Contra Gentiles* (Book 1. Ch. 11):

> The answer to the fourth argument is likewise clear. For man naturally knows God in the same way as he naturally desires God. Now, man naturally desires God in so far as he naturally desires beatitude, which is a certain likeness of the divine goodness. On this basis, it is not necessary that God considered in Himself be naturally known to man,

---

[730] Sancti Thomae de Aquino, *Expositio in Symbolum Apostolorum*, PROOEMIUM — «Fides autem facit quattour bona. Primum est quod per fidem anima coniungitur Deo: nam per fidem anima Christiana facit quasi quoddam matrimonium cum Deo.»

[731] *Summa Contra Gentiles* Lib. III. Caput 38 — «Ex hoc autem quod praedicta Dei cognitione aliquis caret, maxime vituperabilis apparet: designatur enim per hoc maxime hominis stoliditas, quod tam manifesta Dei signa non percipit... Unde et in Psalmo dicitur: *dixit insipiens in corde suo: non est Deus.*»

but only a likeness of God. It remains, therefore, that man is to reach the knowledge of God through reasoning by way of the likenesses of God found in His effects.[732]

How man is to "reach the knowledge of God through reasoning" is then explained further on in Book 3:

> On the other hand, there is another sort of knowledge of God, higher than the foregoing, and we may acquire it through demonstration. A closer approach to a proper knowledge of Him is effected through this kind, for many things are set apart from Him, through demonstration, whose removal enable Him to be understood in distinction from other beings. In fact, demonstration shows that God is immutable, eternal, incorporeal, altogether simple, one, and other such things which we have shown about God in Book One [15-38].[733]

St. Thomas teaches: 1) On the question ($II^a\ II^a$ q. 2. a. 5), *Whether man is bound to believe anything explicitly*, St. Thomas replies to the objection that, "It seems that man is not bound to believe anything explicitly,", saying: «On the contrary, It is written (Hebrews 11:6): "He that cometh to God, must believe that He is, and is a rewarder to them that seek Him.»[734] He then expounds:

---

[732] *Summa Contra Gentiles* Lib. I. Caput 11 — «Ad quartam etiam patet solutio. Sic enim homo naturaliter Deum cognoscit sicut naturaliter ipsum desiderat. Desiderat autem ipsum homo naturaliter inquantum desiderat naturaliter beatitudinem, quae est quaedam similitudo divinae bonitatis. Sic igitur non oportet quod Deus ipse in se consideratus sit naturaliter notus homini, sed similitudo ipsius. Unde oportet quod per eius similitudines in effectibus repertas in cognitionem ipsius homo ratiocinando perveniat.»

[733] *Summa Contra Gentiles* Lib. III. Caput 39 — «Rursus, est quaedam alia Dei cognitio, altior quam praemissa, quae de Deo per demonstrationem habetur, per quam magis ad propriam ipsius cognitionem acceditur: cum per demonstrationem removeantur ab eo multa, per quorum remotionem ab aliis discretus intelligitur. Ostendit enim demonstratio Deum esse immobilem, aeternum, incorporeum, omnino simplicem, unum, et alia huiusmodi, quae in libro primo de Deo ostendimus.»

[734] «Sed contra est quod dicitur ad Heb. XI, *accedentem ad Deum oportet credere quia est, et quod inquirentibus se remunerator est.*»

I answer that, The precepts of the Law, which man is bound to fulfil, concern acts of virtue which are the means of attaining salvation. Now an act of virtue, as stated above (I-II, 60, 5) depends on the relation of the habit to its object. Again two things may be considered in the object of any virtue; namely, that which is the proper and direct object of that virtue, and that which is accidental and consequent to the object properly so called. Thus it belongs properly and directly to the object of fortitude, to face the dangers of death, and to charge at the foe with danger to oneself, for the sake of the common good: yet that, in a just war, a man be armed, or strike another with his sword, and so forth, is reduced to the object of fortitude, but indirectly. Accordingly, just as a virtuous act is required for the fulfilment of a precept, so is it necessary that the virtuous act should terminate in its proper and direct object: but, on the other hand, the fulfillment of the precept does not require that a virtuous act should terminate in those things which have an accidental or secondary relation to the proper and direct object of that virtue, except in certain places and at certain times. We must, therefore, say that the direct object of faith is that whereby man is made one of the Blessed, as stated above (Question 1, Article 8): while the indirect and secondary object comprises all things delivered by God to us in Holy Writ, for instance that Abraham had two sons, that David was the son of Jesse, and so forth. Therefore, as regards the primary points or articles of faith, man is bound to believe them, just as he is bound to have faith; but as to other points of faith, man is not bound to believe them explicitly, but only implicitly, or to be ready to believe them, in so far as he is prepared to believe whatever is contained in the Divine Scriptures. Then alone is he bound to believe such things explicitly, when it is clear to him that they are contained in the doctrine of faith.

2) In *De Veritate* Q. 14 a. 11 St. Thomas elaborates further:

Properly speaking, that is called implicit in which many things are contained as in one, and that is called explicit in which each of the things is considered in itself. These appellations are transferred from bodily to spiritual things. When a number of things are contained virtually in one thing, we say they are there implicitly, as, for instance, conclusions in principles. A thing is contained explicitly in another if it actually exists in it. Consequently, one who knows some general principles has implicit knowledge of all the particular conclusions. One, however, who actually considers the conclusions is said to know them explicitly. Hence, we are also said explicitly to believe certain things when we affirm those things about which we are actually thinking. We believe these same things implicitly when we affirm certain other things in which they are contained as in general principles. Thus, one who believes that the faith of the Church is true, implicitly in this believes the individual points which are included in the faith of the Church. We must note, accordingly, that there are some matters of faith which everyone is bound to believe explicitly in every age. Other matters of faith must be believed explicitly in every age but not by everyone. Still other matters everyone must believe explicitly, but not in every age. And, finally, there are things that need not be believed explicitly by everyone nor in every age.

Then he says which things must be believed by everyone in every age:

> That all the faithful in every age must believe something explicitly is evident from the fact that there is a parallel between the reception of faith with reference to our ultimate perfection and a pupil's reception of those things which his master first teaches him, and through which he is guided to prior principles. However, he could not be so guided unless he actually considered something. Hence, the pupil must receive something for actual consideration; likewise, the faithful must explicitly believe something. And these are the two things which the Apostle tells us must be believed explicitly: "For he that cometh to God must believe that He is, and is the rewarder to them that love Him" (Hebrews 11:6). Therefore, everyone in every age is bound explicitly to believe that God exists and exercises providence over human affairs.

Then St. Thomas elaborates on what must be explicitly professed by the faithful of different rank on different ages:

> However, it is not possible for anyone in this life to know explicitly the whole of God's knowledge, in which our beatitude consists. Yet it is possible for someone in this life to know all those things which are proposed to the human race in its present state as first principles with which to direct itself to its final end. Such a person is said to have faith which is completely explicit. But not all believers have this completeness; hence, there are levels of belief in the Church, so that some are placed over others to teach them in matters of faith. Consequently, not all are required explicitly to believe all matters of faith, but only those are so bound who are appointed teachers in matters of faith, such as superiors and those who have pastoral duties. And even these are not bound to

believe everything explicitly in every age. For there is a gradual progress in faith for the whole human race just as there is for individual men. This is why Gregory says that down the ages there has been a growing development of divine knowledge. Now, the fullness of time, which is the prime of life of the human race, is in the age of grace. So, in this age, the leaders are bound to believe all matters of faith explicitly. But, in earlier ages, the leaders were not bound to believe everything explicitly. However, more had to be believed explicitly after the age of the law and the prophets than before that time. Accordingly, before sin came into the world, it was not necessary to believe explicitly the matters concerning the Redeemer, since there was then no need of the Redeemer. Nevertheless, this was implicit in their belief in divine providence, in so far as they believed that God would provide everything necessary for the salvation of those who love Him. Before and after the fall, the leaders in every age had to have explicit faith in the Trinity. Between the fall and the age of grace, however, the ordinary people did not have to have such explicit belief. Perhaps before the fall there was not such a distinction of persons that some had to be taught the faith by others. Likewise, between the fall and the age of grace, the leading men had to have explicit faith in the Redeemer, and the ordinary people only implicit faith. This was contained either in their belief in the faith of the patriarchs and prophets or in their belief in divine providence. However, in the time of grace, everybody, the leaders and the ordinary people, have to have explicit faith in the Trinity and in the Redeemer. However, only the leaders, and not the ordinary people, are bound to believe explicitly all the matters of faith concerning the Trinity and the Redeemer. The ordinary people must, however, believe explicitly the general articles, such as that God is triune, that the Son of God was made flesh, died, and rose from the dead, and other like matters which the Church commemorates in her feasts.

It is patent from the doctrine presented here that belief in God is of an absolute necessity, and therefore is necessary for all men and in all times to be saved.[735] For faithful of the Church in the time of grace, there is the necessity to profess explicitly the principal mysteries of faith; which St. Thomas expressly qualifies in *II^a II^{ae} q. 2 a.5* as a *necessity*

---

[735] That is, the necessity is absolute for all who have reached the age of reason and are capable of exercising the intellective faculty to actually believe in God. Baptized infants and imbeciles do not have the use of reason but are saved by the grace of the sacrament alone.

of precept. This precept clearly is not applicable to those who labour under invincible ignorance of some of the revealed mysteries; but invincible ignorance of the primary truths of religion (such as the existence of God) is only possible in the feeble minded deprived of the use of reason; and invincible ignorance of the principal revealed truths is possible only in the most ignorant members of the Church, such as those who are illiterate, cut off from civilization, and are totally lacking religious instruction. For a highly educated archbishop and cardinal, and former professor of theology such as Bergoglio, invincible ignorance of any one of the principal truths of faith is absolutely inconceivable. For such a one to deny such primary truths as the necessity of faith — or of any belief in God at all for justification or salvation; or that the Church is bound by divine precept to teach all nations in order to convert them and bring them into to the Catholic faith, is proof beyond all shadow of doubt that such a prelate as Bergoglio is a contumacious heretic, and as such, is an incapable subject of the papacy. Jorge Mario Bergoglio is no pope, because he is an *incapable subject of the papacy* — he is intrinsically incapable of being united to the form of the pontificate, because it is seen as an evident truth that he rejects the Catholic faith which is necessary for a man to be united to the Church, and which is the necessary conforming disposition for a man to be united to the Church as its head. He cannot be the *Vicar of Christ* who openly opposes Christ's teaching with the manifestly visible *dolus* of heretical disbelief.

Against Bergoglio's perverse teaching that even atheists can be without sin, there is the pronouncement of Jesus Christ, who declared, "But this is the judgment: because the light came into the world, and men loved darkness more than the light: it was their *evil works*." (John 3:19)[736] Atheism is not a simple act of unbelief resulting from a mere privation of knowledge, but is an act that is in the nature of an aversion from God. St. Thomas explains in *II^a II^{ae} q. 10 a.1*: 1) «Unbelief may be taken in two ways: first, by way of pure negation, so that a man be called an unbeliever, merely because he has not the

---

[736] «Hoc est autem judicium: quia lux venit in mundum, et dilexerunt homines magis tenebras quam lucem: erant enim eorum *mala opera*.» (Joannes 3:19)

faith.» 2) «Secondly, unbelief may be taken by way of opposition to the faith; in which sense a man refuses to hear the faith, or despises it, according to Is. 53:1: "Who hath believed our report?"» Concerning the first, St. Thomas says, «If, however, we take it by way of pure negation, as we find it in those who have heard nothing about the faith, it bears the character, not of sin, but of a penalty...Hence Our Lord said (Jn. 15:22) "If I had not come, and spoken to them, they would not have sin"; which Augustine expounds (*Tract. lxxxix in Joan.*) as "referring to the sin whereby they believed not in Christ."» Concerning the second, «It is this that completes the notion of unbelief, and it is in this sense that unbelief is a sin.» One who is invincibly ignorant of the Catholic faith is not guilty of the sin of **infidelity**, but as has been explained above, one cannot be excused from sin who professes atheism or any form of disbelief in God.

The cause of atheism is not mere ignorance, since ignorance can be excused if it is inculpable or *invincible*; but it is *spiritual blindness*, which does not excuse, because it is caused by contempt for God and his law. St. Thomas explains:

> Just as bodily blindness is the privation of the principle of bodily sight, so blindness of mind is the privation of the principle of mental or intellectual sight. Now this has a threefold principle. One is the light of natural reason, which light, since it pertains to the species of the rational soul, is never forfeit from the soul, and yet, at times, it is prevented from exercising its proper act, through being hindered by the lower powers which the human intellect needs in order to understand, for instance in the case of imbeciles and madmen, as stated in the first part, (q. 84, a. 7,8.). Another principle of intellectual sight is a certain habitual light superadded to the natural light of reason, which light is sometimes forfeit from the soul. This privation is blindness, and is a punishment, in so far as the privation of the light of grace is a punishment. Hence it is written concerning some (Wis. 2:21): "Their own malice blinded them." A third principle of intellectual sight is an intelligible principle, through which a man understands other things; to which principle a man may attend or not attend. That he does not attend thereto happens in two ways. Sometimes it is due to the fact that a man's will is deliberately turned away from the consideration of that principle, according to Ps. 35:4, "He would not understand, that he might do well": whereas sometimes it is due to the mind being more busy about things which it loves more, so as to be hindered thereby from considering this principle,

according to Ps. 57:9, "Fire," i.e. of concupiscence, "hath fallen on them and they shall not see the sun." In either of these ways blindness of mind is a sin.[737]

In his commentary on Psalm 52 [The fool (*insipiens*) hath said in his heart *there is no God.*], St. Thomas explains, "Above the Psalmist exposes the wickedness of sinners on the part of affection for sin; here he shows their wickedness from contempt of God."[738] In *II^a II^ae* q. 46 a. 1 he distinguishes between stupidity (*stultitia*), which is simple dullness, and "foolishness" (*insipientia*), in the sense of *unwise senselessness*, saying, "But stupidity (*stultitia*) does not seem to be the same as foolishness (*insipientia*), because foolishness is seen to be only about divine things; but stupidity is concerning divine things and

---

[737] II^a II^ae q. 15 a. 1 — «Respondeo dicendum quod sicut caecitas corporalis est privatio eius quod est principium corporalis visionis, ita etiam caecitas mentis est privatio eius quod est principium mentalis sive intellectualis visionis. Cuius quidem principium est triplex. Unum quidem est lumen naturalis rationis. Et hoc lumen, cum pertineat ad speciem animae rationalis, nunquam privatur ab anima. Impeditur tamen quandoque a proprio actu per impedimenta virium inferiorum, quibus indiget intellectus humanus ad intelligendum, sicut patet in amentibus et furiosis, ut in primo dictum est. Aliud autem principium intellectualis visionis est aliquod lumen habituale naturali lumini rationis superadditum. Et hoc quidem lumen interdum privatur ab anima. Et talis privatio est caecitas quae est poena, secundum quod privatio luminis gratiae quaedam poena ponitur. Unde dicitur de quibusdam, Sap. II, *excaecavit illos malitia eorum*. Tertium principium visionis intellectualis est aliquod intelligibile principium per quod homo intelligit alia. Cui quidem principio intelligibili mens hominis potest intendere vel non intendere. Et quod ei non intendat contingit dupliciter. Quandoque quidem ex hoc quod habet voluntatem spontanee se avertentem a consideratione talis principii, secundum illud Psalm., *noluit intelligere ut bene ageret*. Alio modo, per occupationem mentis circa alia quae magis diligit, quibus ab inspectione huius principii mens avertitur, secundum illud Psalm., *supercecidit ignis*, scilicet concupiscentiae, *et non viderunt solem*. Et utroque modo caecitas mentis est peccatum.»

[738] *Commentarium Super Psalmo 52* — «Supra Psalmista arguit nequitiam peccatorum ex parte affectionis ad peccatum; hic arguit eorum nequitiam ex contemptu Dei.»

human things."⁷³⁹ He goes on to explain that, "It is to be known that wisdom, if properly taken, differs from knowledge, because wisdom is about the understanding of divine things, knowledge about the cognition of human things. The fool despises the understanding of divine things, Tob. 21: *withdraw from us, and we do not want knowledge of your ways.* Rom. 1: *the fool is eclipsed,* etc. *Therefore the fool has said,* i.e. he scorned God and the knowledge of God; and this he did in his heart, he said: *there is no God.*"⁷⁴⁰ Thus it is the attachment to sin that causes the spiritual blindness of the atheist, and for which reason the Lord declared, "But this is the judgment: because the light came into the world, and men loved darkness more than the light: it was their *evil works.*" (John 3:19)

In his *Commentary on the Gospel of St. John,* St. Thomas expounds on this theme:

> Therefore, those who do not believe in the Son of God are cut off from salvation, and the cause of their damnation is evident. Here the Lord explains his statement that unbelievers have an evident cause for their condemnation. First, he sets forth the sign which shows this. Secondly, the fittingness of this sign (v. 20). In the sign he sets forth he does three things. First, he mentions the gift of God. Secondly, the perversity of mind in unbelievers. Thirdly, the cause of this perversity. So he says: It is abundantly clear that *whoever does not believe is already judged,* because *the light came into the world.* For men were in the darkness of ignorance, and God destroyed this darkness by sending a light into the world so that men might know the truth: "I am the light of the world. He who follows me does not walk in darkness, but will have the light of life" (below 8:12); "To enlighten those who sit in darkness and in the shadow of death" (Lk. 1:78). Now the light came into the world because

---

⁷³⁹ *II ͣ II ᵃᵉ q. 46 a. 1. arg. 1* — «Sed stultitia non videtur esse idem quod insipientia, quia insipientia videtur esse solum circa divina, sicut et sapientia; stultitia autem se habet et circa divina et circa humana.»

⁷⁴⁰ *Commentarium Super Psalmo 52* — «Sciendum est quod sapientia, si proprie sumatur, differat a scientia, quia sapientia est circa divinorum cognitionem, scientia circa humanorum cognitionem. Vir insipiens contemnit cognitionem divinorum. Tob. XXI: *recede a nobis, et scientiam viarum tuarum nolumus.* Rom. I: *obscuratum est insipiens,* et cetera. *Dixit ergo insipiens,* idest contempsit Deum et scientiam Dei; et hoc fecit in corde suo, dixit: *non est Deus.*»

men could not come to it: for "He dwells in inaccessible light, whom no man has seen or is able to see" (1 Tim 6:16) It is also clear from the perversity of mind in unbelievers who *loved darkness more than the light*, i.e., they preferred to remain in the darkness of ignorance rather than be instructed by Christ: "They have rebelled against the light" (Job 24:13); "Woe to you who substitute darkness for light, and light for darkness" (Is. 5:20). And the cause of this perversity is that *their deeds were evil*: and such deeds do not conform to the light but seek the darkness: "Let us cast off the works of darkness" (Rom. 13:12), i.e., sins, which seek the darkness; "Those who sleep, sleep at night" (1 Thess. 5:7); "The eye of the adulterer watches for the darkness," as we read in Job (24:15). Now it is by withdrawing from the light, which is unpleasant to him, that one does not believe the light… Then when he says, *Everyone who practices evil hates the light*, he shows the appropriateness of the sign he used. First, with respect to those who are evil. Secondly, with respect to the good. So he says: The reason why they did not love the light is that their works were evil. And this is plain because *Everyone who practices evil hates the light*. He does not say, "practiced," but rather practices: because if someone has acted in an evil way, but has repented and is sorry, seeing that he has done wrong, such a person does not hate the light but comes to the light. But everyone who practices evil, i.e., persists in evil, is not sorry, nor does he come to the light, but he hates it; not because it reveals truth, but because it reveals a person's sins. For an evil person still wants to know the light and the truth; but he hates to be unmasked by it. "If the dawn suddenly appears, they regard it as the shadow of death" (Job 24:17). And so he **does not approach the light; and this for fear that his deeds might be exposed.** For no one who is unwilling to desert evil wants to be rebuked; this is fled from and hated. "They hate the one who rebukes at the city gate" (Am. 5:10); "A corrupt man does not love the one who rebukes him" (Prov. 15:12).[741]

---

[741] *Super Evangelium S. Ioannis lectura*, caput 3 lectio 3 — «Qui ergo non credunt in filium Dei, excidunt a salute, et manifesta est in eis causa damnationis. Hic manifestat dominus suam sententiam, scilicet quod causa condemnationis manifesta est in infidelibus: et primo ponit manifestans signum; secundo ostendit signi convenientiam, ibi *omnis enim qui male agit, odit lucem*. In signo autem proposito tria facit: primo enim proponit Dei beneficium; secundo perversitatem mentis infidelium; tertio perversitatis causam. Dicit ergo: manifeste apparet quod qui non credit, iam iudicatus est, quod apparet ex Dei beneficio: quia *lux venit in mundum*. Homines enim erant in tenebris ignorantiae, quas quidem tenebras Deus destruxit, mittens lucem in mundum, ut homines cognoscerent veritatem; infra VIII, 12: *ego*

Thus, atheism and rejection of the true faith in the Gospel of Christ is a sin caused by spiritual blindness resulting from moral corruption. Atheism does not exist as an unsinful natural state but as an unnatural sinful state. Against the objection, «It would seem that unbelief is not a sin. For every sin is contrary to nature, as Damascene proves (De Fide Orth. ii, 4). Now unbelief seems not to be contrary to nature; for Augustine says (De Praedest. Sanct. v) that "to be capable of having faith, just as to be capable of having charity, is natural to all men; whereas to have faith, even as to have charity, belongs to the grace of the faithful." Therefore not to have faith, which is to be an unbeliever, is not a sin.»,[742] St. Thomas counters: «To have the faith is not part of

---

sum lux mundi: qui sequitur me non ambulat in tenebris, sed habebit lumen vitae; Lc. I, 78: *visitavit nos oriens ex alto. Illuminare his qui in tenebris et in umbra mortis sedent.* Sed ista venit in mundum, scilicet lux, quia homo ad eam accedere non poterat: nam *lucem habitat inaccessibilem, quam nemo hominum vidit, sed nec videre potest*: I Tim. VI, 16. Apparet etiam ex perversitate mentis infidelium, qui *dilexerunt magis tenebras quam lucem*, idest, magis voluerunt esse in tenebris ignorantiae quam instrui per Christum; Iob c. XXIV, 13: *ipsi fuerunt rebelles lumini*: Is. c. V, 20: *vae qui ponunt lucem tenebras* et cetera. Cuius quidem perversitatis causa est quia *erant eorum mala opera*: quae a luce dissonant et tenebras quaerunt; Rom. XIII, 12: *abiiciamus opera tenebrarum*, idest peccata, quae tenebras quaerunt; I Thess. ult., 7: *qui dormiunt, nocte dormiunt*; Iob XXIV, 15: *oculus adulteri observat caliginem.* Ex hoc autem aliquis non credit luci, quod ei repugnat, discedendo... Consequenter dicit *omnis enim qui male agit, odit lucem*, ostendit propositi signi convenientiam: et primo quidem quantum ad malos; secundo quantum ad bonos, ibi qui autem facit veritatem venit ad lucem. Dicit ergo: *ideo non dilexerunt lucem, quia erant eorum mala opera*. Et hoc patet, quia *omnis qui male agit, odit lucem*. Non autem dicit egit sed agit: quia si quis male egit, tamen poenitens, et videns se male fecisse, dolet, non odit lucem, sed ad lucem venit. Sed omnis qui male agit, idest in malo perseverat, non dolet, nec ad lucem venit, sed eam odit: non inquantum veritatis quidem est manifestativa, sed inquantum per eam peccatum hominis manifestatur. Diligit enim malus homo cognoscere lucem et veritatem; sed odit per eam manifestari; Iob XXIV, 17: *si subito apparuerit aurora, arbitrantur umbram mortis.* Et ideo non venit ad lucem. Et hoc ut non arguantur opera eius: nullus enim homo, qui non vult malum deserere, vult reprehendi; sed fugit, et odit; Amos V, 10: *odio habuerunt corripientem in porta*; Prov. XV, 12: *non amat pestilens eum qui se corripit.*»

[742] *II*^a *– II*^{ae} *Q. 10 a.1. arg.1* — «Ad primum sic proceditur. Videtur quod infidelitas non sit peccatum. Omne enim peccatum est contra naturam, ut

human nature, but it is part of human nature that man's mind should not thwart his inner instinct, and the outward preaching of the truth. Hence, in this way, unbelief is contrary to nature.»[743] The atheist and the unbeliever are sinners in need of the works of mercy, among which are: 1) To instruct the ignorant, 2) To counsel the doubtful, 3) To admonish the sinners; but in spite of all of Bergoglio's histrionic posturing about "mercy", he shows no mercy whatsoever to those in need of these spiritual works of mercy. When asked, "If an atheist came to you and asked you a fundamental reason for starting to believe what would you answer?" Bergoglio answered, "In front of an unbeliever, the last thing I have to do is try to convince him. Never. The last thing I have to do is talk." It was to save sinners that Christ came into the world and died on the cross, and sent his apostles to preach and make disciples of all nations, baptizing them into the true faith which unites them to God. Justification is by faith, and without faith there is no justification, no sanctifying grace, which, St. Thomas says, is "a certain beginning of glory in us" (*quædam inchoatio gloriæ in nobis*[744]). Without the true faith uniting the soul to the one true God in the charity of sanctifying grace, a soul remains alienated from God on the road to eternal perdition.

This is not difficult to understand. St. Maximillian Kolbe never tired of saying, "There is only one truth and in consequence there can be only one true religion."[745] In that just cited volume of André Fossard, one reads in the writing of the saint:

> It happened not long ago, on the night of April 13-14 this year. The train ran from Warsaw in the direction of Toruń. In front of me a young

---

patet per Damascenum, in II libro. Sed infidelitas non videtur esse contra naturam, dicit enim Augustinus, in libro de Praed. Sanct., quod posse habere fidem, sicut posse habere caritatem, naturae est hominum, habere autem fidem, quemadmodum habere caritatem, gratiae est fidelium. Ergo non habere fidem, quod est infidelem esse, non est peccatum.»

[743] *II^a II^{ae} q. 10 a.1. ad 1* — «Ad primum ergo dicendum quod habere fidem non est in natura humana, sed in natura humana est ut mens hominis non repugnet interiori instinctui et exteriori veritatis praedicationi. Unde infidelitas secundum hoc est contra naturam.»

[744] *II^a-II^{ae} q. 24 a. 3 ad 2.*

[745] André Fossard, *Forget Not Love: The Passion of Maximillian Kolbe*, p. 119.

man was arguing animatedly with two other people about earnings and wealth. I thought to myself: they are probably from the province of Poznań, since, despite having the face of the Slavic features, they went a long way in talking about industry, commerce and earnings. However, I was a little wrong, since one of them, and precisely the one who had the determining role in the conversation, was Jewish. "You will probably be baptized shortly," I said. "No - he answered - one must die in the religion in which he was born". "But what if this religion isn't true?" "For everyone, their religion is the good one, even if I admit I'm not a fervent practitioner." "This is not good! How can there be several true religions? Yet the truth can only be one. In the same matter and under the same aspect, the "yes" and the "no" cannot be true. Yet the various religions differ precisely in the fact that on certain subjects one affirms what another denies ".

In one of his letters St. Maximillian related:

Every month, very regularly, we receive a 64-page periodical entitled: Hikari, or "Light". It is the magazine of the village "Ittoen" (which means: garden of light), founded by the Japanese philosopher Nishida Tenko. Such a character is called the "Japanese St. Francis", while his village is a kind of convent. It is difficult to call it a convent in our meaning, since entire families live in that place. When we landed in Japan five years ago, Mr. Tenko also found out about us and our modest Franciscan life, and visited us, indeed he gave a conference speaking quite benevolently towards us. For this reason in that year, a day very close to the feast of the Father St. Francis, I myself went to "Ittoen" 3. I was received with great cordiality. On one point, however, we could not understand each other, due to the fact that I stubbornly maintained that the truth can only be one and, consequently, there can be no more than one true religion. Almost five years have now passed. They regularly send us their magazine and we regularly exchange them for Kishi. A few months ago the train was quickly taking me to Osaka to buy the card for the Kishi. A middle-aged gentleman approaches me in the carriage and greets me. I recognize him immediately, he is one of the collaborators of Nishida Tenko. Interchangeable questions and answers on health, on the good performance of activities and so on, and in the end a new mention of the theme of religion. "You certainly look down on us, considering us a small entity," he says. "No, absolutely, I appreciate and respect all those who seek the truth, but ... the truth is always and only one". "On the table of Mr. Nishida Tenko there is always the statue of the Immaculate

Conception that you sent us." We had now approached the station to which he was to get off, so we stopped the conversation and said goodbye. However, the news that the Immaculate Conception, from one of his statuettes, turns his gaze towards the founder of that village, has consoled me greatly.

Fr. Maximillian M.

How well the saints, who being filled with the spirit of divine charity, practiced the spiritual works of mercy to the point of heroic virtue, understanding that the mission of the Church is to teach souls the way of salvation and guide them to eternal life. That spirit of mercy animated the priestly life of St Maximillian Kolbe and bore the eternal fruit of salvation for a multitude of souls. It didn't require many words from St. Maximillian to bring about the conversion of the pagan Japanese philosopher, but he did make the effort to speak, and if he had remained silent, Mr. Tenko would have died in Paganism, without the saving grace of Christ. In the cited work, the footnote on Nishida Tenko mentions, "He died on 29 II 1968 at the age of 96. Before dying he received baptism from the hands of Fr. Janusz Koza, O.F.M. Conv." Even more recently, just a few years ago, I read a priest's own account of a conversion brought about by his asking one simple question. The priest, an SSPX missionary in Southeast Asia, was ministering to one of his faithful in a Hong Kong hospital, where he spotted a dying man who, lacking a Christian name, could be seen to be pagan from his name. The priest, having finished ministering to his parishioner went over to the dying man and asked him if he wanted to go to heaven. The man said, "Yes." The priest then instructed the man in the Catholic faith and baptized him; after which the man died. We already know what Bergoglio would have done — he has told us in his own words: "In front of an unbeliever, the last thing I have to do is try to convince him." That spirit which animated St. Maximillian and an immense multitude of missionaries and lay Catholics throughout two millennia to sacrifice themselves for the salvation of souls even unto death, is entirely absent in Bergoglio, who says regarding atheists and unbelievers, "The last thing I have to do is talk," — which is the same as saying, *"Let their souls go to eternal perdition."* Bergoglio's teaching is a stark rejection of the **Supreme Law**, which is: *"The salvation of souls must always be the supreme law in the Church."*

(Canon 1752) His adamant pertinacity in professing and preaching this abominable heresy, which diametrically opposes the explicit teaching of Christ and the bi-millennial doctrinal tradition of the Church by itself demonstrates beyond all conceivable doubt that Jorge Mario Bergoglio is an infidel and a non-Christian — an outsider masquerading as a Catholic, and an intruder who usurps the throne of Peter — an impostor and an Antichrist who, regardless of whether you think he is a valid pope or not, must be "cast out" as Innocent III teaches, "trampled underfoot by men", and "despised by the people"; because "He who does not believe is already judged (John 3)":

> For the servant, according to the Apostle, «stands or falls by his master (Rom. Xiv).» For which reason the same Apostle said; **«Who art thou who judgest another's servant?»** (Ibid.) Whence since the **Roman** as Innocent II teaches **Pontiff has no other master but God,** however so much he should wither away, who can cast him out, or trample him underfoot? Since to him it is to be said: «gather thy case into thy fold?» But let him not wantonly flatter himself of the power, nor rashly glory of the sublimity or honour; because by how much less he is judged by men, that much more he is judged by God. I say less; because he can be judged by men, or rather be shown to be judged, if he plainly should wither away into heresy; because «he who does not believe, already has been judged» (John iii). In this case accordingly it must be understood of him, if the salt loses its savour, it is good for nothing more, but to be cast out, and trampled underfoot by men. — Innocentius III — *Sermo IV De Diversis* «**IN CONSACRATIONE PONTIFICIS**»
>
> Servus enim, secundum Apostolum, «suo domino stat aut cadit (Rom. xiv).» Propter quod idem Apostolus ait; «Tu quis es, qui judicas alienum servum?» (Ibid.) Unde cum Romanus pontifex non habeat alium dominum nisi Deum, quantumlibet evanescat, quis potest eum foras mittere, aut pedibus conculcare? Cum illi dicatur: «Collige causam tuam in sinum tuum?» Verum non frustra sibi blandiatur de potestate, neque de sublimitate vel honore temere glorietur; quia quanto minus judicatur ab homine, tanto magis judicatur a Deo. Minus dico; quia potest ab hominibus judicari, vel potius judicatus ostendi, si videlicet evanescat in haeresim; quoniam «qui non credit, jam judicatus est» *(Joan.* iii). In hoc siquidem casu debet intelligi de illo, *quod si sal evanuerit, ad nihilum valet ultra, nisi ut mittatur foras, et conculcetur ab*

homninibus. — Innocentius III — *Sermo IV De Diversis* «IN CONSACRATIONE PONTIFICIS»

SECTION II

BENEDICT XVI REMAINS THE ONE AND ONLY LEGITIMATE POPE

I have already explained sufficiently that it is a truth of faith that there can be only one pope at any given time in the Church. The Church is a divinely constituted **MONARCHY**, and for there to be monarchical rule, there must be only one who rules as an absolute **MON-arch**. If a **DIARCHY**, or a **TRIUMVIRATE** — or an **ARISTOCRACY**, or a **DEMOCRACY even under a mere figurehead pope** were to be adopted in place of the monarchical governance of the Church, the ecclesial community governed by that body would by that very fact of its defection from the divine constitution of the Church be separated from the body of the true Church instituted by Christ as a **MONARCHY**. There cannot be simultaneously a "pope of action" and a "pope of prayer" — one in possession of the ordinary power of governance as Supreme Pontiff, and the other retaining some aspect of the *munus* he received upon his election to be exercised in the ministry of prayer and suffering as *Pope Emeritus*. As I have explained already, in accordance with the very nature of the papacy as instituted by Christ, when a pope resigns his *office* (i.e. his stable *munus* as pope), there remains with him **nothing** of the Petrine *munus* he received from Christ upon his election to the papacy. As a successor of the apostles, a bishop retains his generic episcopal *munus* even when he gives up his *munus* as ordinary of a diocese and becomes a *Bishop Emeritus*; but when a pope renounces his papal office, the only *munus* he retains, **as one who is still a successor of the Apostles but no longer of Peter as head and chief**, is the **episcopal *munus***, which is ***common to all bishops***, while the papal *munus* is a **unique** *munus* which pertains exclusively and solely to the person who, as successor **not of the Apostles but of Peter in the primacy** actually holds the **supreme** office of *head of the Church and Vicar of Christ*. Thus, a former pope can be a *"Bishop Emeritus of Rome"* like any other *Bishop Emeritus* in virtue of the common episcopal *munus* which he retains even after relinquishing his papal *munus*, but he can never properly be a *"Pope Emeritus"* who retains some aspect of the **Petrine *munus*,** because **one only becomes a former pope by relinquishing the Petrine *munus* totally and unconditionally.** Since Pope Benedict renounced his ministry while expressly stating that the *munus* he received upon his election is not revoked but is "for always", the unique and indivisible Petrine *munus* of the Supreme Pontificate remains exclusively with him as supreme head of the Church — that *munus* which constitutes him as *Vicar of Christ* on earth. What is very telling in this regard is that after seven years of his faux pontificate, Antipope Francis now refuses any longer to appropriate to himself the title of *Vicar of Christ*, and has removed it from the 2020 edition of the *Annuario Pontificio*. LifeSiteNews reported on April 2, 2020, «In a surprise move, Pope Francis has dropped the historic and essential title "Vicar of Christ" from the 2020 Pontifical Yearbook, the Holy See's annual directory, relegating the title to a footnote, calling it a "historical title."» The report goes on to say, «While previous yearbooks listed the title "Vicar of Christ" and the name of the reigning Pope under that title, this year's annual directory simply lists the name "Jorge Mario Bergoglio," the name of the man who became Pope Francis in 2013. Cardinal Gerhard Müller, former prefect of the Congregation for the Doctrine of the Faith, called the change "theological barbarism."» Thus, Bergoglio is clearly seen to be a usurper even of the temporal power he exercises over the Vatican City State, since, "The Temporal Sovereignty of the Pope in the Vatican State is," as Fr. Fahey explains, "a consequence of the Pope's participation in the Spiritual Kingship of Christ as His Vicar on earth."[746]

None of the arguments which claim that Pope Benedict's *Declaratio* validly expressed the intention to renounce his *munus* directly addresses this decisive point, namely, that when Benedict XVI renounced his *ministry*, by distinguishing between the *ministerium* and the *munus*, and between the active and passive aspects of the *munus*, and expressing his intention to continue to exercise the passive aspect of the *munus* even after the juridical cessation of the active exercise of

---

[746] Rev. Denis Fahey, C.S.SP., B.A., D.Pa., D.D. Professor of Philosophy and Church History, Senior Scholasticate, Blackrock College, *The Kingship of Christ According to the Principles of St. Thomas Aquinas*, Dublin 1931.

the *munus* goes into force, he thereby expressed the intention that his act of renunciation of the *ministerium* does not intend the unconditional and total revocation of the *munus* he received upon his election to the papacy on 19 April, 2005. This defectively stated juridical intention renders his act of renunciation utterly equivocal and contradictory, so that it is to no avail to point to Benedict's words which appear to expressly renounce his office or his *munus*, since by the contradictory affirmation of renouncing the *munus* simultaneously made with the negation of renouncing the same already clearly expressed in principle in the *Declartio*, and more explicitly stated afterward by way of clarification at his last public audience, namely, that the renunciation does not revoke the *munus* he received at his election, the apparent renunciation of the office is thereby affirmed and negated in the same juridical act, rendering it null and void.

Arguing against the invalidity of Pope Benedict's renunciation, Fr. Brian Harrison has completely overlooked this point in his arguments, maintaining in his recent article,[747] that when Benedict declared he was renouncing his ministry, the term *ministerium* was intended to be synonymous with *munus*, because (he says), "While resignationists [i.e. those who hold that Benedict's resignation was invalid] claim that in canon law *munus* and *ministerium* have distinct meanings, they are often in practice used synonymously." However, in order that what is juridically intended be intelligibly expressed in a juridical act, the terms used in the document must be understood as they are defined in law, otherwise the juridical intent of the act will not be intelligible, with the consequence that the act will be null and void due to defect of intention. Ecclesiastical laws must be understood according to the proper signification of the terms considered in their text and context[748] (Can. 17; [Canon 18 in the 1917 Code]). Canon 332 § 2 decrees that in order to be valid the pope's renunciation of his *munus* must be "rightly manifested", which means not only that he must follow the correct procedure, but he must also

---

[747] *Is Benedict Still Pope?*, Fr. Brian W. Harrison O.S., *Latin Mass*, Summer 2020.

[748] «Can. 17 — **Leges ecclesiasticae intellegendae sunt secundum propriam verborum significationem in textu et contextu consideratam**; quae si dubia et obscura manserit, ad locos parallelos, si qui sint, ad legis finem ac circumstantias et ad mentem legislatoris est recurrendum.»

rightly express his renunciation in accordance with the letter of the law. In order to rightly express his juridical intent he must properly intend that his words be understood as they are defined and understood in law, otherwise they will be ambiguous or even unintelligible. Therefore, in establishing that for the validity of a papal renunciation it is required that the act be rightly manifested, canon 332 § 2 thereby established the necessity for the renunciation to be expressed in a manner that intends the legal terms employed in the act to be understood as those terms are defined in law. If the pope wishes to deviate from this statutory requirement that his act be rightly manifested in accordance with law, he must make a provision for the exception, since an administrative act has no effect to the extent that it is contrary to an approved law or custom, unless the competent authority had expressly added a derogating clause. (Canon 38)[749] This is why so many papal acts and decrees have ended with a clause saying, *"Notwithstanding anything to the contrary,"* or, *"Notwithstanding any other provisions of law, even incapacitating or nullifying ones."* So if in Benedict's *Declaratio* the term *ministerium* was intended to be synonymous with *munus*, that alone would of itself invalidate the act.

Fr. Harrison then continues his argument in this vein, stating the patent absurdity, "Now, it was indisputably Benedict's intention to use the two words synonymously in his declaration of February 11, 2013." The mere fact that Pope Benedict renounced the *ministerium* but maintains to this day that his *munus* was not revoked, but continues to the present day, contradicts Fr. Harrisons patently false assertion. Again he objects, "At the time Benedict made his declaration all the cardinals, bishops, and faithful — indeed, the whole world understood him to be resigning totally and fully from the papacy." While it is true, as Fr. Harrison says, *"At the time Benedict made his declaration,"* the whole world, (including myself), "understood him to be resigning totally and fully from the papacy," it also needs to be borne in mind that *at the time Benedict made his declaration,* all the

---

[749] «Can. 38 — Actus administrativus, etiam si agatur de rescripto *Motu proprio* dato, effectu caret quatenus ius alteri quaesitum laedit aut legi consuetudinive probatae ontrarius est, nisi auctoritas competens expresse clausulam derogatoriam addiderit.»

cardinals, bishops, and faithful assumed that he had fully resigned the papacy because they had not yet had the opportunity to carefully read the declaration. Even for some time afterward, practically no one had read the document critically and astutely. That assumption, i.e. that he was resigning totally and fully from the papacy, as I have shown, does not stand up to an astute, reading of the document made with a careful and critical analysis of the key passages. Fr. Harrison then objects, «Re. can. 188: A leading commentary explains that this kind of invalidating error would be "a mistaken judgment which affects the essential elements of the resignation."» — This is exactly the kind of error Benedict made in the *Declaratio* when he renounced the *ministerium* but 1) distinguished it from the *munus*, 2) distinguished between the active and passive aspects of the *munus*, 3) expressed his intention to renounce the active aspect, as well as to retain the exercise the passive aspect of the *munus* even after vacating the chair, 4) clarified his intention regarding the object of the renunciation, stating repeatedly thereafter that his *munus* was not revoked; and therefore: The substantial error consists in his belief that the juridical act of renouncing the *ministerium* while retaining some aspect of the *munus* could have the *juridical effect* of vacating of the chair with the consequent loss of power of governance. The reason for this is that the *object* of the act of renunciation was **only** the *ministerium*, which cannot have the effect of vacating the office if the pope expresses the intention to retain any aspect whatsoever of the Petrine *munus*, which remains wholly with the pope until he renounces it absolutely, entirely, and unconditionally. The proposition, "Regardless of the Pope's own intentions, formally renouncing the *ministerium*, but not the *munus*, will not leave Peter's See vacant," is not incorrect as Fr. Harrison believes. Indeed it is correct, if the expressed object of the act is the renunciation of the **ministry *only* while expressly intending in the act the exclusion from that renunciation some aspect of the *munus* which is to be retained**. The office cannot be vacated by an act which expresses the intention to retain any aspect of the *munus*, because a man cannot cease to be pope for so long as he expresses the intention to retain anything of the Petrine *munus* which uniquely belongs to the pope alone. Therefore, the juridical act that expressly intends to renounce only the *ministerium* but retain in any manner the Petrine *munus* cannot have the juridical effect of vacating the Petrine office, even if the resignant intended that the *effect* of the renunciation of the *ministerium* would be to vacate the see by means of the act, because the act is defective if it leaves the resignant in any manner in possession of the *munus*, being that the act itself renounces only what it expressly intends to renounce, and the office is not renounced if the intention to retain anything of the *munus* is expressed therein. Harrison then attempts to support his position with yet another fallacy: «Indeed, in the Wednesday Talk just cited, Benedict also said, "I no longer bear the power of office for the governance of the Church." And that ...power of office" is the indivisible essence of papal authority. Renouncing it is to fully renounce the papacy.» The problem with this argument is that 'the power of office for the governance of the Church' is not the thing Benedict expressly renounced, even if the loss of that power was subjectively intended to be included as an *effect* of the renunciation of the *ministerium*, because the renunciation of the office or its power was not properly expressed as the object of the act, but only the *ministerium*; and even if it had been the proper object, it would have been nullified by his expressly not intending the object of the act to comprehend the entire *munus*. In the cited passage, Benedict only speaks of the loss of the power of governance as being brought about as an effect of his renunciation of the *ministerium*, so that the intended juridical effect of the act was the cessation of the *ministerium*, which he erroneously believed would have the concomitant effect of the vacating of the office and cessation of power of governance — but merely willing the former does not bring about the latter as a concomitant effect even if that is subjectively intended, because the latter is not the expressed object of the act of renunciation. The stated object of renunciation was the *ministerium*, and not the power of governance which he thought he would no longer bear as a consequence of that renunciation of *ministry*.

Continuing in the same vein, Harrison continues, "Worst of all, those who believe Francis is not our pope will lapse into heresy as well as schism the moment Benedict XVI dies." If Bergoglio is not the pope at present while Benedict lives, Benedict's death would not automatically and necessarily cause Bergoglio to be a valid pope. The death of one papal claimant does not of itself necessarily cause the other claimant to automatically become a valid pope, especially if that other one is a heretic. That being the case, if those who now believe Francis is not the pope are not in heresy and schism, then Benedict's death will not necessarily cause them to fall into heresy and schism. Fr. Harrison presumes to speculate about a future hypothetical scenario as if it will certainly and necessarily follow upon the death of Pope Benedict — as if it does not lie within the power of divine providence to bring about an unexpected turn of events, which would cause some other scenario to materialize than that one which Fr. Harrison foresees taking place in the future. So he therefore continues, "For if they're right, the succession of true popes will then, as we have seen, grind to an abrupt and permanent halt." *As we have seen?* No, we have seen no such thing. The see can become temporarily vacant, even for a few years (as has happened in the past); or there can be a period of doubt about the validity of a man's claim on the papal office (as has happened in the past), but a *permanent* vacancy is *impossible*, and there exists no rational foundation to suppose that the death of the legitimate pontiff, Pope Benedict XVI, would necessarily bring the succession of popes to a halt. Such reasoning denies the provident governance of God over the Church. There can and most likely will be a schism, as well as a period of rival claimants vying for rule over the universal Church, and there may well be some years of vacancy without an indubitable pope having a certain claim on the papacy, but there can be no permanent vacancy after Benedict dies — and we cannot simply assume that if Pope Benedict will die before Antipope Francis, that Bergoglio will become an undisputed valid pope, and that there will not be elected in due time a legitimate successor.

* * *

AGAINST THE OBJECTION THAT BENEDICT XVI IS EQUALLY A HERETIC AS BERGOGLIO

There are some who make the objection that, "If Bergoglio is a heretic as you claim, then so also must Ratzinger be considered a heretic." All of them, whether Sedevacantists, or the others who either gullibly believe this Sedevacantist fallacy (such as *Catholic Truth Scotland*), or knowing that it is a Sedevacantist fallacy, propagate it nevertheless in order to confer the appearance of legitimacy on

Bergoglio's faux pontificate and on the heretical anti-church he seeks to erect, and the Masonic agenda he seeks to implement — all of them assert this fallacy not so much to prove that Pope Benedict is a heretic, but to support their indefensible position which claims Bergoglio is not a heretic, and that he is a legitimate pope. I say "indefensible" because, as I have shown, Bergoglio asserts heresy that cannot be excused by any mitigating factors or circumstances, but is of such a nature that whoever would assert it does so evidently with the culpability and *dolus* of formal heresy. The same cannot be said of Pope Benedict XVI. The *indicia* against Ratzinger simply do not add up to the evident fact of manifest formal heresy as they do for the heretic Bergoglio, whose formal heresy, as I have explained, is not known by means of a complex judgment process which arrives at a conclusion after a laborious investigation of evidence, but is known as a fact seen to be evidently true based on immediately evident factual evidence. It can be said that for those who are accustomed to a more Roman, more classical, more south of the Alps sort of theological exposition, there are in Ratzinger's writings some difficult passages in his elaboration of doctrinal points, complex and even recondite expressions which sometimes lead some into the error of thinking he is a heretic. Ratzinger's thought is deeply nuanced and replete with subtle distinctions, and therefore is not always easy reading. I have an original edition of his *Einfühurung in das Christentum*, a work which I first read in 1978, so I am already familiar with his way of thinking. Most people who think he's a heretic do not understand the critical passages in their proper context, nor in their broader context in German theology. As is well known, Joseph Ratzinger is not a Thomist,[750] but is more rooted in the Augustinian

---

[750] Seewald, Peter. Benedikt XVI.: Ein Leben (German Edition). Droemer eBook. Kindle Edition: "Es muss im Frühjahr 1946 gewesen sein, als Läpple seinen 12 Jahre jüngeren Schützling eines Tages beiseitenahm und ihn mit einem Sonderauftrag überraschte, einer Übersetzung. Es ging um Thomas von Aquins Aufsatz Quaestio disputata de caritate, der bislang nur in der lateinischen Originalfassung vorlag. Aber ausgerechnet Thomas! Der Mann mit der »kristallenen Logik«. Allerdings auch mit einem Denken, das Joseph »zu fest in sich geschlossen«, »zu unpersönlich« und letztlich irgendwie unlebendig, statisch und »zu fertig« erschienen war, ohne Dynamik." [It must have been in the spring of 1946 when Läpple took his

theological tradition. In my judgment, that is a major defect in his theology, because it is only by means of the strict application of Thomistic principles as the apparatus of critical analysis and the explication of doctrine, that one can attain to some degree of completeness in the scientific expression of theological truths.

What is worse, Ratzinger's association with that theological movement known to history as the *Nouvelle Théologie* is an undisputed fact of history. Peter Seewald's biography of Benedict XVI relates some interesting testimonies concerning Ratzinger's affinity for *Nouvelle Théologie* and its modernist leanings. In that biography Seewald describes the scene which unfolded when the renowned professor of dogmatic theology, Michael Schmaus rejected Ratzinger's *Habilitationsschrift* for the postdoctoral degree:

> The drama begins when Ratzinger, a promising young theologian, is invited to the annual conference of the "Working Group of German Dogmatists and Fundamental Theologians", which takes place from March 30th to April 1st, 1956 in Königstein im Taunus. For the first time he meets the famous theologian Karl Rahner, 23 years older and considered to be particularly progressive. One was, he stated, immediately "very humanly close". The co-examiner for his habilitation, Professor Schmaus, is also present. What happens now is something like the meltdown of the hope and suffering of the young Ratzinger. "I was struck by thunder," he described the scene later, "a world threatened to collapse for me." The abyss opened up exactly at the minute when Schmaus took the young colleague aside during the conference. "Objectively and without emotion," as Ratzinger recalled, he told his opponent's master student that he had to reject the habilitation thesis. In terms of form and content, it does not meet the applicable scientific standards. He would receive details after the relevant faculty resolution. [...] Ratzinger's work was filled with marginal glosses in all colours, which left nothing to be desired in terms of sharpness. The famous

---

protégé, 12 years his junior, aside and surprised him with a special order, a translation. It was about Thomas Aquinas's essay *Quaestio disputata de caritate*, which so far was only available in the original Latin version. But of all people, Thomas! The man with the "crystal logic". But also with a way of thinking that seemed to Joseph "too tightly closed", "too impersonal" and ultimately somehow inanimate, static and "too finished", without dynamism.]

dogmatist not only criticized Ratzinger's analyses, he also expressed that he considered the young theologian to be a modernist. "Schmaus almost found it dangerous," recalled Eugen Biser, Karl Rahner's successor to the Romano Guardini chair, "Ratzinger was considered a progressive who shook firmly established bastions." [16] Schmaus publicly criticized, "Ratzinger knows how to integrate things in flowery formulations, but where is the heart of the matter? ". [...] Alfred Läpple [Ratzinger's professor in the seminary and lifelong friend - ed] knew that he told the young theologian to the face, "You talk around and avoid precise definitions." Läpple sympathized with the criticism: "Ratzinger is in favor of a theology of feeling. He shies away from clear definitions. *Sic et non* - it is so or it is not so - he never adhered to this medieval motto. He doesn't love the hard definition, but wants to redesign and build it up like an artist builds a painting. And at the end you ask yourself: What did he actually say?" Läpple added: "Schmaus was right that he is too emotional. That he keeps coming up with new words and is happy to move from one formulation to the other." [...] **Some of the professors also spoke of Ratzinger's dangerous modernism, which amounts to subjectifying the concept of revelation, but Söhngen was able to achieve that the work was not rejected but returned for improvement.**[751]

On 28 April 1969, Paul VI announced the foundation of the International Theological Commission, an organ intended to be parallel to the Congregation for the Doctrine of the Faith. On that occasion, the journal *Informations Catholiques Internationales* (n. 336 - May 15, 1969, p. 9), reported the story and gave the list of the 30 theologians chosen for the Commission. Among them was Joseph Ratzinger, with the notation: "Joseph RATZINGER: German, 45 years old: dogmatic theology, ecumenism: formerly suspected by the Holy Office: member of the commission Faith and Constitution of the Ecumenical Council: noted work (in collaboration with Karl Rahner): «Primacy and episcopate»."[752] Seewald mentions that "Even

---

[751] **Seewald, Peter.** *Benedikt XVI.: Ein Leben* **(German Edition). Droemer eBook. Kindle Edition.**

[752] **Joseph RATZINGER:** Allemand, 45 ans: théologie dogmatique, œcuménisme: naguère suspecté par le Saint-Office: membre de la commission Foi et Constitution du Conseil œcumenique: ouvrage remarqué (en collaboration avec Karl Rahner): «Primat et épiscopat».

while working on his doctoral thesis, Joseph realized that his proximity to «Nouvelle Théologie» had entered dangerous territory." The most dangerous principle of the *Nouvelle Théologie* is elaborated by the illustrious Angelicum Thomist Reginald Garrigou-Lagrange O.P. in his article, *La nouvelle théologie, où va-t-elle?*:

> In a recent book by Father Henri Bouillard, *Conversion et Grâce chez Saint Thomas d'Aquin*, 1944, p. 219, we read: "When the mind evolves, *an unchanging truth* is maintained only thanks to a simultaneous and correlative evolution of all the notions, maintaining between them the same relation. *A theology which is not current would be a false theology* [1]". However, in the preceding and following pages it is shown that the theology of Saint Thomas in several important parts is no longer current. For example, Saint Thomas conceived of sanctifying grace as a form (a radical principle of supernatural operations which have the infused virtues and the seven gifts as their next principle): "The notions used by Saint Thomas are simply Aristotelian notions applied to theology" (Ibid., p. 213 sq.). What follows? "By renouncing Aristotelian Physics, modern thought has abandoned notions, schemes, dialectical oppositions which only made sense in terms of it" (p. 224). It therefore abandoned the notion of form. How will the reader avoid concluding: the theology of St. Thomas, no longer relevant, is a false theology. But then how have the Popes so often recommended that we follow the doctrine of St. Thomas? How does the Church say in her Code of Canon Law, can. 1366, n. 2: "Philosophiae rationalis ac theologiae studia et alumnorum in his disciplinis institutionem professores omnino pertractent ad Angelici Doctoris rationem, doctrinam, et principia, eaque sancte teneant". Moreover, how can "*an immutable truth*" be maintained, if the two notions that it brings together by the verb *to be*, are *essentially changeable*? An immutable relationship is only conceivable if there is something immutable in the two terms it unites. Otherwise, you might as well say that an iron spike can immobilize the waves of the sea. No doubt the two notions which are united in an immutable affirmation are at first confused then distinct, such as the notions of nature, person, substance, accident, transubstantiation, real presence, sin, original sin, grace, etc. But if in what they are fundamentally these notions are not immutable, how can the affirmation that unites them through the verb *to be* be immutable? How to maintain that the real presence of the substance of the Body of Christ in the Eucharist requires transubstantiation, if these notions are

essentially changing? How can we maintain that original sin in us depends on a willful fault of the first man, if the notion of original sin is essentially unstable? How to maintain that the particular judgment after death is irrevocable for eternity, if these notions are called to change? And how, finally, to maintain that all these propositions are immutably *true*, if the very notion of truth must change, and if it is necessary to replace the traditional definition of truth (the conformity of judgment with extramental reality and its immutable laws) that proposed in recent years by the philosophy of action: the conformity of judgment with the requirements of action or of human life which is always evolving?[753]

---

[753] Dans un livre récent du P. Henri Bouillard, *Conversion et grâce chez saint Thomas d'Aquin*, 1944, p. 219, on lit: «Quand l'esprit évolue, *une vérité immuable* ne se maintient que grâce à une évolution simultanée et corrélative de toutes les notions, maintenant entre elles un même rapport. *Une théologie qui ne serait pas actuelle serait une théologie fausse*[1]». Or dans les pages précédentes et les suivantes on montre que la théologie de saint Thomas en plusieurs parties importantes n'est plus actuelle. Par exemple saint Thomas a conçu la grâce sanctifiante comme une *forme* (principe radical d'opérations surnaturelles qui ont pour principe prochain les vertus infuses et les sept dons): « Les notions utilisées par saint Thomas sont simplement des notions aristotéliciennes appliquées à la théologie» (*Ibid.*, p. 213 sq.). Que s'en suit-il? «En renonçant à la Physique aristotélicienne, la pensée moderne a abandonné les notions, les schèmes, les oppositions dialectiques qui n'avaient de sens qu'en fonction d'elle» (p. 224). Elle a donc abandonné la notion de *forme*. Comment le lecteur évitera-t-il de conclure: la théologie de saint Thomas n'étant plus actuelle, est une théologie fausse. Mais alors comment les Papes nous ont-ils si souvent recommandé de suivre la doctrine de saint Thomas? Comment l'Église dit-elle dans son Code de droit canonique, can. 1366, n. 2: «Philosophiae rationalis ac theologiae studia et alumnorum in his disciplinis institutionem professores omnino pertractent ad Angelici Doctoris rationem, doctrinam, et principia, eaque sancte teneant». De plus comment *«une vérité immuable»* peut-elle se maintenir, si les deux notions qu'elle réunit par le verbe *être*, sont *essentiellement changeantes*? Un rapport immuable ne se conçoit que s'il y a quelque chose d'immuable dans les deux termes qu'il unit. Autrement, autant dire qu'un crampon de fer peut immobiliser les flots de la mer. Sans doute les deux notions qui sont unies dans une affirmation immuable sont d'abord confuses puis distinctes, telles les notions de nature, de personne, de substance, d'accident, de transsubstantiation, de présence réelle, de péché, de péché originel, de grâce, etc. Mais si dans ce qu'elles ont de fondamental ces notions ne sont pas immuables, comment l'affirmation qui les unit par le verbe être serait-elle

It can be seen in the theology of Joseph Ratzinger that he was to a great extent influenced by this theological current which is unorthodox to the extent that it is ultimately at variance with the perennial mind of the Church's doctrinal magisterium. Ratzinger lost his secure theological moorings by not adhering to the theology of St. Thomas Aquinas, whom he found, (as Seewald relates) «"too tightly closed", "too impersonal" and ultimately somehow inanimate, static and "too finished", without dynamism.»

Another stumbling block which seems to have barred Joseph Ratzinger from the path which leads to a correct understanding of the true content of several articles of faith is his inherited Modernist bias against the distinction between what is natural and supernatural, which to a great degree also infected the thinking of the exponents of *Nouvelle Théologie* (to which Ratzinger associated himself). If I remember correctly, it was Loisy who said that Augustine introduced the idea of the supernatural into Christian theology and ruined everything. Loisy and the Modernists inherited the anti-supernatural bias from the Enlightenment thought, which traces its roots back to the Rationalists, and principally **Spinoza**, whose metaphysics reduced the being of all created reality to the status of mere attributes of one uncreated **Substance**. According to such a monistic concept of substance, which makes no allowance for a multiplicity of created substances, but only for an infinite number of *attributes*, there cannot exist the duality of divine and created nature, but only one nature — one *deus sive natura*, and consequently no divine nature superior to the

---

immuable? Comment maintenir que la présence réelle de la substance du Corps du Christ dans l'Eucharistie requiert la transsubstantiation, si ces notions sont essentiellement changeantes? Comment maintenir que le péché originel en nous dépend d'une faute volontaire du premier homme, si la notion de péché originel est essentiellement instable? Comment maintenir que le jugement particulier après la mort est irrévocable pour l'éternité, si ces notions sont appelées à changer? Et comment enfin maintenir que toutes ces propositions sont immuablement *vraies*, si la notion même de vérité doit changer, et s'il faut substituer à la définition traditionnelle de la vérité (la conformité du jugement au réel extramental et à ses lois immuables) celle proposée ces dernières années par la philosophie de l'action: la conformité du jugement avec les exigences de l'action ou de la vie humaine qui évolue toujours?

nature of created substances. According to this concept, and consequently according to any supposedly scientific understanding of the nature of things founded on it, there exists only **Nature**, outside of which a supernatural realm superior to it is inconceivable. Accordingly, any belief system that bases its understanding of reality on the distinction between Creator and creature, and the resulting substantial duality of the finite determinate nature of created beings and the infinitely superior nature of the uncreated Supreme Being, who in the omnipotent power his infinite Being can and does intervene in a direct and supernatural manner in the spatio-temporal realm of creation, would be considered the product of what Bultmann referred to as a pre-scientific *Weltbild*.[754] While this radical view primarily advanced by Bultmann is certainly not shared by Ratzinger (who has always opposed the Bultmannite theology, but who nevertheless speaks in this vein on page 300 of his *Einführung in das Christentum* with the expression "*von unserem heutigen Weltbild*"), one does nevertheless find a concession to this Bultmannite principle in Ratzinger's *Einführung in das Christentum* where he says regarding Christ's ascension into heaven:

> The talk of the Ascension means to our generation, who were critically awakened by Bultmann, together with that of the descent from hell, the expression of that three-story world view that we call mythical and consider to be definitely overcome. The world is "above" and "below" everywhere just the world, everywhere governed by the same physical laws, everywhere fundamentally explorable in the same way. It has no floors, and the terms "above" and "below" are relative, depending on the observer's location. Yes, since there is no absolute reference point (and the earth certainly does not represent one), one can basically no longer speak of "above" and "below" - or also of "left" and "right"; the cosmos no longer shows any fixed directions. Today nobody will seriously deny such insights. There is no longer a locally understood

---

[754] In his work, *The Science of Historical Theology* (1976), Msgr. John McCarthy thoroughly debunked Bultmann's thesis which considers all scriptural accounts of supernatural or miraculous events to be the mere expression of a mythical, pre-scientific *Weltbild*.

three-storey world. But was it actually intended in these articles of faith about the descent into hell and ascension of the Lord?[755]

It is precisely Ratzinger's own explanation on what is actually intended by these articles of faith which manifest to what extent he reinterprets the articles of faith not according to Bultmann's theology but according to the Modernist principles of the *Nouvelle Theologie*, and in so doing, he implicitly denies the revealed content of these articles by giving them a new meaning. Ratzinger himself sets forth what must be the principle to be applied for the reinterpretation of dogma, namely the Bultmannite principle of "demythologization", when he treats on the *Descent into Hell*: «Perhaps no article of faith is as remote from our consciousness today as this. In addition to the confession of the birth of Jesus from the Virgin Mary and that of the Ascension of the Lord, it most stimulates the "demythologization", which one seems to be able to carry out safely and without offense.»[756] He goes on to say: "We have already made it clear earlier that the journey into

---

[755] *Einführung in das Christentum*, pp. 264-5 (second edition) — "Die Rede von der Himmelfahrt bedeutet unserer von Bultmann kritisch erweckten Generation zusammen mit derjenigen vom Höllenabstieg den Ausdruck jenes dreistöckigen Weltbildes, das wir mythisch nennen und für definitiv überwunden ansehen. Die Welt ist »oben« und »unten« überall nur Welt, überall von denselben physikalischen Gesetzen regiert, überall grundsätzlich auf dieselbe Art erforschbar. Sie hat keine Stockwerke, und die Begriffe »oben« und »unten« sind relativ, abhängig vom Standort des Beobachters. Ja, da es keinen absoluten Bezugspunkt gibt (und die Erde ganz gewiss keinen solchen darstellt), kann man im Grund überhaupt nicht mehr von »oben« und »unten« - oder auch von »links« und »rechts« sprechen; der Kosmos weist keine festen Richtungen mehr auf. Niemand wird heute im Ernst mehr solche Einsichten bestreiten wollen. Eine örtlich verstandene Dreistöckigkeit der Welt gibt es nicht mehr. Aber ist sie denn eigentlich gemeint gewesen den Glaubensaussagen von Höllenabstieg und Himmelfahrt des Herrn?"

[756] *Einführung in das Christentum*, p. 247 (second edition) — «Vielleicht kein Glaubensartikel steht unserem heutigen Bewusstsein so fern wie dieser. Neben dem Bekenntnis zur Geburt Jesu aus der Jungfrau Maria und demjenigen zur Himmelfahrt des Herrn reizt er am meisten zur »Entmythologisierung«, die man hier gefahrlos und ohne Ärgernis scheint vollziehen zu können.»

hell does not actually refer to an outer depth of the cosmos…" So then, what does it refer to? He answers:

> In the basic text, the prayer of the crucified to the God who has forsaken him, there is no cosmic allusion. Rather, our sentence directs our gaze to the depths of human existence, which reaches into the ground of death, into the zone of untouchable loneliness and denied love, and thus encloses the dimension of hell, it carries within itself as a possibility of itself. Hell, existing in the ultimate denial of "being-for," is not a cosmographic determinacy, but a dimension of human nature, its abyss into which it reaches. Today more than ever we know that everyone's existence touches this depth; Since humanity is in the end "one human being", this depth does not only concern the individual, but affects the one body of the human race as a whole, which therefore has to carry this depth as a whole. From here it is to be understood once again that Christ, the "new Adam", undertook to carry this depth and did not want to remain separated from it in sublime untouchedness; on the other hand, of course, it is only now that total refusal in its full depth has become possible.[757]

In his *Einführung in das Christentum*, Ratzinger devotes an entire section to Christ's "Descent into hell" (*»**Abgestiegen zu der Hölle**«*);

---

[757] *Einführung in das Christentum*, pp. 265-6 (second edition) — «In dem grundlegenden Text, dem Gebet des Gekreuzigten zu dem Gott, der ihn verlassen hat, fehlt jede kosmische Anspielung. Unser Satz lenkt unseren Blick vielmehr hin auf die Tiefe der menschlichen Existenz, die in den Todesgrund, in die Zone der unberührbaren Einsamkeit und der verweigerten Liebe hinabreicht und damit die Dimension der Hölle umschließt, sie als Möglichkeit ihrer selbst in sich trägt. Hölle, Existieren in der endgültigen Verweigerung des »Seins-für«, ist nicht eine kosmographische Bestimmtheit, sondern eine Dimension der menschlichen Natur, ihr Abgrund, in den sie hinunterreicht. Mehr denn je wissen wir heute, dass eines jeden Existenz diese Tiefe berührt; da die Menschheit im Letzten *»ein* Mensch« ist, geht diese Tiefe freilich nicht nur den Einzelnen an, sondern betrifft den einen Körper des Menschengeschlechtes insgesamt, das diese Tiefe daher als Ganzes mitaustragen muss. Von hier aus ist noch einmal zu verstehen, dass Christus, der »neue Adam«, diese Tiefe mitzutragen unternommen hat und nicht in erhabener Unberührtheit von ihr getrennt bleiben wollte; umgekehrt ist freilich jetzt erst die totale Verweigerung in ihrer vollen Abgründigkeit Möglich geworden.»

and it is there that he gives his own interpretation of what this article of faith means, beginning with its profession in the liturgy:

> On Good Friday, the crucified Christ remains, but Holy Saturday is the day of the "death of God", the day that expresses the unheard of experience of our time and anticipates that God is simply absent, that the grave covers him, that he no longer wakes up, no longer speaks, so that one no longer even has to deny it, but can simply ignore it. "God is dead and we killed him". This word of Nietzsche belongs linguistically to the tradition of Christian passion piety; it expresses the content of Holy Saturday, the "descent to hell". [758]

Then by reductive interpretation Ratzinger explains away the content of the article of faith to mean only that Jesus died:

> Let us try one more consideration in order to penetrate this multi-layered mystery that cannot be clarified from one side alone. Let us first take note of an exegetical statement. We are told that in our Article of Faith the word "hell" is just a wrong translation for Sheol (Greek: Hades), which the Hebrew uses to describe the state beyond death, which is very vaguely defined as a kind of shadowy existence, thought of more as non-being than being. **Accordingly, the sentence originally only meant that Jesus entered Sheol, that is, that he died.**[759]

---

[758] *Einführung in das Christentum*, (second edition) p. 248 — "Am Karfreitag bleibt immerhin der Blick auf den Gekreuzigten, Karsamstag aber ist der Tag des »Todes Gottes«, der Tag, der die unerhörte Erfahrung unserer Zeit ausdrückt und vorwegnimmt, dass Gott einfach abwesend ist, dass das Grab ihn deckt, dass er nicht mehr aufwacht, nicht mehr spricht, sodass man nicht einmal mehr ihn zu bestreiten braucht, sondern ihn einfach übergehen kann. »Gott ist tot, und wir haben ihn getötet«. Dieses Wort Nietzsches gehört sprachlich der Tradition der christlichen Passionsfrömmigkeit zu; es drückt den Gehalt des Karsamstags aus, das »Abgestiegen zu der Hölle« a."

[759] *Einführung in das Christentum*, (second edition) p. 251 — "Versuchen wir noch eine weitere Überlegung, um in dieses vielschichtige Geheimnis einzudringen, dass von einer Seite allein her nicht aufzuhellen ist. Nehmen wir dabei zunächst noch einmal eine exegetische Feststellung zur Kenntnis. Man sagt uns, dass in unserem Glaubensartikel das Wort »Hölle« nur eine falsche Übersetzung für Scheol (griechisch: Hades) sei, womit der Hebräer den Zustand jenseits des Todes bezeichnet, den man sich sehr undeutlich

Ratzinger interprets the descent into hell in terms that reduce it not merely to the physical experience of death, but to the psychological experience of the connection between the sacrificial death and pain (*in welcher Weise eigentlich Opfer (also Anbetung) und Schmerz zusammenhängen*) which Christ experienced in his death on the cross. This point is elucidated by what is stated in two passages of the previous section:

> The event on the cross is therefore the bread of life "for the many" (Lk 22:19), because the crucified one melted the body of humanity into the yes of adoration. It is therefore completely "anthropocentric", completely human-related, because it was radical theocentrism, the surrender of the ego, and therein the human being, to God. In so far as this exodus of love is the ecstasy of man out of himself, in which he is stretched infinitely beyond himself, as it were torn apart, far beyond his apparently possible extension possibilities, in this respect adoration (sacrifice) is always at the same time the cross, the pain of being torn apart, dying of the grain of wheat, which can only come to fruition in death. But at the same time it is clear that this element of the painful is the secondary, which results from a preceding primary and only has its meaning from it. The constitutive principle of sacrifice is not destruction but love. And only insofar as it breaks up, opens, crucifies, tears, does this also belong to the sacrifice: as the form of love in a world marked by death and selfishness.[760]

---

als eine Art von Schattendasein, mehr Nichtsein als Sein, vorstellte. Demnach hätte der Satz ursprünglich nur bedeutet, dass Jesus in die Scheol eingetreten, das heißt, dass er gestorben ist."

[760] *Einführung in das Christentum*, (second edition) p. 243 — "Das Kreuzesgeschehen ist deshalb Brot des Lebens »für die Vielen« (Lk 22,19), weil der Gekreuzigte den Leib der Menschheit ins Ja der Anbetung umgeschmolzen hat. Es ist deshalb ganz »anthropozentrisch«, ganz menschbezogen, weil es radikale Theozentrik, Auslieferung des Ich und darin des Wesens Mensch an Gott war. Insofern nun dieser Exodus der Liebe die Ekstase des Menschen aus sich selbst heraus ist, in der er unendlich über sich hinausgespannt, gleichsam auseinander gerissen wird, weit über seine scheinbar Möglichen Ausstreckungsmöglichkeiten hinaus, *insofern* ist Anbetung (Opfer) immer zugleich Kreuz, Schmerz des Zerrissenwerdens, Sterben des Weizenkorns, das nur im Tod zur Frucht kommen kann. Aber damit ist zugleich deutlich, dass dies Element des Schmerzhaften das Sekundäre ist, das sich aus einem vorausgehenden

He who carried this separation within himself in order to cancel it out, but who only canceled it because he had it inside him earlier: he reaches from one end to the other. Without leaving the lap of the Trinity, it reaches to the extreme limit of human misery and fills all the space in between. This stretching out of Christ, which the four directions of the cross form meaningful, is the mysterious expression of our own disunity and makes us conform to him «a. The pain is the ultimate result and expression of Jesus Christ's tension from being in God to hell of "My God, why have you forsaken me?". Anyone who has stretched his existence so that he is at the same time immersed in God and immersed in the depths of the godforsaken creature must, as it were, tear apart — he is really "crucified". But this being torn apart is identical with love: it is its realization down to the last (Jo 13,1) and the concrete expression for the vastness that it creates.[761]

Thus, for Ratzinger, the "descent into hell" signifies the psychological trauma of the ultimate loneliness which Christ experienced in his sacrificial death, an experience which in some

---

Primären ergibt und nur von ihm her seinen Sinn hat. Das konstitutive Prinzip des Opfers ist nicht die Zerstörung, sondern die Liebe. Und nur insofern sie aufbricht, öffnet, kreuzigt, zerreißt, gehört auch dieses mit zum Opfer: als die Form der Liebe in einer vom Tod und von der Selbstsucht gezeichneten Welt."

[761] *Einführung in das Christentum*, (second edition) p. 244 — "Er, der diese Trennung in sich getragen hat, um sie in sich aufzuheben, der sie aber nur aufgehoben hat, weil er sie vorhin in sich trug: Er reicht von einem Ende bis zum andern. Ohne den Schoß der Dreifaltigkeit zu verlassen, streckt er sich bis zur äußersten Grenze menschlichen Elends aus und erfüllt den ganzen Zwischenraum. Dieses Sichausspannen Christi, das die vier Richtungen des Kreuzes sinnbilden, ist der geheimnisvolle Ausdruck unserer eigenen Zerrissenheit und macht uns ihm gleichförmig«a. Der Schmerz ist im letzten Ergebnis und Ausdruck des Ausgespanntseins Jesu Christi vom Sein in Gott bis in die Hölle des »Mein Gott, warum hast du mich verlassen? «. Wer seine Existenz so ausgestreckt hat, dass er gleichzeitig in Gott eingetaucht ist und eingetaucht in die Tiefe des gottverlassenen Geschöpfes, der muss gleichsam auseinanderreißen - der ist wirklich »gekreuzigt«. Aber dieses Zerrissenwerden ist identisch mit der Liebe: Es ist ihre Verwirklichung bis ins Letzte (Jo l3,1) und der konkrete Ausdruck für die Weite, die sie schafft."

lesser degree is common to all men, and expressed in the verse of Hermann Hesse which he quotes:

> Seltsam, im Nebel zu wandern!
> Leben ist Einsamsein.
> Kein Mensch kennt den andern,
> Jeder ist allein!

In relation to Christ's sacrificial death, it was even better expressed by the words of Chesterton,

> «It is written, "Thou shalt not tempt the Lord thy God." No; but the Lord thy God may tempt Himself; and it seems as if this was what happened in Gethsemane. In a garden Satan tempted man: and in a garden God tempted God. He passed in some superhuman manner through our human horror of pessimism. When the world shook and the sun was wiped out of heaven, it was not at the crucifixion, but at the cry from the cross: the cry which confessed that God was forsaken of God.»[762]

Ratzinger sums up this thought saying, "All fear in the world is ultimately the fear of this loneliness. From there it can be understood why the Old Testament only has *one* word for hell *and* death, the word Sheol: it regards them ultimately as identical." With these words we arrive at Ratzinger's understanding of the article of faith, *He descended into Hell:* **"Accordingly, the sentence originally only meant that Jesus entered Sheol, that is, that he died."** However, the content of the article of faith, "He descended into hell," is something different, and very precise. The Fourth Lateran Council solemnly professed that Christ descended into hell, and precisely, that *He suffered on the wood of the cross, died, descended into the netherworld, rose from the dead, and ascended into heaven.* **But He descended in soul and rose in the flesh and ascended equally in both** [*in ligno crucis passus et mortuus descendit ad inferos resurrexit a mortuis et ascendit in cœlum.* **Sed descendit in anima resurrexit in carne ascenditque pariter in utroque**]. Thus it was his *soul* that descended to hell *(descendit in anima)*. The *Roman Catechism* explains that:

---

[762] *Orthodoxy* (1908).

In the first part of the article [*Descendit ad inferos*] we are proposed to believe that, after the death of Jesus Christ, his soul descended into hell and remained there as long as the body remained in the sepulchre. With these words we recognize that, at that time, the very person of Jesus Christ was in hell and lay in the tomb, which is not surprising. In fact, as we have often repeated, although the soul had left the body, nevertheless the divinity never separated from the soul or from the body.[763]

The meaning of the article, *He descended into Hell*, does not mean that Christ died or that He was buried, because those things have already been professed in the previous article. The Roman Catechism explains «what is meant here by the term "hell"»:

> ... first of all that it does not mean the "sepulchre", as some, no less impiously than ignorantly, interpreted. In fact, we already learned from the previous article that Jesus Christ our Lord was buried; there was no reason why the Apostles, in drawing up the rule of faith, would repeat the same concept, with a more obscure manner of speech. Here the word in question means those hidden places where the souls of those who have not attained celestial beatitude are. Sacred Scripture offers many examples of this use. In St Paul we read: "In the name of Jesus, let every knee bend, in heaven, on earth, in hell" (Phil 2:10)...[764]

---

[763] *Catechismus Romanus ex decreto concilii tridentini* — Eius igitur priori parte hoc nobis credendum proponitur: Christo iam mortuo, eius animam ad inferos descendisse, ibique tamdiu mansisse, quamdiu eiusdem corpus in sepulcro fuit. His autem verbis simul etiam confitemur eandem Christi personam eo tempore et apud inferos fuisse et in sepulcro iacuisse. Quod quidem cum dicimus, nemini mirum videri debet, propterea quod, ut saepe iam docuimus, quamvis anima a corpore discesserit, numquam tamen divinitas vel ab anima vel a corpore separata est.»

[764] *Catechismus Romanus ex decreto concilii tridentini* — «Sed quoniam articuli explanationi plurimum lucis afferre potest, si parochus prius doceat quid hoc loco inferorum vocabulo intelligendum sit, monere oportet inferos hoc loco pro sepulcro non accipi, ut quidam non minus impie quam imperite putaverunt. Superiori enim articulo Christum Dominum sepultum esse edocti sumus; nec ulla causa erat cur in fide tradenda alio, et quidem obscuriori loquendi genere, idem a sanctis apostolis repeteretur. Verum inferorum nomen abdita illa receptacula significat, in quibus animae detinentur quae caelestem beatitudinem non sunt consecutae. Ita vero sacrae litterae hanc vocem multis in locis usurparunt; nam apud Apostolum

The following paragraph explains precisely and in detail the exact meaning of this dogma:

> These places are not all of the same kind. One is that dark and horrible prison, in which the souls of the damned lie in a perpetual and inextinguishable fire, together with the unclean spirits, which is also called Gehenna, abyss, and in its proper meaning is called hell. Secondly, there is the place of the purgative fire, in which, for a certain time, the pious souls undergo the pains of atonement, so that they can ascend to the eternal homeland, into which nothing polluted will enter. Indeed, the parish priest will insist with renewed diligence on the truth of this doctrine, which the holy councils declare contained in Scripture as in the apostolic tradition, since we live in times in which men do not maintain sound doctrine. Finally, a third place is where the souls of the saints were received before the coming of Jesus Christ our Lord. They enjoyed a quiet residence, without any sense of pain, sustained by the beatific hope of redemption. Jesus Christ descending into hell freed the pious souls, who were waiting for the Saviour in the bosom of Abraham. Nor is it to be supposed that he descended there in such a manner that only his force and power arrived there, but not his soul. But it is entirely to be believed that his soul descended in reality and in presence into hell. We have David's explicit testimony in this regard: "You will not leave my soul in hell" (Ps 15.10).[765]

---

legimus in nomine Iesu omne genu flecti caelestium, terrestrium et infernorum [1] ([1]Flp 2); et in Actis apostolorum divus Petrus testatur Christum Dominum suscitatum, solutis doloribus inferni[2]. ([2]He 2)»

[765] *Catechismus Romanus ex decreto concilii tridentini* — «Neque tamen ea receptacula unius et eiusdem generis sunt omnia. Est enim teterrimus et obscurissimus carcer, ubi perpetuo et inextinguibili igne damnatorum animae simul cum immundis spiritibus torquentur, qui etiam gehenna, abyssus, et propria significatione infernus vocatur. Praeterea est purgatories ignis, quo piorum animae ad definitum tempus cruciatae expiantur, ut eis in aeternam patriam ingressus patere possit, in quam nihil coinquinatum ingreditur[3]. [[3]Ap 21] Ac de huius quidem doctrinae veritate, quam et scripturarum testimoniis et apostolica traditione confirmatam esse sancta concilia declarant, eo diligentius et saepius parocho disserendum erit, quod in ea tempora incidimus quibus homines sanam doctrinam non sustinent. Tertium postremo receptaculi genus est, in quo animae sanctorum ante Christi Domini adventum excipiebantur, ibique sine ullo doloris sensu, beata redemptionis spe sustentati, quieta habitatione fruebantur. Horum

Ratzinger's misinterpretation of the article, (an interpretation that dates back to Nikolaus von Kues a.k.a. Nicolaus Cusanus) hinges on an erroneous understanding of the Hebrew word **Sheol** (שְׁאוֹל): "All fear in the world is ultimately the fear of this loneliness. From there it can be understood why the Old Testament only has one word for hell and death, the word Sheol: it regards them ultimately as identical."[766] While there is indeed some overlapping of meaning between death and hell in the word שְׁאוֹל, it is quite false to say that the Old Testament has only one word for both. In reality there are two different words for "death" and "hell". Thus, "death" in Hebrew: (biblical) מָוֶת [maveth] from the root: מוּת (H4191)]; (modern) מוות [mowet]; and **Sheol** — "hell" (the place of the dead) = שְׁאוֹל [she'ol] The **abode of the dead** is the primary meaning, from which several other meanings are derived. Concerning the word for "death" i.e. *maveth*, (as opposed to *sheol*), one reads in the **Blue Letter Bible**:[767]

> Strong's Number H4194 matches the Hebrew מָוֶת (maveth), which occurs 160 times in 155 verses in the Hebrew concordance of the KJV; The KJV translates Strong's H4194 in the following manner: death (128x), die (22x), dead (8x), deadly (1x), slay (1x).
> Genesis 25:11 — And it came to pass after the death H4194 of Abraham, that God blessed his son Isaac; and Isaac dwelt by the well Lahairoi.
> Judges 16:30 — So the dead which he slew at his death H4194 were more than *they* which he slew in his life.
> Death, dying, Death (personified), realm of the dead:

---

igitur piorum animas qui in sinu Abrahae Salvatorem exspectabant, Christus Dominus ad inferos descendens liberavit. Nec vero existimandum est eum sic ad inferos descendisse, ut eius tantummodo vis ac virtus, non etiam anima, eo pervenerit. Sed omnino credendum est ipsam animam re et praesentia ad inferos descendisse, de quo exstat firmissimum illud Davidis testimonium: *Non derelinques animam meam in inferno*⁴. [⁴Sal 15]»

[766] *Einführung in das Christentum*, (second edition) p. 254 — «Alle Furcht der Welt ist im Letzten die Furcht dieser Einsamkeit. Von da aus ist es zu verstehen, weshalb das Alte Testament nur *ein* Wort für Hölle *und* Tod hat, das Wort Scheol: Beides ist ihm letztlich identisch.»

[767] https://www.blueletterbible.org/lang/lexicon/lexicon.cfm?t=kjv&strongs=h4194.

A. death
B. death by violence (as a penalty)
C. state of death, place of death

Thus, Joseph Ratzinger's erroneous understanding of the meaning of the word *Sheol* perfectly illustrates the point made by St. Thomas in *De Ente et Essentia*, namely, that "a small error in the beginning is great in the end" (*parvus error in principio magnus est in fine*) — because Ratzinger, who always bases his theological opinions in some manner on Scripture, begins with an exegetical error based on an erroneous interpretation of a single Hebrew word, and from that small error in the beginning he arrives at the great error of heretically misinterpreting an article of faith to mean something entirely different than what the article actually professes. Pope Benedict is not a formal heretic. He has always been of an obedient disposition towards the authority of the doctrinal magisterium of the Church. The observation of Ratzinger's former professor and lifelong friend, Alfred **Läpple**, is mentioned in Seewald's biography of Pope Benedict: «**Ratzinger has "always quoted the scriptures and always drawn the bow to the problems and challenges of the present," observed Läpple. "For him there is no good exegesis of a scripture unless one proceeds from the interpretation given by the Church through the Fathers. For him that is *Traditio vivens*, living tradition."**»[768] However, it must also be noted, as Seewald relates, «**Ratzinger took over impartial access to current topics from his master [Söhngen]; the new beginnings shaped by the liturgical movement; the historical-critical examination of tradition; sympathy for the "Nouvelle Théologie"; the ecumenical impulses; the passion for the clear formulation of one's own, albeit different, thinking as a prerequisite for a real

---

[768] Seewald, Peter. *Benedikt XVI.: Ein Leben* (German Edition). Droemer eBook. Kindle Edition — "**Ratzinger habe »immer die Schrift zitiert und stets den Bogen zu den Problemen und Herausforderungen der Gegenwart gespannt«, beobachtete Läpple. »Für ihn gibt es keine gute Exegese eines Schriftwortes, wenn man nicht von der Auslegung ausgeht, die die Kirche durch die Väter davon gegeben hat. Das ist für ihn *Traditio vivens*, lebendige Überlieferung.« **"

dialogue.»[769] It is precisely the influence of the **Nouvelle Théologie** on Ratzinger's own theology that has led him into the material heresy of re-interpreting several articles of the Creed according to a sense which conveys a different meaning than that which has been the meaning of those articles as they have been understood universally and perpetually throughout the past ages by both the hierarchy and faithful in general. The specific examples I have provided here should suffice for this work insofar as they illustrate how Ratzinger has errantly applied the principles of the **Nouvelle Théologie** in his explication of several of the articles of faith in the Creed, without however intending to deviate from the authoritative tradition of the Church.

There can also be seen in Ratzinger's thinking the influence of the *nouvelle théologie* in its blurring of the distinction between nature and grace so prominent in the theology of Henri de Lubac. In some respects it seems to have clearly rubbed off onto Ratzinger's own thinking. In his article, *From Theologian to Pope,* **Francis Schüssler Fiorenza**, (Stillman Professor of Roman Catholic Theological Studies at Harvard Divinity School), explains briefly why, "One can best understand Ratzinger by locating him within the movement known as la *nouvelle théologie* ".[770] Fiorenza rightly points out that "this movement emphasized the integration of nature and grace," — an integration which earned for de Lubac a condemnation of his doctrine in Pius XII's *Humani Generis.* The tendency of that movement was to confuse the distinction between the operation of supernatural principles on nature and the natural operation of principles contained within nature in the blur of what Teilhard de Chardin would call an evolutionary "complexification". In the above cited article, *La nouvelle théologie, où va-t-elle?*, by Reginald Garrigou-Lagrange O.P. one reads on the blurring of that distinction, «On this

---

[769] *Ibid.* — "**Zusammenfassend übernahm Ratzinger von seinem Meister den unbefangenen Zugang zu aktuellen Themen; die von der liturgischen Bewegung geprägten Neuansätze; die historisch-kritische Untersuchung der Überlieferung; die Sympathie für die »Nouvelle Théologie«; die ökumenischen Impulse; die Leidenschaft für die klare Formulierung des eigenen, wenn auch abweichenden Denkens als Voraussetzung eines echten Dialogs.**"

[770] From Theologian to Pope | Harvard Divinity Bulletin Archive

subject in the recent book by Father H. de Lubac, *Surnaturel* (Études historique), 1946, p. 264 [...] we read: "Nothing in St. Thomas announces the distinction that a certain number of Thomist theologians would later forge, between "God author of the natural order", and "God author of the supernatural order,"»[771] and he replies, "On the contrary, Saint Thomas often distinguishes the supernatural ultimate end from the natural ultimate end."[772]

He then elaborates:

> Moreover, Fr. Gaston Fessard S. J. in The November 1945 Studies, p. 269-270, speaks of the "blessed drowsiness protected by canonized Thomism, but also, as Peguy said," buried, "while living thoughts doomed, in his name, to contradiction." In the same review in April 1946, it is said that neo-Thomism and the decisions of the Bible Commission are "a guardrail, but not an answer." And what is proposed instead of Thomism, as if Leo XIII in the encyclical Aeterni Patris had been wrong, as if Pius X in the encyclical Pascendi, in renewing this same recommendation, had gone astray? And where will this new theology go with the new masters it draws inspiration from? Where else does she go in the path of skepticism, fantasy, and heresy? His Holiness Pius XII recently said in a speech published by the Osservatore Romano of

---

[771] "A ce sujet dans le livre récent du P. H. de Lubac, *Surnaturel* (Études historiques), 1946, p. 264 [...] on lit: «Rien n'annonce chez saint Thomas la distinction que forgeront plus tard un certain nombre de théologiens thomistes, entre «Dieu auteur de l'ordre naturel», et «Dieu auteur de l'ordre surnaturel.»"

[772] "Cf. Ia, q. XXIII, a. 1: «*Finis* ad quem res creatae ordinantur a Deo est *duplex. Unus, qui excedit proportionem naturae creatae et facultatem*, et hic finis est vita aeterna, quae in divina visione consistit: quae est supra naturam cujuslibet creaturae, ut supra habitum est Ia, q. XII, a. 4. *Alius autem finis est naturae creatae proportionatus*, quem scil. res creata potest attingere sec. virtutem suae naturae». Item Ia IIae, q. LXII, a. 1: «Est autem *duplex hominis beatitudo*, sive felicitas, ut supra dictum est, q. III, a. 2 ad 4um; q. V, a. 5. Una quidem proportionata humanae naturae, ad quam scil. homo pervenire potest per principia suae naturae. Alia autem est beatitudo naturam hominis excedens. Item *De veritate*, q. XIV, a. 2: «*Est autem duplex hominis bonum ultimum*. Quorum unum est proportionatum naturae... haec est felicitas de qua philosophi locuti sunt... Aliud est bonum naturae humanae proportionem excedens.»"

September 19, 1946: "There is a good deal of talk but without the necessary clarity of concept about a "new theology" which must be in constant transformation, following the example of all other things in the world, which are in a constant state of flux and movement, without ever reaching their term. If we were to accept such an opinion, what would become of the unchangeable dogmas of the Catholic faith?" [...] Moreover, the incarnation of the Word, from this new point of view, would be a moment of universal evolution. The hypothesis of the material evolution of the world is extended to the spiritual order. The supernatural world is evolving towards the full advent of Christ. [...] We thus come to want to change not only the mode of exposition of theology, but the very nature of theology, much more that of dogma. This is no longer considered from the point of view of the faith infused in divine Revelation, interpreted by the Church in her Councils. There is no longer any question of the Councils, but we place ourselves here from the point of view of biology supplemented by the most fanciful rantings which recall those of Hegelian evolutionism, which retained only Christian dogmas in name.

In this we follow the rationalists, and we do what the enemies of the faith desire, we are reduced to ever-changing opinions which no longer have any value. What remains of the word of God given to the world for the salvation of souls?

In these sheets entitled How I Believe, we read, p. 15: "If we Christians want to preserve for Christ the qualities which are the basis of his power and our adoration, we have nothing better or even nothing else to do than to accept the most modern conceptions of Evolution to the end. Under the combined pressure of Science and Philosophy, the World increasingly imposes itself on our experience and our thinking as a linked system of activities gradually ascending to freedom and consciousness. The only satisfactory interpretation of this process is to regard it as irreversible and converging. In this way, a Universal Cosmic Center is defined in front of us, where everything ends, where everything is felt, where everything is controlled. Well, it is in this physical pole of the universal Evolution that it is necessary, in my opinion, to place and recognize the Fullness of Christ ... Evolution by discovering a summit in the world, makes Christ possible, just

like Christ by giving meaning to the World, makes Evolution possible. [773]

---

[773] Reginald Garrigou-Lagrange O.P., *La nouvelle théologie, où va-t-elle?* — "Bien plus, le P. Gaston Fessard S. J. dans *Les Études* de novembre 1945, p. 269-270, parle du «bienheureux assoupissement que protège le thomisme canonisé, mais aussi, comme disait Péguy, «enterré», tandis que vivent les pensées vouées, en son nom, à la contradiction».

Dans la même revue en avril 1946, il est dit que le néo-thomisme et les décisions de la Commission biblique sont «un garde-fou, mais non pas une réponse». Et que propose-t-on à la place du thomisme, comme si Léon XIII dans l'encyclique *Aeterni Patris* s'était trompé, comme si Pie X dans l'encyclique *Pascendi*, en renouvelant cette même recommandation, avait fait fausse route?

Et où va-t-elle aller cette théologie nouvelle avec les maitres nouveaux dont elle s'inspire? Où va-t-elle si non dans la voie du scepticisme, de la fantaisie et de l'hérésie? Sa Sainteté Pie XII disait récemment dans un discours publié par *l'Osservatore romano* du 19 septembre 1946: «Plura dicta sunt, at non satis explorata ratione, «de nova theologia» quae cum universis semper volventibus rebus, una volsemper itura, numquam perventura. Si talis opinio amplectenda esse videatur, *quid fiet de numquam immutandis catholicis dogmatibus, quid de fidei, unitate et stabilitate?*» […] De plus l'incarnation du Verbe, de ce nouveau point de vue, serait un moment de l'évolution universelle. L'hypothèse dé l'évolution matérielle du monde est étendue à l'ordre spirituel. Le monde surnaturel est en évolution vers l'avènement plénier du Christ. […] On en vient ainsi à vouloir changer non seulement le mode d'exposition de la théologie, mais *la nature même de la théologie*, bien plus celle du dogme. Celui-ci n'est plus considéré du point de vue de la foi infuse à la Révélation divine, interprétée par l'Église dans ses Conciles. Il n'est plus question des Conciles, mais on se place ici au point de vue de la *biologie* complétée par des élucubrations des plus fantaisistes qui rappellent celles de l'évolutionnisme hégélien, lequel ne conservait plus des dogmes chrétiens que le nom. En cela on suit les rationalistes, et l'on fait ce que les ennemis de la foi désirent, on là réduit à des opinions toujours changeantes qui n'ont plus aucune valeur. Que reste-t-il de la parole de Dieu donnée au monde pour le salut des âmes?

Dans ces feuilles intitulées *Comment je crois*, on lit, p. 15: «Si nous voulons, nous autres chrétiens, conserver au Christ les qualités qui fondent son puvoir et notre adoration, nous n'avons rien de meilleur ou mêmhe rien d'autre à faire que d'accepter jusqu'au bout les conceptions les plus modernes de l'Évolution. Sous la pression combinée de la Science et de la Philosophie, le Monde s'impose de plus en plus à notre expérience et à notre

Do we not see some tendency towards the same vein of thinking in Ratzinger where he says in the section, *Christ* «the last man» [*3. Christus, »der letzte Mensch«*]:

> When Jesus is called "Adam", this means that he is destined to gather the whole being "Adam" into himself. But this means: that reality which Paul calls "body of Christ", today largely incomprehensible to us, is an inner requirement of this existence, which must not remain an exception, but must "attract" all of humanity (cf. Jn 12, 32). It must be seen as a significant achievement of Teilhard de Chardin that he rethought these relationships from today's view of the world and, despite a not entirely harmless tendency towards biology, he understood them as a whole correctly and in any case made them accessible anew. Let's hear him ourselves! The human monad "can only become fully itself when it ceases to be alone" a. In the background one can hear the thought that in addition to the two orders of the infinitely small and the infinitely large there is a third order in the cosmos that determines the actual drift of evolution: the order of the infinitely complex. It is the actual goal of the ascending process of becoming; it reaches a first climax in the emergence of life, and then progresses further and further to those highly complex structures that give the cosmos a new centre: "As tiny and coincidental as the place that the planets occupy in the history of the star bodies is, so in the end they are the life points of the universe. The axis now runs through it, and from now on the striving for an evolution directed mainly towards the production of large molecules concentrates on it «b. Looking at the world according to the dynamic standard of complexity means «a complete reversal of values. A twist on the perspective.»[774]

---

pensée comme un système lié d'activités s'élevant graduellement vers la liberté et la conscience. La seule interprétation satisfaisante de ce processus est de le regarder comme irréversible et convergent. Ainsi se définit en avant de nous un *Centre cosmique Universel* où tout aboutit, où tout se sent, où tout se commande. Eh bien, c'est en ce pôle physique de l'universelle Évolution qu'il est nécessaire, à mon avis, de placer et de reconnaître *la Plénitude du Christ*... L'Évolution en découvrant un sommet au monde, rend le Christ possible, tout comme le Christ en donnant un sens au Monde, rend possible l'Évolution."

[774] *Einführung in das Christentum*, p. 193 (second edition) — "Wenn nun Jesus »Adam« genannt wird, sagt dies, dass er bestimmt ist, das ganze Wesen »Adam« in sich zu versammeln. Das aber bedeutet: Jene Realität, die Paulus, heute weithin für uns unverständlich, »Leib Christi« nennt, ist eine innere

Then in this context he quotes Teilhard again explaining how man represents an element in relation to some "new and higher synthesis" in this "complexification" from the top:

> I think there is a very central point here; At this point, the dynamic worldview destroys the positivistic idea that is so close to all of us, which sees the permanent only in the "mass", in the hard material. The fact that the world is ultimately constructed and held "from above" becomes visible here in a way that is so impressive - because we are so little used to it. From there access to another text opens up, in order to at least indicate Teilhard's overall view by merging a few fragments. "The universal energy must be a thinking energy, if it is not to be less advanced in development than the goals that are inspired by its effect. And consequently ... the cosmic value attributes with which it surrounds itself in our modern eyes in no way negates the need for us to recognize it as a transcendent form of personality «c. From there, the target point of the whole movement can also be understood as Teilhard sees it: The

---

Forderung dieser Existenz, die nicht Ausnahme bleiben darf, sondern die ganze Menschheit »an sich ziehen« muss (vgl. Jo 12,32). Es muss als ein bedeutendes Verdienst von Teilhard de Chardin gewertet werden, dass er diese Zusammenhänge vom heutigen Weltbild her neu gedacht und trotz einer nicht ganz unbedenklichen Tendenz aufs Biologistische hin sie im Ganzen doch wohl richtig begriffen und auf jeden Fall neu zugänglich gemacht hat. Hören wir ihn selbst! Die menschliche Monade »kann nur ganz sie selbst werden, wenn sie aufhört, allein zu sein«a. Im Hintergrund ist dabei der Gedanke mitzuhören, dass es im Kosmos neben den beiden Ordnungen des unendlich Kleinen und des unendlich Großen eine dritte Ordnung gibt, die die eigentliche Drift der Evolution bestimmt: die Ordnung des unendlich Komplexen. Sie ist das eigentliche Ziel des aufsteigenden Werdeprozesses; sie erreicht einen ersten Höhepunkt in der Entstehung des Lebendigen, um dann immer weiter voranzuschreiten zu jenen hochkomplexen Gebilden, die dem Kosmos eine neue Mitte geben: »So winzig und zufällig der Platz auch ist, den die Planeten in der Geschichte der Sternkörper einnehmen, so bilden sie letzten Endes doch die Lebenspunkte des Universums. Durch sie läuft jetzt die Achse, auf sie konzentriert sich von nun an das Streben einer hauptsächlich auf die Erzeugung von großen Molekülen gerichteten Evolution«b. Die Betrachtung der Welt nach dem dynamischen Maßstab der Komplexität bedeutet so »eine völlige Umkehrung der Werte. Eine Wendung der Perspektive«."

cosmic drift is moving "in the direction of an unbelievable, quasi "monomolecular" state ... where every ego ... is destined to culminate in some mysterious super-ego «d. Man is an end as an ego, but the direction of the movement of being and his own existence shows him at the same time as a structure that belongs to a "super-ego" that does not extinguish him, but embraces him; only in such a union can the form of the future human appear in which human existence will be entirely at its own goal.[775]

Thus it does not suffice for someone to point to one of Ratzinger's propositions and declare it immediately to be heretical, and on that basis judge him to be a formal heretic incapable of holding office, as the Sedevacantists chronically do. If I may borrow an expression from St. Thomas, on some points the Ratzinger theology is not always so much incorrect as it is insufficient; while on other points his doctrines

---

[775] *Einführung in das Christentum*, p. 195 (second edition) — «Ich glaube, dass man hier vor einer sehr zentralen Aussage steht; das dynamische Weltbild zerstört an dieser Stelle die uns allen so nahe liegende positivistische Vorstellung, die das Beständige allein in der »Masse«, im harten Stoff sieht. Dass die Welt schließlich doch »von oben« her konstruiert und gehalten ist, wird hier auf eine Weise sichtbar, die deswegen so eindrücklich ist, - weil wir sie so wenig gewöhnt sind. Von da aus eröffnet sich der Zugang zu einem weiteren Text, um hier wenigstens durch das Zusammenlegen von ein paar Fragmenten die Gesamtsicht Teilhards anzudeuten. »Die universal Energie muss eine denkende Energie sein, soll sie nicht in der Entwicklung weniger weit sein als die Ziele, die von ihrer Wirkung beseelt werden. Und folglich ... heben die kosmischen Wertattribute, mit denen sie sich in unseren modernen Augen umgibt, keineswegs die Notwendigkeit auf, dass wir ihr eine transzendente Form von Persönlichkeit zuerkennen«c. Von da aus kann nun auch der Zielpunkt der ganzen Bewegung verstanden werden, wie Teilhard ihn sieht: Die kosmische Drift bewegt sich »in Richtung auf einen unglaublichen, quasi >monomolekularen< Zustand ..., wo jedes Ego ... dazu bestimmt ist, seinen Höhepunkt in irgendeinem geheimnisvollen Super-Ego zu erreichen«d. Der Mensch ist als ein Ich zwar ein Ende, aber die Richtung der Seinsbewegung und seiner eigenen Existenz erweist ihn zugleich als ein Gebilde, das in ein »Über-Ich« hineingehört, welches ihn nicht auslöscht, aber umgreift; erst in solcher Vereinigung kann die Form des zukünftigen Menschen erscheinen, in der das Menschsein ganz am Ziel seiner selbst sein wird.»

are sometimes materially heretical due only to an incorrect understanding of some primary concepts of the unchangeable dogmas — but not contumacious rejection of the revealed truths themselves. Therefore, if one is to hurl the accusation of heresy at a theologian, the proposition in question must first be shown to properly and literally fall indubitably within the defining parameters of the *indicia* of formal heresy — and not merely be materially heretical, or be interpreted as asserting heresy, merely because it seems to imply heresy without asserting heresy directly and explicitly. It is this kind of defective argumentation that most characterizes the claims that Benedict XVI is a heretic. The root of this kind of error is the failure to strictly qualify the allegedly heretical propositions according to the *indicia* of heresy established by the canonical tradition and jurisprudence of the Roman Church. Secondly, in the absence of clear and indisputable *indicia* of formal heresy, it is absolutely necessary to follow the procedures laid down by the Church's canonical tradition in order to establish not only the fact of objective doctrinal heresy, but then also it is necessary to establish the fact of subjective *pertinacity* in heresy. One cannot simply point to a proposition that seems to say something heretical, and then uncritically declare it heretical, and then judge that there is pertinacity on the basis of a mere presumption in law of *dolus*. Even when there is the matter of heresy already evident, penal law presumes guilt, **but the *presumption* of guilt does not juridically establish the FACT of *public defection from the Catholic faith and the consequent ipso jure loss of office***. Only the evident fact of public defection into formal heresy suffices to establish that the office has been lost *ipso jure*. One cannot simply declare someone a pertinacious heretic on private authority, on the basis of the mere uncritical assumption that a materially heretical proposition (or as the case may be, a seemingly heretical proposition) establishes the fact of pertinacity on the mere basis of the canonical presumption of guilt in penal law. When there is not evident the manifest *indicia of formal heresy*, i.e. both the public, plainly visible, and *evident fact* of objective heresy together with the evident *dolus* of heresy as well; then, on the sole basis of those propositions which constitute the *matter of heresy*, but in the absence of the evidence of *dolus,* which would properly qualify the body of evidence as *indicia* of formal heresy, there would only be *indicia* of

suspicion; and accordingly, there would exist only a *legal presumption of guilt* founded on suspicion, so that defection from the faith could not be immediately judged to be an evident *fact*, but only suspected; and therefore, defection could only be judged a certain fact if and when a *judicial sentence* will have been declared after the prescribed penal process has been completed. That one can privately judge defection into formal heresy to have occurred solely on the basis of the canonical presumption of guilt established only by the matter of heresy, with neither evident *dolus* nor adjudication of the case in a penal process, is the common misconception of all those who misinterpret canon law on this point, and in this manner conclude that you must judge Ratzinger as well as all his Conciliar predecessors guilty of formal heresy if you say that Bergoglio is guilty of formal heresy. The root of this error, as I have explained, is twofold: 1) the failure to distinguish between the clear-cut and manifestly evident *indicia* of formal heresy that exist against Bergoglio but not against Ratzinger, and the lesser degree of *indicia* which are alleged against Ratzinger, but which only qualify as *indicia* of suspicion; and, 2) the failure to grasp that even the founded legal presumption of guilt based on the evident *matter* of heresy which qualifies only as an *indicium* of suspicion, does not establish the *fact* of pertinacity and defection from the faith into formal heresy. Only the plainly evident matter **and** *dolus* of heresy, which manifest the evident *fact* of pertinacity and defection into formal heresy, suffice to fulfil the statutory requirement needed for the *ipso jure* provision on automatic loss of office due to defection from the Catholic faith to take effect. *Indicia* which establish the presumption of guilt are only *indicia* of suspicion, but are not *indicia* of **formal heresy**, which alone suffice to establish the fact of defection from the faith. Since in the absence of what the Church's canonical tradition considers to be certain *indicia* of formal heresy, the burden of proof is not on me to prove Pope Benedict innocent, but is on them who accuse Pope Benedict of formal heresy to prove the accusation of heresy against him, I will not present a lengthy defence of his orthodoxy, but I will provide only a few examples here by way of illustration, which demonstrate the fallacious foundation of the accusations of heresy that are made against Pope Benedict — accusations based in some instances only on material expressions of heresy, but without there having been brought forth any clear-cut and indisputable *indicia* demonstrating pertinacity of formal heresy, which alone suffice to verify that one has defected from the faith.

THE OBJECTION THAT JOSEPH RATZINGER DENIES THE DIVINITY OF CHRIST

It is said by some that Joseph Ratzinger denies the divinity of Christ. The sort of passage the accusers usually point to as evidence of this claim is such as the one found in his *Einführung in das Christentum* which reads:

> If this person is entirely what he does, if he entirely stands behind what he says, if he is entirely for the others and in such self-abandonment yet entirely is with himself; if he is the one, who in losing himself is found (cf. Mk 8:35), then is he not the most human of humans, the fulfilment of humanness per se? May we then resolve Christology in general (= speech about Christ) into theology (= speech from God); mustn't we much more rather passionately reclaim Jesus as *human*, and pursue Christology as Humanism and as Anthropology? Or ought the real man precisely because he is it whole and actual be God, and even God be the true man? Should it be able to be, that most radical humanism and belief in the revealing God meet here, yes merge into one another?[776]

A superficial and fatally defective interpretation of the passage would argue that Ratzinger is here saying that Jesus attained to godhood precisely in the realization of human perfection of self-giving love, but when considered in the full context of his Trinitarian and

---

[776] Joseph Ratzinger, *Einführung in das Christentum*, München, 1968, p. 169 — «Wenn dieser Mensch ganz ist, was er tut, wenn er ganz hinter dem steht, was er sagt, wenn er ganz für die andern und in solchem Sichverlieren doch ganz bei sich selber ist; wenn er der ist, der sich im Verlieren gefunden hat (vgl. Mk 8,35), ist er dann nicht der menschlichste der Menschen, die Erfüllung des Humanen schlechthin? Dürfen wir dann überhaupt Christologie (= Rede von Christus) in Theologie (= Rede von Gott) auflösen; müssen wir dann nicht viel eher Jesus leidenschaftlich als *Menschen* reklamieren, Christologie als Humanismus und als Anthropologie betreiben? Oder sollte der eigentliche Mensch gerade dadurch, dass er es ganz und eigentlich ist, Gott sein und Gott eben der eigentliche Mensch sein? Sollte es sein können, dass radikalster Humanismus und Glaube an den offenbarenden Gott hier aufeinandertreffen, ja ineinander übergehen?»

Christological theology, such an interpretation can be seen to be entirely foreign to Ratzinger's thought. In his trinitarian theology, there is not even a hint of Subordinationism, so that there is preserved a perfect identity between God and Word, yet there is at the same time a distinction between God and Word, making it possible for the man Jesus Christ as Son to be fully God, and that he can also speak of God as his Father. Under the heading *The point of departure of belief in the Triune God* (*Der Ausgangspunkt des Glaubens an den dreieinigen Gott*), Ratzinger explains:

> In Jesus Christ one meet a man who at the same time knows and professes himself as the Son of God. One finds God in the form of the Envoy who is entirely God and not is some intermediary being, who nonetheless with us says to God "Father". This gives rise to a peculiar paradox: on the one hand, this man calls God his Father, speaks to him as a "Thou", that faces him; if this is not supposed to be empty theatrics, but rather Truth, which alone is only worthy of God, then he must be someone else than this Father to whom *he* speaks and to whom *we* speak. On the other hand, however, he himself is the real closeness of God that is meeting us; the mediation of God to us, and this precisely because he himself is God as man, in human form and being: the God with us ("Emmanuel"). His mediation would basically cancel itself and instead of a mediation become a separation if he were other than God, if he were an intermediate being. Then he would not turn us towards God, but convey us away from him. So it follows that he is as the mediator God himself and "Man himself" – both equally real and total.[777]

---

[777] Ratzinger, *Einführung in das Christentum*, pp. 122-123 — "In Jesus Christus trifft man auf einen Menschen, der sich zugleich als Sohn Gottes weiß und bekennt. Man findet Gott in der Gestalt des Gesandten, der ganz Gott und nicht irgendein Mittelwesen ist und der dennoch mit uns zu Gott »Vater« sagt. Damit ergibt sich eine eigentümliche Paradoxie: Einerseits nennt dieser Mensch Gott seinen Vater, spricht zu ihm als einem Du, das ihm gegenübersteht; wenn das nicht leeres Theater sein soll, sondern Wahrheit, wie sie allein Gottes würdig ist, muss er also ein anderer sein als dieser Vater, zu dem *er* spricht und zu dem *wir* sprechen. Andererseits aber ist er selbst die wirkliche, uns begegnende Nähe Gottes; die Vermittlung Gottes an uns und dies gerade dadurch, dass er selbst Gott als Mensch, in Menschengestalt und -wesen: der Gottmit- uns (»Emmanuel«) ist. Seine Vermittlung würde ja im Grunde sich selbst aufheben und statt einer Vermittlung eine Abtrennung werden, wenn er ein anderer als Gott, wenn

Thus, the proposition must be understood in its textual and theological context. First, the theological, in which the divinity of Christ is established on the foundation of trinitarian dogma according to which the Son is *consubstantial* (ὁμοούσιος) with the Father, i.e. of the same *substance* (οὐσίᾱ) as the Father and therefore *consubstantial* and of equal divinity. οὐσίᾱ (ousía) in Attic Greek is ἐσσία (essía) in Doric Greek, and is derived from ὤν (*ṓn*), present participle of εἰμί (*eimí*, "to be"), which in Latin is *esse*. Thus, for the Son to be consubstantial with the Father is to be of the same *esse*, or *"one in being with the Father"* and therefore, the Son as the Word of the Father cannot be anything that is distinct in any manner from God, but is only distinct according to the notional relation of *filiation* through eternal generation by the ingenerate Father within the divine being. In the divine *esse* there can be no real distinction between the divine *being* (ὤν, esse) and the divine knowledge, nor between the divine mind and its operation — between *actus primus* and *actus secundus*, since God is *ipsum esse subsistens* — essential being in which there can be no potentiality, no *actus secundus* but only *actus purus*, and consequently, St. Thomas says, "Whatever is in God is God"[778] — for which reasons God's λόγος cannot be distinct from Himself, and therefore: "the word was with God, and the word was God" [ὁ λόγος ἦν πρὸς τὸν θεόν, καὶ θεὸς ἦν ὁ λόγος] (John 1:1).

In this context of the Son as Word, and Jesus Christ as the incarnate Word, *God himself and «Man himself»* — *both equally real and total*, Ratzinger explains: «Here (as with all of us) there is no "I" that produces words — he has identified himself with his word in such a way that "I" and word are indistinguishable: he *is* word. Likewise, for faith, its work is nothing other than the unconditional merging of oneself into precisely this work; he *does* himself and gives himself; his work is the giving of himself.»[779] From this it follows that, «The person

---

er ein Zwischenwesen wäre. Dann würde er uns nicht zu Gott hin, sondern von ihm weg vermitteln. So ergibt sich, dass er als der Vermittelnde Gott selber und »Mensch selber« — beides gleich wirklich und total — ist."

[778] «quidquid est in Deo Deus est» — [*Super Sent., lib. 1 d. 2 q. 1 a. 3 arg. 4*]

[779] *Einführung in das Christentum*, p. 162 — «Hier ist nicht (wie bei uns allen) ein Ich, das Worte macht — er hat sich so mit seinem Wort identifiziert, dass Ich und Wort ununterscheidbar sind: Er *ist* Wort. Ebenso

is the office, the office *is* the person. The two can no longer be separated: Here there is no reserved space of the private, the "I", which ultimately remains behind its actions and deeds and therefore can at some point also be "out of service"; there is no "I" here separated from its work — the ego is the work and the work is the ego.»[780] The progression of our own consciousness of this unity has for its point of origin our faith in the mystery of the Cross:

> The unfolding of the understanding we call faith happens in such a way that the Christians first hit upon the Identification of person, word and work from the Cross. By it they recognized what is actually and ultimately decisive before which everything else becomes secondary. Therefore, their profession could be restricted to the simple joining together of the words Jesus and Christ – in this connection all was said. Jesus is seen from the cross, which speaks louder than all words: He *is* the Christ – more is not needed. The crucified "I" of the Lord is such a filled Reality, that everything else can step back.[781]

Thus, the very idea of Jesus Christ as Messiah, as King, is revealed in the manifestation of a love that can only be a divine love in the redemptive sacrifice of Christ on the Cross: «If it really is so, if this "I" is believed as pure openness, as total being derived from the

---

ist für den Glauben sein Werk nichts anderes als die Vorbehaltlosigkeit des Sich-selber-Einschmelzens in eben dieses Werk; er tut *sich* und gibt, sich; sein Werk ist das Geben seiner selbst.»

[780] *Ibid.* — "Die Person *ist* das Amt, das Amt *ist* die Person. Beides ist nicht mehr trennbar: Hier ist kein Vorbehaltsraum des Privaten, des Ich, das schließlich hinter seinen Handlungen und Taten verbleibt und deshalb irgendwann auch »außer Dienst« sein kann; hier ist kein von seinem Werk abgetrenntes Ich - das Ich ist das Werk, und das Werk *ist* das Ich."

[781] *Ibid.* p. 165 — «Die Entfaltung des Verstehens, das wir Glauben nennen, geschieht dabei so, dass die Christen zuerst vom Kreuz her auf die Identifizierung von Person, Wort und Werk stoßen. Daran erkannten sie das eigentlich und letztlich Entscheidende, vor dem alles andere zweitrangig wird. Deshalb konnte sich ihr Bekenntnis auf die schlichte Ineinanderfügung der Worte Jesus und Christus beschränken – in dieser Verbindung war alles gesagt. Jesus wird vom Kreuz her gesehen, das lauter redet als alle Worte: Er *ist* der Christus – mehr braucht es nicht. Das gekreuzigte Ich des Herrn ist eine so gefüllte Wirklichkeit, dass alles andere zurücktreten kann.»

Father; if with his whole existence he is "Son" – actualitas of pure service; if – in other words – this existence not only has love, but is love – does it not have to be identical with God, who is love alone? Isn't Jesus, the Son of God, then God himself? Doesn't it then apply: "The word was with God, and it was God" (Jo 1,1)?»[782] In the Gospel, Christ himself foretold his glorification which would be brought about by his crucifixion: "Jesus therefore said to them: When you shall have lifted up the Son of man, then shall you know, that I am he, etc." (John 8:28), and "Now is the Son of man glorified, and God is glorified in him." (John 13:31) Thus the paradox of the Cross is foretold by Christ, as it was mysteriously throughout the Old Testament: "And as Moses lifted up the serpent in the desert, so must the Son of man be lifted up" (John 3:14); "Declare among the nations that the Lord has reigned from the tree" (*Vetus Latina* Psalm 95 v. 10).[783] The paradox of the Cross was encapsulated in writing on the

---

[782] *Ibid.* p. 169 — "Wenn es nämlich so ist, wenn dieses Ich geglaubt wird als reine Offenheit, als totales Sein vom Vater her; wenn es mit seiner ganzen Existenz »Sohn« – actualitas des reinen Dienens – ist; wenn - anders ausgedrückt – diese Existenz Liebe nicht nur *hat,* sondern *ist*- muss sie dann nicht identisch sein mit Gott, der *allein* die Liebe *ist?* Ist Jesus, der Sohn Gottes, dann nicht selber Gott? Gilt dann nicht: »Das Wort war auf Gott hin, und es *war* Gott« (Jo 1,1)?"

[783] Comment by Mons. Antonio Martini (1720 - 1809), Archbishop of Florence: «The whole world with religious fear and trembling presents itself before him, and worship and adore him. The Lord has taken possession of the kingdom: that is, he reigns. He reigned even before his coming on earth by his absolute power: but after his incarnation he reigned by faith, with which he is known, believed, adored. But here I must not fail to note, like the Roman Psalter and various other psalters, not a few Latin Fathers [see St. Augustine, Exp. In ps. 95, 11] and s. Justin martyr [*Apologia Prima* XLI] and s. Ephrem the Syrian, and some Greek edition of the Psalms read: the Lord reigns from the wood, bought the kingdom on the cross where he died (as the Apostle says) *and rose again to have dominion over the living and the dead.* A new and unprecedented way of arriving at the purchase of a kingdom was that which kept Christ from suffering and dying for men. That is: the Lord reigns after the wood. After suffering death on the cross, and later (but risen) he manifested the power given to him by the Father in heaven and on earth. St. Justin[1] accuses the Jews of having removed those two words from the text of the LXX; because (Genebrardo says in this regard) the LXX,

metal plaque affixed to the Cross, which is kept in the *Church of the Holy Cross in Jerusalem* in Rome, which still bears the words engraved in Greek, *Jesus of Nazareth King of the Jews*. Ratzinger comments on this paradox of the Cross in the section, *The Starting Point of the Creed: The Cross*:

> This Execution notice, the death sentence of history, came to exist in paradoxical Unity in the "profession of faith", as the actual starting point and Root point of the Christian faith that Jesus holds for being the Christ: As the crucified one, this Jesus is the Christ, the King. His being crucified is his being King; his being King is the having given himself away (Weggegebenhaben) to men, it is the becoming identical of Word, Mission and Existence even in the giving up of this Existence. His Existence is thus his Word. He *is* Word because he is Love. From the point of view of the cross, faith understands in increasing measure that this Jesus not only did and said *something*, but that in him message and person are identical, yes, that he always really is what he says. John only needed from it to simply draw the ultimate conclusion: If it is so — that is the basic Christological idea of his Gospel — then so is this Jesus Christ "Word"; but a person who is not only has words, but is his word

---

who with prophetic spirit in still other places to illustrate certain passages have added a few words, one can well believe on the testimony of such authors, that they had put those words. I am certainly surprised to see these words, as in the ancient Italic version, taken from the Greek of LXX, which came to light in the early days of the Church. Therefore they are preserved by the Church, and are recited in the hymn of the Passion, and again in the commemoration of the Cross in the Easter Season ". "[1] They have completely suppressed numerous passages of Scripture ... from which it is clear that the one who was crucified was foretold to be God and Man, would be crucified and would die [...] From Psalm 95 they have removed, of the words of David, this brief expression: from wood "(St. Justin, *Dialogue with Tryphon the Jew*, LXXI, 2; LXXIII, 1) St. Alphonsus de' Liguori: "*Commoveatur a facie eius universa terra: dicite in gentibus, quia Dominus regnavit. Commoveatur*, St. Jerome translates *paveat*, let the whole earth be terrified in his presence; tell the nations that the Lord has established his kingdom. St. Justin, St. Augustine, and S. Leo on the word *regnavit*, regnavit read *a ligno*, but the Church no longer makes use of it, except only in the Hymn, Vexilla, etc. *regnavit. a ligno Deus*." [Alfonso Maria de' Liguori, *TRADUZIONE DE' SALMI E DE' CANTICI CHE SI CONTENGONO NELL'OFFICIO DIVINO*, Bassano 1824, p. 251.]

and his work, that is the Logos ("the Word", the meaning) itself; which is from always and forever; which is the foundation the world stands on — if we anywhere encounter such a person, then he is that meaning which holds us all and from which we are all held up.[784]

Thus understood in their theological context, Ratzinger's words, so wrongly interpreted by some to be heretical denial of Christ's divinity, can be correctly understood in their proper textual context:

> So we could accordingly encapsulate the whole thing in the formula: Christian faith is not focused on ideas, but on a person, an "I", and indeed on a such a one that as Word and Son, is defined as total openness. But that leads to a double consequence, in which the drama of faith in Christ, (in the sense of a faith in Jesus as *Christ*, i.e. as Messiah) and its necessary historical progression to the full scandal of faith in the Son (as faith in the true divinity of Jesus) comes to light. If it really is so, if this "I" is believed as pure openness, as total being derived from the Father; if with his whole existence he is "Son" – actualitas of pure service; if – in other words – this existence not only has love, but is love – does it not have to be identical with God, who is love alone? Isn't Jesus, the Son of God, then God himself? Doesn't it then apply: "The word was

---

[784] *Einfühurung in das Christentum,* pp. 164-165: "Dieser Hinrichtungstitel, das Todesurteil der Geschichte, wurde in paradoxer Einheit zum »Bekenntnis«, zum eigentlichen Ausgangs- und Wurzelpunkt des christlichen Glaubens, der Jesus für den Christus hält: Als der Gekreuzigte ist dieser Jesus der Christus, der König. Sein Gekreuzigtsein ist sein Königsein; sein Königsein ist das Weggegebenhaben seiner Selbst an die Menschen, ist das Identischwerden von Wort, Sendung und Existenz in der Drangabe eben dieser Existenz. Seine Existenz ist so sein Wort. Er *ist* Wort, weil er Liebe ist. Vom Kreuz her versteht der Glaube in zunehmendem Maße, dass dieser Jesus nicht nur *etwas* getan und gesagt hat, sondern dass in ihm Botschaft und Person identisch sind, ja, dass er immer schon das ist, was er sagt. Johannes brauchte daraus nur schlicht die letzte Konsequenz zu ziehen: Wenn es so steht — das ist der christologische Grundgedanke seines Evangeliums —, dann ist also dieser Jesus Christus »Wort«; eine Person aber, die nicht nur Wrote hat, sondern ihr Wort und ihr Werk ist, die ist der Logos (»das Wort«, der Sinn) selbst; die ist von immer und für immer; die ist der Grund, worauf die Welt steht — wenn wir irgendwo eine solche Person antreffen, dann ist sie jener Sinn, der uns alle hält und von dem wir alle gehalten sind."

with[785] God, and it was God" (Jo 1,1)? But the reverse question also arises, so that we have to say: If this person is entirely what he does, if he entirely stands behind what he says, if he is entirely for the others and in such self-abandonment yet entirely is with himself; if he is the one, who in losing himself is found (cf. Mk 8:35), then he is not the most human of humans, the fulfilment of humanness per se? May we then resolve Christology in general (= speech about Christ) into theology (= speech from God); mustn't we much more rather passionately reclaim Jesus as *human*, and pursue Christology as Humanism and as Anthropology? Or ought the real man precisely because he is it whole and actual be God, and even God be the true man? Should it be able to be, that most radical humanism and belief in the revealing God meet here, yes merge into one another? I think it turns out that these questions, of the weight of the Church of the first five centuries was shaken, simply out rise to the Christological creed itself; the dramatic The struggle over these questions of that period took place in the ecumenical Councils of that time led to the affirmation of all three questions. Just this triple yes makes the content and the final form of the classical Christological dogmas that was only trying in this way to be loyal to the straightforward original confession of faith in Jesus as the Christ. In other words, The developed Christological dogma admits that the radical being-Christ of Jesus postulates the being-Son and that being-Son includes being-God; only if it is understood in this way does it remain a "logos-like", intelligible statement, while without this consistency one sinks into myth.[786]

---

[785] John 1: 1 — καὶ ὁ λόγος ἦν πρὸς τὸν θεόν, καὶ θεὸς ἦν ὁ λόγος. Commonly translated in English, "and the word was with God, and the word was God." — "with" (πρὸς) — in the sense of local proximity as being present before God: πρὸς τὸν θεόν; translated by Ratzinger as "auf Gott hin".

[786] *Einführung in das Christentum,* pp. pp. 168-170: "Das Ganze könnten wir demnach zusammenfassen in die Formel: Christlicher Glaube ist nicht auf Ideen, sondern auf eine Person, ein Ich bezogen, und zwar auf ein solches, das als Wort und Sohn, das heißt als totale Offenheit, definiert ist. Das führt nun aber zu einer doppelten Konsequenz, in der die Dramatik des Christusglaubens (Im Sinn eines Glaubens an Jesus als *Christus,* das heißt als Messias) und seine notwendige geschichtliche Selbstüberschreitung auf das volle Skandalum des Sohnesglaubens (als Glaube an das wahre Gottsein Jesu) zutage treten. Wenn es nämlich so ist, wenn dieses Ich geglaubt wird als reine Offenheit, als totales Sein vom Vater her; wenn es mit seiner

RATZINGER'S INADVERTENT DENIAL OF TRANSUBSTANTIATION

It is said by some that Joseph Ratzinger consciously denies the dogma of Transubstantiation. The sort of passage the accusers usually point to as evidence of this claim is such as the one found in his *Das Problem der Transsubstantiation und die Frage nach dem Sinn der Eucharistie* which reads:

---

ganzen Existenz »Sohn« - actualitas des reinen Dienens — ist; wenn — anders ausgedrückt — diese Existenz Liebe nicht nur *hat*, sondern *ist*— muss sie dann nicht identisch sein mit Gott, der *allein* die Liebe *ist*? Ist Jesus, der Sohn Gottes, dann nicht selber Gott? Gilt dann nicht: »Das Wort war auf Gott hin, und es *war* Gott« (Jo 1,1)? Aber auch die umgekehrte Frage entsteht, sodass wir sagen müssen: Wenn dieser Mensch ganz ist, was er tut, wenn er ganz hinter dem steht, was er sagt, wenn er ganz für die andern und in solchem Sichverlieren doch ganz bei sich selber ist; wenn er der ist, der sich im Verlieren gefunden hat (vgl. Mk 8,35), ist er dann nicht der menschlichste der Menschen, die Erfüllung des Humanen schlechthin? Dürfen wir dann überhaupt Christologie (= Rede von Christus) in Theologie (= Rede von Gott) auflösen; müssen wir dann nicht viel eher Jesus leidenschaftlich als *Menschen* reklamieren, Christologie alsHumanismus und als Anthropologie betreiben? Oder sollte der eigentliche Mensch gerade dadurch, dass er es ganz und eigentlich ist, Gott sein und Gott eben der eigentliche Mensch sein? Sollte es sein können, dass radikalster Humanismus und Glaube an den offenbarenden Gott hier aufeinandertreffen, ja ineinander übergehen? Ich glaube, es zeigt sich, dass diese Fragen, von deren Wucht die Kirche der ersten fünf Jahrhunderte erschüttert wurde, einfach aus dem christologischen Bekenntnis selbst aufsteigen; das dramatische Ringen jener Periode um diese Fragen hat in den ökumenischen Konzilien von damals zur Bejahung aller *drei Fragen* geführt. Eben dieses dreifache Ja macht den Inhalt und die Endgestalt des klassischen christologischen Dogmas aus, das damit nur dem schlichten Anfangsbekenntnis zu Jesus als dem »Christus« die volle Treue zu halten versuchte. Anders gesagt: Das entfaltete christologische Dogma bekennt sich dazu, dass das radikale Christussein Jesu das Sohnsein postuliert und dass das Sohnsein das Gottsein einschließt; nur wenn es so verstanden wird, bleibt es »logoshafte«, verständige Aussage, während man ohne diese Konsequenz in Mythos absinkt."

Nothing happens physically or chemically through the Eucharist. That is not their level of reality. But a believing stance towards reality also includes the conviction that physics and chemistry do not exhaust the whole of being, that it cannot be said that where nothing physically happens, nothing at all has happened. On the contrary: the real lies behind the physical.[787]

It is not difficult to imagine that only a few centuries ago, Joseph Ratzinger might have been threatened with the stake for saying this, just as John XXII was so threatened by King Phillip VI for having denied to the blessed in heaven the beatific vision before the last judgment; but it is important to understand his meaning before rushing to judgment, since, in his writings on the Eucharist, Ratzinger attempts to uphold the dogma of Transubstantiation rather than attack it. In her dissertation, *Die Eucharistietheologie bei Joseph Ratzinger*, Dr. Daniela Brenner provides some insight into the meaning of this problematic passage. First, she explains why Ratzinger does not interpret the dogma in Thomistic terms:

> The concept of substance in high scholasticism comes too much from the Aristotelian hylemorphism, which he characterizes as "the dualism of matter and form" and which he describes as insufficient because of the excessive intertwining of metaphysics and physics. Instead, Ratzinger argues from the doctrine of creation. From belief in creation "[...] an understanding of substance in accordance with belief could take shape". In his philosophical train of thought he defines the being of the creature in terms of a double substantiality, namely as "being-from-somewhere else" and at the same time "being-in-independence". This is supplemented by the "special way of being oneself", which corresponds to the nature of personal being. Ratzinger classically defines substance as *ens in se existens*. The distinction between "being-from-somewhere else" and "being-in-independence" only means

---

[787] «Physikalisch und chemisch geschieht durch die Eucharistie nichts. Das ist nicht ihre Wirklichkeitsebene. Aber gläubiges Stehen zur Wirklichkeit schließt zugleich die Überzeugung ein, dass Physik und Chemie nicht das Ganze des Seins ausschöpfen, dass also nicht gesagt werden kann, wo physikalisch nichts geschehe, sei überhaupt nichts geschehen. Im Gegenteil: Das Eigentliche liegt hinter dem Physikalischen.»

that the created things that owe their being to another, namely God, are at the same time independent realities and not mere accidents.[788]

Of course, there is not really a "double substantiality" (an absurdity since the nature of primary substance is that it is *primary*), but in the one substantiality of creaturely existence, substances exist as standing in themselves, and therefore as subsisting things precisely because they enjoy a participation in being given to them by the One who is the source of all being. Thus, it is difficult to understand how Ratzinger can say in one work that the notion of mere substance as of what stands in itself is "shattered", but in another he asserts the very unshattered notion of substance precisely as *ens in se existens*. But in order to understand the importance of the notion of substance in the doctrine of transubstantiation, and how Ratzinger's essentially flawed and incoherent notion of substance has led him into an erroneous understanding of that dogma, it will be necessary to consider for a moment his prejudice against the Thomistic-Aristotelian doctrine of substance. Ratzinger's emotional prejudice against Aristotelian philosophy led him to an inverted understanding of the hylomorphic doctrine of substance which is plainly visible in many passages throughout his first major work, *Einführung in das Christentum*, where he wrote in the section on "THE PERSONAL GOD":

---

[788] *Die Eucharistietheologie bei Joseph Ratzinger* — «Der Substanzbegriff der Hochscholastik komme zu sehr aus dem aristotelischen Hylemorphismus, den er „als Dualismus von Materie und Form"[441] charakterisiert und wegen der zu starken Verschlingung von Metaphysik und Physik als ungenügend bezeichnet. Ratzinger argumentiert stattdessen von der Schöpfungslehre her. Aus dem Schöpfungsglauben „könnte [...] ein dem Glauben gemäßes Verständnis von Substanz sich formen"[442]. In seiner philosophischen Gedankenfolge definiert er das Sein des Geschöpfs im Sinne einer doppelten Substanzialität, nämlich als „Sein-von-woanders-her"[443] und zugleich „Sein-in-Selbständigkeit"[444]. Dies werde ergänzt durch die „besondere Weise des Selberseins"[445], die der Wesensart des personalen Seins entspricht.
Ratzinger bestimmt ganz klassisch die Substanz als *ens in se existens*. Die Unterscheidung von „Sein-von-woanders-her" und „Sein-in-Selbständigkeit" möchte nur besagen, dass die geschaffenen Dinge, die ihr Sein einem anderen, nämlich Gott, verdanken, gleichzeitig selbständige Wirklichkeiten sind und nicht bloß Akzidentien.»

In a world that is ultimately not mathematics but love, the minimum is a maximum; that least thing that can love is greatest; the particular is more than the general; is the person, the unique, the unrepeatable, at the same time the final and the highest. In such a far-sighted view, the person is not just an individual, a duplicated copy created by breaking up the idea into matter, but rather a "person". Greek thought always interpreted the many individual beings, including the many individual people, only as individuals. They arise as a result of the breaking of the idea by matter. The multiplied is always the secondary; the real would be the one and the general. The Christian does not see an individual in man, but a person — it seems to me that in this crossing from individual to person lies the whole span of the transition from antiquity to Christianity, from Platonism to faith. This particular being is by no means secondary, which would only give us a fragmentary idea of the general as the authentic.[789]

According to Aristotle, (whose relevant passages on this point are quoted in this work), the individual substance, i.e. the οὐσία, is what is most primary, and every other way that substance is understood is secondary, and depends radically and absolutely on the primary substance, such as *this man* or *this horse*. Thus it is explained on the *Categories* in the **Stanford Encyclopedia of Philosophy**:

> The individuals in the category of substance play a special role in this scheme. Aristotle calls them "primary substances" (*prôtai ousiai*) for

---

[789] *Einführung in das Christentum,* (second edition) p. 117 — «In einer Welt, die letztlich nicht Mathematik, sondern Liebe ist, ist gerade das Minimum ein Maximum; ist jenes Geringste, das lieben kann, ein Größtes; ist das Besondere mehr als das Allgemeine; ist die Person, das Einmalige, Unwiederholbare, zugleich das Endgültige und Höchste. Die Person ist in einer solchen Weitsicht nicht bloß Individuum, ein durch die Zerteilung der Idee in die Materie entstandenes Vervielfältigungsexemplar, sondern eben »Person«. Das griechische Denken hat die vielen Einzelwesen, auch die vielen Einzelmenschen, stets nur als Individuen gedeutet. Sie entstehen infolge der Brechung der Idee durch die Materie. Das Vervielfältigte ist so immer das Sekundäre; das Eigentliche wäre das Eine und das Allgemeine. Der Christ sieht im Menschen nicht ein Individuum, sondern eine Person - mir scheint, dass in diesem Überschritt von Individuum zu Person die ganze Spanne des Übergangs von Antike zu Christentum, von Platonismus zu Glaube liegt. Dieses bestimmte Wesen ist durchaus nichts Sekundäres, das uns nur bruchstückweise das Allgemeine als das Eigentliche ahnen ließe.»

without them, as he says, nothing else would exist. Indeed, Aristotle offers an argument (2a35–2b7) to establish the primary substances as the fundamental entities in this ontology. Everything that is not a primary substance, he points out, stands in one of the two relations (inhering 'in', or being 'said of') to primary substances. A genus, such as animal, is 'said of' the species below it and, since they are 'said of' primary substances, so is the genus (recall the transitivity of the 'said of' relation). Thus, everything in the category of substance that is not itself a primary substance is, ultimately, 'said of' primary substances. And if there were no primary substances, there would be no "secondary" substances (species and genera), either. For these secondary substances are just the ways in which the primary substances are fundamentally classified within the category of substance. As for the members of non-substance categories, they too depend for their existence on primary substances. A universal in a non-substance category, e.g., color, in the category of quality, is 'in' body, Aristotle tells us, and therefore in individual bodies. For color could not be 'in' body, in general, unless it were 'in' at least some particular bodies. Similarly, particulars in non-substance categories (although there is not general agreement among scholars about what such particulars might be) cannot exist on their own. E.g., a determinate shade of color, or a particular and non-shareable bit of that shade, is not capable of existing on its own—if it were not 'in' at least some primary substance, it would not exist. So primary substances are the basic entities—the basic "things that there are" — in the world of the *Categories*.[790]

Brenner then comes straight to the point with Ratzinger's understanding of Transubstantiation based on his own concept of substance, quoting his own words:

> Based on this understanding of substance, this means, applied to the question of transubstantiation, the following: bread and wine are through transubstantiation, «in their essence, in their being, signs, as they were things in their essence before. And they are truly "re-substantialized" in it, in their deepest and most intrinsic nature, in their being, in their true found-in-itself being.»[791]

---

[790] https://plato.stanford.edu/entries/aristotle-metaphysics/#Cate
[791] Brenner, *Die Eucharistietheologie bei Joseph Ratzinger* — Ausgehend von diesem Substanzverständnis bedeutet dies, auf die Frage der Transsubstantiation übertragen, folgendes: Brot und Wein seien durch die

She again hits the nail on the head driving it even deeper, citing the observation of Stefan Oster on the same passage:

> **Stefan Oster notes at this point that Ratzinger's talk of "being a sign" keeps both the physical and the metaphysical level strictly apart and ties in with the Kantian phenomenal level, which he equates with the scholastic level of accidents. With this he intends to guarantee the independence of the physical from the ontological level. If bread and wine remain the same in their physico-chemical composition after the change, there would be no objection to Luther's theory of consubstantiation, according to Ratzinger.**[792]

The error consists in saying that by transubstantiation bread and wine become "in their essence signs", and thus, "as they were things in their essence before", by transubstantiation, "they are truly 'resubstantialized' so that, "in their deepest and most intrinsic nature, in their being, in their true found-in-itself being" they are **signs**. However, if *nothing happens physically or chemically through the Eucharist*, but the *bread and wine* become signs, then **the bread and wine will still exist physically and therefore ontologically as the substances of bread and wine**, so that although they will also exist accidentally as

---

Transsubstantiation, „in ihrem Wesen, in ihrem Sein, Zeichen, wie sie vorher in ihrem Wesen Dinge waren. Und sie sind darin wahrhaft »umsubstanziiert«, in ihrem Tiefsten und Eigensten, in ihrem Sein, in ihrem wahren An-sich getroffen."» The work Brenner cites is, Stefan OSTER, *Person und Transsubstantiation, Mensch-Sein, Kirche-Sein und Eucharistie – eine ontologische Zusammenschau*, Freiburg 2010; and the reference to this passage: "Stefan OSTER, „... anwesend auf personale Weise". Joseph Ratzinger und die Lehre von der Transsubstantiation, in: Rudolf VODERHOLZER (Hg.), Der Logos-gemäße Gottesdienst. Theologie der Liturgie bei Joseph Ratzinger (RS 1), Regensburg 2009, 205-232, hier: 216."

[792] *Ibid.* — «Stefan Oster merkt an dieser Stelle an, dass Ratzinger mit der Rede vom „Zeichensein" sowohl die physikalische als auch die metaphysische Ebene streng auseinanderhält und an die kantische Phänomen-Ebene anknüpft, die er mit der scholastischen Ebene der Akzidentien gleichsetzt. Damit beabsichtige er die Unabhängigkeit der physikalischen von der ontologischen Ebene zu gewährleisten. Sofern Brot und Wein in ihrer physikalisch – chemischen Zusammensetzung nach der Wandlung gleichbleiben, bestünde nach Ratzinger auch kein Einwand gegen die Konsubstantiationslehre Luthers.»

signs, in their essence, they will still remain substantially bread and wine. Hence, if *nothing happens physically or chemically through the Eucharist*, the *substance* of the bread and wine will remain ontologically bread and wine without being transformed into the substance of the body and blood of Christ, and consequently they will not cease to exist substantially as bread and wine in such a manner that there will remain only the *appearance* of bread and wine; yet **transubstantiation** is solemnly defined by the Council of Trent as *that marvellous and singular conversion of the entire substance of bread into the body and the entire substance of wine in the blood* **with only the appearance (species) of bread and wine remaining.**[793] Thus in the Eucharist, although nothing *perceptible* happens physically or chemically through the Eucharist, the physical and chemical structures, elements, and substance of bread and wine actually **cease to exist**, and what remains of them is only the *appearance* of bread and wine. The bread and wine do not become signs, because the bread and wine cease to exist when they are changed into the body and blood of Christ. What becomes a sign is only the *species* of bread and wine. Although he does not intend to deny the dogma of Transubstantiation, he does so inadvertently in such a manner that the matter of heresy is evident in Ratzinger's statements that:

> 1. The reality of the flesh and blood of Christ does not mean an additional substance of the same kind as bread and wine... The presence of Jesus Christ means something essentially different from the presence of physical quantities and therefore does not compete with them. **It means the inclusion of bread and wine in the mighty presence of the Lord**, which meets things in the ground of their being and thus renews and transforms them in their hidden, truly meta-physical depth."[794]

---

[793] «Si quis dixerit in sacrosancto eucharistiae sacramento remanere substantiam panis et vini una cum corpore et sanguine domini nostri Iesu christi negaverit que mirabilem illam et singularem conversionem totius substantiae panis in corpus et totius substantiae vini in sanguinem manentibus dumtaxat speciebus panis et vini quam quidem conversionem catholica ecclesia aptissime transsubstantiatione appellat: a(nathema) s(it).»

[794] Joseph RATZINGER, *Das Problem der Transsubstantiation und die Frage nach dem Sinn der Eucharistie* [153] — «Die Realität von Fleisch und Blut Christi bedeutet nicht eine zusätzliche Substanz von der gleichen Art wie

2. **Bread and wine take part first of all in the general independence of creature being, they have part in the fundamental 'substantiality' that is inherent in what is created as an independent being alongside the divine being. Transubstantiation, however, means that these things lose their creaturely independence, that they cease to simply stand in themselves in the way that is appropriate for the creature and that instead they become pure signs of His presence among us.**[795]

In both of these passages, Ratzinger heretically asserts that by transubstantiation bread and wine are transformed only in their mode of being — the bread and wine continue to exist but in a different way than they existed before, having lost their creaturely independence, they cease to simply stand in themselves as substances, but the bread and wine are included "in the mighty presence of the Lord". But this is a flat contradiction, because if the bread and the wine are only transformed into signs so as to be included in the sacramental presence, then in reality their substance would remain, and they would not change into the substance of the body and blood of Christ, but the substances of bread and wine would become signs of the body and blood in such a manner that the body and blood would not be really present substantially in the sacrament, but would only be symbolically present by way of signification in the substance of the bread and wine. Concerning the first of these two passages,

---

Brot und Wein... Die Gegenwart Jesu Christi bedeutet etwas vom Wesen her anderes als die Gegenwart physikalischer Größen und konkurriert ihnen daher nicht. Sie bedeutet die Einbeziehung von Brot und Wein in die machtvolle Gegenwart des Herrn, die die Dinge in ihrem Seinsgrund trifft und so in dieser ihrer verborgenen, wahrhaft meta-physischen Tiefe erneuert und verwandelt.»

[795] Joseph RATZINGER, *Das Problem der Transsubstantiation und die Frage nach dem Sinn der Eucharistie.* — «Brot und Wein nehmen zunächst an der allgemeinen Selbständigkeit des kreatürlichen Seins teil, sie haben teil an der grundsätzlichen »Substanzialität«, die dem Geschaffenen als einem selbständigen Sein neben dem göttlichen Sein zukommt. Transsubstantiation aber besagt, dass diese Dinge diese ihre kreatürliche Selbständigkeit verlieren, dass die aufhören, in der dem Geschöpf zukommenden Weise einfach in sich selbst zu stehen und dass sie statt dessen zu reinen Zeichen Seiner Anwesenheit unter uns werden.»

Brenner notes that, «he calls attention to the problem of "a coexistence of two substances which could and should both be called" substance "in the same sense" But he describes this as "philosophically and theologically too much in the foreground and superficial".»⁷⁹⁶ And she cites the above quoted passage as evidence that he rejects the notion: "Because in reality the two substances cannot simply be placed next to each other," ⁷⁹⁷ but although he rejects the notion, yet that contradiction is the inescapable logical consequence of his premises. In truth, the bread and wine cannot be *transformed in their hidden, truly meta-physical depth* by God if nothing happens to the *physical substance* of the bread and wine, and thus, the physical nature remaining unchanged, that substance is not changed into the substance of the body and Blood of Christ.

The cause of Ratzinger's error which unintentionally reduces transubstantiation to transignification is his faulty Kantian influenced notion of **substance**. Our knowledge of the physical reality of a thing is not a mere *phenomenon* in the Kantian sense of the term, which reduces our knowledge of things, i.e. the intelligible content of our intuitive knowledge of the essence of things, to a merely subjective *ens rationis* which does not correspond even analogically⁷⁹⁸ to the objective reality of the *thing in itself* (*Ding an sich*), which Kant roughly associated but did not equate with what he called *noumena*,⁷⁹⁹ which are not perceptible to the senses and must therefore, except for the fact of their existence, remain otherwise unknowable to us. Thus, according to the Kantian view, the human intellect would have to be

---

⁷⁹⁶ Brenner, *Die Eucharistietheologie bei Joseph Ratzinger* — «Er verweist jedoch auf Probleme „eines Nebeneinander zweier Substanzen, die man beide im gleichen Sinn »Substanz« nennen könnte und müsste". ⁴⁵⁰ Dies bezeichnet er aber als „philosophisch und theologisch zu vordergründig und oberflächlich"⁴⁵¹.»

⁷⁹⁷ *Ibid.* — «Denn in Wirklichkeit seien die beiden Substanzen nicht schlicht nebeneinander zu setzen.»

⁷⁹⁸ Analogy in the sense that between our abstracted knowledge of the form and the existing form itself, there exists a certain similarity mixed with difference insofar as the object is known according to the mode of the knower in virtue of a proportion or relation of object to object: (Cf. *Summa Theol.*, Iª, q. 13, a. 5, 10, & q. 7; *De potentia*, a. 7.)

⁷⁹⁹ Derived from the Greek, νοούμενον.

considered to have been directly created by God with a fatal defect by which it cannot even properly operate as an intellect, by apprehending the essence of things even in an analogical manner, according to the dictum, *Cognitum autem est in cognoscente secundum modum cognoscentis.*[800] St. Thomas explains in the passage, "For knowledge occurs accordingly as the known is in the knower. But knowledge is in the knower according to the mode of the knower. Whence knowledge of every knower is according to the mode of its nature."[801] Now as is explained below, the proper object first known by the intellect is the *substance* (what Aristotle called οὐσία) of natural things, of which the first apprehension is of their *quiddity*, which is what the thing is, and which constitutes its *essence*, and makes it *what it is*: *to ti ên einai* (τὸ τί ἦν εἶναι) as Aristotle termed it in the *Metaphysics* (1029b), and translated by Cicero into Latin with the single word *essentia*.[802] The essence is ontologically identical to *nature*, which is the *physical reality* — i.e. the *physis* (φύσις) considered under its formal aspect as a principle of motion.[803] Thus, the *physical nature* of a thing which constitutes its *substance* as a being, continues to exist as a *primary substance* for so long as nothing happens to alter its physical nature, its φύσις, and for so long as "Nothing happens physically or chemically

---

[800] *Summa Theol.* Iª q. 12 a. 4 co. — "But the thing known is in the knower according to the mode of the knower."

[801] *Ibid.* «Cognitio enim contingit secundum quod cognitum est in cognoscente. Cognitum autem est in cognoscente secundum modum cognoscentis. Unde cuiuslibet cognoscentis cognitio est secundum modum suae naturae.»

[802] S. Marc Cohen, *Aristotle's Metaphysics*, First published Sun Oct 8, 2000; substantive revision Tue Jul 7, 2020: https://plato.stanford.edu/entries/aristotle-metaphysics/#SubsMattSubj — «'Essence' is the standard English translation of Aristotle's curious phrase *to ti ên einai*, literally "the what it was to be" for a thing. This phrase so boggled his Roman translators that they coined the word *essentia* to render the entire phrase, and it is from this Latin word that ours derives. Aristotle links the notion of essence to that of definition (*horismos*)—"a definition is an account (*logos*) that signifies an essence" (*Topics* 102a3).»

[803] *Nature*, is considered formally as a *principium motus in eo quod est*. St. Thomas takes this definition straight from the Physics of Aristotle (Aristotle, *Physics*, III, I, 201 a 10 s.); and says, «Naturalia enim sunt quorum principium motus in ipsis est.» (*De motu cordis ad magistrum Philippum de Castro Caeli*).

through the Eucharist," nothing happens at all — or as St. Thomas would say, "*Non est sacramentum.*"[804]

According to the dogma of Transubstantiation, the bread and wine cease altogether to exist, and are not changed into signs, but into the body and blood of Christ, so that only the appearance, the *species* of bread and wine remains as signs and nothing of their substance. The species of bread and wine become the signs, not the bread and wine themselves which cease to exist when they are changed into the body and blood of Christ. In this there is no difficulty: *To strengthen a sincere heart faith alone suffices:*

> *Verbum caro, panem verum*
> *Verbo carnem efficit:*
> *Fitque sanguis Christi merum,*
> *Et si sensus deficit,*
> *Ad firmandum cor sincerum*
> *Sola fides sufficit.*[805]

THE OBJECTION THAT JOSEPH RATZINGER DENIES THE RESURRECTION

Pertinacity would be an evident fact in one who would explicitly deny that there is any such a thing at all as a resurrection of the body in the deposit of revelation; but pertinacity would not be evident in one who asserts the material heresy of denying that the resurrection professed in the Creed involves the reconstitution of the human *substance* by means of re-uniting body and soul, if he does not properly understand that according to Catholic dogma, the human *substance* is composed of the animal body and the rational soul. It is a solemnly defined article of faith that the spiritual soul is a *substance*, and that it

---

[804] Klemens Vansteenkiste O.P. explained in his Anglicum lectures that St. Thomas did not speak of sacraments as being "valid" or "invalid", but expressed the idea by saying, "Est Sacramentum," or "Non est sacramentum."

[805] "The Word as Flesh makes true bread into flesh by a word: and the wine becomes the Blood of Christ. And if sense is deficient, to strengthen a sincere heart Faith alone suffices." — St. Thomas Aquinas.

is the *form* of the body,[806] — and what is thereby meant is that being the *form* of the body, the rational soul is the *substantial form* of the body, which by definition exists as the act of matter, and together with the *matter* constitutes a thing as a *substance*; and therefore the resurrection of the dead is necessarily the reconstitution of the two components, the body and soul, which constitute the substance of the person. Without the physical body being restored to life, one cannot even speak of a resurrection of (to use Ratzinger's words), "that which is essential of man, the person,"[807] because what is essential to man in his integral nature is essentially that which constitutes the integral substance of the human person as a *rational animal*, namely, the substantial union of body and soul. Hence, the resurrection of the human being is brought about by the restoration of the union of body and soul. Thus, the resurrection of man can only be brought about by the resurrection of the physical **body,** which brings about the reconstitution of the integral human *substance* by means of the body being brought back into act by the soul — by being reunited with the soul; so that the body and the soul, after their separation at death,

---

[806] **1311-1312 Concilium Viennense:** «Given at Avignon on 13 January in the eighth year. [...] Moreover, with the approval of the said council, we reject as erroneous and contrary to the truth of the catholic faith every doctrine or proposition rashly asserting that the substance of the rational or intellectual soul is not of itself and essentially the form of the human body, or casting doubt on this matter. In order that all may know the truth of the faith in its purity and all error may be excluded, we define that anyone who presumes henceforth to assert defend or hold stubbornly that the rational or intellectual soul is not the form of the human body of itself and essentially, is to be considered a heretic.» «Dat(um) Avinione idus ianuarii anno octavo [...] Porro doctrinam omnem seu positionem temere asserentem aut vertentem in dubium quod substantia animae rationalis seu intellectivae vere ac per se humani corporis non sit forma velut erroneam ac veritati catholicae fidei inimicam praedicto sacro approbante concilio reprobamus diffinientes ut cunctis nota sit fidei sincerae veritas ac praecludatur universis erroribus aditus ne subintrent quod quisquis deinceps asserere defendere seu tenere pertinaciter praesumpserit quod anima rationalis seu intellectiva non sit forma corporis humani per se essentialiter tanquam haereticus sit censendus.»

[807] *Einführung in das Christentum*, (second edition) p. 306 — «Das Wesentliche des Menschen, die Person.»

being reunited, reconstitute the resurrected human *substance*.⁸⁰⁸ This, by strict logical necessity, pertains essentially to the dogma, because otherwise the dogmatic formula of Vienne, which defined that the *substance* of the soul is the form of the body, would be meaningless and therefore false. This is precisely the error of Joseph Ratzinger, a material heresy against the Catholic faith, asserted in his *Einführung in das Christentum*,⁸⁰⁹ where he says, on *The essential immortality of man*:

---

⁸⁰⁸ The Fourth Lateran Council (1215) solemnly professed that after his death on the cross, Christ's *soul* descended to the nether world, and he then resurrected *in the flesh*, and ascended into heaven in both, i.e. **body and soul**, and will come at the end of the world **in both** to judge the living and the dead: «Qui cum secundum divinitatem sit immortalis et impassibilis idem ipse secundum humanitatem factus est passibilis et mortalis quin etiam pro salute humani generis in ligno crucis passus et mortuus descendit ad inferos resurrexit a mortuis et ascendit in cœlum. Sed *descendit in anima resurrexit in carne ascenditque pariter in utroque* venturus in fine sæculi iudicare vivos et mortuos et redditurus singulis secundum opera sua tam reprobis quam electis.»

⁸⁰⁹ *Einführung in das Christentum*, (second edition) p. 306 — «**b) Die wesentliche Unsterblichkeit des Menschen.** Mit den bisherigen Überlegungen dürfte einigermaßen deutlich geworden sein, worum es in der biblischen Auferstehungsverkündigung eigentlich geht: Ihr wesentlicher Gehalt ist nicht die Vorstellung von einer Rückgabe der Körper an die Seelen nach einer langen Zwischenzeit, sondern ihr Sinn ist, den Menschen zu sagen, dass sie, sie selbst, weiterleben; nicht aus eigener Macht, sondern weil sie in einer Weise von Gott gekannt und geliebt sind, dass sie nicht mehr untergehen können. Gegenüber der dualistischen Unsterblichkeitskonzeption, wie sie sich in der griechischen Leib-Seele-Schematik ausspricht, will die biblische Formel von der Unsterblichkeit durch Auferweckung eine ganzmenschliche und dialogische Vorstellung von der Unsterblichkeit vermitteln: Das Wesentliche des Menschen, die Person, bleibt; das, was in dieser irdischen Existenz leibhaftiger Geistigkeit und durchgeisteter Leiblichkeit gereift ist, das besteht auf eine andere Weise fort. Es besteht fort, weil es in Gottes Gedächtnis lebt. Und weil es der Mensch selbst ist, der leben wird, nicht eine isolierte Seele, darum gehört das mitmenschliche Element mit in die Zukunft hinein; darum wird die Zukunft des einzelnen Menschen erst dann voll sein, wenn die Zukunft der Menschheit erfüllt ist.»

With the previous considerations it should become reasonably clear what the biblical Resurrection proclamation actually entails: Their essential content is not the idea of a return of the body to the soul after a long interim but their purpose is to say to men that they, themselves, live on; not under one's own power, but because they are known and loved by God in a way that they can no longer perish. Compared to the dualistic concept of immortality, as is expressed in the Greek body-soul-schematic, the biblical formula of the immortality through resurrection intends to convey a whole human and dialogical notion of immortality: that which is essential of man, the person, remains; what has ripened in this earthly existence of corporeal spirituality and spiritualized corporeality, continues to exist in a different way. It continues to exist because it lives in God's memory. And because it is the man himself who will live, not an isolated soul, that is why the interpersonal human element belongs into the future; therefore the future of the individual will only be full when the future of humanity is fulfilled.

Ratzinger begins by confusing the notion of *resurrection of the dead* (which is a truth of revelation) with that of the *immortality of the soul*, (which is a truth of reason that is also explicitly affirmed in scripture).[810] He speaks of "the biblical formula of the immortality through resurrection," (which does not take place immediately after death, but on the last day) as if it were in some manner opposed to the doctrine of the *immortality of the soul*, which properly denotes a continuation in life of the separated soul, which begins immediately after death and continues until the soul is reunited with the body on the last day. He states plainly that, "the biblical formula of the immortality through resurrection intends to convey a whole human and dialogical notion of immortality," which is "Compared to the dualistic concept of immortality, as is expressed in the Greek body-soul-schematic," according to which it is not "the man himself who will live," but only "the isolated soul" (*weil es der Mensch selbst ist, der leben wird, nicht eine isolierte Seele*). He gives only a description of what

---

[810] Matthew 10:28 — «Do not be afraid of those who *kill the **body*** (ἀποκτεννόντων τὸ **σῶμα**) *but cannot kill the **soul***. (τὴν δὲ **ψυχὴν** μὴ δυναμένων ἀποκτεῖναι) Rather, be afraid of the One who can destroy ***both soul and body*** (καὶ **ψυχὴν** καὶ **σῶμα**) in hell.»

supposedly remains of a man after death according to the biblical conception of resurrection, saying what remains is, "the person," without defining what the person is, or how it is that the person continues to exist immediately after he dies. What remains after death, according to Ratzinger, is "that which is essential of man": **what has ripened in this earthly existence of corporeal spirituality and spiritualized corporeality**" (*was in dieser irdischen Existenz leibhaftiger Geistigkeit und durchgeisteter Leiblichkeit gereift ist*); and that, he says, is "the person," who "continues to exist in a different way." However, when a man dies, between the time of death and the resurrection on last day, there is a *long interval*, and either the dead man ceases altogether to exist until he is raised up on the last day at the resurrection, or his soul continues to exist separated from the body until the soul is reunited with the resurrected body on the last day. Now to say that what is essential of man is the person, and that the person continues to exist in a different way, offers no solution to this question of what remains of a man immediately after death, and does not say what a person essentially is, nor does it explain how the person can continue to exist in a different way after death — because in truth, if the soul does not continue to exist for the duration of that interval between death and resurrection, it cannot be said that the person *continues* to exist during that period of interval. Now if the person is to continue to exist in a different way during that interval, it must continue to exist according to a different mode of being — but for Ratzinger that mode of being is conceived of neither as the continued existence of the immortal soul nor is it conceived of as the *substantial* **"corporeal spirituality and spiritualized corporeality"** of the re-united immortal soul with the mortal body, i.e. the human *substance* created and restored by God to exist by its own proper act of being, but it is conceived of as a mode of being which is not properly its own act of being, but a non-substantial existence of the person in the memory of God: "**It continues to exist because it lives in God's memory.**" However, it is precisely the creature's proper act of being by which God confers substantial being on the creature that distinguishes the created substance from the substance of the Creator, so that if the creature is not a substance, it is not a creature at all, nor can it be said to properly exist, so that the resurrected man, thus conceived, no longer exists as a creature, but exists only as an idea in the mind of God. But an idea that lives in the mind of God is not the eternal life that Christ promised to them to whom He promised that He would raise them up on the last day, because what lives in God's memory is only God's own knowledge of us, but not our knowledge of God. Eternal life consists in the creature's fruition of the divine goodness by the supernatural elevation of the created intellect which enables it to know God by immediate knowledge in the beatific vision: "Now this is eternal life: That they may know thee, the only true God… etc." (John 17:3) However, what lives only in God's memory cannot know God, but can only be known by God. Thus, Ratzinger's concept of human immortality logically would not be a resurrection at all, or even an afterlife of the soul, because it logically implies no manner whatever of a continuation of man's existence as a living being after death, but only of God's memory of that living being which died and no longer lives constituted as a created being in virtue of its own proper act of being, but being deprived of the its own *substantial* act of being at death, it is annihilated and lives on only as an idea in the divine memory. Therefore, if Ratzinger conceives of man's being as a substantial being, then his doctrine logically would imply that man is annihilated at death; and if his being is not considered substantial by its own proper act of being, then man's existence in this world would logically only be conceivable essentially as a mode being of an attribute of the divine substance — and after death that attribute would undergo a modification which would amount to a pantheistic absorption into the *deus sive natura* of Spinoza, which is practically indistinguishable from annihilation.[811] Yet this is not Ratzinger's doctrine, and although he downplays the notion of the human being as a substance, he does not profess the everlasting life promised by Christ to be anything comparable to a pantheistic absorption of man, but describes it in such terms of a real beatitude of a human immortality brought about by the transforming power of God's love: "When the power of love for the other would be so strong somewhere that it would not only have its memory, the

---

[811] **Catholic Encyclopedia** — «Pantheism, if logical, can offer only an impersonal immortality, a future condition in which the individual is absorbed into the absolute—the one infinite being, whether conscious or unconscious. Practically, this differs little from annihilation.» https://www.newadvent.org/cathen/07687a.htm.

shadow of his self, but able to keep himself alive, then a new stage of life would be reached".[812]

Ratzinger does not believe that death results in the annihilation of the human person, but that there exists a natural immortality, but that natural immortality is conceived of in such a manner that it cannot be proven by rational demonstration, but must only be believed in order to avoid the consequence of having to base one's belief in immortality on a non-rational mythological or miraculous foundation:

> Is it not necessary to hold on to natural immortality precisely for the sake of the humanity of faith, because a purely Christologically conceived further existence of man would necessarily slip into the miraculous and mythological? There is no doubt that this last question can only be answered in the affirmative. **But that also contradicts by no means our approach.**[813]

How there can exist a natural immortality of a person whose body dies, but the soul does not survive death and continue to exist separately from the body is a question that Ratzinger makes no attempt to answer in an intelligible manner; nor does he distinguish between the doctrine of the natural immortality of the soul, and the doctrine of the supernatural resurrection of the mortal body re-united to the immortal soul — a true and proper resurrection which can only be brought about by the supernatural intervention of a divine power. How does a "person" whose **"earthly existence" consists of a "corporeal spirituality and spiritualized corporeality" survive the death of the** physical body if there is no imperishable spiritual substance existing as the *form* of the perishable material body — the

---

[812] *Einfühurung in das Christentum*, (second edition) p. 258 — «Wenn die Kraft der Liebe zum andern irgendwo so stark wäre, dass sie nicht nur dessen Gedächtnis, den Schatten seines Ich, sondern ihn selbst lebendig zu halten vermöchte, dann wäre eine neue Stufe des Lebens erreicht.»

[813] *Einfühurung in das Christentum*, (second edition) p. 307 — «Muss nicht gerade um der Menschlichkeit des Glaubens willen an der natürlichen Unsterblichkeit festgehalten werden, weil eine rein christologisch aufgefasste Fortexistenz des Menschen notwendig ins Mirakelhafte und Mythologische abgleiten würde? Diese letzte Frage kann man ohne Zweifel nur bejahend beantworten. Aber das widerspricht auch unserem Ansatz keineswegs.»

soul? How can we even speak of man as a *person* without there being in him that immaterial spiritual component, the *rational soul*, which constitutes his essence as a **person** —a *rationalis naturae individua substantia?*[814] A natural immortality can only be understood as a survival of the separable, spiritual soul after the death of the body if one is to avoid the absurd conclusion that the natural immortality of the person results from a completely natural process of a resurrection of the entire human person. Again, Ratzinger does not distinguish between the philosophical and **biblical** doctrine of the *immortality of the* **soul** (which he dismisses on page 301 as a *"griechische Vorstellung"*[815]) and the revealed dogma of the *resurrection of the* **body**. Both are true and both are infallibly taught as articles of faith, but he wrongly conceives of them as somehow being incompatible with each other. On page 300 he says:

> Before the article on the resurrection of the flesh, we find ourselves in a peculiar dilemma. We have rediscovered the indivisibility of man; we live our corporeality with a new intensity and experience it as an indispensable way of realizing the one human being. From there we can understand anew the biblical message that does not promise immortality to a severed soul, but to the whole person. Out of such a feeling, especially evangelical theology in our century turned emphatically against the Greek doctrine of the immortality of the soul, which is wrongly seen as Christian thought.[816]

---

[814] *Summa Theol.* III^a q. 16 a. 12 arg. 2 — «Sed nihil aliud est persona quam *rationalis naturae individua substantia*, ut dicit Boetius, in libro de duabus naturis.»

[815] *Einführung in das Christentum*, (second edition) p. 302 — «Der griechischen Auffassung liegt die Vorstellung zugrunde, im Menschen seien zwei an sich einander fremde Substanzen zusammengefügt, von denen die eine (der Körper) zerfällt, während die andere (die Seele) von sich aus unvergänglich ist und daher aus sich, unabhängig von irgendwelchen anderen Wesen, weiterbesteht.» [The Greek conception is based on the idea that in man two substances that are alien to one another are joined together, one of which (the body) disintegrates, while the other (the soul) is inherently imperishable and therefore independently of any other Essence, persists.]

[816] *Einführung in das Christentum*, (second edition) p. 300 — «Vor dem Artikel von der Auferstehung des Fleisches befinden wir uns in einem eigentümlichen Dilemma. Wir haben die Unteilbarkeit des Menschen neu

When Ratzinger says on page 255, "Von hier aus erst kann man verstehen, was »Auferstehung« bedeutet. Sie *ist* das Stärkersein der Liebe gegenüber dem Tod,"[817] he does not get to the essence of what resurrection is, because there can be no *Stärkersein der Liebe gegenüber dem Tod* if the *actus primus* of the integral substance of man ceases altogether to exist at death: There can be no *Stärker**sein** der Liebe* (which pertains to *actus secundus*) of the person after death if after death there is no longer any subsistent **Sein** (*actus primus*) of the person at all, except in the limited sense of the subsistent being of the *separated soul* which is powerless to restore being to the integral substance of the human person. If the love he refers to as being stronger than death is God's love, then that love is stronger than death precisely because it has the unique, omnipotent power to create and destroy, and then to restore to being that which had perished — but if that divine power does not restore the body to life, then there is no resurrection, but there could be only some form of incorporeal *afterlife* conceived of as existing in a realm of otherworldly spirits or in the *Sheol* of departed souls. Hence, notwithstanding the magnitude of man's love for God or God's love for man, the imperfect and incomplete immortality of man in the form of a natural continuation of a person's subsistent being is only conceivable if the soul continuing as a separable substance and *vital principle* of the whole person survives the death of the body; while the perfect immortality of the resurrection of the human person in his integral substance is not a natural immortality but a supernatural gift of divine love. However, while Ratzinger affirms the natural immortality of the person, he denies it simultaneously with the logically incoherent assertion, «Where the "communion of saints" is believed, the idea of

---

entdeckt; wir leben mit einer neuen Intensität unsere Leibhaftigkeit und erfahren sie als unerlässliche Verwirklichungsweise des einen Seins des Menschen. Wir können von da aus die biblische Botschaft neu verstehen, die nicht einer abgetrennten Seele Unsterblichkeit verheißt, sondern dem ganzen Menschen. Aus einem solchen Empfinden heraus hat sich in unserem Jahrhundert vor allem die evangelische Theologie nachdrücklich gegen die griechische Lehre von der Unsterblichkeit der Seele gewandt, die man zu Unrecht auch als christlichen Gedanken ansehe.»

[817] "Only from here can one understand what 'resurrection' means. It is love being stronger than death".

the anima separata (the "separateded soul" of which school theology speaks) is ultimately obsolete.»[818] There exists no logical connection between the natural but imperfect immortality of the separated soul and the perfect immortality of the entire human substance, body and soul in the resurrected state of the blessed who are given the supernatural reward of eternal life united to God by the beatific vision, and united to each other in the communion of saints. The former pertains to nature. The latter to grace; but as grace presupposes nature, the souls of the faithful departed await the resurrection of the body which will be accomplished when they will be raised up on the last day by Christ, whose love is stronger than death.

And then there is the question of what exactly is a person according to Ratzinger? Ratzinger speaks of **"that which is essential of man, the person,"**[819] and the person's "special way of being oneself,"[820] but he offers no intelligible alternative definition to the classical definition formulated by Boethius, namely, an *individual substance of a rational nature* — a definition which clearly expresses the essence of a person, which is what a definition must do in order to be a definition (*Definitio declarat essentiam*). And how can there be any other definition expressing what a person *is*, i.e. a definition which expresses the essence, since it is already proven by Aristotle (as is explained below) that "there is no demonstration of the essence of things."[821] Man is a "rational animal," and *that* is what is essential of man; and being *rational* and a *substance*, it pertains essentially to man as defined that he is a *person*. It does not pertain to matter as matter to be rational, so the rational principle in man can only be the *immaterial* soul, which not being composed of matter and form, is a *simple substance* which does not decompose into constituent components in

---

[818] *Einführung in das Christentum*, (second edition) p. 304 — «Wo die »Gemeinschaft der Heiligen« geglaubt wird, ist die Idee der Anima separata (der »losgetrennten Seele«, von der die Schultheologie spricht) im Letzten Überholt.»

[819] *Einführung in das Christentum*, (second edition) p. 306 — «Das Wesentliche des Menschen, die Person.»

[820] «besondere Weise des Selberseins» in *Das Problem der Transsubstantiation und die Frage nach dem Sinn der Eucharistie*.

[821] Aristotle—Works, *Metaphysics*, Book B. 2. p. 2249.

the manner of material things which are generated and corrupted, and therefore the rational soul is according to its nature *immortal*.

That the spiritual soul is a substance which survives the death of the body is a truth of faith proven by reason and authority. The argument by reason for the proof of the immortality of the soul has its origin in Plato's *Phaedo*.[822] St. Thomas begins his proof in I^a *q. 75 a.*

---

[822] «And what do we say of the soul? is that seen or not seen? Not seen. Unseen then? Yes. Then the soul is more like to the unseen, and the body to the seen? That is most certain, Socrates. And were we not saying long ago that the soul when using the body as an instrument of perception, that is to say, when using the sense of sight or hearing or some other sense (for the meaning of perceiving through the body is perceiving through the senses)-were we not saying that the soul too is then dragged by the body into the region of the changeable, and wanders and is confused; the world spins round her, and she is like a drunkard when under their influence? Very true. But when returning into herself she reflects; then she passes into the realm of purity, and eternity, and immortality, and unchangeableness, which are her kindred, and with them she ever lives, when she is by herself and is not let or hindered; then she ceases from her erring ways, and being in communion with the unchanging is unchanging. And this state of the soul is called wisdom?... And to which class is the soul more nearly alike and akin, as far as may be inferred from this argument, as well as from the preceding one? I think, Socrates, that, in the opinion of everyone who follows the argument, the soul will be infinitely more like the unchangeable even the most stupid person will not deny that. And the body is more like the changing? Yes. Yet once more consider the matter in this light: When the soul and the body are united, then nature orders the soul to rule and govern, and the body to obey and serve. Now which of these two functions is akin to the divine? and which to the mortal? Does not the divine appear to you to be that which naturally orders and rules, and the mortal that which is subject and servant? True. And which does the soul resemble? The soul resembles the divine and the body the mortal-there can be no doubt of that, Socrates. Then reflect, Cebes: is not the conclusion of the whole matter this?-that the soul is in the very likeness of the divine, and immortal, and intelligible, and uniform, and indissoluble, and unchangeable; and the body is in the very likeness of the human, and mortal, and unintelligible, and multiform, and dissoluble, and changeable. Can this, my dear Cebes, be denied? No, indeed. But if this is true, then is not the body liable to speedy dissolution? and is not the soul almost or altogether indissoluble? Certainly.»

2 by quoting a passage of Augustine (*De Trin. x, 7*)[823]: "Who understands that the nature of the soul is that of a substance and not that of a body, will see that those who maintain the corporeal nature of the soul, are led astray through associating with the soul those things without which they are unable to think of any nature—i.e. imaginary pictures of corporeal things," and on that basis he states, "Therefore the nature of the human intellect is not only incorporeal, but it is also a *substance*, that is, something subsistent."[824] He then demonstrates the conclusion by pointing out the universality of abstract intellectual concepts which lie beyond the power of corporeal beings to grasp, for which reason:

> It must necessarily be allowed that the principle of intellectual operation which we call the soul, is a principle both incorporeal and subsistent. For it is clear that by means of the intellect man can have knowledge of all corporeal things... Therefore if the intellectual principle contained the nature of a body it would be unable to know all bodies... Therefore the intellectual principle which we call the mind or the intellect has an operation "per se" apart from the body. Now only that which subsists can have an operation "per se." For nothing can operate but what is actual: for which reason we do not say that heat imparts heat, but that what is hot gives heat. We must conclude, therefore, that the human soul, which is called the intellect or the mind, is something incorporeal and subsistent.[825]

---

[823] *Summa Theol.* Iª q. 75 a.2 — «Sed contra est quod Augustinus dicit, X de Trin. Quisquis videt mentis naturam et esse substantiam, et non esse corpoream, videt eos qui opinantur eam esse corpoream, ob hoc errare, quod adiungunt ei ea sine quibus nullam possunt cogitare naturam, scilicet corporum phantasias.»

[824] *Ibid.* — «Natura ergo mentis humanae non solum est incorporea, sed etiam substantia, scilicet aliquid subsistens.»

[825] Iª q. 75 a. 2 co. — «Respondeo dicendum quod necesse est dicere id quod est principium intellectualis operationis, quod dicimus animam hominis, esse quoddam principium incorporeum et subsistens. Manifestum est enim quod homo per intellectum cognoscere potest naturas omnium corporum. Quod autem potest cognoscere aliqua, oportet ut nihil eorum habeat in sua natura, quia illud quod inesset ei naturaliter impediret cognitionem aliorum; sicut videmus quod lingua infirmi quae infecta est cholerico et amaro humore, non potest percipere aliquid dulce, sed omnia videntur ei amara. Si igitur principium intellectuale haberet in se naturam

The argument from authority is drawn from Scripture, from the Fathers, and from the teachings of the infallible magisterium of the Church, both extraordinary and ordinary. For the present purpose, it will suffice to simply present the teaching of the universal magisterium on this point, starting first with the *Roman Catechism*:

1. **Christ's resurrection generated also for us the resurrection of the body** (*Christi resurrectio nobis etiam corporis resurrectionem peperit*):

It should be noted first of all that the resurrection of men in this article is called the "resurrection of the body". This was not done without reason; since the Apostles thus wanted to teach a truth that it is necessary to admit: the immortality of the soul. And, so that no one would believe that the soul dies with the body and that they were both recalled to life, while from many places in the Holy Scriptures the soul is certainly immortal, the article only mentions the resurrection of the flesh. And although often, even in the Holy Scriptures, the word flesh means the whole man, as for example in Isaiah: "All flesh is like hay" (40,6) and in Saint John: "The Word became flesh" (1, 14), however in this place it means the body, to make us understand that of the two parts, soul and body, of which man is composed, the second only, that is the body, is corrupted and returns to the dust of the earth, from which it was drawn, while the soul remains uncorrupted. But since no one is called back to life unless he is dead first, it cannot be properly said of the soul that it rises again. Mention is also made of the flesh to refute the heresy propagated by Hymenaeus and Philetus (2 Tim 2:17), while the Apostle still lived. They asserted that the resurrection mentioned in the Holy Scriptures is not the corporeal, but the spiritual, through which one rises from the death of sin to the life of grace. By the words of the article that error is evidently excluded and the resurrection of the body is confirmed.[826]

---

alicuius corporis, non posset omnia corpora cognoscere... Ipsum igitur intellectuale principium, quod dicitur mens vel intellectus, habet operationem per se, cui non communicat corpus. Nihil autem potest per se operari, nisi quod per se subsistit. Non enim est operari nisi entis in actu, unde eo modo aliquid operatur, quo est. Propter quod non dicimus quod calor calefacit, sed calidum. Relinquitur igitur animam humanam, quae dicitur intellectus vel mens, esse aliquid incorporeum et subsistens.»

[826] «Sed hoc imprimis attendere oportebit, resurrectionem hominum in hoc articulo carnis resurrectionem appellari; quod quidem sine causa factum

2. The body of each one will rise again:

But since the certainty is very important that it is the same and identical body of each of us, although corrupted and reduced to dust, to resurrect to life, the parish priest must carefully explain it. This is the thought of the Apostle when he says: "This corruptible being must clothe himself with incorruption" (1 Cor 15:53), manifestly wanting to indicate his own body by the term this. Job also prophesied of it very clearly saying: "And in my flesh I will see my God; I will see him myself, my eyes will look at him and not another" (19:26). This results from the very definition of the resurrection; in fact, according to Damascene, it is a reference to that state from which you fell (Exp. fidei, 4, 27). Finally, if we consider the reason already indicated above for which the resurrection will take place, there can be no doubt about it. We said in fact that the bodies will be resurrected, so that each one has what is due to his body, according to what he did, both for good and for evil (2 Cor 5:10). Man must therefore necessarily rise in the same body, with which he served God or the devil, to receive the crowns of triumph and prizes with the same body or to suffer pains and tortures.[827]

---

non est. Nam docere voluerunt apostoli id quod necessario ponendum est: animam esse immortalem; quare, ne quis forte eam simul cum corpore interiisse, utrumque vero in vitam revocari existimaret, cum animam plurimis sacrarum litterarum locis immortalem esse plane constet, ob eam rem carnis tantum suscitandae mentio in articulo facta est. Et quamquam saepe etiam in sacris Scripturis caro integrum hominem, ut est apud Isaiam: Omnis caro foenum[2], et apud sanctum Ioannem: Et Verbum caro factum est [3], significet; hoc tamen loco carnis vox corpus declarat, ut duarum partium, animae et corporis, quibus homo constat, alteram tantum, nempe corpus, corrumpi et in pulverem terrae ex qua compactum est redire, animam vero incorruptam manere intelligamus. At vero, cum nemo, nisi mortuus fuerit, ad vitam revocetur, anima proprie non dicitur resurgere. Carnis quoque mentio facta est illius haeresis confutandae causa quae, vivo Apostolo, Hymenaei et Phileti fuit [4], qui asserebant, cum de resurrectione in Scripturis sacris ageretur, non de corporea sed de spirituali, qua a morte peccati ad vitam innocentem resurgitur, accipiendum esse. Itaque his verbis planum fit eum errorem tolli et veram corporis resurrectionem confirmari.»

[827] «Cum vero multum referat nobis certo persuaderi hoc ipsum atque adeo idem corpus quod uniuscuiusque proprium fuit, quamvis corruptum sit et in pulverem redierit, tamen ad vitam suscitandum esse, illud etiam parochus accurate explicandum suscipiet. Haec Apostoli est sententia, cum

The same is taken in the *Catechism of the Catholic Church*, promulgated by Pope John Paul II:

> **365** The unity of soul and body is so profound that one has to consider the soul to be the "form" of the body:²³⁴ i.e., it is because of its spiritual soul that the body made of matter becomes a living, human body; spirit and matter, in man, are not two natures united, but rather their union forms a single nature.
>
> **366** The Church teaches that every spiritual soul is created immediately by God — it is not "produced" by the parents - and also that it is immortal: it does not perish when it separates from the body at death, and it will be reunited with the body at the final Resurrection.²³⁵

In the footnotes, reference is given to the above quoted solemn pronouncements of the Council of Vienne and the Fifth Lateran Council:

> ²³⁴ Cf. Council of Vienne (1312): DS 902.
> ²³⁵ Cf. Pius XII, *Humani Generis*: DS 3896; Paul VI, *CPG* § 8; Lateran Council V (1513): DS 1440.

It will be useful here to take a closer look at the pronouncement of the Fourth Lateran Council, and to give special attention to the passages I have bolded:

> SESSION 8 [Condemnation of every proposition contrary to the truth of the enlightened Christian faith]

---

inquit: Oportet corruptibile hoc induere incorruptionem ²³, ea voce, hoc, proprium corpus aperte demonstrans. Iob etiam de eo clarissime vaticinatus est: Et in carne mea, inquit, videbo Deum, quem visurus sum ego ipse, et oculi mei conspecturi sunt, et non alius ²⁴. Hoc idem colligitur ex ipsius resurrectionis definitione; est enim resurrectio, auctore Damasceno 25, ad eum statum, unde cecideris, revocatio. Denique, si consideremus cuius rei causa resurrectionem futuram paulo ante demonstratum est, nihil erit quod cuiusquam animum hac in re dubium facere possit; Idcirco autem corpora excitanda esse docuimus, ut referat unusquisque propria corporis, prout gessit, sive bonum, sive malum. Hominem igitur ex ipso corpore cuius opera vel Deo vel daemoni servivit, resurgere oportet, ut cum eodem corpore triumphi coronas et praemia consequatur, aut poenas et supplicia miserrima perferat.»

Consequently, since in our days (which we endure with sorrow) the sower of cockle, the ancient enemy of the human race, has dared to scatter and multiply in the Lord's field some extremely **pernicious errors, which have always been rejected by the faithful, especially on the nature of the rational soul**, with the claim that it is mortal, or only one among all human beings, and since some, playing the philosopher without due care, assert that this proposition is true at least according to philosophy, it is our desire to apply suitable remedies against this infection and, with the approval of the sacred council, **we condemn and reject all those who insist that the intellectual soul is mortal**, or that it is only one among all human beings, and those who suggest doubts on this topic. **For the soul not only truly exists of itself and essentially as the form of the human body, as is said in the canon of our predecessor of happy memory, pope Clement V, promulgated in the general council of Vienne, but it is also immortal; and further, for the enormous number of bodies into which it is infused individually, it can and ought to be and is multiplied. This is clearly established from the gospel when the Lord says, They cannot kill the soul**; and in another place, Whoever hates his life in this world, will keep it for eternal life and when he promises eternal rewards and eternal punishments to those who will be judged according to the merits of their life; otherwise, the incarnation and other mysteries of Christ would be of no benefit to us, nor would resurrection be something to look forward to, and the saints and the just would be (as the Apostle says) the most miserable of all people.

And since truth cannot contradict truth, **we define** that every statement contrary to the enlightened truth of the faith is totally false and we strictly forbid teaching otherwise to be permitted. **We decree that all those who cling to erroneous statements of this kind, thus sowing heresies which are wholly condemned, should be avoided in every way and punished as detestable and odious heretics and infidels who are undermining the catholic faith.**[828]

---

[828] **Concilium Lateranense V (1513)** — «Cum itaque diebus nostris quod dolenter ferimus zizaniae seminator antiquus humani generis hostis nonnullos perniciosissimos errores a fidelibus semper explosos in agro domini superseminare et augere sit ausus de natura praesertim animae rationalis quod videlicet mortalis sit aut unica in cunctis hominibus et nonnulli temere philosophantes secundum saltem philosophiam verum id esse asseverant contra huiusmodi pestem opportuna remedia adhibere cupientes hoc sacro approbante concilio damnamus et reprobamus omnes asserentes animam intellectivam mortalem esse aut unicam in cunctis

With these solemn pronouncements and ordinary teachings of the infallible magisterium of the Church in mind, one is confronted with indisputable heterodoxy of Ratzinger's propositions:

> Let us start from verse 50, which seems to me to be a kind of key to the whole: "But I say this, brethren, that flesh and blood cannot inherit the kingdom of God and that what is perishable does not become perishable". [...] Paul teaches, to say it again, not the resurrection of the body, but of the person, and this precisely not in the return of the "flesh-bodies", that is, the biological structures which he expressly describes as impossible (»the perishable cannot become imperishable«), but in the otherness of the life of the resurrection, as it is represented in the risen Lord. [...] But then does the resurrection have no relation to matter at all? And does "Last Day" become completely irrelevant in favour of the life that always comes from God's call? Basically we have already given the answer to this last question with our reflections on the Second Coming of Christ. If the cosmos is history and if matter represents a moment in the history of spirit, then there is not an eternal neutral juxtaposition of matter and spirit, but a final "complexity" in which the world finds its omega and its unity. Then there is a final connection between matter and spirit in which the fate of man and the world is completed, even if today we cannot possibly define the nature of this connection. Then there is a "Judgment Day" in which the destiny of the individual becomes full because the destiny of humanity is fulfilled.[829]

---

hominibus et haec in dubium vertentes cum illa non solum vere per se et essentialiter humani corporis forma existat sicut in canone felicis recordationis Clementis papae v praedecessoris nostri in generali Viennensi concilio edito continetur verum et immortalis et pro corporum quibus infunditur multitudine singulariter multiplicabilis et multiplicata et multiplicanda sit. Quod manifeste constat ex evangelio cum dominus ait: animam autem occidere non possunt.Cum que verum vero minime contradicat omnem assertionem veritati illuminatae fidei contrariam omnino falsam esse definimus et ut aliter dogmatizare non liceat districtius inhibemus omnes que huiusmodi erroris assertionibus inhaerentes veluti damnatissimas haereses seminantes per omnia ut detestabiles et abhominabiles haereticos et infideles catholicam fidem labefactantes vitandos et puniendos fore decernimus.»

[829] *Einführung in das Christentum,* (second edition) pp. 309, 311 — «Gehen wir aus von dem Vers 50, der mir eine Art Schlüssel zu dem Ganzen zu sein

The proposition, "Paul teaches, to say it again, not the resurrection of the body, but of the person, and this precisely not in the return of the "flesh-bodies", that is, the biological structures which he expressly describes as impossible," **is plainly erroneous and heretical, and is refuted by Paul himself.** St. Paul is not saying that the incorruptible resurrection of the flesh and blood bodies in their biological structures is impossible, but that as *flesh and blood*, i.e. the human body in the natural perishable state of its earthly condition cannot undergo the transition to the imperishable state of eternal incorruptibility, while remaining in its natural corruptible earthly state. That transition is only made possible by the divine power of a supernatural grace: "For this corruptible must put on incorruption, and this mortal must put on immortality. So when this corruptible shall have put on incorruption, and this mortal shall have put on immortality, then shall be brought to pass the saying that is written, Death is swallowed up in victory." (1 Corinthians 15:53-55)

Against the explicit definitions of faith, Ratzinger says:

scheint: »Das aber sage ich, Brüder, dass Fleisch und Blut das Reich Gottes nicht erben können und dass Vergängliches nicht zu Unvergänglichkeit kommt«. [309] Paulus lehrt, um es noch einmal zu sagen, nicht die Auferstehung der Körper, sondern der Personen, und dies gerade nicht in der Wiederkehr der »Fleischesleiber«, das heißt der biologischen Gebilde, die er ausdrücklich als unmöglich bezeichnet (»das Vergängliche kann nicht unvergänglich werden«), sondern in der Andersartigkeit des Lebens der Auferstehung, wie es im auferstandenen Herrn vorgebildet ist.[311] [...] Aber hat dann die Auferstehung überhaupt keine Beziehung zur Materie? Und wird der »Jüngste Tag« damit völlig gegenstandslos zugunsten des Lebens, das aus dem Ruf Gottes immer kommt? Auf diese letzte Frage haben wir im Grunde mit unseren Überlegungen zur Wiederkunft Christi die Antwort schon gegeben. Wenn der Kosmos Geschichte ist und wenn die Materie ein Moment an der Geschichte des Geistes darstellt, dann gibt es nicht ein ewiges neutrals Nebeneinander von Materie und Geist, sondern eine letzte »Komplexität«, in der die Welt ihr Omega und ihre Einheit findet. Dann gibt es einen letzten Zusammenhang zwischen Materie und Geist, in dem sich das Geschick des Menschen und der Welt vollendet, auch wenn wir heute unmöglich die Art dieses Zusammenhanges definieren können. Dann gibt es einen »Jüngsten Tag«, in dem das Geschick der Einzelmenschen voll wird, weil das Geschick der Menschheit erfüllt ist.«

The raising of the dead (not the body!), of which the Scriptures speak, is accordingly about the salvation of one, undivided human being, not just the fate of one (possibly secondary) half of the human being. With this it is already clear that the actual core of the resurrection belief does not consist in the idea of returning of bodies, to which we have reduced it in our thinking; this applies even though this image concept is used throughout the Bible.[830]

Ratzinger concludes, "The new world, with the representation of which the Bible closes in the image of the final Jerusalem, is not a utopia, but a certainty that we approach in faith. There is salvation of the world,"[831] — However, whatever that salvation is, or in what does it consist, he does not say precisely, but what he has described does not correspond entirely to the resurrected state to be enjoyed eternally by the blessed in heaven as that is so clearly defined by the ecclesiastical magisterium and unanimously taught by the Fathers and theologians throughout the ages according to the clear and unmistakable sense of Sacred Scripture, expressed in that *"image concept used throughout the Bible"* (diese Bildvorstellung in der Bibel durchgehend verwendet wird), which Ratzinger himself asserts to "consist in the idea of returning of bodies" (in der Idee der Rückgabe der Körper besteht).

---

[830] *Einführung in das Christentum*, p. 302 (second edition) — «Die Auferweckung der Toten (nicht der Körper!), von der die Schrift redet, handelt demgemäß vom Heil des *einen,* ungeteilten Menschen, nicht nur vom Schicksal einer (womöglich noch sekundären) Hälfte des Menschen. Damit ist nun auch schon klar, dass der eigentliche Kern des Auferstehungsglaubens gar nicht in der Idee der Rückgabe der Körper besteht, auf die wir ihn aber in unserem Denken reduziert haben; das gilt, obwohl diese Bildvorstellung in der Bibel durchgehend verwendet wird.»

[831] *Einführung in das Christentum*, p. 312 (second edition) — «Die neue Welt, mit deren Darstellung im Bild des endgültigen Jerusalem die Bibel schließt, ist keine Utopie, sondern Gewissheit, der wir im Glauben entgegengehen. Es gibt eine Erlösung der Welt.»

ON BENEDICT XVI'S ASSERTION THAT THE OLD COVENANT WAS NEVER REVOKED

It is a dogma of the Catholic faith that the Old Covenant was revoked, and indeed, it has perpetually been so professed in the Church *ubique, semper, et ab omnibus*, so at first glance one is inclined to wonder just how it can be possible for people who profess themselves to be Catholics, to at the same time profess against this dogma by asserting that the Old Covenant was never revoked. Already in the preaching of Pope St. Leo the Great (440-461), we read, "Lord you have drawn all things to yourself, because with the rending of the Temple veil, the Holy of Holies has been withdrawn from the unworthy pontiffs, so that the figure would be exchanged for the truth, prophecy for manifestation and the law for the Gospel."[832] The Council of Florence solemnly professed the faith of the Church, that:

> It firmly believes, professes and teaches that the legal prescriptions of the Old Testament or the Mosaic law, which are divided into ceremonies, holy sacrifices and sacraments, because they were instituted to signify something in the future, although they were adequate for the divine cult of that age, once our Lord Jesus Christ who was signified by them had come, came to an end and the sacraments of the new Testament had their beginning. Whoever, after the passion, places his hope in the legal prescriptions and submits himself to them as necessary for salvation and as if faith in Christ without them could not save, sins mortally. It does not deny that from Christ's passion until the promulgation of the gospel they could have been retained, provided they were in no way believed to be necessary for salvation. But it asserts that after the promulgation of the gospel they cannot be observed without loss of eternal salvation.[833]

---

[832] S. Leonis Papae, *Sermo 8* — «*Traxisti, Domine, omnia ad te, quoniam scisso templi velo, Sancta sanctorum ab indignis pontificibus recesserunt, ut figura in veritatem, prophetia in manifestationem et lex in Evangelium verteretur.*»

[833] SESSION 11, 4 February 1442, *Bull of union with the Copts* — «Firmiter credit profitetur et docet legalia veteris testamenti seu mosaice legis que dividuntur in ceremonias sacra sacrificia sacramenta quia significandi alicuius futuri gratia fuerant instituta licet divino cultui illa etate congruerent significato per illa domino nostro ihesu christo adveniente cessasse et novi testamenti sacramenta cepisse. Quemcunque etiam post passionem in legalibus spem ponentem et illis velut ad salutem necessariis se subdentem

Pope Benedict XIV in *Ex Quo Primum*, set forth repeatedly and explicitly citing the definition of Florence, to wit, that the Mosaic covenant has been "revoked" and "abrogated":

> However they are not attempting to observe the precepts of the old Law which as everybody knows have been revoked by the coming of Christ."[834] [...] 61. The first consideration is that the ceremonies of the Mosaic Law were abolished by the coming of Christ[835] and that they can no longer be observed without sin after the promulgation of the Gospel. [...] "Similarly, we profess that the legalities of the Old Testament, the ceremonies of the Mosaic Law, the rites, sacrifices, and sacraments have ceased at the coming of Our Lord Jesus Christ; they cannot be observed without sin after the promulgation of the Gospel. The distinction of clean and unclean foods found in the old Law pertains to the ceremonies which have passed away with the rise of the Gospel. The Apostles' prohibition on food offered to idols, blood, and the meat of strangled animals was suitable at that time to remove cause for disagreement between Jews and Gentiles; but since the reason for this prohibition has ceased to be, the prohibition too has come to an end." [...] 62. The preceding words are from the Profession of Orthodox Faith which Pope Urban VIII required of Orientals, as published in 1642 by the Congregation for the Propagation of the Faith. They are in harmony with the teaching of St. Thomas (*Summa* 1, 2, quest. 103, art. 4, to 3rd). Moreover this teaching is confirmed by ancient documents. St. Gregory II in his capitular letter (chap. 7)... [...] So the Decree for the Jacobites of the Council of Florence reads: "The holy Roman Church firmly believes, professes, and preaches that every creature of God is good and not to be rejected if it is taken with thanks. According to the Lord's

---

quasi christi fides sine illis salvare non posset peccasse mortaliter. Non tamen negat a christi passione usque ad promulgatum evangelium illa potuisse servari duntamen minime ad salutem necessaria crederentur. Sed post promulgatum evangelium sine interitu salutis eterne asserit non posse servari.»

[834] I have not been able to find the original Latin text of the document, but in the Italian version one reads: "però non intendono in nessun modo osservare i precetti dell'antica Legge, che sono stati **abrogati** con la venuta di Cristo, come a tutti è manifesto"."

[835] In the Italian text, the word used is not *abrogated*, as appears in the English translation, but *abolished:* "Le cerimonie della Legge Mosaica sono state ***abolite*** con la venuta di Cristo".

word, a man is not defiled by what enters his mouth. The Church affirms that the distinction made by the Mosaic Law between clean and unclean foods belongs to the ceremonial laws which have passed away with the coming of the Gospel.... [...] 63. The second consideration is that although the ceremonial precepts of the old Law have come to an end with the promulgation of the Gospel [...] 67. The third and final point suggested by the text of the fourth admonition is that Greek priests are not forbidden to use any of the prayers or blessings which are in their Euchologion by reason of references to matters which were subject to the ceremonial precepts of the Old Law. They should, however, do everything with the intention not of obeying the precepts of the old Law, which has now been abolished, but of respecting the new Law of the Church or canonical custom made strong by long and unbroken observance. In dealing with the Greek custom of abstaining from blood and strangled flesh, Lorinus notes that "if the Greeks today abstain from blood on the grounds that they are bound by this law, they are superstitious. This law now binds nobody and its observance savors of the ceremonies of the old Law. [...] 74. But others remarked wisely that some, surely, of the ceremonial rites of the old Law could be observed under the new Law if only they were not done as obligations of the old Law, which was abrogated[836] [...][837]

Thus it is unequivocally clear that according to the solemn and supreme magisterium of the Church, it is a dogma of faith that the Old Covenant has been abrogated by divine ordinance, and has therefore ceased to exist as a legitimate basis for any religious observance by anyone — in a word, it has been **revoked**. The reason, defined at Florence, why the Old Covenant has been abolished, is because it *"signified something in the future,"* and that *something* which it signified was its fulfilment by the Mediator of the New Covenant, Jesus Christ. Thus, before its fulfilment by Christ, the prescriptions of the Old Covenant *"were adequate for the divine cult of that age,"* but then, those Old Testament prescriptions, *"once our Lord Jesus Christ who was signified by them had come, came to an end and the sacraments of the new Testament had their beginning."* It is for reason of this signification that

---

[836] In the Italian version: "che è stata superata" — *superata* is a word that denotes something that has been surpassed, i.e., *superseded*.

[837] Benedict XIV *Ex Quo Primum*, 1st of March 1756.

St. Augustine says, "In the Old Testament the New is concealed, in the New the Old is revealed".[838]

In order to understand why this is so, namely, that the New Covenant is signified by the Old, one must first take into account the original purpose of the first of all covenants, and therefore also the final cause of man and all creation. St. Thomas explains:

> As the end corresponds to the principle, it is not possible to be ignorant of the end of things if we know their principle. Therefore, since the principle of all things is something outside the universe, namely, God, it is clear from what has been expounded above (q. 44. a. 1-2 everything is created by God), that we must conclude that the end of all things is some extrinsic good. This can be proved by reason. For it is clear that good has the nature of an end; wherefore, a particular end of anything consists in some particular good; while the universal end of all things is the Universal Good; Which is good of Itself by virtue of Its Essence, Which is the very essence of goodness; whereas a particular good is good by participation. Now it is manifest that in the whole created universe there is not a good which is not such by participation. Wherefore that good which is the end of the whole universe must be a good outside the universe.[839]

---

[838] St. Augustine, *Quaest. in Hept.* 2,73: PL 34, 623; cf. DV 16. — «Novum Testamentum in Vetere latet, Vetus Testamentum in Novo patet.» In *De Civitate Dei, liber xvi,* cap. XXVII: «Quid est enim quod dicitur testamentum uetus nisi noui occultatio? Et quid est aliud quod dicitur nouum nisi ueteris reuelatio?»

[839] *Summa Theol.* Iª q. 103 a. 2 co. — «Respondeo dicendum quod, cum finis respondeat principio, non potest fieri ut, principio cognito, quid sit rerum finis ignoretur. Cum igitur principium rerum sit aliquid extrinsecum a toto universo, scilicet Deus, ut ex supra dictis patet; necesse est quod etiam finis rerum sit quoddam bonum extrinsecum. Et hoc ratione apparet. Manifestum est enim quod bonum habet rationem finis. Unde finis particularis alicuius rei est quoddam bonum particulare, finis autem universalis rerum omnium est quoddam bonum universale. Bonum autem universale est quod est per se et per suam essentiam bonum, quod est ipsa essentia bonitatis, bonum autem particulare est quod est participative bonum. Manifestum est autem quod in tota universitate creaturarum nullum est bonum quod non sit participative bonum. Unde illud bonum quod est finis totius universi, oportet quod sit extrinsecum a toto universo.»

That extrinsic good, which is the universal end of all creation is the divine goodness: *divina bonitas est finis rerum omnium.* (I*ᵃ* q. 44.a. 4) Therefore, the good that all things seek, and which is the end of all creation, is a participation in the divine goodness: "All things desire God as their end, when they desire some good thing, whether this desire be intellectual or sensible, or natural, i.e. without knowledge; because nothing is good and desirable except forasmuch as it participates in the likeness to God."[840] Thus, all things have been created by God so that they may participate in the divine goodness; and thus, the human race was created in order to participate in a fruition of the divine goodness by a supernatural participation in the divine live by grace, for which reason, the first of all covenants united the entire human race to God, and after the fall of Adam from that grace of original justice, all subsequent covenants were instituted by God for the redemption of the human race and its restoration and to that original state by a *regeneration* of divine grace. This was the first promise given to Adam, the redemption and regeneration of the human race after the Fall (Gen. 3:15), and in this context the end of all subsequent covenants must be understood. Thus, the promise was given to Abraham with circumcision as the sign of regeneration — «Then God said to Abraham, "As for you, you must keep my covenant, you and your descendants after you for the generations to come. This is my covenant with you and your descendants after you, the covenant you are to keep: Every male among you shall be circumcised.» (Gen. 17:9) The means of regeneration itself was promised but not yet given, but circumcision was a sign of regeneration as Augustine says, *"quia circumcisio signum regenerationis"* — and in this context it is explained by him in *De Civitate Dei:*[841]

> Now there are many things called God's covenants besides those two great ones, the old and the new, which anyone who pleases may read and know. For the first covenant, which was made with the first man, is just this: In the day you eat thereof, you shall surely die. Genesis

---

[840] *Summa Theol.* I*ᵃ* q. 44 a. 4 ad 3 — «omnia appetunt Deum ut finem, appetendo quodcumque bonum, sive appetitu intelligibili, sive sensibili, sive naturali, qui est sine cognitione, quia nihil habet rationem boni et appetibilis, nisi secundum quod participat Dei similitudinem.»

[841] https://www.newadvent.org/fathers/120116.htm

2:17 Whence it is written in the book called Ecclesiasticus, All flesh waxes old as does a garment. For the covenant from the beginning is, You shall die the death. Sirach 15:17 Now, as the law was more plainly given afterward, and the apostle says, Where no law is, there is no prevarication, Romans 4:15 on what supposition is what is said in the psalm true, I accounted all the sinners of the earth prevaricators, except that all who are held liable for any sin are accused of dealing deceitfully (prevaricating) with some law? If on this account, then, even the infants are, according to the true belief, born in, not actual but original, so that we confess they have need of grace for the remission of sins, certainly it must be acknowledged that in the same sense in which they are sinners they are also prevaricators of that law which was given in Paradise, according to the truth of both scriptures, I accounted all the sinners of the earth prevaricators, and Where no law is, there is no prevarication. And thus, because circumcision was the sign of regeneration, and the infant, on account of the original sin by which God's covenant was first broken, was not undeservedly to lose his generation unless delivered by regeneration, these divine words are to be understood as if it had been said, Whoever is not born again, that soul shall perish from his people, because he has broken my covenant, since he also has sinned in Adam with all others.[842]

---

[842] *De Civitate Dei liber xvi cap. xxvii* — «Multa quippe appellantur testamenta Dei exceptis illis duobus magnis, uetere et nouo, quod licet cuique legendo cognoscere. Testamentum autem primum, quod factum est ad hominem primum, profecto illud est: Qua die ederitis, morte moriemini. Vnde scriptum est in libro, qui ecclesiasticus appellatur: Omnis caro sicut uestis ueterescit. Testamentum enim a saeculo: Morte morieris. Cum enim lex euidentior postea data sit, et dicat apostolus: Vbi autem non est lex, nec praeuaricatio, quo pacto in psalmo quod legitur uerum est: Praeuaricatores aestimaui omnes peccatores terrae, nisi quia omnes legis alicuius praeuaricatae sunt rei, qui aliquo peccato tenentur obstricti? Quam ob rem si etiam paruuli, quod uera fides habet, nascuntur non proprie, sed originaliter peccatores, unde illis gratiam remissionis peccatorum necessariam confitemur: profecto eo modo, quo sunt peccatores, etiam praeuaricatores legis illius, quae in paradiso data est, agnoscuntur; ut uerum sit utrumque, quod scriptum est, et: Praeuaricatores aestimaui omnes peccatores terrae, et: Vbi lex non est, nec praeuaricatio. Ac per hoc, quia circumcisio signum regenerationis fuit et non inmerito paruulum propter originale peccatum, quo primum Dei dissipatum est testamentum, generatio disperdet, nisi regeneratio liberet: sic intellegenda sunt haec uerba diuina, tamquam dictum sit: "Qui non fuerit regeneratus, interibit anima illa de

Before him and in the same vein, St. Irenaeus writes on the covenants (*Adv. Haer. X*):

> Now by all these one God is shown forth, revealing to men the new dispensation of liberty, the covenant, through the new advent of His Son. [...]
>
> For the living creatures are quadriform, and the Gospel is quadriform, as is also the course followed by the Lord. For this reason were four principal (καθολικαί) covenants given to the human race: **one, prior to the deluge, under Adam; the second, that after the deluge, under Noah; the third, the giving of the law, under Moses; the fourth, that which renovates man, and sums up all things in itself by means of the Gospel, raising and bearing men upon its wings into the heavenly kingdom.** [...]
>
> **Chapter IX.** — For the new covenant having been known and preached by the prophets, He who was to carry it out according to the good pleasure of the Father was also preached, having been revealed to men as God pleased; that they might always make progress through believing in Him, and by means of the [successive] covenants, should gradually attain to perfect salvation. For there is one salvation and one God; but the precepts which form the man are numerous, and the steps which lead man to God are not a few.
>
> **Chapter XVI** — 1. Moreover, we learn from the Scripture itself, that God gave circumcision, not as the completer of righteousness, but as a sign, that the race of Abraham might continue recognisable. For it declares: "God said unto Abraham, Every male among you shall be circumcised; and ye shall circumcise the flesh of your foreskins, as a token of the covenant between Me and you." This same does Ezekiel the prophet say with regard to the Sabbaths: "Also I gave them My Sabbaths, to be a sign between Me and them, that they might know that I am the Lord, that sanctify them." And in Exodus, God says to Moses: "And ye shall observe My Sabbaths; for it shall be a sign between Me and you for your generations." These things, then, were given for a sign; [...] 2. And that man was not justified by these things, but that they were given as a sign to the people, this fact shows,— that Abraham himself, without circumcision and without observance of Sabbaths, "believed

---

genere eius", quia testamentum Dei dissipauit, quando in Adam cum omnibus etiam ipse peccauit.» https://la.wikisource.org/wiki/De_civitate_Dei/Liber_XVI.

God, and it was imputed unto him for righteousness; and he was called the friend of God."

Then, again, Lot, without circumcision, was brought out from Sodom, receiving salvation from God. So also did Noah, pleasing God, although he was uncircumcised, receive the dimensions [of the ark], of the world of the second race [of men]. Enoch, too, pleasing God, without circumcision, discharged the office of God's legate to the angels although he was a man, and was translated, and is preserved until now as a witness of the just judgment of God, because the angels when they had transgressed fell to the earth for judgment, but the man who pleased [God] was translated for salvation. Moreover, all the rest of the multitude of those righteous men who lived before Abraham, and of those patriarchs who preceded Moses, were justified independently of the things above mentioned, and without the law of Moses. As also Moses himself says to the people in Deuteronomy: "The Lord thy God formed a covenant in Horeb. The Lord formed not this covenant with your fathers, but for you." 3. Why, then, did the Lord not form the covenant for the fathers? Because "the law was not established for righteous men." (1 Tim. 1:9) But the righteous fathers had the meaning of the Decalogue written in their hearts and souls, that is, they loved the God who made them, and did no injury to their neighbour. There was therefore no occasion that they should be cautioned by prohibitory mandates (*correptoriis literis*), because they had the righteousness of the law in themselves. But when this righteousness and love to God had passed into oblivion, and became extinct in Egypt, God did necessarily, because of His great goodwill to men, reveal Himself by a voice, and led the people with power out of Egypt, in order that man might again become the disciple and follower of God; and He afflicted those who were disobedient, that they should not contemn their Creator; and He fed them with manna, that they might receive food for their souls (*uti rationalem acciperent escam*); as also Moses says in Deuteronomy: "And fed thee with manna, which thy fathers did not know, that thou mightest know that man doth not live by bread alone; but by every word of God proceeding out of His mouth doth man live." And it enjoined love to God, and taught just dealing towards our neighbour, that we should neither be unjust nor unworthy of God, who prepares man for His friendship through the medium of the Decalogue, and likewise for agreement with his neighbour,—matters which did certainly profit man himself... 5. The laws of bondage, however, were one by one promulgated to the people by Moses, suited for their instruction or for their punishment, as Moses himself declared: "And the Lord commanded me at that time to teach you statutes and judgments."

These things, therefore, which were given for bondage, and for a sign to them, He cancelled by the new covenant of liberty.

In the preceding passages of the two Fathers who wrote most extensively on the covenants, and in unanimity with the other Fathers, three things can be observed: Between the time of Adam and the time of Christ, there were many covenants, but, 1) two principal covenants were given, namely the *Old Covenant*, which is the Mosaic Covenant, and the *New Covenant*, which is the covenant of Jesus Christ, 2) The New Covenant fulfilled the promises of the Old Covenant; and 3) by delivering what was only signified and promised in the Old Covenant, the Old Covenant was made obsolete and became defunct when that which it signified and promised was fulfilled.

Thus, it is not for no reason that the Fathers unanimously teach that the Old Covenant is properly the Mosaic Covenant alone and no other, and that it was revoked: they simply received that doctrine straight out of the New Testament writings of St. Paul ("in Christ it is made void" - 2 Cor. 3:15). In Chapter 8 of Hebrews, the Apostle explains that the Mosaic Covenant is called the Old Covenant precisely because it made old by the New Covenant, and is to be ended: "Now in saying a new, he hath made the former old. And that which decayeth and groweth old, is near its end." On this solid basis of Scripture and Tradition, the Church has defined (Council of Florence) that the Old Covenant is revoked, abolished, and abrogated (cf. Benedict XIV, *Ex quo primum*, 1 March 1756).

St. Thomas concisely sums up the Church's teaching on the relationship between the covenants:

> It must be noted that the good has various degrees, as Dionysius states (Div. Nom. iv): for there is a perfect good, and an imperfect good. In things ordained to an end, there is perfect goodness when a thing is such that it is sufficient in itself to conduce to the end: while there is imperfect goodness when a thing is of some assistance in attaining the end, but is not sufficient for the realization thereof. Thus a medicine is perfectly good, if it gives health to a man; but it is imperfect, if it helps to cure him, without being able to bring him back to health. [...] the Old Law was good... it repressed concupiscence which is in conflict with reason, as evidenced by the commandment, "Thou shalt not covet thy neighbor's goods" (Ex. 20:17). Moreover the same law forbade all kinds

of sin... Consequently it is evident that it was a good law... **the end of the Divine law is to bring man to that end which is everlasting happiness... the prohibition and punishment of sin, does not suffice for the perfection of the Divine law: but it is requisite that it should make man altogether fit to partake of everlasting happiness**. Now this cannot be done save by the grace of the Holy Ghost, whereby "charity" which fulfilleth the law... "is spread abroad in our hearts" (Rom. 5:5): since "the grace of God is life everlasting" (Rom. 6:23). **But the Old Law could not confer this grace, for this was reserved to Christ; because, as it is written (Jn. 1:17), the law was given "by Moses, grace and truth came by Jesus Christ."** Consequently the Old Law was good indeed, but imperfect, according to **Heb. 7:19: "The law brought nothing to perfection."**

Since *The law brought nothing to perfection,* its purpose was fulfilled by its completion by that which it signified, namely Christ, who brought it to perfection by fulfilling what it foretold and promised, namely, the redemption of the human race. For this reason it was necessary for the Old Law to pass away upon its fulfilment by Jesus Christ, with the consequence that since redemption of humanity was accomplished by Christ, salvation can be gained only by faith in Him and obedience to the precepts of the New Covenant mediated by Him, for which reason there is only one valid covenant between God and man, the *new covenant* foretold by Jeremiah (Jer. 31:31-2), mediated by Christ as foretold by Moses (Deuteronomy 18:17-19). In that prophecy in Deuteronomy, ("[17] And the Lord said to me: They have spoken all things well.[18] I will raise them up a prophet out of the midst of their brethren like to thee: and I will put my words in his mouth, and he shall speak to them all that I shall command him. [19] And he that will not hear his words, which he shall speak in my name, I will be the revenger."), God spoke to Moses of *a prophet like to thee,* or *like unto thyself,* which is to say, **the mediator of a covenant**. In *III q. 26 a. 1,* St. Thomas introduces his teaching on this point quoting St. Paul: «It is written *I Tim. II*: "There is one Mediator of God and man, the man Christ Jesus."» He then explains:

> Properly speaking, the office of a mediator is to join together and unite those between whom he mediates: for extremes are united in the mean [medio]. Now to unite men to God perfectively belongs to Christ, through Whom men are reconciled to God, according to 2 Cor. 5:19:

"God was in Christ reconciling the world to Himself." And, consequently, Christ alone is the perfect Mediator of God and men, inasmuch as, by His death, He reconciled the human race to God. Hence the Apostle, after saying, "Mediator of God and man, the man Christ Jesus," added: "Who gave Himself a redemption for all."[843]

In *III q. 1 a.2* St. Thomas explains that for the redemption and restoration of the human race, it was fitting and necessary for God to become incarnate. It was not necessary *absolutely*, "as food is necessary for the preservation of human life," since, as St. Thomas explains, "For God with His omnipotent power could have restored human nature in many other ways." However, it was necessary in a secondary way: «But in the second way it was necessary that God should become incarnate for the restoration of human nature. Hence Augustine says (De Trin. xii, 10): *"We shall also show that other ways were not wanting to God, to Whose power all things are equally subject; but that there was not a more fitting way of healing our misery."*»

The reasons which St. Thomas gives in that same article to explain why it was most fitting that the Son of God should become incarnate are taken mainly from St. Augustine and also St. Leo the Great:

> Now this may be viewed with respect to our "furtherance in good." First, with regard to faith, which is made more certain by believing God Himself Who speaks; hence Augustine says (De Civ. Dei xi, 2): *"In order that man might journey more trustfully toward the truth, the Truth itself, the Son of God, having assumed human nature, established and founded faith."* Secondly, with regard to hope, which is thereby greatly strengthened; hence Augustine says (De Trin. xiii): *"Nothing was so necessary for raising our hope as to show us how deeply God loved us. And what could afford us a stronger proof of this than that the Son of God should become a partner with us of human nature?"*

---

[843] *Summa Theol.* III^a q. 26 a. 1 co. — «Respondeo dicendum quod mediatoris officium proprie est coniungere eos inter quos est mediator, nam extrema uniuntur in medio. Unire autem homines Deo perfective quidem convenit Christo, per quem homines reconciliantur Deo, secundum illud II Cor. V, *Deus erat in Christo mundum reconcilians sibi.* Et ideo solus Christus est perfectus Dei et hominum mediator, inquantum per suam mortem humanum genus Deo reconciliavit. Unde, cum apostolus dixisset, *mediator Dei et hominum homo Christus Iesus,* subiunxit, *qui dedit semetipsum redemptionem pro omnibus.*»

Thirdly, with regard to charity, which is greatly enkindled by this; hence Augustine says (De Catech. Rudib. iv): *"What greater cause is there of the Lord's coming than to show God's love for us?"* And he afterwards adds: *"If we have been slow to love, at least let us hasten to love in return."* Fourthly, with regard to well-doing, in which He set us an example; hence Augustine says in a sermon (xxii de Temp.): *"Man who might be seen was not to be followed; but God was to be followed, Who could not be seen. And therefore God was made man, that He Who might be seen by man, and Whom man might follow, might be shown to man."* Fifthly, with regard to the full participation of the Divinity, which is the true bliss of man and end of human life; and this is bestowed upon us by Christ's humanity; for Augustine says in a sermon (xiii de Temp.): *"God was made man, that man might be made God."*

So also was this useful for our "withdrawal from evil." First, because man is taught by it not to prefer the devil to himself, nor to honor him who is the author of sin; hence Augustine says (De Trin. xiii, 17): *"Since human nature is so united to God as to become one person, let not these proud spirits dare to prefer themselves to man, because they have no bodies."* Secondly, because we are thereby taught how great is man's dignity, lest we should sully it with sin; hence Augustine says (De Vera Relig. xvi): *"God has proved to us how high a place human nature holds amongst creatures, inasmuch as He appeared to men as a true man."* And Pope Leo says in a sermon on the Nativity (xxi): *"Learn, O Christian, thy worth; and being made a partner of the Divine nature, refuse to return by evil deeds to your former worthlessness."* Thirdly, because, *"in order to do away with man's presumption, the grace of God is commended in Jesus Christ, though no merits of ours went before,"* as Augustine says (De Trin. xiii, 17). Fourthly, because *"man's pride, which is the greatest stumbling-block to our clinging to God, can be convinced and cured by humility so great,"* as Augustine says in the same place. Fifthly, in order to free man from the thraldom of sin, which, as Augustine says (De Trin. xiii, 13), *"ought to be done in such a way that the devil should be overcome by the justice of the man Jesus Christ,"* and this was done by Christ satisfying for us. Now a mere man could not have satisfied for the whole human race, and God was not bound to satisfy; hence it behooved Jesus Christ to be both God and man. Hence Pope Leo says in the same sermon: *"Weakness is assumed by strength, lowliness by majesty, mortality by eternity, in order that one and the same Mediator of God and men might die in one and rise in the other — for this was our fitting remedy. Unless He was God, He would not have brought a remedy; and unless He was man, He would not have set an example."*[844]

---

[844] *III q. 1 a.2.*

Since there is but one sole mediator between God and man, Jesus Christ, there can be only one covenant between God and man, namely, the *New and Everlasting Covenant* mediated by Jesus Christ; for which reason, there can exist only one true religion — that one founded by Christ in fulfilment of the scriptures. Since there can only be one true religion, that of the sole mediator between God and man Jesus Christ, **the Jewish religion cannot be the true religion.** St. Alphonsus explains the matter in Chapter III of the Third Part of *Verità della Fede*:

> The Jewish religion cannot be true.
>
> 1. At one time the Jews had true religion, true law and true Church; but after the coming of the Messiah their religion cannot be true anymore, because according to the same prophecies which they accepted as divine, it had to be abolished, and be succeeded by the new law, as Jeremiah foretold (ch. 51. 9. 31): *Ecce dies venient, dicit Dominus, et feriain domui Israel et doinui Juda fœdus novum.* On which words the Apostle then wrote (Hebr. 8. 13.): *Dicendo autem novum, veteravit prius. Quod autem antiquatur et se nescit, prope interitum est.* That then the Messiah has already come, and that this Messiah has been Jesus Christ is already clearly proved in the second part of chapter IV. and the following; and it is based on their own writings, on the miracles of the Saviour and of his disciples, and on the punishment which the poor Jews have suffered for so long for their obstinacy; while the poor see the dominion of Judea lost, the city destroyed, the temple burned, the sacrifices abandoned, and they scattered throughout the earth, without kings, without priests and without altar; all of which was foretold by the prophets: and they see it thus done completely accomplished, and yet obstinate they continue to deny their Saviour. [845]

---

[845] *Verità Della Fede*, Opera Del Beato Alfonso Maria de' Liguori, Tomo Secondo, Parte Terza, Monza, 1823, pp. 63-64: «Non può esser vera la religione Giudaica .1. Un tempo i Giudei ebbero vera religione, vera legge e vera Chiesa; ma dopo la venuta del Messia la lor religione non può esser più vera, perché secondo le stesse profezie da essi accettate per divine, ella dovea abolirsi, ed a quella succedere la nuova legge, come predisse Geremia (c. 51. 9. 31.): *Ecce dies venient, dicit Dominus, et feriain domui Israel et doinui Juda fœdus novum.* Sulle quali parole poi, scrisse l'Apostolo (Hebr. 8. 13): *Dicendo autem novum, veteravit prius. Quod autem antiquatur et se nescit, prope interitum est.* Che poi il Messia sia già venuto, e che questo Messia sia sta to Gesù Cristo

In Chapter IV of the Second Part the Holy Doctor gets to the crux of the matter:

> The Divinity of the Scriptures is also proved by the Prophecies of the coming of the Messiah.
>
> 1. The predicting of the future belongs only to God. Isaiah said: *Annuntiate quae ventura sunt in futurama, et scietis, quia Di estis vos. Isa.* 41. 27. And for the same Prophet the Lord said elsewhere: *Quis similis mei? vocet, et annuntiet. — ventura, et quae futura sunt annuntient eis. Isa.* 44. 7. Whoever is similar to me, says God, should announce future things if he can. Created minds can but foresee, or rather, conjecture the future effects of some natural cause; but to foresee with certainty the effects, totally contingent, this belongs only to God, whose will alone is the cause of these effects. Writers refer to various Oracles, who received the Gentiles from their Idols; but these Oracles were either lies invented by the Idolatrous Priests, or they were also said of ambiguous outcomes, or of things at that time not unknown to the Demons. In Part III. Cap. II. § 1. we will speak of such oracles. On the other hand the Divine Prophecies have already preceded the events long before, and since then they have been fulfilled so individually that he would never have been able to pronounce them, who had not clearly foreseen them. Grotius errs therefore saying that the Prophecies have no strength to persuade Christian truths, but only help to confirm the truths believed. He errs, since the Figures are one thing, the Prophecies another; the Prophecies are those, which are seen to be fulfilled in their natural sense, not at all accomodated; and therefore they have the same strength, which has the truthfulness of God. We omit here to speak of so many other admirable predictions made by the Prophets of the Old Law, and only mention the Prophecies of the Old Testament, which concerned the Messiah, who in the fullness of time was to come to redeem the world. Not only the Prophecies, but all the Sacrifices of the ancient Law, all the solemnities,

---

già si è chiaramente provato nella seconda parte al capo IV. e seguenti; e consta dalle stesse loro scritture, da' miracoli del Salvatore e de' suoi discepoli, e dal castigo che i miseri Giudei soffrono da sì lungo tempo per la loro ostinazione; mentre vedono i miseri il dominio della Giudea perduto, la città distrutta, il tempio bruciato, i sacrificj dismessi, ed essi dispersi per tutta la terra, senza re, senza sacerdoti e senza altare; il che tutto fu predetto da' profeti: ed essi lo vedono compitamente avverato cos' fatti, e pure ostinati sieguono a negare il lor Salvatore.»

and all the Holy Scriptures already coincided with this great Work of the human Redemption. Hence the Apostle says (1. *Cor.* No. 11. *et Coloss.* 2. 17.) that the whole History of the Old Testament is nothing but a Prophecy of Jesus-Christ, and of the New Testament. Some Prophecies are literal of the Messiah: others are mixed with literal, and typical: others are purely typical: and others have been canonized by God himself, having declared that he had given them as figures, 2. Then it cannot be doubted that these Prophecies of the Messiah are really in the Old Testament, because if ever they had been stealthily intruded into the holy Books by Christians, the Jews who deny the coming of the Messiah, and from whom these Scriptures have come down to us, would certainly deny them, and would oppose the false additions made by Christians. But the Jews do not deny them, only they interpret them at their whim for other Persons, and not for the Messiah: however contradicting the Rabbis, who lived before Jesus-Christ, who already explained these Prophecies, as the Christians explain them, accordingly as Oetius *Demonstr. Evang.* and Calmet in his Dissertation of the Messiah show.[846]

---

[846] *Verità Della Fede*, Opera Del Beato Alfonso Maria de' Liguori, DIVISA IN TRE PARTI, Parte II, Napoli 1838, pp. 128-130: «Si prova in oltre la Divinità delle Scritture dalle Profezie della venuta del Messia. 1. Il predire il futuro s'appartiene solo a Dio. Diceva Isaia: *Annuntiate quae ventura sunt in futurum, et scietis, quia Di estis vos.* Isa. 4 1. 27. E per lo stesso Profeta disse altrove il Signore: *Quis similis mei? vocet, et annuntiet.* — *ventura, et quae futura sunt annuntient eis.* Isa. 44. 7. Chi è simile a me, dice Dio, prenunzi se può le cose future. Possono le menti create bensì prevedere, o per meglio dire, conghietturare gli effetti futuri di qualche causa naturale; ma il prevedere con certezza gli effetti, totalmente contingenti, ciò compete solamente a Dio, la sola di cui volontà è la causa di tali effetti, Si riferiscono dagli Scrittori varj Oracoli, che riceveano i Gentili da' loro Idoli; ma questi Oracoli o erano menzogne inventate da' Sacerdoti Idolatri, o pure erano detti di successi ambigui, o di cose in quel tempo non ignote ai Demonj. Nella Parte III. Cap. II. §. 1. si parlerà di tali Oracoli. All'incontro le Profezie Divine son già precedute agli avvenimenti molto tempo prima, e di poi si sono adempite così individualmente, che non avrebbe mai potuto pronunziarle, chi non l'avesse chiaramente prevedute. Erra per tanto Grozio dicendo, che le Profezie non han forza di persuadere le verità Cristiane, ma solo giovano a confermare le verità credute. Erra, poiché altre son le Figure, altre le Profezie; le Profezie sono quelle, che si vedono avverate nel lor senso naturale, non già accomodato; e perciò elle hanno la stessa forza, che ha la veracità di Dio. Noi tralasciamo qui di parlare di tante altre ammirabili predizioni fatte da' Profeti dell'antica Legge, e solamente facciam menzione

The coming of Jesus Christ and his work of redemption is the fulfilment of the messianic prophecies and all that was signified in the Mosaic Law (Matt. 5:17), and his mediation of the New Covenant, as well as the reasons which necessitated the new covenant were foretold in the Old Testament, as is explained in Hebrews 8:

> ⁷ For if there had been nothing wrong with that first covenant, no place would have been sought for another. ⁸ But God found fault with the people and said: "The days are coming, declares the Lord, when I will make a new covenant with the people of Israel and with the people of Judah. ⁹ It will not be like the covenant I made with their ancestors when I took them by the hand to lead them out of Egypt, because they did not remain faithful to my covenant, and I turned away from them, declares the Lord. ¹⁰ This is the covenant I will establish with the people of Israel after that time, declares the Lord. I will put my laws in their minds and write them on their hearts. I will be their God, and they will be my people. ¹¹ No longer will they teach their neighbour, or say to one another, 'Know the Lord,' because they will all know me, from the least of them to the greatest. ¹² For I will forgive their wickedness and will remember their sins no more. ¹³ By calling this covenant "new," he has

---

delle Profezie dell'antico Testamento, che riguardavano il Messia, il quale nella pienezza de' tempi dovea venire a redimere il Mondo. A questa grand'Opera dell'umana Redenzione collimavano già, non solamente le Profezie, ma tutti i Sagrificj dell'antica Legge, tutte le solennità, e tutte le sante Scritture. Onde dice l'Apostolo (1. Cor. no. 11. et Coloss. 2. 17.) che tutta l'Istoria del Testamento Vecchio non è, che una Profezia di Gesù-Cristo, e del Testamento nuovo. Alcune Profezie sono letterali del Messia: altre sono miste di letterali, e tipiche: altre sono puramente tipiche: ed altre sono state da Dio stesso canonizzate, avendo egli dichiarato d'aver le date come figure, 2. Queste Profezie poi del Messia non può dubitarsi, che stiano veramente nel Vecchio Testamento, poiché se mai da' Cristiani fossero state furtivamente intruse ne' sagri Libri, gli Ebrei che negano la venuta del Messia, e da' quali queste Scritture a noi son pervenute, certamente le negherebbero, ed opporrebbero le false agiunzioni fatte da' Cristiani. Ma gli Ebrei non le negano, solamente essi le interpretano a lor capriccio per altre Persone, e non per lo Messia: contradicendo però in tal punto a' Rabbini, che vissero prima di Gesù-Cristo, i quali spiegarono già queste Profezie, come le spiegano i Cristiani, secondo fan vedere l'Oezio *Demonstr. Evang.* ed il Calmet nella sua Dissertazione del Messia.»

made the first one obsolete; and what is obsolete and outdated will soon disappear."

Now for there to be a new covenant, there must be a mediator of it:

> Now the main point of what we are saying is this: We do have such a high priest, who sat down at the right hand of the throne of the Majesty in heaven, 2 and who serves in the sanctuary, the true tabernacle set up by the Lord, not by a mere human being. 3 Every high priest is appointed to offer both gifts and sacrifices, and so it was necessary for this one also to have something to offer. 4 If he were on earth, he would not be a priest, for there are already priests who offer the gifts prescribed by the law. 5 They serve at a sanctuary that is a copy and shadow of what is in heaven. This is why Moses was warned when he was about to build the tabernacle: "See to it that you make everything according to the pattern shown you on the mountain." 6 But in fact **the ministry Jesus has received is as superior to theirs as the covenant of which he is mediator is superior to the old one, since the new covenant is established on better promises.**

On the page preceding the title page of that great three volume work cited above, *Verità della Fede*, St. Alphonsus introduces the foundational principle of the true religion of the New Covenant expressed in the Saviour's own words, "He who does not believe will be condemned." (Qui vero non crediderit, condemnabitur. MARC. CAP. XVI, v. 16.) On these words are founded the dogma the Church professes: "Whosoever will be saved, before all it is necessary that he hold the Catholic faith. Which faith unless every one keep integral and inviolate, without doubt he shall perish in eternity."[847] **Jesus Christ, the Son of God having all power in heaven and on earth (Matt. 28:18) declares that whosoever refuses to believe in Him will be condemned (Mark 16:16), because He is the promised Redeemer of the entire human race (Luke 4:18, Is. 61:1, Matt. 12:18), and therefore, without exception, the grace of that redemption cannot be received without faith in Him,** and in all the saving truths revealed in, by and through Him, which he entrusted to the Church as a repository of those truths to be taught by his

---

[847] Athanasian Creed: «Quicumque vult salvus esse, ante omnia opus est, ut teneat catholicam fidem: Quam nisi quisque integram inviolatamque servaverit, absque dubio in aeternum peribit.»

authority to **all the nations on earth (first the Jewish nation and then the others)**; for which reason **there is *without exception* no salvation for anyone in any other faith or religion outside of the Catholic Church. As there is only one God, there can be only one true religion**, and the reason for this is that: *"There is one Mediator of God and man, the man Christ Jesus."* (I Tim. II) In mediating the New Covenant, He has fulfilled the Old: "Think not that I am come to destroy the Law or the Prophets. I am not come to destroy, but to fulfil." (Matt. 5:17). In fulfilling and bringing to completion all things signified in the Old Covenant, the Old Covenant being completely fulfilled passed away: "For amen I say unto you, till heaven and earth pass, one jot, or one tittle shall not pass of the law, till all be fulfilled." (Matt. 5:18) With the Old Covenant having been fulfilled and therefore brought to an end, the Temple was destroyed and the genealogical records that established the pedigree of the priests of the Levitical tribe were lost forever, bringing the Aaronic priesthood and its temple worship to extinction. Indeed, as a historical reality, the Mosaic Covenant **ceased**, thereby confirming the dogmatic truth defined at Florence, that its *rites, sacrifices, and sacraments have ceased at the coming of Our Lord Jesus Christ.*

THE RATZINGER DOCTRINE ON THE RELATION BETWEEN THE COVENANTS

In a brief article he wrote for *Herderkorrespondenz* 12/2018, *Not Mission but Dialogue,*[848] Pope Benedict XVI wrote:

> The Gospel of **Saint Matthew** ends with the order to the disciples to go out into all the world and make all peoples disciples of Jesus (Mt 28:19). Mission in all peoples and cultures is the commission that Christ has left to His own. It is a matter of making people aware of the "unknown God" (Acts 17:23). Man has a right to know God, because only those who know God can correctly live as humans. **That is why the mission is universal – with one exception: a mission of the Jews was not intended and not necessary simply because they knew the "unknown God"** among all peoples alone. **For Israel, therefore, it was not mission, but the dialogue**, whether Jesus of Nazereth is "the Son of God, the Logos" according to the promises made to his people Israel

---

[848] *Nicht Mission, sondern Dialog*

and, without knowing it, humanity waits. To re-engage in this dialogue is the task that this hour is asking us to do.[849]

I have set in bold the key passage of interest in the cited segment of my translation of the text, which in its stated context is heretical. As a matter of historical fact, the Roman Church has not evangelized the Jewish people as it did so many others throughout two millennia, but that does not mean that «a mission of the Jews was not intended and not necessary simply because they knew the "unknown God" among all peoples alone.» The Church eventually focused its mission to evangelize almost entirely on the Gentiles only because the Jews had first rejected the Church's evangelization of the Jews themselves, and therefore following Christ's instruction, "And whosoever shall not receive you, nor hear your words: going forth out of that house or city shake off the dust from your feet," (Matt. 10:14), the disciples eventually shook the dust from their feet and went forth out of the house of Jacob to evangelize the nations.

As is clear from what is already stated above, Jesus Christ is the *sole mediator between God and man* who mediated the New Covenant as the **head of the entire human race**, i.e. the "Bridegroom" of the whole human race (Matthew 9:15), and the therefore the **New Adam**, i.e. the "last Adam"(1 Cor. 15:45), whose mission did not exclude the Jews, but began with them: "But he answered and said, I am not sent but unto the lost sheep of the house of Israel." (Matthew 15:24) It was to Jews and not Gentiles that Christ

---

[849] «Das Evangelium des Heiligen Matthaus endet mit dem Auftrag an die Jünger, in alle Welt hinauszugehen und alle Völker zu Jüngern Jesu zu machen (Mt 28,19). Mission in allen Völkern und Kulturen ist der Auftrag, den Christus den Seinigen hinterlassen hat. Es geht dabei darum, den Menschen den „unbekannten Gott" (Apg 17,23) bekanntzumachen. Der Mensch hat ein Recht, Gott kennenzulernen, weil nur, wer Gott kennt, das Menschsein recht leben kann. Deswegen ist der Missionsauftrag universal – mit einer Ausnahme: Eine Mission der Juden war einfach deshalb nicht vorgesehen und nicht nötig, weil sie allein unter allen Völkern den „unbekannten Gott" kannten. Für Israel galt und gilt daher nicht Mission, sondern der Dialog darüber, ob Jesus von Nazareth „der Sohn Gottes, der Logos" ist, auf den gemäß den an sein Volk ergangenen Verheisungen Israel und, ohne es zu wissen, die Menschheit wartet. Diesen Dialog neu aufzunehmen, ist der Auftrag, den uns diese Stunde stellt.»

addressed the words, "Therefore I said to you, that you shall die in your sins. For if you believe not that I am he, you shall die in your sin." (John 8:24) It was to "Jews, devout men, out of every nation under heaven" (Acts 2:5) that St. Peter addressed these words: "Do penance, and be baptized every one of you in the name of Jesus Christ, for the remission of your sins: and you shall receive the gift of the Holy Ghost. For the promise is to you, and to your children, and to all that are far off, whomsoever the Lord our God shall call." (Acts 2:38-39) So while it is true, as Pope Benedict says, «Mission in all peoples and cultures is the commission that Christ has left to His own,» it is not true that «the mission is universal – with one exception: a mission of the Jews was not intended and not necessary simply because they knew the „unknown God".» It is not enough just to know God through philosophy or the scriptures to gain salvation, but to be united to God by following Christ, the Son of God, and to receive the sacrament of baptism: "I am the way, and the truth, and the life. *No man cometh to the Father, but by me.*" (John 14:6); and Jesus said to Nicodemus, "a ruler of the Jews" (John 3:1): "Amen, amen I say to thee, unless a man be born again of water and the Holy Ghost, he cannot enter into the kingdom of God." (John 3:5) Thus, it is Christ himself who lays down as a condition for salvation for Jews as well as Gentiles that they have faith in Him, and that they receive the sacrament of water, namely, Baptism the sacrament of faith in Jesus Christ.

In «GRACE AND VOCATION WITHOUT REMORSE: COMMENTS ON THE TREATISE *DE JUDAEIS*», Pope Benedict cites the passage from "A Reflection on Theological Questions Pertaining to Catholic-Jewish Relations on the Occasion of the 50th Anniversary of Nostra Aetate (No. 4)," which says, "the new view of Judaism that developed after the Council can be summarized in two statements". Then he quotes the two statements which are:

> 1) The "theory of substitution," which has hitherto determined theological reflection on this question, should be rejected. This view holds that after the rejection of Jesus Christ, Israel ceased to be the bearer of the promises of God, so that it could now be called the people "who were once your chosen people" (Prayer for the Consecration of the Human Race to the Sacred Heart of Jesus). 2) Instead, it is more

correct to speak of the never-revoked covenant—a theme that was developed after the Council in connection with Romans 9-11.

Concerning the "theory of substitution" mentioned in the text, and which the document claimed "has hitherto determined theological reflection on this question," Benedict observes: «First, it should be noted that there was no "theory of substitution" as such before the Council: none of the three editions of the *Lexikon für Theologie und Kirche* (Buchberger - Rahner - Kasper) contains an entry on the theory of substitution. It is also missing from Protestant lexicons such as *Religion in Geschichte und Gegenwart* (3rd ed.).» It is simply not true that the theory, that *Israel ceased to be the bearer of the promises of God,* "hitherto determined theological reflection on this question." In one of his allocutions I read decades ago, I recall even Bl. Pius IX spoke of allusions to those promises in the letters of St. Paul as being yet to be fulfilled. Nevertheless, there have been isolated instances of what suspiciously sounds almost like a "substitution theory", such as in the sermon of Bossuet who said of the Jews: "Accursed People! Your visitation shall pursue you up to your most remote descendants, until the Lord becomes weary of punishing you and at the end of time takes pity on your wretched remains."[850] However, the idea that the doctrine of the revocation of the Mosaic Covenant would be a consequence of a "theory of substitution" can be seen to be a gross absurdity, in that the Mosaic Covenant was indeed revoked by God, but the promises to the Israelite nation in the other covenants were **unconditional** and therefore **irrevocable**. The kingdom that was taken from them as a punishment for having rejected Christ will indeed be restored to the Jewish nation (Acts 1:6), but not before the time when they will finally submit to the rule of Christ, who is the King of the Jews. (John 19:19)

The objection that says the Old Covenant was never revoked because the promise made to Abraham is irrevocable, is a *non sequitur* rooted in a confused notion of what the term "Old Covenant" means. The Covenant with Abraham is irrevocable, but it is not the Old Covenant. According to rabbinical Judaism and Jewish authors

---

[850] Jacques-Bénigne Lignel Bossuet (27 September 1627 – 12 April 1704) *Sermon for Good Friday*, Complete Works, Vol. II. Page 628.

in general, "The Covenant", i.e. *the Jewish Covenant,* is the Sinai Covenant — the covenant mediated by Moses. It was that covenant of which the prophet Jeremiah spoke, saying it would be replaced by a new covenant: "Behold the days shall come, saith the Lord, and I will make a new covenant with the house of Israel, and with the house of Juda: Not according to the covenant which I made with their fathers, in the day that I took them by the hand to bring them out of the land of Egypt: the covenant which they made void, and I had dominion over them, saith the Lord." (Jer. 31: 31-2).Thus, it is explicitly of only that covenant, the Mosaic Covenant, that it is written in Hebrews of the Old Covenant. It is called the "Old Covenant" precisely because it was made old and obsolete by the New Covenant. However, the pope elaborates in a different vein: "In fact, it is unfortunate that our theology generally sees covenant only in the singular, or perhaps only in a strict juxtaposition of Old (First) and New Covenant. For the Old Testament, "covenant" is a dynamic reality that is concretized in an unfolding series of covenants." He continues a few lines later: "A new stage of covenant theology can be found in the Letter to the Hebrews, which takes up the promise of the new covenant (announced with particular clarity in Jer 31) and compares it with previous covenants." Then the key passage follows: "These are all gathered together under the heading of the "first covenant," which is now replaced by the final, "new" covenant." As I mentioned above, the doctrine of the Fathers follows the clear teaching of Hebrews, according to which, the covenant that was to be replaced was the Mosaic Covenant: "I will make a new covenant with the house of Israel and with the house of Judah: Not according to the covenant that I made with their fathers in the day when I took them by the hand to lead them out of the land of Egypt; because they continued not in my covenant, and I regarded them not, saith the Lord." (Heb. 8: 8-9) Thus, it is explicitly clear that it is the Mosaic Covenant, about which verse 13 says it is made **old**: "Now in saying a new, he hath made the former old." So it is unequivocally the teaching of Scripture and of the Fathers that the "Old Covenant" is the Mosaic Covenant only, and it is a dogma of the Catholic faith clearly taught in the New Testament that the Mosaic Covenant was revoked. Thus, it can be hardly maintained, as Pope Benedict asserts, "The word "revoke" does not belong to the vocabulary of divine action." However, he goes on to say "The formula of the 'never-revoked covenant' may have been helpful in a first phase of the new dialogue between Jews and Christians. But it is not suited in the long run to express in an adequate way the magnitude of reality." He then upholds the Catholic doctrine on the relation of the covenants:

> The whole journey of God with his people finally finds its summary and final figure in the Last Supper of Jesus Christ, which anticipates and carries within itself the Cross and Resurrection. We do not need to discuss the complicated problems of the formation of the two traditions: Mark and Matthew on the one hand, and Luke and Paul on the other. In one case, the Sinai tradition is taken up. What has happened there comes to definitive fulfillment here. Accordingly, the promise of the new covenant of Jeremiah 31 is now a present reality. The Sinai covenant was by its very nature always a promise, an approach to what is final. After all destruction, the new covenant is the love of God that goes as far as the death of the Son. The reestablishment of the Sinai covenant in the New Covenant in Jesus' blood—that is, in his love that vanquishes death—gives the covenant a new and permanently valid form.

In contrast, "Pope" Francis in *Evangelii Gaudium* n. 247 asserts the inexcusable heresy: "We hold the Jewish people in special regard because their covenant with God has never been revoked". Now "their covenant with God" has a definitively fixed meaning, as I have explained — according to the tradition of the ancient Fathers and the Jewish tradition as well, the Jewish Covenant is the Mosaic Covenant. According to Bergoglio, faith in Christ, or any belief in God is not necessary for salvation — According to Bergoglio's creed we can deny Christ and still be saved; but according to Pope Benedict:

> With regard to the Jews, Paul says: "the gifts and the calling of God are irrevocable" (Rom 11:29). To all, Scripture says, "if we endure, we shall also reign with him; if we deny him, he also will deny us. If we are faithless, he remains faithful—for he cannot deny himself" (2 Tm 2:12f).

* * *

COMMENTARY

The defect that can be seen in all of these doctrinal positions is essentially that Ratzinger's arguments arriving at these conclusions involve themselves in an unstated contradiction, such as those especially which are rooted in his faulty understanding of concepts such as substance and form. In *Einführung in das Christentum*, Ratzinger explains:

> Let's conclude the whole thing with an Augustine text that splendidly elucidates what is meant. It can be found in the Commentary on John and follows on from the gospel passage «Mea doctrina non est mea.» - My teaching is not my teaching, but that of the Father who sent me "(7:16). Augustine has in the paradox of this proposition illuminated the paradoxality of the Christian image of God and Christian existence. He asks himself first if it is not pure nonsense, a violation of the elementary rules of logic to say something like this: what is mine is not mine. But he drills deeper, what actually is the "teaching" of Jesus, which at the same time is his and is not his. Jesus is "Word," and so it emerges that his teaching is he himself. If with this insight in mind one reads the sentence again, Then he says, I am not only I; I am not mine at all, but my I is **someone else's**. And so we've passed over from Christology arriving at ourselves: «Quid tam tuum quam tu, quid tam non tuum quam tu - What is so much yours as you, what is so much not yours as you?»[36]. What is so much yours as you yourself and what is so little yours as you yourself? What is most one's own—what lastly really alone belongs to us: one's own "I", is at the same time what is least one's own, for even our "I" we do not have from us and not for us. **The "I" is at the same time that, what I have wholly and what least of all belongs to me.** Thus here once again the concept of bare substance (= that which stands in itself!) is burst and made visible, how a truly self-understanding being apprehends at the same time, that it in being itself does not belong to itself; that it only comes to itself in that it goes away from itself and finds its way back as a relational entity in its primordial originality.[851]

---

[851] *Einführung in das Christentum*, pp. 149-150 (original edition); pp. 147-148 (second edition) — "Beschließen wir das Ganze mit einem Augustinus-Text, der das Gemeinte großartig ans Licht bringt. Er findet sich im Johanneskommentar und schließt an den Satz des Evangeliums an »Mea

What does Ratzinger mean by "durchbrochen"? My first impression was that he might mean "penetrated", but that would then render the use of the expression *sichtbar gemacht* redundant since something becomes visible to the mind when the mind penetrates it, and *"penetrated"* would more properly correspond to the words *eingedrungen* or *durchgedrungen,* so I was compelled to render it as *burst.* The dictionary gives such meanings as *pierced, burst, shattered, penetrated, broken through, etc.* In his translation, J. R. Foster translates it as "shattered". [Thus here again the concept of mere substance (= what stands in itself, is shattered, and it is made apparent how being that truly understands itself grasps at the same time that *in* being itself it does not belong to itself; that it only comes to itself by moving away from itself and finding its way back as relatedness to its true primordial state.] Father José Wisniewski Filho, S.V.D. translates it in Portuguese as "romper-se", which in English is equivalent to *break up, rupture, tear, part, etc.* [Portanto, torna a romper-se o conceito de simples substância (= do que subsiste em si),

---

doctrina non est mea. - Meine Lehre ist nicht meine Lehre, sondern die des Vaters, der mich gesandt hat« (7,16). Augustinus hat am Paradox dieses Satzes die Paradoxie des christlichen Gottesbildes und der christlichen Existenz erhellt. Er fragt sich zunächst, ob es nicht glatter Widersinn, Verstoß gegen die elementaren Regeln der Logik sei, so etwas zu sagen: Das Meine ist nicht das Meine. Aber, so bohrt er weiter, was ist nun eigentlich die »Lehre« Jesu, die zugleich sein und nicht sein ist? Jesus ist »Wort«, und so zeigt sich, dass seine Lehre er selber ist. Wenn man von dieser Einsicht her den Satz noch einmal liest, dann sagt er: Ich bin gar nicht bloß Ich; ich bin gar nicht mein, sondern mein Ich ist eines anderen. Und damit sind wir über die Christologie hinaus bei uns selbst angelangt: »Quid tam tuum quam tu, quid tam non tuum quam tu - was ist so sehr dein wie du selbst und was ist so wenig dein wie du selbst? «[36]. Das Allereigenste -was uns letztlich wirklich allein gehört: das eigene Ich, ist zugleich das am allerwenigsten Eigene, denn gerade unser Ich haben wir nicht von uns und nicht für uns. Das Ich ist zugleich das, was ich ganz habe und was am wenigsten mir gehört. So wird hier noch einmal der Begriff der bloßen Substanz (= des in sich stehenden!) durchbrochen und sichtbar gemacht, wie ein sich wahrhaft verstehendes Sein zugleich begreift, dass es *im* Selbersein sich nicht selbst gehört; dass es nur zu sich selbst kommt, indem es von sich selbst weggeht und als Beziehentlichkeit in seine wahre Ursprünglichkeit zurückfindet."

patenteando-se como um ser racional compreende que não se pertence dentro da sua identidade; que somente chega a si afastando-se de si, regressando, como relacionamento, para a sua verdadeira origem.] **So evidently, according to Ratzinger, the concept of substance as it has been commonly understood is exploded by this consideration, and similarly the commonly understood idea of relation is essentially modified. A few pages earlier (p. 140 in the second edition), Ratzinger says, "With the insight that God is essentially one, but that in him there is the phenomenon of the dialogical, the difference and relatedness of the conversation, the category of relation acquired a completely new meaning for Christian thought. For Aristotle it stood under the "accidents", the accidental conditions of being, which stand out from substance as the sole supporting form of reality."[852]**

In Christian thought the Aristotelian concept of relation really remains entirely valid and remains essentially unchanged insofar as it remains principally understood in its primary and most proper sense as that of an accident predicable of primary being, or *substance*, which is known immediately by the intellect as its proper object. The "completely new meaning for Christian thought" does not change the essential meaning of what a relation is, insofar as the meaning of relation in Christian thought remains essentially a concept of a relatedness, but what changes is not the concept of relation *per se*, but the notion of relation's mode of being *in* the divine substance — the manner in which relations exist in the divine Substance — not as an accident of a substance as its subject, but as a relatedness within the divine Substance, having that Substance as the sole principle of the relations existing between consubstantial supposits, so that the relations exist neither as accidents of a

---

[852] *Einführung in das Christentum*, Second Edition, p. 140 — «Mit der Einsicht, dass Gott substantial gesehen Einer ist, dass es aber in ihm das Phänomen des Dialogischen, der Unterschiedenheit und Bezogenheit des Gesprächs gibt, erhielt für das christliche Denken die Kategorie der Relatio eine völlig neue Bedeutung. Für Aristoteles stand sie unter den »Akzidentien«, den zufälligen Zuständlichkeiten des Seins, die sich von der Substanz als der allein tragenden Form des Wirklichen abheben.»

substance, nor as relation between different substances, but between the different supposits of the one and the same divine Substance. Thus, the notion of substance is hardly "shattered" by this consideration which does not confer on it a new meaning *per se* of what relation essentially is, but relation is given a new meaning regarding its *mode of being in God*; so that it merely underscores the need to properly distinguish the different ways in which the terms "substance" and "relation" can be understood — 1) "substance", namely, uncreated substance as the pure act of essential subsistent being in which there is no potentiality; and created substance which is not essential subsistent being itself, but is brought into being as limited participated being constituted of potentiality and act, and thus a substance which receives its being from God, which therefore exists according to the determined limits of a created principle of act — the *substantial form*, which specifies the essence of the thing by specifically determining its essence according to its specific limitations as participated being; and 2) "relation" which exist as an accident of created substances, but in the divine Substance, in which there exist no accidents, relation exists as an essential attribute because the relations (Paternity, Filiation, Spiration, Procession; *Summa Theol. I^a q. 28.*) have their principle and terminus of action within the undivided divine Substance. (*Summa Theol. I^a q. 40. a. 1-2; q. 41; q. 27 a. 3 ad. 1*[853])

Substance pertains essentially to being in the primary sense of being, so that if there is not substance there is not being. In *Categories* Aristotle distinguishes the different senses of the term *substance*, but in Part 5, (2a11), he explains, "Substance, in the truest and primary and most definite sense of the word, is that which is neither predicable of a subject nor present in a subject;[854] for instance, the individual man or horse." And likewise of "being" there are different but related senses. In *Metaphysics* Γ, he explains:

---

[853] *I^a 27. ad. 1* — «Processio enim quae est ad intra in intellectuali natura, terminatur in processione voluntatis.»

[854] *Categories*, Part 2. p.3 — "By being 'present in a subject' I do not mean present as parts are present in a whole, but being incapable of existence apart from the said subject."

There are many senses in which a thing may be said to 'be', but all that 'is' is related to one central point, one definite kind of thing, and is not said to 'be' by a mere ambiguity... ***there are many senses in which a thing is said to be, but all refer to one starting-point; some things are said to be because they are substances***, others because they are affections of substance, others because they are a process towards substance, or destructions or privations or qualities of substance, or productive or generative of substance, or of things which are relative to substance, or negations of one of these thing of substance itself. It is for this reason that we say even of nonbeing that it is nonbeing.[855]

Accordingly, S. Marc Cohen observes in the *Stanford Encyclopedia of Philosophy*, that the situation is the same with the term 'being':

It, too, has a primary sense as well as related senses in which it applies to other things because they are appropriately related to things that are called 'beings' in the primary sense. The beings in the primary sense are substances; the beings in other senses are the qualities, quantities, etc., that belong to substances. An animal, e.g., a horse, is a being, and so is a color, e.g, white, a being. But a horse is a being in the primary sense—it is a substance—whereas the color white (a quality) is a being only because it qualifies some substance. An account of the being of anything that is, therefore, will ultimately have to make some reference to substance."[856]

Thus, H. Robinson comments, that according to the doctrine of substance in Aristotle, "If substance did not exist it would be impossible for things in any of the other categories to exist. There could be no instances of properties if there were no substances to possess them."[857] Hence, **there could not exist being in any sense if there were not being in the primary sense that, "*some things are said to be because they are substances*"** (*Metaphysics* Γ. no. 2). Therefore being in the primary sense of something that actually exists, can exist only insofar as substance actually exists, **because in their**

---

[855] Aristotle—Works, *Metaphysics*, Book Γ. no. 2, p. 2265.

[856] S. Marc Cohen, *Aristotle's Metaphysics, First published Sun Oct 8, 2000; substantive revision Tue Jul 7, 2020*: https://plato.stanford.edu/entries/aristotle-metaphysics/#SubsMattSubj.

[857] https://plato.stanford.edu/entries/substance/.

primary sense, substance and being are seen to be essentially included in each other, so that if there is no substance there is not being, but only non-being, as is clear from Aristotle's own exposition in *Categories* 5:

> Everything except primary substances is either predicable of a primary substance or present in a primary substance. This becomes evident by reference to particular instances which occur. 'Animal' is predicated of the species 'man', therefore of the individual man, for if there were no individual man of whom it could be predicated, it could not be predicated of the species 'man' at all. Again, colour is present in body, therefore in individual bodies, for if there were no individual body in which it was present, it could not be present in body at all. **Thus everything except primary substances is either predicated of primary substances, or is present in them, and if these last did not exist, it would be impossible for anything else to exist.**[858]

Knowledge of primary substance is primary knowledge, but according to the nature of the intellect, such knowledge is acquired by degrees:

> For since the intellect passes from potentiality to act, it has a likeness to things which are generated, which do not attain to perfection all at once but acquire it by degrees: so likewise the human intellect does not acquire perfect knowledge by the first act of apprehension; but it first apprehends something about its object, such as its **quiddity**, and this is its first and proper object; and then it understands the properties, accidents, and the various relations of the **essence**. Thus it necessarily compares one thing with another by composition or division; and from one composition and division it proceeds to another, which is the process of reasoning.[859]

---

[858] Aristotle—Works, *Categories* 5, p. 6

[859] *Summa Theol.* Iª q. 85 a. 5. — «Cum enim intellectus humanus exeat de potentia in actum, similitudinem quandam habet cum rebus generabilibus, quae non statim perfectionem suam habent, sed eam successive acquirunt. Et similiter intellectus humanus non statim in prima apprehensione capit perfectam rei cognitionem; sed primo apprehendit aliquid de ipsa, puta quidditatem ipsius rei, quae est primum et proprium obiectum intellectus; et deinde intelligit proprietates et accidentia et habitudines circumstantes rei essentiam. Et secundum hoc, necesse habet

Knowledge of primary substance is therefore primary knowledge because it is knowledge of the "first and proper object" **of the intellect, about which the first thing the intellect understands is that a thing** *is*. **Therefore, our first knowledge is knowledge of** *being* **as it exists according to its primary sense, which is the first thing that the intellect apprehends about anything it knows, as St. Thomas explained in the above cited passage:** "For that which first falls in the apprehension is *being*, the notion of which is included in whatsoever one apprehends."[860] The first notion is therefore *being*, which is included in our knowledge of everything we know; but for things to exist at all, they must either be primary substances or be in primary substances, because, (as Aristotle says), **"everything except primary substances is either predicated of primary substances, or is present in them, and if these last did not exist, it would be impossible for anything else to exist."** Thus, our first knowledge of any*thing* apprehended is the knowledge that it *is*, and therefore that first notion of *being* is founded on the first principle of knowledge: "Wherefore the first indemonstrable principle is that "the same thing cannot be affirmed and denied at the same time," which is based on the notion of "being" and "not-being": and on this principle all others are based, as is stated in Metaph. iv, text. 9. ".[861] **This principle, therefore, being the first, is most certain and absolutely true, and is not in the least doubtful because it cannot be demonstrated, as Aristotle proved:**

[p. 2272] There are some who, as we said, both themselves assert that it is possible for the same thing to be and not to be, and say that people

---

unum apprehensum alii componere vel dividere; et ex una compositione vel divisione ad aliam procedere, quod est ratiocinari.»

[860] *Summa Theol.* Iª IIæ q. 94 a. 2. — «Nam illud quod primo cadit in apprehensione, est ens, cuius intellectus includitur in omnibus quaecumque quis apprehendit.»

[861] *Ibid.* — «Et ideo primum principium indemonstrabile est quod non est simul affirmare et negare, quod fundatur supra rationem entis et non entis, et super hoc principio omnia alia fundantur, ut dicitur in IV Metaphys.»

can judge this to be the case. And among others many writers about nature use this language. But we have now posited that it is impossible for anything at the same time to be and not to be, and by this means have shown that this is the most indisputable of all principles. – Some indeed demand that even this shall be demonstrated, but this they do through want of education, for not to know of what things one should demand demonstration, and of what one should not, argues want of education. For it is impossible that there should be demonstration of absolutely everything (there would be an infinite regress, so that there would still be no demonstration); but if there are things of which one should not demand demonstration, these persons could not say what principle they maintain to be more self-evident than the present one. We can, however, demonstrate negatively even that this view is impossible [...] [p. 2274] And it will not be possible to be and not to be the same thing, except in virtue of an ambiguity, just as if one whom we call 'man', others were to call 'not-man'; but the point in question is not this, whether the same thing can at the same time be and not be a man in name, but whether it can in fact. [...] [pp. 2275-2276] And in general those who say this [i.e. There are some who, as we said, both themselves assert that it is possible for the same thing to be and not to be] do away with substance and essence. For they must say that all attributes are accidents, and that there is no such thing as 'being essentially a man' or 'an animal'. For if there is to be any such thing as 'being essentially a man' this will not be 'being a not-man' or 'not being a man' (yet these are negations of it); **for there was one thing which it meant, and this was the *substance of something*.** And ***denoting the substance of a thing means that the essence of the thing is nothing else.*** But if its being essentially a man is to be the same as either being essentially a not-man or essentially not being a man, then its essence will be something else. Therefore our opponents must say that there cannot be such a definition of anything, but that all attributes are accidental; **for this is the distinction between substance and accident – 'white' is accidental to man, because though he is white, whiteness is not his essence. But if all statements are accidental, there will be nothing primary about which they are made**, if the accidental always implies predication about a subject. The predication, then, must go on ad infinitum. **But this is impossible**; for not even more than two terms can be combined in accidental predication. For (1) an accident is not an accident of an accident, unless it be because both are accidents of the same subject.[862]

---

[862] Aristotle—Works, *Metaphysics*, Book Γ. no. 4, pp. 2272, 2274, 2275-6.

The knowledge of the substantiality of being which is founded on this first principle is indubitably true, because it is generally and universally asserted to be so (with the exception of philosophers like Hegel who, as Chesterton observed, are considered by ordinary men to be mad)[863]; and such general knowledge of the ages cannot be false:

> That which is asserted universally, by everyone, cannot possibly be totally false. For a false opinion is a kind of infirmity of the understanding, just as a false judgment concerning a proper sensible happens as the result of a weakness of the sense power involved. But defects, being outside the intention of nature, are accidental. And nothing accidental can be always and in all things; the judgment about savours given by every tasting cannot be false. Thus, the judgment uttered by everyone concerning truth cannot be erroneous. "Now, it is the common opinion of all the philosophers that nothing arises from what is not."[864]

The reason why ordinary men would judge such philosophers to be mad is that their entire doctrine of substance rests on a conception of substance that violates the principle of non-contradiction insofar as it denies the distinction and reality of potentiality and act as the really existing constituent principles of every *ens naturae* known to the human intellect, knowledge which is grounded on the absolutely certain and universally known real distinction between being and non-being.[865] Thus, "*it is the common opinion of all the philosophers that nothing arises from what is not,*" from which principle it necessarily follows:

---

[863] I believe he said that in *The Everlasting Man*.

[864] *Summa Contra Gentiles* 2. Cap. 34 — «Quod enim ab omnibus communiter dicitur, impossibile est totaliter esse falsum. Falsa enim opinio infirmitas quaedam intellectus est: sicut et falsum iudicium de sensibili proprio ex infirmitate sensus accidit. Defectus autem per accidens sunt: quia praeter naturae intentionem. Quod autem est per accidens, non potest esse semper et in omnibus: sicut iudicium quod de saporibus ab omni gustu datur, non potest esse falsum. Ita iudicium quod ab omnibus de veritate datur, non potest esse erroneum. Communis autem sententia est omnium philosophorum ex nihilo nihil fieri.»

[865] An excellent exposition of this point can be found in Gallus Manser's *Das Wesen des Thomismus*.

"Everything that acts, acts insofar as it is in act, just as a man in act makes from a man in potentiality a man in act: whence, since everything is in act through the form, it follows that the form is the moving principle. And thus to move belongs to something insofar as it has form, by which it is in act. Whence, since motion is the act of a thing existing in potentiality, as was stated above, it follows that motion is not of something insofar as it moves, but insofar as it is movable: and therefore in the definition of motion it is placed, that it is the act of the movable insofar as it is movable." — (*Commentary on the Physics of Aristotle*, lib. 3 l. 4 n. 6)[866]

It was Hegel who said, "To be a follower of Spinoza is the essential commencement of all Philosophy."[867] Yet it is in Spinoza's philosophy that there is constructed a doctrine on substance that contradicts the evident truth that *ex nihilo nihil fit*, from which it follows that *"Omne agens agit inquantum est actu."* This universally known and commonly held truth that *nothing arises from what is not*, is founded on the evident truth of the reality of potentiality and act as the constituent principles of the entities of nature, from which all motion depends, since it is because of the real distinction between the two in the constitution of things of nature that it is said, that *since all motion is the act of something existing in potentiality*, and *potentiality can only be reduced to act by that which exists in act*, consequently *all that is moved is movable only by that which is in act; and therefore, the first principle of all motion exists only in a First Mover in which there is no potentiality and no motion but whose* **SUBSTANCE** *is the pure act of subsistent being – ACTUS PURUS, and IPSUM ESSE SUBSISTENS.* Motion can exist only in creatures whose substance is composed of potentiality and act, but all motion

---

[866] *In Physic.*, lib. 3 l. 4 n. 6 — «Omne enim agens agit inquantum est actu, sicut actu homo facit ex homine in potentia hominem actu: unde, cum unumquodque sit actu per formam, sequitur quod forma sit principium movens. Et sic movere competit alicui inquantum habet formam, per quam est in actu. Unde, cum motus sit actus existentis in potentia, ut supra dictum est, sequitur quod motus non sit alicuius inquantum est movens, sed inquantum est mobile: et ideo in definitione motus positum est, quod est actus mobilis inquantum est mobile.»

[867] *Hegel's Lectures on the History of Philosophy*, Section Two: *Period of the Thinking Understanding* Chapter I. — *The Metaphysics of the Understanding*, A 2. SPINOZA.

in nature must have its origin in a Mover which acts insofar as it is in act, and which is not moved (otherwise there would be an infinite regress), and therefore, all motion in nature has its origin in a principle extrinsic to itself, the *PRIME MOVER* who is **GOD**, and who sets in motion the coming into being of all that is seen and unseen. **There can only exist motion in things which have been brought into being by being moved from potentiality to act by an extrinsic moving principle in which there is no potentiality, for which reason, it is evident that there exists a real distinction between the One SUBSTANCE of the Creator, and the multitude of substantial beings He created.** Modern philosophy, which has its real origin in Spinoza, denies this fundamental truth, because it is founded on the axiom that there is only **ONE SUBSTANCE** — **which contradicts the unshakable truth, (founded on our primary knowledge and the first principle of all knowledge), that the very essence of all entities of nature is that they are substances.** In his two volume work on modern atheism (*Introduzione all'ateismo moderno*), Cornelio Fabro traces that common thread of immanentism (which results from the denial of the distinction between divine Substance and created substances) that runs through all modern philosophy, back to Spinoza, who destroys the distinction between Creator and creature by dissolving the distinction between created and uncreated substance, as can be gathered from the clear exposition of Hegel on Spinoza:

> As regards the philosophy of Spinoza, it is very simple, and on the whole easy to comprehend; the difficulty which it presents is due partly to the limitations of the method in which Spinoza presents his thoughts, and partly to his narrow range of ideas, which causes him in an unsatisfactory way to pass over important points of view and cardinal questions. Spinoza's system is that of Descartes made objective in the form of absolute truth. The simple thought of Spinoza's idealism is this: **The true is simply and solely the one substance, whose attributes are thought and extension or nature: and only this absolute unity is reality, it alone is God.** It is, as with Descartes, the unity of thought and Being, or that which contains the Notion of its existence in itself. The Cartesian substance, as Idea, has certainly Being included in its Notion; but it is only Being as abstract, not as real Being or as extension (*supra*, p. 241). With Descartes corporeality and the thinking 'I' are

altogether independent Beings; this independence of the two extremes is done away with in Spinozism by their becoming moments of the one absolute Being. This expression signifies that Being must be grasped as the unity of opposites; the chief consideration is not to let slip the opposition and set it aside, but to reconcile and resolve it. Since then it is thought and Being, and no longer the abstractions of the finite and infinite, or of limit and the unlimited, that form the opposition (*supra*, p. 161), **Being is here more definitely regarded as extension; for in its abstraction it would be really only that return into itself, that simple equality with itself, which constitutes thought** (*supra*, p. 229). The pure thought of Spinoza is therefore not the simple universal of Plato, for it has likewise come to know the absolute opposition of Notion and Being.[868]

Taken as a whole, this constitutes the Idea of Spinoza, and it is just what *pure being* was to the Eleatics (Vol. 1. pp. 244, 252). This Idea of Spinoza's we must allow to be in the main true and well-grounded; **absolute substance is the truth, but it is not the whole truth; in order to be this it must also be thought of as in itself active and living, and by that very means it must determine itself as mind. But substance with Spinoza is only the universal and consequently the abstract determination of mind**; it may undoubtedly be said that this thought is the foundation of all true views — not, however, as their absolutely fixed and permanent basis, but as the abstract unity which mind is in itself. It is therefore worthy of note that thought must begin by placing itself at the standpoint of Spinozism; to be a follower of Spinoza is the essential commencement of all Philosophy. For as we saw above (Vol. I. p. 144), **when man begins to philosophize, the soul must commence by bathing in this ether of the One Substance, in which all that man has held as true has disappeared; this negation of all that is particular, to which every philosopher must have come, is the liberation of the mind and its absolute foundation.** The difference between our standpoint and that of the Eleatic philosophy is only this, **that through the agency of Christianity concrete individuality is in the modern world present throughout in spirit. But in spite of the infinite demands on the part of the concrete, substance with Spinoza is not yet determined as in itself concrete. As the concrete is thus not present in the content of substance, it is therefore to be found within reflecting thought alone, and it is only from the endless oppositions of this last that the required unity emerges. Of substance as such there is nothing

---

[868] *Ibid.*

more to be said; all that we can do is to speak of the different ways in which Philosophy has dealt with it, and the opposites which in it are abrogated. **The difference depends on the nature of the opposites which are held to be abrogated in substance.** Spinoza is far from having proved this unity as convincingly as was done by the ancients; but **what constitutes the grandeur of Spinoza's manner of thought is that he is able to renounce all that is determinate and particular, and restrict himself to the One, giving heed to this alone.**[869]

Thus it is that to deny that created beings are substances is to implicitly deny that they are creatures distinct from God, and ultimately that they even exist as created beings at all, because then, being neither substance nor accident they would either not be anything at all, (and therefore not created), or would exist only in the mind of God as divine ideas (which are not created). Consequently, since the notions of being and substance **in their primary sense, are essentially included in each other,** a statement that would affirm the substantial existence of created beings but implicitly deny that they are substances in the proper sense by discarding their metaphysical constituent principles on the specious pretext that the composition of substances consisting of matter and form pertains to an "obsolete" theory of Greek philosophy is logically reducible to saying that they are and are not substances. Since we can only affirm the existence of beings insofar as we have knowledge of them, and we can only know them insofar as they exist as substances or in substances, our first knowledge of substance is direct and primary. Thus St. Thomas, in *S.C.G. 1 Cap. 3* explains, «**the beginning of all knowledge that the reason perceives about some *thing* is the understanding of the very *substance* of that being** (for according to Aristotle **"what a thing is" is the principle of demonstration**) [*Posterior Analytics* II, 3]» Aristotle explains:

> *Posterior Analytics* Book 1. 2. p. 224 – The premisses must be true: for that which is non-existent cannot be known – […] The premisses must be **primary and indemonstrable**; otherwise they will require demonstration in order to be known, since to have knowledge, if it be

---

[869] https://www.marxists.org/reference/archive/hegel/works/hp/hpspinoz.htm.

not accidental knowledge, of things which are demonstrable, means precisely to have a demonstration of them. The premisses must be the causes of the conclusion, **better known than it**, and prior to it; its causes, since we possess scientific knowledge of a thing only when we know its cause; prior, in order to be causes; antecedently known, this antecedent knowledge being not our mere understanding of the meaning, but knowledge of the fact as well. [...] In saying that the premisses of demonstrated knowledge must be primary, I mean that they must be the 'appropriate' basic truths, for I identify primary premiss and basic truth. A 'basic truth' in a demonstration is an immediate proposition. An immediate proposition is one which has no other proposition prior to it. *Posterior Analytics* Book I. 2. p. 225-226 – So since the primary premisses are the cause of our knowledge – i.e. of our conviction – it follows that we know them better – that is, are more convinced of them – than their consequences, precisely because of our knowledge of the latter is the effect of our knowledge of the premisses.

Thus it is clear why St. Thomas says, **"the beginning of all knowledge that the reason perceives about some *thing* is the understanding of the very SUBSTANCE of that being,"** and Aristotle in *Posterior Analytics* Book II. 3. p. 292 – "definition is of the essential nature or being of something, and all demonstrations evidently posit and assume the essential nature," and therefore in *Metaphysics* Book B. 2. p. 2249, "there is no demonstration of the essence of things." Thus the primary truths, because they are not demonstrable, are not less certain but more certain: *Posterior Analytics* Book I. 2. p. 225-226: "So since the primary premisses are the cause of our knowledge – i.e. of our conviction – it follows that we know them better – that is, are more convinced of them – than their consequences, precisely because of our knowledge of the latter is the effect of our knowledge of the premisses." Of this we can be most certain, that our knowledge of substance is true: *"For that with which the human reason is naturally endowed is clearly most true; so much so, that it is impossible for us to think of such truths as false. [...] Now, the knowledge of the principles that are known to us naturally has been implanted in us by God; for God is the Author of our nature. These principles, therefore, are also contained by the divine Wisdom. Hence, whatever is opposed to them is opposed to the divine*

Wisdom, and, therefore, cannot come from God."[870] The dogmas of the resurrection of the **body**, of the **rational soul** as the **substantial form** of the body, of Tran***substan*ti**ation, and of creation of the world *ex nihilo*, logically presuppose the truth of our natural knowledge of material *substance* composed of *matter and form* so strictly, even to the extent that this notion of substance is included in the very content of the dogmas themselves, so that if the Aristotelian-Thomistic doctrine of substance were to be judged false or "obsolete", and consequently, that according to human science the created entities of nature would accordingly have to be judged not to be substances so constituted, then the truth of those dogmas themselves would necessarily have to be judged to be contrary to the truth of human science, and therefore both true and false. This is quite impossible, since as St. Thomas explains:

> Now, although the truth of the Christian faith which we have discussed surpasses the capacity of the reason, nevertheless that truth that the human reason is naturally endowed to know cannot be opposed to the truth of the Christian faith. For that with which the human reason is naturally endowed is clearly most true; so much so, that it is impossible for us to think of such truths as false. Nor is it permissible to believe as false that which we hold by faith, since this is confirmed in a way that is so clearly divine. Since, therefore, only the false is opposed to the true, as is clearly evident from an examination of their definitions, it is impossible that the truth of faith should be opposed to those principles that the human reason knows naturally. Furthermore, that which is introduced into the soul of the student by the teacher is contained in the knowledge of the teacher—unless his teaching is fictitious, which it is improper to say of God. Now, the knowledge of the principles that are known to us naturally has been implanted in us by God; for God is the Author of our nature. These principles, therefore, are also contained by the divine Wisdom. Hence, whatever is opposed to them is opposed to

---

[870] *Summa Contra Gentiles* 1. Cap. 7 — «Ea enim quae naturaliter rationi sunt insita, verissima esse constat: in tantum ut nec esse falsa sit possibile cogitare. [...] Principiorum autem naturaliter notorum cognitio nobis divinitus est indita: cum ipse Deus sit nostrae auctor naturae. Haec ergo principia etiam divina sapientia continet. Quicquid igitur principiis huiusmodi contrarium est, divinae sapientiae contrariatur. Non igitur a Deo esse potest.»

the divine Wisdom, and, therefore, cannot come from God. That which we hold by faith as divinely revealed, therefore, cannot be contrary to our natural knowledge.[871]

As I explained above, since the notions of being and substance **in their primary sense, are essentially included in each other,** a statement that would affirm the existence of created natural substances but deny that they are substances in the proper sense (i.e. constituted of *potentiality and act* and composed of *matter and form*) is logically reducible to saying that they are and are not substances. Therefore, a statement which affirms the *res naturae* as substances but not as composed of matter and form is evidently false because it contains within itself an implicit contradiction, but it is not by itself an *indicium* of formal heresy; so that if one affirms the truth of the dogmas which presuppose the existence of created substances composed of matter and form (such as man composed of material body and rational soul), but denies that such creatures are thusly composed, one does not necessarily deliberately deny the dogmas by stating simultaneously that created substances exist, and implicitly denying their substantial being by stating that those created beings are not composed of matter and form. Such contradictions in general are plainly false, but not always heretical, and if they sometimes express some heresy, the heresy will not always be immediately evident to all. St. Thomas explains:

---

[871] *Ibid.* — «Quamvis autem praedicta veritas fidei Christianae humanae rationis capacitatem excedat, haec tamen quae ratio naturaliter indita habet, huic veritati contraria esse non possunt. Ea enim quae naturaliter rationi sunt insita, verissima esse constat: in tantum ut nec esse falsa sit possibile cogitare. Nec id quod fide tenetur, cum tam evidenter divinitus confirmatum sit, fas est credere esse falsum. Quia igitur solum falsum vero contrarium est, ut ex eorum definitionibus inspectis manifeste apparet, impossibile est illis principiis quae ratio naturaliter cognoscit, praedictam veritatem fidei contrariam esse. Item. Illud idem quod inducitur in animam discipuli a docente, doctoris scientia continet: nisi doceat ficte, quod de Deo nefas est dicere. Principiorum autem naturaliter notorum cognitio nobis divinitus est indita: cum ipse Deus sit nostrae auctor naturae. Haec ergo principia etiam divina sapientia continet. Quicquid igitur principiis huiusmodi contrarium est, divinae sapientiae contrariatur. Non igitur a Deo esse potest. Ea igitur quae ex revelatione divina per fidem tenentur, non possunt naturali cognitioni esse contraria.»

In regard to the second, someone may hold that something that has always existed cannot be made because such a thing is self-contradictory, just as an affirmation and a denial cannot be made simultaneously true. Still, some people say that God can even make self-contradictories things, while others say God cannot make such things, for such things are actually nothing. Clearly, God cannot make such things come to be, for the assumption that such a thing exists immediately refutes itself. Nevertheless, if we allow that God can make such things come to be, the position is not heretical, though I believe it is false, just as the proposition that the past did not occur is false, about which Augustine says (XXVI *Contra Faustum* cap. 5), "Anyone who says, 'If God is omnipotent, let him make what has happened not to have happened,' does not realize that he is saying, 'If God is omnipotent, let him make true things false insofar as they are true.'" [PL 42, 481.] Nevertheless, certain great men have piously maintained that God can make past events not to have happened, and this was not reputed to be heretical.[872]

Therefore, it cannot be maintained that Joseph Ratzinger is a heretic, on the basis of the specious and false pretext that he has asserted heretical disbelief in dogmas by incorrectly explicating those dogmas which in their proper content include in themselves the notion of created substance composed of matter and form, or that he has explained other dogmas in such a manner that involves his argument in some basic contradiction. He has professed belief in the dogmas, but has explained them in a logically incoherent and

---

[872] *De Æternitate Mundi* — «Secundo modo dicitur propter repugnantiam intellectuum aliquid non posse fieri, sicut quod non potest fieri ut affirmatio et negatio sint simul vera; quamvis Deus hoc possit facere, ut quidam dicunt. Quidam vero dicunt, quod nec Deus hoc posset facere, quia hoc nihil est. Tamen manifestum est quod non potest facere ut hoc fiat, quia positio qua ponitur esse, destruit se ipsam. Si tamen ponatur quod Deus huiusmodi potest facere ut fiant, positio non est haeretica, quamvis, ut credo, sit falsa; sicut quod praeteritum non fuerit, includit in se contradictionem. Unde Augustinus in libro contra faustum: quisquis ita dicit: si omnipotens est Deus, faciat ut ea quae facta sunt, facta non fuerint: non videt hoc se dicere: si omnipotens est Deus, faciat ut ea quae vera sunt, eo ipso quo vera sunt, falsa sint. Et tamen quidam magni pie dixerunt Deum posse facere de praeterito quod non fuerit praeteritum; nec fuit reputatum haereticum.»

sometimes contradictory manner,⁸⁷³ but without directly, immediately, explicitly, and knowingly asserting disbelief in the dogmas themselves, which alone would be an *indicium* of formal heresy that constitutes proof of formal heresy; yet, as I have explained, his exposition on their meaning contain propositions which, considered in themselves, contain material heresy in that the

---

⁸⁷³ Such contradictions are a hallmark of Modernist theology. In this one sees that the influence of Modernism has tainted the theology of Joseph Ratzinger. In his biography of Benedict XVI, Seewald mentioned that Schmaus, "The famous dogmatist not only criticized Ratzinger's analyses, he also expressed that he considered the young theologian to be a Modernist." He also quoted Eugen Biser, Karl Rahner's successor to the Romano Guardini chair, who said, "Schmaus almost found it dangerous," and not only Schmaus, but **"Some of the professors also spoke of Ratzinger's dangerous modernism."** In his encyclical, *Pascendi Dominici gregis*, **(Sept. 8, 1907) subtitled *On the Doctrine of the Modernists*, St. Pius X seemed, to some degree at least, to be describing Joseph Ratzinger's theology twenty years before Ratzinger was born:** *"Having reached this point, Venerable Brethren, we have sufficient material in hand to enable us to see the relations which Modernists establish between faith and science, including history also under the name of science. And in the first place it is to be held that the object of the one is quite extraneous to and separate from the object of the other. For faith occupies itself solely with something which science declares to be unknowable for it. Hence each has a separate field assigned to it: science is entirely concerned with the reality of phenomena, into which faith does not enter at all; faith on the contrary concerns itself with the divine reality which is entirely unknown to science. Thus the conclusion is reached that there can never be any dissension between faith and science, for if each keeps on its own ground they can never meet and therefore never be in contradiction. And if it be objected that in the visible world there are some things which appertain to faith, such as the human life of Christ, the Modernists reply by denying this. For though such things come within the category of phenomena, still in as far as they are lived by faith and in the way already described have been by faith transfigured and disfigured, they have been removed from the world of sense and translated to become material for the divine. hence should it be further asked whether Christ has wrought real miracles, and made real prophecies, whether He rose truly from the dead and ascended into heaven, the answer of agnostic science will be in the negative and the answer of faith in the affirmative — yet there will not be, on that account, any conflict between them. For it will be denied by the philosopher as philosopher, speaking to philosophers and considering Christ only in His historical reality; and it will be affirmed by the speaker, speaking to believers and considering the life of Christ as lived again by the faith and in the faith."*

contrary part of his contradictory assertions are opposed to the dogmas which he does profess, and, due to his faulty understanding of the philosophical concepts which underlie some dogmas, he does not always profess those dogmas according to their proper sense as the Church has defined them. Hence, there are not to be found the *indicia* of formal heresy in the writings of Joseph Ratzinger, who is still at present, Pope Benedict XVI, the Vicar of Christ on earth.

* * *

"POPE EMERITUS"

A pope's valid act of renouncing his *munus* would produce one juridical effect only, namely, that the resignant would cease by that act to be pope, and would no longer in any manner be pope, having entirely relinquished the Petrine *munus*. There would exist nothing in the quality of such an act that would enable the former pope to justify calling himself "Pope Emeritus". That is simply impossible, because it is contrary to the nature of the papacy that a pope could vacate the office and still retain any aspect of the Petrine *munus*. But even if that were possible, then as one who has forfeited all power of governance, he would no longer have any power to create the position of *Pope Emeritus*, being that the juridical act of renunciation would have already deprived him of his jurisdiction. Even if it could validly be done, a renunciation that would not entirely revoke the pope's *munus*, but would effect the vacating of the chair to the extent of causing the cessation of his power of governance and the loss of office, while leaving him with a passive exercise of the Petrine *munus*, would still be only an act of renunciation, and nothing more. It could not have any other valid juridical effect beyond that of vacating the office. It would not by itself canonically create the position in the hierarchy of "Pope Emeritus". On this point, canonist Rosario Vitale, author of *Benedict XVI. The First Pope Emeritus of History,* has explained, "There is still a gap in the law on this topic because, Benedict XVI probably did not have the time to create legislation revolving around it. He could have made a 'motu proprio' or modify Canon 332 paragraph 2. But it's evident that he did not have time or, maybe he let others make this decision." However, a renunciation qualified in such a contradictory manner as Benedict XVI's, cannot in reality produce the juridical effect of the cessation of the power of governance and the vacating of the Apostolic See, while leaving with the resignant pope some passive exercise of the Petrine *munus*, thereby making it possible for him to assume the position of "Pope Emeritus", because the renunciation of the office expressed in such a way that does not intend the total forfeiture of the Petrine *munus* received upon his election to the papacy, is simply incapable of causing the revocation of the *munus* in any manner or degree whatsoever. Due to its contradictory nature, such a renunciation can have no valid juridical effect whatsoever, so that it leaves Pope Benedict in full possession of the Petrine *munus* with the sole consequence that he remains in office as pope with the *full and supreme jurisdiction of the Primacy*. A bishop who validly resigns is still a bishop, and therefore can be called a *Bishop Emeritus*, but a pope who validly resigns his *munus* is simply no longer pope — because he has relinquished the totality of the Petrine *munus*, so that his only remaining *munus* is episcopal and not Petrine. Therefore, a pope having relinquished his *munus* would cease to be pope entirely, nothing of the Petrine *munus* would remain with him, so that he could not in any way be a *Pope Emeritus*, but he could only be a *Bishop Emeritus* equal to and indistinguishable from every other *Bishop Emeritus*. However, since Benedict XVI stated his intention not to totally and unconditionally relinquish the *munus* he received on 19 April 2005, and stands by that decision to this day, his papal *munus* remains with him, with the consequence that Benedict XVI is the only holder of the Petrine *munus* who remains in the fullness of power of the primacy as the Vicar of Christ on earth. The reason for this is that the Petrine *munus* and the episcopal *munus* are of an essentially different nature because the episcopal power and the Petrine power are themselves two distinct and essentially different powers instituted by Christ: the episcopal power and *munus* is *common* to all bishops as successors of the apostles, whereas the papal power and *munus* is *singular* and *unique* to the pope, not as a successor of the Apostles, and not as successor of Peter as an Apostle, but as successor of Peter constituted as head of the Church in the Primacy, so that consequently the totality of the Petrine *munus* by its very nature belongs exclusively to the individual who as the holder of the papal office and its primacy has been given by Christ the *munus* of teaching and governing the universal Church. A validly resigned pope as the former Bishop of Rome, could be legitimately called "Bishop Emeritus", because his bond with his former diocese would be the same as any other Bishop Emeritus, who remains a bishop and successor of the Apostles; but as a former pope he would no longer in any sense be successor of Peter in the Petrine *munus* — his *munus* would no longer be Petrine in any manner whatsoever but entirely *episcopal* as a successor of the Apostles. He would remain a successor of the Apostles just as Peter was an Apostle with the same **apostolic munus** identical to that which he held in common with the other Apostles; but the former pope would no longer have any participation whatsoever in the uniquely singular Petrine *munus* which constituted Peter as the chief over all the Apostles and head of the Church, and is therefore exclusive and proper to the reigning pontiff alone. For the reigning pontiff to cease in the Petrine office by a valid act of renunciation, he must unconditionally and entirely renounce the Petrine *munus* which made him head of the Church, and revert to the simple and subordinate episcopal state as a successor of the Apostles, expressing in his act of renunciation no intention to retain any aspect whatsoever of the Petrine *munus*. If the act is not an unconditional and total renunciation of that *munus*, but is made conditionally in such a manner which intends to retain some aspect of the *munus* he received from Christ when he became pope, then the act is nullified by that condition. The invalidating defect in Benedict's renunciation is the failure to simply and totally renounce the Petrine *munus* which is indivisible, and is inseparable from the primacy, and is thus primatial in it very nature. The invalidity is therefore founded on the substantial error of thinking that the passive and active aspects of the Petrine *munus* can be separated from each other so that they can simultaneously exist in two men, as is in the case with the episcopal *munus*. Therefore, it follows from all these considerations that Benedict XVI is not correctly called *Pope Emeritus*, but he is simply Pope Benedict XVI, *Pontifex Pontificum*, Supreme Pontiff and *Vicar of Christ*. Jorge Mario Bergoglio, is not a true and valid pope, but is an *antipope*, who has rightly abandoned the title of *Vicar of Christ*, whom he cannot represent, and could not represent even if he were otherwise canonically elected, because as one who visibly rejects and heretically opposes the teaching of Christ which the true vicars of Christ have infallibly taught since apostolic times, **Bergoglio** distinguishes himself as an *incapable subject of the papacy*, in whom it is evidently seen that the form of the pontificate cannot exist, due to the contrary disposition in him, which is manifest heresy. **He is *already judged:***

> «In tantum enim fides mihi necessaria est ut cum de cæteris peccatis solum Deum judicem habeam, propter solum peccatum quod in fide commititur possem ab Ecclesia judicari. Nam *qui non credit, iam iudicatus est.* (Joh.3 18)»

Innocentius III — Sermo II De Diversis «IN
CONSACRATIONE PONTIFICIS MAXIMI»

Condemned by his own judgment, BERGOGLIO must be cast out, condemned, and excommunicated:

> Peccatum ergo praelati et aliis damnosum, et sibi est periculosum. Damnosum allis, *quia si sal evanuerit, in quo salietur?* Periculosum sibi; quoniam *ad nihilum valet ultra, nisi ut mittatur foras,* id est ab officio deponatur: *et concucetur ab hominibus,* id est a populo contemnatur. Vel *mittatur foras, et conculcetur ab hominibus,* id est ut excommunicetur et evitetur. Vel *mittatur foras;* quia peccavit in se; *et conculcetur ab homninibus:* quia peccavit in proximum.

Innocentius III — Sermo IV. IN CONSECRATIONE
PONTIFICIS

WHAT MUST BE DONE

What is of the greatest importance in solving the immediate crisis that exists at present — a crisis created by their being in some manner two claimants to the Petrine *munus* — is to bear in mind the principle, *Papa dubius, papa nullus.* Insofar as Jorge Bergoglio can be seen to be a formal heretic he is evidently not a valid pope — and even if one is not entirely convinced that he is a formal heretic, positive doubt at the very least must be admitted in that regard, so that at the very least, as a *papa dubius,* he must not be accepted as a certain pope. If one begins to examine the case of a suspected heretic pope starting from the firm presumption that the individual in question is a valid pope, then the inquiry is over before it even begins, because a valid pope simply cannot be judged. It is entirely useless to present *dubia* to a man who is asserted to validly reign as pope, with the aim of determining whether or not he is a capable subject of the papacy, since, if he is validly constituted as pope, then he is a capable subject who simply cannot be judged by his subjects — not even for heresy, because he is the one who is the supreme judge who decides whether or not any opinion, including his own, is heretical. Hence it is a doomed endeavour to even approach the problem of an actual case of suspected papal heresy by presuming that the suspected papal-heretic is a valid pope, since a valid pope simply cannot be judged by anyone. As I have explained in this work, there exists a direct proportion between the degree of suspicion of heresy and the degree of positive doubt regarding the validity of the heretic's claim on the *munus*. Insofar as there even exists a founded positive doubt, there exists a presumption of nullity of his claim, but, I repeat, if the case begins with a presumption of validity, then the case ends there: *Prima Sedes a nemine iudicatur*. The idea that a valid pope can fall into heresy and cease to be pope is in fact an impossibility, as the great post-Tridentine Doctors, St. Robert Bellarmine and St. Alphonsus de' Liguori already argued, and as I, in the light of *Pastor Æternus*, have proven in this work. Thus, if a man who is even generally believed by most, (albeit with some reservations and in a qualified manner) to be pope — and if he manifests the probable *indicia* of formal heresy, then he is a *papa dubius* to whom it is appropriate to present *dubia* — not as to one who is presumed to be pope, but to one who is presumed in all probability not to be pope. But if a claimant exhibits the *indicia* of **certain formal heresy**, then he falls under the jurisdiction of the Church, to which jurisdiction it pertains, to judge the validity of claims on the papacy when the Apostolic See is seen to be or at least presumed to be vacant. At the present time, that jurisdiction presumably remains with Pope Benedict XVI, since the Apostolic See cannot be presumed to be vacant for so long as Benedict XVI is seen to retain any aspect of his *munus*. If the situation would arise that it cannot be determined with certitude that the See is occupied by a valid pontiff, then it would truly fall within the jurisdiction of the Church to elect a new pope. At any rate, the inevitable eventuality should have been foreseen, just as soon as it became clear that an arrangement would be accepted with two men laying claim on some aspect of the *munus*, that doubts would sooner or later arise about which of the two would be the sole valid holder of the *munus*. Such an arrangement is simply not acceptable, and the cardinals should not have accepted it, and they should not have proceeded to elect a new pope without it being absolutely certain that Pope Benedict had absolutely and unconditionally renounced his *munus* entirely. The unescapable and foreseeable result of such an arrangement in which two claims on the *munus* are accepted is that there will inevitably develop a schism between those who accept the one claim and those who accept the other. If Bergoglio would resign or die while Pope Benedict remains alive, nothing would be resolved by electing a successor of the heretic antipope Bergoglio for so long as Benedict retains his claim on the *munus*, because that successor would also be an antipope. Therefore, in the first place, it falls within the responsibility of Pope Benedict XVI to assert his rightful claim on the Petrine *munus*, and that failing, then to at least juridically arrange for his own successor to be elected. If both of these would fail to materialize, then it would fall within the jurisdiction of Pope Benedict's cardinals to elect his successor when Benedict finally vacates the Apostolic See. It would be much better if Pope Benedict himself would designate the electors of his successor, so that an inevitable schism would be less likely to arise due to doubts about the validity of the conclave that elects his successor. Failure to elect a successor of Pope Benedict would leave the Apostolic See vacant for however so long it would take for a valid successor of Benedict XVI to be elected, since the other claimant, Bergoglio, as a manifestly formal public heretic is certainly incapable of holding the Petrine office, and any heretic elected to succeed him would also be an antipope not only for so long as Benedict XVI survives, but for however long that successor would continue to be a heretic even after Benedict's death. Such an eventuality would result in the maximum damage to the vast multitude of souls who would be seduced into heresy by the false and heretical claimant, who like Bergoglio, would invalidly usurp the papal throne, and who, by exhibiting the *dolus* of his heresy, and his alignment with the enemies of the Church, would manifest his intention to destroy the Church and to deceive even the elect.

TABLE OF CONTENTS

PREFACE 5
PART ONE - DOCTRINAL SUMMARY 7
MANIFEST HERETIC AND SUSPECTED HERETIC 14
DETAILED CRITIQUE OF THE CAJETAN-JOHN
  OF ST. THOMAS THEORY 152
COMMENTARY ON TEXT..212
SALZA & SISCOE DEFEND THE HERETICAL THESIS WITH
  SPOHISTRY AND SUBTERFUGE 216
ST. ALPHONSUS PROVES THAT THE CHURCH CAN NEVER
  JUDGE A TRUE POPE 311
JOHN SALZA AND ROBERT SISCOE REMAIN OBSTINATE IN
  THEIR CONCILIARIST HERESY 315
PART TWO - THE CASE AGAINST BERGOGLIO 362
SECTION I - THE INVALID RESIGNATION OF BENEDICT XVI
  "THE CHURCH WILL BE ECLIPSED. AT FIRST, WE WILL NOT
  KNOW WHICH IS THE TRUE POPE." 362
KEY PASSAGES FROM FR. VIOLI'S LATEST ARTICLE ON POPE
  BENEDICT'S RESIGNATION WITH COMMENTARY 368
JUDGMENT 390
JORGE MARIO BERGOGLIO: HERETIC — INCAPABLE SUBJECT
  OF THE PAPACY 390
— WHO AM I TO JUDGE — 390
THE COUNTERFEIT POPE 396
THE FORMAL HERESY OF JORGE MARIO "FRANCIS"
  BERGOGLIO 405
THE DUBIA..409
The Council of Trent The Fifth Session....................................436
The Council of Trent The Sixth Session....................................437
BERGOGLIO'S MASONIZED RELIGION AIMS TO DESTROY
  CATHOLICISM..501
SECTION II - BENEDICT XVI REMAINS THE ONE AND ONLY
  LEGITIMATE POPE..524
AGAINST THE OBJECTION THAT BENEDICT XVI IS EQUALLY
  A HERETIC AS BERGOGLIO 530
THE OBJECTION THAT JOSEPH RATZINGER DENIES THE
  DIVINITY OF CHRIST 557
RATZINGER'S INADVERTENT DENIAL OF
  TRANSUBSTANTIATION 565

THE OBJECTION THAT JOSEPH RATZINGER DENIES THE
   RESURRECTION 575
ON BENEDICT XVI'S ASSERTION THAT THE OLD COVENANT
   WAS NEVER REVOKED 594
THE RATZINGER DOCTRINE ON THE RELATION BETWEEN
   THE COVENANTS.. 611
COMMENTARY 617
"POPE EMERITUS" 635
WHAT MUST BE DONE 638

www.ingramcontent.com/pod-product-compliance
Lightning Source LLC
Chambersburg PA
CBHW021129230426
43667CB00005B/67